Colorado Christian University
Library
180 S. Garrison
Lakewood, Colorado 80226

REF
BJ
63
E54
1994
VOL.3

RR ETHICS

ETHICS

Volume III
Pessimism and Optimism – Zoroastrian Ethics

A Magill Book
from the **Editors of Salem Press**

Consulting Editor
John K. Roth
Claremont McKenna College

Salem Press, Inc.

Pasadena, California   Englewood Cliffs, New Jersey

Copyright © 1994, by Salem Press, Inc.

All rights in this book are reserved. No part of this work may be used or reproduced in any manner whatsoever or transmitted in any form or by any means, electronic or mechanical, including photocopy, recording, or any information storage and retrieval system, without written permission from the copyright owner except in the case of brief quotations embodied in critical articles and reviews. For information address the publisher, Salem Press, Inc., P.O. Box 50062, Pasadena, California 91105.

∞ The paper used in these volumes conforms to the American National Standard for Permanence of Paper for Printed Library Materials, Z39.48-1984.

Library of Congress Cataloging-in-Publication Data

Ethics / consulting editor, John K. Roth
     p. cm. — (Ready reference)
  "A Magill Book"
  Includes bibliographical references and index.
  ISBN 0-89356-395-1 (set : alk. paper). — ISBN 0-89356-398-6 (v. 3 : alk. paper).
  1. Ethics—Encyclopedias. I. Roth, John K. II. Title: Ready reference, ethics. III. Series
BJ63.E54 1994
170' .3—dc20   94-3995
                                                         CIP

Second Printing

PRINTED IN THE UNITED STATES OF AMERICA

CONTENTS

ALPHABETICAL LIST OF ENTRIES

Volume I

Volume II

Volume III

RR ETHICS

Pessimism and optimism

TYPE OF ETHICS: Theory of ethics

DATE: Pessimism, 1984; optimism, 1985

ASSOCIATED WITH: Pessimism is associated with Martin E. P. Seligman and Christopher Peterson; optimism, with Michael Scheier and Charles Carver

DEFINITION: Pessimism is a negative expectation of the future; optimism is a positive expectation of the future

SIGNIFICANCE: Pessimism and optimism may influence what people expect in certain situations and how they respond to ethical dilemmas

Pessimism and optimism are cognitive explanatory styles (stable tendencies to make particular kinds of attributions concerning positive and negative events). A pessimistic explanatory style looks at uncontrollable events as internal ("It is my fault"), stable ("I will always be this way"), and global ("This is an overall characteristic of mine"). An optimistic explanatory style looks at uncontrollable events as external ("It is someone else's fault"), unstable ("It will be different in the future"), and specific ("Other aspects of myself are different"). When confronted with stressful situations, pessimists believe that they can never gain control, whereas optimists believe that they can maintain control.

Pessimism and optimism are typically measured by means of either self-report scales or content analysis of written or verbal materials. Scales that measure pessimism and optimism are the Life Orientation Test and the Coping Orientations to Problems Experienced (COPE). The COPE has thirteen subscales in three general categories: problem-focused (active coping, planning, suppressing competing activities, restraint, and seeking instrumental social support), emotion-focused (seeking emotional social support, positive reinterpretation and growth, acceptance, turning to religion, and denial), and maladaptive (focusing and venting emotions, behavioral disengagement, and mental disengagement).

Pessimism and optimism carry differing views of basic human nature. Pessimists view humans as basically selfish, aggressive, and cruel. They believe that people are governed by aggressive, even death-seeking instincts. Optimists view humans as basically good, helpful, and cooperative. They believe that people are basically decent and life-affirming. Pessimists assume that nothing will work out, because people cannot be trusted; optimists assume that everything will work out, because people will ultimately behave well.

Pessimism and optimism are related to psychopathology. Pessimism is associated with depression, suicidal ideas and actions, hopelessness about the future, helplessness about the present, feelings of alienation, anxiety, neuroticism, irrational beliefs, and hostility. In contrast, optimism is related to high self-esteem, achievement, and internal locus of control. Thus, pessimism is linked to psychological illness and optimism is linked to psychological health.

Pessimism and optimism are associated with different coping strategies. Pessimists are more likely to cope with stress by focusing on and venting emotion, giving up, disengaging, or denying the stress. Furthermore, pessimists are at relatively greater risk for helplessness and depression when they confront stressful events.

Optimists are more likely to cope with stress by acting, focusing on problems, and seeking social support. Furthermore, optimists are more likely to emphasize the positive in their appraisals of stressful events. For example, when faced with a problem such as a risky operation or a serious continuing struggle with a competitor, they focus on what they can do rather on how they feel. They have a relatively higher expectation of being successful, so they do not give up at the first sign of setback. They keep their sense of humor, plan for the future, and reinterpret the situation in a positive light. They acknowledge their problems and illnesses but have confidence that they will overcome them.

These coping differences have practical implications. For example, optimistic beginning insurance agents sold 37 percent more insurance than did pessimistic agents in their first two years on the job and were more likely to persist through the difficulties of the job and stay with the company.

Pessimists are at increased risk for illness, suicide attempts and completions, and other types of death. For example, in one 1987 study by Christopher Peterson and Martin Seligman, pessimists had twice as many illnesses and made about twice as many visits to doctors as did optimists. In another study of recent heart bypass surgery patients, optimists employed more adaptive coping strategies, recovered faster, returned to normal activities sooner, and attained a higher quality of life than pessimists did. Longitudinal studies suggest that pessimists may suffer more illnesses over their lifetimes and die younger than optimists.

Optimists are relatively more likely to be physically healthy and to live longer. For example, in one study by Sandra Levy and colleagues, women who came to the National Cancer Institute for treatment of breast cancer were followed for five years. On the average, optimists died later than pessimists did, even when the physical severity of the disease was the same at the beginning of the five-year period (Levy et al., 1988). In another study, baseball Hall-of-Famers who had played between 1900 and 1950 were rated on their cognitive explanatory style. Optimists were significantly more likely to have lived well into old age than were pessimists. Perhaps pessimists are more likely to become ill because they stir up negative emotions rather than acting constructively, they have passive rather than active coping efforts, and they have relatively poor health habits.

Optimism and pessimism are learned or developed early in life. In one study it was found that third graders had already developed a habitual explanatory style. Furthermore, third-graders with a more pessimistic explanatory style were more prone to depression and performed more poorly on achievement tests compared to those with a more optimistic style.

Pessimistic explanatory styles may be altered—at least

optimists think so. Cognitive therapy has been successful in teaching depressed, pessimistic people new explanatory styles. This therapeutic approach involves teaching people to replace pessimistic thoughts with more realistic ones. Following this kind of therapy, Aaron Beck and colleagues found that changes in explanatory style were still evident after one year (Beck et al., 1979). Thus, a pessimistic explanatory style may be learned at an early age but can be changed with long-lasting results.   —*Lillian M. Range*

See also Psychology; Self-love; Self-respect.

BIBLIOGRAPHY

Beck, Aaron T., et al. *Cognitive Therapy of Depression.* New York: Guilford Press, 1979.

Folkman, Susan, and Richard S. Lazarus. "Coping as a Mediator of Emotion." *Journal of Personality and Social Psychology* 54, no. 3 (March, 1988): 466-475.

Levy, S. M., et al. "Survival Hazards Analysis in First Recurrent Breast Cancer Patients: Seven-Year Follow-Up." *Psychosomatic Medicine* 50, no. 5 (September-October, 1988): 520-528

Peterson, Christopher, Martin E. Seligman, and George E. Vaillant. "Pessimistic Explanatory Style Is a Risk Factor for Physical Illness: A Thirty-Five-Year Longitudinal Study." *Journal of Personality and Social Psychology* 55, no. 1 (July, 1988): 23-27.

Scheier, Michael F., Jagdish K. Weintraub, and Charles S. Carver. "Coping With Stress: Divergent Strategies of Optimists and Pessimists." *Journal of Personality and Social Psychology* 51, no. 6 (December, 1978): 1257-1264.

Phenomenology of Spirit: Book

TYPE OF ETHICS: Modern history

DATE: Published 1807 as *Phänomenologie des Geistes*

AUTHOR: Georg Wilhelm Friedrich Hegel

SIGNIFICANCE: Hegel elaborates the opposition between morality and ethical life in the *Phenomenology*, thus anticipating the full-scale examination of ethics in his *Philosophy of Right* (1821)

The *Phenomenology* occupies a crucial place in the development of Hegel's thought. It marks his maturation as a philosopher of the highest rank and anticipates within its own unique format every aspect of his later work. Hence, it is important to understand the overarching themes of the book before turning to its examination of ethics.

A major aim of Hegel in the *Phenomenology* is to renew classical Platonic and Aristotelian philosophy from within the modern philosophical tradition. It was only through examination and critique of everything that had been thought since the Greeks that a worldview modeled on theirs could become a viable framework from within which modern people could think and act. In striving to fulfill that aim, Hegel developed a view of the subject who experiences, knows, and acts, which was in conscious opposition to any and all views of subjectivity that were empirical (for example, John Locke), naturalistic (for example, much of the thought of

the Enlightenment), or transcendental (for example, Immanuel Kant). His view was that the acting and experiencing subject is both self-transforming over time (hence, historical) and fundamentally social (in opposition to any and all individualist models).

Thus, in the book's first major section, "Consciousness," Hegel demonstrates that consideration of even the apparently most basic forms of knowing, such as sense perception, produces in the knowing subject an awareness of both itself as knowing and of other knowing subjects. Out of these experiences arises self-consciousness. In Hegel's famous examination of the master-servant relationship in the section "Self-Consciousness," he graphically describes the social yet divided character of human experience.

In the remainder of the *Phenomenology*, Hegel depicts the experiences of this divided human self. In doing so, he examines what are for him the key movements in the development of consciousness in Western culture from the Greeks to Hegel's own time. Stoicism, skepticism, the unhappy consciousness of religion, the development of modern philosophy from Descartes to Kant, the opportunities and perils of freedom in the era of the French Revolution, the phases of religious development in human history—all these are subsumed into Hegel's story of the development of *Geist*, or "spirit." *Geist* is the larger rational plan of which all phases of the development of human consciousness are instances. Each phase is therefore a partial revelation of *Geist*.

Chapter 6 of the *Phenomenology*, in which Hegel examines the development of *Geist* from the Greeks down to his own time, is the section of the book that is germane to ethics. It is structured around a distinction crucial to Hegel's thought, that between morality (*Moralität*) and ethical community (*Sittlichkeit*). Morality is that arena of human life in which the individual is thought of as a subject who is responsible for his or her actions. For Hegel, however, moral life attains its highest realization only within the larger life of a society; this is the realm of ethical community. To be truly morally free therefore requires a society within which that freedom can be expressed.

Here, Hegel's historical reconstruction of Western consciousness becomes crucial. Once there *was* a historically existing ethical community—that of the ancient Greeks—in which the city-state provided for its citizens the essential meaning of their lives. This primal *Sittlichkeit* was lost forever in its original form, however, because of developments within Greek culture itself. Hegel's profound discussion of the tensions between divine law and human law in Sophocles' play *Antigone* exemplifies his view that the Greek ethical world had within it the seeds of its own destruction.

Such a natural ethical system, arising spontaneously out of the early developments of Greek cultural life, was inevitably going to be destroyed, Hegel thought, because the ongoing development of *Geist* toward greater self-consciousness would show such a system to be restricted. Socrates' inquiries initiate the transformation of this first natural *Sittlichkeit*: its original unity was shattered by developments within it as Greek thinkers restlessly searched for universal standards of reason and morality—that is, standards greater than the framework of polis life.

Hegel then went on to describe the standpoint of morality as characteristic of the modern spirit. It is crucial to emphasize that the moral standpoint is, for Hegel, an individualist model of human action. Even when this modern individualist morality is developed to its highest point, at which the individual moral self is seen as identical with the universal law of reason, as in the philosophy of Kant, it is still partial or one-sided in Hegel's view.

Thus, the *Phenomenology* contains a tension in Hegel's ethical thought as it had developed to this point: From a historical point of view, modern morality was superior to Greek ethical community because it was a later, higher stage of *Geist*'s ongoing self-revelation; if modern morality is an advance, however, it is nevertheless a one-sided and partial one, doing scant justice to the social aspects of human communal life. What Hegel would later attempt in the *Philosophy of Right* was the construction of a modern notion of ethical community that would be historically as well as philosophically superior to both Greek ethical life and modern individualist moralities. The reader of *The Phenomenology of Spirit* thus catches the development of Hegel's ethical thought in process and will be led to turn to the *Philosophy of Right* to encounter his resolution of the tension that so provocatively animates the discussion of ethics in the *Phenomenology*. —*Michael W. Messmer*

See also Ethics/morality distinction; Hegel, Georg Wilhelm Friedrich; Kant, Immanuel; Kantian ethics.

BIBLIOGRAPHY

Beiser, Frederick C., ed. *The Cambridge Companion to Hegel.* Cambridge, England: Cambridge University Press, 1993.

Shklar, Judith N. *Freedom and Independence: A Study of the Political Ideas of Hegel's Phenomenology of Mind.* Cambridge, England: Cambridge University Press, 1976.

Taylor, Charles. *Hegel.* Cambridge, England: Cambridge University Press, 1975.

_____. *Hegel and Modern Society.* Cambridge, England: Cambridge University Press, 1979.

Wood, Allen W. *Hegel's Ethical Thought.* Cambridge, England: Cambridge University Press, 1990.

Philo Judaeus (c. 20 B.C.E., Alexandria, Egypt—c. 45 C.E., possibly outside Alexandria, Egypt): Philosopher

TYPE OF ETHICS: Religious ethics

ACHIEVEMENTS: Author of *De opificis mundi* (*The Creation of the World*), *Quod Deus est immutabilis* (*That God Is Immutable*), *De Decalogo* (*On the Ten Commandments*), and many other works

SIGNIFICANCE: Philo combined Old Testament theology with Greek philosophy, especially that of Plato and the Stoics

Philo Judaeus, a Jewish Hellenistic writer from Alexandria, is best remembered as an allegorist who attempted to bridge the gap between Greek philosophy and Hebrew Scripture. Thus, for example, he harmonized Plato's *Timaeus* with the scriptural account of creation by articulating a view that the Logos, or the world of intelligible ideas, existed first as God's thoughts and then as the way in which God leads creatures to know him. Philo wished to reconcile natural knowledge and prophetic knowledge, laws of nature and miracles, and causality and free will.

Philo's attempt to blend Greek and Jewish ideas affected his moral philosophy. On the one hand, his writings are filled with expressions of Jewish piety. In his personal life, he practiced renunciation of the self and sought immediate communion with God through the Logos. On the other hand, much of Philo's teaching shows clear signs of Stoic origins; for example, in the attention that he gives to virtue.

Philo differed from the Stoics in that he did not believe that emotions needed to be rooted out. Again harmonizing Greek philosophy with Hebrew Scripture, Philo held that most people were neither completely virtuous nor completely wicked. God's grace led people to improve. Also, based upon his reading of Scripture, Philo included faith; *philanthropia*, or giving help to those in need; and repentance in his list of virtues. Moreover, he held that God would reward virtuous acts in the spiritual hereafter.

See also Jewish ethics; Plato; Platonic ethics; Stoic ethics.

Physician-patient relationship

TYPE OF ETHICS: Personal and social ethics

DATE: Fifth century B.C.E. to present

DEFINITION: A therapeutic association between the most authoritative of health-care providers and one who solicits medical advice, care, or treatment.

SIGNIFICANCE: The very existence of this relationship raises such fundamental ethical issues as paternalism, autonomy, and informed consent

The two parties to any physician-patient relationship are polarized in numerous respects, which normally include (but are not limited to) educational status, economic status, social status, and health status. The presence of any combination of these differences in status, and the extent to which they prevail, in any particular physician-patient relationship has a decided effect on the relationship itself. This is so because it is precisely these kinds of differences in status that translate into differences in the interests, goals, values, and expectations of the patient and of the physician. Ultimately, these latter differences all too often serve to undermine the success of the physician-patient relationship.

While physician-patient relationships can involve anything from preventive medical examinations of patients whose health status is not noticeably diminished to the treatment of terminally ill patients who are suffering from a significantly diminished health status, Western medical orthodoxy has evolved in such a way as to treat disease and illness after the fact rather than to promote measures and practices that might prevent the onset of disease or illness. Consequently, the vast majority of people in Western cultures who find themselves in a physician-patient relationship as the patient do so only after recognition of their own diminished health status. This, too, has a decided effect on the relationship in question. This is true because the severity of the symptoms of the patient's disease, illness, or injury determines the extent to which the patient has also fallen victim to physiological and/or emotional pain, impairment of the cognitive and reasoning abilities, fear of the unknown, and a perceived loss of control over oneself, one's body, and one's world as one knows it.

For all these reasons, it is not atypical for the physician-patient relationship to engender a very one-sided imbalance of power, and it is precisely this imbalance of power that raises the following fundamental ethical issues that are inherent in the physician-patient relationship: paternalism, autonomy, and informed consent.

Whenever a physician restricts or otherwise impedes a patient's freedom to determine what is done by way of therapeutic measures to herself or himself and attempts to justify such an intrusion by reasons exclusively related to the welfare or needs of the patient, the physician can be construed to have acted paternalistically. To the extent that a physician engages in such paternalistic practices with respect to a patient, the physician is failing to respect that patient's autonomy; that is, the patient's moral right to self-determination.

In spite of the fact that the primary goal of both the physician and the patient should be the restoration of the patient's optimal health status, any differences between the interests, other goals, values, and expectations of the patient as compared to those of the physician within the context of the very same therapeutic relationship set the stage for paternalistic practices on the part of the physician at the expense of the patient's autonomy. Furthermore, the very presence of any or all of the aforementioned by-products of the symptoms of disease, illness, or injury serve only to exacerbate the problem.

For example, an elderly patient with several major medical problems, the combined effects of which indicate that she has only a couple of weeks to live, decides that she wants her kidney dialysis (which is her lifeline because of chronic renal failure) discontinued. Any additional week or so of her life that may be gained by continuing the dialysis is, in her mind, far outweighed both by her own poor quality of life and by the emotional trauma being caused to her loved ones. The attending physician, however, who is committed to a profession that is dedicated to healing and to the sustaining of life, believes firmly that any means of prolonging the life of this patient is justified and should be pursued.

In this case, there would appear to be a conflict of values, if not of expectations and interests, between the physician and the patient, the result of which is paternalistic practices on the part of the physician at the expense of the patient's autonomy. When asked to justify his position, the physician might argue that the patient's cognitive and reasoning abilities have been impaired by the combined symptoms of her many and varied medical problems to the extent that her capacity for effective deliberation concerning her own medical treatment is significantly compromised and that, consequently, the patient is no longer capable of autonomous decision making.

The central question in such a case is whether the patient's decision is consistent with the types of values, interests, and goals that she has expressed throughout her life, or, failing that, whether the patient's decision is the reasonable outcome of a prudent reassessment of her own values, interests, and goals in the light of her present circumstances. The answer to this question should determine whether the patient is any longer capable of autonomous decision making, and consequently, whether questions concerning the transgression of the patient's autonomy should even arise.

Informed consent is intended to be both a moral and a legal safeguard to respect the patient's autonomy and to promote the welfare of the patient. In the medical context, "informed consent" refers to a patient's agreement to and approval of, upon obtaining an understanding of all relevant information, a recommended treatment or procedure that is intended to be of therapeutic value to the patient. The very concept of informed consent raises the following ethical questions.

Given the previously mentioned by-products of the symptoms of disease, illness, or injury (up to and including the impairment of cognitive and reasoning abilities), what percentage of patients, either in the physician's office or in the medical institution, are truly competent to provide their *informed* consent? Given the various respects, already mentioned, in which physicians and their patients are polarized, what constitutes the proper quantity and quality of information necessary for a patient's consent to be truly informed? Given the imbalance of power that normally exists in the physician-patient relationship and the extreme authority status typically afforded physicians, which together pose a serious threat of manipulation of the patient, when, if ever, is a patient's informed consent truly voluntary?

In response to these and other ethical questions that arise within the context of the physician-patient relationship, various models of the relationship have been proposed; however, each of these models has been shown to be flawed (some more than others). Suffice it to say that any model that is proposed for any personal relationship, including that of physician and patient, will fail to the extent that it does not adequately appreciate the singular importance of the individual character of both parties to the relationship. In the final analysis, any attempt to legislate morality is doomed to fail.

—*Stephen C. Taylor*

See also Autonomy; Bills of rights, medical; Bioethics; Death and dying; Diagnosis, ethics of; Euthanasia; Hippocrates; Medical ethics; Institutionalization of patients; Personal relationships; *Principles of Medical Ethics*; Therapist-patient relationship.

BIBLIOGRAPHY

Brody, Howard. "The Physician-Patient Relationship." In *Medical Ethics*, edited by Robert M. Veatch. Boston: Jones & Bartlett, 1989.

Childress, J. F. *Who Should Decide? Paternalism in Health Care*. Oxford, England: Oxford University Press, 1982.

Ramsey, Paul. *The Patient as Person*. New Haven, Conn.: Yale University Press, 1970.

Shelp, Earl E., ed. *Virtue and Medicine*. Dordrecht, The Netherlands: D. Reidel, 1985.

U.S. President's Commission for the Study of Ethical Problems in Medicine and Biomedical and Behavioral Research. *Making Health Care Decisions*. Vols. 1 and 3. Washington, D.C.: Government Printing Office, 1982.

Plagiarism

TYPE OF ETHICS: Arts and censorship

DATE: First modern copyright law passed in England in 1710

DEFINITION: Using words or ideas originally formulated by another author without giving that author appropriate credit

SIGNIFICANCE: Plagiarism is considered to be the theft of another person's ideas

It is often difficult to determine what counts as plagiarism, because groups of people often work on projects as a team. For example, it may be selfish for celebrities not to credit their ghostwriters, but this is not considered plagiarism, because ghostwriters are members of the publisher's staff. In addition, most new ideas are based on combinations of old ideas. In an academic context, students are taught to analyze the sources of their ideas. Therefore, they are expected to provide citations for any direct quotations, paraphrases, and important ideas that are taken from another published author. Failure to do so is plagiarism. Because what a plagiarist steals—credit—is intangible, punishment is usually informal and is based on ethical or social factors. Students who plagiarize are penalized by their schools because teachers want them to learn not to steal in any situation. Professors who plagiarize have violated the social norms of scholarship and therefore their reputations as scholars. In the world of commercial publishing, however, when a plagiarizer robs an original author of profit as well as credit, plagiarism is grounds for a civil lawsuit, and legal penalties can include financial compensation of the injured party.

See also Lying.

Plato (Aristocles; 427 B.C.E., Athens, Greece—347 B.C.E., Athens, Greece): Philosopher

TYPE OF ETHICS: Classical history

ACHIEVEMENTS: Author of *Politeia* (388-368 B.C.E.; *Republic*) and numerous other dialogues

SIGNIFICANCE: Plato developed a theory of justice based upon a division of the soul in which each part performs a distinctive function

Plato's writings are in a dialogue format. He discusses philosophical topics through question-and-answer sessions conducted by Socrates. The Socrates of the Platonic dialogues is very closely modeled after the historical Socrates (469-399 B.C.E.), whose life and death had a tremendous influence upon Plato. The Socrates of the dialogues is, however, at least in part, a fictional character used to impart Platonic themes.

Plato's dialogues are divided into three groups: the early, or Socratic, dialogues; the dialogues of middle age; and the dialogues of old age. The early dialogues employ a particularly rigorous dialectic form. These dialogues frequently deal with ethical topics. In *Protagoras* and *Meno*, Plato asks whether virtue can be taught. In *Protagoras* and *Euthydemus*, he argues both for and against the supposed Socratic doctrine that virtue and knowledge are identical. In *Gorgias*, Plato considers whether it is better to do a wrong than to suffer one. In *Protagoras*, he accepts the hedonistic position that one ought to seek pleasure, but in *Gorgias*, he argues against it. Plato also considers definitions of major ethical terms. He questions the nature of courage, justice, temperance, and piety.

Theory of Forms and Importance of Knowledge for Ethics. Plato is perhaps best known for the theory that true reality belongs to eternal, immutable forms. All other things are poor copies of these realities. According to Plato, there are two "worlds": the world of being and that of becoming. Physical objects and copies of these objects (for example, a horse and the shadow of a horse) belong to the two levels of the world of becoming. These things change, come into being, and perish. Forms (such as beauty and justice) and mathematical concepts belong to the world of being. These entities are eternal and possess more reality than do mutable objects. Everything is made possible by the form of the good.

The theory that more knowledge can be had at higher levels is central to Plato's epistemology and ethics. One important aspect of Platonic ethical theory is that the moral individual strives to obtain more knowledge and thus to come closer to the good.

Two important points are illuminated through this discussion of the moral individual's movement toward the good. The first of these is the Platonic/Socratic doctrine that "to know the good is to do the good." Plato argues that a failure to do good is simply a lack of knowledge. Ignorance causes one to behave wrongly.

Plato also argues that reason is more important for ethics than is pleasure. Reason is primary because one must determine which things bring more or less pleasure. Again, the moral individual is the knowledgeable individual.

Definition of Justice. In *Republic*, Plato puts forward his conception of the ideal state. In book 1, Socrates is concerned with the definition of justice. He believes that justice

Plato (Library of Congress)

is preferable to injustice but needs support for this conviction. He moves the discussion to a different level. If one can discern justice in the larger context of a state, then one should be able to understand the meaning of justice at the level of the individual. Plato thus develops a political model for his theory of justice.

In the same way that the just state is the state in which each individual is doing what he or she does best, so the just soul is the soul in which each "part" is performing its unique function. The soul, according to Plato, has three parts: reason, spirit, and appetites. It is, as he explains in *Phaedrus*, like a charioteer (reason) trying to control two horses, a wayward one (the appetites) and one that can take orders (the spirited one). The charioteer can reach his goal only when the horses are in control. Likewise, the soul is in harmony only when reason controls and sets the goals, the spirited element moves toward the goals, and the appetites are in control.

Plato explains that there is a virtue that corresponds to each division of the soul. Properly functioning reason has wisdom. The spirit that moves in accordance with reason has courage. The appetites, which are under the control of reason, have temperance. All three parts of the soul working in harmony exhibit the virtue of justice. These four cardinal virtues are an important part of Plato's ethical theory. His concern is more with what kind of person one should be than with what kinds of things one should do. Again, to *be* wise is to *do* good.

Place in History. Plato develops an absolutist ethical theory. There is a "right" and a "good" toward which to aspire. He develops this theory to respond to the skepticism and the relativism of the Sophists. One person may be more or less just than another, but each is just in that he or she copies or participates in the form of justice. This form is eternal and unchanging—an absolute.

Alfred North Whitehead (1861-1947) claimed that all philosophy after Plato is a series of footnotes to Plato. This is especially true with regard to ethics. Aristotle (384-322 B.C.E.) developed a virtue-based theory of ethics similar to that described above and yet with its own peculiarly Aristotelian slant. Other ethical theories are patterned after that of Aristotle and, thus, that of Plato. Furthermore, any ethical theory insisting upon absolutes is Platonic.

—*Rita C. Hinton*

See also Absolutes and absolutism; *Apology*; Platonic ethics; *Republic*; Socrates; Sophists; Virtue ethics.

BIBLIOGRAPHY

Annas, Julia. *An Introduction to Plato's "Republic."* Oxford: Clarendon Press, 1981.

Gould, John. *The Development of Plato's Ethics.* New York: Russell & Russell, 1972.

Plato. *The Dialogues of Plato.* 4th ed. 4 vols. Translated by Benjamin Jowett. Oxford: Clarendon Press, 1953.

_____. *The "Republic" of Plato.* Oxford: Clarendon Press, 1942.

Taylor, A. E. *Plato, the Man and His Works.* 6th ed. London: Methuen, 1949.

Platonic ethics

TYPE OF ETHICS: Classical history; Theory of ethics

DATE: 427-347 B.C.E.

ASSOCIATED WITH: Ancient Greek ethics, especially Socrates (c. 470-399 B.C.E.), Sophist ethics (fifth century B.C.E.), and Aristotle (384-322 B.C.E.)

DEFINITION: Plato believed that human beings could be guided, whether by their own reason or wisdom or by good laws, so as to live virtuously

SIGNIFICANCE: Plato's ethics provided the impetus to his theory of forms; his ideas have exerted an ongoing influence on ethical theory by framing the questions that have occupied ethicists and by securing the place of reason in the resolution of ethical issues

The key ethical topics of Plato's dialogues may be listed as follows: the definition of the virtues, most prominently justice, moderation, courage, wisdom, and piety; the so-called Socratic paradoxes (first, that no one sins knowingly, and second, that virtue is knowledge); the inseparability of virtue and happiness (*eudaimonia*); the relation of the virtues to political life; the virtues as subspecies of the idea of the good; and the denunciation of hedonism—that is, the rejection of the popular notion that pleasure is that which produces happiness.

Beyond these topics, which are explicitly identified by Plato, the dialogues address numerous areas of ethical import. These include the existence of the soul, immortality, and life after death (in the dialogue *Phaedo*); rewards and punishments; education; the value of the fine arts; men's duties to the gods, to other men, to their cities, families, and to themselves; the rights and duties of women; and in the story of Gyges and his invisibility ring (*Republic*), the question of whether the moral status of one's conduct should depend on the consequences of that conduct.

History. The event that more than any other turned Plato from politics to philosophy was the trial and condemnation of his teacher, Socrates, in the year 399 B.C.E. In his *Phaedo*, written while he was still in his twenties and poignantly close to the memory of Socrates, Plato described Socrates as the best, most intelligent, and most moral man of his time. After that, Plato determined to take no active part in the radically democratic Athenian judicial or governmental system, which he came to define as the government of those least qualified by temperament and intelligence to rule.

Plato's antidote to what he felt to be the rule of the mob was his concept of government by philosopher-kings, people prepared by lifelong education to be good rulers. In his most famous dialogue, *Republic*, he stated that "Unless philosophers become kings of states or else those who are now kings and rulers become real and adequate philosophers . . . there can be no respite from evil for states or, I believe, for the human race."

This idea antedated by many years the appearance of *Republic*. According to Plato's "Seventh Letter," the search for a king whom he might train in philosophy led him in about 389 B.C.E. to Syracuse, Sicily. Having failed in this attempt to turn the Syracusan tyrant Dionysius I into a philosopher-king, Plato returned to Athens in 387 and in the latter 380's founded his Academy, which J. E. Raven called "a training ground for future statesmen." *Republic* was most likely produced soon afterward, in the early 370's.

Any study of Plato's ethical thought must begin with Socrates' attempts to refute the moral relativism of the sophists. Plato's ethics seems to have evolved beyond his master's, for Plato continued to explore the field in his mature and in his latest dialogues, including *Republic*, *Philebos*, and *Laws*.

The sophists had said that the only ethical standards that were morally binding on an individual's behavior were those that all people agreed to or that followed the laws of nature (*physis*). Most of the rules people live by are, they said, really only local norms or customs (*nomos*) that held little or no moral force. In most cases, therefore, each person is the judge of what is good for himself or herself, and ethics (the ethical measure of *physis*) does not really come into play. Where it is simply a matter of *nomos*, the operative rule was "man is the measure"; that is, what seemed to each individual to be good was, for him, good.

A prime example of a natural law (*physis*) prevalent universally in the world and thus binding on humanity was that of the sophist Thrasymachus, who in *Republic* argued that "might makes right." In the *Gorgias*, Plato makes Callicles of Acharnae articulate the corollary sophist view that local laws were artificial and conventional (mere *nomos*) and framed by the many weak men as a means of keeping the strong under their control.

Definition of the Virtues. Socrates responded (as is known from Plato's earlier, or Socratic dialogues) that individual virtues such as courage (discussed in *Laches*), moderation (*Charmides*), piety (*Euthyphro*), and justice (*Republic*) could be defined for all to understand, so as to place most or all ethical activity under the umbrella of universally accepted standards. The realm in which each person was to be judge of the ethical quality of his own actions was much reduced; sophist ethics was defeated.

The Socratic contribution to ethical thought—essential in Plato's system—was identified by Aristotle, who credited Socrates with laying down the principles of "universal definition and inductive reasoning"; that is, arriving at the universal definition of each virtue by means of a discussion and analysis of particular actions (inductive reasoning).

The Socratic Paradoxes. In developing his own ethical program, Plato took his point of departure from the so-called Socratic paradoxes. The first paradox argues that all men naturally seek to do good but often act wrongly because they mistake evil for good. Men thus commit sin involuntarily and out of ignorance (*Protagoras*). This paradox allows Plato, with Socrates, to define all sin or evil as ignorance and, conversely, to assert that all virtue is knowledge or wisdom: the second paradox.

This knowledge is available to men in general, but ordinary men occasionally err. It thus behooves the best men to acquire knowledge about the virtues, understand their nature, and act on a foundation of knowledge. This is no easy matter and requires a lifelong pursuit of wisdom (*Republic*). Thus, philosophers (seekers of wisdom) will be the wisest and, seeking the good (as all men do), will be less likely to err.

John Gould, in *The Development of Plato's Ethics* (1955), strongly asserts that the goal of Plato's ethical system (virtue, or *areté*) was always to lead to virtuous activity or behavior—for example, justice in the soul will express itself in just action—not merely to arrive at a valid ethical theory. This too was inspired by Socrates, as Plato dramatically demonstrated in the *Crito*, in which his teacher put his ethics into action by accepting the sentence of death as legally binding, refusing to escape from prison when he had the opportunity to do so, and refusing to disobey the state's command that he take poison.

The Teachability of Virtue. Since virtue is knowledge and all men possess an innate capacity for knowledge, then virtue can be taught, and teaching and guidance may direct an individual toward good. On this point Plato seems initially to have wavered, for in the *Meno* Plato has Socrates say that virtue comes rather by chance, while in the *Protagoras* he suggests its teachability. Thus, the moral and political education of youths depends on the identity of virtue with knowledge and therefore on the teachability of virtue.

Plato's Theory of Ideas or Forms as Related to Ethics. When one comes really to know the virtues, it is the immutable, stable, and abiding idea, form, or universal definition of the virtue that one comes to know. In the *Gorgias*, Plato has Socrates make the point that belief or opinion (which Gorgias, as a sophist, teaches) is not a sufficient standard for guiding moral and political life. The idea (or definition) of a virtue is learned by induction from particular case studies of the virtue in action.

In *Republic*, Plato lays out the course of lifelong study whose goal is the attainment of knowledge of the ideas and of the highest of the ideas, which Plato variously calls the idea of beauty, truth, or the good. Intimate knowledge of the ideas of the different virtues allows the guardians of the state to recognize the virtues and their opposites in every action in which they are present.

After a primary education (to age eighteen), the citizens, especially those who will emerge as guardians of the republic, are made to dwell in beautiful surroundings so as to attain to a love of the idea of the beautiful-in-itself. They next serve two years of military service. This is followed by the citizens' higher education, which consists of ten years in "propaedeutic" (preparatory) studies for those who will become the guardians or philosopher kings of the state. The subjects studied in this phase are arithmetic, geometry, astronomy, and harmonics (music). The purpose of this scientific quadrivium is to lead the mind away from material and changing objects of the realm of opinion (for example, two apples, two cubes) to immaterial and immutable realities (for example, the concept of "two" and "cubeness"). Plato had derived from Pythagoras a respect for abstract numbers as unchanging realities. Numbers are akin to the unchanging ideas of the virtues, and this training in correct thinking about numbers, Plato thought, prepared the mind to recognize virtue and vice in action. Many aspiring guardians would be left behind during this phase of education.

The final level of higher education consisted of five years of training in dialectic, also known as the Socratic *elenchos*. Dialectic is the process of repeatedly proposing hypotheses and drawing out consequences used by Socrates in his conversations with his pupils. By this means of interlocution, the pupils were drawn ever closer to the irrefutable and true hypothesis that it had always been the purpose of the session to achieve. Thus, the pupils, future guardians, were trained to brainstorm, together or privately, in the quest for the form or idea that defined and produced knowledge about the virtue in question. This knowledge enabled the guardians to know which human actions claiming to share in the virtue in question were virtuous and which were not. No doubt, other citizens would, at this final plateau, fail to qualify for the ranks of the guardians. Completion of training in dialectic brought the guardians to age thirty-five.

The Overriding Idea of the Good. Some Plato scholars are troubled that in the minor dialogues (*Laches*, among others), the definitions of the virtues sometimes break down when Socrates tests them for their production of happiness in individual or city. That Plato may have done this deliberately in these early dialogues is indicated by the hints of dramatic purpose as opposed to an air of tentative inquiry in their structure and logic.

In *Republic*, Plato himself warns that these early definitions of virtues are not final. The utility of virtue must be related to an ultimate standard or ideal of the good. He devotes much of *Republic* and *Symposium* to achieving this.

For Plato, the forms of the virtues are themselves subcategories of the idea of the good. In reality, moderation, justice, and all the other virtues, including knowledge, are virtues because they participate in goodness. Plato is clear about this in *Republic*, where he calls the good the ultimate aim of life, the final object of desire, and the sustaining cause of everything else. The virtues, whether severally or united under the paradox that all virtue is knowledge, themselves aim at the good.

It is the guardians' vision of the good that enables them to inculcate right opinion, teach virtue, and mold character and institutions in the light of a reasoned concept of goodness in private and public life.

The *Symposium* and other dialogues provide parallels to the idea of the good as final cause by looking, for example, at a hierarchy of friendship, passion, and love culminating in the apprehension of the idea of beauty, which is depicted by Plato as practically identical to the good.

The Relationship of Utility and Pleasure to Ethics. Plato is clear in rejecting Protagoras' dictum that pleasure is to be identified with the good. He denies as well the notion that utility is the source and goal of morality. In *Lysis* and *Symposium*, Plato rejects the theory that the good is desired as a remedy against evil because that would make the good merely a means to an end. For the same reason, he explicitly rejects the hope of immortality as the origin of and reasons for people's morality. In *Republic*, he strenuously opposes the view of Thrasymachus and Callicles that justice is an artificial convention devised by the weak in their conspiracy to neutralize the strong.

In his article "Plato's Ethics," Paul Shorey believes Plato's whole ethical thrust to be a polemic against hedonism: "This doctrine of the negativity of what men call pleasure is the fundamental basis of Plato's ethics." On this basis, Shorey continues, rests Plato's demonstration that virtue and happiness are one. Moreover, pleasures are never pure but always mixed with desire or pain. Finally, Shorey adds, "Pleasure and pain, like confidence and fear, are foolish counselors."

The dialogues devote much space to analyzing the concept of pleasure, which arises in some form in more dialogues than does any other issue. The *Gorgias* and *Philebos* directly oppose the sophist doctrine that defines the good as pleasure and that asserts that true happiness comes from gratifying the sensual appetites. This repudiation of hedonism also appears in *Phaedo* and *Republic*. In *Republic*, where Plato presents the idea of man's tripartite soul, pleasures are ranked as intellectual, energetic, and sensual. Plato allowed the thesis of the *Protagoras* that a surplus of pleasure is good, but only when the pleasure is kept in perspective and is free from all evil consequences. Only in the sense that it suited his ethical system to argue that the virtuous life is the most pleasurable did Plato make Socrates identify pleasure and the good at the end of *Protagoras*. Rather, it is wisdom (*sophia*) that delivers happiness, for wisdom always achieves its object, wisdom never acts in error, and absence of error entails happiness.

Final Developments in Plato's Ethical Thought. In Plato's last years, his ethical approach underwent a change little noticed in discussions of mainstream Platonism. John Gould remarks that in his last work, *Laws*, "Plato the aristocrat, Plato the constructor of systems, Plato the lover of the aesthetic are all represented in their final and most con-

vincing forms, while the ghost of Socrates . . . is no longer present even in the *dramatis personae*."

In *Laws*, the thrust is still the perfection of the individual, but now no longer through the personal acquisition of virtue. Instead, the individual is to be improved by means of ideal legislation whose explicit goal is the control and obliteration of nonvirtuous behavior in the interest of the perfection of society. In this last dialogue of Plato's corpus, the primary virtues are given their own separate existence as *sophrosyne* (moderation or temperance), *dikaiosyne* (justice), *phronesis* (wisdom), and *andreia* (courage), and possession of only one of them is not sufficient.

Plato's thinking has, in fact, undergone a change from that of his Socratic period. In his new ideal state, the legislator will guide his people to virtue by manipulating the distribution of honor and dishonor and by using the pleasures, desires, and passions that motivate people: a kind of nascent behaviorist theory. By using a system of repetitive propaganda to work on popular emotions, he will steer them to virtue (*areté*). Plato's goal was ever the same. What changed in his latter years was his attitude toward human nature, which became more pessimistic. The mistakes of Athenian democracy, rule by the masses, had convinced him that a more thoroughgoing system of controls had to prevail, and this he intended to provide in his new "second-best" state, governed not by philosophers but by law.

—*Daniel C. Scavone*

See also *Apology*; Aristotelian ethics; Aristotle; Boethius, Anicius Manlius Severinus; Cicero, Marcus Tullius; Cynicism; Heidegger, Martin; *Nicomachean Ethics*; Plato; *Republic*; Socrates; Sophists; Stoic ethics; Utopia; Virtue.

BIBLIOGRAPHY

Crombie, I. M. *An Examination of Plato's Doctrines*. London: Routledge & Kegan Paul, 1963. A general work on all aspects of Plato's philosophy, with ninety pages on ethics. Especially useful in tracing Plato's ideas through the early minor dialogues: *Euthyphro, Charmides, Laches, Meno,* and *Euthydemus*.

Gould, John. *The Development of Plato's Ethics*. New York: Russell & Russell, 1972. An excellent survey of the evolution of Plato's ethical views from his youthful days under the influence of Socrates to the fully mature thought of his last dialogues, chiefly *Philebos* and *Laws*.

Grube, G. M. A. *Plato's Thought*. Indianapolis: Hackett, 1980. Perhaps the best introduction to the entire philosophical system of Plato.

Lodge, R. C. *Plato's Theory of Ethics: The Moral Criterion and the Highest Good*. New York: Archon Books, 1966. An interpretation that ignores both solidly based explications of Plato's ethics and Plato himself by subjectively focusing on non-Platonic topics such as "value scales" and "private-spirited artistic creation."

Raven, J. E. *Plato's Thought in the Making*. Cambridge, England: Cambridge University Press, 1965. A highly readable discussion of Plato's life and thought, featuring a generous treatment of his ethics and especially a critique of the views of other premier Plato scholars on important issues.

Rowe, Christopher. *An Introduction to Greek Ethics*. London: Hutchinson, 1976. A short introduction to the field that ranges from Homer to the Epicureans and Stoics.

Shorey, Paul. "Plato's Ethics." In *Plato: A Collection of Critical Essays*, edited by Gregory Vlastos. Vol. 2. Garden City, N.Y.: Anchor Books, 1971. A concise introduction to the major ethical issues considered by Plato from the pen of an important Plato scholar.

_____. *What Plato Said*. Chicago: University of Chicago Press, 1978. A highly acclaimed résumé and analysis of Plato's writings with synopses of and critical commentary on twenty-eight dialogues. Treats ethics in appropriate contexts.

Taylor, A. E. *Plato: The Man and His Work*. 7th ed. London: Methuen, 1960. An indispensable book for any study of Plato's philosophy in English. Provides a thorough discussion of every aspect of Platonism.

Plessy v. Ferguson

TYPE OF ETHICS: Race and ethnicity
DATE: 1896
ASSOCIATED WITH: U.S. Supreme Court
DEFINITION: A historic Supreme Court decision that gave legal sanction to racial segregation in the United States by affirming that separate-but-equal accommodations for blacks and whites were constitutional
SIGNIFICANCE: The decision stands as a landmark, albeit a negative one, in the struggle to defend human and civil rights against racism

Plessy v. Ferguson was provoked by an African-American challenge that argued that an act of Louisiana's legislature was unconstitutional because it violated the Thirteenth and Fourteenth Amendments to the U.S. Constitution. The act in question required all railroads to provide "equal but separate" accommodations for blacks and whites and also forbade intermingling between the two groups.

The Supreme Court's majority opinion concentrated on the Fourteenth Amendment. The Court acknowledged that "the object of the amendment was undoubtedly to enforce the absolute equality of the two races before the law," but the majority opinion also underscored that "in the nature of things, it could not have been intended to abolish distinctions based upon color, or to enforce social, as distinguished from political equality." The effect of this decision was to give legal sanction to segregation in the United States. Significantly, however, the Court's decision was not unanimous. There was a lone dissenter, Justice John M. Harlan, whose minority opinion argued that the U.S. Constitution is "colorblind, and neither knows nor tolerates classes among citizens. In respect of civil rights, all citizens are equal before the law." Justice Harlan's opinion later became the unanimous opinion of the Court in *Brown v. Board of Education of Topeka*, which overturned the separate-but-equal principle.

See also *Brown v. Board of Education of Topeka*; Civil rights movement; Racial prejudice; Racism; Segregation.

Pluralism

TYPE OF ETHICS: Theory of ethics
DATE: Fourth century B.C.E. to present
ASSOCIATED WITH: Aristotle, William James, Amélie Rorty, and Richard Rorty
DEFINITION: The theory of ethics that states that there is no single or unique set of values and principles, but rather a plurality of such sets
SIGNIFICANCE: Pluralism takes a middle path between moral relativism on the one hand (no objective moral principles) and moral monism or universalism on the other (only one moral principle)

Pluralism as it is associated with ethics has had a long history. One can find a precedent in Aristotle for the view that there is no master principle, no moral principle that applies unequivocally to all concrete situations and circumstances. A rule that might apply in one situation might not apply in another. For example, although it may ordinarily be wrong to lie, it could be right to lie if doing so will save someone's life. The moral principle that determines the right thing to do, therefore, is dependent upon the circumstances, and since there are many concrete situations and circumstances, there is a plurality of ways of doing the right thing. As Aristotle would put this, there is a plurality of ways to achieve the good life, and each of these ways entails the actualization of different values and moral principles.

Pluralism is to be distinguished from both monism and relativism. A monist argues that there is an overarching moral principle that unambiguously prescribes what to do in any and every circumstance. An example of such a principle is the utilitarian greatest-happiness principle, which holds that, in every action, one ought to act so as to create the greatest amount of happiness for the greatest number of people. The relativist, however, although agreeing with the pluralist that values depend upon circumstances, claims that there is no objective reason for what is right or wrong other than simply what the people in a given culture or circumstance do. The pluralist believes that there is such an objective reason; thus, even though there is a plurality of ways to achieve the good life, Aristotle nevertheless argues that each way is objectively right precisely because it does achieve the good life. The pluralist, therefore, agrees with the monist that there is to be an objective criterion whereby moral values are to be judged but disagrees with the monist in that the pluralist argues that there is no unique set or system of values that is the only one that satisfies the criteria. Likewise, the pluralist agrees with the relativist that there is a plurality of values but disagrees with the relativist's claim that such values are not legitimated by an objective criterion.

Amélie Rorty, in her essay "The Advantages of Moral Diversity" (1992), argues for a version of Aristotelian pluralism. Like Aristotle, she claims that there is no unique and single conception of what everyone ought to do to achieve the good life. Furthermore, Rorty argues that learning to live and cooperate with others who have different values from our own is beneficial to achieving the good life. A deontologist, who argues that the consequences of an action are not to be considered when determining the moral worth of an action, and a utilitarian, who claims that the consequences are to be considered, will, Rorty believes, when living and cooperating together, keep each other in line; and this keeping each other in line is precisely what Rorty believes to be beneficial for the attainment of the good life.

John Kekes, in his book *The Morality of Pluralism* (1993), holds a position similar to those of Rorty and Aristotle. He also argues that there is a plurality of ways to achieve the good life and that each way requires the realization of often radically different types of values. He also claims that having radically different values present in a society is, as Rorty argued, beneficial both to society and to individuals.

Pluralism is not, however, without its variations. Peter Wenz, for example, in "Minimal, Moderate, and Extreme Moral Pluralism" (1993), accuses the pluralist who argues for the advantages of having radically different, if not contradictory, values coexisting together of promoting incoherence and inconsistency in ethics. This brand of pluralism he labels "extreme pluralism." Rorty and Kekes, however, although calling for the coexistence of radically different values in society, do not call for an individual to hold contradictory values. An individual, they maintain, should sustain a consistent and coherent system of values, whereas society ought to maintain a plurality of values. For this reason, Rorty and Kekes are not to be seen as pluralists of the type that Wenz criticizes.

Christopher Stone, an environmental ethicist who argues for moral pluralism, does hold that an individual ought to maintain radically different values. A father, for example, could be a utilitarian at work but a Kantian deontologist at home with his family. It is this view that, referring explicitly to Stone, Wenz criticizes in his article. Stone's pluralism does promote inconsistency and incoherence and is, by Wenz's definition, "extreme pluralism." A less-extreme pluralism, or moderate pluralism, as Wenz defines it, is roughly the view that Aristotle, Rorty, and Kekes hold; that is, there is a plurality of ways of achieving the good life, yet each way is in itself consistent and coherent. Minimal pluralism, Wenz believes, is true of every ethical theory. In other words, there is no true monistic theory, for monistic theories (such as utilitarianism) do not give a uniquely correct and unambiguous answer in every situation to the question of what one ought to do. There is always a plurality of possible answers, and hence these theories are minimally pluralistic. All ethical theories, Wenz concludes, are to some degree pluralistic.

There are other important philosophers with whom pluralism is associated—most notably, the pragmatists. William James, in *A Pluralistic Universe* (1909), and Richard Rorty, in *Philosophy and the Mirror of Nature* (1979) argue, for example, that what is considered true is simply what is necessary to survive. Truth does not express a relationship of correspondence to reality; instead, truth is determined by the particular goals and needs associated with survival, and because there is a plurality of ways to satisfy these needs, there is a plurality of truths. Truth, like morality, is not one; it is plural. —*Jeff Bell*

See also Aristotle; *Nicomachean Ethics*; Pragmatism; Situational ethics; Teleological ethics.

BIBLIOGRAPHY

Aristotle. *The Nicomachean Ethics*. Translated by David Ross. New York: Oxford University Press, 1980.

James, William. *A Pluralistic Universe*. New York: Library of America, 1987.

Kekes, John. *The Morality of Pluralism*. Princeton, N.J.: Princeton University Press, 1993.

Rorty, Amélie. "The Advantages of Moral Diversity." *Social Philosophy and Policy* 9, no. 2 (1992): 38-62.

Wenz, Peter. "Minimal, Moderate, and Extreme Moral Pluralism." *Environmental Ethics* 15 (Spring, 1993): 61-74.

Pogrom

TYPE OF ETHICS: Race and ethnicity

DATE: Coined 1881

ASSOCIATED WITH: Anti-Semitism under the regimes of the last three Russian czars—Alexander II, Alexander III, and Nicholas II—and later in Hitler's Germany

DEFINITION: Originally a Russian word meaning "destruction" or "devastation"; as an international term, it was applied to coordinated mob attacks by Russians against the lives and property of Jews, and to the systematic persecution of Jews living under the Nazis

SIGNIFICANCE: A pogrom is an expression of religious and racial hatred that is directed toward an easily identified powerless minority and is either approved or condoned by authorities

In modern Russian history, pogrom-like attacks were initially leveled against the Armenians, Tatars, and the Russian intelligentsia. As it is employed in many languages specifically to describe the pillage, murder, and rape of Russian Jews, however, the term "pogrom" denotes three large-scale waves of devastation between 1881 and 1921. Each of these pogroms surpassed the preceding one in scope and savagery and occurred during periods of severe social and political upheaval in Russia. For example, the first pogroms of the 1880's followed the assassination of Czar Alexander II as a result of false rumors about widespread Jewish involvement in the plot. Mobs from more than two hundred towns, inspired by local leaders acting with official support, took part. Pogroms greatly influenced Russian Jewry and history. In their wake, the Russian government adopted systematic policies of discrimination, harassment, and persecution of the Jews. The murder of innocent individuals and whole families was commonplace. This led numerous European anti-Semites to conclude that violence was legitimate and thus helped to pave the way for pogroms to be carried out later in Poland and Germany.

See also Anti-Semitism; Ethnic cleansing; Hitler, Adolf; Nazism; Oppression; Racism.

Police brutality

Type of ethics: Civil rights

Date: 1968 to present

Definition: Police misconduct involving the unnecessary use of force, the excessive use of force, or the use of fatal force

Significance: Friedrich Nietzsche, in *Beyond Good and Evil* and *The Genealogy of Morals*, argued that people can be divided into masters and slaves; police subculture is rooted in what Nietzsche called the "master morality," while the masses possess Nietzsche's "slave morality"; the values and worldviews of these two cultures often clash in violent conflict labeled police brutality

From the beginning, Americans have never fully trusted their government or its officials, even though they must rely upon both. The Fifty-first Federalist Paper argued, "If men were angels no government would be necessary." Human beings are definitely not angels, and they succumb to both good and bad activities. Although checks and balances were written into the U.S. Constitution to limit the "abuse of power" by distributing it between competing branches of government and among federal, state, and local authorities, no comparable safeguards exist to protect citizens against police misconduct. Perhaps this is because the first official U.S. police force was formed in New York in 1844, long after the government was established. A national police force that would prevent local police misconduct has never been established, because of the fear that a U.S. president could use it as a private army or to spy on citizens. Almost all of the 12,000 police forces in the U.S. are local. Their power is virtually absolute and often goes unchallenged. This situation creates a police culture that believes that it is above the law, an attitude that fosters abuse. Therefore, although citizens rely upon the police, they also mistrust them in the belief that informed criticism is the best way to correct misconduct, incompetence, and arbitrariness as well as to encourage a healthy police culture to do its job fairly.

Nietzsche, the Will to Power, and the Police. Nietzsche argued that the human "will to power" makes people seek power and control over others. Those who succeed in this struggle become the master class. They value courage, strength, pride, risk-taking, directness, and sports. Morality, or what is correct in their opinion, becomes associated with the traits possessed by the ruling elite. Morality, for the master class, is not a set of abstract principles.

There is also a slave morality that is based upon values such as humility, justice, self-denial, prudence, and altruism. The slave's morality is reactive; that is, whatever the master class values as good the slave defines as bad. Slaves reject the morality of the master class because they associate it with oppression, evil, and injustice, and they resent the power of the master class. From the slave morality comes not only the concept of justice but also those of guilt and conscience.

Police Culture and Brutality. Police have a unique culture that has its own internal values. When a young officer goes through training at a police academy, he or she typically has every intention of becoming an exemplary officer. Seasoned officers consider such young officers naive. They are ritually introduced to "real police work" by their field training officer. By custom, the training officer's first words to the rookie must be, "Forget everything they taught you at the Academy. This is the real world."

Police culture glorifies the visible symbol of police power: the gun. Target practice becomes a fetish for many officers. Citizens are dehumanized and may become viewed as targets or potential targets rather than human beings. Peer pressure encourages police to socialize together. This isolates them from average civilians and creates an insulated mentality. Most officers ride in patrol cars and spend their days racing from one distress call to another over a large area. This gives them a jaundiced view of citizens, because for eight hours a day the only citizens with whom they interact are either criminals or suspected criminals. In time, some officers begin to view all citizens as either criminals or suspects. They see themselves as besieged, beleaguered, and misunderstood. Out of this view develops the idea that it is "us" against "them." Some sadistic officers use this attitude to divert attention away from their misconduct and to increase group morale. A sense of common identity forms that is based on the degrading of outsiders. Police especially devalue outsiders whom they consider hostile. These people are considered more "them" than others. When stress develops between insiders and outsiders, violence is more likely to occur.

The police believe, understandably, that they are abused and called names often yet receive little money or status from society, despite the danger of their job. This resentment can lead to feelings of anger and powerlessness. One way to regain a sense of power is by exercising elemental power over other human beings. When making arrests, the desire for power may lead police to force suspects to restrict their movement or to stand where they are told to stand. Failure to obey may be swiftly met with violence in an effort to gain power and control. Once such violence starts, it can easily escalate out of control.

The police view themselves as a tight-knit, elite "thin blue line" that protects society from criminal chaos and lawlessness. They fear that they are losing the battle against crime and that a nationwide breakdown of ethical standards and morals forces them to close ranks with fellow officers by developing a cult of secrecy that they call the "code of silence." Confrontational attitudes develop, they claim, in self-defense. Whistleblowers are rare in this culture. Virtually everyone tries to be a "stand-up cop." In addition, in some departments, if an officer reports witnessing brutality carried out by a fellow officer, both officers are suspended without pay. This practice discourages officers from informing the department of misconduct and strengthens the "code of silence."

Police chiefs who make it clear that they respect the code of silence and will ignore charges of brutality leveled against police as long as there is peace and order on the street reinforce this culture and invite brutality. Police learn that they can speed in their cars when they are off duty. If they are stopped and merely show their badges, they are simply told to drive safely and released. A variety of professional courtesies that police extend to fellow officers soon makes them feel that they are "above the law." Officers are reluctant to arrest or even fine fellow police. For many police officers, "good" is whatever makes their jobs less dangerous and easier, even if it involves the unjust violation of others' rights.

By contrast, the majority of citizens believe that officers should protect the rights of citizens and uphold the law, whatever the cost. They reflect Nietzsche's slave morality, and to them it might be better to let a few criminals escape unpunished rather than unjustly accuse, harm, or kill even one innocent citizen. For the masses, justice is of the utmost importance, and if the exercise of justice inconveniences a few police officers or makes their jobs more difficult, then that is a price that must be paid to uphold fair play and protect the innocent.

The Rodney King Case. Thousands of cases of police brutality are filed annually, but the King case is unique because some of the events were captured on videotape. On March 3, 1991, the Los Angeles police stopped a twenty-four-year-old black male motorist named Rodney Glen King after a difficult and dangerous high speed (115 m.p.h.) car chase. Police ordered King to get out of his car, then several officers brutally assaulted King. Four officers in particular took turns clubbing, kicking, and shocking the unarmed King with Taser stun guns, while more than a other officers watched. The officers clubbed King at least fifty-six times, breaking his skull in nine places, breaking his leg, and inflicting many other injuries. Any one of the officers who stood by and watched this beating could have stepped in and stopped it, but none did. Each conformed to group norms and police culture by observing the code of silence while justice was miscarried.

In such a situation, a collective mind takes over and a mob mentality develops. Normal judgment, reasoning, and critical thinking are abandoned. This is made possible by the anonymity of the individual in the crowd. The notion of individual responsibility that normally restrains behavior is gone. Members of the group act rapidly on impulse. In a crowd, behavior gravitates to the lowest common level. Members focus upon what is different—"them." Nothing else matters, and the members attack the outsider. Bystanders who observe such violence and do nothing are in pain but often deny it and cover it up by justifying the violent behavior. Each act such as the King beating changes all who participate in it or witness it. Those who do the beating tend to grow more aggressive. The King beating could have been stopped if one officer had had the courage to defy police culture and call it off, but not a single officer came forward. These officers were prisoners of the master mentality. King became the embodiment of "them," and no officer dared betray "us" during a crisis. It would be King's word against theirs, and because they were all members of a secret society, they would blame the victim.

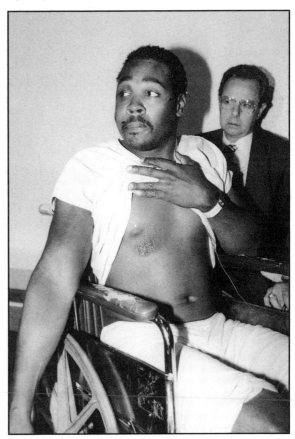

Rodney King displays one of the injuries he received as the result of being beaten by Los Angeles police officers. (AP/ Wide World Photos)

In most cases, an officer's word carries more weight than does a civilian's, as is indicated by the fact that in 1990 the Los Angeles Police Department received more than 2,500 complaints of police brutality, but fewer than fifty cases— less than one-half of one percent—went before a grand jury. In 1987, more than 8,000 complaints of police brutality were filed, yet not one officer broke the code of silence by offering incriminating evidence about another officer. In almost all cases, the victims of police brutality have previously violated some law that has brought them to the attention of the police. Therefore, their credibility is not easy to establish. King was a former convicted felon, even though that should not have mattered in the beating case. In reality, police who engage in misconduct have little to fear under the current system. Police can cover up misconduct by alleging that a suspect was "resisting arrest." King did not plan to press charges, for fear that it would be difficult to prove his case.

Little did either side know that George Holliday had captured more than seven minutes of the savage beating on videotape from his balcony. He sold the tape to television stations, and the beating was seen in millions of homes worldwide. There was definite evidence of police misconduct in this case. Because the arresting officers were white and King was African American, the case became very volatile, and attorney Warren Christopher was asked to head a commission that was established to investigate this case. The Christopher Commission listened to computerized tapes of police transmissions on the night that King was beaten and discovered that the officers were so confident that police culture would protect them that they recorded messages saying, "Capture him, beat him, and treat him like dirt," and "What, did you beat another guy?" Christopher was troubled by the officers' flagrant confidence that "nothing would be done" and that such brutality would be tolerated. Other messages recorded by the commission betrayed open contempt for racial and ethnic minorities and homosexuals. One message recorded during the King incident made reference to "gorillas in the mist," an obvious racial slur. Hospital nurses who treated King stated that the officers who beat him followed him to the hospital to threaten and tease him. These men were driven by the lust for power and control. They were firmly in the grip of Nietzsche's master morality and of the worst elements of police culture.

In the face of irrefutable evidence of police misconduct and brutality, the Christopher Commission sided with the slave morality and called for justice. It noted that, although the problem of police brutality is widespread, a handful of "problem officers" create most incidents. To settle police brutality claims against the city of Los Angeles between 1970 and 1980, the city paid more than $65 million in damages, and the tension created within communities by these cases caused even greater damage. Riots erupted following the trials of the officers who beat Rodney King. These riots destroyed billions of dollars worth of property and cost dozens of people their lives. Society cannot afford continued police brutality. The Christopher Commission was right: the concern for justice must override all other concerns.

Immanuel Kant would have loved this appeal to principle, even though Nietzsche would have been appalled. Unless or until the values cherished by police culture and those embraced by civilian culture are more closely aligned by establishing civilian review boards for police departments and rewarding police for preventing crimes through community service programs, then these two value systems will clash, and the result may too often be police brutality. In the absence of curbs on police power, a healthy mistrust of the police can only make them less brutal and more efficient, effective, and determined to do right for the citizens who employ them. A Nietzschean analysis of police brutality makes this clear. —*Dallas L. Browne*

See also Abuse; Criminal punishment; Justice; Professional ethics; Violence.

BIBLIOGRAPHY
Barker, Thomas, and David L. Carter. *Police Deviance.* 2d ed. Cincinnati, Ohio: Anderson, 1991.
Brenner, Robert N., and Marjorie Kravitz, eds. *A Community Concern: Police Use of Deadly Force.* Washington, D.C.: United States Department of Justice, 1979.
Donner, Frank. *Protectors of Privilege: Red Squads and Police Repression in Urban America.* Berkeley: University of California Press, 1990.
Dudley, William, ed. *Police Brutality.* San Diego: D. L. Bender, 1991.
Elliston, Frederick, and Michael Feldberg, eds. *Moral Issues in Police Work.* Totowa, N.J.: Rowman & Allen, 1985.
Lundman, Richard J., ed. *Police Behavior: A Sociological Perspective.* New York: Oxford University Press, 1980.
Nietzsche, Friedrich. *Beyond Good and Evil.* Translated by R. J. Hollingdale. New York: Penguin Books, 1990.
_____. *The Genealogy of Morals.* Translated by Horace B. Samuel. New York: Macmillan, 1924.
Skolnick, Jerome H., and James J. Fyfe. *Above the Law: Police and the Excessive Use of Force.* New York: Free Press, 1993.
Stratton, John G. *Police Passages.* Manhattan Beach, Calif.: Glennon, 1984.

Political correctness

TYPE OF ETHICS: Politico-economic ethics
DATE: Mid- to late 1960's; reapplied in 1990's
ASSOCIATED WITH: Columnists, political commentators, and professors with a variety of political perspectives
DEFINITION: A hegemony of orthodox ideas about race and gender; the intolerant treatment of those who differ with that orthodoxy
SIGNIFICANCE: An example of the way in which an ethical judgment of what is desirable behavior and thought can be used to justify the suppression of alternative viewpoints

Political correctness, or PC, is a pejorative term used to describe a phenomenon particularly prevalent in American universities in which those who claim to seek a more pluralistic and equitable society attempt to suppress traditional views about ethnic minorities, women, and homosexuals in favor of more radical ones. Among the ideas discredited by the politically correct are suggestions that gender roles have been in any way mutually agreed upon or have yielded mutual benefits, that homosexuality may be morally wrong or physically unnatural, and that the preferential treatment of minorities

EXAMPLES OF THE POLITICALLY CORRECT LEXICON	
Politically Incorrect Terms	**Politically Correct Terms**
Negro, black	African American
Indian	Native American, American Indian
Oriental	Asian American
Mexican American	Chicano/Chicana, Latino/Latina
colored people	people of color
homosexual	gay or lesbian
disabled	differently abled
handicapped	physically challenged
reverse racism	ethnocentric revitalization
reverse discrimination	affirmative action

through affirmative action is an unjust means of attaining equity. Also subject to censure are traditional designations for minority and other groups that have not been chosen by those groups. Political correctness is enforced by threats of expulsion and censure, by mandatory "sensitivity sessions" for students, and by codes that restrict free speech.

See also Academic freedom.

Political liberty

TYPE OF ETHICS: Politico-economic ethics
DATE: Coined 1832
ASSOCIATED WITH: Political theorists, especially John Stuart Mill and the utilitarian movement of the nineteenth century
DEFINITION: A human state of being distinguished by the absence of coercion or constraint imposed on one by another individual or by the society of which one is a member; in such a state, one is neither prevented from acting as one would choose nor compelled to act otherwise than one would choose
SIGNIFICANCE: Encompasses the basic democratic freedoms, such as freedom of speech, and is fundamental to the ethical implications of theories of social justice

As defined above, "political liberty" is to be conceived of as a negative freedom—that is, a freedom *from* external coercion or constraint. It is this conception of political liberty that has been fundamental to the tradition of such Western ideas as individualism and liberalism in both political philosophy and political theory. The classic expression of this conception of political liberty is John Stuart Mill's *On Liberty* (1859).

In practice, however, political liberty almost always refers to a positive freedom—that is, a freedom *of* some specific kind of good or some specific type of activity. Examples of the latter include some of the basic democratic liberties: freedom of thought, freedom of expression, freedom of as-

sembly, freedom of religious pursuits, freedom of political participation, and so forth; freedom of property acquisition and disposal is an example of the former. Although this second conception of political liberty is dependent on the initial one, every particular freedom that can be associated with this positive conception involves some form of individual or social activity with respect to which the right to *choose on one's own* is acknowledged as both socially and morally significant.

It is important not to confuse the two very different ideas of human abilities and political liberties. To conflate what one *can* do with what one is *at liberty* to do makes little or no sense. The fact that a member of a particular society is unable to vote on election day because of, for example, major medical surgery is irrelevant to whether that same individual, as a member of that society who satisfies all voting eligibility requirements, is at liberty to vote. In other words, just because this individual was unable to vote and, in fact, did not vote does not in any way mean that this individual was not free to vote. This same irrelevancy between what one can do and what one is at liberty to do also holds true for a member of a particular society who is, in fact, able to vote, but who is not allowed to vote merely because this individual happens to be a member of a particular segment of the society each of the members of which is systematically prohibited from voting. That is, just because this individual was not at liberty to vote—that is, not allowed to vote—does not in any way mean that this individual was not able to vote. In neither of these cases does one's ability (or lack thereof) to vote have anything to do with one's freedom (or lack thereof) to vote.

Fundamentally, political liberty must be construed as a balance between the exercise of authority of the society over its members, on the one hand, and the liberty of choice and of effectual action that individual members of the society are allowed to exercise, on the other. That is, individual liberty and governmental authority are the two sides of the same political coin; the more there is of either one, the less there must be of the other. Within this framework, questions of conflict concerning the political liberties of the individual, justice, and the well-being of the society as a whole naturally arise.

In political theory, both the kinds of particular political liberties and the degree to which each ought to be acknowledged by the government to be granted to individuals depend upon a whole host of factors, such as one's conception of both human nature and human rationality, one's conception of the relationship between an individual's right to autonomy and a sense of the appropriate degree of latitude to be granted to governmental authority, and one's conception of what ought to be the purpose of both the government itself and its social and political institutions (for example, whether the fundamental reason for the very existence of government and its social and political institutions is to promote human happiness or satisfaction; to provide for the peace, security, and any or all associated rights of each member of the society; or to provide for the development in each member of the society of some particular conception of human excellence).

In practice, too, both the kinds of particular political liberties and the degree of which each ought to be acknowledged by the government to be granted to individuals depend upon a vast array of circumstances, not the least of which is the form of government that has been established. For example, the differences between both the number and the extent of political liberties granted to individuals under a totalitarian régime as compared to a democracy are usually obvious.

Even in representative democracies according to which individual members of the society are allowed a wide latitude of autonomy, however, it is possible for political leaders to engage in a more insidious type of political coercion than that typically found in totalitarian societies. In order for a democracy to be effective, its individuals need access to more, rather than less, and accurate, rather than inaccurate, information relevant to political decision making. To the extent that those in positions of political power, presumably for reasons of self-interest, deny to members of the society the quantity and quality of information necessary to well-informed political decision making (for example, through manipulation of the media of communication and distortion or denial of relevant information), however, to precisely that extent is that democracy being undermined and to precisely that extent are the members of such a society being denied their political liberties. In the final analysis, political liberty means liberty of choice and of effectual action; consequently, to the extent that this insidious type of political coercion is perpetrated against the members of such a society, the menu of viable options available to them is artificially diminished, which, in turn, diminishes their freedom both of choice and of effectual action, and ultimately denies them at least some of their political liberties.

—*Stephen C. Taylor*

See also Freedom and liberty; Libertarianism; Mill, John Stuart; *On Liberty*; Politics; Power.

BIBLIOGRAPHY

Berlin, Isaiah, ed. *Two Concepts of Liberty*. Oxford, England: Clarendon Press, 1958; reprinted in *Four Essays on Liberty*. Oxford, England: Oxford University Press, 1969.

Griffiths, A. Phillips, ed. *Of Liberty*. Cambridge, England: Cambridge University Press, 1983.

Mill, John Stuart. *On Liberty* (1859); reprinted in *Essays on Ethics, Religion and Society*. Vol. 10 in *Collected Works*, edited by J. M. Robson. Toronto, Canada: University of Toronto Press, 1969.

Pelczynski, Z. B., and John Gray, eds. *Conceptions of Liberty in Political Philosophy*. London: Athlone Press, 1984.

Raphael, D. D. *Problems of Political Philosophy*. 2d rev. ed. London: Macmillan Education, 1990. See especially Chapter 3.

Ryan, Alan, ed. *The Idea of Freedom*. Oxford, England: Oxford University Press, 1979.

Political realism

TYPE OF ETHICS: Politico-economic ethics
DATE: Articulated in 1513
ASSOCIATED WITH: The sixteenth century Italian Renaissance politician Niccolò Machiavelli, author of *The Prince*, a book of advice for rulers
DEFINITION: The view that leaders of nations should act in their own best interests in order to gain and maintain power
SIGNIFICANCE: Raises the question of whether governments have a responsibility to behave ethically toward their citizens and toward other countries

Critics of political realism say that a leader who is a political realist is likely to be a tyrant who is uninterested in the welfare of the citizens of her or his own nation and other nations. Such a leader is also likely to gain support by using political rhetoric to trick others into believing that her or his actions do serve their interests. Such a leader abdicates the responsibilities of considering the interests of others and telling them the truth. Defenders of political realism say that a realistic reading of history shows that practicality rather than ethics is the principle guiding the behavior of governments and leaders. For example, leaders have always used cruelty in order to make people fear and obey them. Some defenders of political realism say that ethics are simply not relevant to government and that behaving ethically would hamper a leader's ability to get things done. Other defenders say that political realists follow a competitive ethic, wherein those who are best at the games of power are the most successful leaders.

See also Machiavellian ethics; Realpolitik.

Politics

TYPE OF ETHICS: Politico-economic ethics
DATE: 600 B.C.E. to present
DEFINITION: The art of governing
SIGNIFICANCE: Makes explicit the practical social implications of ethical principles

The standard view of politics' relation to ethics is captured in H. B. Acton's famous aphorism: "Power tends to corrupt, and absolute power corrupts absolutely." The first part of Lord Acton's aphorism identifies a danger inherent in the political process. Since political ends can be achieved only by the exercise of power, power is concentrated in the hands of politicians. Unfortunately, as much of history illustrates, politicians have often diverted power away from its proper use, despite the institution of checks and balances to prevent abuses.

The second part of Acton's aphorism makes the more cynical claim that the political process is inherently immoral. Since power is the ability to do work, however, it follows from that claim that the ability to do work is immoral. From this conclusion follows the odd conclusion that only the completely impotent are moral. The conclusion is odd because it creates a paradox: While most people think that governments do perform valuable functions, Acton's aphorism would lead one to believe that governments are immoral to the extent they are able to perform those functions.

This paradox indicates that the relationship between ethics and the political process involves more than simply the existence or nonexistence of power. Power is central to government, but the questions of exactly how much and what types of power governments should have and to what ends that power should be put have generated a number of political theories. Many of those theories have been put into practice, and although the political arena contains many instances of hypocrisy, lying, disloyalty, and thievery, there is evidence that in both theory and practice politics has been and continues to be influenced greatly by ethics.

The Influence of Ethics. Aside from the amount of corruption that exists in governments, part of the difficulty in seeing the influence of ethics is the diversity of opinions about what in fact is ethical. Debates exist about whether morality is essentially religious or secular, relative or universal, altruistic or egoistic. Such differences of opinion make it easy for those on one side of a debate to see those on the other as immoral. Another part of the difficulty is that even those who agree about what is ethical may disagree about the proper methods to be used to achieve it. Some may believe that the end justifies the means—that is, that it is justifiable to lie to a rival politician if doing so achieves a good goal—while other advocates of the same end may reject that premise.

The complex relationship between ethics and politics can be captured in three pairs of related questions: questions of ends (What is good? What does this politician think is good?); questions of means (Does the end justify the means? Does this politician think the end justifies the means?); and questions of integrity (Is this politician or system practicing what is good? Is this politician or system practicing what he, she, or it thinks is good?). A judgment about the influence of ethics on politics is a result of answers to these questions.

Ethics and Government. Government is a social institution that formulates and enforces rules. In both the content of its rules and its method of enforcing them, government is unique. Other social institutions formulate rules, but the rules that they formulate apply only to those who participate in that institution. For example, a baseball league is a social institution that formulates rules, but its rules apply only to those who play in the baseball league. A government's rules, by contrast, apply to all members of the society. Other social institutions also enforce their rules, but the maximum penalty for violating a rule is to be disassociated from the institution. If, for example, one violates the rules of baseball, one may be kicked off the team. A government, by contrast, is the only social institution that enforces its rule by the use of physical force. If one violates a government's rules, it

may confiscate one's property, restrict one's liberty, or even kill one.

Since government is the only social institution that makes universal rules that are backed up by the use of physical force, the content of those rules is of special importance. What rules are so important that everyone should follow them? What rules are so important that if they are violated the drastic resort of physical force is appropriate?

The only way to answer these questions is by appealing to ethics. Politics, accordingly, is an institutionalization of an ethics. This fact is easier to recognize in political theories: Plato, Thomas Hobbes, and John Locke, for example, appeal to (conflicting) ethical principles and moral evaluations of human nature in defending their political theories. Despite corruption, however, most political practice also illustrates the application of ethics.

Three Historical Examples. The influence of ethics on political practice can be seen in the three systems that dominated the twentieth century: Marxism (or international socialism), fascism (or National Socialism), and capitalism (or constitutional democracy). Each system has had enormous practical influence on political theory and practice, and each puts into practice a set of explicit principles that its advocates believe to be moral.

Collectivism. Marxism and fascism are versions of collectivism. Collectivism defines morality socially, holding that the welfare of the group is primary and, accordingly, that individual interests are subordinate to those of the group. Collectivists admonish individuals not to be self-interested; that is, not to put their personal interests above group interests but to sacrifice their interests for the welfare of the group.

Depending on how the group is defined, versions of collectivism arise. Some versions hold that the family is the proper group and that individuals should devote their lives to serving their families. Other versions hold that the group to which individuals should sacrifice is the tribe, the nation, the race, the working class, or the ecosystem. The common denominator in all these versions of collectivism is that individuals are not ends in themselves.

Largely through the influence of G. W. F. Hegel (1770-1831), collectivism dominated nineteenth century German philosophy. The two most prominent versions of collectivism to arise after Hegel were Marxism and fascism.

Marxism. "From each according to his ability, to each according to his need." Marx's slogan, from his *Critique of the Gotha Program*, is the clearest statement of the fundamental ethical principle of his version of collectivism. According to the principle, individuals are not ends in themselves. They should see themselves as servants of the needs of others, and they should devote their lives to serving others' needs to the best of their ability. As long as someone has an unfulfilled need and I, for example, have the ability to fill it, I have a duty to sacrifice my personal interests and devote myself to fulfilling that need. To the extent that I shirk my duty, I am acting unethically. To the extent that the society I live in allows me to shirk my duty, the society is unethical.

Marx noted that Western societies often pay lip service to altruistic principles; in practice, however, they encourage the pursuit of self-interest, the profit motive, and capitalism. What is needed to make society ethical, Marx argued, is a radical shift away from the individual to the collective, from the private to the social.

In defining "social," Marx takes the broadest possible view. Society, he argued, should not be conceived along familial, racial, religious, or ethnic lines. If, for example, I define the moral society racially, then I will see myself as a servant of my race; if service to my race is of the highest moral significance, then I will view members of other races as having less moral significance. Such attitudes can only foster racial conflict. If I define myself as an individual, then I will hold my own interests to be of the highest significance, but this will lead me into conflict with other individuals and will lead to a competitive society. To prevent these conflicts, Marx argued, individuals must learn not only to define themselves primarily as social, not individual, beings but also to conceive of society as including the entire human race. Only then, Marx believed, would socialism be realized. Marxism, accordingly, defends socialism by appealing to collectivist ethical principles, which it hopes to apply internationally.

Fascism. In the twentieth century, "fascism" was the name adopted by a group of Italians to designate their new version of socialism. The leader of this group, Benito Mussolini, had for many years been a Marxist socialist before deciding that substituting "the Italian people" for "the working class" would give socialist ideas a better chance of success in Italy, for then they would be able to draw upon the nationalistic loyalty of most Italians. "Fascism" also labels the political system of Germany during the 1930's and 1940's, under Adolf Hitler's National Socialism. In both countries, fascists applied collectivist ethical principles to politics. The core doctrine was expressed clearly by Alfred Rocco, a leading Italian fascist. Fascism stresses, he said, "the necessity, for which the older doctrines make little allowance, of sacrifice, even up to the total immolation of individuals, in behalf of society. . . . For Liberalism [i.e., individualism], the individual is the end and society the means; nor is it conceivable that the individual, considered in the dignity of an ultimate finality, be lowered to mere instrumentality. For Fascism, society is the end, individuals the means, and its whole life consists in using individuals as instruments for its social ends."

In their insistence upon the morality of collectivism, the fascists agreed with the Marxists. "There is more that binds us to Bolshevism [the dominant Russian version of Marxism] than separates us from it," declared Hitler. Like the Marxists, the Italian and German fascists believed that capitalism was evil because of its individualism, its tolerance of the profit motive, and its emphasis on pursuing private interests. Hitler defined National Socialism as "idealism," as the system in which each individual "willingly subordinates his own ego to the life of the community and, if the hour demands it, even sacrifices it."

The fascists disagreed with the Marxists about some important points. While the Marxists defined the moral community internationally and economically, the fascists defined it nationally and racially. While the Marxists attacked all religions, the fascists focused their attacks almost exclusively on Judaism. Despite these differences, the fundamental thesis of Marxism and fascism is the same: Both have the same collectivist view of the relationship between the individual and the society. Both Marxists and fascists could accept the following statement from *Mein Kampf*: "each activity and each need of the individual will be regulated by the party as the representative of the general good."

By the mid-1930's, years before the beginning of World War II, the National Socialists had put into practice many standard socialist economic policies. Medicine was socialized, a modern welfare system was instituted, and the goal of complete equality of income was being sought. German industrial production was regulated and directed by the central government; while owners maintained legal possession of their enterprises, government bureaucrats set production goals and controlled wages, prices, and interest rates. Additionally, since private interests were not to be trusted to serve the public good, the Reichskulturkammer instituted a sweeping censorship covering what was taught in schools, what books were published, and what appeared on radio and in films, plays, and newspapers. The important point is that all these policies were instituted by appealing to collectivist ethical principles: *Gemeinnutz vor Eigennutz!* ("The common interest before self-interest") was the standard slogan justifying Nazi policies.

Since socialism requires that individuals subordinate their private interests to the good of the group, and since under Hitler the designated group was the German nation, "National Socialism" was an appropriate name for Hitler's political program.

It is sometimes argued that dictators such as Lenin and Stalin in the Soviet Union and Hitler and Mussolini in Germany and Italy were simply cynical power seekers who mouthed collectivist and socialist slogans without really believing them, but this idea is not plausible. If one is young, cynical, and seeking power, the most likely route to power is by infiltrating the established, already-powerful political parties (or the military). The least likely route to power is to join a fringe political group, since fringe groups rarely have any influence. Fringe groups attract only people who are committed to the causes for which the group stands. Yet the Communist and National Socialist Parties were, when Lenin, Stalin, and Hitler joined them, tiny and far from power. Therefore, it is likely that these men believed in the principles that they preached.

While collectivist ideas were most influential in eastern Europe, Italy, and later in Asia, they also had an impact in the West. In the late nineteenth and early twentieth centuries, it was common for intelligent American and English students to spend some time studying in Germany, which was at the time the world's leading intellectual nation. While in Germany, the students were naturally exposed to the latest collectivist theories. As Friedrich Hayek noted, "Many a university teacher during the 1930's has seen English and American students return from the Continent uncertain whether they were communists or Nazis and certain only that they hated Western liberal civilization."

Individualism and Capitalism. In the West, however, classical liberal ideas had retained a strong hold. Classical liberalism emphasizes the importance of the individual and tends to see social institutions as valuable to the extent that they leave individuals free to pursue their values. Individuals are ends in themselves, according to this view, and not means to the ends of other individuals or to groups.

By deemphasizing or rejecting collectivism, individualists tend to reject or at least be suspicious of any claims upon the individual to sacrifice life, liberty, or well-being. In politics, this individualist ethic leads to the view that the role of the government is not to exact sacrifices from individuals to serve a collective good, but to protect the lives and liberties of individuals as they pursue their personal conceptions of the good life. In economics, individualists tend to advocate a free market, since a free market decentralizes political power, leaving investment, buying, and selling decisions in the hands of private individuals. In this way, advocates of capitalism's limited government and free markets have tended to appeal to individualist ethical principles in support of their political policies.

Conclusion. Ethics has had a broad influence in the history of modern and contemporary politics. Many conflicting ethical theories have contributed to that influence, but in terms of their influence on modern and contemporary political affairs those ethical theories fall into two major categories: individualist and collectivist. The moral slogan of individualism, "Every individual is an end in himself," stands in contrast to the moral slogan of collectivism, "From each according to his ability, to each according to his need." The principle of individualism provides moral support for capitalism; the principle of collectivism provides moral support for socialism.

Historically, it can be seen that to the extent that the politicians in power were committed to an ethic that holds individual interests to be immoral or at least subordinate to collective interests, they believed it to be improper to leave economic and political power in private hands. Accordingly, their ethics dictated that power must be concentrated in public hands, and therefore a centralization of political and economic power resulted.

By contrast, to the extent that the politicians in power were committed to an ethic that holds individuals' pursuits of their own interests to be moral, then the politicians believed it to be proper to leave power in hands of those private individuals and to see their role as politicians as secondary and supportive. Accordingly, their ethics dictated that power must not be concentrated in public hands, and therefore a decentralization of political and economic power resulted. —*Stephen R. C. Hicks*

See also Capitalism; Communism; Fascism; Marxism.

BIBLIOGRAPHY

Hitler, Adolf. *Mein Kampf.* Translated by Ralph Manheim. Boston: Houghton Mifflin, 1971. The original manifesto of National Socialism. Hitler is very explicit about the collectivist principles of ethics upon which National Socialism depends.

Macchiavelli, Niccolò. *The Prince.* New York: Knopf, 1992. A classic work in the "cynical" tradition of ethics and politics. The author provides practical guidance to politicians by advocating the use of immoral methods to achieve and maintain power.

Marx, Karl, and Friedrich Engels. *The Communist Manifesto.* New York: Bantam, 1992. A clear and brief survey of the principles of communism, with special emphasis on what Marx and Engels see as the moral failings of capitalism.

Peikoff, Leonard. *The Ominous Parallels.* New York: Stein & Day, 1982. A clear and detailed exposition of the philosophical and historical roots of German National Socialism.

Rand, Ayn. "What Is Capitalism?" In *Capitalism: The Unknown Ideal.* New York: New American Library, 1966. A series of essays by Rand and others defending capitalism on moral grounds.

Sterba, James P. *How to Make People Just.* Totowa, N.J.: Rowman & Littlefield, 1988. An introductory survey of a broad range of political theories, showing the ethical presuppositions of each. The author also defends a moderate version of socialism.

Poll tax

TYPE OF ETHICS: Civil rights

DATE: Abolished in the United States in 1964

ASSOCIATED WITH: Voting rights; Twenty-fourth Amendment

DEFINITION: A poll tax is a form of capitation, or head tax, which people must pay before being allowed to vote

SIGNIFICANCE: Poll taxes raise the ethical questions of whether it is proper to make people pay for the right of voting and whether such taxes disfranchise the poor

Poll taxes existed in the United States from the earliest colonial times. They were usually quite small and did not act to discourage many people from voting. In the years following the Civil War, the poll tax system was refined in the Southern states for the purpose of disfranchising black voters. The tax remained small, but it had to be paid for every election in which the potential voter might have voted. This tax effectively disfranchised nearly all black voters. Because the election laws in the United States are made by state governments, a constitutional amendment was needed to do away with poll taxes. In 1964, the Twenty-fourth Amendment abolished the payment of such taxes as a condition for voting in federal elections.

See also Constitution, U.S.; Suffrage.

Pollution

TYPE OF ETHICS: Environmental ethics
DEFINITION: Environmental contamination resulting from human processes
SIGNIFICANCE: Pollution's causes and effects both have ethical components

Further Definition. Pollution must be viewed in the light of natural versus human-based events. A natural event is part of the fundamental cycle of Earth processes that maintain a balance of building up and wearing down, of destruction and recovery. A volcano may spew tons of ash into the atmosphere and darken the sky so much that weather patterns are changed. Mudflows precipitated by loose debris and rapidly melting glaciers clog waterways on which nearby ecosystems rely. Lava kills everything in its path. Despite these drastic, destructive changes, natural processes will clear the air to reestablish customary weather patterns, will create more glaciers whose runoff will establish new river ecosystems, and will produce fertile soils to support life in areas where it was destroyed.

Pollution is the introduction of agents by humans into the environment in quantities that disrupt the balance of natural processes. Its possible detrimental effect on human life is not part of pollution's definition. Neither are human ignorance or lack of foresight, which may greatly influence the course and severity of pollution.

Ethics is a dimension specific to pollution that is not characteristic of natural processes. Humankind has the intellectual capacity to affect its course, and is itself affected morally by pollution's existence.

Pollution started when humans began manipulating the environment. Although pollution is usually characterized as chemicals or by-products of synthetic processes, this characterization is not entirely accurate. Waste from herds of domestic animals, for example, is a natural product, but it causes many environmental problems. Introducing aggressive nonnative species into an established ecosystem is also pollution, since such species frequently overwhelm the natural system's balance and displace native species. It has even been asserted that the human species itself is a pollutant, since it is both an aggressive species and nonnative to many habitats that it occupies and exploits.

In considering pollution created by manufacturing and daily human activities, there is no uncontaminated ecosystem. Even beyond Earth's known biosphere, humankind sends objects into outer space, and those that become defunct or were never intended to return are dubbed "space junk." Invisible pollutants cannot be overlooked. Various types of synthesized and concentrated radiation—from ultra-low-frequency sound waves to sonic booms; from artificial lighting in classrooms, offices, and along highways to nuclear radioactivity—bombard and vibrate the molecules of the land, the air, and the inhabitants. As a result of all these different contaminants, plant and animal species suffer from aborted embryos, deformed offspring, poor health, shortened lives, and death. Among those suffering is the human species.

History. Since pollution has an ethical dimension, why has humanity not exercised its moral strength in preventing or halting it?

Part of the answer is ignorance. It is not until environmental damage is recognized—usually by detecting injury to some species of plant or animal—that humankind realizes that pollution has occurred.

When gasoline-powered cars were introduced, it never occurred to proponents of modern transportation that the admittedly malodorous exhaust could possibly place large numbers of people in dire respiratory straits, let alone cause Earth to face global warming. Even when auto exhaust was recognized as a major contributor to the unsightly haze of smog, scientists had not yet developed sensing and testing equipment that would give them knowledge of the scope of the air pollution problem.

Another reason that humankind's moral capacity has not been a force in preventing pollution is lack of foresight. This issue illustrates two kinds of humanity's arrogance. Many people assume that humankind has the power and intelligence to solve every problem it recognizes. Many people also have the unrealistic, erroneous belief that there are segments of society that cannot be affected by the dangers that everyone else faces.

When nuclear power plants were developed, the designers were aware that lethal by-products would be generated, and planners incorporated holding ponds and other storage areas in the building complexes. They had not yet developed any means for the safe disposal of nuclear waste, assuming that they would be able to do so as necessary at some future date. Since these designers recognized most of the possible problems of such facilities, did they assume that they were invulnerable to those problems?

Another factor in the pollution situation is the human population's exponential growth. The relationship between technological development and increased human survival has so far been linked in an endless circle. If the human population was only one percent of what it is now, with a corresponding ratio of contaminants in the environment, pollution would be no less real, though it might not seem as serious.

Discussion. The ethics of the survival of life on Earth are shaped by the immediate danger presented by environmental pollution. Most people presume that the survival of the human species is the most important issue. Some reject this conclusion as blatant, homocentric speciesism and argue that the survival of human life is inherently no more urgent or legitimate than the survival of any other species.

Many people realize, without making claims for the necessity of human survival, that it is dependent on uncountable plant and animal species surviving and upon an environment unsullied enough to support them. All these considerations are based on human acceptance of responsibility for the future. Is humankind responsible for the future? Should humankind assume any responsibility for it?

Perhaps human arrogance causes humankind to presume that such a responsibility exists. Could it be that human history is merely a natural part of evolution on earth? Are humankind's effects on the environment part of the natural scheme of things to which the environment will eventually adapt? Will that adaptation include mass extinctions and the subsequent development of other life forms capable of tolerating the changes that humankind has wrought?

Is humankind responsible for all future generations of life? Is humankind morally liable for the future of Earth itself? If humankind does accept any of these responsibilities, what are the exigent considerations?

Given the history of discovering pollution by hindsight, it would seem logical that humankind should not introduce any further agents, unknown or known, into the environment. If additional contamination by known pollutants is to be stopped, it cannot be done without accepting the moral consequences of the human misery and death that will follow as a result of the loss of jobs and the decreased availability and less efficient distribution of food and other human necessities.

As with most moral issues, the pollution dilemma has no easy answers. Yet if humankind is to persist, there can be no avoiding the ethical considerations involved in a possible solution to the problems of pollution. —*Marcella T. Joy*

See also Earth, human relations to; Environmental ethics; Future-oriented ethics; Gaia; Nature, rights of; Responsibility; *Silent Spring*; Sociobiology; State of nature; Technology.

BIBLIOGRAPHY

Allsopp, Bruce. *Ecological Morality.* London: Frederick Muller, 1972.

Partride, Ernest, ed. *Responsibilities to Future Generations: Environmental Ethics.* Buffalo, N.Y.: Prometheus Books, 1981.

Rolston, Holmes, III. *Environmental Ethics: Duties to and Values in the Natural World.* Philadelphia: Temple University Press, 1988.

Scherer, Donald, ed. *Upstream/Downstream: Issues in Environmental Ethics.* Philadelphia: Temple University Press, 1990.

Silver, Cheryl Simon, with Ruth DeFries. *One Earth, One Future: Our Changing Global Environment.* Washington, D.C.: National Academy Press, 1990.

Poona Pact

TYPE OF ETHICS: Civil rights
DATE: September 25, 1932
ASSOCIATED WITH: Mohandas Karamchand Gandhi

DEFINITION: A compromise measure that rescinded the Communal Award, thereby guaranteeing joint legal representation with the general population to the Untouchables, the lowest-status group of people in India, who previously had been represented only as a separate group

SIGNIFICANCE: The Poona Pact drew attention to the plight of the Untouchables, whose lives were (and are) severely circumscribed by the strictures of the Hindu caste system, in which they are considered "outcastes" (members of no caste) who are vile and impure

The Independence Movement in India accelerated when Mohandas Karamchand Gandhi returned from South Africa to India in 1915 and brought with him the weapon of *satyagraha*, or "truth force." He had developed satyagraha to protest nonviolently the Boers' refusal to recognize the validity of traditional Indian marriages. He also used moral force to attempt to end the oppression of East Indians by the South African white minority government. Gandhi joined the Indian National Congress, a Hindu-dominated independence movement, and convinced the organization to join forces with Mohammed Ali Jinnah, whose Muslim League also wanted independence for all of India under a policy that Jinnah labeled *khilafat*. Gandhi persuaded both groups to boycott British-made products, to strike, and to engage in a general policy of noncooperation with Britain. The British initially responded with force to suppress this movement. In 1932, when this response failed, British prime minister Ramsay MacDonald announced constitutional proposals known as the Communal Award, which were viewed as conciliatory measures.

The Communal Award provided for separate electorates for Muslims, Europeans, Anglo-Indians, Sikhs, Christians, upper-caste Hindu Indians, and Untouchables. For several thousand years Hindus have been divided into four major castes. Each caste performs specific jobs that its members monopolize. Members of a caste tend to marry within their caste. The *brāhmins*, who are considered the highest caste, tend to be priests, rulers, landowners, and intellectuals. At the very bottom of this social hierarchy are the Untouchables. They are outcastes who are considered so low and vile that to touch them pollutes a person. They are stigmatized, held in contempt, discriminated against, and assigned the least desirable work, housing, and food.

Gandhi believed that the British were using the classic strategy of "divide and rule," viewing the attempt to segregate Untouchable voters in the Communal Award as a bid to divide the Hindu community and to grant power to either the Muslim or the European minority. Either scenario would have fragmented the independence movement and delayed independence. Gandhi believed that communal separatism could be avoided if a secular government were created. Gandhi vowed to fast until he died unless the Communal Award's establishment of separate electorates for various classes of Indian society was rescinded. Gandhi was a *vaiśya* (a member of the merchant caste); therefore, his vow to resist, with his life if necessary, segregating Untouchables on a separate election roll was revolutionary. No member of a privileged caste had ever proposed such an act. Gandhi's action threatened the caste-based system of segregation, discrimination, and exclusive privilege. He fasted until separate representation for Untouchables was rescinded. The key to the victory was Indian unity, which Gandhi forged through the "Poona Pact." By means of this pact, the entire Hindu community voted on each candidate. As a result, Untouchables were also guaranteed their fair share of seats in schools and representation throughout Indian society.

For decades, Britain had denied colonial subjects the right of self-determination on the grounds that they were racially and mentally inferior, and thus incapable of enlightened self-rule. Gandhi's Poona Pact, coupled with his noncompliance campaign, constituted a direct challenge to the colonial order. Both actions assumed that all people had certain basic rights, and that assumption defied the British notion of native inferiority. Gandhi was able to unite Muslims and Hindus by appealing to the Hindu doctrine that each individual must find his or her own path to God. Gandhi also effectively utilized the Muslim tradition of tolerance for neighbors who practiced different religions, as long as peace was maintained. This appealed to Jinnah and the Muslim community, who wanted Pan-Indian unity. Although Gandhi did not wish to abolish the caste system entirely, because it had so thoroughly permeated Indian society, his efforts on behalf of the Untouchables pointed out the unfairness of the concept of untouchability.

See also Bigotry; Caste system, Hindu; Gandhi, Mohandas Karamchand; Human rights

Population control

Type of ethics: Environmental ethics

Dates: From antiquity; implemented by government in 1952

Definition: Population control is an attempt to limit human population by various means

Significance: Attempts to limit population growth to prevent the population from depleting the earth's limited resources and to improve the quality of life worldwide

The human population, like that of other creatures, is limited in growth by its biotic potential, the maximum rate at which a species can produce offspring given unlimited resources and ideal environmental conditions. At this rate of growth, the population would grow slowly only to increase rapidly to produce an exponential curve. Neither humans nor any other species in a given ecosystem can indefinitely grow at their biotic potential, since one or more factors always act as limiting agents. The maximum population size an ecosystem can support indefinitely under a given set of environmental conditions is called that ecosystem's carrying capacity.

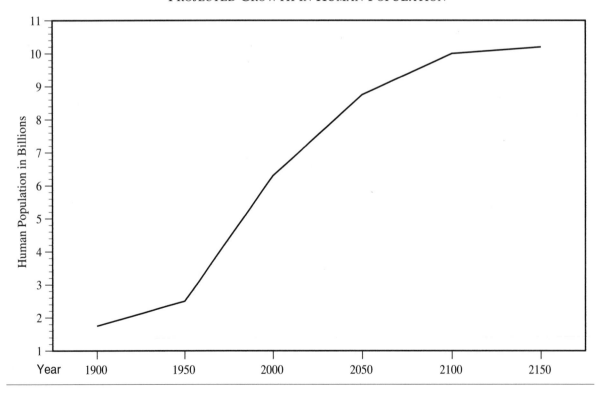

PROJECTED GROWTH IN HUMAN POPULATION

Growth Potential. Human population has continued to grow as Earth's carrying capacity for humans has been extended as a result of human cleverness, technological and social adaptations, and other forms of cultural evolution. People have altered their ecological niche by increasing food production, controlling disease, and using large amounts of energy and material resources to make habitable those parts of the world that are normally not so.

Observers believe a wide range of populations is possible. Some observers believe that people have already gone beyond the carrying capacity point at which all the earth's inhabitants can be fed, sheltered, and supported. Estimates on the low end of population are that only 1.2 billion people can be supported to U.S. dietary standards and only 600 million at the U.S. rate of energy consumption. These numbers are likely low, since the U.S. rate of food and energy use is high. The higher estimate for human carrying capacity is 45 billion people on a diet similar to U.S. dietary standards, made possible by cultivating all available land, using nuclear power for energy, and mining much of the earth's crust to a depth of 1.6 kilometers for resources. An even higher estimate for human carrying capacity is 157 billion if diets are based solely on grains.

The human population continues to grow, regardless of what the carrying capacity may be. The world population doubles every thirty-five years at growth rates of the 1970's and 1980's. If the population were controlled to zero population growth, the world population would continue to grow for several generations because of decreasing death rates.

Ethical Concerns. Ethically, most nations favor stabilized or low population growth, because problems of peace, poverty, racism, disease, pollution, urbanization, ecosystem simplification, and resource depletion become harder to solve as the population increases. At the same time, many less-developed nations feel that population control, coupled with the continued status quo of international economic order, poses a dire threat to already oppressed people. These nations insist that for population control to become accepted, there must be a reorganization of economic and political power. These nations argue that people are the most vital of the world's resources and that problems of resource depletion and pollution can be solved by human ingenuity and technology. It is argued that the more people there are, the more likely it is that these problems will be solved. Economic growth would be stimulated because with more people there would be more production.

In contrast, others argue that, ethically, the world population should be limited because most people would be added to the least-developed countries, where education, health, and nutrition levels are so low that continued rapid population growth would condemn millions to an early death. Though technological advances do not come only from people who are well educated or paid, nations that favor limited population growth feel that encouraging rapid birth rates in the hope that someone may be born to solve the world's pollution and resource problems is an inhumane way to preserve the lives of people who already exist. Nations that encourage better education, nutrition, health care, and work opportunities for a smaller population feel that, ethically, that approach has a greater chance of making needed technological breakthroughs without adding to human suffering.

Methods of Population Control. Because most nations favor limited population growth, controlling the human population is primarily done by controlling the birth rate. Two approaches to controlling the birth rate of the human population are economic development and family planning. It is argued that economic development may not be able to help the least-developed countries lower their birth rates, since economic development for these nations is more difficult than it is for those nations that developed in the nineteenth century. In these least-developed countries, expanded family planning programs may bring a more rapid decrease in the birth rate than can economic development alone.

Family planning is a purely voluntary approach whereby information and contraceptives are provided to help couples have the number of children they want when they want to have them. Between 1965 and 1985, family planning was claimed to be a major factor in reducing the birth rates of China, Mexico, and Indonesia. In the same period, moderate to poor results of family planning occurred in the least-developed countries, such as India, Brazil, Bangladesh, and many countries in Africa and Latin America. India started the world's first national family planning program in 1952. Its population then was 400 million; by 1985, it had grown to 765 million, and it is projected to be 1 billion by 2000.

Many people believe that effective population control must include a combination of economic development and the use of methods that go beyond voluntary family planning. Among these methods are voluntary abortion and increased rights, education, and work opportunities for women.

—*David R. Teske*

See also Birth control; Environmental ethics; Malthus, Thomas; Zero Population Growth (ZPG).

BIBLIOGRAPHY

Ehrlich, Anne H., and Paul R. Ehrlich. "Needed: An Endangered Humanity Act?" In *Balancing on the Brink of Extinction,* edited by Kathryn A. Kohm. Washington, D.C.: Island Press, 1991.

Fritsch, Albert J., et al. *Environmental Ethics: Choices for Concerned Citizens.* Garden City, N.Y.: Anchor Press, 1980.

Hardin, Garrett. *Naked Emperors: Essays of a Taboo-Stalker.* Los Altos, Calif.: William Kaufmann, 1982.

Miller, G. Tyler, Jr. *Environmental Science: An Introduction.* Belmont, Calif.: Wadsworth, 1986.

Newland, Kathleen. *Women and Population Growth: Choice Beyond Childbearing.* Washington, D.C.: Worldwatch Institute, 1977.

Pornography

Type of ethics: Sex and gender issues

Date: 1864

Associated with: Obscenity and its regulation; U.S. Supreme Court; antipornography movements encompassing feminist and religious concerns

Definition: While no single definition is universally accepted, the term "pornography" generally refers to sexually explicit materials intended to arouse a reader or viewer; "porno" (from Greek *porne*) refers to prostitutes and their patrons, and "graphy" refers to writing or drawing

Significance: Pornography is a concept with moral, political, and legal dimensions; its definition, regulation, and effects are contested, and feminist, civil libertarian, and moral perspectives on the issue are divergent

Supreme Court Justice Potter Stewart made the comment in *Jacobellis v. Ohio* (1964) about obscenity that "I know it when I see it." While many scholars and laypersons have made light of the statement, his famous words encapsulate the problematical nature of the debate about pornography. Since pornography eludes common definition, its impact on society and individuals is also passionately debated.

Conflicting perspectives on pornography from conservative, libertarian, and feminist standpoints reflect in condensed form broader societal, political, and legal debates on modern-day issues relating to morality, censorship, and women's rights.

In the United States, where the First Amendment to the U.S. Constitution assumes preeminent status to expression as a "preferred freedom," the pornography debate is strongly tied to jurisprudential arguments about the limits of free expression. Jurisprudence in this area raises questions about the correct "balance" between freedom and equality and the appropriate emphasis on individual rights versus community values and morality.

The terms "pornography" and "obscenity" are sometimes used interchangeably. Some scholars, however, distinguish between obscenity, which is the legal term, and pornography, which is a broader term. Obscenity refers to nonwholesome sexually explicit materials that contradict societal norms. Pornography may include both socially unacceptable, lewd material and sexually explicit erotica consisting of materials that are sexually explicit but not necessarily "offensive" to societal values.

Brief History of Regulation. Excavations of ancient Greek artifacts reveal art depicting sexually explicit and even violent sexual acts (see Eva Keuls' *Reign of the Phallus,* 1985). In Greek and Roman times and in England until the seventeenth century, censorship was practiced primarily to control objectionable religious (blasphemous) and political (heretical) writings. While norms in most societies have shunned open displays of sexuality, written materials of any kind have been largely unavailable to the masses except in the last several centuries.

The English case *King v. Sedley* (1663) is often cited as a precursor of modern obscenity law. While the case did not deal directly with the distribution of obscene materials, it provided the legal and theoretical basis for modern obscenity law. Sir Charles Sedley was penalized by the court for standing nude and drunk on a tavern balcony. He spoke to a crowd below, using profane language, and poured urine on the bystanders beneath him. For offending public morality, he was fined and jailed.

Obscenity regulation was rare until the beginning of the nineteenth century, when government regulation of sexual morality became more common. By one estimate, there were approximately three obscenity prosecutions yearly in England between 1802 and 1857. By the mid-1850's, urbanization, expansion of the market for popular books, and Victorian moral standards combined to explain increased interest in and dissemination of sexually explicit materials. The regulation of such materials likewise increased. In 1857, for example, Lord Campbell's Act, which banned the dissemination of obscene works, was enacted.

In the English case of *Regina v. Hicklin* (1868), the court provided a definition of obscenity that shaped English, Canadian, and American law in this area well into the 1950's. The obscene publication *The Confessional Unmasked* was invidiously anti-Roman Catholic, purporting to describe the sexual depravity of Catholic priests. Chief Justice Alexander Cockburn's obscenity test in this case struck at any materials, including those devoid of religious or political assault, that "deprave and corrupt those whose minds are open to such immoral influences, and into whose hands a publication of this sort may fall." This test is generally viewed as extremely restrictive, since it regulates materials that "corrupt" even the most susceptible members of society, as opposed to restricting materials that corrupt the mythical "average" person used in later tests.

An 1815 Pennsylvania case was the first obscenity case decided in the United States. Generally, very little obscenity regulation occurred in the United States until passage of the Comstock Act in 1868 by the New York legislature, which prohibited the dissemination of obscene literature. A federal law regulating mailing of obscene works was passed in 1875, and most states passed antidissemination laws during the late 1800's.

Judges applied the Hicklin test until about 1933, when most U.S. jurisdictions relied upon a modified test devised by federal court judges in the case of *United States v. One Book called Ulysses.* Judges in the *Ulysses* case, which did not reach the Supreme Court level, declared obscene only those sexually explicit works that, on the whole, had a prurient effect on average readers. This less-restrictive definition protected some sexually explicit works with literary merit.

Two major Supreme Court decisions have shaped obscenity law. In 1957, the landmark case of *Roth v. United States* established that obscene materials are outside of limits of

First Amendment protection. Since the First Amendment holds that "Congress shall make no law . . . abridging freedom of speech or of the press," *Roth* constituted an important ruling on the issue, suggesting the limits of protected content. The decision defined obscenity in terms of "whether to the average person, applying contemporary community standards, the dominant theme of the material taken as a whole appeals to the prurient interest." In 1973, the Supreme Court refined its definition in *Miller v. California.* Regulation of hard-core pornography was the primary aim of the decision, which specified "patently offensive representations or descriptions of ultimate sexual acts, normal or perverted, actual or simulated," and "patently offensive representations or descriptions of masturbation, excretory functions, and lewd exhibition of the genitals."

The Court's guidelines for judging obscene work, set down in *Miller,* are: "(a) whether 'the average person, applying contemporary community standards' would find that the work, taken as a whole, appeals to the prurient interest (Roth), (b) whether the work depicts or describes, in a patently offensive way, sexual conduct specifically defined by the applicable state law, and (c) whether the work, taken as a whole, lacks serious literary, artistic, political or scientific value."

The *Miller* case raised questions about why government should be able to decide which material has value. Some scholars argue that such decisions about value should be left to the marketplace and to individual consumers. Critics, including dissenting justices, also expressed concern about *Miller*'s definition of obscenity, which they viewed as insufficiently precise and clear.

In contradistinction, the regulation of child pornography is almost universally accepted. Because of the special vulnerability of children, the legal system has allowed greater protection for children from the harms of pornography. In *New York v. Ferber* (1982), the Supreme Court upheld a statute banning pornography in which children are used as models or actors. The Court accepted broader regulation of child pornography in comparison with other forms, permitting government prohibition of works that only in incidental part (not as a whole) are graphic as well as materials that may possess "serious artistic, literary, scientific or educational value," and works that may not arouse "prurient" thoughts in average individuals.

Conservative Views on Pornography. Clear justifications for allowing government regulation of obscenity are often lacking in Supreme Court decisions on the subject. Stated definitions and rationales for obscenity regulation, however, suggest underpinnings in conservative thought.

Conservatives, who support strong regulation and enforcement of obscenity law, seek to preserve societal values and morals in the interest of the general welfare. From the 1960's through the 1980's, support by conservatives for obscenity regulation was grounded in a commitment to traditional family roles and values. From the conservative stand-point, pornography threatens those values, since it depicts, and may arguably promote, sexual relationships outside of marriage as well as unusual and societally condemned sexual practices depicted in pornography.

For example, the 1986 *Final Report of the Attorney General's Commission on Pornography* suggested that "it is far from implausible to hypothesize that materials depicting sexual activity without marriage, love, commitment, or affection bear some causal relationship to sexual activity without marriage, love, commitment or affection."

Thus, obscenity, in the conservative view, compromises the integrity of the community by precipitating a decline in religious and moral values among its members.

Support for pornography regulation by conservatives also rests on the assertion that pornography degrades human relationships and depreciates the individuals depicted by the pornography. Sexual acts in pornography are reduced to their purely physical dimensions; they are depicted as animalistic rather than presented in the context of consensual and loving human relationships.

Pornography regulation is also justifiable when expression harms individuals, according to the conservative view. The 1986 *Attorney General's Report,* for example, documents many cases in which individuals, usually women, were adversely affected by pornography—as participants in its production or victims of its effects. Possible links between pornography and violence against women and children have been investigated by social scientists, who have reached mixed conclusions in experimental studies.

Liberals' Support for Free Expression. Conservatives' support for obscenity regulation in the interests of society and community often conflicts with liberals' support for individual freedom of consenting adults to self-expression and choice in what they read or see.

Generous free speech rights are also defined within the framework of the "marketplace of ideas" wherein ideas compete for acceptance. Theoretically, weak or harmful ideas will falter within the marketplace and lose acceptance. The theory places faith in individual citizens to judge astutely the merits of the ideas presented.

Free speech rights may also be justified by democratic aims. Free speech and expression are particularly valued in democratic societies, such as the United States, in order to promote effective citizenship and participation in government. Confidence in the ability of individuals to make wise choices is an essential part of democratic society.

Some scholars also support maximum expression rights as a function of the need for tolerance in a democracy, particularly one with a diverse, pluralistic, and multicultural population. Unusual, unpopular, and abhorrent ideas should be tolerated with the expectation that tolerance will be reciprocated. Thus, from this perspective, citizens must tolerate some obnoxious, even harmful, expression.

Obscenity regulation is sometimes defended on the basis that, unlike vilified, objectionable speech with political significance, obscenity is "low value" expression, outside the ambit of the political and intellectual expression intended to be protected by the First Amendment.

Others justify pornography on the basis of overlooked positive functions that it might provide, including a possible sexually therapeutic effect for inhibited or sexually dysfunctional individuals or couples. Pornography may also provide informational benefits. The norm of sexual privacy impedes dissemination of information about sexuality, which may hamper self-expression and understanding of sexuality.

While mindful of the potential harms of pornography, liberals contend that the harms must reach a high threshold to justify regulation. Liberals are, therefore, skeptical of social scientific evidence suggesting harms of pornography. They support regulation only when nearly definitive proof of harm can be mustered.

The National Commission on Obscenity and Pornography (1970) embraced libertarian views that pornography's harms are relatively limited. At that time, available social scientific evidence suggested the absence of a connection between pornography usage and violence. This finding has been modified by subsequent studies.

Anti-Pornography Feminist Position. While in virtual agreement that pornography degrades women, feminists are divided in their views about the regulation of pornography.

In the 1980's, feminist scholars reconceptualized pornography as a civil rights issue, thus juxtaposing the values of equality for women against the free expression rights of individuals. Feminists such as Catharine MacKinnon, who, with Andrea Dworkin, wrote a civil rights ordinance that addressed the pornography issue, contend that liberals' preoccupation with free speech rights is myopic in that it underestimates the harms of such expression to women. In 1986, the MacKinnon-Dworkin ordinance was declared unconstitutional in federal courts.

Defining pornography in terms of its harms to women, feminists, such as MacKinnon, have also pointed out that while the analogy of the marketplace of ideas with regard to free expression might be appropriate if all citizens had equal access to and voice in the marketplace, the analogy fails when the distribution of power in society is unequal. Socially, politically, legally, and economically, according to this argument, women have less power and voice than do men within a patriarchy, and therefore their arguments are less likely to be viewed as credible.

In feminist "dominance" theory, Catharine MacKinnon argues that because men have defined social reality and legal theory, issues such as pornography, sexual assault, and sexual harassment may be defined and viewed differently by women and men, yet the male perspective on these issues is more frequently the preferred one.

Furthermore, concepts such as neutrality and objectivity, which are integral tools in legal interpretation, have been characterized in feminist and postmodern theory as, in practice, upholding the views of the socially powerful. For example, the "contemporary community standards" guideline in *Miller* is rejected by MacKinnon as irrelevant to feminist concerns because women are pervasively devalued and dehumanized as sex objects, making such subordination of women an accepted part of the culture—befitting "contemporary community standards."

Specific harms attributable to pornography are cited in the civil rights ordinance as well as in feminist literature. The cited harms primarily affect women. For example, the ordinance recognizes the potential for women and children to be coerced into performing in pornography productions as well as abused, beaten, threatened, and tortured. Linda Marchiano, who appeared in the pornographic film *Deep Throat,* contends that she performed in the film under duress and that she was severely beaten and abused while making the film.

The 1986 *Attorney General's Report* also contains numerous examples of victim testimony citing the use of coercive and misleading tactics to force women and children to perform in the production of pornographic materials.

Feminists have also rekindled the argument that pornography use is linked with sexual assault. Such causal connections are supported by anecdotal evidence that some assailants model their crimes on ideas found in pornographic materials. In addition, certain findings by social scientists suggest that pornography exposure can affect attitudes toward women and that, in laboratory settings, exposure to sexually violent pornography is correlated with increased aggression toward women.

The most pervasive harm of pornography to women, as presented in feminist theory, is that it reinforces the subordination of women by men. In pornography, women are depicted as sexual objects whose purpose is to provide pleasure to men. MacKinnon and Dworkin argue that pornography asserts that women desire to be battered, humiliated, and beaten. It eroticizes male domination of women, including violence against women. A common theme of pornography involves a woman who is raped and at first resists, but later enjoys it. Social science research cited in the 1986 *Attorney General's Report* shows that nonoffender college males, who were not generally aroused by sexually aggressive pornography, were aroused by rapes in which the victim appeared to enjoy the assault. Furthermore, such arousal was shown to be correlated with acceptance of rape myths.

The objectification of women in pornography mirrors societal attitudes about women, whose importance is judged on the basis of sexual attractiveness and availability. From this standpoint, pornography is symptomatic of women's situation, limiting women's opportunities and making it difficult for women's full capabilities to be equally recognized.

Summary. Divergent perspectives on pornography derive from different emphases on the values of community, individual freedom, and equality. The conservative perspective places primary emphasis on morality and the general welfare, while increasingly demonstrating additional concern for the harms to individuals correlated with exposure to pornography or its users. The concern over harm is shared by feminists, who place strong emphasis upon the need for equality and women's rights. Liberals stress the value of individual free expression rights, which are central to a democratic society, suggesting that these rights be cautiously balanced against the claims of harms to individuals or the general welfare. —*Mary A. Hendrickson*

See also Bill of Rights, U.S.; Censorship; Common good; Freedom and liberty; Freedom of expression; Rape; Sexuality and sexual ethics.

BIBLIOGRAPHY

Clor, Harry M. *Obscenity and Public Morality: Censorship in a Liberal Society.* Chicago: University of Chicago Press, 1969. While somewhat dated, this volume supplies a lucid and comprehensive argument in support of obscenity regulation.

Donnerstein, Edward, Daniel Linz, and Steven Penrod. *The Question of Pornography: Research Findings and Policy Implications.* New York: Free Press, 1987. This volume is useful for its summary and analysis of social science "effects" studies that consider possible links between pornography and violence.

Downs, Donald Alexander. *The New Politics of Pornography.* Chicago: University of Chicago Press, 1989. Downs explores the new challenges of feminist and conservative analyses of pornography to obscenity doctrine.

Dworkin, Andrea. *Letters from a War Zone: Writings, 1976-1989.* New York: E. P. Dutton, 1988. Essays written during the period indicated, including several on the topic of pornography from law journals and speeches. Written from a feminist perspective.

Lederer, Laura, ed. *Take Back the Night: Women on Pornography.* New York: William Morrow, 1980. A collection of essays exploring various aspects of the pornography issue as it affects women.

MacKinnon, Catharine A. *Feminism Unmodified: Discourses on Life and Law.* Cambridge, Mass.: Harvard University Press, 1987. A series of essays from the perspective of feminist jurisprudence, several of which explicate feminist views of current obscenity doctrine. An exegesis in support of a civil rights approach to pornography regulation that recognizes pornography's harms to women.

Olen, Jeffrey, and Vincent Barry. *Applying Ethics: A Text with Readings.* 4th ed. Belmont, Calif.: Wadsworth, 1992. The text discusses principles of "moral" and "good" reasoning. Includes essays that apply ethics to social issues. Pornography is one of the topics considered.

United States Attorney General's Commission on Pornography. *Final Report of the Attorney General's Commission on Pornography.* Nashville, Tenn.: Rutledge Hill Press, 1986. The conclusions of this commission conflict with those of the 1970 presidential commission's report. This report highlights the harms of pornography and suggests stronger enforcement and regulation.

Post-Enlightenment ethics

TYPE OF ETHICS: Modern history
DATE: Nineteenth century to present
ASSOCIATED WITH: Politico-economic ethics and natural rights
DEFINITION: Thinking influenced by the eighteenth century Enlightenment, which was characterized by a skeptical view of traditional values and relied heavily upon reason and science in striving for universal human progress
SIGNIFICANCE: Influenced the rise of modern democratic governments, the scientific revolution, and the formation of the social sciences

The term "Enlightenment" took its place in the English language in the seventeenth century. Its frequent employment did not occur, however, until the twilight of the movement to which it is applied. Immanuel Kant's 1784 essay *What Is Enlightenment?* made the term applicable to the philosophical movement that was centered in France and Germany from the middle of the seventeenth century to the dawn of the nineteenth century.

The Enlightenment has bequeathed to succeeding ages the methodical study of human relations. The social sciences became the offspring of the Enlightenment. Although these disciplines were not a part of the movement proper, they were spawned by the Enlightenment *philosophes'* struggle to improve society.

The Enlightenment was a sharp break with the dominant view of life that was prevalent during the Middle Ages. In medieval society, belief was the chief means by which humanity operated. Thus, both the church and superstition held unquestioned authority in most circles. The Enlightenment, however, introduced a rejection of traditional doctrines, whose validity largely rested upon their longevity. The Enlightenment's questioning and probing method was conducive to the growth of science and its application to the political and social realms.

Generally, the Enlightenment tended to reject the restraints that had been placed on medieval thinking. The movement's free thinking not only expanded beyond metaphysical constraints but also dismissed them as being irrelevant and incomprehensible in determining what is ethical. The narrow focus of medieval scholasticism was replaced by an interdisciplinary pursuit of knowledge. Philosophy became the medium through which Enlightenment thinkers examined history, politics, science, and other fields.

Chief Tenets. The Enlightenment set forth the employment of free reason, which involved the analysis and evaluation of existing institutions and doctrines. This movement subjected traditional authority to examination and interrogation. The motive behind the probing was a belief in progress. Unlike the thinkers of the *ancien régime*, thinkers of the post-Enlightenment era believed that human effort was the chief contribution to progress. Some *philosophes* believed in it so fervently that they conceived of a heaven on Earth that was a product of humanity's designs.

Kant called the statement *sapere aude* ("dare to know")

the Enlightenment's motto. Indeed, a chief objective of the movement was self-knowledge. The way to knowledge, according to the *philosophes*, was through experience. Since humanity was a part of nature, experience through that medium was possible. Hence, for Enlightenment thinkers, nature became the great teacher. This belief in experiential knowledge became known as empiricism.

The focus on the knowledge of humankind put a new emphasis on humankind's motivation and nature. Instead of taking the medieval view of humankind's preoccupation with otherworldly rewards, the *philosophes* conceived of humanity as being motivated by such temporal concerns as appetite, fear, and pride. This view ushered in the era of rational scientific materialism.

Thus, post-Enlightenment ethics have sought to reform society. It is believed that societal redemption will improve individuals who are influenced by the social environment in which they live. Hence, the Enlightenment and its following generations have focused their attention on life in the present rather than a life to come.

There is a temptation to dismiss the Enlightenment as being atheistic, but to do so would be inaccurate. Only in a few extreme cases were attempts made by Enlightenment thinkers to disprove the existence of a supreme being.

Instead, the *philosophes* were areligious. Although religion did not hold sway over them as it had over the medievalists, most of the Enlightenment's leaders did ascribe to various elements of religious teachings in their personal faith. For example, many of them were deists and therefore believed in God as creator but not in divine immanence in history.

Influence on Religion. Many post-Enlightenment Protestant theologians have synthesized this movement with orthodoxy to form a theology that is at odds with John Calvin's doctrine of predestination and Martin Luther's bondage of the will. Modern Protestantism accentuates personal accountability. The individual is believed to be able to exercise choice regarding his or her eternal destiny. Such a view was readily accepted by Puritan New England. The American colonists were rebelling against the authority of the Church of England. Their belief in the freedom of conscience was confirmation of a crucial link with an important tenet of the Enlightenment.

New England continued to abide by Calvinism's belief in hard work and thrift. The region also, however, came to incorporate the Enlightenment's teachings. As a result, American Protestantism, so far as salvation was concerned, moved toward an Arminian theology in which human individual freedom of choice was stressed.

The Enlightenment's view of humanity called for something other than a metaphysical solution to the problem of bringing into being a moral society. The *philosophes* devised a system that emphasized human choice. Providing a quasi-link with the rigidity of medieval theology, however, the Enlightenment did believe that laws could be found in na-

ture. They believed that the laws that brought order to the physical environment could be studied and used in the social arena to form a moral society.

Thus, although the Enlightenment did emphasize individual freedom, it did not advocate anarchy. Natural law was believed to contain principles that would ensure societal advantages that included the recognition of the equality of human beings and the right to pursue happiness. While it was individualistic in its accentuation of freedoms, it was at the same time a submission to natural laws that called for order and continuity in both the physical and the social environment.

The *philosophes* believed that it was possible and even desirable that society should exist without religious supervision. They did not, however, advocate the abolition of religion as a necessity. Instead, they called for religious tolerance. Arguments in favor of this position particularly were characteristic of the English Protestants. Consequently, the post-Enlightenment United States (a former English colony) has adopted an official stance of separation of state and church. By not having a state religion, the country attempts to tolerate all faiths and to ensure personal freedom of religion.

Influence on Science. With its probing nature, the Enlightenment was conducive to scientific investigations. Its rejection of unquestioned authority created a climate for scientific explorations, experiments, and resulting discoveries and inventions. This ushered in the Industrial Revolution, which has not only transformed but also expanded the world's economies. Out of this technological growth came the belief that human beings were capable of shaping life's conditions. The optimistic view of progress swayed the post-Enlightenment world away from a reliance upon fate. The post-Enlightenment world has come to depend more on human ingenuity to explain the causes of phenomena, including explanations for destructive storms, floods, and other natural disasters. The modern world is not inclined to attribute such events to acts of divine justice or the inevitable. Instead, it looks for causative factors and preventive measures that will deter or minimize future damages. Thus, the post-Enlightenment world depends on human effort rather than on religion or superstition to explain the unknown.

Unfortunately, post-Enlightenment manipulators have applied some of the *philosophes'* scientific cataloging to justify classism, racism, and ethnocentrism. By classifying humanity into various segments, these individuals have used the *philosophes'* efforts to bring about order to create disunity among human beings. By going beyond the species of *Homo sapiens* and classifying humans into races and classes, the post-Enlightenment manipulation introduced a stratified chain of being for humanity. This doctrine subverted the Enlightenment's attempt to recognize the equality that nature had decreed. Hence, scientific racism became a perverted use of the Enlightenment's doctrines.

Influence on Philosophy. During the Middle Ages, philosophy and theology were one. Because of the Church's domination, it was considered sacrilegious to conduct speculative thinking that was independent of religious dogma. The few medievalists, such as Peter Abelard, who exercised some degree of free thought were ostracized and persecuted. The Enlightenment's philosophy, however, exemplified human reason as the avenue to truth. In fact, the Enlightenment's *philosophes* were also scientists; that is, they studied nature in the belief that it contained laws that brought order to the universe. This concept led them to classify and organize information into a system. As a result, the *philosophes'* most important form of publication was the encyclopedia, in which they cataloged scientific and philosophical knowledge. Natural law was perceived as governing not only the physical environment but also society.

This was a clear divorcement from medieval thinking. The *philosophes* did not believe that ethics could be mastered by studying metaphysics or religion. Thus, for ethics to be comprehended, it was believed that the student had to abandon metaphysics and religion. The Enlightenment viewed these disciplines as explanations for the imponderable.

The *philosophes*, again unlike the medievalists, did not concern themselves with otherworldly rewards and punishments. Instead, their focus was humanity's present situation. Thus, they attempted to discover natural laws that spoke to human behavior, government, and individual freedoms.

Because of this emphasis, the post-Enlightenment world has turned its attention toward the improvement of society. Disciplines such as sociology and psychology came of age because of the Enlightenment's scrutiny of humanity's problematic situation. The systematic study of these problems was a fundamental component of the development of the social sciences. The post-Enlightenment world has been much more understanding and helpful in treating mental disease. While the medievalist was prone simply to dismiss a disturbed person as one possessed by a demon, modern science has searched for the physical and psychological causes of mental disturbance. The net result of the advent of such social sciences has been the emergence of a more humane way of dealing with such patients.

The *philosophes'* views were widely dispersed. Their philosophy reached far beyond western Europe. The United States was particularly receptive to the positions expostulated by Montesquieu, Voltaire, Locke, and others. These Enlightenment thinkers came to have a basic and profound impact upon the American Revolution and the democratic government that was formed in the aftermath.

Influence on Politics. The Enlightenment had a tremendous impact in the governmental sphere. Its philosophy of natural law became the basic argument for individual freedom, including the pursuit of happiness. Thus, the Enlightenment declared that the governed did not exist for the benefit of the governor. Jean-Jacques Rousseau espoused the view that government was really a contract between the governed and the governor, who had reciprocal responsibilities.

Opposing arbitrary authority and the divine right doctrine, the *philosophes* held that a citizen had rights that included expectations of the government.

Furthermore, the Enlightenment gave credence to the doctrine of the right to revolt. Whenever the government infringed upon citizens' individual freedoms, the citizens were justified in overthrowing that government.

While this doctrine legitimated the American and French revolutions in the eighteenth century, it was paradoxical to its contemporary practices of slavery and colonialism. Thus, while the Enlightenment ushered in a new era that was characterized by emphasis upon individual freedoms, it did not provide a clean break with the despotic past. Many of the violations that subverted the human being's pursuit of happiness would continue for many years, even in lands where the Enlightenment's principles had been formally adopted as the basis for government. These continued violations illustrated that many of the *philosophes* were overoptimistic. Their hope for an earthly utopia has continued to elude humanity even though reforms and democratic ideals have become diffused throughout the post-Enlightenment world.

Influence on Social Stratification. Among the doctrines set forth by the Enlightenment was the equality of human beings. This idea was a radical departure from the medieval practice of feudalism. Under the *ancien régime*, a vassal would swear his fealty to a nobleman. The vassal was subservient to the nobleman in every way imaginable. His major assignment was to render service and obeisance unto his lord (the nobleman). In no way did the serf consider himself to be on an equal par with his master.

The Enlightenment was an integral part of the modernization of the Western world. As the growth of the middle class occurred, feudalism's structure of nobility and serfdom was challenged. Thus, the Enlightenment challenged this archaic stratification and at the same time served as an apologetic mechanism for the emerging middle class. In this way, the Enlightenment helped to pave the way for the spread of both democracy and capitalism. The Enlightenment's teachings regarding natural law and equality undermined the feudal structure. Thus, socially, post-Enlightenment society tended to be fluid. In modern democratic society it is reasonable to expect social and economic mobility. American optimism especially made the modern citizen believe that economic and social improvement is a reasonable expectation and perhaps even a right.

Yet despite the post-Enlightenment world's optimistic expectations, social stratification continues. Certainly, modern stratification in the industrialized countries is not as drastic as the plight of the medieval serf as contrasted with the comfortable life of the aristocratic nobility. Yet the dream of a classless society has proved to be an unrealistic aspiration. Even communism's imposition of a uniform dress code (as in the case of China) has not proved to be successful in producing a totally egalitarian society. Thus, the unattainable goal of a utopia free of classism again demonstrates the unrealistic expectations of some of the *philosophes*.

In fact, the post-Enlightenment world has not completely obliterated feudalism. The remains of this medieval institution can certainly still be found in the military and in the business world's corporate culture. Despite this structure, however, the Enlightenment has influenced these modern organizations. There are rules that the rulers are expected to follow, and if they do not, they can be replaced. Thus, despite the military and corporate hierarchy, the post-Enlightenment world does demand personal accountability from all.

Contribution. Post-Enlightenment ethics are characterized by an appreciation for individual freedoms, democratic government, and an optimistic belief in human progress. As a result, society has become less staid and evasive of human accountability. Post-Enlightenment ethics do not ascribe blame for accidents and disasters to God or fate. Instead, human ingenuity and negligence are cited as factors in bringing about either success or failure. Such thinking has given birth to two opposing positions. Fatalists have used aspects of the Enlightenment to classify humanity into groups that range from the primitive to the most advanced. By doing so, they have maintained the inequities that were part of the *ancien régime*. Such misuse of the Enlightenment has subverted its aspiration for a totally reformed society. Yet the Enlightenment has also helped to inspire democratic ideals and universal fraternity. Since these noble ideals are not fully attained, it might be said that the Enlightenment is still in progress. —*Randolph Meade Walker*

See also Enlightenment ethics; Natural rights.

BIBLIOGRAPHY

Capaldi, Nicholas. *The Enlightenment: The Proper Study of Mankind*. New York: G. P. Putnam's Sons, 1967. This work provides a comprehensive overview of the dominant themes of the Enlightenment and the ways in which they differed from those of the *ancien régime* against which they were set.

Cassirer, Ernst. *The Philosophy of the Enlightenment*. Translated by Fritz C. A. Koelln and James P. Pettegrove. Boston: Beacon Press, 1955. This specialized study examines the Enlightenment's thinking. The prominent concepts of the movement are explained in a clear and understandable manner. Defends the new thinking in the light of the Romantic movement's characterization of it as "shallow Enlightenment."

Commager, Henry Steele. *The Empire of Reason: How Europe Imagined and America Realized the Enlightenment*. Garden City, N.Y.: Anchor Press/Doubleday, 1977. The contention of this book is that the Enlightenment originated in Europe but did not reach its fruition until it was incorporated in Anglo-America.

Crocker, Lester G. *Nature and Culture: Ethical Thought in the French Enlightenment*. Baltimore: The Johns Hopkins University Press, 1963. A valuable specialized study of the place of ethics in the Enlightenment's teachings. It contends that a homogeneity of thought on human nature and morals disappeared with the breakup of medieval Christian metaphysical teachings.

Gay, Peter. *The Enlightenment: An Interpretation*. New York: W. W. Norton, 1977. This is the definitive text on the Enlightenment. It examines the *philosophes'* world and explains why their demands and expectations were made.

Koch, Adrienne, ed. *The American Enlightenment: The Shaping of the American Experiment and a Free Society*. New York: George Braziller, 1965. Complete with an introduction that gives a comprehensive interpretation of the American Enlightenment, this work is a collection of primary sources. It includes letters, autobiographies, and other writings of some of America's key Enlightenment figures, such as Benjamin Franklin and Thomas Jefferson.

Palmer, R. R. *The Age of the Democratic Revolution: A Political History of Europe and America, 1760-1800*. Princeton, N.J.: Princeton University Press, 1959-1964. This volume offers a synthesis of political history on both sides of the Atlantic. It provides an important connective understanding of the various movements for democratic reform that were staged in Europe as well as America, demonstrating that the birth of democracy was not an isolated event.

Potsdam Conference

TYPE OF ETHICS: Modern history

DATE: July 17 to August 2, 1945

ASSOCIATED WITH: U.S. president Harry S Truman, Soviet Premier Joseph Stalin, and the Cold War

DEFINITION: Occurring soon after the total defeat of Germany, this was the last meeting of the Allied leaders of Great Britain, the Soviet Union, and the United States during World War II (1939-1945)

SIGNIFICANCE: Longstanding ideological and ethical differences between the United States and the Soviet Union emerged to solidify the territorial and economic dismantling of Germany and lay the foundations of the Cold War

In the Berlin suburb of Potsdam, the Allied powers met from July 17 to August 2, 1945, to strengthen their resolve to defeat Japan and to decide how to put the world back together after the shattering experience of World War II had ended. Stalin, who had been cunning and brutal in securing control at home, was bent on exploiting Russia's victory after the war. Truman, the naive idealist who believed implicitly in his country's innate goodness, had faith in the principle of international cooperation. Great Britain sided with Truman, who demanded that free elections be held in eastern European countries that, it was charged, had unfairly been made satellites of the Soviet orbit of control. Stalin refused. War damages, or reparations, were another crucial issue. The Soviets wanted to rebuild their war-torn economy with German industry; the United States feared that it would be saddled with the entire cost of caring for defeated Germans. Each side ended up taking reparations from its zone of occupation, and Germany was divided in two

Winston Churchill (left), Harry Truman (center), and Joseph Stalin at the Potsdam Conference. (National Archives)

without input. The growing antagonism between the United States and the Soviet Union resulted in the Cold War.

See also Cold War; Stalin, Joseph; Truman Doctrine.

Poverty and wealth

TYPE OF ETHICS: Politico-economic ethics

DATE: From antiquity

DEFINITION: Wealth is an abundance of worldly riches and a high and secure standard of living; poverty is the relative lack of wealth

SIGNIFICANCE: All people are entitled to live lives of material and psychological prosperity; unfortunately, the distribution of prosperity throughout the world is grossly unequal, and no solution to the problem is in sight

The First and Third Worlds. Generally speaking, the First World consists of the Western capitalist countries and various other relatively well-to-do countries such as Australia and Japan, all of which opposed the communist bloc countries during the Cold War. The Second World consists of the former Soviet Union and the other communist bloc countries that opposed the United States and other Western countries during the Cold War. The Third World consists

primarily of those African and Asian countries that were not aligned with either side during the Cold War. The problem of poverty is particularly acute in the Third World countries.

Third World countries cover 60 percent of the world's land surface and include 70 percent of the world's population. Its constituent countries are much less homogeneous than are the First World countries, since they represent a wide variety of social, economic, cultural, political, and geographical environments. Unfortunately, what Third World countries do have in common is a marked socioeconomic disadvantage that manifests itself in weak economies, overpopulation, and widespread poverty.

In the Third World, poverty is pervasive both relative to First World countries and on an absolute level. State welfare systems are either inadequate or nonexistent, and for that reason millions of people are malnourished and die in periodic famines. Housing and shelter are often inadequate.

Third World countries have weak economic systems that are characterized by low agricultural productivity; an undeveloped industrial base; limited technology; limited purchasing power; overreliance on a small number of export products, making their economies particularly vulnerable to fluctuations in supply and demand; and reliance on foreign investments and the importation of industrial equipment (see Pacione, 1988).

Third World countries also have demographic deficiencies, such as low life expectancy at birth, high rates of infant mortality, large families, rampant disease, and high rates of infection. These countries also tend to have incompetent governments that are characterized by poor administration, widespread corruption, lack of opportunity and high unemployment, glaring inequities between social classes, a disproportionate concentration of wealth and power in the hands of a ruling elite, and insufficient resources devoted to social programs and education (impoverished sub-Saharan countries continue to spend two to three times as much on armaments as on education. Because of such inequities, the best-educated segment of the population may leave; for example, in the 1980's, one-third of Africans with a post-secondary education emigrated to Europe.

is made on the backs of the poor." Therefore, if the developed countries are hoarding all the wealth and this wealth is generating poverty in the undeveloped nations, poverty can be wiped out by redistributing the wealth from developed to undeveloped nations. Examples of this theory being put into practice include the Peace Corps, foreign aid, and low-interest loans or grants that are provided by the World Bank and the International Monetary Fund.

The concept of redistribution may be ethically laudable, but it has not worked in practice, as is indicated by the growing disparity between developed and undeveloped nations. The zero-sum theory says that significant improvement in the well-being of the Third World can occur only if a significant decline in the well-being of the First World occurs simultaneously. A similar rationale works on a smaller scale for the powerful interest and economic groups within Third World countries that have monopolized the wealth of those countries. Clearly, these nations and groups

COMPARISON OF WEALTH-RELATED FACTORS BETWEEN FIRST AND THIRD WORLD COUNTRIES			
Measure	**Years Covered**	**First World**	**Third World**
Per capita food production (in units)	1980-1985	102-108	100-103
Total fertility rate (lifetime children per woman)	1950-1985	2.8-2.0	6.2-4.1
Population growth rates (percentage of increase)	1955-1990	1.3-0.5	2.0-1.8
Infant mortality rates (infant deaths per 1,000 live births)	1950-1985	56-17	159-92
Life expectancy at birth (years)	1950-1985	65-73	41-57
World exports	1963-1985	82-79	4-12
(Percentage of market)	1985-1992	79-81	12-1

It is obvious that there is an enormous disparity between the First World and the Third World in terms of the distribution of wealth and power, and this disparity appears to be growing, according to the 1992 report of the United Nations Development Program. Income disparities between the richest and the poorest 20 percent of countries have more than doubled during the past thirty years. Currently, the average income gap is more than 140 to 1 ($22,808 to $163). In terms of control over economic activity, in 1989, the richest 20 percent of nations controlled between 80 and 95 percent of total gross national product, world trade, commercial lending, domestic savings, and domestic investment. The poorest 20 percent of countries controlled between 0.2 and 1.4 percent of economic activity.

Ethics and the Wealth of Nations. Most Third World countries are in a relationship of unequal exchange with the countries of the developed world. One theory maintains that the way to decrease this inequality is to redistribute wealth. Central to this strategy is the belief that economic interaction is a zero-sum game; that is, that as one nation acquires more wealth and becomes richer, another nation loses wealth and becomes poorer. As Marjorie Kelly (1992) put it: "Wealth

have not been willing to undertake such a level of redistribution. In fact, the data suggest that they are accumulating an even greater share of the wealth. According to Jacob Needleman (1991), "The outward expenditure of mankind's energy now takes place in and through money." Marjorie Kelly observed that one of the consequences of this single-minded accumulation of money is that "we have come to lack a sense of financial obesity: a cultural consensus that enough is enough and too much is grotesque . . . we lack any . . . revulsion to vast sums of money."

Kelly argues that a solution to this problem may be to recognize that equality of wealth is impossible to achieve. Kelly suggests that one solution might be to encourage the creation of wealth that does not cause poverty, creating a win-win situation, an ethically earned prosperity that also makes others prosperous. For example, a product is sold by a company to customers who become prosperous by using the product. Kelly's idea is interesting, but it is not clear on what scale a win-win situation could operate globally. In addition, the success of such a strategy hinges on—as Kelly noted—a duty on the part of the wealthy to care for those who do not have wealth. The fact that affluent nations are becoming wealthier and the Third World is sinking deeper into poverty suggests that Kelly's sense of duty has not yet achieved recognition or high priority. —*Laurence Miller*

PER CAPITA GROSS DOMESTIC PRODUCT, 1988	
First World countries	**Amount**
United States	$20,000
West Germany	$18,000
Third World countries	
Ivory Coast	$960
Thailand	$915
Ghana	$410
Kenya	$370
Tanzania	$258
Burma	$200

See also Capitalism; Communism; Economic analysis.

BIBLIOGRAPHY

Berberoglu, Berch. *The Political Economy of Development.* Albany: State University of New York Press, 1992.

Kelly, Marjorie, et al. "Are You Too Rich If Others Are Too Poor?" *The Utne Reader*, no. 53 (September-October, 1992): 67-70.

Osterfield, David. *Prosperity Versus Planning.* New York: Oxford University Press, 1992.

Pacione, Michael, ed. *The Geography of the Third World: Progress and Prospect.* New York: Routledge, 1988.

Smeeding, Timothy M., Michael O'Higgins, and Lee Rainwater, eds. *Poverty, Inequality, and Income Distribution in Comparative Perspective.* Washington, D.C.: Urban Institute Press, 1990.

Power

TYPE OF ETHICS: Theory of ethics

DATE: 420 B.C.E.

ASSOCIATED WITH: Thrasymachus, Niccolò Machiavelli, Thomas Hobbes, Friedrich Nietzsche, and Michel Foucault

DEFINITION: The ability or capacity to control, influence, dominate, or exercise authority over other persons or things

SIGNIFICANCE: Determining how to define power and its uses will help identify the difference between its legitimate use and its exploitative and oppressive use

Power is often confused with authority, but power is distinct from authority. In general, power implies an ability or capacity of some sort. More particularly, power implies an ability or capacity to exercise influence, control, or dominion over others. Authority is the legitimate right to use power. Not every-one, however, believes in the separation between power and authority. Despots, tyrants, and dictators eschew legitimacy and wield authority like a sword. Vladimir Ilich Lenin viewed the rule of the Communist Party, the dictatorship of the proletariat, as being based on brutal force, unlimited by any laws or rules. Mao Tse-tung identified power with authority. One has authority because one has power to rule. "Political power grows out of the barrel of a gun," said Mao. This article will focus on the sources and nature of power.

Power as Knowledge. Power has been identified with knowledge, freedom, justice, and political authority. In Plato's allegory of the cave, knowledge is likened to the power that emancipates slaves of sensory perception from the darkness of ignorance to the bright light of intellectual knowledge. Francis Bacon claimed that knowledge is power. In the *Advancement of Learning* (1605), he wrote, "For there is no power on earth which setteth up a throne or chair of estate in the spirits and souls of men, and in their cogitations, opinions, and beliefs, but knowledge and learning."

Power as Freedom. Thomas Hobbes, Baruch Spinoza, Immanuel Kant, and Jean-Paul Sartre understood freedom to be the source of power. Hobbes argued that the social contract came about by means of the surrender or alienation of natural freedom to society. Hobbes wanted to place all power in the hands of the sovereign. Spinoza identified freedom as power—power to act, power for self-preservation. Spinoza defined power as *conatus*, the special propensity or capacity of a thing to perform; in short, the freedom of self-preservation. Kant postulated that human beings have free will to impose laws upon themselves; that is, human beings have moral autonomy or freedom, which is the source of power. Sartre believed that freedom was the power of self-determination.

Power as Political Authority. The Greek Sophist Cratylus, a skeptic and relativist, claimed that the law of right is the law of the strongest; in other words, power is right, power is justice. This ethic was taken over by the argumentative Sophist Thrasymachus. Plato's *Republic* opens with a discussion between Socrates and the aged Cephalus over the meaning of life, which leads to the question of the just life. Having asked for a definition of justice, Socrates receives a reply from Polemarchus, son of Cephalus, who argues on the authority of the Greek poet Simonides that justice is to give to each what is owed. In the course of the discussion, a frustrated and impatient Thrasymachus charges into the debate. Justice, he argues, is whatever brings advantage to the stronger or to established rule. At the end of the argument, Thrasymachus winds up defending injustice as being more valuable than justice, because injustice can be used to the advantage of the stronger. In effect, Thrasymachus defines justice as power.

John Locke. John Locke identified political power with legitimate authority. In the *Second Treatise of Government* (1690), Locke differentiated political power and despotical power. The difference consisted in the fact that political power is legitimate authority, whereas despotical power is arbitrary. Political power is founded on the social contract, in which self-rule is willfully handed over to society for the common good and for protection. Despotical power is simply arbitrary power over other persons.

Karl Marx. Karl Marx claimed that political power can be explained in terms of economic relations of property ownership; therefore, he viewed power in capitalist society as exploitation. For Marx, private property is the source of social power. Marx believed that private property ownership patterns created asymmetrical relations of power resulting in the development of two classes: the exploiting class and the exploited class. The property-owning classes are the exploiting classes because they exploit the labor power of the non-owning classes. Workers must enjoy freedom from servitude and must be propertyless. The reason that capitalist power is exploitative is that capitalist society must constantly renew its conditions of existence by ensuring that a sizable percentage of the population remains propertyless and therefore subordinate to the dominant class. The worker has no choice, if he or she wants to survive, but to appear on the labor market as a commodity to be bought and sold. Power over others, therefore, grows out of unequal property relations.

Max Weber, unlike Marx, found sources of power outside the economic realm. Power may flow from the possession of economic or political resources. High positions may also confer power.

Machiavelli. Niccolò Machiavelli (1469-1527) wrote *The Prince* (1513) and dedicated it to Lorenzo de Medici, hoping to attract the attention of the Medicis. *The Prince* has been called a grammar of power, and for good reasons. The book was written about the acquisition of absolute power. *The Prince* was taken from the *Discourses*, which set forth several principles: the superiority of the democratic republic, reliance upon mass consent, organic unity, the role of leadership in achieving cohesiveness, the imperative of military power, the use of national religion to unify the masses and to cement morale, the will to survive and ruthless measures, the cyclical rise and fall caused by the decadence of the old and reinvigoration of the new. Though *The Prince* can be studied in the context of the Mirror of Princes Literature, a genre that flourished during the Middle Ages and depicted princely virtues, it signified a revolutionary turn in political thinking by rejecting ethics and metaphysics and espousing political realism. Machiavelli refused to imagine human beings as they ought to be; instead, he employed as his starting point the realistic acknowledgment of human beings as they are. Machiavelli believed that ideals and ethics were ineffective in government. Chapters 15 through 19 of *The Prince* are the most radical. These chapters deal with the qualities that a prince ought to possess. The prince is advised to disregard the question of whether his actions should be called virtuous or vicious. The choice of action, Machiavelli claims, depends not upon ethics but upon circumstances.

Machiavelli was not concerned with good or evil, but with effective government; not with virtues, but with *virtù*, or vitality. Chapter 14 stresses the primacy and necessity of brute power being employed for strategic ends—in other words, war. For Machiavelli, the prince has no other aim but war. The prince is counseled to learn war through action and study and to know and defend even in peacetime.

Thomas Hobbes. Thomas Hobbes (1588-1679) defined the nature of political power in *Leviathan*, which contains a powerful argument on behalf of strong government. Hobbes wrote *Leviathan* while exiled in Paris from the English Civil wars. Hobbes's aim was to unite Church and state into one powerful structure. Holding to a mechanical view of the universe, he naturally constructed his theory of human nature on the basis of mechanistic principles. For example, he depicted the human mind as a function of the nervous system. Chapter 13 contains the famous passage called the "Naturall Condition of Mankind." Hobbes claimed that the state of nature is a state of war because of human equality (for example, a small man could kill a big man with a rock). Human life in this natural state is "solitary, poore, nasty, brutish, and short." Power is socially and equitably distributed. In order to gain mutual protection, and because human beings enjoyed a natural rational propensity to seek peace, a commonwealth was in order. Such a commonwealth would be formed by a compact in which each individual agreed to allow as much liberty to others as he or she would expect to enjoy. By forming a compact and mutually renouncing individual freedom and power, the members of society would grant absolute power to the sovereign. Only the government, then, could assign rights and determine justice.

Friedrich Nietzsche. Friedrich Nietzsche (1844-1900), in *The Dawn* (1881), *The Gay Science* (1882), *Beyond Good and Evil* (1886), *The Will to Power* (1901), and *Thus Spoke Zarathustra* (1883), made power an interpretative principle of human behavior and morality. The will to power is at the heart of his philosophy. He pointed out a dualistic morality—a slave morality, or herd morality, versus a master morality. The slave morality was guided by resentment against the successful, wealthy, and powerful. The Superman (Übermensch) appears as the Nietzschean hero who affirms life and recalls Goethe's Faust, who symbolized the ever-striving, never satisfied power of the human spirit. "Dead are all gods; now we will that superman live." Superman is the goal of history. In *The Antichrist*, Nietzsche defined the good as power. "What is good? Everything that heightens the feeling of power in man, the will to power, power itself."

Michel Foucault. Foucault was one of the brightest luminaries to grace the French firmament of intellectual thought in the twentieth century, and his influence can be felt throughout the academic world of the West. His major contribution to social thought was the stimulation of new thinking about power. This concept is central to his social and political critique. In it, he thinks he has found the Archimedean point with which to understand the systems and structures of rationality, political authority, and science. However one may conceive of Foucault's use of the concept of power, there is no way to interpret his project of contemporary historical analysis without tackling the ineluctable idea of power.

Power for Foucault is not some kind of substance. It is neither an essence composed of definable qualities nor an ontological category representing some real entity. Instead, power is an abstract configuration, an abstract possibility of relations of force. Foucault conceives of power in essentially nominalistic terms. "Power in the substantive sense, *le pouvoir*, doesn't exist. . . . In reality power means relations, a more-or-less organized, hierarchical coordinated cluster of relations." Relations within the social body make the presence of power ubiquitous. This is the case because Foucault views power coterminously with the conditions of social relations. What is revolutionary about Foucault is his localization of the mechanisms of power in the apparatuses outside the state. He locates power, or "micro-powers," on the mundane, quotidian level of familial relationships, kinship systems, local administrations, and so forth. He cautions, therefore, that unless the mechanisms of power that function outside the state are changed, nothing in society will be changed. Foucault then locates power at every point of society. In fact, he contends that the functioning of the state depends on concrete power relations diffused throughout the social body. Power functions at myriad points of social contact and has myriad effects.

Foucault thinks of power as having "capillary" forms of existence—the capillaries being the points at which power enters and invests itself in individuals. It is at this level that power becomes productive of social knowledge.

The functioning of power creates new bodies of knowledge. Power and knowledge are inexorably connected. One cannot exist without the other. Power is constrained to produce knowledge, and knowledge cannot escape engendering more power. Foucault doesn't mean the same thing by power/knowledge that the Frankfurt School meant by reason/domination. Foucault is not trying to unmask the oppressive systems of the dominant classes. Instead, he is attempting to locate the points of intersection of power and knowledge as they are dispersed strategically throughout the social body.

What part does the individual play in the process of the determination of power within the social body? Foucault seems rather ambiguous concerning the individual subject and the problem of subjectivity. On the one hand, he says that it is the position of the subject that exercises power, not the individual; on the other, he says that power is exercised in the very bodies of individuals. The effects of power invest themselves in the bodies of individuals. Biopower (also called political technology) and biopolitics refer to the control of species and the control of the body. Political technology leads to the categorization of human species and converts the human body into an object to be manipulated (dis-

ciplinary power). The aim is to create a docile and productive body. Biopolitics depicts the individual as an object of political concern for the purpose of normalization.

In *Discipline and Punish* (1979), Foucault presents power as the force of normalization and the formation of knowledge. Normalization and knowledge invest the body, the individual, the masses, and the body politic. "The soul is the effect and the instrument of a political anatomy; the soul is the prison of the body." Through knowledge, power moves to a new level. Knowledge is power over people that ends up normalizing people and standardizing them in the factory, school, prison, hospital, or military.

Power is not built up of individual wills. Individuals and subjects are not particular powers, they do not possess power, and power does not emanate from them. Yet all individuals are subjects in a universal struggle in which everyone fights everyone else. There is, for Foucault, no such thing as an oppressor/oppressed polarity such as the Marxist class struggle between the proletariat and the bourgeoisie. Forms of rationality other than the economic enmesh themselves in the institutions and domains of society, engendering effects such as sexism and racism.

At his inaugural address at the Collège de France, France's most distinguished academic institution, Foucault presented a discourse about discourse entitled "L'Ordre du discours." In it, Foucault argues that the production of discourse is controlled by procedures of exclusion, sexual and political prohibition, taboo, ritual, and the right to speak. The will to knowledge leads to a system of exclusion that relies on institutional support. Procedures arise for the control of discourse, systems of restriction, conditions, and rules of access. The number of those allowed to participate is small. Ritual defines qualifications, gestures, behavior, and circumstances. Societies of discourse preserve discourse within a restricted group.

For Foucault, then, power is a heuristic principle, or explanatory rule, for understanding social practices. He corrected the too-long-held view that power is exclusively repressive or constraining. In fact, what Foucault demonstrated was the insidious way in which power produces conformity, legitimizes political power, and creates exclusionary forms of knowledge.   —*Michael Candelaria*

See also Foucault, Michel; Hobbes, Thomas; *Leviathan*; Locke, John; Machiavelli, Niccolò; Machiavellian ethics; Marxism; Nietzsche, Friedrich.

BIBLIOGRAPHY

Foucault, Michel. *Discipline and Punish: The Birth of the Prison.* Translated by Alan Sheridan. New York: Vintage Books, 1979. This work concerns itself with the expression of power in penal institutions and the development of disciplinary techniques that can convert the body into a docile instrument.

_____. *Power/Knowledge: Selected Interviews and Other Writings, 1972-1977.* Edited by Colin Gordon. Translated by Colin Gordon et al. New York: Pantheon

Books, 1980. Essays and interviews that concentrate mostly on the issue of power and its pervasive presence in every area of human life, especially in human bodies. It also deals with penal institutions, the Panopticon of Jeremy Bentham, health institutions, and the history of sexuality.

Hobbes, Thomas. *Leviathan*. Edited by C. B. Macpherson. Harmondsworth, England: Penguin Books, 1968. This masterpiece of political literature contains a powerful argument for a strong authoritarian government. Its subjects include social contract theory, the state of nature, the mechanistic view of human nature, naturalistic ethics, and the unity of Church and state.

Machiavelli, Niccolò. *The Prince*. Edited by Quentin Skinner and Russell Price. Cambridge, England: Cambridge University Press, 1988. This masterly analysis of power was written during a time when there was a growing need for the centralization of the Italian city-states, an increasingly nationalistic ethos, and a restoration of the Medicis to power in Florence. Although *The Prince* was written to gain favor with the Medicis, its aim was to describe how principalities are won, held, and lost.

Nietzsche, Friedrich. *The Portable Nietzsche*. Edited and translated by Walter Kaufmann. New York: Viking Press, 1984. Most of the works contained here are new translations by Kaufmann. Included are the entire text of *Thus Spoke Zarathustra* and selections from works such as *Beyond Good and Evil*. Also includes letters and notes.

Pragmatism

Type of ethics: Theory of ethics

Date: First used publicly 1898

Associated with: American philosophers Charles Sanders Peirce, William James, John Dewey, and George Herbert Mead

Definition: A theory of meaning, truth, and conduct in which objects, ideas, and events are understood dynamically in terms of their potentialities to guide action toward intelligent ends

Significance: Rejects formal, absolute principles for an experimental, contextual attitude toward values, stressing the importance of education, communication, social cooperation and democracy

Pragmatism was initiated by Charles Sanders Peirce (1838-1914) and William James (1842-1910) and developed by John Dewey (1859-1952) and George Herbert Mead (1863-1931); it has been revived since the 1970's. Responding to Darwinism, Peirce and James viewed thought as a process within the whole context of life-activity. In his foundational essays "The Fixation of Belief" (1877) and "How to Make Our Ideas Clear" (1878), Peirce argued that thinking arises from a disturbance in action and aims at producing a belief that more successfully guides future action. Beliefs are not mental states but organic dispositions or habits. James popularized the term "pragmatism" first in 1898 and then in the famous lectures published as *Pragmatism* (1907).

For Peirce, pragmatism was a general theory of meaning, while James stressed the view that "truth" means "workability." Mead explored the implications for social psychology. John Dewey developed it into a rich theory of human existence and conduct, including ethical, social, and political philosophy, often known as "instrumentalism" but more correctly called "Cultural naturalism." (Instrumentalism, the theory of intelligent inquiry, is part of Dewey's general theory of experience, ranging from prereflective feelings to refined aesthetic and religious meanings.)

Dewey begins by seeing humans as living organisms acting within and responding to their environments. People are neither predetermined mechanisms nor purely independent. Action is a feedback process of learning, operating within certain constraints but capable of a variety of developments. As cultural beings, people also live in a social environment in which the experience of others shapes their own conduct. The process of learning, then, offers a third alternative for moral theory. "Morals means growth of conduct in meaning," says Dewey. "It is learning the meaning of what we are about and employing that meaning in action."

For Dewey, ethics deals with all human action. It legitimately involves obtaining reliable information; broad experience; skills in communication, cooperation, and deliberation; educational and political organization; and the creation of new values and ideals. Ethics, in short, is the art of rendering human existence as meaningful and intrinsically fulfilling as possible.

Like any art, ethics is concerned with the techniques whereby its aim may be realized. In this sense, it is experimental and gains insight from the success of the scientific method. Dewey denied that ethical problems should be handed over to the social sciences or some managerial elite, but he hoped that the cooperative, experimental attitude of science could be widely inculcated for framing tentative solutions to social problems that leave many human lives devoid of hope or meaning. By seeing the moral life as capable of being guided by a variety of intelligently undertaken experiments instead of as the subject matter for formal principles of ethical judgment, Dewey thought, it might be possible to improve the human condition.

Out of native impulses, desires arise, leading to actions that form habits. Habits "constitute the self," becoming one's character. They lead to certain kinds of further action that may cause reevaluation of past desires, a transformation or enlargement of them with respect to their objects, or a deepening of their meaning with broadened experience. Though Dewey agrees with Aristotle that action and habit are the basis of character, he finds no one fixed and defining virtue. The self is a process, Dewey states: "[I]t is impossible for the self to stand still, it is becoming and becoming for better or worse. It is in the *quality* of becoming that virtue resides. We set up this and that end to be reached, but *the* end is growth itself." Although he rejects absolute values, Dewey is no subjective relativist; instead, he is a contextual pluralist. The good self is one that is informed about its world, grasps the tendencies of situations, and deliberates well about possible ends and the means required to realize them.

Deliberation includes the imaginative search for ideals of conduct and the discovery of new values. Only in a derivative sense is it understood as the mere search for means to preselected ends. Two children fighting over a ball may discover the game of catch, discovering the new value of co-operative play and friendship, transforming the old values of possessiveness and dominance. Deliberation is not primarily a private affair; one deliberates alone because one has deliberated aloud with others. Ethical reasoning, then, is no calculative or rule-bound procedure but is fraught with imagination, dialogue, and dramatic interpretation. It aims to understand the meaning of a present situation by determining its tendencies and the possible values that they realize. An event gains meaning within an overall process. By seeing the actual in the light of the possible, one can make intelligent choices and critically evaluate one's conduct. One can grow intelligently. This is Dewey's understanding of freedom.

A society incorporating such behavior would provide the most secure basis for democracy as a way of life. Civilization would be no abstract ideal but would concretely aim at every means possible to realize conditions whereby human beings could lead inherently significant lives.

—Thomas Alexander

See also Dewey, John; James, William; Peirce, Charles Sanders.

BIBLIOGRAPHY

Dewey, John. *The Collected Works: The Early Works, The Middle Works, The Later Works*. 37 vols. Edited by Jo Ann Boydston. Carbondale: Southern Illinois University Press, 1967-1992.

_____. *Human Nature and Conduct*. Vol. 14 in *The Collected Works: The Middle Works*, edited by Jo Ann Boydston. Carbondale: Southern Illinois University Press, 1985.

_____. "Philosophies of Freedom." In *The Collected Works: The Later Works*, edited by Jo Ann Boydston. Vol. 3. Carbondale: Southern Illinois University Press, 1984.

_____. *Theory of Valuation*. Vol. 13 in *The Collected Works: Later Works*, edited by Jo Ann Boydston. Carbondale: Southern Illinois University Press, 1988.

_____. "Three Independent Factors in Morals." In *The Collected Works: The Later Works*, edited by Jo Ann Boydston. Vol. 5. Carbondale: Southern Illinois University Press, 1985.

Dewey, John, and James H. Tufts. *Ethics*. 2d rev ed. Vol. 7 in *The Collected Works: The Later Works*, edited by Jo Ann Boydston. Carbondale: Southern Illinois University Press, 1985.

Gouinlock, James. *John Dewey's Philosophy of Value.* New York: Humanities Press, 1972.

Prescriptivism

TYPE OF ETHICS: Theory of ethics
DATE: Coined in 1952 by Richard Mervyn Hare
ASSOCIATED WITH: Richard Mervyn Hare
DEFINITION: The theory that the main meaning and purpose of moral language is to prescribe or command
SIGNIFICANCE: Prescriptivism implies that ethical knowledge as such does not exist

Hare's view has received at least five important criticisms. First, his view that morality consists only of commands implies that ethical knowledge is impossible, since a command, unlike an indicative statement, cannot be true. Second, his view that anyone who accepts a moral statement and can act on it will obey the command has counterexamples in apathetic and evil people who knowingly refuse to do what they admit is ethically required. Third, the great variety of uses of moral claims makes it unlikely that they can all be reduced to imperatives. Fourth, F. E. Sparshott believes that Hare neglects the fact that any morality must incorporate "those rules of conduct that seem necessary for communal living." Fifth, P. H. Nowell-Smith reduces Hare's theory to the absurd by exposing its implication that "Nothing that we discover about the nature of moral judgments entails that it is wrong to put all Jews in gas-chambers."

In ethics and religion, prescriptivism sometimes refers not to Hare's theory but to the theory that the only justifications for moral claims are the commands of some authority (such as God). Socrates criticized this view in Plato's *Euthyphro*, where he suggested that an act was not good only because God commanded it but that God commanded the act because it was independently good.

See also Hare, R. M.

Price fixing

TYPE OF ETHICS: Business and labor ethics
DATE: Made illegal in the United States on July 2, 1890
ASSOCIATED WITH: Theories of marketplace behavior
DEFINITION: Agreement by sellers of a product or service to charge the same price
SIGNIFICANCE: Because consumers have little power in bargaining over prices, many theorists believe that it is unfair for sellers to get together to set high prices

Concepts associated with price fixing go back at least to ancient Greece. Philosophers argued about how a "just price," one that was fair to both consumers and producers, could be identified. Debates concerning the ethical issues involved in setting prices concerned the relative power of consumers and producers in the marketplace and behavior that constituted fair play. Opponents of price fixing argued that producers are likely, if allowed, to set prices that give them high levels of profit that are not justified by costs or risks taken in business.

The Sherman Antitrust Act, signed into law on July 2, 1890, forbade contracts, combinations of business, or conspiracies in restraint of trade. Exactly what constituted a restraint of trade remained to be decided by the courts, but price fixing was soon declared illegal under the act. The price fixing laws of the United States are more stringent than are those of other countries. Many countries do not forbid the practice, and some well-known trade organizations, such as the Organization of Petroleum Exporting Countries, exist primarily to fix prices. Even the United States allows some forms of price fixing, such as guaranteed minimum prices for farm products and minimum wages. These exceptions are seen as benefiting sellers of products or services that society has an interest in protecting.

See also Antitrust legislation; Monopoly; Profit economy; Sales, ethics of.

Pride

Type of ethics: Personal and social ethics
Associated with: Individualism, egoism, and humility
Definition: A highly positive evaluation of one's own worth
Significance: Argues that humans ought to be ambitious and strive for excellence of character and, having achieved it, should justifiably feel self-esteem

John Stuart Mill noted that pride is "a name which is given indiscriminately to some of the most and to some of the least estimable feelings of which mankind is capable." Pride has been identified as a proper reward for moral achievement and as a key element in a healthy psyche, and it has been blasted as a destructive emotion and as one of the "seven deadly sins."

The core of pride is a high sense of one's own moral value. One dimension of this is moral ambitiousness—a desire to achieve excellence of character. People speak, for example, of taking pride in their work; that is, of being committed to the achievement of quality. This forward-looking dimension of pride complements its backward-looking dimension as a sense of self-satisfaction for what one has achieved. People speak, for example, of feeling proud of having done a good job, of having succeeded at a challenging task.

History. Aristotle held pride, or "greatness of soul," to be the "crown" of the virtues. Pride, he argued, follows from the achievement of virtue. Anyone who has worked hard to achieve excellence of character will feel a justified sense of self-worth. Excellence of character and the pride that goes with it also translate into a certain style of action: The proud person not only does excellent things but also does them with grace and dignity. Magnificence characterizes the great-souled person in both character and action.

Aristotle's was a highly optimistic account of what was possible for human beings. Later thinkers often accepted a more pessimistic view of human nature, and therefore deemphasized pride or even condemned it as a sin. The Christian tradition has many prominent representatives of this view. Emphasizing human helplessness in the face of Original Sin, Christians argued that pride is unjustified. Since humankind is sinful and weak, humility is proper. Pride was condemned as rebellion against God, because it involves a sense of self-worth and competence, and those who feel self-worth and competence will not feel dependent upon God to save them from sin.

The modern era has been an heir to the Greek and Christian traditions, and many modern thinkers seek a middle way between them. Between the extremes of pride and humility lies modesty—thinking oneself neither great nor worthless. Such middle ways can be found in David Hume's advocacy of a "well-regulated pride" and Adam Smith's advocacy of magnanimity tempered with self-denial and a ready sympathy for the woes of others.

Criticisms. Pride requires that one (a) achieve excellence of character, (b) evaluate one's character accurately, and (c) act in accordance with one's evaluation. Opponents of pride argue that one or more of these conditions cannot or should not be satisfied. As noted above, Christians argue that since humans cannot achieve moral goodness by their own efforts, (a) is impossible. Others argue that humans chronically overestimate their achievements, so (b) is wishful thinking, and a dose of modesty or humility is a useful corrective. Still others argue that one ought to be self-deprecating about oneself so as not to hurt the feelings of others, or so as not to appear to be vain or a braggart.

Defenders of pride reject these arguments. Humans have free will, so they can regulate their thoughts and actions. Accordingly, they can act consistently in a way that allows them to achieve excellence of character and a fulfilled life, and this is what one should do: Happiness depends on excellence of character, and excellence of character is acquired by one's own efforts. This process of forming one's character means objectively evaluating one's thoughts and actions throughout one's life, reaffirming those that are good and changing those that are not. Once one has achieved excellence of character, simple justice requires that one reap the reward for one's achievement: pride.

False Pride, Vanity, and *Hubris*. True pride should be distinguished from false pride, vanity, and *hubris*. Everyone knows people who never miss an opportunity to brag about some achievement, whether real or imagined. A braggart may appear to be proud, but chronic bragging indicates a lack of pride: The braggart feels a desperate need for the approval of others, feeling self-worth only when that approval is received. Therefore, the braggart publicizes his or her accomplishments or, failing that, exaggerates or invents some. Clearly, there is a huge difference between self-evaluation based on actual accomplishment and self-evaluation based on deluded praise or praise extorted from others.

Vain people depend for their feeling of self-worth upon superficial or secondary characteristics, such as having a glorious family history, a slim figure, or a wonderful head of hair. While such things can be pleasant or desirable, vain people place them at the core of their self-evaluation and therefore expect inappropriate amounts of admiration from others.

Hubris is presented in classical Greek mythology and

drama as the flaw of wanton activity flowing from an over-estimation of one's worth. The man of *hubris* acts as though he has power and worth beyond his station, and because of his flaw he inevitably meets a tragic end. *Hubris* is distinguished from pride by reference to the accuracy of one's self-evaluation. The man of *hubris* misjudges his power and worth, and since he cannot live up to or control the outcomes of his deeds, he ends in disaster. The proud woman, by contrast, judges her considerable powers accurately and has the excellence of character necessary to use her powers confidently, gracefully, and successfully. —*Stephen R. C. Hicks*

See also Self-respect; Selfishness; Virtue.

BIBLIOGRAPHY

Aristotle. *Nicomachean Ethics*. Edited by G. Ramsauer. New York: Garland, 1987.

Augustine. *Confessions*. Translated by Henry Chadwick. New York: Oxford University Press, 1991.

Bernard (Abbot of Clairvaux). *The Steps of Humility*. Translated by George Bosworth Burch. Notre Dame, Ind.: University of Notre Dame Press, 1963.

Rand, Ayn. "The Objectivist Ethics." *The Virtue of Selfishness*. New York: New American Library, 1964.

Smith, Adam. *The Theory of Moral Sentiments*. Indianapolis: Liberty Classics, 1976.

Principles of Medical Ethics

TYPE OF ETHICS: Bioethics
DATE: Adopted 1957
DEFINITION: The American Medical Association (AMA) guidelines on professional conduct, consisting of basic principles, supplemented by opinions and commentary on specific cases and questions
SIGNIFICANCE: Set professional standards of conduct that are applicable to all U.S. physicians

In 1957, the AMA replaced its *Code of Ethics*—which had, since the organization's founding in 1847, stated the duties that American physicians owed to their patients, their society, and to one another—with a statement of moral principles, supplemented by commentary. The reform was consonant with the appeal to basic moral principles by the 1948 Nuremberg Tribunal and the World Medical Association. It also lessened physicians' malpractice liability under the explicit obligations stipulated by the *Code* and, at the same time, provided a more flexible format for advising physicians on conduct. The *Principles* require physicians to provide competent, compassionate medical service, respectful of human dignity; to deal honestly with patients and colleagues; to expose fraud and deception; to respect the law; to respect the rights of patients and to safeguard their confidences; to respect the rights of colleagues and other health care professionals; to advance scientific knowledge; to share information with patients, colleagues, and the public; and to recognize a responsibility to contribute to the community.

See also American Medical Association (AMA); Bills of rights, medical; Medical ethics.

Principles of Medical Ethics with Annotations Especially Applicable to Psychiatry

TYPE OF ETHICS: Psychological ethics
DATE: First published September, 1973, in *The American Journal of Psychiatry*
ASSOCIATED WITH: The American Medical Association and the American Psychiatric Association
DEFINITION: An addendum to *Principles of Medical Ethics* that addresses unique issues confronting psychiatrists
SIGNIFICANCE: Describes the ethical issues confronting practicing psychiatrists and defines what constitutes ethical conduct

The 1973 statement of *Principles* recognized that, although psychiatrists have the same goals as all physicians in adhering to the American Medical Association's code of ethics, psychiatrists also face particular ethical questions that differ in kind and degree from those of other medical specialties. The annotations given in the *Principles* were viewed as being open to revision from time to time to reflect current issues and problems. An extensive revision was published in 1986. The most relevant sections of the 1973 document dealt with contractual relationships with other mental health professionals and physicians; the waiving of confidentiality; and speaking out on social issues not related to psychiatry. The thrust of the document was that psychiatrists must maintain the trust of their patients and other medical and nonmedical professionals. The 1986 revision maintains this basic thrust, but its seven sections contain much more lengthy, detailed, and specific annotations and focus in particular on the various aspects of the psychiatrist-patient relationship, such as confidentiality, consultation with other psychiatrists, honesty, and so forth.

See also *Ethical Principles of Psychologists*; Medical ethics; *Principles of Medical Ethics*; Psychology.

Prisoner's dilemma

TYPE OF ETHICS: Theory of ethics
DATE: Created 1950
ASSOCIATED WITH: Russell Hardin, Mancur Olson, and others
DEFINITION: An ethical dilemma that sheds light on the possibilities for individual cooperation toward collective goals
SIGNIFICANCE: Individual self-interest may prevent collective action that all individuals perceive is in their self-interest, leaving each individual in a less optimal situation than would have been the case if everyone had cooperated

The prisoner's dilemma was originally developed as a thought experiment in 1950. It has since become synonymous with a whole class of ethical and social problems involving the conflict between individual rationality and collective action aimed toward serving common goals.

Structure: Two-Person Problem. The problem begins with two prisoners, A and B, who are arrested for a crime. A clever district attorney, not having enough evidence to convict either defendant, offers each of them a deal separately. If both individuals confess to the crime, then both will receive a lesser sentence of three years. If neither confesses to the crime, they will be convicted of a lesser charge, which carries a five-year sentence. If one confesses and the other does not, however, then the prisoner who confesses will receive a sentence of ten years and the other prisoner will go free. It would appear that both prisoners would be well-advised to confess to the crime and receive a three-year sentence; certainly, both would prefer this result to the one in which neither confesses and both receive a five-year sentence. Yet each prisoner's protection of his own self-interest will lead to the less preferred result.

Consider prisoner A's position. If prisoner B does not confess, prisoner A receives a sentence of ten years if he confesses and five years if he does not confess; hence, prisoner A should not confess under these circumstances. If prisoner B does confess, then prisoner A receives a sentence of five years if he confesses but goes free if he does not confess; hence, prisoner A should not confess under these circumstances either. Since prisoner B has only these two choices, prisoner A's individual rationality compels him to avoid confessing, regardless of what prisoner B does. Similarly, prisoner B should avoid confessing, regardless of what prisoner A does. Both prisoners therefore receive five-year sentences for not confessing, even though both would prefer the three-year sentence they would receive if both confessed. Note that communication between the two prisoners will not help this problem. Even if the two could speak to each other, each would find it in his interest to try to convince the other to confess and to avoid confessing himself.

The ethical dimensions of this problem arise because both prisoners know they would be better off if they would coordinate their efforts and cooperate in their strategy, but their individual self-interest leads them to a less optimal result. One of the first applications of this problem to a real-life situation concerned the control of nuclear weapons. Consider two nations, A and B, in a nuclear arms race. Each nation knows that these weapons are horribly expensive to build and maintain; each nation also has sufficient firepower to destroy the other nation. Yet if one nation gains a significant edge in building nuclear weapons, it will be able to destroy the other nation's weapons in a first strike and dictate terms for peace by threatening the now-defenseless nation with a second destructive strike. Both nations may agree that to build new nuclear weapons is senseless, since the opposing nation will simply build more weapons to match the increase; as a result, they will have the same strategic balance, but will be much poorer and will not be able to use their resources for other important domestic priorities such as social welfare and job creation.

It would seem that the two nations should agree to stop building arms. Yet consider nation A's interests. If nation B does not stop building arms, nation A can stop and risk conquest or can keep building and maintain the status quo. Under these circumstances, nation A will continue building arms. If nation B does stop building arms, nation A can stop and maintain the status quo or can keep building arms and conquer nation B. Under these circumstances, nation A will continue building arms. Since nation B must be expected to think in the same way, the arms race will escalate and both nations will waste resources to maintain the status quo, even though both sides realize they would be better off with fewer weapons (and, therefore, lower costs for the creation and maintenance of arms).

Structure: Multi-Person Problem. A second ethical application of the general prisoner's dilemma, discussed by Mancur Olson and Russell Hardin, among others, extends the problem to more than two parties and discusses individual efforts toward collective action approved by all members of a group. In this scenario, an individual is asked to contribute to a group effort. A common example used is the placement of catalytic converters on cars to reduce pollution. Assuming that it costs $400 to add a converter to a car and that each individual believes that it is worth paying the money to clean up the air, it seems reasonable to believe that all individuals would order converters for their cars. Yet the individual contemplating this action considers two circumstances. If everyone else does not add a converter, then the individual can pay $400 to add a converter without making the air significantly cleaner (since one person's car produces very little pollution) or can choose not to add the converter and avoid paying the price. Under these circumstances, the individual should not order the converter. If everyone else does add a converter, then the individual can pay $400 to add a converter without adding appreciably to cleaner air (since one car produces insignificant amounts of pollution) or he can not add the converter and enjoy cleaner air without paying the price. Once again, the individual should not order the converter under these circumstances. The one difference between the two-party situation and the multi-party situation with the prisoners' dilemma is that it would be in the interest of the individual in the second situation to order the converter only if his contribution made the difference between the success or failure of efforts to clean up the air. Unfortunately, the chances of such a situation occurring are so small in most cases of large groups that it would not provide sufficient incentive to contribute to solving the problem. As a result, all individuals agree that it would be worth the money to contribute $400 for cleaner air, but none of the individuals does so, and the effort fails.

Proposed Solutions. Two solutions have been posited to both situations. The first involves coercing, or forcing, all individuals to cooperate toward the common goal. In the case of pollution controls, for example, the federal government sets emission standards that must be met for individuals to drive their cars; they are forced to add catalytic converters to their cars. A problem with this solution is that it requires some authority to compel the parties to cooperate; in the example involving nuclear weapons, however, there is no authority that exists that has the power to compel nations to halt an arms race.

A second solution is to give selective incentives to only those persons who cooperate. All individuals who contribute to public television, for example, receive handbags with the PBS logo, which only contributors can obtain. Such selective incentives may include cheaper vacations, group medical or life insurance benefits, or other incentives. The problem with this solution is that in most cases a group must already exist to provide selective incentives; one cannot obtain group health insurance rates, for example, if one does not have a group to insure. This solution does not explain how groups are started in the first place.

Neither solution addresses the central ethical problem of the prisoner's dilemma: that self-interested individuals may be prevented from participating in collective action that all understand is in the general interest. Therefore, self-interest alone may not compel people to contribute to the general welfare in many cases, even when individuals realize that their self-interest would be better served if everyone contributed to the collective goal than if no one did.

—*Frank Louis Rusciano*

See also Common good; Dilemmas, moral; Paradoxes in ethics.

BIBLIOGRAPHY

Abrams, Robert. *Foundations of Political Analysis: An Introduction to the Theory of Collective Choice.* New York: Columbia University Press, 1980.

Barry, Brian, and Russell Hardin. *Rational Man and Irrational Society?* Beverly Hills: Sage Publications, 1982.

Hardin, Russell. *Collective Action.* Baltimore: The Johns Hopkins Press for Resources for the Future, 1982.

Hirsch, Fred. *The Social Limits to Growth.* Cambridge, Mass.: Harvard University Press, 1976.

Jervis, R. *The Logic of Images in International Relations.* Princeton: Princeton University Press, 1970.

Olson, Mancur. *The Logic of Collective Action.* Cambridge, Mass.: Harvard University Press, 1965.

Rapaport, Anatol, ed. *Game Theory as a Theory of Conflict Resolution.* Boston: D. Reidal, 1974.

Privacy

TYPE OF ETHICS: Civil rights

ASSOCIATED WITH: Constitution of the United States; U.S. Supreme Court

DEFINITION: The constitutional right of privacy protects the individual from unwarranted government interference in intimate personal relationships or activities

SIGNIFICANCE: "Privacy" as a civil right implies that there is a zone of individual autonomy in which people ought to be free to behave as they wish; the dimensions of this zone are among the most controversial issues in philosophy and law

John Stuart Mill wrote, "[T]here is a sphere of action in which society, as distinguished from the individual, has, if any, an indirect interest; comprehending all that portion of a person's life and conduct which affects only himself, or if it also affects others, only with their free, voluntary and undeceived consent and participation" (*On Liberty*, 1859). The "sphere of action" in which society has only an indirect interest is a matter of intense controversy. As Otis H. Stephens and John M. Schab II said in *American Constitutional Law* (1993),

> The debate over the constitutional right of privacy is ultimately a debate between two sharply divergent views of the law. In the libertarian view, the law exists to protect individuals from one another. In this view, morality is not in and of itself a legitimate basis for law. The classical conservative view, on the other hand, sees law and morality as inseparable and holds that the maintenance of societal morality is one of the essential functions of the legal system.

Constitutional Basis of Privacy Rights. There are several provisions in the Bill of Rights that explicitly protect privacy. The Third Amendment prevents forced quartering of soldiers in people's homes. The Fourth Amendment protects against unreasonable searches and seizures on the basis that people have a "reasonable expectation of privacy." The Fifth Amendment protects the privacy of people's minds by prohibiting compulsory self-incrimination, and the First Amendment ensures freedom of conscience in political, religious, and associational matters. The due process clause of the Fifth Amendment protects substantive as well as physical liberty. Proponents of greater privacy rights have argued that the words of the Ninth Amendment, which suggests that there are unspecified rights "retained by the people," provides additional justification for expanding constitutional rights of privacy.

Although Justice Louis Dembitz Brandeis dubbed "the right to be let alone" "the most comprehensive of rights and the right most valued by civilized men," the first explicit recognition of a constitutional right of privacy by a majority of the Supreme Court took place in *Griswold v. Connecticut* (1965). An 1879 Connecticut law forbade the sale or possession of birth control devices and also made "assisting, abetting, or counselling" another in the use of such devices unlawful. Estelle Griswold, the director of Planned Parenthood in Connecticut, was arrested for violating this statute three days after Planned Parenthood opened a clinic in New Haven. Griswold was convicted and fined $100. After several intermediate appeals, the Supreme Court agreed to hear Griswold's case. After argument, the Connecticut law was declared unconstitutional. Justice William O. Douglas, writing for the majority, found that "specific guarantees in the Bill of Rights have penumbras, formed by emanation from those guarantees that help give them life and substance. Various guarantees create zones of privacy . . ." In sum, Douglas' argument was that the First, Third, Fourth, Fifth, and Ninth Amendments, when taken together in the light of the Court's earlier decisions, created a new independent right of privacy that was violated by Connecticut when it attempted to deny people access to birth control devices. Although Douglas' opinion was carefully limited to "marital privacy," it was widely read to go beyond the rights of married couples, and when a similar issue arose a few years later in Massachusetts, the Court extended the *Griswold* holding to unmarried persons.

Eight years after *Griswold*, the Supreme Court enormously extended the right to privacy when it decided in *Roe v. Wade* that the right of privacy covers a pregnant woman's decision whether to have an abortion. In this case, the Court struck down a Texas statute that prohibited all abortions except for the purpose of saving the life of the mother. Justice Harry A. Blackmun's opinion recognized, however, that there is a state interest in the preservation of fetal life, and therefore the right to abortion is qualified—it is absolute only in the first trimester of pregnancy, the period in which the fetus is not yet viable. *Roe v. Wade* has occasioned immense political and juridical controversy since 1973. The American public has been sharply divided over the abortion issue, and judicial and legislative struggles still continue twenty years after the Court's decision. The right announced in *Roe v. Wade* has been slightly modified in several subsequent Supreme Court decisions, but despite several serious challenges, its fundamental principle still stands.

Roe v. Wade was the high-water mark of the constitutional right of privacy. The Supreme Court has not pressed it further and, indeed, held in *Bowers v. Hardwick* (1986) that there is no constitutional right to engage in homosexual sodomy. The Court explicitly reserved decision on whether there is a right, marital or otherwise, to engage in heterosexual sodomy.

Some public safety issues also raise privacy issues. Recreational drug use, motorcycle helmet and automobile seatbelt laws, prostitution, suicide, and euthanasia are all issues that implicate privacy rights and with which courts and legislatures will increasingly have to deal.

—Robert Jacobs

See also Bill of Rights, U.S.; Civil rights; *Dronenburg v. Zech*; First Amendment; Gay rights; Privacy, invasion of; *Roe v. Wade*; Sexual revolution.

BIBLIOGRAPHY

Mill, John Stuart. *Utilitarianism, Liberty, and Representative Government.* New York: E. P. Dutton, 1950.

Stephens, Otis H., and John M. Scheb II. *American Constitutional Law.* Minneapolis: West, 1993.

Privacy, invasion of

TYPE OF ETHICS: Civil rights

DATE: Coined 1890

ASSOCIATED WITH: Boston lawyers Samuel D. Warren and Louis D. Brandeis

DEFINITION: Exposure of one's private life, especially by the media

SIGNIFICANCE: Once privacy had been acknowledged as a legal concept, the media had to respect the more private areas in a person's life

In 1890, two Boston lawyers, Samuel D. Warren and Louis D. Brandeis, published an article on the right to privacy in the *Harvard Law Review.* The article deplored the sensationalistic tactics used by the press at that time, which violated the average person's notions of privacy. Gradually, during the next century, such invasions of privacy were incorporated into an articulated concept in tort law. The earliest kind of privacy invasion was known as appropriation, the use of another's name or likeness for commercial purposes without that person's consent. Two other types of invasion of privacy—intrusion upon another person's seclusion and placing a person in a false light—developed later. A last kind of invasion of privacy—the one to which Warren and Brandeis referred—is the publication of private information about a person. Today, if such information is newsworthy or is a matter of public record, the media may publish it. Since opinions differ regarding what is newsworthy, however, this type of invasion of privacy remains most vexing for citizens and media alike. Generally, though—supermarket tabloids notwithstanding—because the right of privacy is now recognized by law, the media can no longer publish whatever it wishes to without consequence.

See also Accuracy in Media (AIM); Fairness and Accuracy in Reporting (FAIR); Journalistic ethics; Libel.

Private vs. public morality

TYPE OF ETHICS: Beliefs and practices

DATE: From antiquity

DEFINITION: A doctrine holding that private morality and public morality often diverge from each other, thus creating ethical dilemmas for the public individual who must "weigh" both when making hard choices that affect many other people

SIGNIFICANCE: Philosophers have attempted to combine the concepts of private and public morality in order to create an ethical society and state

In *Moral Man and Immoral Society* (1932), Reinhold Niebuhr argued that there are sharp, major distinctions between the moral, ethical "rules" of behavior for individuals, on the one hand, and for social groups, political and business leaders, and the state and nation, on the other hand. Actually, Niebuhr's thought on the issue was not original, for consideration of this ethical problem dates from antiquity. The most famous philosopher to address it was Niccolò Machiavelli, who taught political rulers how to be "bad" ethically so that they could be "good" in their calling. Such leaders, then, may lie, break promises, use violence, engage in deceit, give and take bribes, and even commit murder if such actions are necessary to hold and augment power. Another who drew distinctions between personal morality and public morality was Martin Luther, who talked of an "earthly realm" and a "spiritual realm" as if they were absolutely different entities. Max Weber also argued that there was a sharp split between personal and public ethics, while pointing out that the public "person"—all leaders in politics, business, the military, and so on—may have to use dubious means to achieve "good."

Twentieth century political analysts such as George Kennan, Charles Frankel, and Arthur Schlesinger have argued that *realpolitik* is the only thing that counts in government and in diplomacy. Frankel perhaps spelled it out best. He held that the moral rules of individuals in their personal lives are definitely not the rules that should guide people in performing complex social, political, or economic roles.

Interestingly, J. Fred Buzhardt, legal counsel to the morally condemned ex-president Richard Nixon, who resigned his office in disgrace, once asked whom the members of society would prefer as a leader—did they want a competent "scoundrel" or an "honest boob?" In this view, the picture of private versus public morality is darkly painted. Is it necessary to choose between ethically upright "boobs" and dishonest, lying, cheating criminals and near-criminals? The implication of Buzhardt's question is, of course, that the ethical, honest, sincere person is too naive to assume a leadership role in politics, business, education, and so on. Instead, there is room in the elite leadership class only for liars and thieves.

Machiavelli and J. Fred Buzhardt, then, endorse unethical public behavior as the norm and ethical behavior as bizarre. Such thinkers are themselves taking an immoral position by clinging to views that, over time, have caused much harm. Therein lies the problem. Public morality has been defined by those who speak for immorality, some of whom would tolerate all corruption and abuse if such practices were to lead to success. Actually, the later scandals in American "public" life have demonstrated that the country does not need competent scoundrels but should return to honesty, lest American civilization experience a permanent decline.

Consider a few facts. During the Vietnam War, four different presidents at some point lied to the public, as did some of their generals. Had the truth been told, might America have avoided that long, costly, and lethal imbroglio? In the Watergate scandal of the 1970's, lawyers, one-time Central Intelligence Agency operatives, and their minions committed such crimes as breaking and entering, burglary, and illegally "bugging" phones—all this for political and economic gain. When the scandal became public, lies abounded in such great number that many people think that the public may never know the exact extent of the wrongdoing.

In the late 1980's and 1990's, more scandals abounded. Corporate executives of the Chrysler Automobile Company ordered mechanics to "roll-back" speedometers so that used cars could be sold as new cars. Executives of many savings and loan associations and commercial banks looted their own depositors, their own "businesses," and forced the future's taxpayers to pick up the tab. Many congresspersons also showed their true character when they corruptly mismanaged their post office, restaurant, and bank. Former presidents Ronald Reagan and George Bush became mired in the "Irangate" arms-for-hostages controversy and a possible coverup. A person need only read a big-city newspaper regularly to find example after example of corruption and immorality in politics, business, and other public fields.

There are those who believe that public leaders should be held morally accountable for their actions, just as individuals are held accountable in private life. Perhaps public leaders should examine their lives and ask such questions as: Have I lied, cheated, stolen, broken promises, deceived, or taken bribes today? —*James Smallwood*

See also Luther, Martin; Machievellian ethics; Morality; Niebuhr, Reinhold; *Realpolitik*; Watergate break-in.

BIBLIOGRAPHY

Brennan, Joseph G. *Ethics and Morals.* New York: Harper & Row, 1973.

Cahn, Edmond. *The Moral Decision: Right and Wrong in the Light of American Law.* Bloomington: Indiana University Press, 1955.

Childs, John L. *Education and Morals.* New York: Appleton-Century-Crofts, 1950.

Durkheim, Émile. *Professional Ethics and Civic Morals.* London: Routledge & Kegan Paul, 1957.

Fleishman, Joel L., and Bruce L. Payne. *Ethical Dilemmas and the Education of Policymakers.* Hastings-on-Hudson, New York: Hastings Center, Institute of Society, Ethics, and the Life Sciences, 1980.

Halsey, Margaret. *The Pseudo-ethic: A Speculation on American Politics and Morals.* New York: Simon & Schuster, 1963.

Holmes, Samuel J. *Life and Morals.* New York: Macmillan, 1948.

Joad, C. E. M. *Guide to the Philosophy of Morals and Politics.* New York: Random House, 1937.

Sellers, James. *Public Ethics: American Morals and Manners.* New York: Harper & Row, 1970.

Webber, Robert E. *The Moral Majority: Right or Wrong?* Westchester, Ill.: Cornerstone Books, 1981.

Pro-choice movement

TYPE OF ETHICS: Sex and gender issues

DATE: Late 1960's

ASSOCIATED WITH: The feminist movement that emerged in the 1960's

DEFINITION: A coalition of persons and groups, secular and religious, that wish to keep abortion legal, unrestricted, and available to all women

SIGNIFICANCE: One side in the debate about the morality of abortion and the relationship of fetal rights to women's rights

Throughout history, a major means by which men have controlled women and restricted their rights is the control of human reproduction. Abortion rights have become a central concern of the women's rights movement. The movement argues that women must have total control over their bodies, including their reproductive processes, if they are to be able to function as free, equal members of society.

History. Abortion has been practiced throughout history and across cultures. Formulas for abortion appear in Chinese

A pro-choice demonstrator. (Sally Ann Rogers)

medical texts dating from 3000 B.C.E. and in Islamic texts in the Middle Ages. Regular reference to abortion appear in Greek and Roman texts and early Christian literature. Regardless of societal tolerance or prohibition, women have resorted to abortion to terminate unwanted pregnancies even though many of the techniques used have threatened their lives and health.

The modern pro-choice movement has its roots in the women's rights movements of the early twentieth century in the United States and Europe. Responding to legal prohibitions against disseminating information about birth control, women such as Margaret Sanger incorporated demands for reproductive rights into the movement. Building on this base, the feminist movement in the United States in the 1960's established a pro-choice coalition to support abortion rights. Included were demands that the legality of abortion be restored (abortion had been legal in the United States until the latter half of the nineteenth century). In 1973, with the Supreme Court decision *Roe v. Wade*, prohibitions against abortion during the first trimester of pregnancy were ruled unconstitutional and only limited restrictions were permitted during the second trimester of the pregnancy. In the ruling, a woman's "right to privacy" in such matters was upheld as having greater legal standing than fetal rights or the right of states to intervene in the reproductive life of women. The Court's decision generated an immediate protest and the establishment of a coalition of religious groups that designated themselves as the "pro-life movement." This movement has worked to limit and even abolish the legal right to abortion. Such limitations have included the removal of federal funding for abortions, the establishment of required waiting periods before abortions can be performed, and parental and paternal notification and/or consent. A number of such restrictions were upheld by the Court in the 1980's and early 1990's.

These new restrictions have revitalized the pro-choice movement and expanded the coalition to include a number of secular and religious groups. The term "pro-choice" was consciously employed during this period to affirm the belief in the primacy of women's right to choose. While persons in this coalition have a wide range of viewpoints pertaining to the morality of abortion, they are united by their belief that abortion should and must remain legal. By the 1980's, the movement had become more proactive, stating that a pro-choice environment requires guaranteed medical care for expectant mothers and young children, guaranteed minimum adequate income that assures proper nutrition and housing for children, job-security guarantees for pregnant women, and federally mandated maternity leaves. Only such rights, it is argued, allow women to exercise free choice in response to pregnancy.

Ethical Arguments. Because of the disparity of beliefs of those who constitute the pro-choice movement, there are no moral arguments that are universally accepted. The most prominent and widely used arguments follow. (1) Drawing on the concept of "developmentalism," fetal life is recognized as human life and as having value. Value accrues, however, as humans develop. A woman, as a fully developed person living in a network of relationships in which she is valued, has rights that take precedence over fetal rights in situations of conflict. (2) Since many pregnancies occur without the consent of the woman involved (rape, incest, contraceptive failure, ignorance), the fetus has no more right to use the woman's body than the state or a stranger has a right to use her organs, without consent, for transplant purposes. (3) Since women are the ones primarily affected by pregnancy and childbirth, they legitimately retain the right to decide whether to terminate a pregnancy. Only legal access to safe abortions assures women control of their own lives. (4) Confronted with unwanted pregnancies, many women will resort to abortion whether legal or not. (250,000 to 1,000,000 illegal abortions were performed annually in the United States in the years prior to its legalization.) Illegal abortions are often unsafe, leading to the death or sterility of the mother. Since abortion cannot be stopped, it should be legal, medically safe, and easily accessible. (5) Failure to provide federal funding for low-income women is discriminatory and leads to unwanted births, further impoverishment, and in some cases life-threatening attempts at self-induced abortion. (6) Since some pregnancies result in the development of severely defective fetuses, the mother, as the party most affected by the birth of such a child, should have the right to decide whether such a pregnancy should be continued. (7) In an overpopulated world suffering from resource depletion and environmental pollution, women should have the right to use abortion as a means of population control when they view it as a morally preferable choice.

—*Charles L. Kammer III*

See also Abortion; Pro-life movement; Sexism; Women's liberation movement.

BIBLIOGRAPHY

Boston Women's Health Book Collective. *The New Our Bodies, Ourselves: A Book by and for Women.* Rev. ed. New York: Simon & Schuster, 1992.

Feinberg, Joel, ed. *The Problem of Abortion.* 2d edition. Belmont, Calif.: Wadsworth, 1984.

Harrison, Beverly Wildung. *Our Right to Choose: Toward a New Ethic of Abortion.* Boston: Beacon Press, 1983.

Petchesky, Rosalind Pollack. *Abortion and Women's Choice: The State, Sexuality, and Reproductive Freedom.* Rev. ed. Boston: Northeastern University Press, 1990.

Tribe, Laurence H. *Abortion: The Clash of Absolutes.* New York: W. W. Norton, 1992.

Pro-life movement

TYPE OF ETHICS: Sex and gender issues; bioethics

DATE: Early 1960's to present

DEFINITION: The pro-life movement believes that it is always inappropriate to carry out abortions, because the right to life is inherent in every human being from the moment of fertilization of the human ovum

SIGNIFICANCE: The pro-life movement seeks to prevent the abortion of any fetus from the time at which the human ovum is fertilized, because pro-lifers view fertilization as the event that produces a human being; hence, their ethical judgment is that abortion is murder, a crime that is always wrong.

Ethical conflict over abortion has grown hugely since the 1960's, when the pro-life movement began. The first members of this movement were Catholics, whose views were supported by the Catholic church. Since then, the movement has spread, and it now numbers among its proponents people from every religion, race, and walk of life. All these people view any abortion as being murder because they see the fetus as becoming a human being at the moment of conception, when sperm and egg fuse. Pro-life responses to abortions vary from peaceful methods that include demonstrations and attempts to dissuade women seeking abortions to active demonstrations at abortion clinics that sometimes lead to physical confrontations involving pro-life demonstrators, clinic staffers, and patients seeking to obtain abortions. In some cases, abortion clinic staffers have been threatened with physical violence, abducted from their homes or workplaces, and subjected to various levels of physical harm by pro-life zealots.

The end goals of the pro-life movement are to seek for the fertilized ovum the same rights that persons who have been born enjoy. It is deemed by many or most pro-lifers that the United States Constitution should be amended. A version of the amendment supported by several pro-life members of Congress states that "the paramount right to life is vested in each human being, from the moment of fertilization without regard to age, health or condition of dependency."

Concepts and Methodology. The basic pro-life concepts about abortion, from several sources, indicate the following ethical judgments: (1) the fetus at any stage in its growth from fertilization on is a human being in every sense of the word, (2) an abortion thus kills a person and is murder, and (3) anyone who condones abortion condones murder and is a criminal. According to some members of the movement, such people deserve "anything that happens to them." The action techniques of the pro-life movement vary greatly, and many are codified by pro-life manifestos such as *Closed: Ninety-nine Ways to Stop Abortion* (Scheidler, 1985).

Such manifestos list numerous operational procedures, including sidewalk counseling of pregnant women, picketing and demonstrations at abortion sites, disseminating leaflets and getting pro-life literature into libraries, advertising in the news media, using sit-ins, picketing the homes of abortionists, going into politics, and using horror stories to frighten women who are seeking abortions. Fortunately, many manifesto writers point out that violence should not be used, because it constitutes using evil to fight evil. Yet there have been regrettable instances in which this belief has not been shared by some pro-lifers, who have destroyed

property, abducted abortionists, threatened a shooting war, and, in one case, killed a doctor who performed abortions.

Historical Aspects. The conflict over abortion is as old as humankind. The ancient Greek and Roman philosophers codified the use of abortion. For example, Plato favored the use of abortion when it was for society's good, and Aristotle defined human life as beginning only forty or ninety days after the conception of a male or female fetus, respectively. With the development of Christianity, strong antiabortion sentiment arose and began to flourish. In more modern times, English common law stated that abortion was legal until mothers felt movement in the womb—"quickening"—and this view persisted well into the eighteenth century.

By the twentieth century, the abortion debate became quiescent, and many abortions were made legal by the 1950's. In the 1960's, with most Americans favoring therapeutic abortion, the pro-life movement began and evolved to include religious, medical, and lay proponents. At first, the pope and numerous Catholic functionaries preached a pro-life manifesto that was not backed by the Protestant churches. In the 1970's, however, various protestant clerics began to support the idea.

A number of physicians, including Jack Wilke, have been long-time leaders of the movement. Wilke, in fact, wrote a 1970's "abortion handbook," illustrated with pictures of mutilated fetuses, that earned eminence for his pro-life National Right to Life Committee. By the 1980's, the polarization between pro-life and pro-abortion factions had grown hugely, and the debate has since then become more and more acrimonious. It is not clear what will happen; however, verbal—and sometimes physical—battle lines have been drawn.

Pro-life lobbies in Washington, D.C., have sought to pass the amendment alluded to earlier. In addition, Randall Terry's well-known Operation Rescue has sought to prevent abortions and close abortion clinics. Documents have also been written by prominent lawyers propounding the legality of the rights of the unborn. Some splinter groups among pro-life proponents have warned their adversaries that a shooting war awaits them. A serious confrontation seems to be inevitable.

Conclusions. The ethical issue that focuses the actions of the pro-life movement is that it is never appropriate to stop the occurrence of a human life. The advocates of this viewpoint warn that if their point of view is unheeded, the consequences of such unethical decision making will lead to the practice of genocide. In contrast, those who favor abortion for "appropriate reasons" fear that its criminalization will lead to other restrictive legislation that will diminish human rights and produce many other forms of related human persecution. It seems possible that an ethical compromise could give both sides some of their desires. One model for use could be that of western Europe, in which respect for every human life is promised and abortion is permitted under conditions that are deemed appropriate and ethical.

—*Sanford S. Singer*

See also Abortion; Bioethics; Birth control; Christian ethics; Family; Jewish ethics; Pro-choice movement; Right to Life.

BIBLIOGRAPHY

Cozic, Charles P., and Stacy L. Tipp, eds. *Abortion: Opposing Viewpoints.* San Diego, Calif.: Greenhaven Press, 1991.

Faux, Marian. *Crusaders: Voices from the Abortion Front.* Secaucus, N.J.: Carol, 1990.

Merton, Andrew H. *Enemies of Choice.* Boston: Beacon Press, 1981.

Paige, Connie. *The Right to Lifers.* New York: Summit Books, 1983.

Rice, Charles. *No Exceptions.* Gaithersburg, Md.: Human Life International, 1990.

Scheidler, Joseph M. *Closed: Ninety-nine Ways to Stop Abortion.* San Francisco, Calif.: Ignatius Press, 1985.

Professional ethics

TYPE OF ETHICS: Business and labor ethics

DATE: 1970's

ASSOCIATED WITH: Normative ethics, applied ethics, and occupational ethics

DEFINITION: The normative discipline that deals with distinctive ethical obligations arising for those in professional occupations, including but not limited to medicine, law, and kindred fields

SIGNIFICANCE: In Western society, professionals, unlike nonprofessionals, have special responsibilities toward their clients, toward their occupations, and toward the public; ethical theory should explain these responsibilities

Professional ethics undertakes to examine the special ethical obligations and problems that people who work in professional occupations have because of their professional status. It seeks to reach normative conclusions about these; that is, it considers how professionals *ought* to behave in their professional work, not merely how they *do* conduct themselves. In order to accomplish this goal, it must consider the various professions in their historical, legal, and social contexts in society. Relative to differently organized societies, or relative to different eras in Western society, it may need to reach different conclusions concerning professional conduct.

Every occupation (at least every legal one) involves its own characteristic ethical obligations. Thus, firemen have a special obligation to rescue people from burning buildings even when it is dangerous to do so, and farmers have a special obligation to see that the foodstuffs that they produce are safe to consume. All such special obligations presumably could be discussed in the field of occupational ethics.

In order for professional ethics to be a distinctive field in its own right, it needs to differ from occupational ethics. The special ethical obligations of professionals need to be seen as differing in their source and character from those of nonprofessional workers. This can come about only if professional ethics is based on a conception of the professions that succeeds in demarcating them ethically from other occupations.

The term "profession" is used in a variety of ways in the English language, and most of these do not embody conceptions that are suitable for grounding professional ethics as a field in its own right. To forestall confusion that may generate doubt about the legitimacy of professional ethics, it will be useful to review several of these widespread uses before focusing on a more appropriate one.

Some Uses of the Term "Profession." When people ask "What is your profession?" this is often merely a polite way of asking one's occupation. In this usage, the terms "profession" and "occupation" are synonyms.

Another frequent use, which is familiar from sports, contrasts professional with amateur standing: To be a professional in an activity is to make that activity one's principal career, from which one expects to derive income.

In another sense, professional work is work that is done skillfully. "They do a professional job," people say of workers who perform knowledgeably and well.

The term "profession" generally carries a favorable connotation, and sometimes it is used merely to express the speaker's approval of an occupation and the desire that it be accorded high status. Thus, when someone says "Realtors are professionals!" often no factual information is involved, and the speaker is merely voicing approval of the occupation and seeking to enhance its standing in the minds of hearers.

In sociology, professions often have been discussed, and many descriptive criteria of professionalism have been put forward. These include the following: the work is white-collar, above-average education is required, above-average pay is received, there is an explicit code of ethics to which those in the occupation subscribe, entry is limited by licensing procedures, those in the occupation have an association that is dedicated to maintaining standards, the service provided is indispensable for the public good, those in the occupation work as independent practitioners, and income does not depend much on the deployment of capital. Typically, a sociologist studying professionalism establishes a particular list of such factors and then stipulates that an occupation is to count as a profession only if it accords with at least several factors on that list.

None of these widespread ways of understanding the term "profession" is satisfactory as a basis for normative professional ethics, because each of these definitions picks out as professions some set of occupations that, from the standpoint of normative ethics, do not differ significantly from the occupations it classifies as nonprofessions. If professional ethics is to be viewed as a field in its own right, it is necessary to employ a conception of what professions are that is more normatively oriented than are any of the conceptions noted above.

A Historically Based Conception. How did certain occupations first come to be called professions? Considering the history of the term may lead toward a conception that is suitable for the purposes of professional ethics.

The Latin term *professionem* originally meant the making of a public declaration. In medieval Latin, it came to mean the taking of religious vows. The English word "profession" comes directly from the Latin, and until the sixteenth century it too meant only the public taking of religious vows. After that, however, it came to mean an occupation in which learned knowledge is applied to the affairs of others, especially medicine, law, divinity, and university teaching.

The linkage between oath taking and distinctively professional occupations arose because of the procedures of the medieval universities. In them, students prepared for one of four careers; they could become physicians, lawyers, clerics, or university teachers. At various stages in the course of study, and especially at its conclusion, the student was required publicly to take religious oaths. These oaths affirmed general loyalty to the doctrines of the Church and to the discipline of the university, and specific commitment to the special ethical standards of the learned occupation being entered into. Such oaths, devised by persons who already belonged to the occupations in question, carried with them the threat of divine retribution should they be violated; thus, they served as fairly effective means for constraining new entrants to respect the ideals of service that had been established for these occupations.

Because they had taken these oaths, members of these four occupations came to have special ethical obligations that were different in origin and nature from those incurred in other occupations.

Applying the Conception to Modern Life. Downplaying its religious aspect, this conception of professions nowadays can be regarded as postulating an understanding between society and those in a profession, a bargain from which both sides benefit. This understanding may be spelled out explicitly, at least in part, but often in modern times it is left largely unstated and is taken for granted. Society accords certain valuable advantages to the members of the occupation, and they in return pledge themselves to promote certain goals that have value to society.

The chief benefit that society grants to members of the occupation is the right to a considerable measure of control over their own activities. This includes the right of those in the occupation to define for themselves that standards of performance should be obeyed in it and their right to organize their own disciplinary procedures for enforcing those standards. They may also be granted the right to restrict entry into the occupation by imposing licensing requirements (this may well have the effect of reducing competition and keeping fees high). It will be especially appropriate for society to grant these privileges to the members of occupations that are highly technical and require extensive knowledge. Outsiders will be unable to make reliable judgments about how those in such occupations ought to conduct themselves; therefore, the setting of standards and the enforcement of discipline may best be left to the specialists within.

In return for granting these privileges, society receives from the members of the occupation higher-quality service and the curbing of certain types of self-interested exploitation of their expertise by those in the occupation. The ethical requirements that the profession imposes upon itself fall under three headings: responsibilities toward clients (or patients), responsibilities toward the profession itself, and responsibilities toward society. Usually, the interests of the client will be accorded high priority, and the professional's technical skills will be viewed as the cient's to command, for any reasonable purpose. Responsibilities toward the profession itself will aim at enhancing the excellence of the profession's services and maintaining its standing in the eyes of the public. The responsibilities to society, though not negligible, will usually be accorded a distinctly lower priority.

If all goes well, both society and those in the profession will benefit from such a bargain. The ethical status of professionals will thereby become differentiated from that of nonprofessionals, whose conduct is not governed by bargains of this type.

In U.S. society, medicine and law are traditionally the paradigmatic examples of professions in this sense. Other occupations deserve to be classified as professions if they strongly resemble medicine and law in having this type of ethical structure. Whether an occupation counts as a profession will not be a black-or-white matter, however, but will be a question of degree.

Free Enterprise Versus Communism. This contrast between the ethics of professionals and those of nonprofessionals makes sense within a society that has an individualistic ideology such as the free-enterprise system, which prevails in the economic life of the United States. Such an ideology makes it ethically permissible for workers to aim at promoting their own individual advantage, when they are in occupations which have not entered into any professional-type bargain with society. Such nonprofessional workers are supposed to be ethically bound by the law and by the requirements of minimal decency (which prohibit lies, fraud, murder, assault, and the like). In addition, they are ethically bound by any explicit promises they have made to others; for example when an employee contracts to obey an employer's orders in doing work of certain kinds. Aside from these limitations, however, nonprofessional workers in an individualistic society are ethically free to act as they please, seeking their own advantage. (Society permits them this ethical latitude because doing so encourages them to work harder and more efficiently, which ultimately benefits society.) There arises a contrast between their ethical situation and that of professionals, whose conduct is constrained by self-imposed ethical commitments of the kind already mentioned, which are quite unlike employment contracts.

In a communistic society, this difference between professionals and nonprofessionals would not exist. Under communism, the ideology would be that every worker, whether physician or coal miner, always should be striving above all to promote the well-being of society. Consequently, there would be no special group of professional occupations whose ethics would contrast significantly with the ethics of other occupations.

Medicine as a Profession. In Western society, medicine has had a professional character since ancient Greek times, when physicians took the Hippocratic oath, pledging to protect their art and to use their medical skill only for the promotion of health. Although medicine has changed enormously over the years, modern physicians are rightly expected to retain some of the Hippocratic spirit of dedication to healing, righteousness, and service. For example, in an emergency, even a physician who is off duty is ethically bound to provide medical aid to injured persons who would not otherwise be treated (this is not the case with nonprofessional workers, such as farmers or fire fighters, who have no general obligation to provide services that have not been contracted).

Some writers who discuss medical ethics include in it wide-ranging public policy questions concerning how best to organize the delivery of health care in society. This is potentially misleading, in that it may suggest that defects in the system of health-care delivery exist only because physicians are not fully discharging their ethical responsibilities. It should not be supposed that increasing the ethical dedication of physicians will be the only, or even the best, way to perfect the structure of a health-care system. To deal with its problems, legislators must make wise public policy decisions.

A particularly controversial topic in medical ethics is whether it is permissible for physicians to end the lives of terminally ill patients who request it or to assist them in committing suicide. On the one hand, the Hippocratic tradition commits the physician to using medical skill only to heal and to preserve life; on the other hand, suffering patients sometimes desire to die, and some compassionate physicians think that it would be proper to provide such service. Prevailing opinion within the American Medical Association has opposed the latter view as setting too dangerous a precedent, and U.S. law has forbidden such action by physicians. In The Netherlands, however, euthanasia has been legally accepted and has been widely practiced.

Law as a Profession. In the United States, law as a profession has been dominated by the American Bar Association (ABA). Its Canons of Professional Conduct serve as an explicit statement of the way in which U.S. lawyers conceive of their professional responsibilities.

According to this statement, the lawyer is "an officer of the court." This phrase expresses the idea that the lawyer is a part of the justice system and therefore has an obligation to uphold that system and to promote its efficient functioning.

The ABA views the lawyer as having a primary responsibility to the client, whose prerogative it is to decide what legal action is to be undertaken. The lawyer's task is to provide accurate legal information and then to carry out the client's wishes. It is the lawyer's duty to keep strictly confidential what the client has revealed in the course of consultation, and the lawyer cannot legally be forced to divulge such information.

One vexing issue in legal ethics is how far the lawyer may go in promoting the client's cause by means that seem shady yet that are not illegal. For example, in a criminal defense, may the lawyer permit the client to give testimony that the lawyer has good reason to believe is untruthful? As an officer of the court, the lawyer ought not to countenance perjury, yet the lawyer also has an obligation to advance the client's case, and the client's questionable testimony may do this. In such cases, two responsibilities clash, and lawyers differ among themselves about how far to go.

Is Business a Profession? As education in business management has advanced, the field has become more and more complex and technical. Intricate mathematical analyses and strategies have become available to assist and guide the business executive. This development has encouraged some writers to say that business has now become "professionalized."

Business ethics, however, remains different from professional ethics. Under the free-enterprise system as it exists in the United States, it is ethically permissible for businesspersons to make pursuit of their own advantage their primary goal, as long as they do not break the law or violate minimal standards of decency. Professionals, however, have additional ethical obligations that further limit their pursuit of self-interest; they ought not to be as single-minded in their profit-seeking as businesspersons may be.

Various Other Occupations. Architecture, engineering, accounting, military science, and many other occupations partake of the character of professions in varying degrees. Those engaged in these occupations possesses technical skills and provide them to those who need them. Because these skills are so technical, it is difficult for outsiders to evaluate their use; therefore, associations in these occupations establish codes of conduct and seek to maintain high standards. The degree of professional independence is less, on the whole, than that prevailing in medicine and law, but the professional paradigm does make sense in respect to these occupations.

When architects, engineers, or accountants (especially certified public accountants) are independent practitioners taking on clients, their status is more strongly professional. When the practitioner is an employee of a business enterprise, the employer naturally exercises considerable control over the way in which work is carried out, and independence is diminished. Even so, the practitioner who has a will to do so may be able to maintain independence by rejecting any orders that are contrary to professional canons.

Journalism: A Controversial Occupation. Journalism is an occupation whose status has been especially controversial. Many journalists have come to regard themselves as subject to very special ethical imperatives that make journalism a profession rather than a business activity. They think of themselves as charged by society with the vital task of conveying news, and, more specifically, of exposing wrongdoing by prominent persons. (They have sometimes spoken of journalism as constituting a "fourth branch of government.")

A special test of this conception of journalism as a profession arises when journalists claim a legal right to preserve the confidentiality of their sources. For example, suppose an employee in a government department reveals to a journalist classified information about improper activity within that department. The government then seeks to prosecute the leaker and demands that the journalist reveal this person's name. The journalist perhaps refuses to do so, claiming a privilege of confidentiality that is, supposedly, analogous to the lawyer's privilege of keeping confidential what clients have said in legal consultation. Many journalists have thought they ought to have such a privilege; the U.S. Congress and the courts, however, have refused to grant it to them, and journalists who refuse to cooperate with legal authorities risk criminal prosecution.

Against the view that journalism is a profession, it can be pointed out that it is not an occupation requiring extensive scholarly education. Furthermore, it would probably be imprudent for society to hand over to journalists the kind of power to set their own standards and regulate their own activities that physicians and lawyers are granted. To do so might give journalists more political control over society than they should have.

Conclusion. From time to time, society should ask itself whether the tacit bargains that have been struck with professional groups are working out well. If they are not, and the balance has shifted away from the best interests of society in certain areas, then renegotiation may be appropriate.

Modern trends in medicine and law have been away from the older pattern of individual practitioners. More and more physicians and lawyers are becoming employees of large organizations. As employees, they must accept direction from their employers; therefore, they tend to be less independent than was the case in the past. This decreasing independence diminishes their distinctively professional status but does not eliminate it. —*Stephen F. Barker*

See also Hippocrates; Law; Medical ethics; Military ethics.

BIBLIOGRAPHY

Bayles, Michael. *Professional Ethics.* 2d ed. Belmont, Calif.: Wadsworth, 1989. Attempts to find a common structure in the ethical issues confronting many different occupations.

Callahan, Joan C., ed. *Ethical Issues in Professional Life.* New York: Oxford University Press, 1988. A wide-ranging anthology of writings about various occupations.

Goldman, Alan. *The Moral Foundations of Professional Ethics.* Totowa, N.J.: Rowman & Littlefield, 1980. An opinionated but stimulating philosophical analysis of basic issues, especially those concerning law and medicine.

McDowell, Banks. *Ethical Conduct and the Professional's Dilemma.* New York: Oxford University Press, 1991. Discusses the professional's conflict of interest over providing excessive services.

Pellegrino, Edmund D., et al., eds. *Ethics, Trust, and the Professions.* Washington, D.C.: Georgetown University Press, 1991. A lively collection of essays on philosophical, sociological, and international aspects of professions.

Profit economy

TYPE OF ETHICS: Politico-economic ethics
DATE: 1600's
ASSOCIATED WITH: Adam Smith, capitalism, and Karl Marx
DEFINITION: A social system designed to allocate efficiently the scarce resources of a society by allowing individuals to pursue their own self-interest and to accumulate the wealth gained from that pursuit
SIGNIFICANCE: A profit economy is thought to maximize individual autonomy and is considered a just social system because it is said to lead to the increased benefit of the entire community and because profit is thought to be related to merit

The purpose of economic activity is the satisfaction of wants. The question of which wants and whose wants should be satisfied is a problem of social justice. A profit economy determines how resources are to be allocated, what goods will be provided, and which wants will be satisfied by encouraging individuals to act in ways that they believe will enhance their own self-interest. In a profit economy, firms will act to maximize their profits and households will act to maximize their income, since firms and households are motivated by the desire to accumulate wealth. It is the ability to accumulate wealth that has raised questions about the justice of a system based on profit. Utopian thinking, which is based on the idea of economic equality, considers the getting of profit as the getting of more than one rightfully deserves, resulting in an unjust and preferential system. Supporters of a profit economy counter that in the real world, if profit is not to be had, little will be done. Furthermore, it is argued that a profit economy functions particularly efficiently, creating wealth that over time, will benefit all.

See also Monopoly; Profit taking.

Profit taking

TYPE OF ETHICS: Business and labor ethics
DATE: Nineteenth century to present
ASSOCIATED WITH: Investors, speculators, and insider trading
DEFINITION: Broadly, converting one's investment in securities or property to cash after realizing a profit
SIGNIFICANCE: Often involves profit gained by illegal means or profit gained unfairly at the expense of others

In its broadest context, profit taking simply refers to the action of an investor in cashing in an investment and realizing whatever profit has been made. There are at least three circumstances, however, in which profit taking raises ethical questions. Especially during the 1980's, when corporate restructuring became commonplace, insider or management buyouts and firms "going private" often meant that investors with privileged knowledge about a company would offer stockholders more than the market value for their shares but less than the true value of those shares. Then, sometimes after only a brief period of reorganization, the investors would "go public" again, sell some or all of their shares at a considerably higher price, and thus engage in profit taking. Such practices raised questions of a conflict of interest on the part of the managers involved, who were operating in their own interest rather than upholding their fiduciary responsibility to the company's shareholders. A second circumstance that raises ethical questions occurs when an investor realizes excessive profit from a transaction based on some standard of social acceptability, and a third such circumstance occurs when an investor gains profit by using unreasonable economic power.

See also Insider trading.

Progressivism

TYPE OF ETHICS: Theory of ethics
DATE: Early twentieth century
ASSOCIATED WITH: Reform movements, populism, public reform, muckraking, scientific efficiency, and Theodore Roosevelt
DEFINITION: A concern with the state of society and a conviction that human compassion and scientific investigation can expose societal problems and solve them
SIGNIFICANCE: Holds that society, through the efforts of volunteer agencies and political institutions, is responsible for and capable of addressing its ills and directing progress for the future

Although lacking a definitive ideology with common tenets, progressivism evolved in the late nineteenth century as a unique American philosophy that was intended to counter the economic and social ills of the Industrial Revolution and a burgeoning urban society. The philosophy formed the basis for a large-scale reform movement, led by young, educated professionals, that embraced all levels of society and encompassed diverse ideologies. The unifying forces for this movement were a belief that humankind had evolved sufficiently to control the course of human development through reform, dispelling the prevailing assumption of a fixed unalterable order beyond human control, and the belief that reform was to be accomplished through a democratically controlled government. Progressives emphasized systems, planning, management, predictability, collective action, the scientific method, and the value of expert opinion. Beginning with the Theodore Roosevelt Administration in 1901, the U.S. government initiated and sponsored legislation and amendments to cure the ills of society, make society more democratic, and provide equality for all Americans.

See also James, William; Pragmatism.

Promiscuity

TYPE OF ETHICS: Personal and social ethics
DATE: From antiquity
DEFINITION: Expansive and undiscriminating sexual behavior, such as becoming sexually active at a young age or having sex with many partners
SIGNIFICANCE: Although promiscuity per se is morally neutral, it may have several serious and negative outcomes; for example, dishonesty, sexually transmitted diseases, unwanted pregnancy, abortion, and the proliferation of single-parent households

The Sexual Revolution. The change in sex habits of Americans since the end of World War II has been described as leading to unlimited sexual freedom. Contraceptive devices had provided nearly complete protection from pregnancy, and changing and more relaxed attitudes about sex had mitigated the stigma of premarital and extramarital sex, sex with multiple partners, and having children out of wedlock. It seemed the American society had indeed become more promiscuous.

An extensive study of sexual behavior by Albert D. Klassen, Colin J. Williams, and Eugene E. Levitt (1989) concluded, however, that there was no evidence suggesting any far-reaching changes in sexual norms. Patterns of traditional sexual behavior were neither significantly reduced nor reversed. The authors concluded that a "sexual revolution" had not occurred in the United States.

Promiscuity. The conclusion that no sexual revolution has occurred does not imply that promiscuity does not exist. Klassen et al. pointed out that norms contradicting the traditional ones have emerged and that commitment to the traditional norms may not be as strong as in the past.

Another extensive study of American sexual patterns and behavior by Sam Janus and Cynthia L. Janus (1993) does provide a measure of how extensive promiscuity is. Their data suggest that promiscuous behavior occurs frequently. To cite some of the statistical information gathered by Janus and Janus:

1. Twenty-six percent of women and 40 percent of men aged 18 to 38 at the time of the survey became sexually active by age 14.

2. Forty to 63 percent of men from age 18 to age 65 and older at the time of the survey said that sexual experience before marriage was important. For women, the figure ranges from 25 to 56 percent.

3. Sixty percent of men have had relations with 1 to 30 partners, 21 percent with 31 to 60, and 18 percent with 61 or more. For women, the figures are 81, 9, and 7 percent.

4. Eighteen percent of men have had one extramarital affair, 38 percent have engaged in extramarital affairs rarely, and 29 percent often had extramarital sex. For women, the figures are 27, 38, and 12 percent.

5. Twenty percent of men, regardless of income level, have had sex with prostitutes, whereas the figures for women range from 3 to 8 percent. Most of these people

used the services of a prostitute occasionally (25 to 63 percent), rather than once (6 to 50 percent) or often (7 to 31 percent).

Promiscuity and Ethics. In Africa, premarital and extramarital sex are common. For example, a survey in Zimbabwe revealed that 40 percent of married men had had extramarital sex within the past year (the actual figure is probably higher). Part of the reason for this high frequency is that there is a cultural expectation that married men can have other relationships, and these relationships are accepted by the wives. (This attitude is changing because of the AIDS epidemic in Africa.) Ethically, promiscuity per se is neither good nor bad but depends on the culture in which it occurs. Unfortunately, often accompanying promiscuity are the following outcomes, which can only be viewed as negative:

Dishonesty. Where promiscuous behavior is not condoned—for example, in marriage—it is usually conducted without the partner's awareness. Lying and deceitfulness are commonly used by the one having the relationship in order to keep it secret. This breach of trust and of the bonds of marriage is hardly noble and virtuous behavior.

Role Models. For better or worse, professional athletes are the true heroes of American culture, and therefore their behavior sets a powerful example. When, for example, famous basketball players brag publicly about having sex with more than ten thousand women or contract AIDS in the course of having sex with hundreds of women, or the mistress of a baseball player is rewarded with extensive coverage in *Playboy*, legitimate questions can be raised about the kinds of examples that these heroes provide.

Sexually Transmitted Diseases (STD). The more persons with whom an individual has sex, the greater that individual's chance of contracting a sexually transmitted disease. According to a report released in 1993 by the Guttmacher Institute, 20 percent (56 million) of all Americans have an STD. Of the 12 million new cases diagnosed each year, about 90 percent involve people under age 25. By March of 1992, 139,269 adults and adolescents and 1,954 children had died from AIDS in the United States (not all as a result of promiscuous sex). The AIDS epidemic in Africa is even worse.

Other Effects of Promiscuity. The 1993 Kids Count Data Book claims that the status of adolescents is "deteriorating." Aside from STD, almost 9 percent of all babies in 1990 were born to single teenagers, and teenagers also accounted for about 25 percent of all abortions. Marilyn Gardner used these data to claim that "Early sexual activity can exact a terrible price from promising young lives . . . too many find themselves shackled by unplanned pregnancies, abortions, single motherhood, infections or infertility."

It would seem, then, that promiscuity is what is called in ethics a quandary; that is, a moral question about which ethical analysis produces a single undisputed answer: On balance, promiscuity is bad. To avoid the pejorative connotation of the term "promiscuity," social scientists often refer to "sexual networking" or "a pattern of multiple partners." Since promiscuity is not neutral in its effects, however, perhaps the pejorative connotation is desirable.

—Laurence Miller

See also Acquired immunodeficiency syndrome (AIDS); Sexual revolution; Sexual stereotypes; Sexuality and sexual ethics; Sexually transmitted diseases.

BIBLIOGRAPHY

Janus, Sam. *The Death of Innocence*. New York: Morrow, 1981.

Janus, Sam, and Cynthia L. Janus. *The Janus Report on Sexual Behavior*. New York: J. Wiley, 1993.

Klassen, Albert D., Colin J. Williams, and Eugene E. Levitt. *Sex and Morality in the U.S.* Middletown, Conn.: Wesleyan University Press, 1989.

Posner, Richard A. *Sex and Reason*. Cambridge, Mass.: Harvard University Press, 1992.

Weeks, Jeffrey. *Sex, Politics and Society*. 2d ed. New York: Longman, 1989.

Promises

TYPE OF ETHICS: Personal and social ethics

DEFINITION: A promise is a declaration that one will or will not do something

SIGNIFICANCE: Raises the question of whether it is ever ethically justifiable to break a promise

Every society is organized according to various kinds of rules and standards for behavior. Humans' social nature, limitations, and similar needs, along with the scarcity of objects, goods, or conditions such as food, wealth, and jobs, serve to create situations of conflicts that moral and other rules seek to resolve or minimize. There are many implied agreements, or moral rules, that allow people to live safely and to have meaningful relationships with others. These include agreements not to harm one another, not to lie or cheat, to obey laws, to treat others with dignity, and to keep promises.

In earlier times, one's promise, or "word," was part of one's reputation. Many promises and agreements were made verbally or by shaking hands. Some promises, such as personal ones, are still made that way, but many are written down as formal contracts and agreements. This is because such promises tend to be more complex and because fewer and fewer people actually honor their promises.

To understand the concept of promising and the breaking of promises, two basic and opposed approaches to morality must be examined: nonconsequentialist and consequentialist views.

Nonconsequentialist views, which oppose the breaking of promises at any time, are typified by Kantian duty ethics. Immanuel Kant (1724-1804) would argue that people should not universalize the breaking of promises, because if everyone should break promises, then promises would no longer have any meaning. Universalizability is based on the equality and rationality of persons. It means that one would be willing to be on the receiving end of a moral action. This concept is also expressed by the golden rule (Do unto others as you would have them do unto you), which is part of many religious and nonreligious codes of ethics.

Whether one keeps or breaks promises has an effect on human relationships, and one of the main arguments against breaking promises is that breaking them can destroy or undermine personal relationships. If a person promises to do something, most people will tend to believe that person's word. If the promise is broken, the relationship with that person is weakened, because trust is a central element of vital relationships. The lack of trust that develops makes rapport more difficult to achieve in the future.

A second argument against the breaking of promises is the idea that if a person breaks a promise and gets away with it, it becomes easier to break other promises. It can become a habit that is hard to break. Third, breaking a promise can have serious effects on other people's lives. In some situations, people make decisions that can greatly affect their lives based on promises that are made to them. For example, someone may quit one job for a promised job and end up with no job at all.

The destruction of general social trust is a fourth reason for not breaking promises. Much of what people do is based on promises and agreements. Once these promises and agreements break down, social trust breaks down. One example of such a situation is the lack of trust that people have regarding promises made during political campaigns. A final argument against breaking promises involves the loss of personal integrity of the one breaking the promise. Breaking a promise not only hurts one's reputation with others but also causes the loss of one's own self-esteem.

What if the consequences for everyone affected would be better if a promise were broken? Consequentialist theories argue that whether a promise should be kept depends on the end results. Consequentialists believe that one should always act to maximize happiness and minimize pain for all involved. Breaking a promise is acceptable if the greatest good consequences would be the result of that act.

One argument favoring the breaking of promises has to do with changed circumstances. One who has made a promise should have the right to break it if the circumstances under which it was made have changed. Another defense of promise breaking involves the arising of moral conflicts. For example, protecting human life should take precedence over keeping a promise. Promise breaking should also be allowed when promises are made in unusual situations. For example, a promise made to satisfy someone on his deathbed can be broken later for good reasons.

Finally, in the spirit of the Latin phrase *caveat emptor* ("let the buyer beware"), recipients of promises should beware. They should not assume that promises will be kept.

—*Cheri Vail Fisk*

See also Consequentialism; Deontological ethics; Integrity; Kant, Immanuel; Teleological ethics; Trustworthiness; Universalizability.

BIBLIOGRAPHY

Adler, Mortimer J. *The Time of Our Lives: The Ethics of Common Sense.* New York: Holt, Rinehart & Winston, 1970.

Barnsley, John H. *The Social Reality of Ethics: The Comparative Analysis of Moral Codes.* London: Routledge & Kegan Paul, 1972.

Cunningham, Robert L., ed. *Situationism and the New Morality.* New York: Appleton-Century-Crofts, 1970.

Hare, R. M. *Applications of Moral Philosophy.* Berkeley: University of California Press, 1972.

Property

TYPE OF ETHICS: Theory of ethics

DEFINITION: Goods over which individuals or groups have legal control

SIGNIFICANCE: Property arrangements determine the extent to which individuals control their own lives

Human beings need material goods to survive. Therefore, whoever controls the production and distribution of material goods controls human survival. The legal arrangements that societies enact for the control of material goods—property—are based on ethical principles regarding the proper relationship between the individuals who must ultimately consume the goods and the societies of which they are a part. Historically, three broad ethical approaches have shaped legal arrangements for the control of property: the individual, the collective, and the monarchic.

Individualism. Individualist ethics argue that each individual is an end in himself or herself. Each individual should have control of his or her own life and be responsible for his or her own well-being. Accordingly, individualists argue that each individual should have legal control over whatever property he or she produces or acquires; in other words, the right to private property should be a fundamental social principle. Economically, a free enterprise system results from the recognition of private property rights. In such a system, the moral standard at work is self-responsibility and individual achievement, and the property arrangements in the individualist society reflect this standard.

Collectivism. Collectivist ethics argue that individuals are subordinate to the larger social group of which they are a part. The larger social group varies depending on the version of collectivism that is advocated: The group may be defined in national, tribal, racial, or cultural terms. Common to all versions of collectivism is the principle that individuals exist primarily to serve the welfare of society as a whole; therefore, collectivists argue that society as a whole (or its representatives) should have legal control over all property in society. Control of a portion of society's property may be delegated to various individuals, but ultimate control remains with society as a whole. Economically, some form of socialist economy should result. In such a system, the moral standard at work is the value of the individual to the society, and the property arrangements within the collectivist society reflect this standard.

Monarchism. Monarchist ethics argue that some single individual (or, in aristocratic variations, a small number of individuals) is inherently superior to the rest of the individuals in the society. Accordingly, most individuals in the society exist primarily to serve the monarch (or the aristocratic class), and therefore the monarch should retain ultimate control over all property. Whether an individual has control of much, little, or no property thus depends upon the will of the monarch. Economically, some form of command economy should result. In such a system, the moral standard at work is the value of the individual to the monarch, and the property arrangements within the monarchist society reflect this standard.

Mixed Systems. Historically, most societies' property arrangements have been mixtures of two or more of the above principles. In some tribal societies, for example, most property is controlled communally, while some is controlled individually. Since no individual has control over the use of enough property to ensure his or her existence, however, an individual's survival is controlled by the tribe. Individuals whom the tribe holds to be valuable are granted greater control over property, both as a sign of favor and in the hope that they will use it to benefit the tribe, while individuals for whom the tribe no longer has a use—such as the deformed, the aged, and those who are deemed troublemakers—are denied access to the tribe's property. In this way, the primary moral standard at work is the value of the individual to the tribe, and the property arrangements within the tribe reflect this standard.

Most contemporary Western societies are a mixture of individual and collective property arrangements. Much property is owned and controlled by private individuals, but the use to which individuals can put their property is often controlled collectively by, for example, zoning laws; in some cases, a private individual's property rights can be overridden by eminent domain.

Connection to Civil Rights. Individual property rights are sometimes contrasted with other categories of individual rights—most often, civil rights such as the rights to freedom of religion, freedom of speech, freedom of association, and the freedom to vote. In some accounts of rights, civil and property rights fall into two fundamentally different categories; advocates of such accounts use such a distinction to argue for a mixed system of rights—for example, that all property should be controlled collectively, while individuals should retain the full range of civil rights. Others argue that there is no fundamental distinction between civil and property rights; they will argue, for example, that the right to freedom of speech means very little if one has no right to own a printing press.

Intellectual Property. Most philosophical discussion has focused on material property; for example, tools, real estate, machines, and animals. Increasingly, however, many of the values that contribute to human life require primarily intellectual (rather than physical) work for their production. Accordingly, individualist societies have evolved legal mechanisms to protect individuals' rights to the fruits of their intellectual labors, once they have been translated into physical form. Copyrights exist to allow individuals to control the use of the written works or art works that they have produced, industrial trademarks are registered and protected by law, and patents are issued to protect individuals' control over their inventions, such as new machines or drugs. Scientific advances continue to raise questions about the proper scope of such rights—for example, as biotechnology makes possible the creation of new life forms.

—*Stephen R. C. Hicks*

See also Capitalism; Communism; Intellectual property; Socialism.

BIBLIOGRAPHY

Blumenfeld, Samuel, ed. *Property in a Humane Society.* LaSalle, Ill.: Open Court, 1974.

Hamilton, Alexander, James Madison, and John Jay. *The Federalist Papers.* New York: Washington Square Press, 1976.

Locke, John. *Two Treatises of Government.* Cambridge, England: Cambridge University Press, 1960.

Macpherson, C. B. *The Political Theory of Possessive Individualism.* London: Oxford University Press, 1964.

Rand, Ayn. "Patents and Copyrights." In *Capitalism: The Unknown Ideal.* New York: New American Library, 1967.

Prudence

TYPE OF ETHICS: Personal and social ethics
DATE: Fifth century B.C.E.
ASSOCIATED WITH: Virtue ethics
DEFINITION: A state of character or principle of action concerned with determining the most effective means of achieving long-term benefits for oneself, and sometimes also for the groups of persons to which one belongs
SIGNIFICANCE: Prudence has a long history as a virtue that is necessary for living ethically, as well as a shorter history as a principle competing with ethics

In twentieth century ethical theory, there are two quite different ways of understanding prudence and its relationship to ethics. According to one, prudence is a virtue that is essential to an ethical life. According to the other, prudence is a principle that is distinct from, and often opposed to, ethics. The best approach to understanding these two conceptions of prudence is to look at their history. Since prudence has been examined during most of its history in languages other than English, it is helpful to identify the non-English ancestors of the term "prudence."

For most of the leading ethical theorists of ancient Greece, ancient Rome, and the Roman Catholic tradition, prudence is understood to be one of the four cardinal (principal) virtues. In the *Republic* (c. 390 B.C.E.), Plato uses the Greek word "*sophia*," which is usually translated into English as "wisdom," and Greek words meaning justice, courage, and temperance to name the four chief virtues (states of character) of both good persons and good communities. For Plato, persons with the virtue of *sophia* are those who exercise forethought in determining what is best, both for themselves and for the communities to which they belong, and whose rational faculties are in command of their other faculties. Plato's student Aristotle distinguishes, in his *Nicomachean Ethics* (c. 330 B.C.E.), *sophia* and *phronēsis*. For Aristotle, a person with the virtue of *phronēsis* is able to deliberate rationally about which actions best achieve the end of a good human life. *Phronēsis* was later translated into Latin as *prudentia*, from which the English word "prudence" is derived. Philosophers in the Stoic and Epicurean traditions, both Greek and Roman, also developed theories of the cardinal virtues.

Drawing from many of his predecessors in the Greco-Roman and Judeo-Christian traditions, Thomas Aquinas provides a detailed account of the virtue of prudentia in his *Summa Theologica* (c. 1270). He defines *prudentia* as "right reason applied to action" and explains that it is concerned, not with determining ends, but with determining the means to the end of a good, complete human life. Following Aristotle, he discusses three subvirtues of *prudentia*: *euboulia*, or good deliberation; *synesis*, or good judgment in ordinary cases; and *gnome*, or good judgment in exceptional cases. He distinguishes *prudentia* from false *prudentia*, which enables one to determine well the means to an immoral end, and from incomplete *prudentia*, which falls short of complete *prudentia* in one way or another. He explains that *prudentia* is concerned with both the good of individuals and the good of the families and communities to which they belong, and he offers a detailed analysis of the vices, or negative states of character, that are opposed to *prudentia*.

The shift in the understanding of prudence that occurred between the thirteenth and twentieth centuries was part of a larger shift in the understanding of the relationship between ethical obligation and the good of persons who perform ethical actions. Whereas the dominant view in ancient and medieval ethics was that being ethical is usually good both for ethical persons themselves and for those who are affected by their actions, the history of modern ethical theories is one of increasing emphasis on the obligation to benefit other persons at the expense of self-interest. The Prussian philosopher Immanuel Kant played a major role in developing the belief that prudence (in German, *Klugheit*) and ethics often oppose one another. In *Laying the Foundation of the Metaphysics of Morals* (1785), he distinguishes "rules of skill," which describe the means to ends that people could desire; "counsels of prudence," which describe the means to an end that all people do in fact desire (their own happiness); and "commands of morality," which tell people which actions they should perform because they are good actions, regardless of what ends are desired. For Kant, what makes an action moral is that it is motivated by a desire to perform a moral action, not that it has certain intended or actual consequences. In his *Critique of Practical Reason* (1788) and *Perpetual Peace* (1795), Kant writes that there

are clear boundaries between prudence and ethics, and that actions motivated by the desire to achieve happiness directly oppose morality. Kant's theory is, therefore, a departure from those traditions that understand prudence to be one of the virtues, without which one cannot be ethical.

The history of eighteenth to twentieth century ethical theory in the English-speaking world also includes a shift toward the belief that prudence and morality are in competition with, or opposed to, each other. Jeremy Bentham, in his *Introduction to the Principles of Morals and Legislation* (1789), understands ethics in terms of a distinction between duty to self and duty to others. He associates prudence with the former, but is somewhat tentative in calling it a duty at all: "The quality which a man manifests by the discharge of this branch of duty (if duty it is to be called) is that of *prudence*." In *The Methods of Ethics* (1874), Henry Sidgwick goes beyond Bentham by calling *phronēsis* "practical wisdom" and classifying it as an "intellectual virtue," and then classifying prudence as a "self-regarding virtue." Though Sidgwick allows that "prudence may be said to be merely wisdom made more definite by the acceptance of self-interest as its sole ultimate end" and that "it is a strongly supported opinion that all valid moral rules have ultimately a prudential basis," he is a contributor to the separation of prudence from ethics.

In twentieth century English-language discussions of ethics, it is common to find "prudence" used both as the name of a principle that is in competition with ethics and as the name of a virtue that is essential to an ethical life. For example, William K. Frankena writes, within a single paragraph in *Ethics* (1973), both that "morality must be contrasted with prudence" and that "it may also be that prudence is a moral virtue." Some twentieth century writers attempt to minimize confusion by following Sidgwick in using "practical wisdom" as the English name of the virtue *phronēsis/prudentia*.

—*David W. Lutz*

See also Altruism; Egoism; Self-interest; Self-love; Virtue ethics.

BIBLIOGRAPHY

Aristotle. *The Nicomachean Ethics*. Translated by J. E. C. Welldon. Buffalo, N.Y.: Prometheus Books, 1987.

Kant, Immanual. *Foundations of the Metaphysics of Morals and What Is Enlightenment*. 2d rev. ed. Translated by Lewis White Beck. New York: Macmillan, 1990.

Plato. *The Republic of Plato*. 2d ed. Translated by Allan Bloom. New York: Basic Books, 1991.

Sidgwick, Henry. *The Methods of Ethics*. 7th ed. Chicago: University of Chicago Press, 1962.

Thomas Aquinas, Saint. *The Summa Theologica*. 2d ed. Translated by Lawrence Shapcote. Chicago: Encyclopedia Britannica, 1990.

Psychology

TYPE OF ETHICS: Psychological ethics
DATE: 1960's to present

ASSOCIATED WITH: American Psychological Association, American Psychological Society, and U.S. Government Office of Protection from Research Risks

DEFINITION: Psychologists have established ethical guidelines for research (animal and human) and for applied practice (therapeutic and work settings)

SIGNIFICANCE: Research ethics prevent the physical, mental, or emotional abuse of subjects; ethics for practitioners ensure that clients' best interests receive priority over practitioners' personal and business considerations

When most people think of psychologists, they think of psychotherapists. These are licensed psychologists who have a private practice with individual clients or who work in settings such as hospitals, substance abuse clinics, or victim services centers. Psychotherapists (or clinical psychologists) have as their main goal helping their clients to achieve a better sense of balance, self-esteem, or mental health. To achieve this goal, they use a variety of therapeutic techniques and follow ethical guidelines intended to ensure that the clients' best interests are being met as well as possible.

Not all psychologists, however, are therapists. Psychologists are found in a variety of nonclinical settings where they must follow ethical guidelines as they apply their psychological knowledge and skills. Research psychologists must ensure the well-being of their animal or human experimental subjects, while psychologists who work in industrial, educational, and government settings try to ensure the well-being of those with whom and for whom they work: employees, students, and citizens in general.

The American Psychological Association (APA), the largest U.S. professional organization for psychologists, has formulated and published ethical guidelines for psychologists in each of these settings. It also maintains several committees that answer questions, make suggestions, and sometimes investigate psychologists who have been reported for malpractice or other unethical behavior.

Ethics in Therapy. The relationship between therapist and client is complex and potentially fraught with ethical dilemmas. In many instances, the reason the client is seeking help is, in and of itself, sensitive information; clients may be embarrassed or ashamed about a problem or behavior, such as phobia, bulimia, or sexual dysfunction. In other circumstances, a client may feel that his or her job, marriage, or even personal liberty may be in jeopardy if the issues that are brought up in therapy somehow become public knowledge. Clearly, one of the primary concerns of any clinician is to establish an open and trusting relationship with the client, and in most cases, that can be done only when confidentiality is ensured.

Therapists try to ensure confidentiality whenever possible, but a promise of complete confidentiality may put the therapist at risk for other kinds of ethical infractions. What if, for example, a client reports repeated fantasies of murdering his ex-girlfriend and the therapist feels that the reported fantasies may be based upon a real motive and plan? What if

the client brings up a history of child abuse and then admits to being a perpetrator as well as a victim? These and other such ethical quandaries are more than hypothetical, and, after a real case in which a client did murder his ex-girlfriend, the California Supreme Court ruled that the privilege of therapist-client confidentiality, like the privilege of doctor-patient confidentiality, has its limits. In cases in which it appears that the public welfare is endangered (whether it be a particular individual or the public at large), a therapist is ethically and legally required to report his or her assessment of the situation to appropriate authorities who may be able to protect the endangered individual or individuals. Rarely, however, are such decisions either straightforward or without cost.

Another attribute of the client-therapist relationship that makes it difficult to make clear-cut ethical judgments is the fact that the relationship of the therapist to the client may be, at one time or another, that of an objective expert, a friend, an authority figure, a role model, or a variety of other things; and behavior that is appropriate in some kinds of relationships may not be appropriate in others. In addition, since therapeutic sessions often involve intense emotion, there is always the potential for one or both parties to interpret the emotion as personal rather than situational and to respond to that emotion in an inappropriate way. It is not always possible to know when each type of role could be helpful and when it could be harmful; thus, it is impossible to come up with clear guidelines. Most psychologists, however, acknowledge the dangers inherent in playing multiple roles and realize that it is the psychologist, rather than the client, who should always be on the alert for such dangers.

A common but undesirable type of relationship between therapist and client is one of client emotional *dependence* upon, or *indebtedness* to, the therapist. While in such a relationship, the client may make it easy for the therapist to take undue advantages that are not in the client's best interest—for example, overcharging, extending the period of therapy beyond what is necessary, accepting favors, or even entering into a sexual relationship with the client. Such outcomes are antithetical to the goal of developing a better sense of self-esteem and well-being in the client, and they should be avoided at all costs; once developed, however, such relationships are often difficult to undo without additional psychological pain or damage.

Licensed therapists are also expected to maintain professional standards in other areas, such as maintaining and upgrading their education and competence, avoiding conflicts of interest, being able to make appropriate referrals when necessary, and being truthful in their advertising and other public statements.

Ethics in the Courtroom. Psychologists are more and more frequently being called as expert witnesses in the courts. One increasingly common practice is the use of psychologists to present evidence about the validity of certain types of testimony. Psychologists may address, for example, the accuracy (or lack thereof) of eyewitness testimony of witnesses of different ages (as in child abuse cases), or of memory elicited while the witness was under hypnosis, or the likelihood of different types of errors made by "lie detectors." They may also be asked to address special issues such as child development (as in custody cases), victimology, post-traumatic stress disorder, or "brainwashing." Testimony should be unbiased and, to be accepted by the court, should be based upon accepted knowledge and standards.

Psychologists are also sometimes called upon to make judgments that could affect a person's legal status. As expert witnesses in court, they may be asked to give their opinion on a person's mental status and ability to stand trial ("competence"), on a person's likely mental status at the time of a crime ("sanity"), or on the likelihood that a particular convicted criminal will respond positively to treatment or rehabilitation. This type of testimony cannot, like the types discussed above, be based solely upon accepted scientific standards and "facts"; because each case is unique, the psychologist must rely on clinical and personal judgment as well as scientific and statistical data.

Clearly, the impact of such judgments can be of great consequence, both to the public and to the person being judged. Therefore, both ethical and legal guidelines exist in order to help psychologists (and others involved in the criminal justice system) make decisions about a person's psychological competence and legal status. Despite U.S. society's long, traditional belief in personal liberty and the pursuit of happiness, that liberty can be taken away if a person is perceived to be a threat to himself or herself or to the public; whenever such drastic measures are considered, the ethical as well as the practical consequences must be addressed.

In some cases, a person is perceived to have lost the capacity to make free, rational choices—not as a result of incarceration, but as a result of severe physical or mental illness. Psychologists must often testify regarding a person's mental status and abilities when questions arise regarding the legitimacy and enforceability of a contested will, contract, or other legal document, or the involuntary commitment of an individual to a mental treatment facility. Both ethical and legal guidelines exist that allow a guardian or other legally designated individual to make decisions in the best interests of an "incompetent" individual, but it is difficult to determine when, if ever, a person should lose the legal right to make decisions, even when those decisions may seem irrational to an observer.

Although it is a minority opinion, some psychologists share the view of Thomas Szasz, who argues that all psychiatric and psychological diagnoses of mental disorders are simply negative labels that the majority give to those in the minority who have a different view, or kind of life. Szasz argues that simply because someone may be statistically abnormal and doesn't function the way that society expects, that does not make him or her any less of a person, even

in terms of legal rights and status. Clearly, what one considers "ethical" depends substantially upon one's philosophy.

Ethics in Education and the Workplace. Unlike clinical psychologists, psychologists in educational and industrial settings are unlikely to be working with clients with mental illness, yet there exist in these settings many sensitive issues that require ethical consideration. Perhaps foremost among these are the issues surrounding testing. Students, workers, or potential job applicants may be tested for a variety of things, including honesty, aptitudes and abilities, attitudes, and personality. Such tests are thought to predict academic or job performance and are thus often used to "track" people into particular classes or careers.

One of the most controversial ethical issues surrounding testing is the phenomenon of labeling. Although many of the tests used in academic and industrial settings do have predictive validity (that is, they can predict people's performance at better than chance levels), no test is perfect, so sometimes a person's performance is estimated at a much lower level than it actually is. Since the tests are thought to measure stable attributes of individuals, they are usually not given more than once; thus, a person whose test score underestimated his or her abilities would likely be tracked into an area that would underutilize that person's skills and understimulate his or her intellect. Once the person is labeled as unlikely to succeed in other, perhaps more demanding areas, it is unlikely that such opportunities will be made available. At the same time, the person may *self-label* and enter into what is called a "self-fulfilling prophecy"; the person will assume that the test is accurate and that he or she is not cut out for other kinds of challenges, and thus will not try more challenging things. Since many skills really reflect the phrase "use it or lose it," if the person ceases to try new things and practice skills, his or her competence level may truly drop. Thus, as a result of being labeled by a test, the person may in fact become more like what the test originally (incorrectly) suggested.

The ethical quandary surrounding test use is whether the benefits that the tests confer to the educational or business institution outweigh the potential losses to the individuals being tested. Since some tests are statistically valid, they can save institutions time and money by tracking people quickly and efficiently into areas in which they will perform well; they also can be beneficial for those students or workers who are unhappy and want professional advice about what kind of study or job may suit them better. The costs of labeling someone, however, are unmeasurable.

As an example, consider honesty testing. Some honesty tests, such as the polygraph test, are statistically better than chance at ferreting out dishonest individuals as long as the tester/interpreter is honest and well trained. By giving a polygraph test to all potential employees, a business may save thousands of dollars by screening out some people who might embezzle, steal equipment, or sell company secrets.

For each dishonest person who is caught by polygraph testing, however, there are several honest people who will also be weeded out and labeled by the test. Although the institution may save money by giving the test, many innocent (honest) people will suffer—they will not get the job, they may have something negative put in their files, or they may even be told that they failed the test, and may become depressed, hopeless, angry, or otherwise emotionally scarred. Because of these human costs, the U.S. Congress has outlawed the use of polygraphs in some settings, but where they are still allowed, the psychologists involved must consider the ethical issues each time the test is administered.

Unlike the polygraph test, not all tests used in educational and work settings are even statistically valid. Sometimes tests go out of date as society and culture change. Even those that are valid for one population (for example, adult males) may not be valid for another population (for example, adolescent males). Good psychologists must constantly keep up to date about the strengths, weaknesses, and limitations of the tests they use. Like their clinical counterparts, industrial and educational psychologists must realize that their tests are not always accurate, that there are dangers in mislabeling just as there are in misdiagnosing, and that a person is more than the sum of his or her test scores.

Ethics in Research. Psychologists who do research are subject to federal regulations that ensure that subjects' rights are not abused. According to federal guidelines, each research institute must set up an ethics committee to monitor animal research and another to monitor human research. Each committee must include not only research scientists but also at least one individual who has studied ethics and at least one person who can represent the views of the local community. Research using both animal and human subjects must be approved by the relevant committees before it is begun.

Researchers using animal subjects must ensure that animals are housed, fed, and transported in a humane manner; government-employed veterinarians make unannounced visits to make sure that each facility is operating in compliance with federal animal welfare guidelines. Researchers must also ensure that animals' pain and suffering is minimized, and that all alternative research techniques have been considered before any painful procedures are planned. The number and species of animals that are used must also be justified. On an annual basis, each committee presents a summary report of the institution's research activities to the federal government.

Researchers using human subjects must do much more in order to get a project approved by the local committee. Each researcher must demonstrate that all subjects are informed, in writing, of all possible risks of participation; that each subject signs a written consent form (or has a legal guardian sign instead); that subjects are never pressured to participate in a study and know that they are free to withdraw from the study at any time; that counseling is available for anyone who does somehow feel injured by participation in the study; that all data are kept confidential at all phases of the study; and that all subjects receive a written "debriefing" at the end of the study, which not only thanks them for their participation but also gives them any information about the study that may have been withheld or disguised in the consent form.

Withholding or disguising information in the consent form is called "deception." Deception is kept at a minimum but sometimes is necessary in order to prevent subject bias. For example, subjects may sign up to participate in a study that is supposedly on reading, but is really on helping behavior. While the subjects are sitting in what they think is a waiting room, the experimenter may stage an "accident" and observe how many subjects try to help the accident "victim" and under what conditions. It is likely that subjects would behave in a different way under these fairly realistic circumstances if they knew that the "accident" was staged and that they were really in a study of helping behavior. All research deception must be approved by the ethics committee in advance, and the debriefing must explain to the subjects why the deception was necessary. Studies that involve major or prolonged deception are generally not approved, even though they might provide useful information.

—Linda Mealey

See also Animal research; Behavior therapy; *Ethical Principles of Psychologists*; Experimentation, ethics of; Family therapy; Group therapy; Hypnosis; Institutionalization of patients; Intelligence testing; Mental illness; Milgram experiment; Science, ethics of; Sex therapy; Therapist-patient relationship.

BIBLIOGRAPHY

American Psychological Association. "Ethical Principles of Psychologists." *American Psychologist* 36 (June, 1981): 633-638. Principles one through eight cover ethics for practicing psychologists, number nine is on research using human participants, and number ten is on research using animals.

Keith-Spiegel, Patricia, and Gerald P. Koocher. *Ethics in Psychology: Professional Standards and Cases.* New York: Random House, 1985. Co-written by one of the original formulators of the ten ethical principles (see previous entry), this book gives detailed descriptions, justifications, and examples regarding APA ethical guidelines for therapy, testing, advertising, publishing, finances, and conflicts of interest.

Meyer, Robert G., E. Rhett Landis, and J. Ray Hays. *Law for the Psychotherapist.* New York, N.Y.: W. W. Norton, 1988. Organized as a handbook for practicing therapists, this text is still accessible to nonprofessionals. Covers many sensitive areas, including courtroom testimony, involuntary commitment, treatment issues, and malpractice.

Rubinstein, Joseph, and Brent Slife, eds. *Taking Sides: Clashing Views on Controversial Psychological Issues.* 5th ed. Guilford, Conn.: Dushkin, 1988. Each edition of this series, which is reedited approximately every three years, includes a "yes" and a "no" essay from experts debating a variety of controversial issues in psychology; includes ethical issues, such as research ethics, therapy effectiveness, behavior modification, intelligence testing, the insanity defense, and the consequences of diagnostic labeling.

Szasz, Thomas Stephen. *Thomas Szasz: Primary Values and Major Contentions*. Edited by Richard E. Vatz and Lee S. Weinberg. Buffalo, N.Y.: Prometheus, 1983. An excellent summary of Szasz's works, their critiques, and his rejoinders. Puts Szasz's views in the contexts of "psychiatric wisdom" and conventional public thinking.

Psychopharmacology

TYPE OF ETHICS: Psychological ethics
DATE: 1949
ASSOCIATED WITH: The diagnosis and treatment of mental disorders
DEFINITION: The discipline that studies the effect that drugs have on emotional states, including mood, thought, and behavior
SIGNIFICANCE: Raises questions involving informed consent, efficacious treatment, freedom of choice, and exposure to risk

While many physicians and biologically oriented psychiatrists have had a long-standing commitment to the use of psychotropic medications for the treatment of some emotional disorders, others have questioned its use in particular cases. From an ethical perspective, some people have questioned whether such interventions are demonstrably superior to other treatment forms—such as psychotherapy, for example—in view of the known side effects of medications. In addition, it is not always clear that patients are able to give fully informed consent, and it is not always clear that patients are fully informed of all the risks inherent in psychopharmacological interventions.

History. While the use of psychoactive drugs designed to treat mental disorders is relatively recent, the use of drugs as pain relievers and sleep producers goes back for many hundreds of years. Alcohol and opiates are good examples of drugs that have been used for such purposes. The use by the medical community of drugs to treat mental symptoms goes back to the 1840's, when bromides were first used to treat anxiety. Later in the nineteenth century, Sigmund Freud, the father of psychoanalysis, suggested that cocaine was a psychoactive drug that could be helpful, and in the first part of the twentieth century barbiturates were introduced to treat anxiety. Alan Gelenberg, Ellen Bassuk, and Stephen Schoonover point out in their book The Practitioner's Guide to Psychoactive Drugs (1991) that in 1949, with the synthesis of chlorpromazine, the medical community began to focus on the use of drugs to treat mental illness. At about the same time that chlorpromazine was developed, reserpine (another tranquilizer synthesized from the root of the plant *Rauwolfia serpentina*) came into use. Lithium chloride was used as early as 1940, but its ability to counter manic behavior was not established until 1949 and lithium itself was not approved for use in the United States until 1970.

Prescription Privileges. While physicians and some other health professionals (for example, nurse practitioners and optometrists) do have the authority to prescribe medications, nonphysicians, including psychologists, do not have prescription privileges, although on the federal level psychologists have legally prescribed within the Indian Health Service. In the 1990's, there has been a spirited debate among psychologists regarding whether prescription privileges should be sought by psychologists on a state-by-state basis. The focus of the argument has been on psychotropic medications and their judicious use. Some people have argued that nursing home residents are often treated with drugs that are designed to treat mental disorders when, in fact, most of these patients are not mentally ill. Conversely, while there is agreement that some children with symptoms of hyperactivity and/or attention deficit disorder should be treated with psychotropic medications, it is important to diagnose such problems carefully, since such problems may involve parents' ineffectiveness in coping with the child.

Objections to the Prescription of Psychotropic Drugs. In his book *Toxic Psychiatry* (1991), Peter Breggin argues that many patients may not have been fully apprised of the negative (addictive and dangerous) side effects of many psychotropic medications. In addition, he argues that the use of drugs even for the severely mentally ill is not unequivocally supported by research and that the results of positive drug studies are countermanded by evidence that some psychotropic drugs cause brain impairment. Mary Lee Smith, Gene Glass, and Thomas Miller, in their book *The Benefits of Psychotherapy* (1980), analyzed 112 experiments that studied the separate and combined effects of drug therapy and psychotherapy. They found that even for serious psychological disorders, psychotherapy was nearly even with drug therapy in terms of overall effectiveness. While drug therapy and psychotherapy taken together produced greater effects than did either drug therapy or psychotherapy alone, the effects of these therapies in combination were only slightly greater than their separate effects.

The Combined Use of Pharmacotherapy and Psychotherapy. In his book *The Psychotherapist's Guide to Psychopharmacology* (1990), Michael J. Gitlin raises the question of whether there are negative interactions between drug therapy and psychotherapy. To the extent that successful drug therapy reduces symptoms, some patients may not wish to continue in psychotherapy for their emotional problems. There is also concern that dependence on drugs may make patients unusually passive and relatively unwilling to explore their problems in psychotherapy. Finally, some patients may become distressed at the notion that they could benefit from medications in addition to psychotherapy, since they may perceive medications as a kind of crutch. Some patients, however, are convinced that they have some kind of chemical imbalance that needs to be "fixed" by means of psychotropic drugs. These patients do not believe that it is important to explore their problems in psychotherapy.

Gitlin also describes who should have a medication consultation. He points out that patients with such psychiatric symptoms as delusions, hallucinations, or psychosis should be considered, as well as patients with appetite or sleep disturbances and those with significant suicidal tendencies. Patients with significant medical disorders and patients with a family history of more than minor psychiatric disorders are candidates for drug therapy. Finally, patients presenting confusion, concentration problems, and other cognitive symptoms are also good candidates for medication consultations.

The Right to Refuse Treatment. In his book *Law, Psychiatry, and Morality* (1984), Alan Stone raises an important moral and ethical issue. Should hospitalized mentally ill patients be required to take antipsychotic medications? Critics of forcing hospitalized patients to take antipsychotic medications argue that this is an invasion of privacy or that these drugs are mind altering and thus violate First Amendment rights. It is known, for example, that some antipsychotic drugs can affect speech and thought. Stone cites a case in which the court was asked to decide whether the state can impose the use of antipsychotic drugs in the absence of an emergency. In that case (*Rogers v. Commissioner of Mental Health*), a federal judge decided that the patient did have the right to refuse medication, since the patient was not likely to harm himself or others. Stone argues that the real issue that should be addressed is whether a patient's mental illness will respond to antipsychotic medications, rather than assuming that antipsychotic drugs are chemical restraints. Some organizations, such as the National Association for the Mentally Ill, strongly agree with Stone. Others, including many psychologists, agree with the judge's decision. Time will tell how this topic will be resolved. —*Norman Abeles*

See also Institutionalization of patients; Psychology; Therapist-patient relationship.

BIBLIOGRAPHY

Breggin, Peter. *Toxic Psychiatry.* New York: St. Martin's Press, 1991.

Gelenberg, Alan J., Ellen L. Bassuk, and Stephen C. Schoonover, eds. *The Practitioner's Guide to Psychoactive Drugs.* 3d ed. New York: Plenum, 1991.

Gitlin, Michael J. *The Psychotherapist's Guide to Psychopharmacology.* New York: Free Press, 1990.

Smith, Mary L., Gene V. Glass, and Thomas I. Miller. *The Benefits of Psychotherapy.* Baltimore: The Johns Hopkins University Press, 1980.

Stone, Alan A. *Law, Psychiatry, and Morality.* Washington, D.C.: American Psychiatric Press, 1984.

Public interest

TYPE OF ETHICS: Personal and social ethics
DATE: The earlier equivalent terms "common good" and "common interest" occur in Plato's *Republic* and Aristotle's *Politics* (fifth century B.C.E.); "public interest" was used by Jeremy Bentham in 1843
ASSOCIATED WITH: Theories of the role of government, including intervention in matters of economic and environmental concern
DEFINITION: Actions or attitudes that serve to promote the well-being of the public rather than that of individuals
SIGNIFICANCE: Raises the question of how far the public interest should outweigh private and special interests, inasmuch as the public interest, by definition, is everyone's interest

For Plato and Aristotle, the concept of public interest arises together with the following fundamental questions: What is justice? What is the best structure of society? What is the proper role of government? The same concept, under the term "commonwealth," underlies the social contract theories of Thomas Hobbes (*Leviathan*, 1652), John Locke (*Second Treatise of Government*, 1689), and nineteenth century progressivism. In 1907, U.S. president Theodore Roosevelt signed the Pure Food and Drug Act, quieting decades of outcry against dangerous consumer products that were perceived as resulting from unregulated pursuit of the profit motive. The 1930's saw renewed interest in the government's mission to benefit society, and a plethora of public-interest legislation resulted. In the 1960's and 1970's, legislation addressed to public health and safety introduced a new level of regulation of private enterprise, fueled by the growing consumer and environmental movements. In response to business objections, there was a partial rollback of regulation in the 1980's. The longer-term trend, however, has been the evolution of a closer identification between private enterprise and public needs, partly reversing the traditional view that free enterprise and the public interest are inherently at odds.

See also Consumerism; Environmental Protection Agency (EPA), U.S.; Whistleblowing.

Punishment

TYPE OF ETHICS: Beliefs and practices
DATE: From antiquity
DEFINITION: The practice of punishing (for example, fining, restraining, flogging, or executing) offenders for the sake of retribution, deterrence, incapacitation and/or rehabilitation
SIGNIFICANCE: Universally employed as a mechanism of social control, punishment has been the subject of intense debate and remains ethically problematic

Punishment, along with crime, appears to be as old as human society. Punishment involves doing harm to supposed offenders in order to prevent the harm caused by crime. It is a crucial means used to promote social control, order, and, presumably, justice. While punishment has been endemic to human society, it is morally problematic in theory as well as practice. Therefore, it retains the status of a necessary evil. A society in which punishment is clearly obsolete has yet to evolve.

History of the Concept. The idea and practice of punishment are as old as civilized societies. Various histories make it clear that punishment has been a basic component of human society, past and present. Indeed, one measure of advancing civilization has been the codification of law, including criminal offenses and sanctions. Punishment is treated conceptually in Western philosophy, at least from the time of Plato, and is prominent in Asian philosophy as well (for example, the Chinese Legalists). The Bible and the Qur'ân contain many passages and parables involving punishment. With the coming of the Enlightenment (in the eighteenth century), social reformers sought to rationalize and humanize punishments, making penalties proportional to offenses and arguing against particularly brutal sanctions. The Ninth Amendment to the United States Constitution, for example, prohibits (though it does not define) "cruel and unusual" punishment.

Types of Punishment. Punishment may be classified into several types. Corporal punishment involves physical sanctions such as beating, flogging, or the amputation of limbs. Capital punishment involves the execution of offenders and is limited to the most heinous of crimes. Incarceration, the most common contemporary sanction for serious offenders, involves forced restraint in a prison setting. (Incarceration also may involve forced labor, though this has become less common.) Less-serious offenders may be subjected to fines, house arrest, probation, or community service.

Moral Bases for Punishment. Punishment involves doing harm to people, restraining their freedom, inflicting pain, or even taking their lives. Because of this, it requires moral justification. The primary justification is "retributive justice" (or just deserts). This means that the harm of punishment may legitimately be inflicted because the victims of punishment *deserve* punishment. In addition, punishment may be defended as a "deterrent." The swift and certain punishment of offenders discourages other people from breaking laws. Two defenses of punishment try to minimize the harm inherent in the concept. "Incapacitation" suggests the morally neutral restraint of prolific criminals until they have passed the age of peak criminal activity. "Rehabilitation" suggests that punishment can be beneficial. Here, restraint is used to reform the offender in a way that serves his or her best interests as well as society's. The problem with these last two rationales is that both involve the radical restraint of freedom. (In addition, incapacitation involves massive allocation of social resources and rehabilitation has yet to be proved effective in practice.)

Moral Dilemmas. Punishment is morally problematic in both practical and theoretical terms. In practice, the criminal sanction is often utilized to punish real or imagined "political" crimes against autocratic or tyrannical regimes. It is also sometimes meted out by unruly mobs, as in vigilante justice. In addition, real-life punishment is often brutal, even for minor offenses. The remedies for these ills are guarantees of due process and, as mentioned above, the prohibition of cruel punishments. Even when it is formally correct, however, the criminal process is disconcertingly imperfect.

Theoretically, punishment is marred by the problematic nature of culpability and criminal responsibility. Punishment can be legitimate only if offenders deserve to be punished. To be so deserving requires the presumption of free will. Free will, however, is philosophically and sociologically problematic. Where free will is not assumed (as, for example, in cases of criminal insanity), criminal responsibility is mitigated to the extent that temporarily insane defendants may even escape punishment or medical restraint altogether. While insanity is the extreme case, people are compelled in their behavior by all sorts of factors. Thus, free will is not an absolute. Indeed, its very existence is impossible to prove. There are also important social limits to the concept of criminal culpability, particularly where crime is heavily associated with a segment of the population that is in a disadvantaged social position. In such a case, social responsibility becomes confounded with criminal responsibility. As a result, the entire criminal process, including punishment, becomes morally suspect.

The Limited Effectiveness of Punishment. In addition

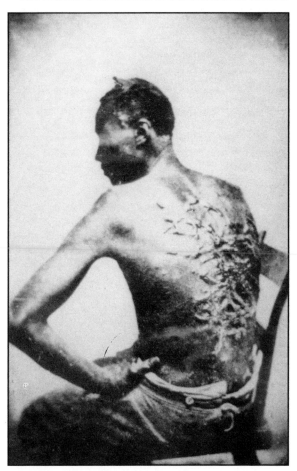

An African American slave displays the results of a whipping by an overseer in 1863. (National Archives)

to the moral dilemmas of punishment, there are practical limits to punishment's effectiveness as a means of maintaining order. Punishment is, at best, only one-half of the equation when it comes to social order. The other half is the availability to all strata of society of sufficient rewards for legal pursuits. Societies that permit crime-producing socio-economic disparities are not able to ensure social order by means of the criminal sanction. This means that a society can simultaneously have harsh punishments and high crime rates, as exhibited by the United States during the last third of the twentieth century. Thus, punishment is most accurately seen only as a corollary means of maintaining social order, one that complements the teaching of solid social values and an abundance of opportunity for legitimate gain.

The Future of Punishment. Despite its moral and practical limits, punishment appears to be an indispensable mechanism for dealing with certain kinds of behavior. For centuries, utopian thinkers have held out the hope for a society so well ordered that punishment would become obsolete. Such a condition has yet to emerge. Until it does, people can still attempt to minimize the role of punishment in preserving order and producing justice.   —*Ira Smolensky*

See also Amnesty International; Bentham, Jeremy; Capital punishment; Criminal punishment; Law; Mercy; Social justice and responsibility; Torture.

BIBLIOGRAPHY

Barnes, Harry E. *The Story of Punishment: A Record of Man's Inhumanity to Man.* 2d rev. ed. Montclair, N.J.: Patterson Smith, 1972.

Drapkin, Israel. *Crime and Punishment in the Ancient World.* Lexington, Mass.: Lexington Books, 1989.

Foucault, Michel. *Discipline and Punish: The Birth of the Prison.* Translated by Alan Sheridan. New York: Vintage Books, 1979.

Garland, David. *Punishment in Modern Society: A Study in Social Theory.* Chicago: University of Chicago Press, 1990.

Matson, Johnny, and Thomas M. DiLorenzo. *Punishment and Its Alternatives: A New Perspective for Behavior Modification.* New York: Springer, 1984.

Packer, Herbert L. *The Limits of the Criminal Sanction.* Stanford, Calif.: Stanford University Press, 1968.

Paul, Ellen F., et al., eds. *Crime, Culpability, and Remedy.* Cambridge, Mass.: Blackwell, 1990.

Primoratz, Igor. *Justifying Legal Punishment.* Atlantic Highlands, N.J.: Humanities Press, 1990.

Ten, C. L. *Crime, Guilt, and Punishment: A Philosophical Introduction.* New York: Oxford University Press, 1987.

Van den Haag, Ernest. *Punishing Criminals: Concerning a Very Old and Painful Question.* Lanham, Md.: University Press of America, 1991.

Quinlan, Karen Ann (Mar. 29, 1954, Scranton, Pa.—June 11, 1985, Morris Plains, N.J.): Focus of ethical controversy

TYPE OF ETHICS: Bioethics

ACHIEVEMENTS: The removal of Quinlan's respirator helped the fight for the right to die

SIGNIFICANCE: Karen Ann Quinlan's death is important in discussions regarding whether there is a difference between active and passive euthanasia

On April 15, 1975, Karen Ann Quinlan, then twenty-one years old, was taken to a hospital in a critical comatose state. She had had a few drinks, passed out, and temporarily quit breathing. There was a small amount of alcohol in her body as well as a nontoxic level of aspirin and Valium. Part of her brain had died because of oxygen depletion. She was moved to St. Clare's Hospital in Denville, New Jersey, where it was determined that she had extensive brain damage. Karen began to deteriorate physically and coiled into a fetal position. She was attached to an MA-1 respirator. In July, her parents asked that the respirator be removed and signed papers absolving the hospital from legal liability. The doctors refused. Karen was twenty-one, so her parents were not her legal guardians. Joseph Quinlan went to court to be appointed guardian so that he could have the respirator removed. The lower court ruled against the Quinlans, but the New Jersey Supreme Court ruled in their favor. Six weeks later, Karen was still on the respirator; however, the doctors agreed to wean her from it. She continued to breathe without the respirator. In June, 1976, she was moved to a nursing home where she was given high-nutrient feedings and antibiotics. She lived for ten years in a persistent vegetative state. Her case is important in discussions of the right to die, the ordinary/extraordinary care distinction, the active/passive euthanasia distinction, and the need for a living will.

See also Euthanasia; Life and death; Right to die.

Qur'ân: Muslim holy book

TYPE OF ETHICS: Religious ethics

DATE: Revealed to Muḥammad between 609 and 632

SIGNIFICANCE: The Qur'ân, the holy book of the Muslim religion, which was revealed to the Prophet Muḥammad by God through the angel Gabriel over a period of twenty-two years, is the primary source of Muslim ethics

Origin. Muslims believe that the Qur'ân was revealed by God to the Prophet Muḥammad through the angel Gabriel. At the age of forty, Muḥammad began to receive messages from God. Muḥammad had the habit of retiring to secluded places outside Mecca in order to pray and think. It was during one of these periods of seclusion that the angel Gabriel first appeared to Muḥammad. Gabriel shook Muḥammad several times and ordered him to repeat after him, to "recite in the name of the Creator" (the literal meaning of the word *qur'ân* is "to recite"). Muḥammad's relationship with the angel Gabriel was to last the rest of his life, and the Qur'ân was revealed piece by piece. The actual compilation of the holy book was undertaken by the third caliph, ʿUthmân.

Form. The Qur'ân contains 114 chapters, or *sûras*, which are further divided into thirty parts, or *ajza*. The order of the chapters, which is not chronological, was decided by Zayd ibn Tabi, who was one of Muḥammad's close associates. Zayd is believed to have collected all the verses from various sources—some in written form and others orally, from those who knew them by heart. Some scholars believe that the current form of the Qur'ân took shape many centuries after the death of the Prophet Muḥammad. The accepted belief among Muslims, however, is that the book was compiled in its original form by the order of caliph ʿUthmân. When the compilation had been completed, ʿUthmân sent copies to the principal centers of the Muslim empire—Damascus, Basra, and Kufa—ordering that all previous versions be destroyed. According to one account, the people of Kufa preferred another version that had been compiled by Ibn Masʿud.

Contents. Orthodox Muslims believe that Islam is a complete code of life and that the Qur'ân contains answers for all conceivable questions. The Qur'ân is the fundamental authority on all matters. (If no clear answer is found in the holy book, the next source is the *ḥadîth*, or sayings, that grew up around the life of the Prophet Muḥammad.) The Qur'ân is written in verse, and it is considered to be the ultimate example of Arabic poetry—a standard against which all other literature must be judged. It deals with all kinds of subjects, ranging from property and family law to the way in which prisoners should be treated during a war. The book is written with remarkable fluency and great style, and with a wide range of vocabulary. Because of the Qur'ân's literary quality, many skeptics challenged Muḥammad's claim that he did not know how to read and write. Several Christian and Jewish scholars claimed that Muḥammad borrowed concepts from their religions and had help from scholars in presenting his message to his followers. Muslims, however, claim that only a divine message could be so beautiful and poetic.

It is a fact that Muḥammad traveled extensively for business purposes. He is said to have visited several centers of knowledge of the time, including Palestine, Egypt, and Lebanon. These are the places where he is said to have met scholars and to have learned about other religions. Western scholars believe that this is how Muḥammad formulated his ideas.

One important concept contained in the Qur'ân is that the other so-called "religions of the book"—Christianity and Judaism—are valid because they are based on true prophets such as Moses and Jesus, who were sent by God. According to Islamic belief, God sent various prophets to show people the true path. After some time had passed, the people would be led astray by Satan, and God would send another prophet. Muslims believe, however, that God chose Muḥammad to bring the final message of God for all people. One of the five pillars of Islam is the belief that there is no God but Allah, and Muḥammad is the prophet of Allah; there will be no prophets after Muḥammad.

Some of the most important ideas of Islam are similar to those of Judaism and Christianity. Both Judaism and Christianity are monotheistic, and in both the ideas of heaven and hell are similar to those found in Islam. Many of the episodes described in the Qur'ân are the same as those found in the Old Testament; for example, the versions of the story of Abraham's willingness to sacrifice his son at God's command and the story of Noah's Ark are quite similar in the two books. One of the central themes of the Qur'ân is the day of judgment, which is described in various verses throughout the book. On that day, all human beings will be resurrected and made to answer for all their actions on Earth. Muslims will be expected to have followed the dictates of Islam to the letter.

There are various ways of interpreting parts of the Qur'ân, and these have led to the development of various schools of thought within Islam. Although there are two main sects in Islam—Sunnîs and Shî'ites—there are also several subsects that differ in fundamental ways regarding certain cru-cial concepts. In the modern Islamic world, for example, there is fierce debate regarding women's rights, laws of inheritance, interest-free banking, and many other subjects. There is a major struggle between a desire for modernity and the requirement to follow Islamic precepts to the letter. At present, Iran and Saudi Arabia represent Orthodox Islam, whereas Turkey and Egypt represent a more pragmatic, modern variety of Islam. —*Khalid N. Mahmood*

See also Ḥadîth; Islamic ethics; Muḥammad al-Muṣtafâ; Shî'a; Sunnîs.

BIBLIOGRAPHY

Ali, Ahmed. *Al-Qur'an: A Contemporary Translation.* 2d rev. ed. Princeton, N.J.: Princeton University Press, 1988.

Cragg, Kenneth, and R. Marston Speight. *The House of Islam.* 3d ed. Belmont, Calif.: Wadsworth, 1988.

Denny, Frederick Mathewson. *Islam and the Muslim Community.* San Francisco: Harper & Row, 1987.

Esposito, John L. *Islam: The Straight Path.* New York: Oxford University Press, 1988.

Râbi'a al-'Adawiyya (712, Basra, Iraq—801, Basra, Iraq): Mystical poet

TYPE OF ETHICS: Religious ethics
ACHIEVEMENTS: Composed numerous influential poems inspired by the absolute love of God; is one of the most important women in Islamic ethics
SIGNIFICANCE: She was a formative influence in the development of devotional Sufism, and her life is a popular epitome of devotion to God

Râbi'a's life is a metaphor for her thought: She was a slave who was set free by her master. She was a joyful ascetic who was freed from attachment to or desire for things of this world, even from the selfish desires of attaining Paradise and avoiding Hell. Her life was completely filled with immediate love of God for God's own sake. Hers was a jealous God who would countenance no other loves: There was no remaining room for marriage, worldly gain, self, or even any special reverence for the Prophet Muḥammad. She produced no treatises or other lengthy works, but her brief sayings, her short poems in awe and celebration of God's beauty, and stories of her life made a dramatic impact and played an important part in transforming the severe asceticism of early Sufism into a mysticism focused on divine love. She inspired devotional poets such as al-Rûmî and was celebrated by 'Aṭṭâr as "a second spotless Mary." She remains a popular ideal of devotion to God.

See also Islamic ethics; al-Rûmî al-Balkhî, Maulânâ Jalâl al-Dîn; Sufism.

Racial prejudice

TYPE OF ETHICS: Race and ethnicity
DATE: From antiquity
DEFINITION: Unequal valuation of persons on the basis of race
SIGNIFICANCE: Diminishes respect for persons and promotes social injustice

Racial prejudice stems from the mistaken notion that superficial physical differences among people reflect inherited differences in character, personality, motivation, intelligence, and potential. Racial prejudice leads to interpersonal conflict and to discrimination in housing, jobs, and services. Laws designed to end the effects of prejudice have been enacted in many countries, though large numbers of people continue to harbor prejudiced views.

Racial prejudice is often confused with ethnocentrism, the presumed superiority of one's own culture over the cultures of other people. Traditional animosity between the Chinese and Japanese, for example, is sometimes interpreted as racist, but this hostility is more likely the result of cultural bias.

History. On the basis of historical records, it is difficult to distinguish racial prejudice from nationalism and ethnocentrism. An undoubted case of racial prejudice, however, developed among the Tutsi, Hutu, and Twa peoples of Rwanda and Burundi during the fourteenth century. This region was originally settled by the Twa, who were very short hunters and potters. At some time before the 1300's, the Hutu, who were agriculturalists of medium stature, moved into the region and asserted dominance over the Twa. Then the Tutsi, who were unusually tall people, immigrated to the area and assumed sovereignty over *both* the Hutu and the Twa. Physical stature played an important role in the development and maintenance of this prejudicial hierarchical system.

Racial prejudice also played a role in the histories of South Africa and the United States, countries in which white European settlers achieved cultural dominance over indigenous, darker-skinned peoples. The South African system of apartheid, which was dismantled during the early 1990's in response to years of political turmoil and international boycott, was designed by the ruling Dutch colonialists to maintain separate white and black cultures. Blacks and other nonwhites, who accounted for more than four-fifths of the population, experienced restrictions in travel, education, land ownership, and voting privileges.

In the United States, centuries of tension and misunderstanding between whites and Native Americans developed into bitter racist resentments during the nineteenth century. As a result, Native Americans were forcibly removed by the federal government to reservations where they still live. Racial prejudice was also directed against Hispanics, Asians, African Americans, Jews, and other ethnic minorities in America. White supremacist organizations such as the Ku Klux Klan used beatings, lynchings, and other terrorist tactics to maintain the low social status of racial minorities. In response to the social activism of the 1950's and 1960's, however, the Civil Rights Act of 1964 outlawed racial segregation and other forms of discrimination in public establishments. Despite this and other government reforms, white supremacists continue to foster racial prejudice in America.

One of the most chilling examples of racial prejudice resulted in Nazi Germany's attempt to exterminate the Jews during the 1930's and 1940's. Adolf Hitler believed that Jews were innately inferior to Germans and other members of the so-called Aryan race. Because Jews competed for food and other resources that his own "superior" people deserved, Hitler believed that it was his duty to eliminate Jews and other unworthy competitors. Hitler's intense race hatred led to the systematic killing of millions of Jews during the Holocaust. Similar genocidal campaigns have been mounted by the Turks against the Armenians, the Iraqis against the Kurds, and the Serbians against the Bosnian Muslims.

Justifications for Racial Prejudice. While social scientists believe that racial prejudice is a learned response, the roots of racial prejudice often remain obscure. The justifications used by people to defend racist attitudes, however, are well documented. Ironically, the most influential justifications for racial prejudice have come from two unlikely sources: science and religion.

Racial prejudice was almost universal among western Europeans and Americans during the 1800's. White scientists felt compelled to provide empirical evidence for the assumed superiority of their race. Craniometricians, for example, believed that brain size and intelligence were causally linked—the larger the brain, the more intelligent the person. Despite a lack of objective support for this hypothesis, craniometry became very popular. Brains of famous people were measured, compared, and preserved after their owners' deaths, and the average cranial capacities of skulls from people of different racial groups were computed. The results suggested that whites were more intelligent than members of other races. When I.Q. tests were developed during the early twentieth century, these were also employed by psychologists to reinforce the notion of white superiority. Recent studies have shown that attempts by craniometricians and psychologists to provide scientific support for racist views were flawed by unconscious bias or outright fraud.

Religious notions have also provided powerful justifications for prejudiced attitudes, especially against African Americans. For example, biblical fundamentalists have taught that the descendants of Noah's son Ham developed "inferior" traits such as dark skin and kinky hair as the result of a divine curse. Others have ascribed the origin of these traits to the activities of the devil. Still others believed that blacks originated as a result of sinful cross-breeding between humans and animals. Because of distorted ideas such as these, many white Christian congregations in America refused to admit African Americans to their services, denominationally operated hospitals denied care to dark-skinned patients, and church schools closed their doors to black children.

Eradicating Racial Prejudice. Deeply ingrained racial prejudice is difficult but not impossible to eradicate in individuals and societies. The mass media can play an important role in reshaping societal attitudes. Political activism can promote legislative changes favoring nondiscriminatory practices. Children can learn to appreciate racial diversity if they are taught the value of human variation early in life. Individuals can overcome prejudice by associating with members of other racial groups on a regular basis.

—*James L. Hayward*

See also Apartheid; Bigotry; Civil rights movement; Genocide; Racism.

BIBLIOGRAPHY

Ehrlich, Howard J. *The Social Psychology of Prejudice.* New York: John Wiley & Sons, 1973.

Gould, Stephen J. *The Mismeasure of Man.* New York: W. W. Norton, 1981.

Kevles, Daniel J. *In the Name of Eugenics: Genetics and the Uses of Human Heredity.* New York: Alfred A. Knopf, 1985.

Stein, George J. "Biological Science and the Roots of Nazism." *American Scientist* 76 (January/February, 1988): 50-58.

Watson, Peter, ed. *Psychology and Race.* Chicago: Aldine, 1973.

Racism

TYPE OF ETHICS: Race and ethnicity
DATE: Fifteenth century to present
ASSOCIATED WITH: Civil rights and human rights
DEFINITION: The belief that humanity is divided into stratified, genetically different stocks, called races; according to its adherents, racial differences make one group superior to another
SIGNIFICANCE: Racism became a justification for slavery in the Western Hemisphere and for the subsequent denial of human and civil rights to people of color

The concept of race is an invention of the early modern world. The ancient and medieval worlds did not identify persons by race. Individuals were recognized during these earlier periods in geographic terms. Hence, an African would be called Ethiopian or Egyptian as opposed to being called black or negro.

Origin. Racial emphasis came into use as a support for imperialism and its accompanying institution of slavery. Although the origin of the word "race" is obscure, experts believe that it began as a loose description of similar groups. This description originally was not restricted to biologically similar people. For example, in 1678, John Bunyan in *Pilgrim's Progress* wrote of a "race of saints."

The first English record of the use of the word "race" was in 1508. In that year, William Dunbar in a poem spoke of "bakbyttaris if sindry racis" (backbiters of sundry races).

It was not until 1684 that the term "race" was used to designate skin color and other distinguishable physical features. It was then used by the Frenchman François Bernier, who used his experiences as a traveler and physician to employ such an application.

It appears, however, that such classifications did not become commonplace immediately. It was only after science adopted the concept of race as an explanation for human variation that it became a broadly accepted tenet.

Citations of Earlier Prejudices. Some scholars, such as Winthrop Jordan and Joseph Harris, have documented evidence of racial prejudice all the way back to the earliest contact between whites and nonwhites. These actions appear to be based more on geographic differences than on color differences. For example, fantastic fables about Africans circulated among Europeans. Equally preposterous stories about Europeans, however, circulated in the ancient and medieval world among Europeans. Thus, such views seem to be the products of encounters between different peoples in an age that was characterized by superstition and fear of the unknown.

Scientific Application. The year 1798 has been cited as marking the beginning of scientific racism. This later form of racism was not restricted to skin color alone. It was used to slight Jews and Catholics as well as nonwhite people. In its earliest use, scientific racism was employed mainly as a justification of economic inertia. Thus, it was said that human deprivation could not be relieved through charitable donations. According to the proponents of scientific racism, government volunteer agencies or individuals would simply be throwing money away if they were to spend it on the segment of humanity that was hopelessly and irretrievably at the bottom of the social and economic status of society.

This employment of a pseudoscientific justification for racism was expanded with the introduction of Social Darwinism in the late nineteenth century. Purveyors of this doctrine imported Charles Darwin's theory of evolution from biology and placed it into a social context. Whereas Darwin himself had only theorized about species, the Social Darwinists declared that one race was superior to another because it had evolved further and faster than had the inferior group. A chain of evolutionary progress was created that placed the black race at the bottom and whites of the Nordic pedigree at the summit of humanity. Thus, black people were portrayed as animalistic, subhuman, and therefore incapable of higher thought, while Nordic Europeans were said to be natural leaders.

The use of science to prop up racism has probably been the most pernicious development in the history of racism. When zoology, anatomy, and other fields of scientific study advanced explanations of human differences, they were given serious hearings. Consequently, the layperson has accepted the scientist's word as authoritative in spite of its theoretical and unproved claims.

Religious Application. From the beginning of the European enslavement of Africans, religion was an element in the process. As early as 1442, Pope Eugenia IV granted absolution to Portuguese seamen who, under the direction of Prince Henry the Navigator, took African "souls" and sold them. Within ten years, however, it became unnecessary to ask for absolution, because Pope Nicholas V gave the king of Spain his blessing to enslave "pagans." Christopher Columbus' writings show that he used this same justification for the enslavement of Native Americans.

Chapels were included in most of the slave factories, also known as "castles," which were erected along the west coast of Africa. Their presence was indicative of organized Christianity's approval of slavery.

At first, the Spanish provided for enslaved Africans to be manumitted upon their conversion to Christianity, since it was considered wrong for one Christian to hold another Christian in bondage regardless of the bondsman's race. As conversions to Christianity became commonplace among African slaves, however, manumissions became uncommon. At least by the middle of the seventeenth century, Europeans began to identify black skin with a lifetime of slavery.

The Bible was used to "prove" that blacks were a cursed people. A favorite scriptural citation for this purpose was Noah's curse upon his grandson Canaan because his father Ham had mocked his own father Noah (Genesis 9:20-27). This scripture was given a racial interpretation by the slavocracy's hermeneutists. They declared that Ham was the father of the black race and that Noah's specific condemnation of Canaan should be expanded to include all black people.

Thus, religious justification for the enslavement of blacks evolved from the belief that it was immoral for a Christian to enslave another Christian, regardless of race, to the nineteenth century idea that the African was eternally condemned to be a servant of others. By the nineteenth century, proponents of slavery declared that it simply was the natural order for the African to be "a hewer of wood and drawer of water" for the more advanced races.

This progression is illustrative of slavery and the resulting racism's evolving ethics. As the "peculiar institution" became more prevalent, the argument to legitimate it—especially from a religious perspective—became more vindictive toward nonwhite lands.

Sermons were preached to both slaves and their masters regarding the merits of African chattel property. Especially in the southern United States, both whites and blacks were taught that anyone who espoused any form of equality between the races was actually guilty of violating the divine order of nature. Such indoctrination was extremely effective, and people's attitudes did not change when laws were passed stating otherwise. Religious justifications for racism have continued to be employed by individuals and by such hate groups as the Ku Klux Klan in the United States long after the passage of the Emancipation Proclamation, the Thirteenth Amendment to the Constitution, and even the Civil Rights Bill of 1964.

Cultural Application. Both slavery and imperialism used cultural arguments to control other races. The doctrine of the "white man's burden" said that Europeans had a moral responsibility to expose deprived nonwhites to the superior culture of the whites. Thus, Africans who were kept on a plantation were thought to benefit from their close association with their masters. It was said that Africans, if left alone, would languish in retrogressive ignorance and backwardness. White. new Racism

This paternal view was not unique to American slavery. Both Europe and the United States used the concept of the white man's burden to justify the usurpation of the lands of nonwhite people. In each territory, the indigenous people were characterized as savage and uncivilized. Only exposure to the white man's superior culture would save such people.

This attitude of superiority legitimated the takeover of others' lands. It was believed that the white man knew best what to do with those lands. His takeover therefore not only helped the real estate to be put to better use but also better served the native people.

This view reflected the belief that many whites held during the age of imperialism. They saw themselves as God's gift to humanity. Officially, this concept came to be known as "manifest destiny." This meant that the imperialists believed that they had a mission to expand beyond others' borders to uplift those people to the imperialists' level.

This view of a neglected or minimal culture among nonwhite people was predicated upon a Eurocentric view of history. This meant that unless Europeans were leading and shaping a culture, it was not worthy of study. This attitude was arrogant and discriminatory in its highlighting of historical contributions. Anything of note that had been done by nonwhite people was ignored, while every important aspect of human civilization was always in some way considered a product of white genius. Such a polemical view of culture helped to solidify white supremacy and the existence of racism.

Economic Application. Similar to the use of culture was the introduction of economics as a prop for racism. During slavery, the argument was advanced that the institution was necessary for the benefit of black people. It was declared

nomic boon to blacks. They pointed to postbellum vagabondage and government dependency among freed slaves as proofs that black people were better off on the plantation, where they were given food, clothing, and shelter.

Such writers never considered that it was the years of exploitation and neglect on the plantation that had contributed to the freed slaves' deplorable condition. Also, they never addressed the freed slaves and antebellum free blacks who, in the face of tremendous difficulties, still managed not only to support themselves and their families but also to become entrepreneurs, landowners, and employers, sometimes even of whites.

This squalid "colored only" store is one result of the racism that became institutionalized in the southern United States. (National Archives)

that they were childlike and incapable of self-support. As long as they remained on the plantation, they had a haven that protected them from want. Slavery's defenders in the face of abolitionists' demands used this argument to portray slavery as being quite advantageous to the slaves. Even after the Civil War, many southern historians continued to use the economic argument to show that slavery was an eco-

In the twentieth century, economics was used as a defense for South Africa's apartheid policy and the continued business transactions carried on there by American and European corporations. In the wake of an international call for divestiture, these companies argued that their continued operation in South Africa was for the good of the blacks and colored people at the bottom of the economic ladder. Divestiture would deprive these two groups of a livable wage. Therefore, it was prudent for nonwhite people to continue to work for these corporations while the corporations used their influence to effect change.

The South African argument was as paternalistic as the American slaver's position. In both instances, the true benefactors of exploited labor declared that they had a higher mission than that of simple selfishness. Instead, they declared that their activities were for the good of nonwhite workers, who could not fend for themselves without white paternalism.

Social Application. After the American Civil War and Reconstruction, Jim Crow laws were instituted throughout the southern United States. These laws segregated society on the basis of race in practically every area of life. Except in menial jobs, blacks could not enter white restaurants, hotels, schools, or any other "white only" public facility. When they were allowed in the same buildings as whites, African Americans had separate, well-defined places such as balconies or basements to occupy.

Most southern states reinforced their segregation policies with laws that prohibited interracial marriages. Propagandists repeatedly warned that having one drop of negro blood meant that one was a negro. To the racist, amalgamation was a deadly sin.

Resulting from such hysteria was a negrophobia that frequently manifested itself in the worst imaginable forms of brutalization. In the late nineteenth century and the first half of the twentieth century, it was common for African Americans to be lynched. The most common offense was the violation of white women, real or imagined. Frequently, it was the latter. A celebrated case of this sort occurred when fourteen-year-old Emmett Till was murdered in Money, Mississippi, in 1955. Apparently, his only offense was that he called a white woman "baby."

Institutional Application. With the massive urbanization of African Americans in the United States in the twentieth century and the resulting residential segregation in cities, the stage was set for the emergence of institutional racism. This form of racism was more covert than was individual racism, which was emotional and blunt. Institutional racism resulted in a denial of equal access to goods and services by predominantly black sections of the cities. For example, higher prices and less-desirable products were more often found in the predominantly black and Hispanic inner cities than in the white suburbs.

Since this type of discrimination manifested itself through institutions and was not individually accountable, many people were simply oblivious to its existence. In addition, because of diminished interracial contact in urban areas, many suburbanites, as a result of ignorance of the ways in which societal institutions discriminate, are prone to blame deplorable living conditions within inner cities on the residents' lack of initiative and concern rather than on institutional biases.

Nevertheless, institutional racism can at least help to explain a disproportionate number of nonwhites being unemployed, underemployed, and incarcerated in prisons. Despite affirmative action policies and legal gains that have taken place during the twentieth century, African Americans and other minorities are excluded and ignored by many institutions, such as employers, lenders, and investment agencies. A prime example is the absence of stockbrokers' and other investment advertisements in African American-oriented media.

Expansion. Although racism had been sporadically applied to various groups from its inception, its primary application had been toward blacks of African ancestry. In their role as America's permanent bondspeople, African Americans were ridiculed and ostracized in a way that condemned everything that associated with them. In the post-World War I world, however, racist attitudes began to be manifested toward others on a systematic basis. By the 1920's, the Ku Klux Klan had begun campaigns against not only the African American but also Asians, Jews, Catholics, and all persons born outside the United States. The hatred that had originally been primarily aimed at African Americans overflowed to such an extent that it found other victims as well. Anyone who was not white, Anglo Saxon, and Protestant was susceptible to racism's venom.

The following decade of the 1930's saw this expansion reach global proportions. The rise of Adolf Hitler's Nazi regime in Germany was based upon the concept of Aryan supremacy. All other groups were considered inferior and unfit. Unfortunately, this form of expanded ethnic bigotry reached such an extent that 6 million Jews perished at the hands of the Nazis during World War II.

New Conflicts. Many African American leaders have argued that it is impossible for black people to be racist. They believe that they can be prejudiced, but not racist, because they lack the power to enforce their prejudice.

While this position has been advanced by the African American left, the white right has charged that group with reverse racism. White some conservatives contended that government affirmative action programs and the preferential treatment accorded minorities since the passage of civil rights legislation victimize whites in the same way that nonwhites previously were discriminated against by white supremacists.

Efforts to Eradicate Racism. Persons of goodwill have seen the wisdom in freeing humanity of racial bigotry. Although racism has been opposed since its inception, the most celebrated and concentrated efforts began with the modern Civil Rights Movement, which began with the bus boycott in Montgomery, Alabama, in 1955. Under the nonviolent leadership of Martin Luther King, Jr., racism was exposed as morally wrong. King's philosophy accentuated the brotherhood of humanity and love for one's neighbor, regardless of race, nationality, or ethnicity.

By developing an integrated coalition and marching

peacefully under King's leadership, King's followers erected a workable model of human cooperation that could be emulated throughout the world. In contrast, those who brutalized these nonviolent protesters with police dogs and fire hoses convinced many people throughout the world that racism was an insidious evil that should be stamped out.

As a result, people have become more reluctant to be known as racists. Instead, racially sensitive issues have been adopted as code words to describe positions. Racism continues to flourish, but it has become more institutional than individual.   —*Randolph Meade Walker*

See also Apartheid; Civil rights; Human rights; King, Martin Luther, Jr.; Slavery.

BIBLIOGRAPHY

Banton, Michael, and Jonathan Harwood. *The Race Concept.* New York: Praeger, 1975. A general discussion of the evolution of the idea of race. Although it allows that the origin of the race concept is obscure, it is certain that the prevalent use of racial divisions of humanity coincided with the spread of early slavery.

Barzun, Jacques. *Race: A Study in Superstition.* Rev. ed. New York: Harper & Row, 1965. An interesting refutation of Nazi teachings that addresses the expanded use of race beyond color applications. A scholarly exposure of scientific racism's absurdity.

Chase, Allan. *The Legacy of Malthus: The Social Costs of the New Scientific Racism.* New York: Alfred A. Knopf, 1977. A thorough treatment of scientific racism. Discusses its destructive effects and offers a means for its eradication.

Conrad, Earl. *The Invention of the Negro.* New York: Paul S. Eriksson, 1967. A revealing look at the newness of the despised status of the Negro. This work contends that black Africans did not suffer extreme degradation until the slave trade became big business in the Americas.

Jordan, Winthrop D. *White Over Black: American Attitudes Toward the Negro, 1550-1812.* New York: W. W. Norton, 1977. A thoroughly documented study of early European perceptions of black Africans. This study provides an interesting contrast to Conrad's thesis. It contends that racism produced slavery.

Rain forests

TYPE OF ETHICS: Environmental ethics

DATE: Late twentieth century to present

DEFINITION: Large wooded areas characterized by more than one hundred inches of rainfall annually and tall evergreen trees that provide a high canopy

SIGNIFICANCE: The ability to resolve the conflicting demands placed upon the rain forests provides a framework for the resolution of future ecological versus economic dilemmas

The rain forests provide indigenous peoples and the world with a rich source of actual and potential benefits. In their natural state, the rain forests act as filters for the global atmosphere, provide habitats for animal and plant species, and provide food for humans. The rain forests are also harvested as a source of fuel, with the resulting cleared land providing a rich soil for farming. Finding a balance between altering the rain forests for temporary benefit and using them in their natural and sustainable state is the heart of the rain forest debate.

In their naturally occurring state, the rain forests of the world act as watersheds for the surrounding land. The rich soil and dense foliage of the forests act as a natural sponge capturing rainfall and runoff. These trapped waters are slowly released, recharging aquifers, streams, and natural reservoirs. It is this trapping and slow releasing of water that controls both flooding and erosion in the forests and surrounding areas. When the rain forest is clear-cut and removed, streams, lakes, rivers, and other natural waterways are quickly filled with runoff sediment and lost. Along with playing an important role in the water cycle, the rain forest is critical in the conversion of carbon dioxide into oxygen. The loss of one of the earth's natural air filters cannot be replaced in any manner. This loss threatens not only to affect local areas but also to have global air-quality effects. With the removal of rain forests, the local area immediately is affected by an alteration in the moisture content of the air and a disturbance in the water cycle. The long-term effects of this disturbance could be the development of arid savannah or desert.

Although the rain forests cover slightly more than 7 percent of the land mass of the world, they provide habitats for more than 50 percent of the animal and plant species found on the planet. The destruction of plant life in the rain forest not only threatens the water cycle and the planet's carbon dioxide/oxygen cycle but also removes plant species that may provide important medical benefits. This loss of potential medicines is another example of local action's having worldwide effects. Rain forest plants have already contributed aspirin and many other pharmaceuticals, some of which are used in the treatment of leukemia and Hodgkin's disease. The loss of this rich pharmaceutical research possibility is not recoverable in any way.

The reasons for rain forest destruction are myriad; primarily, however, it is a matter of economics and survival. Nearly half of all the trees cut in the forests are used for fuel to cook and heat homes. The vast majority of rain forests are found in less-developed countries where alternative fuels such as fossil fuels, solar power, or hydroelectric power are not available in remote and isolated areas. Yet while the forests provide a rich supply of fuel, local people nevertheless are not able to cut and secure adequate fuel supplies to meet their basic survival needs. Although globally there exist several other fuel sources, local people lack the economic strength to secure these sources of fuel. As a result, the forests are cut and sold for timber products, providing poor communities with a bit of economic freedom. The newly cleared land, with its rich and fertile soil, is used for farming until it is depleted of all nutrition—usually, within five years. Although the agricultural use of the land is limited to such a short duration, it again provides the community with much-needed economic benefits. After the soil has been used to exhaustion, the farmer cuts more of the forest, sells the timber, and farms the new land until it also is depleted. When the trees have been cut and the soil has been depleted, the forest on that land is gone and the soil can no longer support the life that existed upon it six or seven years earlier.

Clearly, the economic benefits derived from using the forests in such a destructive short-term manner are enough to drive the process on. It is important to present to local people a means of using the forest in its natural and sustainable state that will provide them comparable economic benefit for the long term. There are several possibilities, such as harvesting and selling fruits and nuts from the forests, tourism, and a tax for the use of the rain forests for medical research.

It is the resolution of this dichotomy—the forest in its natural state providing water, oxygen, medicine, and habitat versus the economic and existence needs of local peoples—that must be effected. It is estimated that one tree, over a period of fifty years, provides $196,250 worth of benefits by producing oxygen, reducing erosion, recycling water, and creating habitats. The same tree, when sold for lumber, is worth approximately $600. The $600 is actual and usable currency, however, while the nearly $200,000 value exists in the form of benefits. It is the need for hard currency that must be addressed if preservation of the rain forest is to occur and continue. This economic need must be addressed not only by world leaders but also by indigenous peoples. Ultimately, the entire world will suffer the consequences of rain forest destruction; however, it is the local people who will be the first to suffer; and the local people have little economic capability to adjust. —*Tod Murphy*

See also Ecology; Environmental ethics; Global warming; Greenhouse effect.

BIBLIOGRAPHY

Aiken, S. Robert. *Vanishing Rain Forests: The Ecological Transition in Malaysia.* New York: Oxford University Press, 1992.

Kilaparti, Ramakrishna, and George M. Woodwell, eds. *World Forests for the Future: Their Use and Conservation.* New Haven, Conn.: Yale University Press, 1993.

Miller, Kenton, and Laura Tangley. *Trees of Life: Saving Tropical Rain Forests and Their Biological Wealth.* Boston: Beacon Press, 1991.

Park, Chris. *Tropical Rainforests.* New York: Routledge, 1992.

Pimm, Stuart. *The Balance of Nature? Ecological Issues in the Conservation of Species and Communities.* Chicago: University of Chicago Press, 1991.

Rand, Ayn (Feb.2, 1905, St. Petersburg, Russia—Mar. 6, 1982, New York, N.Y.): Novelist and philosopher
TYPE OF ETHICS: Modern history

ACHIEVEMENTS: Author of *The Fountainhead* (1943), *Atlas Shrugged* (1957), *The Virtue of Selfishness: A New Concept of Egoism* (1964), and *Capitalism: The Unknown Ideal* (1966)
SIGNIFICANCE: A major advocate of rational egoism and laissez-faire capitalism

Rand advocated an ethics of rational self-interest. The hero of her best-selling *Atlas Shrugged* states, "I swear—by my life and my love of it—that I will never live for the sake of another man, nor ask another man to live for mine." The moral purpose of anyone's life is his or her own happiness; he or she exists to serve no other individual or group. The moral standard by which one guides one's actions is set by the objective requirements of human life. Thus, Rand rejected two common theses in ethical theory: that selfless sacrifice is moral and that acting in one's self-interest means doing whatever one feels like. She rejected as "moral cannibalism" any form of altruism—that is, any claim that the selfless sacrifice of some humans for the benefit of others is moral. She also argued that, since feelings are not tools of cognition, they are not reliable guides to action; hence, one must rationally define the principles of action that will allow one to achieve the values necessary to sustain one's life.

Rand extended her ethics to politics. In a social context, an individual's achievement of values requires freedom from coercion. Hence, every individual has a right to his or her own life, liberty, and property, and these rights provide a moral foundation for free enterprise and constitutionally limited government.

See also Egoism; Objectivism; Selfishness.

Rape

TYPE OF ETHICS: Sex and gender issues
DATE: From antiquity
DEFINITION: Sexual intercourse forcibly imposed on one person by another person without the consent of the victim
SIGNIFICANCE: Rape is an unethical, reprehensible act that has devastating effects on its victims

Rape is legally defined as any form of sexual intercourse forcibly imposed by one or more persons upon another person without the consent of the victim or victims. Mary Koss and Mary Harvey (1987) consider rape to represent the end point of a continuum of sexual victimization that includes attempted rape (the attempt to use force or the threat of force to have sexual intercourse without the victim's consent); sexual harassment (nonconsensual sexual intercourse obtained through the abuse of power or authority by the offender in a job or school setting); sexual imposition (the use of force or threats to obtain sexual acts other than intercourse, such as kissing); and sexual contact (nonconsensual touching of the victim's intimate body parts).

Koss and Harvey (1987) distinguish five types of rape: stranger rape (the rapist is unknown to the victim); acquaintance rape (the rapist is recognized by the victim); date rape

(rape occurs during a consensually agreed upon social encounter); marital rape (one spouse is sexually assaulted by the other); and child sexual abuse (sexual contact that occurs to a child as a result of force, threat, deceit, or the exploitation of an authority relationship).

Incidence of Rape. In the vast majority of cases, the rapist is male and the victim is female. The Federal Bureau of Investigation's definition of rape specifies that the victim is female, and according to Koss and Harvey (1987), 100 percent of reported rapes involve a male offender and female victim. Consequently, almost all the rape literature focuses on female victims, although the dynamics of rape are similar when the victim is male.

Rape is a persistent, serious, and frequently occurring social problem. The number of reported rapes increased more than fivefold from 1960 to 1989 (from 16,680 to 94,504); however, the number of reported rapes is undoubtedly significantly lower than the true number, because most occurrences are never reported. Koss and Harvey (1987) did a number of studies that revealed much higher rates than those officially reported. For example, in one study, 44 percent of the interviewed sample reported rape or attempted rape, and the report rates for other forms of sexual victimization were less than 1 percent. A study of female adolescents between the ages of 11 and 17 in 1976 and 1977 revealed that 1 to 2 percent reported sexual assault by peers. Two percent translates into 540,000 sexual assaults nationwide. If children are considered, Koss and Harvey (1987) cite data that one-fifth to one-third of all women have had a sexual encounter with an adult male during childhood.

The incidence of rape is geographically influenced. Larry Baron and Murray A. Straus (1989) found significant differences in the frequency of rape among individual states. The states with the highest incidences of rape had five to ten times as many cases of rape compared to the states with the lowest incidences. Although the incidences of reported rapes have increased dramatically in all states over the years, this incidence ratio of five to ten has remained quite constant. Rapes occur much more frequently (rapes per 100,000 population) in the West, followed by the South, the North Central region, and the Northeast. Within each state, rape occurs more frequently in urban than in rural areas, and states with a high ratio of males to females show higher rates of rapes. Rape rates were not related to the degree of income inequality in a state or to the percentage of a state's population that is black, the percentage of individuals aged 18 to 24, the percentage of single males aged 15 or older, or the level of unemployment.

Characteristics of the Rapist. Susan Brownmiller (1975) made the interesting observation that when other crimes of violence are compared to rape, the rapist falls midway between aggravated assault and robbery—the rapist is "the man in the middle." The typical rapist has the following characteristics: he is slightly younger than the assaultive offender and slightly older than the robber; uses less physical force than the assaulter but more than the robber; drinks less prior to the rape than the assaulter but more than the robber; is less likely to commit rape in his neighborhood than assault, but does not commit robbery. Rape is also more frequently committed against a total stranger than is assault but less frequently than is robbery. Brownmiller believes that rape "borrows" from these two other crimes; rape is an act of sexual assault and robbery (the rapist "acquires" the woman's body).

Brownmiller (1975) also pointed out that the rapist has the least sharp image, and generalizations about rapists are difficult to come by. Rape is committed primarily by young poor men, and its victims tend to be young poor women. Otherwise, research comparing rapists to other groups (such as convicts, other sex offenders, college males) has not supported significant psychological differences between these groups. In fact, along almost every dimension examined with sophisticated psychological tests, rapists are not significantly different from other males. This fact, combined with their wide variety of backgrounds, prevents making any sweeping generalizations.

Ann Wolbert Burgess' (1985) review of her and others research suggests that a more meaningful way of typing rapists may be in terms of their motivation to commit rape. Burgess distinguishes four motivations for rape:

(1) *Aggression.* Rape is an aggressive activity that enhances the rapist's sense of power, masculinity, or self-esteem, or permits him to express feelings of mastery and conquest. He tends to be manipulative and impulsive, maintains unstable interpersonal relationships, and lacks a sense of empathy. (2) *Anger.* Rape is committed out of anger and contempt toward women and allows the rapist to hurt, humiliate, and degrade his victim. He may also, however, feel some concern for his victim and may even attempt restitution. (3) *Sadism.* The sadistic rapist is sexually aroused in response to violence, and the act of his assault, which is very brutal, may be bizarre. (4) *Impulsivity.* Rape is but one part of a pervasive exploitative, predatory, and antisocial lifestyle in an individual with an extensive criminal history.

Theories of Rape. On the face of it, it might seem that the frequency with which rape occurs is perplexing. There are easier, often perfectly legal and less risky ways to satisfy motives of aggression, anger, sadism, and impulsivity. Why then do women so frequently become the objects of these motives? A number of theories have been developed, and these are now briefly reviewed.

Psychiatric Theory. This theory has dominated explanations of rape since the 1930's. (This is not to say that the theory is correct; vehement objections have been raised against it, which will be discussed). Diana Scully and Joseph Marolla state that psychiatry explains rape as being caused by, singly or in combination: (1) irresistible impulse, (2) mental disorder, (3) momentary loss of control caused by use of alcohol and drugs, and (4) victim precipitation. In the irresistible impulse, rape is seen as an expression of an urge beyond the rapist's self-control, without logic or reason, and is experienced as a strong and overpowering drive to rape.

To view rape as a mental disorder is to explain it as a significant impairment in normal personal and social functioning. The impairment is most probably caused by faulty upbringing that produced an abnormal childhood; in particular, a sadistic personality and a hatred of the rapist's mother. The basis of the sadistic personality is a combination of the motives of sex and aggression, the two key motives in Freud's psychoanalytic theory. Sexual intercourse becomes bound to aggression. The rapist's mother, to whom the rapist was sexually attracted as a child as part of his oedipal wish, is simultaneously seductive and rejecting. The rapist never resolves his oedipal wish and grows up sexually attracted to his mother but also has strong feelings of aggression toward her. The offender displaces his aggression upon a woman via the act of sex. Symbolically, the rape forces his seductive but rejecting mother into submission. Additionally, some psychoanalysts believe the rapist to be a latent homosexual, which contributes to his hostility toward women.

The use of alcohol or drugs by rapists prior to the rape has been mentioned frequently in the literature. Consumption of alcohol presumably removes or reduces social restraints, allowing the sexual-aggressive drive to overwhelm rapists and lead them to commit rape. Alternatively, the rapist may claim that, although he was not under the influence of drugs, his victim was, thus inviting the rapist to take sexual advantage of her.

Victim precipitation refers to the rape victim's being functionally responsible for the rape by behaving in a way that provokes the rapist to rape her. Commissive behavior would actively encourage the rape by, for example, encouraging but then denying a sexual advance at the last possible moment or by voluntarily agreeing to drink with or ride in a car with the rapist. Omissive behavior involves failing to use preventive measures, such as failing to react sufficiently strongly to sexual overtures or dressing in a sexually suggestive way so as to attract attention and encourage sexual advances. All these acts to invite the rapist are, according to psychoanalysis, expressions of a universal, unconscious, masochistic wish on the part of women to be raped and humiliated.

The evidence to support these psychiatric-psychoanalytic theories is flimsy at best and in most cases nonexistent. The great majority of rapes are premeditated rather than the result of an irresistible impulse. The relationship between rape and alcohol or drugs as a releaser of sexual inhibitions has not been empirically demonstrated. There is also no evidence whatsoever firmly linking rape to latent homosexuality or the family dynamics described by psychoanalysis.

Biological Theories. According to Randy Wilsen, Nancy Wilsen Thornhill, and Gerard Dizinno, rape is a behavior that is performed by men who are relatively unsuccessful

A rally to promote public awareness of rape. (S. A. Rogers)

in competing for the status and resources necessary to attract and successfully reproduce with desirable mates. Rape is a category of sexual conflict in which males seek to control female sexual behavior and therefore is placed squarely in the purview of comparative biology and evolutionary theory. Rape is an evolved mating strategy used by those males ("big losers") who otherwise would not be able to compete with more successful males. What once may have been an adaptive behavior is now maladaptive, however, since the adaptive costs of reproduction exceed its benefits.

The authors base their theory on a comparative study of forced sexual intercourse in animals and certain statistical data about rape—that it is directed primarily at young (hence fertile), poor women primarily by young, poor ("big losers") men. This evolutionary theory is interesting. The authors have made predictions from their theory that have been supported. The theory is very new, however, and needs to be tested further. Also, making analogies between human and animal behaviors and selecting certain data on rape that support the theory are open to criticism. For example, that rapists are mostly poor young men may not necessarily mean that they rape because they are "big losers"; it may be that they rape because it is a safe way of displacing antagonism and resentment at their social status onto women or as a way of asserting their masculinity as a substitute for their lack of economic success.

Societal and Cultural Theories. It was noted previously that there are large differences in the rates of rape among individual states and between regions of states. Through complex statistical analyses, Baron and Straus (1989) accounted for these differences in terms of three sociocultural variables: gender inequality, pornography, and social disorganization. Specifically, the lower the status of women relative to men, the higher the rate of rape. Gender inequality is part of a social milieu that is conducive to rape. Also, the higher the circulation of pornographic literature, the higher the rate of rape. The authors interpret this finding to suggest that pornography is more likely to be part of "a hypermasculine or macho culture pattern" that condones violence and force, believes in male supremacy, and degrades women. The level of social disorganization is directly related to the level of rape. The social forces that control violent behavior are weakened. In a sociocultural milieu characterized by sexism and violence, loss of social control permits easier outlet for rape.

Baron and Straus have identified important social contributors to rape that suggest that rape is more than simply a psychiatric problem confined to the individual male and his upbringing or a biologically based behavior.

Feminist Theory. This theory stands in stark contrast to psychiatric theory and is, in part, a reaction against the psychiatric explanation of rape. According to Burgess and Maggie Humm, rape is an act of social control as well as a social institution that perpetuates the patriarchal domination of women and functions to keep women in their place through sexual degradation, violence, and assault. Rape is viewed as the logical conclusion of sexism and is an especially pernicious form of social control and coercion because it constantly reminds women of their vulnerability to men. Rape is a cultural and social behavior that is institutionalized in law and custom and is the symbolic expression of a white male hierarchy. Rape is an extension of normal sexual aggression acted out within the context of male sexual expectations and hostility toward women.

Feminist theory thus views rape as normative rather than deviant, as does psychiatric theory. Traditional male socialization encourages males to associate dominance, strength, virility, and power with being masculine, but submissiveness, passivity, weakness, and inferiority with being feminine. Thus women are viewed from legal, social, and religious contexts as male property to do with what they will.

Accompanying this attitude is the development by males of what Scully and Marolla refer to as a "vocabulary of motive" to diminish their responsibility and justify and excuse rape. For example, the psychiatrist Benjamin Karpman stated that rapists were sick but were not responsible for their behavior. They did not *consciously* and deliberately rape. Rather, they were victims of a disease from which they may suffer more than their victims. Therefore, since the rapist is "sick," he cannot be held responsible for his behavior. As another example, linking rape to latent homosexuality serves to place rapists in a group of deviant outsiders. By segregating rapists from "normal" men, the label of latent homosexuality serves to protect the interests of males.

Feminist theory has been criticized for a lack of data to support its contentions. Rather, it is supported by no more than "ideological furor." For example, if rape is normal, socially sanctioned behavior, then it would be predicted that rapists should be equally represented in all walks of life and age categories. The data show, however, that rapists are mostly young, poor males.

However valid feminist theory eventually proves to be, it has been of critical importance in the consciousness raising of males (or at least some males) concerning how they regard and act toward women. For example, in their 1984 textbook *Abnormal Psychology*, David L. Rosenhan (a psychiatrist) and Martin E. P. Seligman (a clinical psychologist) state:

> Rape is a major crime, an act for which it is imperative that society hold the individual responsible, punishing him accordingly. If we were to include rape as a *disorder* . . . , there would be some tendency to excuse the act and lighten the burden of the rapist's individual responsibility—even if there was not a shred of evidence other than the rape itself that indicated psychological abnormality. The acts of murder, assault and theft are not automatically thought of as psychological disorders unless there is additional evidence of abnormality, and we believe rape should be thought of in the same way. The expression "only a sick man could have done that," when applied to rape . . . seems to us deeply and insidiously confused.

Ethical Issues. Ross Harrison observed that "Rape is obviously bad, indeed a horrific thing. It belongs to the real world in which people are hurt, humiliated and abused . . . it is unproblematic that rape is a bad thing." A 1983 study of rape in New Zealand stated, "Rape is an experience which shakes the foundations of the lives of the victims. For many its effect is a long-term one, impairing their capacity for personal relationships, altering their behavior and values and generating fear."

The Constitution of the United States guarantees each citizen the right to "life, liberty, and the pursuit of happiness." Clearly, rape violates the basic civil rights of the victim. Although most rapes do not end in the murder of the victim (this occurs in a fraction of 1 percent of the cases), the victim's liberty and freedom of choice are taken away during the commission of the act. The victim may be robbed of happiness, since the aftermath of rape can be devastating. The symptoms and signs of rape trauma are well documented: physical (injury, disease); emotional (anxiety, fear, depression, shame, anger); cognitive (flashbacks, memories, impaired concentration); psychological (lessened self-esteem, disruption in social relations, withdrawal, isolation, aggression); sexual (sexual attitudes, impaired sexual functioning). Rape, then, represents a total assault on the very being and essence of what it is to be a person. Rape is what is called in ethics a quandary, a moral issue that, upon analysis, yields a single undisputed answer. Rape is horrifying and is not to be tolerated, and the rapist must be held responsible for his act.
                                                          —Laurence Miller
See also Abuse; Sexual abuse and harassment; Violence.

BIBLIOGRAPHY
Baron, Larry, and Murray A. Straus. *Four Theories of Rape in American Society*. New Haven, Conn.: Yale University Press, 1989. A detailed and excellent discussion of the sociocultural factors that influence rape.

Brownmiller, Susan. *Against Our Will*. New York: Simon & Schuster, 1975. A seminal work of the feminist theory of rape. Powerful, compelling, and convincing.

Burgess, Ann Wolbert, ed. *Rape and Sexual Assault: A Research Handbook*. 3d ed. New York: Garland, 1991. Provides thorough, comprehensive presentations of rape and its relationship to social institutions and issues.

Koss, Mary, and Mary Harvey. *The Rape Victim: Clinical and Community Approaches to Treatment*. Lexington, Mass.: Stephen Greene Press, 1987. Defines rape; also discusses rape trauma and social and community issues.

Tomaselli, Sylvana, and Roy Porter, eds. *Rape*. New York: Basil Blackwell, 1986. Discusses various interpretations of rape, including feminism, philosophical issues, popular culture and art, psychoanalysis, and mythology.

Rawls, John (b. Feb. 21, 1921, Baltimore, Md.): Philosopher
TYPE OF ETHICS: Modern history
ACHIEVEMENTS: Author of *A Theory of Justice* (1971)

SIGNIFICANCE: Presented an argument for an egalitarian theory of justice, based on social contract theory
John Rawls, who has taught at Harvard University since 1962, is best known for *A Theory of Justice*. In that book, Rawls defended a theory of justice that sought to strike a compromise between the democratic ideals of equality and liberty. The theory was in the social contract tradition associated with John Locke and Jean-Jacques Rousseau, but Rawls introduced the idea that the contract would establish abstract principles of justice rather than specific laws or arrangements. Rawls's contract was a hypothetical one involving agents who have been idealized in certain ways to create what he called an "original position."

Rawls argued that the agents in this original position should be ignorant of their own abilities and prospects in order to ensure that the principles they choose will be fair ones. The result, he argued, would be egalitarian principles that would maximize the position of the worst-off persons rather than maximize overall utility and that would protect certain basic liberties. Rawls is also known for the idea that any theory should be judged on the basis of whether it is the result of a process of "reflective equilibrium" in which one considers competing theories and their implications, testing these against one's intuitions about general principles and cases.

See also Social justice and responsibility.

al-Razi, Abû Bakr Muḥammad ibn Zakariya

(c. 864, Rayy, Iran—c. 925, Rayy, Iran): Philosopher and physician
TYPE OF ETHICS: Religious ethics
ACHIEVEMENTS: Author of *Kitab al-jami al-kabir*, a comprehensive medical encyclopedia in twelve volumes; *Al-Tibb al-ruhani* (c. 920; *The Book of Spiritual Physick*, 1950), his principal ethical treatise; and the apologetic *Al-Sirat al-falsafiya* (c. 920; *The Philosopher's Way of Life*, 1926)
SIGNIFICANCE: As a trained philosopher and a practicing physician, al-Razi epitomized to his contemporaries and later generations of Muslim intellectuals the man of knowledge devoted to both the ethical aspects of medicine and metaphysical speculations concerning life itself
Early in his life, al-Razi was educated in the fields of traditional Arabic literature, mathematics, astronomy, and philosophy. In the formation of his religious ideas, it is probable that a distinctly nonorthodox teacher, Iranshahri, played a major role. As a physician, al-Razi displays in his medical treatises the careful, methodical temperament of the empiricist, though a sense of genuine empathy is always present. According to al-Razi, some humans have been endowed with divine reason to awaken their souls to ultimate spiritual return with the Creator; others have not. Just as the Creator never seeks to harm humans, people too ought to seek only their own and others' betterment. Al-Razi believed in the transmigration of souls, the sacredness of all life, and the universal possibility

of salvation through reason and philosophy, the latter position being fiercely opposed by religious scholars of his own day.

See also Bioethics; Islamic ethics; Medical ethics.

Realpolitik

TYPE OF ETHICS: International relations
DATE: Established 1848
ASSOCIATED WITH: German Chancellor Otto von Bismarck
DEFINITION: In international affairs, *realpolitik* means that governments should be guided by their own practical interests, meet facts and situations as they arise, and use any practical means to achieve their ends
SIGNIFICANCE: After the overthrow of Napoleon Bonaparte in 1815, European governments tried to prevent war; in the 1850's, however, war was accepted as a means necessary to achieve a purpose; it was not viewed as glorious or as an end in itself, but as one of the tools of the statesman

Though Otto von Bismarck became the most famous practitioner of *realpolitik*, *realpolitik* was by no means confined to Germany. The failure of the 1848 revolutions throughout Europe dashed the dreams and visions of a humane nationalism, aspirations for liberalism without violence, the ideas of a peaceful and democratic republican commonwealth. The most immediate and far-reaching consequence of the failure of the 1848 revolutions was a new toughness of mind. Idealism was discredited and conservatives were more willing to exercise repression. It became a point of pride to be realistic and to be willing to face facts as they were. The future was to be determined by present realities rather than by ideas of what ought to be.

See also Machiavellian ethics.

Reason and rationality

TYPE OF ETHICS: Theory of ethics
DATE: Fifth century B.C.E. to present
DEFINITION: The faculty that integrates and differentiates perceptual information
SIGNIFICANCE: Raises the issue of whether reason has a fundamental or secondary role in morality

Common sense holds that being reasonable is a good thing. Being reasonable means taking account of all relevant evidence when deciding what to believe and do, and when establishing principles by which to live. It means settling disagreements by appeal to evidence, which involves being willing to change one's mind based on the evidence. If one is rational, one will discover what is true and false, and if one discovers what is true and false, one will be able to act so as to live the good life. In short, reason is commonly held to be the primary method of learning truths, including truths about morality; accordingly, rationality is held to be a virtue.

Rational theories of morality are marked by several features. They hold that (1) there are moral facts; (2) that those facts are universal, or true for everyone; (3) that reason is capable of identifying those facts; and (4) that disagreements over moral issues are resolvable by rational investigation.

Such accounts of morality, however, face challenges by accounts that hold that morality is not fundamentally rational.

Irrationalism. One problem is the seeming interminability of debates about moral issues. If moral truths are rationally verifiable, why are moral disagreements so rampant? In genuinely cognitive disciplines, such as mathematics and science, methods exist with which to settle disagreements rationally, but it seems that no such methods exist in morals.

A second problem is the emotionalism that moral issues evoke. Since many people cannot be swayed from their moral beliefs by appeals to reason, perhaps morals are based on some nonrational source.

The Is/Ought Problem. A third consideration is the famous "is/ought" problem. David Hume (1711-1776) argued that normative ("ought") conclusions cannot be deduced from descriptive ("is") premises. In a valid argument, terms cannot appear in the conclusion that do not appear in the premises. Therefore, if morality is concerned with facts, then normative conclusions must be deduced from fundamental statements of fact that contain "ought" terms. Sensation is the only fundamental source of factual information, however, and people do not seem to sense goodness and badness, merely colors, sounds, and so on.

Following Hume's reasoning, G. E. Moore (1873-1958) argued that any attempt to derive moral statements from physical, biological, or psychological facts commits the "naturalistic fallacy."

While irrationalists agree that morality is not fundamentally rational—that, at most, reason helps to figure out how to satisfy moral commitments made on a nonrational basis—they disagree about the fundamental source of moral commitments.

Religious irrationalism holds that God's commands are the source of morals. Many religions hold that ethics is a matter of obeying divine commands, whether one understands them or not. The story of Abraham in the Hebrew Scriptures (Genesis 22) is an example. God commands Abraham to sacrifice his son Isaac. From a rational perspective, obeying would be immoral: It would mean murdering an innocent boy, and it would cause Abraham and his wife great emotional suffering. Yet all Abraham believes that he needs to know is that God has commanded, so he is prepared to kill. Hence, morality for Abraham means obeying without question commands that do not necessarily make sense.

Secular irrationalism comes in several varieties. According to emotivists, such as Bertrand Russell and A. J. Ayer, moral statements express attitudes that are based on subjective emotional states. According to existentialists, such as Albert Camus and Jean-Paul Sartre, moral attitudes are based on arbitrarily chosen commitments.

Irrationalism is thus strongly linked with moral relativism—the thesis that moral values are not universal. If morals are not rationally based, then consistency is not necessary. If morals are based on subjective emotions, faith, or arbitrary commitments, then, since these are highly variable, morals will be highly variable.

Reason's Role. For rational theories of ethics, then, the challenge is to find and validate a rational source of ethics. The history of ethics contains four major types of attempts to do so.

Intuitionists hold that good and bad are properties of external things themselves, in the same way that colors, textures, and sounds are properties of things. Just as people have sense organs to detect color and sound properties, they have a moral sense to detect moral properties. Moral properties are therefore independent of subjective states, they can be identified accurately, and thus they provide data for rational moral reflection and action.

Hedonists hold that moral properties are based on facts about human nature itself: Humans are born with pleasure/pain mechanisms. What causes sensations of pleasure and pain is not a matter of subjective choice. Sensations of pleasure and pain provide the data for rational moral reflection and action. Morality is a matter of calculating which actions will maximize pleasures and minimize pains.

Kantians hold that morality is based on the nature of reason itself. Noumenal reason projects a priori laws to one's phenomenal self. Since one is human, one should act in accordance with one's distinguishing feature: reason. Since reason demands consistency, morality means using one's reason to determine which maxims of action are consistently realizable, and then acting according to those maxims.

Objectivists hold that morality is based on relational facts about human nature and its environment. Human beings are organisms of a specific nature, and their nature and their environment jointly specify requirements that must be satisfied for them to survive. Good thus is identified fundamentally with what is necessary for survival, and bad with that which leads to death. Reason is a capacity whose function is to identify those survival requirements and to direct the actions of the organism in ways appropriate to fulfilling them.

—Stephen R. C. Hicks

See also Hedonism; Intuitionist ethics; Kant, Immanuel; Rand, Ayn.

BIBLIOGRAPHY

Camus, Albert. *The Myth of Sisyphus.* Translated by Justin O'Brien. New York: Knopf, 1955.

Hare, R. M. *Freedom and Reason.* Oxford: Clarendon Press, 1963.

Kierkegaard, Søren. *Fear and Trembling.* Translated by Walter Lowrie. Garden City, N.Y.: Doubleday, 1954.

Redlining

TYPE OF ETHICS: Business and labor ethics
DATE: 1970's
ASSOCIATED WITH: Banks and insurance companies
DEFINITION: The systematic exclusion of residents of certain areas, especially low-income, inner-city neighborhoods, from home mortgage lending and property insurance coverage

SIGNIFICANCE: Redlining is an unjust practice, critics charge, because it denies opportunities to those who could qualify for financial services simply because they reside in particular areas; it results in *de facto* discrimination

In looking for an efficient way to screen out high-risk applications for home mortgages, rehabilitation loans, and home and auto insurance, banks and insurance companies adopted the practice of "redlining," which involves excluding entire low-income neighborhoods from consideration or charging excessively high prices in these areas. Predictably, the burden of these practices fell most heavily on poor African Americans, and civil rights organizations charged that this amounted to systematic discrimination.

Congress passed the Community Reinvestment Act in 1977, followed by the Home Mortgage Disclosure Act, to deal with redlining and the more general problem of directing loans and insurance coverage to low-income areas. The former requires banks and thrifts to make a certain proportion of their loans in the areas where their depositors live, and the latter requires them to report their mortgage lending by census tract. The question remains, however, how much responsibility banks should take for providing loans to low-income borrowers as a matter of social policy, especially if such loans conflict with sound business practice.

See also Civil rights; Discrimination.

Relativism

TYPE OF ETHICS: Theory of ethics
DATE: Sixth century B.C.E. to present
ASSOCIATED WITH: The Greek sophists, John Mackie, and Bertrand Russell
DEFINITION: The belief that there are no absolute or universal moral standards and that what is morally right or wrong is relative to an individual, group, or culture
SIGNIFICANCE: Represents a rejection of the traditional view that there are objective moral standards

Ethical relativism is related to but distinct from general philosophical relativism and epistemological skepticism. According to this position, the human mind is incapable of attaining any genuine or objective truth. Hence, knowledge is subjective and "relative" to the knower.

The ethical relativist is skeptical of determining some truth about moral matters. This position can be traced to the Greek sophists, who were the objects of Socrates' criticism in Plato's famous dialogues. Thus, sophists such as Callicles and Gorgias contended that morality was relative and that what was right for one person or group was not necessarily right for another. They rejected ethical universalism, the notion that what is morally right and wrong is basically the same for everyone, viewing ethical or moral judgments as matters of convention or personal taste. In contrast to the sophists, most philosophers, such as Plato, Aristotle, Thomas Aquinas, Immanuel Kant, G. W. F. Hegel, and so forth have decisively rejected this extreme position and embraced the idea that there are universal, moral absolutes transcending time and place. Some contemporary thinkers, however, have resurrected the position of moral skepticism and relativism.

In general, it is possible to distinguish between two types of ethical relativism: cultural relativism and the more extreme individualistic relativism. The latter represents the viewpoint that moral values or norms differ among individuals within a society or culture. In other words, moral judgments are purely subjective; they are simply a matter of one's personal tastes or an individual's conscience. If someone believes that euthanasia is morally permissible, one's judgment in this regard must be considered valid and tenable. Likewise, if someone else considers euthanasia to be wrong, that too is a reasonable judgment. Thus, extreme relativists accept that valid ethical judgments can be inconsistent with one another.

This notion of extreme relativism is expressed in the work of contemporary ethicists such as John Mackie. In *Ethics: Inventing Right and Wrong* (1977), Mackie argues that there is nothing truly good or bad or right or wrong. Rather, these categories must be "invented" in order to have any ethics. Mackie believed that the seeds of this position could be found in the works of his predecessors, such as David Hume and Thomas Hobbes. For Mackie, moral language, with its reference to "right" and "wrong," creates the illusion of objectivity, but in reality objectivity in the realm of ethics is impossible.

Cultural relativism represents the more moderate viewpoint that moral values differ from one society or culture to another. It admits that within a society some valid moral standards are possible, but those standards will sometimes differ from one culture to another. As a result, principles that are considered central and vital in one society might be on the periphery of another culture's value system. Moreover, the cultural relativist proclaims that there are no fixed or immutable standards that can serve as the ultimate guide to a society's moral code. All moral norms are conditional, completely dependent on time, place, and circumstances.

Cultural relativists also differentiate between descriptive cultural relativism and normative cultural relativism. The former version of relativism is summed up in the incontrovertible proposition that moral beliefs and practices differ from one culture to another. It affirms the findings of anthropologists and historians who have discovered that different peoples have different values. For example, while some societies practice polygamy, others prohibit the practice. Similarly, a society's moral values may evolve over the course of time. Slavery was once legal and was commonly accepted in American society, but now it is regarded as offensive and grossly immoral. The descriptive relativist simply uncovers and "describes" this cultural diversity, along with a society's evolving standards.

Normative cultural relativism represents the philosophical position that there are no transcultural, universal moral norms and that prevailing moral judgments in different cultures are equally valid. Thus, the moral judgment "bribery is wrong" in one culture is just as valid as the judgment "bribery is right" in another culture. According to normative ethical relativism, each moral judgment must include a qualifier such as the following: "Bribery is wrong *in society X.*" To a certain extent, the normative relativist regards moral values as equivalent to customs in that both have only local validity instead of universal validity. The normative relativist adheres to the dictum "when in Rome do as the Romans do" when it comes to matters of custom and morality.

On the surface, normative cultural relativism seems to be plausible, especially since it is quite apparent that different societies do have different moral codes, but there are some salient difficulties with this position as well as with the more extreme view of individualistic relativism. It should be remarked that if there is no absolute standard of some sort and all moral codes are valid, it becomes impossible to criticize other cultures or contend that the morals of some societies are inferior to those of other societies. Is it possible to accept the notion that all moral systems and norms are on the same level? In addition, if one embraces cultural relativism, the notion of moral progress becomes unintelligible. Progress implies improvement, but if there is no general, independent, transcultural standard, how can one judge that a country or culture has indeed made any progress in its moral life?   —*Richard A. Spinello*

See also Anthropological ethics; Morality; Sophists.

BIBLIOGRAPHY

Brandt, R. B. *Ethical Theory.* Englewood Cliffs, N.J.: Prentice-Hall, 1959.

Ladd, John. *Ethical Relativism.* Belmont, Calif.: Wadsworth, 1973.

Leiser, Burton. *Custom, Law, and Morality.* Garden City, N.Y.: Anchor Books, 1969.

Mackie, John. *Ethics: Inventing Right and Wrong.* Harmondsworth, England: Penguin Books, 1977.

Rachels, James. *The Elements of Moral Philosophy.* New York: Random House, 1986.

Religion

TYPE OF ETHICS: Theory of ethics
DATE: Fifth century B.C.E. to present
DEFINITION: A study of the relationship between ethical norms and religious experience
SIGNIFICANCE: Addresses the relationship between religion and ethics; tries to determine whether religion necessarily is the same as or motivates ethics

The relationship of religion to ethics is controversial, especially in cultures influenced by Islam, Christianity, or Judaism. The range of opinion is wide. For some, religion destroys ethics. For others, ethics depends upon religion. For still others, religion and ethics are the same.

Religion might destroy ethics in two ways. Perhaps an omniscient God makes morality pointless, since it does away with the freedom of persons to do other than God has foreseen. A loving, forgiving deity may render obedience to moral laws optional from a practical point of view. Ethics might depend upon religion because religion provides the only effective motivation for persons to obey moral law, as opposed to pursuing their own self-interest. Perhaps God's will determines legislatively right and wrong action, in which case religion and ethics are identical.

Ethics and morality will herein be considered synonymous. Influential persons have argued for a sharp theoretical distinction, claiming that ethics is the broader notion, including much that falls outside of morality. This author agrees with Julia Annas that this distinction is not so much theoretical as historical, serving unnecessarily to separate ancient and modern ethical work.

Difference Arguments. That religion and ethics are not co-identical can be shown in at least four ways.

The first way is to note that the connection between religion and ethics in any particular society is a matter of convention. Greek polytheism and Christianity will be used to illustrate this point.

In Plato's (429-347 B.C.E.) dialogue *Euthyphro*, a priest of Apollo in Athens suggests to Socrates (470-399 B.C.E.) that piety is what is loved by the gods. This is the conventional answer to the question "What is piety?" in fifth century Athens.

Socrates then asks whether piety is pious because it is loved by the gods or is loved by the gods because it is pious. The difference is enormous. Something carried is so because someone carries it, not vice versa. The priest, Euthyphro, becomes convinced that piety is loved by the gods because it is pious. Socrates points out that this communicates that the gods love piety, but not why they love piety or what piety is. Euthyphro is thrown into confusion, not knowing how to cope with the consequences of admitting criteria for piety that are not religious. Piety is a Greek virtue. The difference between this virtue and what the gods love shows at least that arguments separating ethics and religion were known to Plato, though Athenian convention considered them identical.

The argument in *Euthyphro* is generalizable. In a Jewish, Christian, or Islamic context, it involves the awareness that answering the question "Why should I obey God's commands?" with "Because He is good" involves a vacuous circularity unless the word "good" is defined in terms other than those of obedience to God. Therefore, criteria of goodness must be independent of an awareness of divinity. Also, if people possess such criteria, they are in a position to judge good and evil on their own, without consulting divine commandments. This does not mean that the divine commands do not embody norms that are in fact good according to human criteria. They may embody such norms, which raises the second difference argument.

A second way to show that ethics and religion are different is to recognize that all nonprimal world faiths accept the Mosaic decalogue's ethical prohibitions against lying, stealing, murder, and adultery. A "nonprimal world faith" is one of the following: Islam, Christianity, Judaism, Buddhism, Confucianism, and Taoism. Clearly, these religions do not share religious doctrines or beliefs. Different religions embrace the same code of ethics.

Huston Smith, in his influential book *The World's Religions* (1991), refers not only to these ethical prohibitions as common denominators of world faiths but also to their shared endorsement of three basic virtues: humility, charity, and veracity. There are three common aspects of traditional religious vision as well: Things are more integrated than they seem, better than they seem, and more mysterious than they seem. Smith uses the phrase "wisdom tradition vision" rather than "traditional religious vision" in order to include Western philosophy up to Descartes in his analysis of commonalities. This shows that ethics is much more stable in its content than is religion and is therefore different from religion.

P. H. Nowell-Smith states that cultural relativism is based on the failure to recognize this distinction between religion and ethics. "If these are lumped together, it is easy to pass from the true premise that religious rules are everywhere different to the false conclusion that moral rules are different too."

A third way to separate religion and ethics is to note that connections between them are generally absent from primal, or pretechnological, societies. The ideas that primal peoples derived their beliefs concerning right and wrong from shamans or holy people who spoke for the gods, and that religion and ethics were separated only in later, more complex and secularized stages of development in those societies are clearly mistaken. One might use the Australian Aborigines as an example to undergird this point, but one might as easily use the ancient Greeks and Romans, the Vikings, the Druids, the Japanese (Shinto), or any of a dozen Native American tribes.

The Australian Aborigines use a word that means, so far as anyone can tell, "everywhen." Everywhen is the time an individual spends engaged in activity that is central to the survival or flourishing of the clan-grouping. The essential things are food, shelter, procreation, and such. When I, as an Aborigine, build my house according to the ancient plan, or hunt, or fish, or produce children, I become the first person ever to accomplish these acts successfully, and therefore one of a number of first persons. First persons are not gods to be imitated. The time difference between myself and the first persons is gone when I enter everywhen, as my children will, and their children after them. In these sacred, eternal acts, I overcome the accidents and misfortunes that occur as the normal seasons pass. This is my religion.

The Aborigines are quite aware of linear time. Their notion of everywhen accomplishes the same religious work for them that the last judgment of God accomplishes for Muslims and Christians: the domination of linear history. Linear, causal history contains much injustice, accident, disease, and disaster. In it, good things happen to bad people and bad things happen to good people. Religion must offer hope in

The first meeting of the World Conference of Churches, which took place in Evanston, Illinois, on March 21, 1949, was a major event in the modern history of religion. (National Archives)

the form of an understanding that dominates these facts, or it is not a successful religion.

The critical thing to note regarding any connection between ethics and religion for the Aborigines is that judgments concerning where I am entitled to build my house, where I can hunt or fish, and with whom I produce children, are not related to everywhen. These are ethical decisions made among humans, by humans, and for humans. No one speaks for the archetypes on these matters. Religion proper has nothing to say about them, and only points to the necessity of the acts themselves.

Thus, primal societies do not exhibit the kind of connection between religion and ethics that some developmental views present. They also do not subsume ethical commandments under religious teaching, as the nonprimal world faiths do. This is obscured in nonprimal religions by the fact that all but one (Hinduism) were founded by some individual. Such an individual is, of course, an integrated human being, usually highly so. He exhibits ethical as well as re-

ligious integration in his expressions, judgments, and so on, clouding the fact that religion and ethics are different.

A fourth way to show ethics and religion to be different is to consider the problem of saying just what ethical system is required by any specific religion; for example, Judaism and/or Christianity. The Judeo-Christian religion has operated, and operates today, as a religious basis in vastly different societies or cultures. Any such religion will offer behaviors that are relatively independent of particular, specific forms of social life. It will also exhibit enormous flexibility regarding moral standards in different cultures and at different times. Historically, Judeo-Christianity has served as the religion of Hebraic tribalism, Hellenistic aristocracy, Roman imperial monarchy, Constantinian bureaucracy, the Third Reich, and American republican capitalism. As MacIntyre says, "it will perhaps come as a relief to consider that the whole problem of Christian morality is to discover just what it is."

It is perhaps worth noting that the comparative stability

of ethical norms as opposed to religious beliefs pointed out in the second difference argument above can be rendered inconsequential by classifying a group as nonhuman, as the Third Reich did in the case of the Jews, in order to kill them without violating the prohibition against murder.

Taken together, the difference arguments make identity claims hard to defend. This does not mean that individuals who recognize the difference do not themselves integrate religious and ethical beliefs and norms. Plato presents Socrates as not accepting the conventional wisdom, or the institutional understanding of a priest, regarding piety. Just as clearly, Socrates accepts piety as a personal virtue. Plato's Socrates also exhibits religious beliefs when speaking for himself and not engaged in dialectic, particularly in *Phaedo*.

Dependence Arguments. One need not stray from Plato for a model for arguments that render ethics dependent upon religion for motivation. Plato entertains this line of thought in *Republic*, his utopian rendering of the ideal state.

The religion of the Greeks was contained in the narratives and poetry of Homer, Hesiod, and others. These stories were considered by Plato as unsuitable subject matter for the education of the young in *Republic* (377a–392c), because they present the divine as capricious, immoral, and even cruel. The divine nature must be, for Plato, good, not a source of evil. This brings to the fore Plato's attitude toward the truth. It should be noted that the Greek word *pseudos* need not have the deprecatory connotations of "false" or "lying." The stories *(mythoi)* told to children are in general fictitious *(pseudoi)*. What Plato insists upon is that these stories be "true" by not misrepresenting the divine character.

In *Republic* (382a–389b), there is a discussion to the effect that, although outright lying is despicable, "spoken falsehood" may be useful; for example, militarily or to save a friend from himself or herself. This passage ends with an analogy to medical practice: as medicine should be administered by a physician only for the good of the patient, so also falsehoods should be employed by rulers only for the good of the state. Not long after (414d–e), Plato passes into a myth for his own purposes. His practical, ethical purposes in this myth are to bind persons to both their land and one another. The myth has it that the rulers, guardians, and workers sprang full-grown from mother earth, who nurtured, formed, and educated them.

This sequence of passages has long been used to question or condemn Plato's ethics. Such condemnation has prompted heartfelt defenses also, such as that of Francis Cornford, who despises those who would "suggest that he [Plato] would countenance the lies, for the most part ignoble, now called propaganda." These reactions are extreme because Plato is toying with the controversial notion that a religious creation story is necessary to provide a level of solidarity and fellow-feeling that might serve to glue humans together in community, actual or utopian, and motivate them to follow ethical norms.

Plato is *not* here countenancing propaganda of any crude sort, since he clearly intends for both the guardians and rulers to be convinced of the truth of the myth. Neither group is particularly credulous, and Socrates does not express much confidence in his ability to secure their belief.

This argument and others like it concern motivation, not ethical content. Ethical content is fairly constant between religious cultures. Dependence arguments harp on motivating persons through religion to observe ethical content. Some say that only religion will work, while others say that religion is unnecessary or irrelevant. It is in this standoff that destruction arguments become relevant.

Destruction Arguments. Some who claim that religion is unnecessary for or irrelevant to ethical motivation are neutral about or committed to a religious point of view, but others are not. Some are convinced that religion is the cause of most ill will and violence between persons in the world. They catalog the historical abuses of secular power by ecclesiastical authorities. They cite the enmity in Northern Ireland between Protestants and Catholics. They cite fanatical acts by Christian or Islamic fundamentalists. They are morally nauseated by these facts. Their nausea motivates them to mount arguments that religion destroys ethics, such as those mentioned at the beginning of this article. Quite naturally, such persons react strongly against any suggestion that ethics is dependent upon religion, because the two tend in opposite directions in their minds.

The two sides of this conflict will never touch. One side clings to direct experience with the divine. The other clings just as tenaciously to the trouble caused by organized, and therefore politically effective, religious groups, not to mention clinging to objections to the metaphysics of religious beliefs. Intelligent religious folk are not motivated to refute claims that religion has been the cause of all manner of evil in the world, because it does not threaten the status of their direct experience with the divine. For religious folk, the fact that such experience becomes perverse when constituted as a conflict-producing political platform is a manifestation of human corruption, not divine corruption. This response sometimes incenses those who want religious people to take responsibility for the carnage their religious organization causes, presently or historically. But this is heat, not light. Closed religious people hide behind their belief that without God, all is permitted. Closed humanists hide behind their belief that all religious people have been lobotomized. The two groups never speak directly to each other.

Is there any hope for resolution, anything better than this heated darkness? Some religious persons and humanists think there is a positive answer: Thomism. Although Thomas Aquinas was a Catholic theologian, open, secular persons are not put off by Thomism. MacIntyre says, "Aquinas' theological ethics is such as to preserve the nontheological meaning of the word good." This is true, for Aquinas defines good as "that toward which desire tends." MacIntyre allows Aquinas' faith because, in it, calling God good is naming him as the object of desire. This means that God and good are not defined in terms of each other. Therefore, "'God is good' is a synthetic proposition, and to cite God's goodness is to give a reason for obeying his commandments." This reason, the nature of goodness, is naturally desired and as available to non-believers as believers, so both groups have access to accurate beliefs about goodness. Believers must regard unbelievers as possessed of natural reason, because of, not in spite of, their own faith. God created this natural reason, acknowledged or not, in every person. Believers and unbelievers are even in terms of practical rationality and can learn from each other in making ethical decisions. MacIntyre, in turn, does not consider religious folk ethically irrelevant; only their religious beliefs are ethically irrelevant.

Clearly it matters more, regarding ethics, whether a religious person is open or closed than whether he or she is religious or nonreligious. The same is true of a nonreligious person. MacIntyre goes as far as to say, "Thomist Christianity . . . exhibits more of a kinship with certain kinds of secular rationalism than with certain kinds of Christian irrationalism."

Thomism is Aquinas' version of Aristotle. Neither of these thinkers separates virtue from happiness, acting well from doing well. Modern ethicists, religious and nonreligious, have separated virtue and happiness. Modern ethics texts take the crucial issue to be the reconciliation of altruism with self-interest. This presupposes that to be virtuous is not to be happy, if "happy" means satisfying one's natural desires, and that to be happy is to be not virtuous. The invention and acceptance of modern individualism by Martin Luther, Niccolò Machiavelli, Thomas Hobbes, and Immanuel Kant was necessary to accomplish this separation. Modern individualism presupposes that basic opposition between self-centeredness and virtuous behavior that prompts requiring virtuous behavior to be motivated by the power of religion. According to Hobbes *and* Luther, humanity is depraved by nature. Aquinas and MacIntyre refuse to allow this presupposition.

Of course, Thomism cannot be expected to solve much in Islamic or Jewish cultures unless it is properly translated. Such translation and synthesis await an appropriate time or champion. It is difficult, however, to ignore a sophisticated, open theology in a time of oppression and violence caused partly by closed religion. The significance of Thomism is underrated in the Academy's postmodern reflection in proportion to the overrating of the necessary demise of religion and/or closed humanism. —*Joe Frank Jones III*

See also Altruism; Atheism; God; MacIntyre, Alasdair; *Republic*; Revelation; Selfishness; Thomas Aquinas.

BIBLIOGRAPHY

Annas, Julia. "Ethics and Morality." In Encyclopedia of Ethics, edited by Lawrence C. Becker and Charlotte B. Becker. New York: Garland, 1992. A brief but useful article on the subject.

Gilby, Thomas. "Thomism." In *The Encyclopedia of Philosophy*, edited by Paul Edwards. New York: Macmillan, 1967. A brief but excellent introduction to Thomism, with an explanation of its attractiveness to nonreligious ethicists and statesmen.

Hudson, Yeager. "The Independence of Ethics from Religion." In *The Philosophy of Religion*. Compiled by Yeager Hudson. Mountain View, Calif.: Mayfield, 1991. Contains useful discussion of primitive societies, developmental issues, and Thomist natural law. Hudson fleshes out the relation between rational and religious ethics in a manner acceptable to religious Thomists and secular rationalists alike.

MacIntyre, Alasdair. *A Short History of Ethics*. New York: Macmillan, 1966. A historical study of how ethical thinking in the West got where it is. It is standing the test of time well.

Nielsen, Kai, and Hendrik Hart. *Search for Community in a Withering Tradition: Conversations Between a Marxian Atheist and a Calvinian Christian*. Lanham, Md.: University Press of America, 1990. For those interested in pursuing the relation between ethics and religion in postmodern dialogue.

Nowell-Smith, P. H. "Religion and Morality." In *The Encyclopedia of Philosophy*, edited by Paul Edwards. New York: Macmillan, 1967. Excellent discussion, with more room for detail than the present article, but without serious consideration of the rapprochement offered by Thomism.

Plato. *The Republic of Plato*. Translated by Francis M. Cornford. Oxford: Clarendon Press, 1941. This attempt to make Plato's *Republic* accessible to Greekless readers is still worthy of admiration.

Smith, Huston. *The World's Religions*. San Francisco: HarperCollins, 1991. Acknowledged almost universally in the West as the best, most accurate, brief textbook on world religions.

Republic: Book

TYPE OF ETHICS: Classical history

DATE: Fifth century B.C.E.

AUTHOR: Plato

SIGNIFICANCE: Plato's most important work continues to influence philosophers and ethicists

Republic consists of a lengthy discussion of the advantages of choosing justice rather than injustice. In order to persuade his interlocutors, Socrates, the protagonist of *Republic*, uses every rhetorical device available to him, blending images and arguments into a whole that is worthy of the name "cosmos." Included in the work are fictional regimes, noble lies, an analogy of the good, allegories exposing human ignorance, geometrical explanations of knowledge, an image of the soul in speech, and a myth. The interlocutors, however, remain skeptical. They see no reason to believe that the soul has conflicting powers that are in need of intelligent governance, and they doubt that a philosopher king would rule the city more successfully than would a greedy tyrant who might agree to satisfy the interlocutors' own greed.

Framed among the most refined set of images available to philosophy, Socrates' failure to persuade is also a success.

So rich is Socrates' ability to demonstrate the truth of his claim that it has provoked innumerable commentaries. The power of the dialogue lies in its drama. Captured at the end of a religious festival, Socrates is forced to argue the merits of justice and the disadvantages of injustice. Under the tyrannical rule of Cephalus, who believes that justice is good only for those whose appetites have become dull with time, Socrates gives in to his craving for arguments and must find a way out of his own injustice. Cephalus leaves the discussion and hands his power to his son Polemarchus, who claims that justice is good for collecting debts. Thrasymachus, a guest, believes that justice proves advantageous for strong persons who can use justice to subdue the weak.

Aware that justice has been shattered and that each speaker has taken from it what suits his preference, Socrates does justice to justice. Since justice requires the ordering of many parts into a unity governed without tyranny and with concern for the well-being of both the parts and the whole, the philosopher must attempt to educate his interlocutors. The hardest to persuade are Thrasymachus and Adeimantus, who are men of appetites; like the appetites that govern them, they are insatiable unless they are restrained but are also fragile and can be destroyed easily by excessive discipline. In respect to the city, the larger picture of the soul, this is tantamount to saying that Socrates must convince the artisans, or the masses, to accept the rule of the philosopher king. Appetites and artisans respond to whatever appears to be pleasurable. The philosopher, therefore, must carefully select images that are simultaneously appealing and restraining. The story of Gyges and the tale of Er meet this need, awakening desire for the pleasures of justice and rejection of the pain that follows injustice. Spiritedness, in turn, receives a strong dose of fiction. Intelligence thrives on the divided line. In order to educate whole souls and entire cities, one must use didactic devices that function as a whole. *Republic* itself is that whole. It should be kept in mind, however, that this whole is not available to the dramatis personae of the work. Therefore, the fact that the interlocutors are not persuaded by Socrates does not diminish the power of the drama. *Republic* is written in the first person and is presumed to be Socrates' recollection of past events. In fact, only the unnamed audience must be truly persuaded.

Socrates' instruction relies on two parallel triads that are presumed to share a common virtue:

Soul	City	Virtue of each
Intelligence	Ruler	Wisdom
Spiritedness	Guardians	Courage
Appetites	Artisans	Moderation

Justice is the virtue of the city and the soul taken as a whole. Training into moderation proceeds through imitation, courage comes about through fictions, and wisdom (rational thought)

arises from the study of music and geometry. Geometry satisfies intelligence's desire to look into the nature and structure of things, and music prepares intelligence to govern the many, forming a beautiful unity that never neglects the well-being of its parts. Justice, then, is learned through music. Presumably, music keeps intelligence in touch with the whole soul, for "someone properly reared in rhythm and harmony would have the sharpest sense of what has been left out or what is not a beautiful product of craft or what is not a fine product of nature." When intelligence matures in reason, or *logos*, music takes the form of dialectic. This claim makes good sense if one recalls that Greek is a language with pitch and rhythm.

Dialectic harmonizes. If one analyzes the divided line musically, one notices that its center is a continuous note that is interrupted by pauses marked by the lines that divide images from sensations and thoughts from truths. At the end of sensation, one sees a longer pause that is analogous to the rest that is inspired in the soul by the trust that seeing an object causes. When the object that is being observed causes a contrapuntal sensation, the soul, which is provoked to think, continues the melody. The sensation in question provokes thought by "tending to go over to the opposite." Seeing the index finger, the middle finger, and the little finger, one is satisfied to call them fingers. One pauses. Their relationship, however, gives mixed messages, calling the index finger both large and small. What is required is a measure, a gathering of the parts into a harmonious whole that is analogous to the organization that is required by the parts of the city and the powers of the soul. The dialectician is the one who grasps the explanation of the being, or *ousia*, of each thing and unifies the many according to their nature. He provides a melody, conducts the orchestra, and hears and cherishes every note that is played, but never imposes an interpretation on the players. He governs by minding his own business. That minding of one's own business precisely defines what justice is. It should not surprise one then, that the best ruler of both the city and the soul is the philosopher king.

—*Anne Freire Ashbaugh*

See also Plato; Platonic ethics.

BIBLIOGRAPHY

Annas, Julia. *An Introduction to Plato's "Republic."* Oxford, England: Clarendon Press, 1981.

Crombie, I. M. *An Examination of Plato's Doctrines*. London: Routledge & Kegan Paul, 1963.

Plato. *The Dialogues of Plato*. 4th ed. 4 vols. Translated by Benjamin Jowett. Oxford, England: Clarendon Press, 1953.

_____. *The Republic of Plato*. Oxford, England: Clarendon Press, 1942.

Research, industrial

TYPE OF ETHICS: Scientific ethics

DATE: Twentieth century

DEFINITION: A collection of principles and practices followed by industrial and manufacturing concerns that engage in research to improve processes and develop new products

SIGNIFICANCE: Ethical industrial research seeks to maintain intra- and intercompany integrity, to deal honestly with the public, and to treat company research personnel fairly

More than fifty years ago, the sociologist Robert Merton stated the norms of the scientific research community: communality, organized skepticism, originality, universality, and disinterestedness. To these should be added self-motivation, an openness in sharing results, and a readiness to change when objective evidence calls for it. To some degree, all these ethical norms are challenged by the practice of industrial research. The discussion that follows identifies some of these challenges, both to the individual and to the corporation.

The Individual Scientist. People with research degrees (usually Ph.D.'s) in the sciences are accustomed from their university experience to being their own bosses in choosing and executing research projects. In industry, by contrast, they are assigned a research problem and must report regular progress to a boss who reports to a higher boss, on up to the research director, with results appearing not in professional journals, but only in internal reports. The problem is less acute in very large, research-oriented companies, where the projects are correspondingly larger and more interesting. In companies with very small research operations, the problems can be depressingly trivial (for example, it is difficult to care how to lengthen the time it takes corn flakes to become soggy in milk). It is also less uncomfortable for graduates without university research training to be trained in a particular company's laboratory and absorb the company's goals with the training. Nevertheless, nearly all industrial researchers occasionally feel that they are compromising true science and must find their own way to be comfortable with this.

Research Practices Within a Corporation. Companies must make money to survive. The problem for the research division, then, is to do as wide-ranging and complete research as possible within budgetary restraints. The urge to cut off research projects that do not pay off quickly must be resisted, as must the urge to stop a successful project the instant a product becomes possible. A more pernicious ethical problem is that of actually doing the research. Chemical procedures have sometimes been made up out of whole cloth, because "we know that's how they'd come out anyhow," and products have been represented as research breakthroughs that were nothing of the kind. Patent policy is worth mentioning: American firms customarily claim patent protection not only for a specific invention, the patent's subject, but also for any similar device or process that can be related to it, thus closing out research efforts by other firms. A topic that is too large to deal with here is the ethical handling of animals in industrial laboratories.

Relations with Other Corporations. All companies examine competitors' products with the idea of improving their own or claiming a share of the market. So long as this practice does not infringe patents, it is legitimate. What is not legitimate is deliberate industrial espionage—hiring a firm to place a person on the competitor's payroll to ferret out secrets of process or formulation that can be obtained in no other way. Equally unethical is the hiring away of key employees to exploit their privileged knowledge. Some firms have explicit policies that forbid this practice; many require professional employees to sign contracts that forbid their working for a competitor for a specified time after leaving the company. A separate issue of marketing that touches on the research side is that of firms that compete, not by improving manufacturing and distribution processes to reduce costs, but by blitzing competitors with a steady flow of new products. A weak firm can be driven out of business by such practices.

Responsibility to Customers. Customers need to know a great many things that only the industrial research laboratories can tell them—for example, about product safety. The Food and Drug Act was passed in 1906 to ensure the purity of foods and the safety and efficacy of drugs; even so, many errors have been made that have stemmed from careless, if not unethical, practices: the pediatric syrup of sulfa drugs marketed in the late 1930's that used toxic ethylene glycol as solvent; the grossly teratogenic drug thalidomide, which was withdrawn from the market in the 1960's; diethylstilbestrol, which is carcinogenic in women even to the second generation; and a host of other drugs and food additives, some quietly taken off the market when studies that should have been done in the original research showed unacceptable side effects. Environmental effects should be investigated (although these cannot always be anticipated); for example, pesticide residue toxicity, chlorofluorocarbon depletion of the ozone layer, and so forth. Finally, customers need to know that new research products are genuine innovations: Could the ingredients of a new two-drug pill have been prescribed separately more cheaply? Will this new research-hyped cosmetic really make one sixteen years old again? Do automotive gimmicks such as rectangular headlights or hideaway headlights make a car safer or mechanically superior? Though some of these examples border on marketing and salesmanship, many relate to the research laboratory.

Conclusion. As the foregoing discussion indicates, industrial research deviates in many respects from pure research. Nearly all these points of deviation call for ethical decisions. No attempt has been made here to say what decisions should be made; the purpose of this article is descriptive rather than prescriptive.

—*Robert M. Hawthorne, Jr.*

See also Business ethics; Science, ethics of.

BIBLIOGRAPHY

Amato, Ivan. "The Slow Birth of Green Chemistry." "Can the Chemical Industry Change Its Spots?" and "Making Molecules Without the Mess." *Science* 259 (March 12, 1993): 1538-1541.

Blevins, David E. "University Research and Development

Activities: Intrusion into Areas Unattended? A Review of Recent Developments and Ethical Issues Raised." *Journal of Business Ethics* 7 (September, 1988): 645-656.

Carboni, Rudolph A. *Planning and Managing Industry-University Research Collaborations.* Westport, Conn.: Quorum Books, 1992.

Kornhauser, William. *Scientists in Industry: Conflict and Accommodation.* Berkeley: University of California Press, 1962.

Vagtborg, Harold. *Research and American Industrial Development.* New York: Pergamon Press, 1976.

Wilks, Stephen. "Science, Technology and the Large Corporation." *Government and Opposition* 27, no. 2 (Spring, 1992): 190-212.

Research, weapons

TYPE OF ETHICS: Scientific ethics

ASSOCIATED WITH: Government, civilian, and military research

DEFINITION: Initiating research or consolidating existing knowledge into the production of weapon systems

SIGNIFICANCE: Raises the following questions: Under what ethical justification does science proceed in the development of more efficient weapons? If the weapons are used, does responsibility for the outcome belong to the inventors or the users?

The ethical stance used to justify research into developing more efficient weapon systems is nearly the same as that used to justify standing military forces—defense. The theory is that a society with a well-trained and well-equipped military force is the one best prepared to defend itself from outside aggression. Historically, the most efficient means to promote a military force's victory is to provide it with quality leadership and supply it with weapon systems superior to those of the adversary. Traditionally, any participation in the defense of one's nation and its people is seen as a moral, noble, and patriotic act. These reasons often motivate members of the scientific community to participate in defense projects in much the same way that they inspire other people to enter diplomatic or military service.

Ethical justification for any defense-oriented service to one's nation is readily accepted if the motivating provision is to provide protection of way of life, family, sovereignty, territorial integrity, political agenda, or philosophical belief. On occasion, however, the missions of defensive weapons have been redefined or new weapons have been sought for purely offensive purposes in order to foster a society's political, territorial, or philosophical agenda. While the use of such weapons may be ethically and morally justified by those seeking to expand their political or philosophical influence, these weapons present many science professionals with an ethical dilemma involving their personal beliefs and the demands of their vocation: Do their personal or professional ethics conflict with the research that society demands of them, and if so should they withhold their expertise and skills or should they set aside personal beliefs and allow the ends to justify the means?

In an idealistic world, science professionals would work only on projects that conformed to their personal ethical standards. As a community, science professionals abide by a code of ethics governing scientific methodology, and adherence to this code influences their dedication, discipline, and loyalty in the pursuit of scientific goals. As individuals, however, science professionals are like all other citizens in that they are members of society and by their choice of vocation have become providers of unique services to that society: They are educators, inventors, engineers, physicians, explorers, and theoretical and applied researchers in all fields. For this reason, science professionals have been asked throughout history to help solve problems for humanity. In most instances, society's requests of science pose little ethical difficulty: finding cures for disease, improving crop yields, designing safe products.

Another of society's requests, however, is that science professionals commit their knowledge and skills to aid in the defense of their society. As a result, many scientific discoveries are transformed into weapons systems providing more effective means for nations to defend themselves. Intellectually, science professionals participating in weapons research projects know that their work, if used, may cause the death of other living things, but this knowledge is complicated by a paradox: Technologies specifically developed for weapon systems have resulted in products that improve the quality of life, and, conversely, research done for totally benign purposes has resulted in very effective weapons. Some examples are lasers, whose use has revolutionized both medical surgery and the delivery of explosive ordnance; computer systems that speed computations and communication yet also control weapons systems; materials research that provides energy savings, durability, and protection in commercial packaging as well as for armored vehicles; and aircraft designs that improve the performance of both civilian and military aircraft. The multiple uses of modern technologies make it nearly impossible to predict their long-term applications.

Science professionals understand that the specialized educations and skills that they possess do not come with an inherent moral or ethical code, and each time they consider participating in a research project, their decision to participate or not is based on their perception of the research's possible ramifications. Each individual's choice may be influenced by theological beliefs, personal values, professional agendas, political motives, emotions, patriotism, or societal demands. These personal values have influenced many science professionals to turn away from all weapons research. After World War II, many scientists and engineers, appalled by the massive civilian casualties resulting from the uncontrollable destructive force of tactical nuclear weapons, refused to continue working on weapons research. Other science professionals, who are opposed to the use of tactical nuclear weapons but aware of their society's defensive needs, have chosen to engage in "smart bomb" research, designing nonnuclear explosive ordnance that can be directed to point-specific military targets with minimal danger to civilian noncombatants.

Science professionals understand that the discoveries, inventions, and technologies that arise from their scientific inquiries are in themselves amoral. They view their input in the development and perfecting of new weapon technologies as something quite separate from the production and use of these technologies. Science and military professionals do not operate with *carte blanche* in the field of weapons research. It is society and its representatives, based on their interpretation of perceived threats, that establish a weapons research agenda. Society utilizes the services of science and military professionals to ensure that its defense agenda is fulfilled. It is also society that instructs these professionals to use weapon systems to make war. All too often, society proves reluctant to accept the ethical burdens and responsibilities resulting from war, and science and military professionals find themselves blamed for the efficiency with which they have carried out the will of their nation.

—*Randall L. Milstein*

See also Military ethics; Nuclear energy; Research, industrial; Science, ethics of.

BIBLIOGRAPHY

Barke, Richard. *Science, Technology, and Public Policy.* Washington, D.C.: Congressional Quarterly, 1986.

Bronowski, Jacob. *Science and Human Values.* Rev. ed. New York: Harper & Row, 1965.

Dyson, Freeman. *Disturbing the Universe.* New York: Harper & Row, 1979.

Florman, Samuel C. *Blaming Technology: The Irrational Search for Scapegoats.* New York: St. Martin's Press, 1981.

Lakoff, Sanford A., ed. *Science and Ethical Responsibility.* Reading, Mass.: Addison-Wesley, 1980.

Rose, Hilary, and Steven Rose, eds. *The Political Economy of Science: Ideology offin the Natural Sciences.* London: Macmillan, 1976.

Responsibility

TYPE OF ETHICS: Beliefs and practices
DATE: Fourth century B.C.E. to present
ASSOCIATED WITH: Action theory, metaphysical presuppositions of moral reasoning, and problems of freedom and determinism
DEFINITION: Intentionally causing an event to occur with the ability to either act or refrain; the awareness of doing or the memory of having done the action when held accountable in a judgment context of shared relevant moral values
SIGNIFICANCE: Responsibility is a precondition for moral regard; persons are judged morally praiseworthy or blameworthy only if they are responsible for their actions

The concept of responsibility is a focus of long-standing dispute in metaphysics and moral philosophy. There is widespread disagreement about whether and in what sense persons are morally responsible for their actions. Some philosophers believe that to be morally responsible an agent must be free. Others think that responsibility obtains independently of the question of free will. Among those who regard freedom as essential to responsibility there are various theories about whether and in what sense persons are free. To understand the philosophical background of dispute about the concept of responsibility, it is necessary to sketch out the main lines of controversy and evaluate the strengths and weaknesses of some of the most influential positions.

Freedom and Responsibility. It is commonly said that persons can reasonably be held responsible for what they do only if their actions are done freely. In moral evaluation and legal decision making, persons are usually excused from responsibility for their actions if the evidence suggests that they acted without the ability or opportunity to choose to act differently.

Severely mentally retarded or insane persons and persons under extreme duress are routinely exempted from moral responsibility. The law similarly draws commonsense distinctions between murder in the first degree and manslaughter, in which an agent is said to have acted in the heat of passion. The idea is that under circumstances of extraordinary confusion or stress, the average person is not capable of acting freely; therefore, moral responsibility is at least temporarily diminished or suspended. A victim coerced by threat of violence to commit a moral offense in conditions in which most persons would find they have no choice but to comply is often seen as a mitigating circumstance absolving the agent of moral responsibility. The same reasoning applies to the exclusion of severely mentally retarded or insane persons from the category of moral responsibility. Persons with such disorders are usually judged unable to reason about their actions and the consequences of those actions. They are thought not to act freely or to act with such limited freedom that they cannot be considered moral agents, and their actions are not judged morally right or wrong. More morally and legally controversial cases concern substance abuse addicts and others under the influence of biochemical compulsions who may be involved in wrongful actions but who seem to lack the necessary self-control to be considered responsible.

Determinism. If these examples prove that responsibility entails freedom, then moral responsibility for action is problematic. There are scientific and philosophical reasons for doubting that humans are free enough in a deeper metaphysical sense to support the traditional concept of moral responsibility. The freedom to choose to act or to refrain from acting is challenged by causal, logical-semantic, and theological kinds of determinism. These theories maintain, on different grounds, that persons cannot act otherwise than they in fact do. Logical-semantic determinism holds that agents are determined in what they do by the eternal abstract truth conditions of propositions describing their future actions. Theological determinism makes similar claims from the assumption of God's perfect omniscience of what agents will do and how they will choose to act. Since causal determinism is thought to pose the most serious threat to free action, however, it is convenient in what follows to limit discussion to it. Causal determinism arises from the conception of human beings as physical systems, subject, like other macrophysical entities, to deterministic natural laws. If persons are determined by the laws of physics, then they are no more free to choose and act than nonliving things are. If moral responsibility entails causal freedom, then persons are not morally responsible.

There is a spectrum of degrees of freedom and responsibility in the ordinary, nonphilosophical, sense. It begins, on the low end, with nonhuman animals and severely retarded or insane persons, who are believed to have no moral responsibility at all. Then come addicts and persons under the direction of psychopathological compulsions; they are intermediate cases, who are typically thought to have some, but less than normal, moral responsibility. Finally, there are normal human adults, who, other things being equal, are usually regarded as morally responsible agents. If nonhuman animals, the severely retarded, and insane persons lack responsibility, and if addicts and compulsives have diminished responsibility because they cannot exercise sufficient self-control, the same reasoning coupled with philosophical arguments for determinism suggests that no one anywhere in the spectrum is morally responsible. If human beings are merely complicated physical systems, then even norman human adults are not freely in control of what they do. They cannot do other than what they do, but are merely manipulated through body chemistry and the environment by the same cause-and-effect relations that govern all other natural phenomena in the universe. If this is true, and if moral responsibility entails causal freedom, then no person is morally responsible, and there is no justification for regarding normal human adults as more morally responsible than nonliving things, nonhuman animals, the severely retarded or insane, addicts, or compulsives.

Accordingly, to preserve moral responsibility in the light of the challenge of determinism, some philosophers have argued that freedom is not necessary for moral responsibility. They interpret responsibility as mere accountability. By this they mean that to be morally responsible is to be the person causally responsible for a certain event, capable of explaining one's reasons for acting, and perhaps able and willing to accept approval for a good result and accept blame for or rectify an unwanted outcome. It is in this pragmatic sense that airlines are held responsible for damage to a passenger's luggage, and it is at this level that legal responsibility generally functions, without raising deep metaphysical issues about whether airline employees act freely in the sense of being causally undetermined.

Metaphysics of Responsible Action. There are two main types of theories of moral responsibility, which can be referred to as compatibilist and incompatibilist. Compatibilist theories of responsibility hold that responsibility is independent of the problem of freedom, or that responsibility is logically compatible with causal determinism, so that agents can be responsible in the pragmatic sense even if they are not free. Incompatibilist theories insist that whether agents are morally responsible logically depends on whether and in what sense they are free, and that responsibility is logically incompatible with causal determinism. Incompatibilism further divides into responsibilist and nonresponsibilist theories. Responsibilist incompatibilism is the position that responsibility is incompatible with determinism but that agents are responsible precisely because they are not causally determined. Nonresponsibilist incompatibilism is the view that responsibility is incompatible with determinism, but since agents are causally determined, they are not responsible. Nonresponsibilist incompatibilism implies that an agent's feeling of responsibility, sometimes manifested as pride, guilt, or stirrings of conscience, is illusory.

The distinction is reflected above in cases involving compatibilist responsibility, such as an airline's collective accountability for a passenger's luggage, and the incompatibilist judgment that if agents are not causally free in a deeper metaphysical sense, then they are no more responsible for what they do than are nonhuman animals or even nonliving physical things. The advantage of compatibilism is that it assumes no burden of challenging the modern scientific world outlook according to which all natural phenomena are supposed to be reductively causally explainable by the laws of physics. Yet it preserves a pragmatic sense in which it is intelligible to hold normal human adults responsible, while morally excusing and excluding from responsibility nonhuman animals, the severely retarded or insane, and related commonsense and legally recognized exceptions. The advantage of responsibilist incompatibilism, if it can be convincingly defended, is that it accords with traditional moral thinking about the dignity of mind and the difference between human beings and other natural systems, and especially with the conception that an agent in acting responsibly could have chosen to act differently. From the standpoint of responsibilist incompatibilism, compatibilism offers an intellectually unsatisfying diluted sense of responsibility that is insufficient to sustain moral judgment and justify the social mechanisms of praise and blame, reward and punishment. From a nonresponsibilist incompatibilist standpoint, such judgments and practices cannot be justified, because they are based on false assumptions about the freedom of action.

To resolve the metaphysics of freedom and responsibility requires an investigation of concepts in philosophical psychology or the philosophy of mind. The freedom of the will is accepted by substance dualist theories of mind, in which the mind or soul is said to be a spiritual substance distinct from the body's material substance. If the mind is immaterial, then it is causally free and undetermined by causal necessity. Unfortunately, substance dualism cannot satisfactorily explain causal interaction between body and mind. If mind and body are causally independent of each other, and if only the body is subject to causation, then the mind cannot be causally responsible, and hence cannot be morally responsible, for actions involving body movements. If, however, mind and body are identical, and if the body, like other purely physical systems, is subject to causal determinism, then so is the mind; therefore, the problem of the causal determinism of action remains on incompatibilist assumptions to threaten moral responsibility. The dilemma is that if the mind is part of the body's causal nexus, then it is causally determined and therefore not morally responsible for its actions; if the mind is not part of the body's causal nexus, then the mind is not causally responsible, and again therefore not morally responsible for its actions.

There is another theory of mind that allows both mind-body causal interaction and incompatibilist freedom of will and moral responsibility. Instead of regarding mind as a spiritual substance distinct from but somehow interacting with the body's physical substance, persons can be understood as physical substances with both physical and nonphysical aspects, or properties. This alternative to classical substance dualism is known as aspect, or property, dualism. If the mind is not an immaterial substance, then the problem of its causal interaction with the material body does not arise. If mental properties are irreducible to purely physical properties, then there is a sense in which persons are not merely physical entities. The nonphysical or physically irreducible properties of persons constitute an aspect of persons by virtue of which they do not fully fall under deterministic causal laws. The difference between the mind and ordinary purely physical systems postulated by this kind of theory permits minds to be causally undetermined in the contracausally free ethical decision making for which they are morally responsible.

Taking Responsibility and Holding Others Responsible. There are social as well as metaphysical dimensions of the concept of responsibility. To be judged morally responsible for the consequences of an action, an agent must intend to act, intend that the action result in the consequences for which the agent is responsible, and be aware of or remember having done the action when held accountable for it. A shared sense of values in taking responsibility and holding others responsible is also presupposed. These factors impose additional intentional conditions on the concept of moral responsibility.

The importance of these additional conditions can be illustrated by a commonsense example. Suppose that an agent freely decides to turn on a light switch. The agent is responsible for the immediate action of turning on the light but not necessarily responsible for its further unforeseen consequences. If turning on the light enables a killer to see a victim in the room, then the agent's turning on the light may

in some sense be causally responsible for the victim's murder. If the agent has no knowledge that the killer is present or that the person in the room might be a target for murder, however, and has no acquired responsibility to act as the victim's guardian, then the correct judgment seems to be that the agent is at most partly causally responsible, but not morally responsible, for the victim's death. This condition can be formulated by saying that an agent must intend the consequences of an action in order to be morally responsible for it. The agent in the example intends to turn on the light and is, as far as moral considerations are relevant, morally responsible for doing so. The agent does not intend that the victim be killed, however, and therefore is not morally responsible for the fact that this occurs in part as a consequence of turning on the light. The killer intends to murder the victim and is morally responsible for that action, for which the light's being turned on merely affords an opportunity.

A related though more controversial condition is that the agent recognize or be aware of doing an action or of its effects at the time when held responsible for it. Persons who have committed what would otherwise be regarded as a moral offense are sometimes acquitted of responsibility by the consideration that they have no memory of having so acted. If an agent acts and then suffers amnesia permanently affecting memory of the action, it may be inappropriate to hold the person morally responsible thereafter, even if at the time the agent would have been rightly judged morally responsible. It seems pointless to praise, blame, reward, or punish persons for actions they have no memory of doing.

It may be equally pointless to hold persons morally responsible, in the sense of morally praising, blaming, rewarding, or punishing them, if they do not share at least some of the relevant values of those judging them. This is a normative condition that can be explained as the agent's intending to do an action in a certain way, as a morally good, bad, or indifferent act. The light switcher may intend to turn on the light as a morally indifferent act. The killer presumably intends to murder the victim as a morally wrong act. If, however, the killer has values so different from those of the persons who judge the murder that the act is not intended to be something morally wrong, but instead something morally good or indifferent, and if there is no prospect of altering the killer's behavior or values by moral censure or punishment, then, regardless of legal proceedings taken against the person for the safety of others, it may be inappropriate to regard the killer as morally responsible. A more realistic example concerns the incompatible attitudes of those persons who value the private possession of property and those who share all things in common. If members of two such opposite cultures meet and the sharers take and use a possessor's property, it is arguably unjustified to hold the sharers morally responsible for committing an act of theft. The fact that moral responsibility is seldom overridden by normative considerations testifies to prevailing agreement among human cultures at least about the most basic moral values. The normative element is nevertheless an important part of the complete philosophical analysis of the concept of moral responsibility.

Limits of Responsibility. If there are some things for which agents are morally responsible, there are still others for which they clearly are not responsible. Some existentialist philosophers maintain that each person is morally responsible for the intended consequences of their acts, then an individual who accepts the existence of the universe becomes morally responsible for it.

The existentialist argument seems confused. Agents are morally responsible only for intended events for which they are causally responsible, provided that memory and normative conditions are also satisfied. Accepting the fact that the world exists does not make the agent causally responsible

Many of the defendants in the Nuremberg Trials (some of whom are shown here) claimed that they were only following orders and therefore were not responsible for their own actions. (National Archives)

sible for the state of the entire universe, including its past history and future.

The exact meaning of this extravagant thesis is obscure, but the claim seems to be that in accepting the fact that the universe exists, the individual participates in the fact of its existence in such a way as to comply with and constitute the universe as existent. The individual's acceptance is an intentional mental act, involving the person as agent in adopting a certain attitude toward the world. The consequence of the act is that the universe exists and would otherwise not exist for the individual who accepts the fact. If per-

for its existence, and the agent certainly cannot be causally responsible and hence not morally responsible for any part of the world's past history. Assuredly, no human agent correctly remembers having caused the universe to exist. In the present analysis of moral responsibility, there is no sound basis for existential guilt, despair, and anxiety about the state of the world as the burden of one's personal responsibility. By the same token, no person can be morally responsible for what another does, except insofar as an agent acts as an instrument of another's will. This is not an exception to the analysis, but an application of the definition of moral responsibility by which a person is indirectly but still ultimately causally responsible for an event undertaken by another person acting as delegate.   —*Dale Jacquette*

See also Accountability; Coercion; Conscience; Determinism and freedom; Dignity; Existentialism; Freedom and liberty; Future-oriented ethics; Intention; Mental illness; Moral responsibility; Moral status of animals; Punishment; Self-control; Social justice and responsibility; Values.

BIBLIOGRAPHY

Berofsky, Bernard. *Freedom from Necessity: The Metaphysical Basis of Responsibility*. London: Routledge & Kegan Paul, 1987. A detailed discussion of the metaphysical presuppositions of moral accountability. Philosophical analysis of addictive and compulsive behavior, necessity, unalterability, autonomy, and psychopathology.

Edwards, R. B. *Freedom, Responsibility and Obligation*. The Hague: Martinus Nijhoff, 1970. Examines central issues of the concept of responsibility as it relates to the problem of human freedom.

Fingarette, Herbert. *On Responsibility*. New York: Basic Books, 1967. An exact but nontechnical inquiry into the role of responsibility in practical reasoning, including the development of self-realization and the sense of responsibility and guilt.

Fischer, John M., ed. *Moral Responsibility*. Ithaca, N.Y.: Cornell University Press, 1986. A useful collection of papers by contemporary philosophers on the nature of agency and responsibility for action.

Glover, Jonathan. *Responsibility*. London: Routledge & Kegan Paul, 1970. A balanced treatment of theoretical and practical topics. Emphasizes problems in the traditional conflict between determinism and moral responsibility, blameworthiness, and excusability, with special application to mental illness and criminal responsibility.

Jacquette, Dale. *Philosophy of Mind*. Englewood Cliffs, N.J.: Prentice-Hall, 1994. Discusses property dualism as a solution to the mind-body problem and its implications for contracausal freedom of will and action, moral responsibility, and the dignity of mind.

Shotter, John. *Social Accountability and Selfhood*. Oxford, England: Basil Blackwell, 1984. An investigation of the concept of responsibility to others and the development of the sense of responsibility from the standpoint of developmental psychology.

Revelation

TYPE OF ETHICS: Beliefs and practices

DEFINITION: Divine disclosure

SIGNIFICANCE: If God exists and has revealed himself to humans, then he may have disclosed matters of moral significance, and the very nature of human moral experience may justify the expectation that God has revealed himself

While the earliest reflections on the nature of ethical conduct were rooted in religion, the philosophical treatment of ethics has led many people to assume the autonomy of ethics. This is the idea that ethics is not in any way dependent on revelation. Thus, a wedge has been driven between moral philosophy and theological or revealed ethics. There are, however, interesting and persistent questions about a possible relation between the two.

Since revelation means, at the highest level of generality, divine disclosure, questions about the relationship between revelation and ethics are part of a larger network of more general questions about the relationship between God and morality. Those questions that focus expressly on the significance of revelation for the moral life arise for any religious tradition that holds that God has revealed himself in some way that bears upon the human moral situation, but revelation may be understood in different ways.

The Meaning of Revelation. First, revelation may take the form of general information about divine reality gleaned from the pattern of the natural world order created by God. Here, divine truth is disclosed indirectly through the effects of divine activity—especially the activity of creation. This is often called "general revelation." Some philosophers, such as Thomas Aquinas, have argued that general revelation is an ample source of knowledge about the foundations, principles, and sanctions of ethics. This view is known as the natural law tradition in ethics.

Second, revelation may refer to an intersubjective encounter between God and humanity that is entirely lacking in the overt transmission of any truths. The propositional content of what may be called "personal revelation" is at most implicit in the divine-human encounter. The possibility of basing ethics on revelation depends on what is concretely implied by the character of one's religious experience. It would be difficult to justify the universalizability of moral principles derived in this fashion since religious experience is in principle a very private matter.

Third, revelation may be understood as the direct divine disclosure to humans of truths in propositional form. The great "revealed religions"—Judaism, Christianity, and Islam—hold that their respective scriptures are a deposit of divine revelation. Theologians have called this sense of divine revelation "special revelation" to distinguish it from general revelation. It is special revelation that is usually in view in discussions about the relationship between revelation and ethics.

Is Ethics Based on Revelation? There are at least three views about the general relationship between revelation and ethics. First is the view that a system of ethics must be based on (special) revelation. This claim is defended by a developed account of the implications of divine sovereignty and of human sinfulness and by the attempt to refute all secular systems of ethics. The sovereignty of God implies that the content of morality is determined by the will of God. Moreover, human depravity involves rebellion against the will of God, resulting in a failure even to know the will of God. Finally, all secular theories of ethics provide empirical evidence of the corruption of human thought about ethics.

A second approach affirms the complete, or nearly complete, autonomy of ethics. Goodness cannot be determined by the will of God, for it can be meaningfully asked: Is the will of God itself good? Those who define goodness in terms of God's will are no better off than those who define goodness in terms of some natural property such as pleasure. To define goodness, which is an irreducible property, in terms of something else is always a mistake.

The suggestion that ethics is autonomous must be qualified. For, as G. E. Moore (who first attacked the naturalistic fallacy) observed, one's metaphysics will have a bearing upon the practical question "What ought I to do?" "If, for instance, Metaphysics could tell us not only that we are immortal, but also, in any degree, what effects our actions in this life will have upon our condition in a future one, such information will have an undoubted bearing upon the question what we ought to do. The Christian doctrines of heaven and hell are in this way highly relevant to practical Ethics" (Moore, *Principia Ethica*). Since revelation might provide the sort of metaphysics that Moore refers to here, one cannot strictly rule out the bearing of revelation upon ethics, even if goodness is a nonnatural and unanalyzable property.

In any case, there is an important difference between that which *makes* an action right or wrong and the way in which one is to *know* that the action is right or wrong. One is an *ontological problem*; the other is an epistemological question. Even if the moral quality of an action is not ontologically determined by the will of God, God, if he is omniscient and wills the goodness of humans, may elect to reveal the nature and content of that morality which does not strictly depend upon his will.

According to the third view, ethics enjoys a limited range of autonomy from special revelation, though ethics is supplemented or completed by special revelation. Natural law theories are typical examples of this approach. To be sure, they envision a link between revelation and all correct ethical thinking, but much of the content of a true ethical system can be known without the aid of special revelation, since general revelation is also an important source of moral knowledge.

Three Additional Questions. Does moral experience establish a need for revelation? Background knowledge about the existence and nature of God, together with an awareness that humans are faced with a complex set of moral difficulties, may be thought to justify the expectation of some further revelation from God that would address the moral needs and concerns of the human community.

This raises a second question: Is God a member of the moral community? If God exists, then it is quite possible that God himself is a member of the moral community, and that human persons have moral obligations toward God as well as toward other humans. It may even be that God has moral responsibilities toward humans about which it would

be useful for humans to know. Suppose, for example, that God should make a promise to act in a certain way on behalf of humans and thus obligate himself to them. How should humans know of his promise apart from revelation, and what would be the force of a promise of which humans were not aware? Suppose, further, that the promise takes effect only if humans act in a particular way. In that case, the conditions must be revealed as well.

Finally, it needs to be asked, What effect might revelation have upon moral theory? If it turns out that there is a good argument for the need for revelation given the quality of human moral experience, then people can expect that any revelation answering this need will deeply inform, perhaps even overturn, much of human moral theory. The supposition of a revelation that addresses human moral experience implies that morality may be deeply affected by revelation.

H. Richard Niebuhr has noted four changes to the moral law caused by divine revelation: (1) the prescriptive force of the moral law is discovered to be absolute in that humans are revealed to be beholden to the sovereign of the universe; (2) the application of the moral law is discovered to be wider ranging than any secular ethics and timelessly in force; (3) the moral law is discovered to be unexceptionable, providing an external corrective to any corruptible human system of morality; and (4) the eventual transformation of human persons into freely loving agents is discovered to be a real possibility.   —R. Douglas Geivett

See also Atheism; Christian ethics; Divine command theory; Epistemological ethics; Ethical monotheism; God; Golden rule; Immortality; Islamic ethics; Jesus; Jewish ethics; Moore, G. E.; Muḥammad, al-Muṣṭafâ; Natural law; Naturalistic fallacy; Religion; Secular ethics; Ten Commandments; Universalizability.

BIBLIOGRAPHY

Adams, Robert M. *The Virtue of Faith*. New York: Oxford University Press, 1987.

Brunner, Emil. *The Divine Imperative*. Translated by Olive Wyon. Philadelphia: Westminster Press, 1947.

Grisez, Germain. *Christian Moral Principles*. Vol. 1 in *The Way of the Lord*. Chicago: Franciscan Herald Press, 1983.

Gustafson, James M. *Ethics from a Theocentric Perspective*. 2 vols. Chicago: University of Chicago Press, 1981-1984.

Henry, Carl F. H. *Christian Personal Ethics*. Grand Rapids, Mich.: Baker Book House, 1977.

McInerny, Ralph. *Ethica Thomistica*. Washington, D.C.: Catholic University of America, 1982.

Mitchell, Basil. *Morality: Religious and Secular*. Oxford, England: Clarendon Press, 1985.

Moore, G. E. *Principia Ethica*. Cambridge, England: Cambridge University Press, 1966.

Niebuhr, H. Richard. *The Meaning of Revelation*. New York: Macmillan, 1970.

Swinburne, Richard. *Revelation: From Metaphor to Analogy*. Oxford, England: Clarendon Press, 1992.

Revenge

TYPE OF ETHICS: Personal and social ethics

DATE: From antiquity

DEFINITION: A response in kind for a wrong done to one-self; punishment inflicted in retaliation for an offense

SIGNIFICANCE: Revenge may well be an inherent human motive; therefore, society must justly control the dispensation of revenge if the thin veneer of civilization is to be maintained

Revenge as Need. Pietro Marongiu and Graeme Newman proclaim in *Vengeance* (1987) that "Vengeance has the power of an instinct. The 'lust for vengeance,' the 'thirst for revenge' are so powerful that they rival all other human needs." Revenge is a form of the universal motive of aggression in which reciprocity is sought to avenge injuries to oneself or to restore a sense of equality.

Revenge is often considered to be neurotic, aberrant behavior. In the words of the psychoanalyst Karen Horney, "Every vindictiveness damages the core of the whole being," implying resentment, spite, malice, or righteousness. Revenge is the basest of human motives. At the other end of the continuum stands forgiveness, the act of pardoning another person for any unpleasant or hostile behavior committed against oneself. In contrast to revenge, forgiveness is good and represents the noblest manifestation of human nature.

The Function of Revenge. The dichotomy between revenge and forgiveness obscures certain facts about the place of revenge in the human psyche, according to Susan Jacoby (*Wild Justice*, 1983). If revenge is a universal human need, then to forgive requires conscious suppression of the need to make others suffer as one has suffered. Humanity's long history is characterized by injury being inflicted on and sustained by others. That humanity seems to prefer revenge to forgiveness gives revenge a certain importance.

In fact, both Jacoby and Marongiu and Newman argue that revenge is not abnormal or aberrant behavior but a legitimate human need. Underlying this legitimacy is, as Jacoby says, "the profound sense of moral equilibrium impelling us to demand that people pay for the harm they have done to others." Revenge serves both moral and utilitarian roles. It is an example to society and a means of dealing with an offender. By making an example of an offender through revenge, society demonstrates to its members that certain behaviors are serious violations of the social order, are morally repugnant, and will produce unpleasant consequences for the perpetrator. Thus, revenge has deterrent, exemplary (it shows the public that society's well-being is being addressed), and moral aspects. In 1976, the U.S. Supreme Court legitimized the death penalty by proclaiming that revenge was an acceptable legal objective. That capital punishment was appropriate under certain circumstances reflected society's belief that some crimes are so terrible that the only adequate penalty for them is death.

The Doctrines of Pollution and Proportionality. The use of the term "revenge" may produce a disquieting sense of unease and discomfort. "Revenge" seems to be pejorative. If the words "justice, restitution, punishment or retribution" are substituted for revenge, however, the pejorative connotation disappears. Looked at in this way, the issue is not whether revenge is aberrant or evil behavior, but the establishment of a just and proper relationship between the nature of the act and the severity of the revenge. Finding such a relationship has been an ongoing matter of concern in literature, religion, and law since antiquity.

The two key concepts in striking this appropriate balance are the doctrines of pollution and proportionality. In ancient times, revenge was carried out as an individual vendetta or at the tribal level. The religious and political doctrine of pollution that developed among the ancient Greeks and Hebrews viewed certain acts, such as murder, as offenses against the whole society. This doctrine was an important point of transition between tribalism and written law. By means of this doctrine, the primacy of the state and of its gods and laws over the individual and tribe in enforcing punishment for acts of pollution was established.

The doctrine of proportionality states that the revenge extracted for an act of pollution shall be neither excessive nor trivial but shall match or be proportional to the seriousness of the act. This statement establishes a distinction between constructive revenge and destructive revenge. Limits are placed on the imposition of extreme forms of legalized revenge for lesser transgressions by forbidding penalties greater than the original crime and making the punishment fit the crime. "If men strive, and hurt a woman with child, so that her fruit depart from her . . . and he shall pay as the judges determine . . . thou shalt give life for life, eye for eye, tooth for tooth, hand for hand, foot for foot, burning for burning, wound for wound, stripe for stripe" (Exodus 21:22-25).

Revenge as a Quandary and a Dilemma. The doctrines of pollution and proportionality establish that certain acts shall be met by revenge meted out by the state and that this revenge shall be proportional to the offending act. Pollution is relatively straightforward in that there will be a relatively high level of agreement among people regarding what acts pollute. Proportionality is often very difficult to determine, however, as is indicated by the wide variation in prison sentences handed out for the same crime in different states and the controversy surrounding the issue of capital punishment. Thus, the pollution aspect can be viewed as a quandary (a question for which no single undisputed answer or consensus can be attained), but the proportionality aspect is often a dilemma (in which more than one ethical position is possible). Since revenge seems to be inherent in the human condition, these issues will have to be faced continually.

—Laurence Miller

See also Criminal punishment; Justice; Mercy; Violence.

BIBLIOGRAPHY

Ayers, Edward L. *Vengeance and Justice*. New York: Oxford University Press, 1984.

Bowers, Fredson Thayer. *Elizabethan Revenge Tragedy.* Gloucester, Mass.: Peter Smith, 1959.

Hallett, Charles A., and Elaine S. Hallett. *The Revenger's Madness.* Lincoln: University of Nebraska Press, 1980.

Jacoby, Susan. *Wild Justice.* New York: Harper & Row, 1983.

Marongiu, Pietro, and Graeme Newman. *Vengeance.* Totowa, N.J.: Rowman & Littlefield, 1987.

Reverse racism

TYPE OF ETHICS: Race and ethnicity

DATE: Late 1960's and early 1970's

DEFINITION: The use of government-sanctioned preferential treatment to benefit historically oppressed races; an attitude adopted by members of a minority that the majority is racially inferior

SIGNIFICANCE: An example of the use of unjust means to effect a just solution to an intractable social problem

Reverse racism is a term attributed to government-supported programs designed to remedy past injustices caused by racial discrimination. Remedies such as hiring quotas and affirmative action favor one race at the expense of random members of another race to make up for privileges that the second race once enjoyed at the expense of the first. In the simplest terms, such policies have been questioned on the basis of whether two wrongs can make a right. The term "reverse racism" has also been applied to racial consciousness-raising methods among minority groups that use the denigration of the majority racial group as a means of attaining intraracial solidarity. These methods are practiced by minority political and religious figures such as the Nation of Islam's Louis Farrakhan and academics such as Leonard Jeffries, head of the African-American Studies Department of City College of New York, who has told his classes that the lack of melanin in the skin of whites has rendered them inferior to blacks.

See also Political correctness; Racism.

Revolution

TYPE OF ETHICS: Politico-economic ethics

DATE: Seventeenth century to present

DEFINITION: A violent overthrow of the political and social order that occurs within a concentrated period of time and transforms not only the politics but also the values of a society

SIGNIFICANCE: Revolutions ordinarily involve a repudiation of the past, especially the immediate past, including its social norms and conventions, and raise an expectation of significant improvement in the immediate future

In the latter part of the twentieth century, the term "revolution" has been invoked so frequently as to lose its currency. The word has come to be used to describe dramatic changes in virtually any area of human activity. Thus, one may read about a revolution in fashion, a sexual revolution, a women's revolution, or a revolution in the arts. While revolution in its traditional sense may involve change in any or all of these activities, it is a term whose classical application is properly limited to a few events of enormous political and social magnitude. It is not to be confused with a rebellion, a revolt, or a *coup d'état*, in which only political power is transferred from one group to another. While it includes a shift in political power, its transforming effects are not limited to politics. They involve rapid and enduring social, cultural, and economic change as well as political change.

In its original sense, the word "revolution" had nothing to do with politics or with violent or rapid social and political change. Rather, the word was part of the scientific vocabulary and meant to return to a proper, prescribed course. Therefore, for example, in 1543, a posthumously published book by the Polish astronomer Nicholas Copernicus was titled *The Revolutions of the Celestial Spheres.* Copernicus was using the word "revolution" in its accepted sense—something proceeding according to a proper, prescribed course. The planets, he contended, proceeded according to such a course around the sun. Revolution, then, meant literally revolving. In retrospect, Copernicus' book was revolutionary in a more modern sense—it transformed the human view of the world by postulating a theory of heliocentric universe in place of the geocentric universe that was dominant until that time.

The association of the term "revolution" with the political events of the seventeenth century began to transform the term's meaning. Even then, the word continued to retain its earlier meaning of persisting in a prescribed course or returning to a designated course from which there had been a departure. The events of 1688-1689 in England provide an example of this usage. They were called the Glorious or Bloodless Revolution, by which was meant that, after the improper actions of King Charles II and James II, England returned to its proper, designated course with the replacement of King James II by William and Mary.

In this sense, revolution was political but conservative; that is, the revolutionaries were restoring things, returning them to a proper course. The American Revolution was also sometimes justified in this way. Americans thought that they were deprived first of the "rights of Englishmen"—then of the "rights of man." They were restoring something that they claimed they already had but that King George III had allegedly taken from them. Insofar as war for American independence was not accompanied by a radical social transformation, some historians argue that it was not a revolution in the classic sense.

The French Revolution, which began in 1789, became the model for revolution, not only for historians but also for later revolutionaries of the nineteenth and twentieth centuries. They would try to emulate the French Revolution. Even the Chinese, who began their revolution in the second decade of the twentieth century, thought first in terms of the French example, and the French Revolution was only later displaced by the model of the Russian, or Bolshevik, Revolution of 1917.

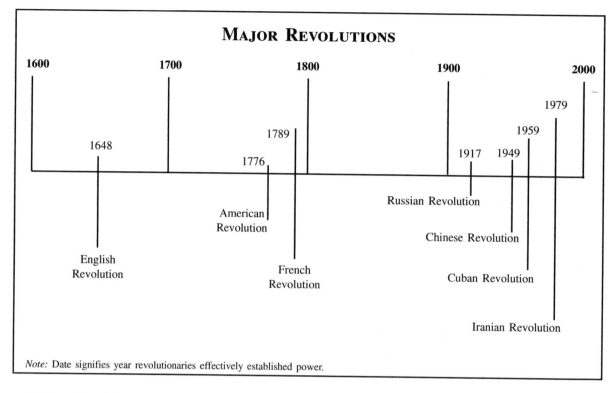

MAJOR REVOLUTIONS

Note: Date signifies year revolutionaries effectively established power.

The French Revolution, even in its early stages, was characterized by Edmund Burke, its harsh critic, as a social revolution, "a revolution in sentiments, manners and moral opinions." It challenged and overturned the values of society. What was most appalling to Burke was that the French Revolution rejected the past. The French Revolutionary generation rather quickly adopted the phrase "old régime" to designate the society that it was rejecting. The revolutionaries were sweeping away the old order of privilege and inequality and were replacing it with something new and, presumably, better. The best example of this repudiation of the past was the attempted institution, however unsuccessful, of a new calendar. The French Revolutionaries established the year 1 to be dated from the beginning of the Republic in 1792. History was starting over. Religion and the Church were repudiated. The social order of the old society was abolished. Even established fashion changed, as with the *sans culottes* (those who wore no britches), who repudiated the dress that was associated with the corrupt aristocracy.

The extent to which the past is repudiated may differ with different revolutions, but it is not only the political order that is transformed. Along with their repudiation of the past, revolutionaries need a vision of a future, however vague. They must be convinced that they are building a better world. The vision of the future may be drawn from the writings of a generation of social critics, as the French Revolutionaries drew upon the *philosophes* of the eighteenth century, or from a more systematic theory of society, such as that of Karl Marx and Vladimir Lenin, whose work influ-

enced the Bolshevik revolutionaries in Russia in 1917. Although they are influenced by theories developed in the past, revolutions are future oriented, insofar as they are ordinarily conceived as inaugurating a period of enduring progress, equality, and justice. In this connection, revolution is related to the humanism of the Western tradition, since revolutionaries assume that humankind can improve the human condition. This optimism and fervor are evident in the sense of passion and zeal that is displayed by revolutionaries and even those nonparticipant contemporaries who are transported by the intensity of their times. So, for example, William Wordsworth could write of 1789, "Bliss was it in that dawn to be alive/ But to be young was very heaven."

Revolutionaries have often been aware of the importance of their own times and instilled with a sense of the righteousness of their actions. Accordingly, their deeds are often accompanied by eloquent justifications, such as the American Declaration of Independence or the French Declaration of the Rights of Man and Citizen.

Revolution has been a modern phenomenon, insofar as it requires an organized state against which to rebel. While it was also a Western phenomenon, it has in the twentieth century been transported to other areas of the world, such as China. Given their dimensions and their transforming effects, revolutions are relatively rare. Many historians would include the English Revolution of the 1640's along with the American and French Revolutions in the following century among the few pre-twentieth century revolutions. In the twentieth century, after the Russian Revolution, the upheavals in China and Cuba qualify as revolutions given the magnitude of the social change that they generated. The Iranian Revolution appears to be unique in that it was not future oriented. It rejected the immediate past, which had been influenced and supposedly corrupted by the West, in order to return to a more purified condition that ostensibly obtained before Western influence was exerted.

—Abraham D. Kriegel

See also Marxism; Political liberty; Social contract; Socialism.

BIBLIOGRAPHY

Arendt, Hannah. *On Revolution*. New York: Viking Press, 1963.

Best, Geoffrey, ed. *The Permanent Revolution: The French Revolution and Its Legacy*. Chicago: University of Chicago Press, 1989.

Billington, James. *Fire in the Minds of Men: Origins of the Revolutionary Faith*. New York: Basic Books, 1980.

Brinton, Crane. *The Anatomy of Revolution*. Rev. and exp. ed. New York: Vintage Books, 1965.

Dunn, John. *Modern Revolutions: An Introduction to the Analysis of a Political Phenomenon*. Cambridge, England: Cambridge University Press, 1972.

Right and wrong

TYPE OF ETHICS: Theory of ethics

DATE: From antiquity

DEFINITION: In the sense used here, right means conforming to the facts and to the truth, to what is just, to what is proper; a true standard; qualities that constitute moral propriety; honesty. Wrong, then, is the opposite: immoral, unethical, not in accord with high standards, dishonest, not proper, not according to truth or facts

SIGNIFICANCE: Like the concepts of honesty, truth, and justice, the concepts of "right" and "wrong" are central to the development of an ethical philosophy

Since the days of the ancient Greek philosophers Socrates, Plato, and Aristotle, thinkers have searched for a way to distinguish between right and wrong. One twentieth century thinker who adopted and further developed the Aristotelian position was William D. Ross. He made the case for intuitionism, arguing that the moral convictions of well-educated, reasonable, and thoughtful people were the data of ethics, just as sense perceptions are the data of the sciences. He rejected both ethical subjectivism and utilitarianism, arguing instead that duty was the key to ethics. For Ross, right and good had distinct objective qualities. The former had to do with acts, while the latter had to do with motives.

Another modern philosopher who accepted Ross's argument was James Rachels, who added that morality—the attempt to discern right from wrong, good from bad—must be guided by reason. One should do whatever one has the best reasons for doing while keeping in mind the worth and interests of all those people who will be affected by one's actions. When considering a course of action, the conscientious moral individual will analyze the possible choices, measuring the implications of certain choices. After such deliberation, the moral individual will take the best possible course of action. Not all thinkers, however, agree with the above appeal to reason.

The Problem of Ethical Subjectivism. Scholars such as Ross and Rachels refused to accept subjectivism, which holds that everything is relative. To a subjectivist, nothing is right or wrong. Rather, moral judgments about good and bad and right and wrong are simply personal opinions based on an individual's "feelings" and nothing more. Even "truth" to an individual is truth according to "feelings." Thus, subjectivists reject the role of reason in making moral judgments. Furthermore, cultural subjectivism or relativism addresses a similar point, arguing that morals and values vary from culture to culture. Thus, there is no one standard of right and wrong. Regarding both ethical and cultural subjectivism, Ross and Rachels responded that reason and reasons are central, for truths in morals are truths of reason; that is, moral judgments that are correct must be backed by better reasons than an alternative judgment. Subjectivists are right that feelings and opinions are important to an individual, but to consider only those factors in making judgments is, in effect, to opt out of moral thinking, for moral thinking must weigh the reasons for and consequences of potential actions.

Right, Wrong, and Religion. In the United States, most laypersons would list ministers, priests, and rabbis if they were asked to name moral "experts." Unfortunately, such laypersons regard morality and religion as inseparable when, in fact, religious leaders appear to be no better and no worse judges than are people in other "walks" of life. Nevertheless, many people embrace what some theologians call the divine command theory, which holds that what is morally right is commanded by God and what is wrong is condemned and forbidden by God. A positive result of such a view is that it immediately solves the problem of subjectivism.

Atheists and agnostics reject the divine command argument. Even the noted Christian Thomas Aquinas (c. 1225-1274) rejected it. One reason why philosophers object to the theory is that it poses an unsolvable dilemma, for the following question must be asked: Is conduct right because God commands it or does God command it because it is right? To answer the question, one might take the example of truthfulness. The Hebrew God commands it in the book of Exodus; therefore, people should be truthful because God orders them to be so. It is God's command that makes telling the truth necessary, and without such a command, truth would be neither right nor wrong, neither good nor bad. This view makes God's commands seem arbitrary, meaning that God could have given another command (to lie, for example) that would then have been right. Such logic reduces the goodness of God to unintelligible nonsense, for believers think that in addition to being all-knowing and all-powerful, God is also all-good.

A second analysis of the divine command theory takes another path. God commands truthfulness, other virtues, and right action simply because they are right. Thus, he commands people not to lie, not to kill, not to steal, and so on because such actions are simply wrong, while their opposites are simply right. This views avoids the dilemma mentioned in the above paragraph. The goodness of God is maintained. Upon reflection, however, one sees that this second view abandons the theological definitions of right and wrong, for it is saying that there are standards of right conduct and right thinking that are independent of God and that rightness existed prior to God's affirmation of it.

Because of the above contradictions, most theologians do not stress the divine command theory. Instead, they embrace the theory of natural law, which holds that reason determines moral judgments of right and wrong. Were the natural law theory to end there, modern philosophers such as Ross and Rachels could likely accept the position. Theologians explain, however, that God is still involved, for he is a perfectly rational entity. He created a rational order in the universe and gave humans the power to be rational and to use powers of reason. Thus, in this view, moral questions of right and wrong still depend on God.

The natural law theory seems to hold up well in minor matters but appears to falter whenever moral dilemmas emerge. Since the 1970's, for example, an ongoing struggle has been waged on the issue of abortion. Good, sincere, reasoning people have disagreed on the subject. Many religious people are on opposite sides of the issue. Whither the natural law theory? It does not provide the answer. A further criticism includes the fact that if God gave humans the power to reason, he obviously did not give all people equal reasoning skills. Simple observation demonstrates that not all people are equal when it comes to intelligence, skills, and so on.

Right, Wrong, Psychological Egoism, and Ethical Egoism. Any "system" of morality discerns rights and wrongs and also asks people to behave unselfishly. Before one acts, one must consider the consequences. Will anyone be hurt by the course of action? Unless one can answer no, a proposed action should be forestalled. Psychological egoism attacks the just-stated point. Once widely held by philosophers, psychologists, and others, the theory of human nature holds that, indeed, people will act selfishly as they pursue their own self-interest. Furthermore, the theory holds that it is unreasonable to expect people to act otherwise, for pure altruism has never existed except in myth.

Psychological egoism leads to a reinterpretation of motives for being right and good. For example, if a wealthy man or woman donates much time and money to charitable work that benefits hundreds or thousands of people, that person is really only showing his or her superiority, for he or she is publicly demonstrating how successful he or she is. The unspoken statement is this: "Look at me. Not only can I take adequate care of myself, but I have much left over and will share with those who are failures and who are therefore inferior to me."

Perhaps another person, John Doe, also gives money to charity. His motive is likely selfish, for his religion teaches him that he will be rewarded in heaven, and John is trying to buy his way in. Or, again, a hero saves several families from a burning apartment complex. Had it not been for her valor, all would have perished in a most horrible way. While the mayor gives the hero the key to the city, a psychological egoist points out that the hero acted not out of concern for the innocent families but to gain public notoriety.

According to legend, even Abraham Lincoln was a psychological egoist. Once, while aboard a stagecoach, he remarked to a fellow passenger that he thought most men were motivated by selfishness. Just as the passenger was collecting his thoughts to rebut Lincoln's statement, the stage passed over a bridge and the two heard a sow below the bridge making horrible noises. Her piglets were mired in water and mud and stood in danger of drowning. Lincoln called out to the driver to stop, then got out of the coach, ran down to the immobile young pigs, and got them safely to a dry bank. As Lincoln climbed back into the coach, the other passenger asked him what had happened to selfishness. Abe supposedly replied that if he had not saved the pigs, he would have worried about it for days.

The moral of the above stories is that it is precisely the unselfish person who derives great satisfaction from helping others, whereas the truly selfish person does not. If one wishes for others to be happy (or fed, or given health care, or given a job, or saved from a burning building) and acts on that thought, then one is indeed unselfish and altruistic. Psychological egoism is only the act of reinterpreting "right" motives to make them seem "wrong," while straining the English language and the meaning of its words.

A close cousin of psychological egoism, ethical egoism says that there is only one principle of conduct: self-interest. All questions of morality, of right and wrong, of good and bad must be subordinate to that principle. Occasionally, however, it might be that one cooperates with others, keeps promises, completes duties and so on because one's self-interest might be compatible with the self-interest of others. Furthermore, ethical egoism also sees a boundary between self-interest and self-indulgence. Indulgence might lead to a life of drug use, drinking, gambling, and so on; ethical egoists would frown on all such lifestyles, arguing that such vices are definitely not in a person's true self-interest.

Ayn Rand was one thinker who embraced a form of ethical egoism. She argued that striving for one's own self-interest is the only way one can make one's life valuable. True altruism, she argued, would lead one to see that one's own life was nothing but a "thing" to be sacrificed for the sake of doing good deeds for others. Altruism, she concluded, does not "teach" one how to live one's life, only how to sacrifice it. Although Rand was not a trained philosopher, her ideas, which were most popular in the 1960's and 1970's, still have some force.

Among the problems of Rand's view is the problem of extremism. In her writings, she pushed ideas to their absolute extremes. To her, altruism implied that one's life had no value at all because one had to sacrifice everything upon *any demand* made by others; for example, when considering the starving poor, one would give all one's food and all one's money to those unfortunates and would then, of course, become one of them. Altruism does not necessarily push one to that extreme. One can help others within reason. Additionally, ethical egoism cannot be correct, for it cannot provide true solutions to the many different people whose self-interests are in conflict. In real conflicts, all cannot "win" unless moral rules are adopted, which Rand condemned.

Right, Wrong, Utilitarianism, and the Social Contract. Utilitarians in the mold of David Hume (1711-1776), Jeremy Bentham (1748-1832), and John Stuart Mill (1806-1873) hold that one should follow the course that brings the greatest good to the greatest number; in other words, one should follow a course that will create happiness for the greatest number. The problem? Utilitarianism can soon lead to hedonism, a philosophy that accepts no moral rules whatsoever. Whatever feels good and makes one happy is all that counts.

With extreme utilitarianism, all moral rights and rules are tossed aside. Consider, for example, the case of Mr. X, who lives in a small town where everyone knows everyone else. All other adults in town hate Mr. X because he is always dirty, never takes a bath, and shows up for all occasions in tattered clothes; worse, there is always alcohol on his breath. What an awful example he is to the youngsters in the community, especially since the children love him, for he always has time to stop and tell them stories about elves, fairies, and leprechauns. One morning the police find Mr. X shot to death. A strict, no-exceptions utilitarian would conclude that the murder of X was right, for it brought happiness to the adults of the community and it saved the children from the influence of a degenerate. In this way, extreme utilitarianism can be used to condone murder.

Those who believe that they can find rules for right-wrong, good-bad in the social contract may be close to the mark in developing a moral ethical society. They hold that people are naturally social and want to live among their kind for mutual benefits such as group protection from danger, companionship, a more interesting social and cultural life, and so on. When people enter the social contract, however, they agree that certain moral rules are necessary if the group is to survive and flourish. Personal violence and murder are not permitted, nor are untruthfulness, theft, child abuse, adultery, and so on. Those vices are not permitted because they would tear the group-society asunder.

Right, Wrong, and Immanuel Kant. Aspects of Kant's philosophy can, in a manner of speaking, be used to buttress the argument for the social contract theory of right and wrong. His categorical imperatives remain potent in this modern age. His imperatives are not relative and are unchanging over time. He held that people should say and do things that could be accepted as "universal" laws that could be followed by all people, everywhere. Thus, is it right or good to steal the goods of others? No, for society would revert to violent chaos if all stole from all. Can one be a habitually violent person, perhaps even a murderer? No, for if everyone behaved in that way, the war of one against all and all against all would commence as society collapsed. One should not lie because that would be an announcement that universal lying was permissible. Yet such behavior would be self-defeating, for if all people lied, no one would ever believe anyone again, including the first liar who started it all. Modern philosophers will not press Kant's views to the extreme, however, for they hold that exceptional circumstances may, if only rarely, mitigate any of his imperatives.

Conclusions. There are many approaches to finding an answer to the question of moral right-wrong, good-bad, and several are complementary. Modern philosophers such as Ross and Rachels stress that ethics is a product of reason, not merely of feelings or opinions. Certainly, they are correct. Many voices call for less selfishness, holding that one must also think of others and their welfare if they will be affected by an action. Concern for others, then (even to the point of Abe Lincoln's altruism), is desired. Certainly, this, too, is correct. The utilitarian's belief in the greatest good for the greatest number can also be a guide, but one with limits—limits that must include concern for duty and justice. Equally, the social contract's view of moral rules for civilized living, rules that can hold a society together, are also valid. Finally, all of Kant's categorical imperatives (with room for exceptions) could be interwoven with the ideas of reason, good, and the social contract to add more strength to the doctrine of right and wrong. Rejected then would be relativism of any kind, egoism in any form, and reliance on God, for God's true commands are unknowable.

—James Smallwood

See also Integrity; Morality; Sin; Virtue.

BIBLIOGRAPHY

Adler, Mortimer J. *Desires, Right and Wrong: The Ethics of Enough.* New York: Macmillan, 1991. Adler focuses on the ethics of right and wrong and on overwhelming desires that tempt "right." He ends by arguing for moderation or for what he called the ethics of "enough."

Black, Donald. *The Social Structure of Right and Wrong.* San Diego: Academic Press, 1993. This up-to-date volume examines social conflict, conflict management, and social control—all within the framework of right and wrong.

Cabot, Richard C. *Honesty.* New York: Macmillan, 1938. After generally examining honesty and "right" thinking and behaving, Cabot examines wrongs under such headings as prevarications, self-deceit, and dishonesty.

_____. *The Meaning of Right and Wrong.* New York: Macmillan, 1936. This volume began Cabot's examination of various ethical issues and problems relating to the idea of "right" and "wrong."

Greider, William. *Who Will Tell the People: The Betrayal of American Democracy*. New York: Simon & Schuster, 1992. A journalist rather than a trained philosopher, Greider nevertheless does a good job of exposing many of the wrongs in American society, including government and business scandals. He seems to conclude that there are many more wrongs in modern America than there are rights.

Payne, Robert. *The Corrupt Society: From Ancient Greece to Present-day America*. New York: Praeger, 1975. Writing just after the Watergate scandal of the 1970's, Payne examines frauds, falsehoods, dishonesty, and other wrongs as well.

Rachels, James. *The Elements of Moral Philosophy*. New York: Random House, 1986. A trained philosopher, Rachels examines various issues in ethical moral philosophy, including such elements as relativism, utilitarianism, and the question of right and wrong.

Taylor, A. E. *The Problem of Conduct*. New York: Macmillan, 1901. This older work is still valuable because Taylor focuses on dishonesty and other wrong behaviors while upholding ethical behavior.

Right to die

TYPE OF ETHICS: Bioethics

DATE: Coined December, 1935

ASSOCIATED WITH: Karen Ann Quinlan, The Hemlock Society, and the Society for the Right to Die

DEFINITION: The right to refuse medical treatment, even if death would result

SIGNIFICANCE: Brought end-of-life medical decisions into the public debate and also helped to bring medical ethics outside the exclusive purview of doctors

"Right to Die" was the title of a debate in *Forum* on legalizing euthanasia. Later, the term was used to refer solely to *voluntary* euthanasia. Viewed narrowly, the right to die is merely the application of autonomy-based legal principles of self-determination and informed consent developed in the nineteenth century: If treatment cannot be given without consent, even for the individual's own good, then the individual must have a right to refuse treatment. During the 1970's and 1980's, the right to die was used in this sense, as a synonym for voluntary *passive* euthanasia.

History. After World War II, several factors led to the recognition of the right to die. Medical advances and social prosperity reduced sudden deaths, resulting in a growing elderly population, greater incidence of senility, and greater incidence of death from degenerative diseases. Meanwhile, health care costs soared and smaller, more dispersed families led to increased institutionalization of the elderly. By means of respirators and other forms of technology, life could be continued indefinitely despite failing organs. Though the number of patients in "a limbo between life and death" had increased, these issues remained private as physicians dis-

continued treatment or withheld resuscitation for some hopelessly ill patients. With the advent of transplants, however, particularly heart transplants, the established definition of death became inadequate. Public debate began with a Harvard committee's 1968 recommendation that brain death be included in the "definition" of death. Meanwhile, civil and human rights movements emphasizing self-determination, bodily integrity, and individual empowerment were reflected in a movement away from "mercy killing" to a focus on voluntary euthanasia.

Then, in 1975, the case of Karen Ann Quinlan galvanized the public consciousness in the battle for end-of-life decision-making control. The family sued to have Karen, who was in a persistent vegetative state (a coma with minimal brain function and no anticipated recovery of consciousness), removed from a respirator. The New Jersey Supreme Court held in 1976 that under the Constitution, acceptance or refusal of any treatment was to be made by the patient, or in the case of incompetency, by her guardians in accordance with her expressed desire. *Quinlan* also suggested that "ethics committees" could assist families and physicians in medical decision making. Such committees, staffed by physicians, ethicists, and lawyers, later became common.

Afterward, courts consistently found a "right" to die in the common law or federal or state constitutions. In 1990, the U.S. Supreme Court confirmed a federal constitutional "liberty" basis for the right to refuse life-sustaining treatment, including possibly artificial nutrition and hydration.

Ethical Issues. Society has long held legal and moral prohibitions against the taking of human life. Early discussions centered on whether allowing a human being to die when that death could be prevented or forestalled was tantamount to killing. In 1957, Pope Pius XII distinguished between permissible forgoing of treatment in "hopeless cases" and active euthanasia, which was killing or suicide, but who was to determine which was which? The pope intimated that the individual's duty to accept, and society's duty to provide, medical treatment extended to ordinary treatment but not to extraordinary (or "heroic") measures. Though popular in the 1970's, these categories were later dismissed as unworkable. Other attempts to distinguish killing from permitting "natural death," distinguishing between withholding and withdrawing treatment and between acts and omissions, were also rejected as morally indefensible and tending to discourage the initiation of treatment. Committing suicide cannot be distinguished from refusing treatment on the basis of an action versus nonaction distinction. Thus, the fundamental question is whether an individual should ever be allowed to forgo life-sustaining treatment.

The right to die is often justified along utilitarian grounds and opposed on the basis of deontological, beneficence-based principles. Some utilitarians oppose any euthanasia, however, believing that the harms from potential abuse and from accepting incursions into the sanctity of life outweigh the benefits. Conversely, some deontologists support the

RIGHT TO DIE LEGISLATION	
1968-1974	Florida introduces the first death-with-dignity or right-to-die bills allowing execution of a document directing treatment withdrawal with confirmation of terminal illness; 1974 bill only passes the House.
1969, 1973-1974	Voluntary euthanasia bills are introduced in Idaho, Montana, and Oregon, but are not passed.
1971-1974	Various bills permitting execution of a declaration that an individual does not want his or her life prolonged through extraordinary or artificial means are presented in California, Delaware, Maryland, Massachusetts, Washington, and Wisconsin; none passes.
1973	The American Hospital Association adopts a "Patient's Bill of Rights" that includes the right to reject medical treatment, even if it would result in death. Also creates the role of patient ombudsman to ensure that patient's rights are respected.
1974	Euthanasia Society of America (later called Society for the Right to Die) is reactivated to promote legalization of living will and passive euthanasia. In 1967, members had established the tax-exempt Euthanasia Education Council, which was dedicated to public education. Before publicity about the *Quinlan* case in 1975, the Council had distributed 750,000 copies of its living will. During the next year-and-a-half of publicity over *Quinlan*, 1.25 million copies were requested. The enforceability of these living wills, however, remained at issue.
October, 1976	The first living will law, the California Natural Death Act, is enacted. Effective January 1, 1977, individuals could, through a signed and witnessed document, direct in advance that medical treatment be withheld. Several defects in the law would plague other living will statutes. It applied only when death was "imminent" and not to patients in an irreversible coma who could be sustained indefinitely with respirators and feeding tubes. Ambiguous language suggested that death had to be imminent even if the patient were placed on life support. Curiously, the directive was not binding unless the patient executed or reexecuted the document fourteen days after being diagnosed as terminal; the document had to be reexecuted every five years. The law also did not address the withholding of artificial nutrition and hydration and did not apply during pregnancy.
1977	After *Quinlan*, fifty bills are introduced in thirty states and signed into law in seven states: Arkansas, Idaho, Nevada, New Mexico, North Carolina, Oregon, and Texas.
1983	Although many states had living will laws (thirty-six by 1985), their applicability was usually limited to decisions about life support withdrawal for terminal patients. Thus, in 1983, the President's Commission for the Study of Ethical Problems in Medicine recommended the use of Durable Powers of Attorney (formal, written proxy designations that are effective even after the principal becomes incompetent) for health care decisions. At the time, only Delaware had a similar provision—in its living will statute.
1990	The Patient Self-Determination Act passes, requiring all health care institutions to provide patients on admission with information about their rights under state law to make medical treatment decisions, to accept or refuse treatment, and to prepare advance directives; the Act also requires institutions to furnish their own written guidelines implementing those rights. Additionally, each state must prepare and distribute to health care providers written descriptions of its laws.
November, 1991	Washington State voters defeat ballot Initiative 119 by a 54 percent to 46 percent vote despite substantial support in early polling; the law would have strengthened the existing legislation on advance directives and would have permitted physician-assisted suicide.
1992	California amends its living will law to apply to irreversible comas, to make it clear that the imminence of death is determined without the use of life support, that artificial nutrition and hydration is life-prolonging medical treatment that may be terminated, and to eliminate the need for reexecution of the document. The California amendments were based on the Uniform Rights of the Terminally Ill Act, which had been adopted by several other states. This model act was also being revised into a comprehensive act that would eliminate the confusion created by the states' piecemeal approach on advance directives.

(continued)

	RIGHT TO DIE LEGISLATION (CONTINUED)
November, 1992	California voters reject an "aid-in-dying" ballot initiative, Proposition 161, by a vote of 54 percent to 46 percent. Its proponents cite the 46 percent voter approval as a victory in itself.
By mid-1993	Forty-seven states (all except Massachusetts, Michigan, and New York) and the District of Columbia have passed living will legislation. All allow some advance direction on medical treatment, but many differences exist.
	Every state (except Alabama) and the District of Columbia either expressly authorized the appointment of a proxy for health care decisions or had general durable power of attorney statutes interpreted to permit appointment of a health care proxy. Many statutes expressly cover the withholding or withdrawing of life-sustaining treatment, though some permit it only if the principal has executed a living will, is terminally ill, is in an irreversible coma or the document expressly authorizes that power. Many of the statutes provide a sample power-of-attorney form; in a few states, that is the only acceptable form. Many of the laws allow the principal to give directions or guidelines for medical decisions. The statutes are fairly uniform, although there is disagreement on the proxy's powers over artificial nutrition and hydration, with some statutes permitting and others prohibiting that authority, while the majority are silent on the issue. Another area of disagreement is the ability of the agent to make decisions for a pregnant woman.
	More than half the states had laws indicating who was to make medical decisions in the case of an incompetent patient without a designated proxy and where a living will was not effective. Though some apply only in specific situations (for example, only to patients in nursing homes or only to cardiopulmonary resuscitation), most apply to all medical decision making. Many explicitly mention consent to withhold or withdraw life support. Most have a priority list of persons who are to act as surrogate decision makers, usually court-appointed guardians, spouses, parents, adult children, siblings, and other relatives. A few leave the ultimate decision to the physician, who only needs to consult with the family.
By August, 1993	Four state legislatures (Maine, Michigan, New Hampshire, and Vermont) consider laws permitting medically assisted suicide.

right to die by defining "benefit" to encompass not only prolonged life but also freedom from suffering, or the protection of individuals' liberty interests. Some suggest that autonomy cannot be overridden, others that decisions in extremis are not autonomous.

Opponents of euthanasia often argue the "slippery slope"—that allowing some to die will lead to further "justified" endings of lives. Some cite various eugenics movements as evidence for this view. Proponents counter that all moral choices involve drawing lines with a potential for abuse. Another objection raised is that the slippery slope entails accepting a recognized evil, disregarding the autonomy, dignity, and suffering of the dying patient in favor of possible future evils.

Some argue that human life is inviolable and that acceptance of a decision to forgo any amount of life necessarily requires a societal recognition that some lives are not worth living. Others counter that this inviolability is negated by causes throughout history that have been deemed worthy of self-sacrifice. Some fear that passive euthanasia will insidiously change the treatment of the elderly and dying; individuals may be subtly coerced into dying because they perceive themselves as burdens to their families, or because they see others who are younger, healthier, or even in comparable positions refusing treatment.

Passive euthanasia for the terminally ill enjoys overwhelming societal and judicial support, though popularity in the polls does not foreclose the need to address the ethical concerns surrounding the issue. The public and the media characterize the issue as one of not unduly "prolonging life" or of allowing individuals to die "naturally" and "with dignity"; such characterizations beg the question of what is a dignified and natural death in the context of advancing medical technology.

Even if passive euthanasia is acceptable, a number of issues remain unresolved: Can the right be invoked on behalf of incompetent patients? For formerly competent individuals, treatment decisions can be made on the basis of previously expressed wishes. For the never competent (including children), recognizing an equal right to refuse treatment produces thornier questions of how to carry out that right without committing involuntary euthanasia.

Is a slow, painful, and lingering death or an indefinite existence under sedation dignified? Can artificially administered nutrition and hydration be withheld to hasten the end? Are feeding tubes or intravenous drips another form of medical treatment? Is it dignified to allow individuals to starve to death? Does the right to die include the right to assistance in suicide? Finally, should the right to die be extended to individuals suffering from painful chronic or degenerative illnesses?
—Ileana Dominguez-Urban

1 RIGHT TO LIFE / 757

See also Euthanasia; Life and death; Medical ethics; Quinlan, Karen Ann; Right to life.

BIBLIOGRAPHY

Beauchamp, Tom L., and Seymour Perlin. *Ethical Issues in Death and Dying*. Englewood Cliffs, N.J.: Prentice-Hall, 1978.

Humphry, Derek, and Ann Wickett. *The Right to Die: Understanding Euthanasia*. New York: Harper & Row, 1986.

Meisel, Alan. *The Right to Die*. New York: John Wiley & Sons, 1993.

Rothman, David J. *Strangers at the Bedside: A History of How Law and Bioethics Transformed Medical Decision Making*. New York: Basic Books, 1991.

Russell, O. Ruth. *Freedom to Die: Moral and Legal Aspects of Euthanasia*. New York: Human Sciences Press, 1975.

United States President's Commission for the Study of Ethical Problems in Medicine and Biomedical and Behavioral Research. *Deciding to Forgo Life-Sustaining Treatment*. Washington, D.C.: GPO, 1983.

Right to life

TYPE OF ETHICS: Bioethics

DATE: Early Christian era to present

DEFINITION: The right-to-life concept seeks to apply ethical principles from various standpoints to identify whether it is ever appropriate to carry out an abortion

SIGNIFICANCE: Seeks appropriate and ethical methods to assure the human fetus the right to life owed to every human; opposes abortion, which is viewed as murder

Ethical conflict over abortion has faced humanity throughout history. On the one hand, sociological problems, maternal health, woman's rights, and the fear of overpopulation have led many people to espouse abortion. On the other hand, religious and biological issues have led others to favor antiabortion (right-to-life) concepts. Finding sensible, ethical solutions to the problem of abortion is essential to society. Appropriate solutions must satisfy mothers, prevent the murder of humans still in the uterus, and avoid exploitation of individual population sectors while permitting abortions that are deemed acceptable.

Methodology and Concepts. Many nonabortive birth control methods are widely used. These include abstinence; coitus interruptus (male withdrawal); rhythm (intercourse during safe portions of the menses); pessaries (for example, condoms); birth control pills; and surgical intervention by tubal ligation or vasectomy. Despite these methods, many unplanned pregnancies present the moral dilemma of whether to abort.

Those favoring abortion argue that it is fitting during the time period when a fetus is not a person, though precisely when humanity occurs is uncertain. Many people argue that any abortion is correct when carrying a fetus to term will cause a mother death, severe psychological damage, or impinged human rights. Another point of view is that when a fetus is found to be severely physically or mentally damaged, abortion is merited. Still other abortion advocates note that abortion stops overpopulation.

The antiabortion viewpoint—right to life—also varies greatly. Some advocates preach that sexual abstinence is the only suitable birth control method and that conception always engenders the right to life. Others believe that once egg and sperm join, the human-to-be has been produced, and that the abortion of unborn people—they claim that tens of millions of such operations have been carried out—exceeds the worst planned race or religious genocide ever carried out. At the other end of the right-to-life group spectrum are those who espouse factoring into the decision the age—yet to be determined—at which a fetus becomes a person, potential problems for the mother, and societal aspects.

History. Many people believe that abortion is a product of modern medicine and that the debate—nowadays very antagonistic—regarding whether to abort and why or when to do so is a modern phenomenon. This belief is the result of clashes between pro-choice and pro-life factions who espouse appropriate abortion and no abortion, respectively. In fact, the Greek, Roman, and Jewish philosophers of antiquity codified abortion and its use. For example, Plato and Aristotle favored abortion when it was for the good of society, and Aristotle defined human life as present forty or ninety days after conception for males and females, respectively. Neither philosopher, however, would have set those times as upper limits for abortion.

With the development of Christianity, strong antiabortion sentiment arose (for example, Roman Emperor Constantine outlawed abortion). As the power of Christianity grew, so did sanctions against abortion. Even among theologians, however, there were—and continue to be—various degrees of condemnation. Some declared that any abortion was murder, others saw it as murder beginning forty days after conception (a holdover from Aristotle?), and some believed that abortion was acceptable to save a mother's life.

In more modern times, English common law stated that abortion was legal until mothers felt movement in the womb—"quickening"—and this view persisted well into the eighteenth century throughout the British Empire and the nations that arose from it. Hence, in the colonial United States, quickening was viewed as the time when abortion became illegal. On this basis, despite the unchanged view of Christian ministers and priests, abortion became a common mode of birth control. The practice, which was so widespread that abortionists often advertised their services in newspapers, led to antiabortion sentiment. First, the American Medical Association (c. 1850) condemned it. Soon, feminist movements joined in, denouncing abortion as a tool of male domination.

This segment of the abortion debate was relatively mild and died out by the twentieth century. In fact, it was so quiescent that beginning in the 1950's, many abortions were made legal, a legality supported by the American Medical Association, the National Organization for Women, many states, and the federal government. Adding to the popularity of abortion legality was fear—fanned by the media—that population growth would soon cause the world to starve to death.

It was at this time, with most Americans in favor of therapeutic abortion, that the right-to-life movement came into being. The polarization between pro- and antiabortionists has grown hugely, and the debate has become more and more radical. In 1973, the Supreme Court case *Roe v. Wade* assured women the right to decide whether to terminate pregnancy. Then, in 1988, in *Webster v. Reproductive Health Services,* the Supreme Court reversed its position. The attempts by Operation Rescue to stop legal abortions by picketing and by harassing those choosing abortion and physicians performing abortion have further confused the issue, polarizing public opinion even more.

Conclusions. Two thorny ethical issues concerning abortion are whether it is ever appropriate to stop the occurrence of a human life and whether a woman should determine what happens to her body. Advocates of both issues propose that if their point of view is unheeded, the consequences, aside from unethical decision making, will cause horrible outcomes for society. Antiabortionists state that the murder of fetuses will lead to other equivalent crimes (such as genocide). Those who favor abortion fear that following absolute criminalization will come restrictive legislation that will diminish human rights and produce a paradigm of minority persecution. It seems possible that both these views are extreme and that ethical compromise could give both sides some of their desires, with much flexibility. One model for use could be that of western Europe, which promises respect for every human life and permits abortion under conditions deemed appropriate in a well-thought-out, ethical fashion. Abortion programs also must be designed so that inequities (such as limitation to less-advantaged classes) are avoided and informed consent is guaranteed. —*Sanford S. Singer*

See also Abortion; Bioethics; Birth control; Christian ethics; Family; Jewish ethics; Pro-choice movement; Pro-life movement.

BIBLIOGRAPHY
Merton, Andrew H. *Enemies of Choice.* Boston: Beacon Press, 1981.
Paige, Connie. *The Right To Lifers.* New York: Summit Books, 1983.
Rice, Charles E. *No Exceptions.* Gaithersburg, Md.: Human Life International, 1990.
Rosenblatt, Roger. *Life Itself.* New York: Random House, 1992.
Whitney, Catherine. *Whose Life?* New York: William Morrow, 1991.

Robotics

TYPE OF ETHICS: Scientific ethics
DATE: 1940's to present

ASSOCIATED WITH: Automation, artificial intelligence, and computer technology
DEFINITION: The science and technology of creating machines that perform human activities
SIGNIFICANCE: The existence of machines that are capable of replacing humans in various activities has a far-reaching impact on society and may redefine humankind's role in the world

The word "robot" was first used in *R.U.R.,* or *Rossum's Universal Robots,* a 1921 play by Karel Čapek, to describe machines that perform the work of humans. The word is derived from the Czech word *robota,* which means slave labor. The play is a story of mechanical laborers who revolt against their human masters.

The science of robotics draws on two technologies: automatic machine control and artificial intelligence. Devices for automatic machine control, which are called servomechanisms, work by feeding information about the machine's location, speed, and direction back to a control unit that automatically makes adjustments.

By the 1950's, mathematicians began to explore the possibilities of modeling human logic and behavior in computer programs. In 1956, John McCarthy, then at Dartmouth College, gave this discipline its name—artificial intelligence. The first artificial intelligence researchers began to program computers to play games, prove mathematical theorems, and even play the role of ersatz psychologist. Later efforts focused on the building of robots. The first patent for an industrial robot was awarded to Joseph Engelberger in 1961. The machine, which was called the Unimate, used a feedback control system that was attached to a computer. The Unimate robots were first used to control die-casting machines.

Robotics Development. Robotics continues its development via two approaches to design. The first of these is the top-down approach, which focuses on a specific task to be done by the machine. Industrial robots that pick parts from a bin or do welding from a fixed position on a factory floor are examples of top-down design. Computer programs called expert systems also employ the top-down approach to perform tasks focused in a narrow field—such as identifying mineral deposits or advising doctors about blood diseases—by consulting a body of knowledge in the form of rules.

A more difficult approach to robot design is the bottom-up approach, in which the goal is to build general-purpose machines. Robots of this type tend to be mobile, use a camera system to visualize the world around them, and may be programmed to accomplish a variety of tasks. Computer programs for these machines simulate learning by adding observations and experience to their model of the world.

Ethical Issues. The ethical issues of robotics arise from several areas. The most obvious involves concern about the social consequences of replacing human labor with machine labor. Large-scale factory automation has resulted in the permanent loss of millions of unskilled jobs throughout the industrialized world. As robots continue to be refined and used in more applications, they will replace humans in jobs requiring ever greater degrees of skill. The economic benefits of robot automation reach a point of diminishing returns when the social costs of the unemployed workers—government subsidies, poverty, crime, and political unrest—become too high.

Some experts think that general-purpose humanoid robots will remain too expensive ever to reach widespread use. They contend that society will work itself through an inevitable turbulent period in the wake of the robot automation of industry and evolve into a period in which skilled workers are used instead of robots.

Others believe that advances in computer and robotics technology will inevitably lead to a convergence of the specialized, expert approach and the general-purpose, mobile, artificial intelligence approach. Such a convergence would lead to the development of a self-aware machine with a sophisticated model of its world and the ability to increase its knowledge. Other ethical issues arise from the prospect of robots becoming more and more like humans in appearance and behavior. Such issues raise questions that have no answers, because there is no way to know what will happen until sentient machines actually make their appearance.

By 1993, chess computers were playing at tournament level, and it was predicted that they would beat all human players within a few years. How will humans adjust to machines that surpass their own intelligence? Given the possibility of intelligent, humanlike robots, what should be their place in human society? Will they be allowed to coexist with people, with their fundamental rights protected by law, or will they be a disposable race of slaves?

Many questions have been raised about the legal status of intelligent robots. If they are accorded rights under the law, should they also have responsibilities? Who would be blamed if a robot's "negligence" caused an accidental death? Could robots manage human workers, serve on juries, or run for elected office? Could they vote?

What kind of ethical principles should be built into robots? Science fiction author Isaac Asimov began to explore this issue in the 1940's with a series of stories about intelligent robots. Asimov's robots had "positronic brains," circuits based on the Three Laws of Robotics, whose principles were protecting the well-being of humans, obeying human orders, and self-preservation, in that order.

Some robotics experts predict that intelligent machines will eventually be capable of building other, more intelligent machines. As the future unfolds, people may confront some very disturbing prospects if the machines they have created become more intelligent and powerful than they are themselves. Because machine technology develops millions of times faster than biological evolution, the capabilities of robots could someday so far surpass human ones that the human race could become extinct—not because of war, pestilence, or famine, but because of a lack of purpose.

—*Charles E. Sutphen*

See also Artificial intelligence; Computer technology; Dominion over nature, human; Sentience.

BIBLIOGRAPHY

Berliner, Hans. "Losing the Human Edge." *Byte* 18 (May, 1993): 282.

Lees, John. "An Esoteric Ethical Excursion." *Creative Computing* 9 (August, 1983): 162-163.

Minsky, Marvin, ed. *Robotics*. Garden City, N.Y.: Anchor Press/Doubleday, 1985.

Moravec, Hans. *Mind Children*. Cambridge, Mass.: Harvard University Press, 1988.

Winston, Patrick Henry. *Artificial Intelligence*. 2d ed. Reading, Mass.: Addison-Wesley, 1984.

Roe v. Wade

TYPE OF ETHICS: Sex and gender issues

DATE: 1973

ASSOCIATED WITH: U.S. Supreme Court

DEFINITION: The Court's decision gave constitutional protection to a woman's right to obtain an abortion throughout her pregnancy (although states may regulate it or prohibit it at the point of fetal viability, which is approximately the third trimester), under the Fifth, Ninth, and Fourteenth Amendments to the United States Constitution

SIGNIFICANCE: This controversial landmark decision in constitutional law continues to raise ethical questions regarding personal autonomy and reproductive choice as balanced against respect for and preservation of human life; it also leaves unanswered questions regarding the role of the U.S. Supreme Court in finding the solutions to these dilemmas

Roe v. Wade was provoked by an unmarried, pregnant Texas woman, Jane Roe, who wished to obtain an abortion that was not necessary to save her life. She challenged the Texas statute, which prohibited all nontherapeutic abortions, claiming that the statute violated her liberty and her right to privacy under the Fifth, Ninth, and Fourteenth Amendments to the United States Constitution. The United States Supreme Court, in a seven-to-two vote, struck down the Texas statute and all other statutes like it. Justice Harry Blackmun, the author of the majority opinion, concentrated on the right of privacy that he found in the Ninth and Fourteenth Amendments, saying that the right to privacy was broad enough to encompass a woman's decision to terminate her pregnancy without interference from the state. He qualified this decision, however, by recognizing the state's interest in protecting human life, holding that after the point of viability of the fetus, the state's interest in the health of the woman and the human life she carries overrides a woman's right to terminate her pregnancy and that the state may then prohibit all abortions necessary to save a woman's life. In the opinion of the Court, however, during the first two trimesters of pregnancy, a woman's interests outweigh the interests of the state. The dissenting opinion of Justice White, however, frames the ethical dilemma of the court in a much more precise way. He stated, "At the heart of the controversy are those pregnancies which pose no threat to the mother. The court apparently views the convenience or whim of the mother more than the continued existence and development of the life she carries. Whether or not I might agree with those values, I find no constitutional warrant for imposing such an order of priorities on the people and on the legislature of the states. In a sensitive area such as this, over which reasonable men may easily and heatedly differ, I cannot accept the Court's exercise of its clear power of choice by imposing a constitutional barrier to state efforts to protect human life and by investing women and doctors with the constitutionally protected right to exterminate it. This issue should be left for the people and the political processes people have devised to govern their affairs."

There are three considerations to be taken into account when considering the ethics of abortion. Abortion involves the status, value, or rights of unborn human life. The question of whether a fetus is a person and when life begins was ignored in *Roe v. Wade*; it is, however, an essential question in the ethical considerations of abortion, for if a fetus is a person upon conception, then abortion is equivalent to murder, and the right to life would have first priority over any choice of the mother. The second consideration is the welfare of pregnant women. The right of these women to have self-determination in their own reproductive capacity is a vital consideration in the abortion dilemma, as is protection from the physical, mental, and social harm that would result from an unwanted pregnancy. The third ethical consideration in the abortion decision is the interests of others who are not directly involved in the abortion decision but who are concerned as well. This includes the father of the fetus, the family members of the mother and father, the religious and civil communities, and perhaps population control experts as well. Each of these is a value to be respected. The ethical dilemma of abortion arises in precisely those situations in which all values cannot be given equal support or in which the support of one precludes the support of another. Disagreements regarding the morality of abortion arise from differing evaluations of the priorities of the considerations involved, based on philosophy, experiences, religious training, attitudes toward life and family, and the moral value that one seeks to observe.

The majority view, as written by Justice Blackmun, is now the law of the land, and has provided the citizenry with abortion on demand. Whether this is a matter of reproductive freedom that has made society more free and open and a better, less oppressive place to live or a decision that has led to a complete lack of respect for life, the decision concerning abortion and the role of *Roe v. Wade* in society is a decision that each person must make according to his or her own code of morals and values.   —*Amy Bloom*

See also Abortion; Bioethics; Right to life.

BIBLIOGRAPHY

Faux, Marian. *Roe v. Wade: The Untold Story of the Landmark Supreme Court Decision.* New York: Macmillan, 1988.

Frohock, Fred M. *Abortion: A Case Study in Law and Morals.* Westport, Conn.: Greenwood, 1983.

Garfield, Jay L., and Patricia Hennessey, eds. *Abortion: Moral and Legal Perspectives.* Amherst: University of Massachusetts Press, 1985.

Krason, Stephen M. *Abortion: Politics, Morality, and the Constitution: A Critical Study of Roe vs. Wade and Doe vs. Bolton and a Basis for Change.* Lanham, Md.: University Press of America, 1984.

Petchesky, Rosalind P. *Abortion and Woman's Choice: The State, Sexuality, and Reproductive Freedom.* Boston: Northeastern University Press, 1984.

Rubin, Eva R. *Abortion, Politics, and the Courts: Roe vs. Wade and Its Aftermath.* Westport, Conn.: Greenwood, 1982.

Rousseau, Jean-Jacques (June 28, 1712, Geneva—July 2, 1778, Ermenonville, near Paris, France): Philosopher

TYPE OF ETHICS: Enlightenment history

ACHIEVEMENTS: Author of *Du contrat social: Ou, Principes du droit politique* (1762; *A Treatise on the Social Contract: Or, The Principles of Political Law,* 1764), *Julie: Ou, La Nouvelle Héloïse* (1761; *The New Héloïse,* 1761), and *Émile: Ou, De l'éducation* (*Émilius and Sophia: Or, a New System of Education,* 1762-1763)

SIGNIFICANCE: Emphasized the ethical values of liberty, emotion, nonviolence, and simplicity; held that human purity derived from God and nature, and stressed the worthiness of children and women

Rousseau's philosophical writings and novels, all of them rich in ethical content, inspired a major shift in Western thought during the eighteenth century and part of the nineteenth century. They substantially undercut the Age of Reason and inspired a new Age of Romanticism. In the process, Rousseau's eighteenth century lifestyle and work influenced manners and morals, the reevaluation of education, conceptions of the state and of politics, and the reassertion of religious values. His philosophical genius led the way to new views of human nature, liberty, free creative expression, violence, the character of children, and the vital human and cultural importance of women.

Foundations of Rousseau's Ethics. Rousseau's ethics were rooted in his moral and religious perceptions about human nature, human behavior, and human society. In *Discourse on the Sciences and the Arts* (1750), *Discourse on the Origin of Inequality* (1755), and *Social Contract* (1762), he systematically traced his thoughts on each of these subjects. Humanity, Rousseau believed, was fundamentally good. Originally living alone, simply, and in a state of nature, humanity was free, healthy, and happy. As a result of living in society, however, humanity acquired property along with the aggressiveness required for securing and defending

Jean-Jacques Rousseau (Library of Congress)

that property. Depraved conditions, ignoble passions, and vices soon were rampant: pride in possessions, false inequalities, affectations, greed, envy, lust, and jealousy, which were attended by insecurity, personal violence, and war. Thus, although humanity was by nature good, society itself was innately corrupt. Humanity, Rousseau concluded, had been corrupted by society. What most educated eighteenth century observers viewed as the rise of civilization, Rousseau viewed as its decline.

Rousseau's own experiences were responsible for this assessment of society, even though the assessment itself was laced with idealism. He had begun life orphaned, poor, and vagrant. Unhappily struggling through menial posts and an apprenticeship, he subsequently rose to notoriety, thanks to the help of generous and sensitive patrons, many of them women. He became familiar with sophisticated intellectuals and with the rich, yet eventually he abandoned this level of society for a life of simplicity and honest, if irrational, emotions. His style and philosophy repudiated society's standards, its affectations, its belief in the indefinite improvement of humanity, and its philosophical addiction to stark reason and utilitarianism.

Rousseau's Social Contract. Rousseau believed that humanity had descended from a natural state of innocence to an artificial state of corruption—a state made worse by what he regarded as the stupidity and self-delusion of most of his contemporaries. He fully understood that any hopes of returning to humanity's ancient innocence were chimerical. Nevertheless, the values that he cherished—freedom, simplicity, honestly expressed emotions, and individualism— were still in some measure attainable as the best of a poor bargain. In his *Social Contract*, he indicated how the liberty that humanity had lost in the descent to "civilization" could be recovered in the future.

Recovery could be achieved by means of humanity's acceptance of a new and genuine social contract that would replace the false one to which Rousseau believed humanity was chained. Thus, while humanity was born free and was possessed of individual will, its freedom and will had become victims of a fraudulent society. People could, however, surrender their independent wills to a "general will"; that is, to Rousseau's abstract conception of society as an artificial person. In doing so, people could exchange their natural independence for a new form of liberty that would be expressed through liberal, republican political institutions. The general will, a composite of individual wills, pledged people to devote themselves to advancing the common good. The integrity of their new social contract and new society would depend upon their individual self-discipline, their self-sacrifice, and an obedience imposed on them by fear of the general will.

Religious and Educational Ethics. The history of republican Geneva, Rousseau's birthplace, imbued him with a lifelong admiration of republican virtues, but neither the eighteenth century Calvinism of Geneva nor Catholicism, Rousseau believed, fostered the kind of character that would be required for the republican life that he imagined under the "Social Contract." In his view, Catholicism, for example, directed people's attention to otherworldly goals, while Calvinism had succumbed to a soft and passive Christianity that was devoid of the puritanical rigor and innocence that had once characterized it and that Rousseau admired. Rousseau, on the contrary, advocated the cultivation of this-worldly civil values that were appropriate for a vigorous republican society: self-discipline, simplicity, honesty, courage, and virility. His proposed civic religion, stripped of much theological content, was intended to fortify these values as well as to enhance patriotism and a martial spirit.

Rousseau's educational ideas, like his religious proposals,

sought to inculcate republican civic virtues by directing people toward freedom, nature, and God. Small children were to be unsaddled and given physical freedom. Children from five to twelve were to be taught more by direct experience and by exposure to nature than by books. Adolescents should learn to work and should study morality and religion. Education, Rousseau argued in his classic *Émile*, should teach people about the good in themselves and nature, and should prepare them to live simple, republican lives.

—*Clifton K. Yearley*

See also Citizenship; Corruption; Courage; Honor; Obedience; Self-control; Social contract; State of nature.

BIBLIOGRAPHY

Broome, J. H. *Rousseau: A Study of His Thought.* New York: Barnes & Noble, 1963.

Grimsley, Ronald. *Jean-Jacques Rousseau.* Brighton, England: Harvest Press, 1983.

Guéhenno, Jean. *Jean-Jacques Rousseau.* 2 vols. Translated by John and Doreen Weightman. London: Routledge & Kegan Paul, 1966.

Havens, George R. *Jean-Jacques Rousseau.* Boston: Twayne, 1978.

Royce, Josiah (Nov. 20, 1855, Grass Valley, Calif.— Sept. 14, 1916, Cambridge, Mass.): Philosopher

TYPE OF ETHICS: Modern history

ACHIEVEMENTS: Author of *The World and the Individual* (1899-1901) and *The Philosophy of Loyalty* (1908)

SIGNIFICANCE: An important American philosopher, Royce developed an ethic based on his "philosophy of loyalty," which emphasized that human beings are not isolated individuals but are members of communities

After teaching in San Francisco and at the University of California at Berkeley, Royce moved to Cambridge, Massachusetts, in 1882 and distinguished himself as a professor of philosophy at Harvard University. There he became close friends with the American pragmatist William James, although Royce's philosophy differed fundamentally from that of his famous colleague.

Royce's philosophical idealism stressed that a human self is a center of purpose and striving; therefore, human life involves suffering and a struggle with evil. Royce affirmed, however, that in facing these obstacles courageously, in achieving success wherever one can, and in recognizing that one's relationship with the Absolute, or God, entails the overcoming of every evil, one can experience positive meaning and joy.

According to Royce, such human fulfillment depends on loyalty, which he defined as "the willing and practical and thoroughgoing devotion of a person to a cause." Not all causes are good ones, but Royce believed that the act of being loyal is good whenever it does occur. He concluded that the most fundamental principle of the moral life ought to be that of being loyal to loyalty. This principle points toward a community where all individuals are free, where they use their abilities and cultivate their interests, and where all these persons and factors encourage and support one another.

See also Common good; Idealist ethics; Loyalty; Social justice and responsibility; Universalizability.

al-Rûmî al-Balkhî, Maulânâ Jalâl al-Dîn (c. Sept. 30, 1207, Balkh, near modern Mazar-i Sharif, northwestern Afghanistan—Dec. 17, 1273, Konya, Asia Minor): Mystical poet

TYPE OF ETHICS: Religious ethics

ACHIEVEMENTS: Author of the *Mathnavî* and numerous other mystical and philosophical poetical works

SIGNIFICANCE: The most influential mystical poet in the Persian language and the eponymous founder of the Mevlevî Sufi order

Al-Rûmî was an extraordinarily prolific Persian poet, best known for his *Mathnavî*, which is arguably the most important single work in Persian literature. Although the *Mathnavî* is massive in scope (26,000 verses), it focuses on al-Rûmî's primary concerns: the longing of the soul for its beloved and the loss of self in a love for God so absolute that only God exists. He emphasized the cycle of the origination of all things from God and their return through extinguishing the self. The highest possible achievement of the soul is longing for God, beyond which there is annihilation of individuality. Al-Rûmî frequently reworked traditional stories or used metaphors of intoxication and/or human love, and, disdaining discursive thought and logical argument, he saw himself as being in the spiritual tradition of al-Ḥallâj, Sanâ'î, and ʿAṭṭâr.

Biography. Al-Rûmî's family left Balkh when he was quite young, fleeing the invading forces of Genghis Khan. In 1228, he moved to Konya, where his father, the noted theologian Bahâ' al-Dîn Walad, taught. Al-Rûmî took over those teaching duties after his father's death. In 1244, he met the famed Sufi Shams al-Dîn Tabrîzî in Konya (they may have met previously in Syria), and the two became inseparable partners in the rapture of absolute, mystical love of God. This relationship seems to have been the cause of al-Rûmî's turn to mystical poetry. Al-Rûmî's relationship with Shams dominated his life, eclipsing responsibilities to family and students, who exiled Shams to Syria. Al-Rûmî's eldest son, Sultan Walad, recalled Shams because the separation was heartbreaking for al-Rûmî. Their previous behavior resumed, leading another of al-Rûmî's sons to conspire successfully with his students to murder Shams. Soon thereafter, al-Rûmî entered into a similar relationship with Salâh al-Dîn Zarkûb.

Legacy. After al-Rûmî's death, Sultan Walad organized the Mevlevî (Turkish for al-Rûmî's title, *maulânâ*, or master) order of Sufis, in which dancing in circles is an important spiritual exercise. The Mevlevî (the "whirling dervishes" of European writers) have been a significant popular, devotional alternative to more legalistic Islamic orthopraxy, and al-Rûmî's tomb remains a focus of popular religion and pilgrimage. His poetry was influential as far away as Bengal and has remained influential to the present day. Among those moved by his poetry were the Mughal Emperor Akbar, the Chistî Sufi saint Nizâm al-Dîn Auliyâ, and the twentieth century poet Muhammad Iqbal.

See also al-Ḥallâj, al-Ḥusayn ibn Mansûr; Islamic ethics; Sufism.

Russell, Bertrand (May 18, 1872, Trelleck, Monmouthshire, Wales—Feb. 2, 1970, near Penrhyndeudraeth, Wales): Philosopher

TYPE OF ETHICS: Modern history

ACHIEVEMENTS: Author (with Alfred North Whitehead) of *Principia Mathematica* (1910-1913), *On Education* (1926), *Education and the Social Order* (1932), *Why I Am Not a Christian* (1957), and many other significant works in philosophy

SIGNIFICANCE: Although primarily a logician, Russell developed a subjectivist ethical position in the belief that human beings could choose good over evil

Russell's early work centered on mathematics and logic, culminating in the publication of *Principia Mathematica*, but twice he was dramatically drawn into issues of values and ethics. The first occasion came in 1901, when a "quasi-religious experience" brought home to him the isolation of the individual and led to his advocacy of humane policies in education, the punishment of criminals, and personal relationships. He published an essay, "A Free Man's Worship" (1903), but was too involved in his work on logic to devote much time to these ideas. The second and lasting shift was prompted by World War I, which he opposed, though he would later support the opposition of Nazism in World War II. The horrors of the war prompted Russell to consider how humankind might change. He was convinced that the key was education, because childhood experience molded adult attitudes, including the acceptance of violence. In his writings and at Beacon Hill School, which he founded, he advocated the disciplined but kindly treatment of students. Ultimately, however, he realized that values were matters of opinion, and he never found an objective way to prove that his values were best. He argued powerfully for his humane approach to education, sexual relationships, and other aspects of life in such works (in addition to those previously named) as *Marriage and Morals* (1929), *Religion and Science* (1935), and *Human Society and Ethics* (1955).

See also Humanism.

Sales, ethics of

TYPE OF ETHICS: Business and labor ethics

DATE: From antiquity

ASSOCIATED WITH: Marketing ethics

DEFINITION: The application of principles of moral behavior to the relationship between buyers and sellers, in its broadest meaning covering all aspects of marketing

SIGNIFICANCE: In every age, sellers have been accused of using their power in the marketplace to take advantage of buyers, raising questions about the rights of both groups

The selling of goods and services has long been the subject of moral and, sometimes, theological concern. Economic theorists at least since the time of Adam Smith have assured people that when a buyer and a seller with equal knowledge of a product reach agreement and a transaction occurs in the marketplace, the situations of both buyer and seller are improved; otherwise, one or the other would not have agreed to the transaction. Nevertheless, since both buyer and seller are seeking to maximize their positions and since their interests are diametrically opposed, one seeking the lowest possible price and the other seeking the highest, it is natural to expect each to try to take advantage of the other, sometimes unfairly. The problem is rooted in whether buyer and seller have equal knowledge; as products and services have become increasingly complex and as manufacturers and sellers have grown into multibillion-dollar corporations, equal knowledge, and therefore equal power, in the marketplace has become the exception rather than the rule.

Marketing Ethics. The ethics of marketing, a broader and more current interpretation of sales, can be viewed in terms of the natural dimensions of the marketing function. The first concerns the safety and appropriateness of the product or service being marketed, normally considered under the subject of product liability. Here the question is: Who has responsibility and liability for any harm done to individuals or to society by the product? This has become an enormously complex and rapidly changing area of the law and of moral concern as well. Traditionally, common law and social thought relied on contract theory, which holds that buyer and seller come as equals to the marketplace and, once the deal has been struck, the buyer is responsible for the product, including any harm it might cause. Especially since the 1950's, however, more and more of the responsibility and liability have been placed on the seller and, particularly, the manufacturer. It has been argued that the manufacturer has the most knowledge of the product, is in the best position to prevent harm from occurring, and is better able to bear the financial liability for harm than is the buyer, especially when the latter is an individual consumer. No longer is it necessary to show that manufacturers have been negligent in any way; they are now expected to anticipate any potential hazards or possible misuse by customers.

Pricing and Promotion Issues. Ethical questions can arise also in the pricing function of marketing. Here the question is whether a price is considered fair, especially when the product is a necessity such as a basic food item, housing, or medical care. The introduction of revolutionary pharmaceutical products—for example, Burroughs Wellcome's AZT for the treatment of AIDS patients and Genentech's TPA for heart attack victims—has often triggered complaints that the manufacturer's high price puts an unfair burden on the buyer. Some retailers have been accused of unfairly charging prices in low-income areas that are higher than those that they charge in more affluent neighborhoods for the identical merchandise.

Sophisticated advertising and other promotional tactics are often the subject of ethical questioning. Critics charge that advertisers, usually the manufacturers, manipulate and exploit consumers, and thus use unfair means to encourage them to buy. Manufacturers and some social scientists respond that unless the advertising is actually dishonest, and

Making exaggerated claims for products is a common unethical technique used to increase sales. (Library of Congress)

therefore illegal, consumers cannot be coerced by legal advertising messages into buying anything that they do not really want to buy. This issue takes on added significance when so-called "vulnerable" groups are the target. Cigarette companies have been criticized for targeting African Americans and women; breweries for targeting young, inner-city African Americans for high-alcohol-content beverages; breakfast cereal and toy manufacturers for targeting children; and door-to-door sellers of safety devices for targeting the elderly. Other ethical questions raised about advertising include the promotion of inappropriate values; for example, materialism and the exploitation of women by emphasizing sex.

In the distribution function of marketing, ethical questions are raised when retailers close up stores in inner-city areas of urban centers (for example, after the Los Angeles riots of May, 1992), when major food retailers collect "slotting fees" from manufacturers just for agreeing to carry new products, and when direct marketers buy and use confidential demographic and consumer behavior information in compiling lists of potential customers.

Corrective Action. Action to correct these ethical problems comes from three sources. First, various industries and business associations agree to exercise self-restraint through company-wide or industry-wide codes of conduct and through the formation of organizations such as the Better Business Bureaus to monitor corporate behavior. Second, dozens of watchdog consumer organizations, such as the Center for Auto Safety, Co-op America, and the Center for Science in the Public Interest, have been formed to guard consumers' interests and call attention to what they perceive as improper behavior on the part of sellers. Third, since the 1970's, many laws have been passed to help protect consumers, such as the Consumers Products Safety Act, the Child Protection and Safety Act, and the Hazardous Substances Act at the federal level. —*D. Kirk Davidson*

See also Consumerism; Marketing.

BIBLIOGRAPHY

Galbraith, John Kenneth. *The Affluent Society*. 3d ed. New York: Houghton Mifflin, 1976.

Hunt, Shelby D., and Lawrence B. Chonko. "Marketing and Machiavellianism." *Journal of Marketing* 48 (Summer, 1984): 30-42.

Laczniak, Gene R., and Patrick E. Murphy. *Marketing Ethics: Guidelines for Managers*. Lexington, Mass.: Lexington Books, 1985.

Levitt, Theodore. "The Morality (?) of Advertising." *Harvard Business Review*, July-August, 1970: 84-92.

Smith, N. Craig, and John A. Quelch. *Ethics in Marketing*. Homewood, Ill.: Richard D. Irwin, 1993.

SALT treaties

TYPE OF ETHICS: International relations
DATES: SALT I, May 26, 1972; SALT II, June 18, 1979
ASSOCIATED WITH: U.S. presidents Richard Nixon and Jimmy Carter and Soviet president Leonid Brezhnev
DEFINITION: The Strategic Arms Limitation Treaties, or SALT treaties, were designed to curb the U.S.-Soviet arms race in strategic nuclear weapons and to place limits on the development of antiballistic missile defenses
SIGNIFICANCE: Began the process of nuclear weapons reduction

After several years of preliminary efforts, negotiations between the United States and the Soviet Union regarding reducing strategic nuclear weapons began on November 17, 1969. Several factors spurred both states toward an agreement. The United States was anxious to stop the steady Soviet buildup of intercontinental ballistic missiles (ICBMs), which in 1970 for the first time exceeded those of the United States. By the early 1970's, the Soviet Union was approaching numerical parity with the United States in the total number of strategic nuclear delivery vehicles. For its part, the Soviet Union was anxious to avoid a competition with the United States in building antiballistic missile (ABM) defenses. In 1967, the U.S. Lyndon Johnson Administration decided to proceed with a pilot ABM system, as did the succeeding Nixon Administration. Another factor was that both countries had committed themselves to nuclear weapons reductions as part of their effort to persuade nonnuclear weapons states to sign the Nonproliferation Treaty. Finally, during the early 1970's, the two superpowers were moving toward improved relations, which both sides recognized would be dramatically symbolized by significant arms control agreements.

Between November, 1969, and May, 1972, seven negotiating sessions were held, alternating between the cities of Helsinki and Vienna. Completion of the SALT I package was not achieved until May, 1972, when Richard Nixon and Leonid Brezhnev met in their first summit session in Moscow. The fundamental compromise of SALT I was embodied in two agreements: an ABM Treaty limiting defensive weapons (the primary concern of the Soviet Union) and a moratorium on the deployment of offensive weapons (the principal U.S. objective).

The ABM Treaty was the more important of the two agreements. It provided that each party would refrain from building a nationwide antiballistic missile defense and would limit the construction of ABM site defenses to only two specific sites. (Subsequently, the treaty was modified to limit site defense to a single site.) The site defenses were intended to permit both sides to protect their national capitals and one ICBM site. The Soviet Union had already begun construction of an ABM defense of Moscow, and the United States was free to do the same for Washington, D.C. (which it never did). An important provision of the ABM Treaty stipulated that "Each Party undertakes not to develop, test, or deploy ABM systems or components which are sea-based, air-based, space-based, or mobile land-based." More than a decade later, this prohibition would be used to criticize as illegal the proposal of the Reagan Administration for a "strategic defense initiative." The ABM Treaty, which was rati-

SALT TREATIES TIME LINE	
September 18, 1967	U.S. Secretary of Defense Robert McNamara announces U.S. limited ABM system
July 1, 1968	U.S. President Lyndon Johnson announces preliminary SALT discussions
November 17, 1969	SALT negotiations begin in Helsinki
May 26, 1972	SALT I agreements are signed in Moscow
July 1, 1972	Moratorium on offensive missiles begins
September 30, 1972	ABM Treaty ratified by United States
October 3, 1972	SALT I agreements take effect
November 21, 1972	SALT II negotiations begin
November, 1974	Ford-Brezhnev accord begins at Vladivostok summit
March 12, 1977	U.S. President Jimmy Carter endorses comprehensive plan
October 1, 1977	Missile moratorium expires
June 18, 1979	SALT II Treaty is signed in Vienna
December, 1979	Soviet Union invades Afghanistan
January, 1980	U.S. President Jimmy Carter withdraws SALT II Treaty from Senate
March, 1983	U.S. President Ronald Reagan proposes Strategic Defense Initiative (Star Wars)

fied by the United States on September 30, 1972, is of unlimited duration, although it is subject to review every five years.

The other part of SALT I was an Interim Agreement not to construct any new fixed, land-based ICBM missile launchers for a five-year period beginning July 1, 1972. This five-year moratorium was formalized as an Executive Agreement rather than as a treaty. Both parties could modernize and replace their strategic offensive missiles and launchers, but they could not increase their total number. Thus, the United States was limited to 1,054 ICBMs and the Soviet Union to 1,618. A protocol to the Interim Agreement limited the United States to a maximum of 710 submarine-launched ballistic missiles (SLBMs) and the Soviet Union to 950 launchers. The rationale for this agreement was that while both parties possessed a different mix of weapons, they were nevertheless roughly in a state of parity. While in certain categories of missiles the Soviet Union possessed more, the United States had the advantage of technological superiority. It was assumed that before the moratorium expired, both governments would negotiate a follow-on agreement (SALT II) that would begin the process of inventory reduction.

SALT II proved to be considerably more difficult to negotiate than SALT I had been. In October, 1977, the five-year moratorium ended and no follow-on agreement was in sight. Both governments unilaterally and simultaneously announced their intention to abide by the constraints of the Interim Agreement, pending a new accord. Not until May, 1979, was SALT II completed, and then it was never ratified. There were three principal reasons for the protracted negotiations of SALT II. First, during the 1970's, technological improvements in weapons systems made verification of an agreement extremely difficult. The development of cruise missiles by the United States, the deployment of mobile launchers by the Soviet Union, and the deployment of mul-

tiple independently targeted reentry vehicles (MIRVs) by both sides required intrusive and cooperative monitoring measures that both sides were reluctant to accept. Second, the détente relationship of the early 1970's collapsed as the decade passed. Soviet-American conflicts in the Third World fueled suspicions that the Soviet Union was determined to expand at Western expense. Soviet-Cuban involvement in Angola and Ethiopia in the mid- to late 1970's particularly angered the United States. The Soviet invasion of Afghanistan in December, 1979, induced U.S. president Jimmy Carter to abandon the effort to ratify SALT II. Third, negotiations were complicated by domestic politics, particularly in the United States. President Nixon was disabled by the Watergate crisis, which forced his resignation in 1974. President Carter was slow to move the negotiations because of both overambition to produce drastic cuts and diplomatic ineptitude.

In 1974, President Gerald Ford met Leonid Brezhnev in Vladivostok to devise a general framework for a SALT II treaty. They agreed that each side would be permitted a total of 2,400 strategic delivery vehicles, of which 1,320 could be MIRVs. Five years later, under a different American administration, an agreement was reached. It was signed by Carter and Brezhnev at a summit meeting in Vienna.

Unlike SALT I, SALT II is a long and complicated agreement. The documents include a Treaty to remain in force through 1985, a Protocol of three years' duration, and a Joint Statement of Principles to serve as a guideline for future negotiations. The main terms of the agreement can be summarized as follows: a ceiling of 2,400 strategic launchers, to decline to 2,250 by 1981; a limit of 1,320 on MIRV missiles and bombers; a further subceiling of 1,200 for MIRVs, ICBMs, and SLBMs; a further subceiling of 820 for MIRV ICBMs; a limit on the number of warheads on MIRV missiles; limits on the deployment of mobile missiles and cruise missiles; and a limit on Soviet production of the Backfire bomber.

By the time SALT II was signed, relations between the superpowers had deteriorated, making ratification in the United States politically difficult. Ronald Reagan, who was elected U.S. president in 1980, opposed the ratification of SALT II, though throughout his administration he adhered to its provisions (as did the Soviet Union). In the 1980's, U.S.-Soviet relations radically improved, and subsequently the two states did agree on arms control measures that went breathtakingly beyond both SALT I and SALT II. The threat of nuclear devastation was substantially reduced by these agreements.   —*Joseph L. Nogee*

See also Cold war; International law.

BIBLIOGRAPHY

Arms Control and Disarmament Agreements: Texts and Histories of Negotiations. Washington, D.C.: U.S. Arms Control and Disarmament Agency, 1982.

Newhouse, John. *Cold Dawn: The Story of SALT*. New York: Holt, Rinehart & Winston, 1973.

Stanford Arms Control Group. *International Arms Control: Issues and Agreements*. 2d ed. Stanford, Calif.: Stanford University Press, 1984.

Talbott, Strobe. *Endgame: The Inside Story of SALT II*. New York: Harper & Row, 1979.

Wolfe, Thomas. *The SALT Experience*. Cambridge, Mass.: Ballinger, 1979.

Sanctions

TYPE OF ETHICS: International relations
DATE: Seventeenth century to present
DEFINITION: A legal mechanism by which governments punish other governments that have violated international law or that have engaged in domestic practices considered offensive to other nations
SIGNIFICANCE: Provides a means to encourage compliance with international law short of war

International relations are marked by the lack of centralized mechanisms for maintaining order and punishing violations of international law. For this reason, states, in both their individual capacities and as collective groups, have relied on sanctions to punish offending governments. Sanctions take a variety of forms, including the imposition of trade boycotts and embargoes, the freezing of assets held in foreign banks, the suspension of foreign aid or investment activity, the breaking of diplomatic relations, the establishment of blockades, and even the limited use of military force. Economic sanctions are not always effective in achieving compliance from the offending government. Their success is most likely when a large number of states that have commercial and economic ties to the offending state act quickly and firmly to impose sanctions, when the offending state is economically weak and unable to withstand the sanctions, and when third parties are unlikely to come to the offender's assistance. Historically, sanctions took the form of unilateral retaliation by the injured state against the offender.

In the twentieth century, with the rise of international organizations such as the League of Nations and the United Nations, sanctions have been adopted as a multilateral mechanism for taking action against renegade states that violate international law.

History. Sanctions have always been present in international relations as a means of punishing violators of international law. In effect, an injured state, having no capacity to appeal to a higher authority, relied on its own resources to take action against governments that injured it by violating treaty obligations or customary international law. Several principles, however, placed ethical, moral, and legal constraints on how states could use retaliatory force and how much force they could use as a sanction against the offender. Three basic principles were involved. First, it was assumed that one could retaliate legally only when the action was in response to a prior illegal action or provocation. Second, it was assumed that the injured party would allow some time to resolve the dispute peacefully. Third, it was required that any retaliation would be proportional in character and degree to the original offense. Excessive retaliatory force was considered illegal, and restraint in the course of retaliation was expected.

With the emergence of global and regional collective security organizations in the twentieth century, governments moved toward the multilateral use of sanctions. Collective security organizations require their members to resolve disputes among themselves peacefully; that is, to avoid the use of force against one another. When a member of a collective security treaty such as the United Nations illegally uses force against another member, other member states are expected collectively to resist and punish such aggression. Sanctions are typically employed to deal with such situations, although the severity of the sanctions and their effectiveness have varied substantially in actual practice, and in many instances there has not been adequate consensus to employ any sanctions at all. This happens when there is doubt about which state was actually the author of aggression, and in cases in which a clear aggressor has powerful allies that will oppose efforts by collective security bodies such as the United Nations to take any action. In such cases, individual states are free to impose sanctions of their own against a state that has violated international law. Multilateral sanctions, in other words, have not replaced self-help by individual states but have supplemented it. When, how, and whether sanctions are imposed ultimately depends more on political realities than on ethical, moral, or legal considerations.

Ethical Issues. International relations are marked primarily by the principle that states are sovereign. This principle calls for nonintervention in the domestic affairs of a state. It calls for each state to recognize the independence, territorial integrity, and equality of other states. How then can sanctions be justified against a state? When should sanctions be imposed? Under collective security treaties to which governments have voluntarily subscribed, sanctions are justified when one state violates the territorial integrity of another state and, at least under the United Nations Charter, when such violations threaten international peace and security. In other words, if states have a right to territorial integrity and noninterference in their domestic affairs, then they have a duty to respect other states' independence and territorial integrity. Where clear-cut aggression occurs, sanctions are ethically, morally, and legally justified. The U.N. Security Council can act only if a majority of its members (that is, nine states, including the five permanent members who have veto power) agree to impose sanctions. If they fail to do so, then states are left to decide how to proceed to protect their rights and interests.

One of the most ticklish issues concerning sanctions turns on the question of their use against states for actions that are primarily domestic in character and that may not clearly threaten international peace and security. May the international community, for example, interfere in the domestic affairs of a state to punish it for mistreatment of its own citizens? States have, for example, imposed sanctions on their own, and at the request of the United Nations, to oppose South Africa's domestic policy of apartheid. Sanctions were imposed on Rhodesia when a white minority unilaterally declared independence in the 1960's. Such cases are, however, rare. Usually, sanctions are imposed when the domestic actions of states begin to have serious international consequences. When domestic instability produces civil war, refugee flows into neighboring states, boundary incursions, and the like, then states are more likely to impose sanctions.

Another problem with economic sanctions is that they often hurt the innocent population of a country without damaging or removing the culpable government, as has happened in Iraq. For how long should states impose sanctions that are hurtful to the innocent? Here, ethical and humanitarian considerations must be weighed in the balance with political judgment.

Conclusion. Sanctions are imposed by states for many reasons. Sometimes they are meant to punish an aggressor, sometimes to pressure an outlaw state into compliance with international law, sometimes to prevent the further spread of conflict, and sometimes simply to express the moral indignation or outrage that the people and government of one country feel about the actions of another country's government. In the latter case, the imposition of sanctions fulfills its purpose in the very act of implementation even if the offending state fails to desist from its objectionable behavior.

—*Robert F. Gorman*

See also Deterrence; Economics; International law; Intervention; Limited war; Power; Sovereignty; War and peace.

BIBLIOGRAPHY

Bennett, A. LeRoy. *International Organizations: Principles and Issues.* 5th ed. Englewood Cliffs, N.J.: Prentice-Hall, 1991.

Daoudi, Mohammed, and Munther Dajani. *Economic Sanctions: Ideals and Experience.* London: Routledge & Kegan Paul, 1983.

Harrelson, Max. *Fires All Around the Horizon: the UN's Uphill Battle to Preserve the Peace.* New York: Praeger, 1989.

Henkin, Louis, et al. *Right v. Might: International Law and the Use of Force.* New York: Council on Foreign Relations Press, 1989.

Hufbauer, Gary C., and Jeffrey Schott. *Economic Sanctions Reconsidered: History and Current Policy.* Washington, D.C.: Institute for International Economics, 1985.

Śaṅkara (c. 788, Kāladi Village?, Kerala, India, west coast of Malabar, India—820, Kedārnāth, India): Philosopher

TYPE OF ETHICS: Religious ethics

ACHIEVEMENTS: Wrote commentaries on the Prasthānatraya, which consists of the Upaniṣads, the Bhagavad Gītā, the Vedānta Sūtra, and many other works; he founded four *mathas*, or monasteries, in India, in Mysore Province of southern India, in Puri in the east, Davaraka in the west, and Badarinath in the north

SIGNIFICANCE: Advocated monistic or Advaita Vedānta philosophy, which explains how to achieve the ultimate reality, or Brahman

Śaṅkara is the most influential philosopher of the Advaita, or nondualistic, school of Vedānta philosophy in India. He was considered the incarnation of the god Śiva. His view is representative of the main teachings of the Upaniṣads, which do not portray any consistent view of the universe and of reality. Śaṅkara detected a synthesis underlying the Upaniṣads and insisted on interpreting them in a single coherent manner. He tried to revive the intellectual speculation of the Upaniṣads through his reaction against the ascetic tendency of Buddhism and the devotional tendencies stressed by the Mimāṁsa school. The central position of Śaṅkara's philosophy is that all is one; only the ultimate principle has any real existence, and everything else is an illusion (*māyā*). The basic teaching of Advaita Vedānta is that the direct method of realization of Brahman is the path of knowledge, which consists of getting instruction from a teacher, reflecting on its meaning, and meditating on truth with single-minded devotion. For Śaṅkara, philosophical discrimination and renunciation of the unreal are the basic disciplines for the realization of Brahman. Finite humanity can catch a glimpse of Brahman through a personal god, who is the highest manifestation of the infinite.

The self, or ātman, according to Śaṅkara, is pure subject and is never an object of consciousness. It is not a duality; it is different from the phenomenal, the spatial, the temporal, and the sensible. It is assumed to be foundational but it is in no sense a substance. Self is the ever-existent and self-existent first principle. It is not something that is unknown. One must come to the realization that one is Brahman. This is self-knowledge, the knowledge of self being the self of all things. One must realize one's identity as Brahman, for Brahman is knowledge. Self-knowledge and realization are one and the same.

From the level of Brahman, nothing is seen to be real—not the existential self that people view as ego, not the worlds, and not the universes.

According to Advaita Vedānta philosophy, the highest good consists in breaking down the bonds that shut one out of the reality that one is. It is only the realization of Brahman that can give one permanent satisfaction. Śaṅkara wrote, "Attaining the Knowledge of Reality, one sees the universe as the nondual Brahman, Existence-Knowledge-Bliss Absolute." It is not possible for everyone to achieve this highest state, yet everyone can try to achieve it progressively, through his or her inner light. It is up to the individual to choose any course of action (karma) that is of value to that person. When one clings to the world, one looks for rewards for action and feels disappointed when the objects of desire are not achieved. This applies even to praiseworthy actions such as worship and giving alms. If these actions are performed with desire or attachment, they cause bondage. Therefore, nonattachment must be cultivated if one wants to progress to the highest good.

It is often believed that Śaṅkara discourages the performance of duties and advocates the discipline of nonaction for the realization of truth. This is not true, however, because Śaṅkara's position is that because of māyā, or ignorance, one does not recognize one's true nature and finds oneself involved with the relative world of good and evil, life and death, and other pairs of opposites. Therefore, one tries to avoid evil and to do good, rising and falling according to the results of one's actions. Gradually, one discovers that it is impossible to attain lasting happiness and peace by clinging to rewards and realizes that work performed in the spirit of surrendering the results to God, in the spirit of calm, unattached by love or hate, by reward or punishment, purifies the heart and makes it inclined toward the cultivation of meditation and self-knowledge. The liberated person engages in service to humanity but not in an egoistic way, because a liberated person is above good and evil, above morality.

Release from the wheel of birth and rebirth comes through jñāna, or knowledge or insight, which lifts one out of one's individuality into the oneness of the infinite. At the beginning stage, one learns the art of concentration through the worship of the personal God and acquires purity of heart through performance of unselfish duties. In the next stage, one acquires knowledge of Brahman and realizes the impersonal absolute. The way of devotion (bhakti mārga) must be transcended if one is to realize the supreme good, the realization of self as Brahman. It is at this level that one becomes liberated from the endless sufferings of the world. This level can be achieved during one's lifetime. This freed soul does not have anything more to achieve but still continues to work for the welfare of the world. The liberated person does not negate his or her relationship to the finite world, since there is a direct relationship between the spiritual and the ethical. The freed soul (jivan-mukta) follows the moral code set down by his or her society, because he or she is unattached and freed from desires.

—Krishna Mallick

See also Hindu ethics; Upaniṣads; Vedānta.

BIBLIOGRAPHY

Deussen, Paul. *The System of the Vedanta*. Translated by Charles Johnston. Chicago, Ill.: Open Court, 1912.

Hiriyanna, Mysore. *The Essentials of Indian Philosophy*. London: Allen & Unwin, 1949.

Koller, John M. *The Indian Way*. New York: Macmillan, 1982.

Radhakrishnan, Sarvepalli. *Indian Philosophy*. 2 vols. New York: Macmillan, 1958.

Smith, Huston. *The Religions of Man*. New York: Harper & Row, 1958.

Santayana, George

(Dec. 16, 1863, Madrid, Spain—Sept. 26, 1952, Rome, Italy): Philosopher, poet, novelist

TYPE OF ETHICS: Modern history

ACHIEVEMENTS: Wrote *The Life of Reason: Or, the Phases of Human Progress* (1905-1906), *Scepticism and Animal Faith* (1923), and *Realms of Being* (1927-1940), among other works

SIGNIFICANCE: Santayana posited an evolution of ethics that led to lifestyles that emphasized detachment, contemplation, kindness, faith, and a sense of irony about human failings

A materialist and a gentle skeptic, George Santayana expressed himself as sensitively in his extensive formal and philosophical writings as he did in his poetry and novels. Pushing doubt as far as he could, he ended his explorations believing that everything could be doubted except, possibly, faith. Such "animal faith" sprang, he explained, from humankind's survival instincts. Santayana's somewhat Platonic ideal world arose from primitive magic and science and took a higher form in religion. The ethics that he derived from his philosophizing were explained as the results of a three-phase historical evolution. Early, or prerational, morality, although culturally rich, was crude and without consistent application. Its refinement, rational morality, was a vital outgrowth of humankind's general adherence to the dictates of reason and, as the nineteenth century well understood, to a belief in progress. The horrendous effects of two world wars, however, supplanted the positivism of rational morality with postrational pessimism. With little that was positive distinguishing this world, humankind's attention shifted to the promise of otherworldliness—for Santayana, the sad end of ethical development. After years of teaching at Harvard University, Santayana, the recipient of an inheritance, took up residence in Rome, thereafter exemplifying a lifestyle that conformed with his ethics. It was a contemplative existence marked by a kindly, tolerant skepticism and detachment. Able to cultivate the interrelated values of science, art, and religion, he came as close as a doubter could to assessing the benefits of his ideal society.

See also Morality; Pessimism and optimism.

Sartre, Jean-Paul (June 21, 1905, Paris, France—Apr. 15, 1980, Paris, France): Philosopher, playwright, novelist

TYPE OF ETHICS: Modern history

ACHIEVEMENTS: Author of *L'Être et le néant* (1943; *Being and Nothingness*, 1956), *L'Existentialisme et un humanisme* (1946; *Existentialism*, 1947), and various plays and novels reflecting existentialist themes

SIGNIFICANCE: The leading proponent of modern existentialist thought, Sartre departed from traditional ethical theory with his subjectivist perception of human morality

At the heart of Sartrean ethics is the same basic premise that defines Sartre's larger existentialist philosophy: that humanity makes itself. There is no created human nature and thus no prescribed grounds for behavior apart from what the individual chooses. This is not to say that ethics was peripheral to Sartre, or simply an afterthought. Even during the formative days of his philosophical career, before World War II, he emphasized the need for "authenticity" in human behavior, which is one of the cardinal tenets of his theory of morality.

His first novel, *Nausea* (1938), is the story of a young scholar seeking to learn more about an obscure historical figure, and his research leads him to face the universal human tendency to distort real identity. For Sartre, this "unauthenticity" precluded genuine morality by denying the most elemental truth. Sartre's experiences in World War II—witnessing the defeat of France by Germany and his own imprisonment in a Nazi camp—further convinced him that morality must emanate from candidly facing the truth about one's existence.

Existence Precedes Essence. In Sartre's thought, there was no higher being, no God who had created human nature, and thus no transcendent basis for ethics. "There is no human nature," he wrote, "since there is no God to conceive it." Candidly atheistic, Sartre turned away from traditional religion. An individual, he argued, exists before he or she has a nature (essence), and the essence that a person acquires is the result of his or her own choices and their translation into action. The pivotal emphasis is upon action, for intentions alone do not shape essence.

If this seems to place Sartre clearly within a relativist genre of ethics, other factors qualify the apparent radical individualism of his thinking about morality. The first is his unflagging zeal for human responsibility. Although one does shape one's own essence, one is also responsible—for the sake of authenticity—to be consistent with the goals of one's chosen way of life. For example, one who eschews dishonesty can hardly spend his or her life lying or otherwise deceiving others. Responsibility in Sartrean ethics is tantamount to commitment, a view that has an interesting correlation with more conventional ethical thinking in the Judeo-Christian and other great major religious traditions.

A second dimension of Sartrean ethical thought that limits extreme relativism and individualism is Sartre's perception of "bad faith" (*mauvaise foi*). It is bad faith, to Sartre, to pretend—particularly to oneself—to be something that one

is not. Social role-playing such as "being" a student, professor, worker, or attorney is one level of such bad faith, but so is assuming that one's being is exhausted by such a definition. People are more than the social roles they play, and morality is much more than being good at performing the expected behavior patterns. Although there is no one in the final analysis to help one make choices, one is responsible to one's past and anticipated future to be sincerely what one is.

Furthermore, Sartre defined individual existence in terms of broader human existence. Just as a person is the product of the past, he or she is also relational. The surrounding world of things, as well as other people, is an integral part of one's existence and therefore morality. In the play *No Exit*, the characters are in hell, which is symbolized by a small room where each is subjected to the piercing gaze of the others. One of them, Ines, is a lesbian who is responsible for the death of her friend's husband. Like Garcin, a deserter, and Estelle, a child-killer, Ines can find no escape from the others' eyes and presumed judgment. No less a philosopher than Immanuel Kant had raised similar moral issues, but he did so in terms of the question of whether a person could legitimately want his behavior to be universal. Kant's "categorical imperative," as it is called, assumed a universal transcendent moral order. Sartre did not, but neither did he advocate behavior that did not in some sense aid the existence of others. If Sartre thus seemed to approximate such concepts as love and universal moral premises, he remained humanistic in his ethical theory. The significance of others in one's ethics is that they also objectively exist and are part of the individual's responsibility.

Being-for-Itself. Basic to this line of ethical reasoning is Sartre's distinction between being-for-itself (*pour-soi*) and being-in-itself (*en-soi*). Being-in-itself is the type of existence that defines things. A rock's essence and being are identical. There is no self-conscious reflection, no selfhood at stake. In short, there are no choices to be made by things. Human existence is radically different, a being-for-itself; that is, the human mode of existence is one of active choices and bearing the responsibilities for the outcome of those choices. In that sense, it is being-for-itself. Humanity also exists "*en-soi*," however, and this dual nature demands responsibility. A tree or rock cannot decide, either for itself or for other things, what to do or be. Humans can and must. The individual is in the present, facing the de facto past and facing a future that requires continued decision making and acting on those decisions responsibly.

Implications for Ethical Conduct. In the Sartrean view of human life, nothing counts more than responsibility. Indeed, responsibility is the essence of being human. With no higher moral order either to shape one's essence or by which to judge one's actions, one must face squarely individual responsibility as well as the possible impact that one's behavior might have on others. Sartre's own estimation of the ethical implications of his ideas focused on the notion that the individual's quest for being is related to that of humanity as a whole. People are, he argued, agents "by whom the world comes into being." Lacking in Sartrean ethics is a transcendent source of value, but there are good reasons in the existentialist perspective to love, to help others, and to discipline one's actions.　　　　　—*Thomas R. Peake*

See also Existentialism.

BIBLIOGRAPHY

Greene, Norman Nathaniel. *Jean-Paul Sartre; the Existentialist Ethic*. Westport, Conn.: Greenwood Press, 1980.

Meszaros, Istvan. *Search for Freedom*. Vol. 1 in *The Work of Sartre*. Atlantic Highlands, N.J.: Humanities Press, 1979.

Nass, Arne. *Four Modern Philosophers: Carnap, Wittgenstein, Heidegger, Sartre*. Translated by Alastair Hannay. Chicago: University of Chicago Press, 1968.

Richter, Liselotte. *Jean-Paul Sartre*. Translated by Fred D. Wieck. New York: Frederick Ungar, 1970.

Warnock, Mary. *Existentialist Ethics*. New York: St. Martin's Press, 1967.

Schopenhauer, Arthur (Feb. 22, 1788, Danzig, Poland—Sept. 21, 1860, Frankfurt am Main): Philosopher

TYPE OF ETHICS: Modern history

ACHIEVEMENTS: Author of *Die Welt als Wille und Vorstellung* (1818; *The World as Will and Idea*, 1833-1886)

SIGNIFICANCE: Arthur Schopenhauer's pessimistic philosophy advocated an ethics of asceticism, yet his emphasis on the primacy of will influenced both will-to-power thinkers and modern existentialists

Financial independence enabled Schopenhauer to devote his life to philosophy, and he developed his pessimistic system as a follower of Immanuel Kant. In *The World as Will and Idea*, he identifies the will as the Kantian thing-in-itself that comprehends the external world through the mental constructs of time, space, and causality. As Schopenhauer understood it, will comprises intellect, personality, and the potential for growth and development. Although powerful, it is not free but is controlled by causation like all else that exists. Confronting a meaningless existence and a godless universe, Schopenhauer concluded that ethical behavior requires withdrawal from the pleasures of life in favor of contemplation. The individual must tame the will so that it becomes less insistent on its egoistic desires, which lead only to further desires. Where others are concerned, the proper attitude is compassion, since they too suffer an identical fate. The truth of Christianity, according to Schopenhauer, lies in its early emphasis on renunciation of the world and an ascetic life. Although he failed to clarify how this asceticism could be achieved in the absence of freedom, Schopenhauer's work includes a strong suggestion. Because human actions are explicable through motives, he equates motive with cause. Thus, causation may be rooted in intellectual concepts. As the individual recognizes the futility of existence, he or she can become compassionate toward others and accept the futility of desire.

See also Asceticism; *Beyond Good and Evil*; Pessimism and optimism; Will.

Schweitzer, Albert (Jan. 14, 1875, Kaysersberg, Germany—Sept. 4, 1965, Lambaréné, Gabon): Theologian, missionary

TYPE OF ETHICS: Modern history

ACHIEVEMENTS: Author of *Kulturphilosophie* (1923; *Philosophy of Civilization*); winner of the 1952 Nobel Peace Prize

SIGNIFICANCE: A first-rate theologian who was always interested in public affairs, Schweitzer used his keen abilities as an analyst to explore the ways in which civilization had become "self-destroying"

In his early adulthood, Albert Schweitzer was an organist, a music scholar, and a world figure in theological studies. In 1905, Schweitzer began studying to be a physician so that he could be a mission doctor in equatorial Africa. In 1913, he opened a clinic in Gabon, doing much of the building with his own hands. He lived there for most of the rest of his life. His work in Africa caused Schweitzer to contemplate world civilization as a whole. He developed an ethics that he called "Reverence for Life." Schweitzer believed that life itself was of the highest value, but that life is harsh and self-destructive. People should treat every form of life with the same reverence that they afford their own. They should do this by trying to reach their own highest level of perfection and by helping their society reach perfection. These two goals are often contradictory: In raising the individual, one must keep in mind one's responsibilities to the society. In addition, because humans destroy something or someone by their every act, every action taken to attain perfection also results in destruction. This awareness drove Schweitzer's philanthropy but also made him an unhappy man.

See also Ahiṁsā, Morality.

Science, ethics of

TYPE OF ETHICS: Scientific ethics

DEFINITION: The various ethical issues related to scientific research and procedures

SIGNIFICANCE: Seeks to examine the impact of science on society, the individual, and on ethical issues; in addition, seeks to develop an appropriate code of ethics for those conducting scientific research and to develop appropriate standards for the funding of science research

Issues. Science, ethics, and philosophy interact in a range of arenas. The development of ethical standards—that is, codes of behavior that govern moral decisions—has been a major issue for the great philosophers and thinkers of their time. Traditionally, metaphysical hypotheses and religious beliefs have governed the attempts of humankind to fathom the unfathomable, to come to grips with mortality, and to hold themselves to a set of standards of conduct. The science of the twentieth century has influenced this search, in some cases incorporating, in some cases rejecting, religion as a part of that effort.

The writings of Albert Einstein epitomize the attempt to reconcile science with religion. In this century, Einstein holds a central place because of his groundbreaking ideas on theoretical physics. He writes, "To know what is impenetrable to us really exists, manifesting itself as the highest wisdom and the most radiant beauty which our dull faculties can comprehend only in their most primitive forms—this knowledge, this feeling, is at the center of true religiousness."

At the same time, the achievements of science and technology have posed their own moral dilemmas. For example, the theory of relativity, developed by Albert Einstein in the early twentieth century, set the stage for the development of the atomic bomb. In the face of a creation with such awesome destructive potential, however, the question is posed: To what extent should scientists involve themselves in the ultimate consequences of their research?

For this generation and for generations to come, the advances in the fields of genetics and biomedicine are likely to give rise to similar dilemmas. The much-seen film *Jurassic Park* (1993) focused the popular consciousness on the risks inherent in bioengineering technology. With all their inherent potential for good, genetic technologies may carry as yet unknown risks and consequences.

The limited amount of funding available for science research has forced both scientists and those responsible for science policy to make choices regarding which projects to fund. Should "big" projects such as the Human Genome Project or the Superconducting Supercollider (SSC) be funded or should many smaller but important projects receive government or private monies? Where should these "big" projects be located? Should basic research be targeted in the hope of eventual payoff or should applications research be the major focus? Are political and economic concerns playing a too-important role in the funding process? To what extent should science and mathematics education be considered a priority?

In the late 1980's and early 1990's, the spotlight turned on ethical conduct and misconduct in science research. A major challenge to both the scientific community and the community at large is this: What is the appropriate response to scientific fraud and misconduct? What should be the response to the "gray areas" of even more problematical situations of conflict of interest or "honest mistakes"?

Philosophical Issues. As a guide in an attempt to deal with the range of ethical issues involved in scientific research, the scientific community and the community at large might look to philosophical thinkers who have dealt with issues in this field. In fact, from antiquity through the beginning of this century, the great thinkers of their times concerned themselves with issues not only of philosophy, ethics, and morality but also with those of science. Aristotle, René Descartes, and Immanuel Kant made major contributions not only to philosophy but also to the sciences. Wolfgang von Goethe, although best known for his literary works, also wrote extensively on the natural sciences.

At the same time, science has had a major, sometimes even a revolutionary, impact on the values and the world view of society. The theories of Galileo and Isaac Newton on planetary motion and the views of Charles Darwin on the evolution of species had that kind of revolutionary impact. Similarly, the development of the atomic bomb strongly influenced the political and social climate of the latter half of the twentieth century. It is likely that major advances in computer science and bioengineering now taking place will have their impact well into the twenty-first century. It is equally likely that scientists and society will have to deal with the ethical dilemmas posed by the positive and negative capabilities of these technologies.

The analysis of moral and ethical decisions in science might make use of following principles of ethics and philosophy.

The value neutrality of science is epitomized by the vision of the scientist as the ceaseless seeker motivated only by the search for truth. This theory has its basis in features first introduced in the seventeenth and eighteenth century. The theory of the scientific method, which is known as inductivism, has relied on this concept and postulates that science begins with the collection of data, goes on to generalize about laws and theories, and makes predictions that can be proved. The theory of inductivism had its roots in the writings of Francis Bacon in the sixteenth and seventeenth century and in the empiricist theories developed by David Hume in the eighteenth century. The inductivist view was supported by the Cambridge school of Bertrand Russell in the early twentieth century and the Vienna circle of the 1920's and 1930's.

Critics of the Vienna circle and of inductivism have included Karl Popper. Popper maintains that the concepts and postulates (which are ultimately proved or disproved by experimentation) are the products not necessarily of observations but of potentially "unjustified (and unjustifiable) anticipations, by guesses, by tentative solutions to our problems, by conjectures. The conjectures are controlled by criticism; that is, by attempted refutations, which include severely critical tests." The source of the hypothesis is irrelevant; the originator of the hypothesis or postulate joins in the criticism and testing of the hypothesis that he or she has proposed. Popper is considered to have inaugurated the current era in the philosophy of science.

Misconduct in Science. The embarrassment of the "honest mistake" is far surpassed by the violation of the ethos of science of the outright fraud. Fraud in science impugns the integrity of the research process and destroys the trust on which scientific achievement is built. At the same time, intentionally fraudulent actions undermine the confidence of society and the body politic in science and scientific inquiry. Potentially, the effects of fraud may be horrific; if, for example, a medical treatment should be based on fraudulent results.

Many scientists base their codes of conduct on the example of role models and on what some have termed the "school of hard knocks." A more systematic approach has been contributed by professional organizations who have contributed their expertise. A recent contribution is a 1989 publication of the National Academy of Science, *On Being a Scientist*. Other resources include a 1992 report, likewise from the National Academy of Sciences, called *Responsible Science: Ensuring the Integrity of the Research Process*. These publications and others often cite as examples of fraud and misconduct the actions of William Summerlin at Sloan-Kettering in the 1970's; those of John Darsee at Harvard and those of Stephen E. Breuning in Pittsburgh in the early 1980's; and those of Thereza Imanishi-Kari and Nobel laureate David Baltimore in the late 1980's.

A well-known and rather tragic example of fraud was that of William Summerlin. In the early 1970's, William Summerlin came to the Sloan-Kettering Institute as the chief of a laboratory working on transplantation immunology. A laboratory assistant noticed that the supposedly black grafts on white mice could be washed off with ethanol. It turned out that Summerlin had used a black felt-tipped marker to mimic the appearance of black grafts. Additional discrepancies regarding Summerlin's results on corneal transplantations led an internal committee to recommend that Summerlin take a medical leave of absence and to condemn Summerlin's behavior as irresponsible.

In the early 1980's, John Darsee had worked under the supervision of Eugene Braunwald, a well-known cardiologist at Harvard University. At Harvard, three coworkers apparently observed Darsee fake data for an experiment. An internal investigation for the next few months found no discrepancies. A subsequent National Institutes of Health (NIH) investigation, however, demonstrated that virtually every paper that Darsee had produced was fabricated.

Another episode involved a professor at the University of Pittsburgh, Stephen E. Breuning, who had become prominent for his expertise in the medical treatment of mental retardation. In 1983, Breuning's former mentor, Robert Sprague, questioned the veracity of his student's research. Eventually, it turned out that much of Breuning's data came from experiments that had not been performed on subjects that had not even been tested.

An exceptionally disturbing case was that of Thereza Imanishi-Kari and Nobel laureate David Baltimore of MIT. A postdoctoral fellow at Imanishi-Kari's laboratory, Margot O'Toole, uncovered evidence that Imanishi-Kari may have fabricated certain results appearing in a paper in *Cell* on gene transplantation, a paper that was also coauthored by Baltimore. University inquiries at MIT dismissed O'Toole's concerns, but a few years later the concerns resurfaced, resulting in ultimate retraction of the *Cell* paper and investigations by the NIH, Congressman John Dingell, and the Secret Service. While the U.S. attorney in the case declined to prosecute Imanishi-Kari, as of this writing, clouds continued to obscure her career and that of Baltimore.

In the late 1980's and the early 1990's, more than 200 allegations of misconduct in science were received by the U.S. government. One study has indicated that approximately 40 percent of the deans of graduate schools knew of cases of misconduct at their institutions. A recent survey sponsored by the American Association for the Advancement of Science likewise indicated that during the first ten years, 27 percent of scientists indicated that they had personally encountered incidences of falsified, fabricated, or plagiarized research.

In fact, by the late 1980's and into the early 1990's, articles on misconduct in science continued to constitute the vast majority of references on science ethics produced by computerized literature searches. In the late 1980's, incidents of apparent fraud, plagiarism, and misconduct drew the attention of the Subcommittee on Oversight and Investigations of the U.S. House of Representatives, chaired by Congressman John D. Dingell. The threat not only to the research process but also to the autonomy of the scientific community posed by examples of abuse has challenged scientists to develop ways of dealing with misconduct within their ranks. Congressman Dingell himself acknowledged the drawbacks of resolving issues of misconduct in the congressional hearing. "Encouraging science to police itself is far preferable to the alternatives . . . But with every case [which is] is covered up or mishandled, pressure builds for such extreme measures."

Certain instances of apparent fraud violate any accepted standards of moral or ethical conduct. Many other situations, however, fall into what might be termed a "gray area."

For example, a vexing question concerns the allocation of credit for scientific achievements. The bitter dispute between Newton and Gottfried Wilhelm Leibniz over who first discovered the calculus is paralleled by the twentieth century quarrel between Robert Gallo, the renowned AIDS researcher at the NIH, and his counterpart at the Pasteur Institute, Luc Montagnier, over the discovery of the AIDS virus.

Also in what might be termed a "gray area" are issues of "conflict of interest." (Outright bribery to promote fabrication of results would violate most standards of conduct.) By the late 1980's and early 1990's, doubts over the degree to which scientists' findings might be influenced by funding sources led journals such as *Science*, *JAMA*, and the *New England Journal of Medicine* (NEJM) to adopt standards of disclosure for potential conflicts of interest. The *JAMA* and *NEJM* standards stressed financial conflicts; the *Science* standards also include a range of other relationships that might possibly have influenced the scientist's work. The possibility of abuse inherent in these kinds of standards has led to a "backlash" as scientists and physicians engaged in medical research talked of a "New McCarthyism in Science" and evoked the possibility that not only financial conflicts but also such factors as religion and sexual orientation might be included in the disclosure standards. Kenneth J. Rothman, writing in the *Journal of the American Medical Association*, cites Popper (*The Open Society and Its Enemies*, 1966) in noting the impossibility of achieving full objectivity in any scientific endeavor.

Equally problematical for the scientist—and also in a "gray area"—are the new ethical problems created by scientific discoveries. Are scientists responsible for the ethical and moral uses of their discoveries? For example, should decisions about the use of the atom bomb have been in the hands of the scientists or, as actually occurred, in the hands of the politicians? Should scientists attempt to exert any kind of control over the uses of their discoveries?

A tradition of political neutrality governed science from the seventeenth century through World War I. Bacon, for example, conceived of science as a "new instrument." The chemist Robert Hooke warned the founders of the Royal Society of London that their business was to "improve the natural knowledge of things, not meddling with Divinity, Metaphysics, Moralls, Politicks, Grammar, Rhetorick or Logic." World War I, however, disrupted the tradition of neutrality as technological solutions not only made up for the losses of raw materials caused by the war but also played a major role in enhancing the lethal effect of explosive and chemical weapons.

Political authorities continued to come into the scientific arena with the advocacy by the Stalin regime of the 1930's and 1940's of the genetic theories of T. D. Lysenko. Nazi Germany purged its Jewish and left-wing scientists. Some disapproving scientists left the country, but others remained, adhering to a tradition that held no place for social responsibility and hoping to exert influence on the Nazi regime. World War II gave impetus to research in a range of areas, as synthetics replaced raw materials and new drugs such as penicillin became available. Refugee scientists from Nazi Germany encouraged preliminary research on an atomic bomb. The ensuing success of the Manhattan Project resulted in the explosion of the atomic bombs over Hiroshima and Nagasaki, which was followed by the development of atomic capability by the Soviet Union in 1949.

The dilemma for scientists is this: To what extent should they concern themselves with the ultimate consequences of their discoveries? Is scientific knowledge and discovery an inherent good? Are the risks of scientific and technological advances as important as the potential benefits?

The challenges posed by the development of the atomic bomb are paralleled by issues raised by the scientific advances of the 1980's and 1990's. The development of computer and electronic technology raises some important issues of privacy and the possibility of social control. Equally problematical are issues raised by advances in the biological and medical sciences.

An additional ethical issue concerns the eradication of racism and sexism in science. For example, a particularly shocking example of racism involved the Tuskegee syphilis experiment. During a forty-year study that received federal funds, African American victims of syphilis were denied treatment even after penicillin became available. The apparent justification was that the denial of treatment was essential to the study of the progress of the disease.

A challenge for researchers is to design studies of common illnesses (for example, myocardial infarction, diabetes) that not only provide sufficient data on the white middle-class male population but also include information on which to base the treatment of minority and female patients.

Allocation of Resources. Scientific research in the United States is funded to a large extent by the U.S. government. Major corporations, such as large pharmaceutical companies, support much of the rest. What are the implications of these facts?

The marriage of science and government dates back to World War II and Vannevar Bush, who then headed the Office of Scientific Research and Development. In the system that evolved, research proposals are initiated by the researcher, who usually works in a university or institute setting. At the same time, funding was a federal responsibility, and although some research was taking place in government laboratories, most basic research was undertaken in universities. There arose not a single funding agency, as envisioned by Bush, but a multiplicity of agencies—responsible for funding basic research.

By the late 1980's, the numbers of individuals involved in basic research had increased, while the pool of dollars available stayed the same. The result was that a far smaller proportion of grant proposals were being funded. For example, in 1980, the NIH approved up to one in three "meritorious" grants for funding, while by the 1990's, fewer than one in five grants received approval. The system in place through the latter half of the twentieth century has achieved scientific productivity, as measured by the numbers of citations; prestige, measured by the numbers of Nobel Prizes; and some degree of economic productivity.

In the late 1980's and early 1990's, the lessened availability of funding and the potential for political abuse and "porkbarrel" science led some experts to question the current criteria for funding science research. At the same time, the costs of new technologies and issues relating to the use of those technologies have led some people to question the direction of public policy on science issues. This position has yet to be adopted by public policymakers. The direction of governmental policy at the beginning of the 1990's is reiterated by Donna Shalala, Secretary of the federal department of Health and Human Services. Shalala states, "The last thing we should try to do is try to curb technology in our attempt to deal with costs or to slow down our investment in research. . . . The issue is how you use technology, far more than whether we should keep producing technology. Rather than beating up on technology, we need to get scientists and administrators to think about the more appropriate use of it."

—*Adele Lubell*

See also Bacon, Francis; Bioethics; Darwin, Charles Robert; Descartes, René; Environmental ethics; Hume, David; Manhattan Project; Military ethics; Nazism; Psychology.

BIBLIOGRAPHY

Bell, Robert. *Impure Science: Fraud, Compromise and Political Influence in Scientific Research.* New York: John Wiley & Sons, 1992. The author claims to document how some members of the scientific community have fostered influence, misconduct, and fraud in scientific research. The volume is most valuable for its account of some less-well-known examples of alleged fraud or misconduct.

Committee on Science, Engineering, and Public Policy (U.S.). Panel on Scientific Responsibility and the Conduct of Research. *Responsible Science: Ensuring the Integrity of the Research Process.* 3 vols. Washington, D.C.: National Academy Press, 1992-1993. A comprehensive volume that attempts to delineate issues around integrity in science research and devise appropriate procedures for dealing with misconduct.

Dingell, J. D. "Shattuck Lecture: Misconduct in Medical Research." *New England Journal of Medicine* 328 (June 3, 1993): 1610-1615. Congressman Dingell is best known for his role as chairman of the Subcommittee on Oversight and Investigations of the U.S. House of Representatives. Dingell played a major role in governmental investigation into scientific misconduct in the late 1980's and early 1990's. The article is the address he gave to the Massachussetts Medical Society in Boston in May 1992.

Gillies, Donald. *Philosophy of Science in the Twentieth Century.* Cambridge, Mass.: Blackwell Scientific, 1993. The author discusses some important trends in the philosophy of science in the twentieth century. He particularly focuses on the ideas of Karl Popper, with whom Gillies studied during the late 1960's.

Martino, J. P. *Science Funding.* New Brunswick, N.J.: Transaction, 1992. This volume documents the history and current status of trends in the funding of scientific research, from Vannevar Bush to the present.

Mosedale, F. E., ed. *Philosophy and Science.* Englewood Cliffs, N.J.: Prentice-Hall, 1979. Includes the writings of philosophers, scientists, and others on important issues in science. Many selections discuss ethical and moral concerns. A drawback of the collection is that readings from the 1980's and 1990's are not included.

National Academy of Sciences. Committee on the Conduct of Science. *On Being a Scientist.* Washington, D.C.: National Academy Press, 1989. A booklet that offers the beginning and active scientist an introduction to the ethos of science.

Scorched-earth policies

TYPE OF ETHICS: Military ethics

DATE: First described by Herodotus in 440 B.C.E.

DEFINITION: Destruction of the natural environment, particularly food resources, as a deliberate means of waging warfare

SIGNIFICANCE: Places humankind's long-term responsibility for the environment in conflict with short-term national advantage, and raises the issue of the morality of bringing the impact of war home to noncombatants

In its narrow sense of setting the grass of the plains on fire, the practice of scorched-earth warfare is particularly associated with the steppelands of Russia and the Ukraine. The first attested example of the practice occurred during a war between the Scythians and the Persians in 512 B.C.E. (recorded by Herodotus in 440 B.C.E.). The Scythians, a nation of nomadic horsemen, lured the Persian army of Darius ever deeper into the steppe by retreating before the Persians. Some Scythians then doubled back, destroying the grass and poisoning the wells along the Persians' original route, believing that this would prevent the Persian cavalry's escape (since their horses would be deprived of food). As the Scythians candidly recalled, however, their plan backfired. The Persians escaped by retracing their footsteps, despite the devastation they encountered.

Analogous tactics were used more than two millennia later. During the Russian retreat before the invading army of Napoleon Bonaparte in 1812, the Russians themselves burned Moscow and the croplands along the route of Napoleon's advance. When the tide of battle turned, the French army had to retreat through a devastated countryside that offered no food or shelter. This successful use of the scorched-earth policy as a patriotic and defensive tactic (enhanced by Leo Tolstoy's epic depiction of Russian sacrifices during 1812 in his historical novel *War and Peace*, 1867-1869) lent it an enduring positive aura, at least in the Russian context.

More typically, however, scorched-earth tactics used defensively have backfired. If one goes along with environmentalist Arthur Westing's interpretation that deliberate destruction of the land by other means, such as flooding, is also scorched-earth policy (*Warfare in a Fragile World—Military Impact on the Human Environment*, 1980), then the most cataclysmic example in the twentieth century occurred during the Second Sino-Japanese War (1937-1945). In 1938, as a defensive measure, the Chinese dynamited a major dam on the Yellow River. This temporarily halted the Japanese advance and resulted in several thousand Japanese casualties; in the long run, however, several hundred thousand Chinese, mainly civilians, drowned, and damage from flooding continued for a decade.

Scorched-earth tactics used offensively have tended to be successful in the short run. Major incidents of deliberate crop destruction as a means of offensive warfare have abounded throughout history. During the Peloponnesian War (431-404 B.C.E.), the Spartans repeatedly destroyed the Athenian grain crops (and, not incidentally, won the war); the Athenians did not choose to employ a tactic that until then had been used only by barbarians. Widespread crop destruction, in large part deliberate, accompanied the ravages of the Huns, the Vandals, and the Mongolian conquests (1213-1224). The Mongolian conquerors of Mesopotamia destroyed the ancient irrigation works on which agriculture had depended for millennia, and the Fertile Crescent became a desert. In the Thirty Years' War (1618-1638), the majority of Czech casualties (up to 75 percent of the population of Bohemia) resulted from starvation and disease caused by crop destruction.

The use of scorched-earth tactics increased in the modern era, and it came to be morally justified as a humane means of bringing war to a swifter conclusion. The theory was formulated in the American context during the American Civil War (1861-1865) by two Union generals, Philip Sheridan and William Tecumseh Sherman. One of the many ways in which this war transformed civilization was an increased consideration of all factors that contributed to the war effort, including food itself. As part of a conscious policy of bringing the war home to the civilians who supported the soldiers, in order to make the war end quickly, Sheridan oversaw the destruction of about 700,000 hectares of agricultural land in the Shenandoah Valley, and Sherman's troops laid waste to about 4 million hectares of rural Georgia (1864). As a result, the war did indeed end quickly. In view of the success of these tactics, they were incorporated into U.S. policy during the U.S.-Indian Wars (1865-1898) and again during U.S. intervention in the Philippine Insurrection (1899-1903).

The apotheosis of the scorched-earth policy as a fast way to end a war, justified by the idea that there would be fewer total casualties, was the atomic bombing of Hiroshima and Nagasaki in Japan in 1945. This action immediately ended Japanese participation in World War II, but it raised ethical questions that cannot be easily answered.

The ultimate scorched-earth policy would be a nuclear war, after which the affected parts of the earth would be so scorched as to be uninhabitable for thousands of years. The ultimate scorched-earth policy thus brings one back to the discovery made by the cunning Scythians who may be credited with inventing it in the first place: It tends to backfire. Defenders who employ the tactic find that they have a tiger by the tail: Both immediately and in the long run, they may do far more damage to themselves than to the invading enemy. Those who employ scorched-earth tactics offensively stand to lose on many counts: They put themselves in an extremely weak position in world opinion, since the policy will justifiably be termed barbaric; they are destroying the earth's resources, thereby impoverishing themselves as well as others; and they are moving in the direction of total war, which tends to blur distinctions not only between combatants and noncombatants but also between the opposing sides. —*D. Gosselin Nakeeb*

See also Bioethics; Means/ends distinction; Military ethics; War and peace.

BIBLIOGRAPHY

Chandler, D. G. *The Campaigns of Napoleon.* New York: Macmillan, 1966.

Levandowsky, Michael. "Environmental Consequences of Nuclear War." In *Security vs. Survival: The Nuclear Arms Race*, edited by Theresa C. Smith & Indu B. Singh. Boulder,

Colo.: Lynne Rienner, 1985.

Liddell Hart, B. H. *Sherman: Soldier, Realist, American.* New York: Dodd, Mead, 1929.

Nash, J. R. *Darkest Hours: A Narrative Encyclopedia of Worldwide Disasters from Ancient Times to the Present.* Chicago: Nelson-Hall, 1976.

Westing, A. H., ed. *Environmental Warfare: A Technical, Legal, and Policy Appraisal.* London: Taylor & Francis, 1984.

_____, *Warfare in a Fragile World: Military Impact on the Human Environment.* London: Taylor & Francis, 1980.

Scott v. Sandford

TYPE OF ETHICS: Modern history
DATE: 1857
ASSOCIATED WITH: U.S. Supreme Court
DEFINITION: The Court placed limits on Congress' ability to control slavery and ruled that African Americans were not eligible to become U.S. citizens
SIGNIFICANCE: The decision strengthened slaveholders' claims that they had unlimited property rights to slaves

Scott v. Sandford was the result of a suit for freedom by the slave Dred Scott. Scott's master had taken Scott to serve him during an army posting in the northern part of the Louisiana Purchase, where slavery had been prohibited by Congress. Eventually, Scott's master returned Scott to the slave state of Missouri. Scott sued for his freedom on the basis of his residence in a territory where slavery did not exist. Chief Justice Roger B. Taney ruled that Scott was still a slave and that Congress had no authority to prohibit slavery in American territories. Congress had denied southerners "due process of law" under the Fifth Amendment by singling out their property, and not that of northerners, for restriction. Furthermore, Taney ruled, the case was not properly before the Supreme Court. No person of African descent—whether slave or free—was a citizen of the United States with rights to bring suit in federal court. This case strengthened the power of slaveholders and undercut antislavery activists who were seeking a general abolition of slavery in U.S. territories.

See also Bill of Rights, U.S.; Citizenship; Civil rights; Slavery.

Scottsboro case

TYPE OF ETHICS: Race and ethnicity
DATE: 1932
ASSOCIATED WITH: U.S. Supreme Court
DEFINITION: The Court held that states must provide counsel for indigent or ignorant defendants in capital cases
SIGNIFICANCE: The Court held for the first time that a state criminal trial was defective under the due process clause of the Fourteenth Amendment because deprivation of counsel in a capital case denies the defendant a fair hearing

The Scottsboro case (*Powell v. Alabama*) was one of several

A scene from one of the Scottsboro trials. (National Archives)

sensational cases that arose from the arrest and trial of seven young black men for the rape of two white women in Alabama. The men were quickly tried and sentenced to death in an atmosphere of great public excitement; units of the Alabama National Guard had to be called up to prevent the defendants from being lynched. At trial, no effective assignment or employment of counsel had been made, as the Supreme Court later found. The Court, by a vote of 7-2, decided that the trial court's failure to assure effective representation of the defendants had deprived them of a fair hearing. Since notice and hearing are the central elements of due process, the convictions were reversed. This case provided a particularly significant precedent because the Court showed itself willing for the first time to invoke the due process clause of the Fourteenth Amendment to hold that a state criminal proceeding had deprived a defendant of a fundamental right.

See also Civil rights; Due process.

Second Sex, The: Book
TYPE OF ETHICS: Sex and gender issues
DATE: Published 1949 as *Le Deuxième Sexe*
AUTHOR: Simone de Beauvoir
SIGNIFICANCE: The text, an attempt to explain why women as a class remain oppressed, rejects the essentialist view that gender traits are dependent upon biology

Beauvoir rejects the Aristotelian position that women, because of their biological characteristics, must play a limited role in society. She further rejects Freudian psychology's position that woman's natural state is passive while man's is active because of the physical characteristics of the genitalia. She posits that women are limited primarily by the conditioning imposed on them by a male-dominated society, not by any biologic weakness or inferiority. Because the behavior of human beings is based in large part on rationality and choice, instead of on instinct, Beauvoir suggests that human behavior is not fixed and immutable but should be based on the individual's rational decision to behave in a particular way in a given situation. Beauvoir then expands on that stance, using Sartre's belief that to be fully human, each person must be free to choose what he or she will become and that the process of choosing never ends. She further asserts that the sexual identity assigned to girls by modern Western society, which prepares them primarily to become wives, mothers, and housewives, destroys women's creative potential and leads to self-alienation and destruction of the psyche.

See also Sexism; Sexual stereotypes.

Secular ethics
TYPE OF ETHICS: Theory of ethics
DATE: c. 450 B.C.E. to present
DEFINITION: The theory that ethical principles originate in nature
SIGNIFICANCE: Denies the validity of appeals to supernatural sources for ethics

"If God is dead, then everything is permitted." Toward the end of the nineteenth century, Fyodor Dostoevski expressed his despair at the disrepute into which religious ethics had fallen. The enormous prestige of science had led many thinkers to believe that science had supplanted religion as the proper source of answers to questions about the universe and humanity's place in it. Ethics, many believed, should follow the path of other disciplines—such as astronomy, physics, and biology—

and become secular; that is, shorn of its traditional religious context.

Traditional religious ethics claim that without a god, ethics is meaningless. Three considerations motivate this claim. First, the fact that humans have argued about ethics for several millennia without reaching agreement is evidence that humans are not able to discover, by their own efforts, what is good and bad. Second, the fact that many people do things that they believe are unethical is evidence that humans are weak by nature and therefore are not competent to be good by their own efforts. Third, the fact that many evil-doers are never brought to justice is evidence that humans are not competent to administer justice effectively. Without a god, therefore, humans would wallow in ignorance and sin, and evil would often triumph over good. Accordingly, the religious account argues, a being greater than humanity—a powerful, knowledgeable, and good being—is needed to tell humans what to do, to make sure they do it, and to administer ultimate justice.

Criticisms of Religion. One major difficulty of the religious view is proving the existence of a god. Even supposing that the existence of a god could be proved, however, religion still would face serious difficulties. For, even if there is reason to believe there is a god, why should humans do what that god says?

The fact that the god was powerful would not guarantee that what it said was in fact good, for it could be both powerful and evil or both powerful and uninformed. To do what it says simply because it ordered one to do so would be to commit a logical fallacy—the appeal to force.

The fact that the god was knowledgeable also would not be a sufficient guarantee—for it could be both knowledgeable and evil—and to do what it says simply because it is knowledgeable would be to appeal to authority.

Finally, that the god is good cannot be determined without circularity, for the religious approach claims that humans do not know what is good before the god tells them so; they would have to know what was good, however, before they could judge whether the god was good and therefore whether they could trust its commands. If humans can distinguish good and evil, then they do not need a god to tell them which is which, but if humans cannot distinguish good and evil, then they have no way of knowing whether a god is telling them to do good things or bad things.

According to these objections, religion fails to ground ethics rationally. Advocates of religion may reject rationality and fall back on faith, but irrational faith is a precarious thing. Without evidence, one has no way of knowing whether one's faith is true, and therefore one has no way of knowing whether the principles upon which one acts are moral. Since different individuals believe different things on the basis of faith, faith leads to social difficulties. Without appealing to rationality and evidence, members of different faiths cannot resolve disagreements peacefully. History provides ample evidence that disagreements over articles of faith regularly lead to violence.

The above epistemological criticisms are sometimes supplemented by criticisms of the central content of religious ethics. By placing the sources of value in a supernatural realm, religion devalues life on earth. Evidence for this view can be found in the fact that virtually all religions emphasize sacrifice rather than achievement, suffering rather than pleasure, and self-denial rather than self-affirmation.

Secular Sources. These criticisms of religious ethics have given impetus to secular accounts of ethics. By appealing to natural phenomena, secular approaches try to solve the problems that have traditionally motivated religious ethics.

One such problem is finding a source for universal ethical principles; that is, principles that are true for everyone. Religion attempts to solve this problem by claiming that a god establishes rules and stipulates that they hold for everyone. Some secular theorists (relativists) attempt to solve this problem by rejecting the assumption that there are universal ethical principles. Relativists argue that ethics is based on individual or group feelings or traditions. If ethics is primarily a matter of feeling, however, then the obvious fact that feelings vary radically rules out universality. If ethics is primarily a matter of social traditions, history and anthropology provide evidence of a wide range of radically different social traditions.

Other secular theorists, however, accept the challenge of finding a universal source for values by identifying natural facts that are universal. For example, some theorists (Hedonists) note that all humans have a pleasure/pain mechanism, and therefore they argue that people should define "good" and "bad" in terms of pleasure and pain. Other theorists (the Kantians) note that all humans have a rational faculty, and therefore they argue that morality should be defined in terms of the rational consistency of action. Other theorists (objectivists) note that all humans have the same fundamental survival needs, and therefore they argue that people should define "bad" in terms of what leads to death and "good" in terms of that which makes human life possible.

—*Stephen R. C. Hicks*

See also Aristotle; Existentialism; God; Hedonism; Kant, Immanuel; Mill, John Stuart; Nietzsche, Friedrich; Rand, Ayn; Relativism; Religion; Sartre, Jean-Paul.

BIBLIOGRAPHY

Smith, George. *Atheism: The Case Against God.* Buffalo, N.Y.: Prometheus, 1979.

Warnock, Mary. *Existentialist Ethics.* New York: St. Martin's Press, 1967.

Sedition

TYPE OF ETHICS: Politico-economic ethics

DATE: Alien and Sedition Acts passed in the United States in 1798

DEFINITION: Sedition is the crime of inciting the public to change the government by unlawful means

SIGNIFICANCE: The crime of sedition as it originated in England encompassed defamation of the royal family or the government or the inciting of rebellion; so broad a definition of the crime necessarily implicates the freedoms of conscience and speech

The first sedition laws in the United States were the Alien and Sedition Acts of 1798, which were passed during the administration of John Adams. These laws defined sedition very broadly; many believed them to be unconstitutional. They were certainly impolitic and unpopular, and they were repealed under the Jefferson administration in 1801. In the United States today, sedition consists of advocacy of the illegal or violent overthrow of the government; it is more than mere defamation of the government or government officials. Because the essence of sedition is speech or publication, the crime as it is defined in most American jurisdictions always involves free speech issues. By the latter part of the twentieth century, rules set by the U.S. Supreme Court made it nearly impossible to convict anyone of sedition unless the government could show that the defendant's speech or publication explicitly advocated illegal acts and that it created a "clear and present danger" that the acts would take place. These rules place so heavy a burden on the prosecution that there were no successful federal sedition prosecutions in the United States between 1953 and 1993.

See also Constitution, U.S.; First Amendment; Sedition Act of 1798.

Sedition Act of 1798

TYPE OF ETHICS: Media ethics

DATE: 1798

ASSOCIATED WITH: President John Adams

DEFINITION: One of four "Alien and Sedition Acts" designed to suppress domestic opposition to Federalist policies during a period of European anti-American aggression

SIGNIFICANCE: Challenged the First Amendment rights of free speech and a free press, an attempt that ultimately served to broaden the scope of both concepts and limit governmental restraint of political dissent

The Sedition Act was prompted by Federalist fears that growing Republican opposition to Federalist policy would weaken popular support and lead to the end of Federalist control at a time when the United States was caught between rival international powers. The Act sought to apply the English common-law tradition of "seditious libel" by making it unlawful to "write, print, utter, or publish . . . any false, scandalous, or malicious writing . . . against the government of the United States . . . or to bring [it] . . . into contempt or disrepute." On that basis, ten newspaper editors were convicted, one of them a Congressman, by courts made up exclusively of Federalist judges. Advocates justified the Act by interpreting the First Amendment as pertaining only to "prior restraint," meaning that the government could not prevent the publication of dissent but could prosecute the result. Opponents protested that the First Amendment prevented the government from sup-

pressing political speech at any stage, and they pronounced the Act unconstitutional. Republican opposition was carried out through the Kentucky and Virginia Resolutions (written by Thomas Jefferson and James Madison, respectively), which asserted the right of states to "nullify" unwanted federal intrusions on individual rights. The Act expired with the inauguration of Thomas Jefferson, and no subsequent attempt to suppress political dissent has ultimately been successful.

See also Constitution, U.S.; First Amendment; Freedom of expression; Politics; Sedition.

Segregation

TYPE OF ETHICS: Race and ethnicity; Civil rights; Legal and judicial ethics

ASSOCIATED WITH: Race and ethnic relations

DEFINITION: Physical separation of one group from another

SIGNIFICANCE: Segregation of minorities in the United States was a negative social and economic practice that kept the country from achieving "liberty, freedom, and equality," promises upon which the nation was founded; the practice consigned millions of people to "second class" citizenship

Segregation, historically, was born in the colonial era when the "majority" practiced de facto segregation. When most blacks were slaves, free blacks suffered de facto segregation in housing and social segregation based on "custom" and "folkways." As the Northern colonies abolished slavery, de facto segregation sometimes became de jure separation supported by local ordinances and/or state law.

As long as the South maintained slavery, that institution "regulated" race relations, and de jure segregation was not needed. In 1865, however, the Southern slaves were set free and legal segregation made its appearance. After the Civil War, most Southern states passed legislation known as Black Codes, which resembled the old Slave Codes. Under the new codes, social segregation was often spelled out. For example, most states moved immediately to segregate public transportation lines. By the end of Reconstruction (1865-1877), race lines had hardened, and social segregation was the rule rather than the exception.

Unsuccessful Challenges. Some African Americans challenged segregationist laws. In 1896, blacks from Louisiana sued a public transportation company (railroad) that operated segregated passenger cars, as stipulated by Louisiana's state laws. Black leaders argued that the state laws and the railroad's actions violated the Thirteenth and Fourteenth Amendments to the Constitution. The case, *Plessy v. Ferguson*, reached the United States Supreme Court, which ruled that segregation was "legal" as long as "separate but equal" facilities were made available for minorities. A lone dissenter, Justice John M. Harlan, who happened to be a white Southerner, rejected the majority opinion, saying that the Constitution should be "color-blind" and that it should not tolerate "classes" among the citizens, who were all equal.

Despite Harlan's dissent, the *Plessy* decision gave abso-

Segregated entrances such as this stairway at a Mississippi movie theater were common before the civil rights movement of the 1950's and 1960's. (Library of Congress)

lute legal sanction to a practice that many states, including some in the North, were already practicing by custom and tradition—*Plessy* "froze" segregation into the highest law of the land. Thereafter, segregationists, especially those in the South, used their legislatures to pass a host of new laws that extended the supposed "separate but equal" doctrine to all areas of life. For example, restaurants, hotels, and theaters became segregated by law, not only by custom. Railroad cars and railroad stations divided the races; hospitals, doctors' offices, and even cemeteries became segregated. Some Southern state laws called for segregated prisons, while prisons in other states took criminals from both races but separated them within the facility. At least one state passed a law that forbade a white and a black prisoner to look out the same prison window at the same time. If the prisoners were physically close enough to look out at the same time, they were too close to please segregationists.

As the United States matured during the twentieth century, segregation was extended whenever "technology" made it seem necessary. For example, in 1915, Oklahoma became the first state in the Union to require segregated public "pay" telephone booths. When motor cars were first used as a "taxi" service, taxi companies were segregated—a "white" taxi serving whites only and a "black" taxi serving African Americans only. Public water fountains became segregated, as did public restroom facilities.

Another problem became associated with segregation. Often, there was *no* separate facility for blacks, who were denied service altogether. For example, as late as the 1960's, President Lyndon B. Johnson's personal maid and butler-handyman experienced difficulty traveling by car from Washington, D.C., back to Johnson's Texas home. There were few if any "motels" along the way that would rent rooms to African Americans.

Successful Challenges. Eventually, the National Association for the Advancement of Colored People (NAACP) launched new attacks against segregationist laws—especially in circumstances in which no separate facilities existed for African Americans.

For example, in *Gaines v. Missouri* (1938) and *Sweatt v. Painter* (1949; a Texas case), the Supreme Court ruled that blacks could attend white law schools because no separate school was available *in state* for African Americans. In 1950, in *McLaurin v. Oklahoma*, the NAACP tested the same concept and won another court battle. As *McLaurin* showed, the University of Oklahoma had admitted a black student to its graduate program but then had segregated him on campus. After the high court ruled that such segregation was unfair and illegal because it denied "equal" education, Thurgood Marshall of the NAACP became even more determined to challenge segregation. He did so successfully when, in *Brown v. Board of Education of Topeka* (1954), the Court declared segregated public education illegal.

If segregation was unjust and unconstitutional in education, it seemed clear that it was also unjust in other areas of life. Thus, in 1955, under the leadership of Martin Luther King, Jr., and others, a nonviolent protest movement took to the streets and eventually won victories that included new laws such as the Civil Rights Act of 1964 and the Voter Registration Act of 1965.

Ultimately, a limited social and economic "revolution" occurred that condemned segregation and, in part, created a new American society. —*James Smallwood*

See also Apartheid; Bigotry; Caste system, Hindu; Integration; Racial prejudice; Racism; Slavery.

BIBLIOGRAPHY

Blauner, Bob. *Racial Oppression in America.* New York: Harper & Row, 1972.

Branch, Taylor. *Parting the Waters: America in the King Years, 1954-1963.* New York: Simon & Schuster, 1988.

Feagin, Joe R., and Clairece Booner Feagin. *Racial and Ethnic Relations.* 4th ed. Englewood Cliffs, N.J.: Prentice-Hall, 1993.

Forman, James. *The Making of Black Revolutionaries.* 2d ed. Washington, D.C.: Open Hand, 1985.

Garrow, David J., ed. *We Shall Overcome: The Civil Rights Movement in the United States in the 1950's and 1960's.* 3 vols. Brooklyn, N.Y.: Carlson, 1989.

Powledge, Fred. *Free at Last? The Civil Rights Movement and the People Who Made It.* Boston: Little, Brown, 1991.

Sitkoff, Harvard. *The Struggle for Black Equality, 1954-1992.* New York: Hill & Wang, 1993.

Self-control

TYPE OF ETHICS: Personal and social ethics
DATE: Seventh century B.C.E. to present
ASSOCIATED WITH: Stoicism; virtue ethics

DEFINITION: The reasoned, disciplined moderation of passion and behavior so as to avoid harmful or immoral excess

SIGNIFICANCE: A personal virtue fundamental to the accomplishment of goals and the development of other virtues

The concept of self-control as a modern moral and psychological trait is directly rooted in the Greek concept of *sōphrosynē*, which is usually translated as "temperance," although there is no exact English equivalent. Although a number of concepts capture facets of what the Greeks meant by *sōphrosynē*—balance, limit, proportion, order, equilibrium, harmony, restraint, moderation, sobriety—none defines it completely. Yet the concept of self-control, complemented by self-knowledge, lies at its core, being a virtue crucial to the achievement of order and moderation in life. In contrast to it is *hybris*, the vice of arrogance, excessive behavior, unrestrained passion, and other extremes.

Sōphrosynē was not only a personal virtue for the Greeks but a civic one as well; in addition to being a standard of individual behavior and character, it was, especially for Athenians, a measure of the political and social health of the *polis*, lying between the extremes of tyranny and anarchy. Just as the individual was responsible for maintaining the proper order among the elements of the soul by means of the intelligent control of its baser parts, the rulers were responsible for maintaining the proper order among the various segments of society by the wise governance of its lower echelons. Plato utilizes this concept of self-control in his *Republic*. An individual must control the influence of spirit (feelings) and passion (desire) by subjecting them to the constraints of reason (intelligence), the highest element of the soul. The philosopher-king, using the judgment that comes from philosophical wisdom, must maintain order among the lower elements of society so that the self-control proper to a virtuous individual is amplified in the polis as a whole.

Aristotle understands self-control, the virtue of "temperance," more narrowly. In the *Nicomachean Ethics*, self-control is marked by the disciplined enjoyment of eating, drinking, and sexual intercourse, as opposed to the correlative vices of excessive indulgence and insufficient sensitivity to physical pleasure. Although Aristotle cites temperance as a separate virtue, however, it possesses a generic component that is fundamental to the other virtues as well. Every Aristotelian virtue requires self-control. For example, courage is the exercise of bravery in the right way at the right time for the right reason and to the right degree. To misjudge the proper measure of courage—to be brave to the point of foolhardiness, or to be cowardly when courage is required—is to be wrongly controlled by either ambition on the one hand or fear on the other, which happens when one loses control over oneself and allows intelligent judgment to be subdued by one's nonrational faculties.

Sōphrosynē was central to Stoic moral teaching during the Hellenistic period. The Stoics viewed it as essentially the exercise of wise and practical judgment in matters of indulgence and abstinence, preserving the traditional Greek association between sōphrosynē and self-control. The Romans eventually absorbed sōphrosynē into their ethical canon, where it figures prominently in the writings of Cicero, who identifies *temperantia*, or "self-control," as its most important component and contrasts it to *luxuria* United States ("excess") and *avaritia* (greed), which he believed were the worst vices of Roman citizens. Early Christianity, although at first eschewing anything associated with paganism, eventually assimilated sōphrosynē, along with other classical virtues, into its own ethical structure, since these virtues were consistent with Christian ethics. Christians made chastity the defining feature of sōphrosynē, however, almost eclipsing its other aspects.

Sōphrosynē was absorbed by the modern mind in essentially its original Greek form, with a continued emphasis on self-control. It is recognizable in Michel de Montaigne's essay "Of Husbanding Your Will," in which Montaigne extols the virtues of a moderate lifestyle: "One must moderate oneself between hatred of pain and love of pleasure; and Plato prescribes a middle way of life between the two." Undue absorption with personal and public affairs is to be avoided if one wishes to live serenely. In addition, the more possessions one acquires, the more likely one is to suffer the bad luck that is an inherent aspect of material acquisition and ownership. One's energy should be expended chiefly on what one can control; namely, oneself and one's personal affairs: "The range of our desires should be circumscribed and restrained to a narrow limit . . . and moreover their course should be directed not in a straight line that ends up elsewhere, but in a circle whose two extremities . . . terminate in ourselves." Balance and moderation are the keys to tranquillity.

Because of its inward, quasi-psychological nature, self-control, like some of the other traditional virtues of character, has been largely neglected by most modern philosophers. Some thinkers, however, have attempted to reinstate consideration of the traditional virtues as an essential feature of moral discourse. Anthony Quinton (1993), for example, defines moral character as self-control or self-discipline, which is required to maintain one's determination toward a goal and to avoid being distracted by "passing impulses" and unproductive pursuits. It is the essential element in moral development, even though the self-control necessary to good moral character may be used for bad purposes as well. According to Quinton, modern people would do well to emulate the vigorous moral rectitude of the Victorians, whose incorporation of self-control into their character made them worthy models of moral uprightness.   —*Barbara Forrest*

See also Character; Stoic ethics; Temperance; Virtue ethics.

BIBLIOGRAPHY

Aristotle. "Nicomachean Ethics." In *Introduction to Aristotle*, edited by Richard McKeon. 2d rev. ed. Chicago: University of Chicago Press, 1973.

Montaigne, Michel de. "Of Husbanding Your Will."

Translated by Donald M. Frame. In *Great Books of the Western World*, edited by Mortimer J. Adler. 2d ed. Chicago: Encyclopaedia Britannica, 1990.

North, Helen F. "Temperance (Sōphrosynē) and the Canon of the Cardinal Virtues." In *Dictionary of the History of Ideas: Studies of Selected Pivotal Ideas*, edited by Philip P. Wiener. Vol. 4. New York: Charles Scribner's Sons, 1973.

Plato. "Charmides." In *The Collected Dialogues of Plato*, edited by Edith Hamilton and Huntington Cairns. Translated by Lane Cooper et al. Princeton, N.J.: Princeton University Press, 1984.

_____. "Republic." In *The Collected Dialogues of Plato*, edited by Edith Hamilton and Huntington Cairns. Princeton, N.J.: Princeton University Press, 1969.

Quinton, Anthony. "Character and Culture." In *Vice and Virtue in Everyday Life: Introductory Readings in Ethics*, edited by Christina Sommers and Fred Sommers. 3d ed. Forth Worth, Tex.: Harcourt Brace Jovanovich College Publishers, 1993.

Self-deception

TYPE OF ETHICS: Personal and social ethics

DATE: From antiquity

ASSOCIATED WITH: Social scientific studies of neurosis, unconscious motivation, self-attribution, and irrational action

DEFINITION: One deceives oneself by avoiding full acknowledgment of some important fact (about oneself or the world) that one tacitly admits, together with evading the recognition that one is doing so

SIGNIFICANCE: Self-deception can blind one to past moral transgressions, facilitate imminent immoral conduct, and prevent the achievement of authentic self-knowledge

A person is tempted to self-deceive whenever the reasons for accepting some thought as true are better than the reasons for not accepting it and the person does not want the thought to be true. If the individual in such a situation avoids acknowledging a fact that is supported by evidence because of the intimated advantage of doing so, then the person self-deceives. Since this act violates a basic principle of rational cognition (to assent to what is supported by the evidence), the self-deceiver will further self-deceive about the very activity of self-deceiving. Hence, people who in fact are deceiving themselves will vehemently deny to themselves and to others that they are doing so. In this general process, the person need not fully embrace utter falsehoods. Self-deception essentially occurs by avoiding the recognition of some important and well-supported conception. The person can be held accountable for this evasion because there is tacit awareness of the good reasons for not evading acknowledgment; "deep down," the self-deceiver "knows better." This paradoxical nature of being self-deceived is manifested in inconsistencies in conduct and in speech; on some occasions, action will be based on what is "really known," and on other occasions, it will be based on self-deception.

Self-deception is morally problematical for three reasons. First, it is a practice of untruthfulness, and to the extent that being truthful is inherently good, self-deception is always wrong. This is true even if the deceiving involves a morally neutral issue.

Second, deceiving oneself can have deleterious effects on one's conscience and the ability to understand oneself. Conscience is corrupted because self-deception (especially if it is habitual) can involve overlooking moral failures in one's past and avoiding consideration of moral obligations to which one is bound in the present. The ability to understand oneself is damaged because self-deception (again, especially if it is habitual) can direct attention away from realities of oneself that are important but are very difficult to accept.

Third, self-deceiving can have harmful effects on others. Being able to deceive oneself about a topic greatly facilitates deceiving others about that same topic (by masking from them one's own disbelief). In addition, deceiving oneself about the harm that one is causing for others makes it easier to harm them (by precluding scruples arising from one's own conscience). If this type of self-deceiving becomes habitual, then one can become completely oblivious to the harmful effects of one's conduct on others.

A prevalent type of self-deception with deleterious effects on self and others involves not taking responsibility for one's own actions. People tend to deceive themselves concerning how able they are to act in a manner other than the manner in which they act when they do something wrong. Shunning avowal of the immediately evident reality of their own free will, they focus instead on how "pressing" their needs and wants appear to be to them. This type of self-deceiving subverts the sense of being in control of one's own impulses, which in turn results in those impulses being less controlled. It thereby becomes likely that the individual does whatever he or she wants to do, in spite of obvious immorality and harm to others.

The diminishment in self-control brought on by chronic self-deception about one's own responsibility can also affect the degree of control that one has over the very impulse to deceive oneself. This in turn can make it difficult to distinguish voluntary self-deception from pathological self-delusion. In the latter case, the person is incapable of admitting the truth and is not subject to moral censure. Only if a person is able to abstain from self-deception and admit to the truth is the act of self-deception subject to moral evaluation. If it is controllable and wrong, it should be avoided.

In order to avoid deceiving oneself, one must be aware of the subjects about which there is temptation to deceive oneself. Since all people want to think highly of themselves and want to avoid making costly sacrifices, the strongest enticements to self-deceive arise when people assess their moral imperfections or are subject to demanding moral obligations. To prevent self-deception when one confronts such topics, it is necessary to keep clearly in mind the good of authentic self-understanding and the evils that can result from deceiving oneself. There are, however, issues about which a measure of self-deception could be harmless or even beneficial. For example, if one deceives oneself into thinking that one is less afraid than one actually is about delivering an impending public address, then one may be better able to deliver the speech. Nevertheless, in such situations, self-deception is rarely the only means available to achieve the beneficial results. Since self-deceiving can become a habit and habitual self-deception carries with it the dangers noted earlier, it is probably best to always avoid deceiving oneself. —*Mark Stephen Pestana*

See also Existentialism; Hypocrisy; Integrity; Lying; Sartre, Jean-Paul; Self-righteousness; Truth.

BIBLIOGRAPHY

McLaughlin, Brian P., and Amelie Oksenberg Rorty, eds. *Perspectives on Self-Deception.* Berkeley: University of California Press, 1988.

Martin, Mike W. *Self-Deception and Morality.* Lawrence: University Press of Kansas, 1986.

Mele, Alfred R. *Irrationality: An Essay on Akrasia, Self-Deception, and Self-Control.* Oxford, England: Oxford University Press, 1987.

Murphy, Gardner. *Outgrowing Self-Deception.* New York: Basic Books, 1975.

Sartre, Jean-Paul. *Being and Nothingness.* Translated by Hazel E. Barnes. New York: Washington Square Press, 1966.

Self-interest

TYPE OF ETHICS: Personal and social ethics
DATE: Fourth century B.C.E. to present
ASSOCIATED WITH: Seventeenth century British philosopher Thomas Hobbes
DEFINITION: A concept used to pick out those motives or reasons for acting that are beneficial to or to the advantage of the person (agent) performing the action; used in contrast to altruism
SIGNIFICANCE: Acting from self-interest is seen either as a legitimate ethical motive that is to be encouraged or as an illegitimate reason for acting that is to be avoided; any ethical theory must address this issue and adopt one of the two alternatives

Though Plato in his *Republic* was the first to raise the issue of the role that self-interest plays in ethics, it was Thomas Hobbes's treatment of the concept in *Leviathan* (1651) that cast the discussion of the relationship between ethics and self-interest in modern terms.

Varieties of Self-Interest. Philosophers generally speak of two kinds of self-interest: enlightened and unenlightened. This distinction is made by those who think that self-interest has a significant contribution to make to ethics. Interests can be classified as being either short-term or long-term, and sometimes what may be in one's short-term interest may not be in one's long-term interest. Short-term interests are those that are immediate consequences of the action performed and are of immediate benefit to the individual who is acting.

Long-term interests, however, are future consequences of the action, and the benefit to the individual may not matter for quite some time. Almost no one would advocate that one should pursue short-term interests exclusively. Rather, those who believe that self-interest and ethics are related encourage the pursuit of long-term interests. Emphasizing the pursuit of long-term as opposed to short-term interests is called enlightened (or rational) self-interest, while emphasizing the pursuit of short-term interests is called unenlightened self-interest.

Relationship of Self-Interest to Ethics. One can appreciate the different positions regarding the relationship between self-interest and ethics by reflecting on the answers to the following question. Do the demands of enlightened self-interest ever correspond to the dictates of ethics?

There is a theory of ethics that answers this question in the affirmative: egoism. This theory claims that self-interest plays a crucial role in determining ethically appropriate action. There are two kinds of egoism, depending in part on the role that is assigned to self-interest.

Psychological Egoism. This theory claims that human beings by their very nature must act in their own self-interest. According to this view, human beings cannot help but act in their own interest. That is how they are constituted.

Technically, this is not an ethical theory but rather a scientific or psychological theory about human nature. In fact, a psychological egoist would contend that ethics as traditionally conceived is impossible, since traditional ethics requires a person to act altruistically, to act in the interests of others, and human beings are simply psychologically incapable of doing that. Psychological egoism advocates that ethics should be revamped to take into account this important fact about human nature. Once this is done, the goal of this redefined ethics is to persuade people to pursue enlightened rather than unenlightened self-interest. Thomas Hobbes is the person most often associated with psychological egoism.

Ethical Egoism. The other brand of egoism is called ethical egoism. In contrast with psychological egoism, ethical egoism is a traditional ethical or normative theory that acknowledges that people have the ability to act altruistically. It contends that, although people can act in the interests of others, they should not. Ethical egoism claims that one should pursue one's enlightened self-interest exclusively. It contends that the only time one should take into consideration the interests of others is when it is in one's interest to do so.

A number of reasons have been offered by ethical egoists to explain why one should act in one's own self-interest. For one thing, it just makes good sense. People should know what is in their own interest better than they know what is in the interest of others, and it is always good to act on as much information as possible. For another, if everyone pursued his or her own interests exclusively and did not meddle in other people's business, everyone would be better off.

Two major branches of ethics—namely, utilitarianism and deontological ethics—answer the above question in the negative. They both claim that acting solely in the light of one's own self-interest is never ethically acceptable. They contend that one of the goals of an ethical theory is to persuade an agent to put aside self-interested pursuit, whether enlightened or not, and act altruistically. These groups, however, deal with self-interested behavior in different ways.

Utilitarianism. Utilitarianism claims that, in determining what the morally appropriate action is, one should take into consideration the interests of everyone who is affected by the action, and no one person's interest should count more than anyone else's. The right action is the one that will produce the greatest good for the greatest number of people. Notice that this theory still uses the concept of self-interest, though in a much-diminished capacity. One's interests do matter, but they matter only as much as everyone else's. This theory requires that one may have to sacrifice one's interest for the interests of others (the common good).

Deontological Theories. Both egoism and utilitarianism determine right and wrong by looking at the consequences of an action. Deontological theories look to something other than consequences to determine right and wrong. For that reason, these theories go a step further than utilitarianism does, banishing self-interest in any form. According to these theories, acting in self-interest automatically removes the agent from the ethical realm. Self-interest is something that must be controlled or defeated in order for true ethical behavior to take place.   —*John H. Serembus*

See also Altruism; Egoism; Hobbes, Thomas; Human nature; *Leviathan*.

BIBLIOGRAPHY

Edwards, Paul, ed. *The Encyclopedia of Philosophy*. New York: Macmillan, 1967.

Gauthier, David P., ed. *Morality and Rational Self-Interest*. Englewood Cliffs, N.J.: Prentice-Hall, 1970.

Hobbes, Thomas. *Leviathan: Or the Matter, Forme, and Power of a Commonwealth Ecclesiastical and Civil*. Edited by Michael Oakeshott. New York: Collier Books, 1962.

Olson, Robert. *The Morality of Self-Interest*. New York: Harcourt, Brace & World, 1965.

Rachels, James. *The Elements of Moral Philosophy*. 2d ed. New York: McGraw-Hill, 1993.

Self-love

TYPE OF ETHICS: Personal and social ethics

DATE: Fifth century B.C.E.

DEFINITION: The pursuit of actual or apparent goods for oneself

SIGNIFICANCE: Self-love is considered by different writers to be essential to an ethical life, to be the greatest opponent of ethics, or to lie somewhere between these extremes

The best approach to understanding the relationship between self-love and ethics is to study its history. Aristotle, in his *Nicomachean Ethics* (c. 330 B.C.E.), addresses the question of whether ethical or unethical persons love themselves more. His answer is that, although most people believe that unethical persons love themselves more than do ethical persons, precisely the opposite is actually true. He defends this position by making an analogy between self-love and the friendship of two persons. The type of friendship he has in mind is not a superficial one, but rather a strong relationship between two ethically mature persons. He identifies five characteristics of such a friendship: (1) wishing and doing what one believes to be good for the friend; (2) wishing the friend to continue living; (3) finding it pleasant to spend time with the friend; (4) desiring the same things as does the friend; and (5) sharing the friend's sorrows and joys.

Aristotle then writes that if one is ethical, one will have an analogous relationship with oneself: (1) wishing and doing what one believes to be good for oneself; (2) wishing oneself to continue living; (3) finding it pleasant to spend time with oneself; (4) having consistent desires; and (5) sharing one's own sorrows and joys consistently. Aristotle then contrasts this type of self-love with the self-love of one who is unethical: (1) wishing and doing for oneself what is pleasant to the senses, rather than what is good for oneself; (2) hating one's own life, because of painful memories of evil actions; (3) seeking the company of other persons in order to be distracted from the memory of past evil actions and the expectation of future evil actions; (4) having inconsistent desires; and (5) being torn by the internal conflict of both regretting one's evil actions and remembering them as pleasurable.

Aristotle goes on to explain that most people have false beliefs about self-love. There is a sense in which "selfish" people, those who seek the greatest share of such contested goods as money, honors, and bodily pleasures for themselves, love themselves. This is what most people mean by "self-love." It is, however, an inferior type of self-love that deserves condemnation. In contrast, persons who sacrifice the inferior goods of money, honors, and bodily pleasures in order to benefit others are the ones who genuinely love themselves. Aristotle believes that this is true even in the case of what most people consider the ultimate sacrifice: that of one's life. He maintains that the true self-lover prefers dying in defense of friends and country to living a long life with the memory of having been a coward.

These two types of self-love, sometimes distinguished from each other and sometimes not, appear frequently within post-Aristotelian discussions of ethics. For example, both of the following passages are found in Saint Augustine's *City of God* (426):

> The two cities were created by two kinds of love: the earthly city was created by self-love reaching the point of contempt for God, the Heavenly City by the love of God carried as far as contempt of self.

God, our master, teaches two chief precepts, love of God and love of neighbor; and in them man finds three objects for his love: God, himself, and his neighbor; and a man who loves God is not wrong in loving himself.

Although one could conclude that Augustine is inconsistent, a more reasonable conclusion (perhaps supported by the fact that he uses different Latin words for "love" in the two passages) is that there is a qualitative difference between the two self-loves.

In more recent ethical theory, however, the trend is toward viewing self-love as being opposed to ethics. Joseph Butler, in his *Fifteen Sermons Preached at the Rolls Chapel*, maintains that both the "principle of benevolence" and the "principle of self-love" are natural to human persons. Furthermore, he does not see them as being in competition with each other: "Though benevolence and self-love are different; though the former tends most directly to public good, and the latter to private: yet they are so perfectly coincident, that the greatest satisfactions to ourselves depend upon our having benevolence in a due degree; and that self-love is one chief security of our right behavior toward society." He also states, however, that in his discussion of these two principles, "they must be considered as entirely distinct." He explains that "there can no comparison be made, without considering the things compared as distinct and different."

Though Butler argues at length that benevolence and self-love promote each other, many of his successors maintain that the two principles are indeed distinct and that they frequently oppose each other. This understanding of the relationship between self-love and ethics is quite different from Aristotle's. For Aristotle, people are confronted with the choice between loving themselves improperly and loving themselves properly. Because to love oneself properly is to love others, however, one does not have to choose between proper self-love and love of others. According to what has become the dominant position of eighteenth to twentieth century ethical theory, however, one is confronted with a choice between loving oneself and loving others. Although few writers hold that one should have no self-love, many argue that ethics requires that one decrease one's self-love and increase one's love for others.

One example of a twentieth century writer who is committed to what is now the dominant view is William K. Frankena. Despite the fact that both Saint Augustine and Joseph Butler were Christian bishops, and even though the mainstream of the Christian moral tradition has considered proper self-love to be the basis of obedience to the biblical command "love your neighbor as yourself," Frankena writes in *Ethics* (1973): "In the Judeo-Christian tradition, self-love, even of an enlightened kind, has generally been regarded as the essence of immorality, at least when it is made the primary basis of action and judgment." Although there is room to debate the meanings of "enlightened self-love" and "primary basis," Frankena's statement is at best misleading and at worst false.
—*David W. Lutz*

See also Altruism; Egoism; Prudence; Self-interest.

BIBLIOGRAPHY

Aristotle. *The Nicomachean Ethics*. Translated by J. E. C. Welldon. Buffalo, N.Y.: Prometheus Books, 1987.

Augustine, Saint, Bishop of Hippo. *The City of God*. Translated by Marcus Bods. New York: Modern Library, 1983.

Butler, Joseph. *Fifteen Sermons Preached at the Rolls Chapel and A Dissertation upon the Nature of Virtue*. London: G. Bell, 1964.

Sidgwick, Henry. *The Methods of Ethics*. 7th ed. Chicago: University of Chicago Press, 1962.

Thomas Aquinas, Saint. *The Summa Theologica*. Translated by Laurence Shapcote. 2d ed. Chicago: Encyclopaedia Britannica, 1990.

Self-preservation

TYPE OF ETHICS: Personal and social ethics

ASSOCIATED WITH: Stoicism, Thomas Aquinas, Thomas Hobbes, David Hume, and Immanuel Kant

DEFINITION: Activity in which a being works to perpetuate its existence

SIGNIFICANCE: The natural and instinctive inclination toward self-preservation is sometimes cited to support the contention that human life is of fundamental value

On July 20, 1993, Pennsylvania logger Don Wyman found himself trapped in the wilderness, his left leg broken and pinned underneath a fallen tree. For an hour, Wyman called for help and attempted to dig his leg out, both to no avail. Aware that he was continuing to lose blood from his injuries, the trapped logger began pursuing what he perceived to be his only chance to escape. Using a bootlace as a tourniquet, Wyman proceeded to amputate his leg just below the knee with a pocket knife. Thus freeing himself from the tree, he crawled two hundred yards up a steep slope to a bulldozer, drove the bulldozer some three hundred yards to his pickup truck, and drove the truck to a farm two miles away, where an ambulance was called.

The case of Don Wyman is a dramatic illustration of the drive for self-preservation that is a fundamental inclination of human nature. Interestingly, philosophers reflecting on this natural inclination have reached very different conclusions concerning its moral significance. Especially noteworthy in this regard is the contrast between the advocacy of suicide by Stoicism and the absolute prohibition of suicide by some schools of natural law morality.

Stoic philosophers such as Zeno of Citium (c. 340-265 B.C.E.) and Cleanthes of Assos (c. 303-232 B.C.E.) were committed to following the demands of nature and were equally aware of the inclination for self-preservation that permeates the natural order. In the case of human beings, they understood the inclination for self-preservation as a demand to perfect one's nature. Taking rationality to be definitive of human nature, the Stoics advocated the soul's complete governance by reason as the epitome of virtue. Strong passions and appetites, however, were symptomatic of a diseased soul and thus were regarded as states of mind that needed to be expunged in the quest to achieve true virtue. Because a soul's attachment to the affairs and goods of the external world is what causes it to be governed by emotions and desires, the Stoics prescribed a rational indifference to the vicissitudes of life. So strong was their commitment to this indifference that the Stoics saw the rational choice of one's own death as a morally legitimate expression of indifference to the affairs of the world, a conviction upon which both Zeno and Cleanthes are believed to have acted. Though it is not obviously inconsistent, it is at least ironic that a philosophy that recognizes the natural inclination toward self-preservation as a basic moral principle should come to the conclusion that suicide is a morally permissible option.

Also recognizing the natural inclination toward self-preservation, Thomas Aquinas (c. 1223-1274) and other natural law moralists reach the conclusion—in direct opposition to that of the Stoics—that it is always impermissible to commit suicide. According to the natural law ethics of Aquinas, God has created the natural order according to a plan and has placed within natural beings a tendency to work toward the fulfillment of that plan. Human beings, like all other natural beings, have divinely implanted inclinations that point the way to their fulfillment. Unlike other natural beings, however, human beings have been given the gift of freedom and thus can choose to act either in accordance with God's plan or in opposition to it. In order to live a virtuous life, then, human beings must reflect upon their God-given nature and freely act so as to fulfill that nature. Insofar as he viewed the drive for self-preservation as one of the fundamental inclinations of human nature, Aquinas arrived at the conclusion that it is always impermissible intentionally to terminate or shorten one's own life.

In order to understand fully Aquinas' position, it is important to note that he did think that there are circumstances in which it would be morally permissible to perform an action that one foresees will result in one's own death. For example, it would be morally praiseworthy for a soldier to throw himself or herself on a hand-grenade to save the lives of fellow combatants. That such cases do not contradict the absolute prohibition of suicide is found in the fact that a true case of suicide requires that one intend to kill oneself, whereas the heroic soldier intends only to save the lives of others and does not intend his or her own death.

One of the strongest objections to the natural law defense of an absolute moral prohibition of suicide is that formulated by the Scottish philosopher David Hume (1711-1776). Hume maintained that the inclination for self-preservation is not a fundamental inclination, because it is grounded in the more comprehensive inclination to achieve happiness. Therefore, suicide does not violate a human beings' natural inclinations if the continuance of the individual's life promises more hardship than happiness. —*James Petrik*

See also Euthanasia; Hume, David; Kevorkian, Jack; Self-interest; Stoic ethics; Thomas Aquinas.

BIBLIOGRAPHY

Beauchamp, Tom L., and Seymour Perlin, eds. *Ethical Issues in Death and Dying*. Englewood Cliffs, N.J.: Prentice-Hall, 1978.

Brody, Baruch A., ed. *Suicide and Euthanasia: Historical and Contemporary Themes*. Dordrecht: Kluwer, 1989.

Horan, Dennis J., and David Mall, eds. *Death, Dying, and Euthanasia*. Frederick, Md.: University Publications of America, 1980.

Kant, Immanuel. *The Moral Law: Kant's Groundwork of the Metaphysic of Morals*. Translated by H. J. Paton. London: Hutchinson, 1978.

Novak, David. *Suicide and Morality: The Theories of Plato, Aquinas, and Kant and Their Relevance for Suicidology*. New York: Scholars Studies, 1975.

Self-regulation

TYPE OF ETHICS: Business and labor ethics

DATE: A movement of the late nineteenth and twentieth centuries

ASSOCIATED WITH: The National Association of Securities Dealers (NASD), the American Institute of Certified Public Accountants (AICPA), and the Institute of Chartered Financial Analysts (ICFA)

DEFINITION: Self-regulation is an attempt by business and professional organizations to regulate the ethical conduct of their members, thereby avoiding or augmenting formal government regulation

SIGNIFICANCE: Self-regulation represents a voluntary commitment by individuals to adhere to a specific set of ethical standards

In the late nineteenth century, social critics began to promote increased government regulation of business, industry, and various professions. In an attempt to stave off additional government intrusion into commercial affairs, many Self-Regulatory Organizations (SROs) were formed. SROs function as private rule-making and enforcement bodies that govern the activities of their members. Exemplary among such SROs is the American Institute of Certified Public Accountants (AICPA), which was founded in 1887 to self-regulate the accounting profession. The AICPA states that its mission is to "provide standards of professional conduct and performance," "monitor professional performance," and "promote public confidence in the integrity, objectivity, competence, and professionalism" of public accountants. SROs such as the AICPA possess the power to censure or disbar their members from practice if they violate professional standards of conduct. Proponents of SROs contend that voluntary professional organizations are inherently more capable of encouraging ethical behavior than is a centralized government agency. Critics of SROs charge that the organizations merely act in the self-interest of their members rather than in the interest of society at large.

See also Professional ethics.

Self-respect

TYPE OF ETHICS: Personal and social ethics

DATE: Eighteenth century to present

ASSOCIATED WITH: The eighteenth century philosopher Immanuel Kant; modern moral psychology; and modern social, political, and ethical theory

DEFINITION: Recognition of and regard for one's dignity and intrinsic value as a human being and for the rights that one's humanity confers

SIGNIFICANCE: Regarded by Kant as the most important of one's duties to oneself and as the necessary condition for fulfilling one's duties to others

According to Immanuel Kant, self-respect is the most important of one's moral duties to oneself and is the prerequisite for the fulfillment of one's duties to others. To transgress this duty is to forfeit the intrinsic worth that one possesses as a human being. Being human confers upon one a uniquely significant status: One possesses the gift of reason, and only rational beings can engage in moral deliberation. Consequently, only rational beings can recognize the concept of duty and act in recognition of universal moral law. Since the moral law commands the respect of rational beings by virtue of its absolute power over them, each rational being must acknowledge and respect this power of recognition in every rational being. One owes one's fellow humans respect as rational, moral, beings; likewise, one owes oneself respect insofar as one is human and, therefore, rational and moral.

There are actions that result in the forfeiture of one's self-respect and the respect of others. Drunkenness robs a person of dignity insofar as it makes that person an object of ridicule, unable to act responsibly or to exercise the powers of rational deliberation. "Cringing servility" is likewise degrading, and it detracts from one's special status as human, as does lying. A liar, though possibly harming no one, becomes tainted by the intrinsic vileness of the lie. One who becomes the instrument or plaything of another, and who may do so for gain or profit, forfeits the respect that humans owe to themselves and to which they are entitled from others. Since all persons are equal by virtue of their common humanity, any act that places a person in a subservient position relative to someone else diminishes that person's self-respect. Accepting favors or charity places one in a permanently subordinate position relative to one's benefactor, a position in which the recipient remains even after repaying the debt. Suicide, however, is the most serious violation of one's duty to oneself because it constitutes the use of oneself as an instrument, a means to an end, violating the supreme moral duty to treat every human being, including oneself, as an end rather than a means. To end one's life, even to escape intolerable suffering, is an abuse of the ennobling freedom that gives humans the capacity for virtue. Finally, just as this freedom is the source of human virtue, so is it also the source of human depravity, which springs from actions that not only dehumanize the perpetrators but also degrade them below the level of animals. Such an action is the *crimen carnis contra naturam*, an unnatural crime of the flesh, exemplified by an offense so abominable that it arouses nausea and contempt in one who merely contemplates it. In the light of the potential for depravity through the abuse of humanity's freedom, each person has a special responsibility to use that freedom to bring credit to himself or herself as an individual representative of humanity, for when one degrades oneself individually, one degrades humanity as a whole. According to Kant, respect for humanity as exemplified in oneself reveals one's respect for the moral law.

From the standpoint of modern moral psychology, self-respect may be viewed as being somewhat different from "self-esteem." Whereas self-respect is rooted in the moral quality of one's character, self-esteem refers to a positive assessment of oneself that may come from traits such as appearance, personality, talents, and so forth. The difference is evident in the fact that a negative appraisal of oneself with respect to characteristics such as physical appearance or talent does not necessarily result in an unwillingness to recognize one's value and rights as a human being.

Self-respect, in addition to being an important theme in modern moral psychology, occupies a prominent place in the ethical thought of modern moral philosophers after Kant. Thomas Hill, Jr., allows self-respect to retain its Kantian significance when he contrasts it with servility. Servility, which is marked by a refusal to insist on respect from others and by a willingness to submit to public humiliation, is morally blameworthy when it springs from laziness, timidity, or the desire to retain some relatively unimportant advantage. The moral wrongness of this kind of servility results from the fact that in refusing to stand up for one's rights, one devalues oneself as a human being. In doing so, one devalues the moral law, which humans have a unique duty to uphold.

Self-respect serves as an important component in a well-ordered society, according to John Rawls in *A Theory of Justice* (1971). Rawls distinguishes self-respect as the most important primary good, a primary good being something that a rational individual would want regardless of the kind of life the person lives or whatever else that person wants. The just society, in recognizing the importance of each individual, provides a strong foundation for self-respect. A person who has a secure sense of self-worth is more likely to carry out life plans successfully, since the value of those plans is derived to a significant degree from the self-respect that comes from having one's personal value acknowledged by society.

—Barbara Forrest

See also Character; Dignity; Duty; Guilt and shame; Kant, Immanuel; Psychology.

BIBLIOGRAPHY

Darwall, Stephen L. "Two Kinds of Respect." In *Ethics and Personality: Essays in Moral Psychology*, edited by John Deigh. Chicago: University of Chicago Press, 1992.

Deigh, John. "Shame and Self-Esteem: A Critique." In *Ethics and Personality: Essays in Moral Psychology*. Chicago: University of Chicago Press, 1992.

Didion, Joan. "On Self-Respect." In *Slouching Towards Bethlehem*. New York: Noonday Press, 1990.

Hill, Thomas, Jr. "Servility and Self-Respect." In *Vice and Virtue in Everyday Life: Introductory Readings in Ethics*, edited by Christina Sommers and Fred Sommers. 3d ed. Fort Worth, Tex.: Harcourt Brace Jovanovich College Publishers, 1993.

Kant, Immanuel. *Lectures on Ethics*. Translated by Louis Infield. Edited by Lewis W. Beck. New York: Harper & Row, 1963.

Rawls, John. *A Theory of Justice*. Cambridge, Mass.: Belknap Press, 1971.

Self-righteousness

Type of ethics: Personal and social ethics
Date: Sixth century B.C.E. to present
Associated with: The Bible and numerous philosophers
Definition: Confidence in one's own righteousness, especially in comparison with others who are deemed unrighteous
Significance: The negative connotation often associated with the concept raises the question of whether one may properly think of oneself as moral through one's own efforts

Self-righteousness can be condemned as involving either or both of two moral faults: hypocrisy (one does not measure up to one's avowed standards) or pride (one treats others with disdain or makes ostentatious displays of one's accomplishments). In the first case, one's claim to being righteous is vitiated by unacknowledged moral faults; in the second case, by behavior toward other persons designed to make them feel inferior and/or to enhance one's own self-image by comparison. Christian thinking has typically opposed finding one's righteousness in oneself in favor of finding it through faith in Jesus. Self-righteousness can, however, be understood more positively as the reasonable conviction that one indeed does adhere of one's own will to a defensible moral code and thus deserves self-approval. Such self-approval, however, does not warrant requiring others to accept that judgment. Also, Jesus' condemnation of the Pharisees as hypocrites for attending to external rather than internal matters of law and morality (Matt. 23) points to the possibility of self-deception that is inherent in thinking of oneself as righteous.

See also Hypocrisy; Pride; Self-deception.

Selfishness

Type of ethics: Personal and social ethics
Associated with: The ethical theory of egoism and the twentieth century novelist and philosopher Ayn Rand
Definition: The concern with and pursuit of one's own interests and desires without regard to or in conflict with the interests and desires of others
Significance: Selfishness is a characteristic that is considered alien to ethical behavior and, hence, is something that ethical theories discourage

Selfishness is construed as a vice or character flaw. All one has to do to see this is to reflect on the common usage of the term. To be labeled "selfish" is to be censured and held in low regard. Such labeling is a condemnation. Ethical theorists also share this disdain, though Ayn Rand with her philosophical theory of objectivism may appear to be an exception. The role that selfishness plays in her ethical theory will be discussed below.

If someone is acting selfishly, that person is not acting ethically. Traditionally, the goals of ethics and those of selfishness are antithetical. Even those theories of ethics that advocate acting in one's own interest—namely, the various versions of egoism—would never endorse constant selfish behavior. For this reason, it will be helpful to explore the relationship between selfishness and self-interest.

Selfishness and Self-Interest. Are acting selfishly and acting self-interestedly identical? Critics of egoism, which is the ethical theory that claims that one should always act in one's own interest, answer this question in the affirmative. They find egoism morally repugnant because they find selfishness morally repugnant. Certainly, selfish behavior does involve some form of self-interested behavior. A selfish act is performed because the person expects to satisfy some current need or desire. Does self-interested behavior, however, necessarily involve selfish behavior? In other words, can there be behavior that is self-interested yet unselfish? Defenders of egoism say yes. For example, they insist that it is not in one's interest to act purely selfishly all the time, though there are some egoists who maintain that it is acceptable to act selfishly on occasion. Egoists distinguish between short-term and long-term self-interests.

Short-term Versus Long-term Interests. Short-term interests are those that are met immediately, while long-term interests are those that will be satisfied in the future. When one acts selfishly, one is acting on the basis of short-term self-interests exclusively. When one acts selfishly, one does not take into account the impact of the pursuit of one's short-term interests on others; hence, one does not take into account the impact on one's own long-term interests. Since interfering with others in their pursuit of their interests may lead them to hinder one's own pursuit of future interests, such interference may have a negative impact on one's long-term interests. What this means, then, is that acting selfishly, though it is in one's short-term interest to do so, may have consequences that will hinder the pursuit of one's long-term interests. Conversely, it may be in one's long-term interest to act unselfishly, since acting unselfishly would not anger others and would give them no reason to interfere with one's future goals. Thus, an egoist could simultaneously advocate the exclusive pursuit of self-interest and avoid the charge of selfishness by insisting that it is the pursuit of one's long-term as opposed to short-term self-interest that is at the heart of egoism. Aiming for the long-term is described as acting in one's rational self-interest. This means that it is not generally rational to act selfishly, although an egoist could still advocate selfish behavior as long as that behavior did not interfere with one's long-term interests.

Ayn Rand and Objectivism. In *The Virtue of Selfishness* (1961), Ayn Rand seems to be contradicting the claim made at the start that ethics views selfish behavior with disdain and contempt. It seems that she encourages selfish behavior, believing that it is at the core of true ethical behavior. By calling selfishness a virtue, she seems to be sanctioning that kind of behavior.

It turns out, however, that her position is not far from that of the ethical mainstream. Her title is intended to capture and hold the reader's attention. As a title for a treatise on ethics it is misleading. What she is really advocating is that the definition of selfishness should be stripped of all its negative connotations. She suspects that there has been some kind of moral conspiracy on the part of the ethics of altruism, which advocates that one needs sometimes to put one's own interests aside and act for the interests of others, and which demeans and belittles anyone who dares to act in his or her own interest exclusively.

The goal of her theory, known as objectivism, is to expose this conspiracy and to show that there is nothing wrong with acting in one's own interest exclusively. What does selfishness, denuded of its negative connotations, look like? It is nothing other than what traditional egoists call rational self-interest. Hence, her position on selfishness is consistent with the ordinary one, and her own ethical theory is just another version of egoism. Though she claims the contrary, the point is essentially a semantic one. For Rand, then, selfish behavior and self-interest are identical, but selfishness should be stripped of its negative connotations. For traditional egoists, however, selfishness, and self-interest are not identical. They discourage selfishness and encourage the pursuit of rational self-interest. —*John H. Serembus*

See also Egoism; Objectivism; Self-interest; Self-love.

BIBLIOGRAPHY

Campbell, Richmond. *Self-Love and Self-Respect: A Philosophical Study of Egoism.* Ottawa, Canada: Canadian Library of Philosophy, 1979.

Gauthier, David P. *Morality and Rational Self-Interest.* Englewood Cliffs, N.J.: Prentice-Hall, 1970.

Olson, Robert. *The Morality of Self-Interest.* New York: Harcourt, Brace & World, 1965.

Rand, Ayn. *The Virtue of Selfishness: A New Concept of Egoism.* New York: New American Library, 1964.

Rescher, Nicholas. *Unselfishness: The Role of the Vicarious Affects in Moral Philosophy and Social Theory.* Pittsburgh: University of Pittsburgh Press, 1975.

Sentience

TYPE OF ETHICS: Animal rights
DATE: First used seventeenth century
ASSOCIATED WITH: Philosopher Peter Singer and the animal rights movement
DEFINITION: Consciousness; specifically, the capacity to feel pain and pleasure
SIGNIFICANCE: Sentience is sometimes taken to be a necessary and sufficient condition for moral standing

Derived from the Latin verb *sentire*, meaning to feel or perceive, the term "sentient" was used as early as 1632 to describe a being as conscious. The concept of sentience (the quality of being sentient) became crucial to the animal rights movement after Peter Singer took it to be a necessary and sufficient condition for having interests in his book *Animal Liberation* (1975). Singer's view was that all (and only) beings that are capable of feeling pain or conscious suffering have interests that matter from the moral point of view. The question "Which beings are sentient?" is answered by using an analogy. The more relevant behavioral and/or neurophysiological similarities there are between a given organism and a human being, the stronger is the case for saying that the organism is sentient. In *Animal Liberation*, Singer speculated that (with the exception of cephalopods like octopi, squid, and cuttlefish) probably only animals above the phylogenetic "level" of mollusks (such as clams, oysters, and scallops) are conscious. While excluding insects, this does include crustaceans (such as shrimp and lobsters).

Many who have examined the available evidence have concluded that although all vertebrates probably are capable of feeling pain, invertebrates probably are not (again, with the exception of cephalopods).

See also Animal consciousness; Animal research; Animal rights; Moral status of animals; Pain; Singer, Peter; Vivisection.

Sex therapy

TYPE OF ETHICS: Psychological ethics
DATE: 1966
ASSOCIATED WITH: William H. Masters and Virginia E. Johnson
DEFINITION: The treatment of people who are experiencing sexual problems
SIGNIFICANCE: Sex therapy may be unethical if it is conducted inappropriately

Sexual therapy was pioneered by Masters and Johnson (1970), although other therapists have also created many important techniques. Sex therapy generally focuses on reducing performance anxiety, changing self-defeating expectations, and fostering sexual skills or competencies. Both sex partners are often involved in therapy, although individual treatment is possible. Because sexual dysfunction may be linked to drug effects, sex therapists must be knowledgeable to some degree about pharmacology. Sex therapists educate the couple and guide them through a series of homework assignments. They also treat interpersonal problems.

Three main sexual disorders treated by sex therapy are arousal and erectile disorders, premature ejaculation, and inhibited orgasm. Two causes are predominant: people's tendency to adopt a spectator role during intercourse, which causes them to examine their own performance; and the fear of performing inadequately. Either of these problems can create inhibitions against enjoying the normal sensations that lead to sexual satisfaction.

Arousal and erectile disorders are of two types: primary and secondary erectile dysfunction. Primary erectile dysfunction means that a man has never had an erection of sufficient strength for sexual intercourse. Fear and unusual sensitivity or anxiety regarding sexual incidents that have happened early in life may contribute to primary erectile dysfunction. Secondary erectile dysfunction means that the man has had successful sexual intercourse in the past but now fails to achieve penile erection in 25 percent or more of his sexual attempts. Secondary erectile dysfunction can be a vicious cycle: One or a few incidents of impotence can lead a man to become overanxious and abnormally sensitive, so that the next attempts at intercourse are also failures. Next, an interpersonal component enters the picture. Almost any response by the man's partner exacerbates the problem. If she continues to be physically affectionate, he may interpret her actions as a demand for sexual intercourse, a demand that he fears he is unable to satisfy. If she is less affectionate physically, he may defensively interpret her behavior as a rejection of his sexually inadequate self.

Sensate focus, which is a basic element of treatment of arousal and erectile disorders (as well as inhibited orgasm), involves directing attention away from intercourse and toward other behaviors that feel pleasurable to the partner, such as caressing the neck or massaging the back. Intercourse is initially forbidden by the therapist, so these exercises take on importance, allowing the couple to experience sexuality in a relaxed, non-performance-oriented manner. Gradually, more and more involved sexual activities are allowed, and the couple is eventually told that intercourse is permissible. Typically, such treatment is successful. Improvement rates for primary erectile dysfunction are about 60 percent, and for secondary erectile dysfunction they are 74 percent.

Premature ejaculation occurs when a man cannot delay ejaculation long enough to satisfy his sexual partner during at least half of his sexual encounters. Premature ejaculation is usually caused by emotional and psychological factors. The most common treatment is the squeeze technique, in which the man's sexual partner stimulates him manually until he signals that ejaculation is about to occur. Then, the partner firmly squeezes the tip of his penis to inhibit orgasm. When he feels that he has control, stimulation is repeated. Gradually, he acquires the ability to delay orgasm sufficiently for satisfactory intercourse.

Inhibited orgasm is of two types: primary and secondary. Primary orgasmic dysfunction means that a woman never achieves an orgasm through any method of sexual stimulation. Though many causes are physical, more often they are psychological and are grounded in extreme religious orthodoxy, unfavorable communication about sexual activities, or some childhood trauma. Secondary orgasmic dysfunction is the inability of a woman who has achieved orgasm by one technique or another in the past to achieve it in a given situation. Secondary orgasmic dysfunction may occur when a woman is unable to accept her partner because she finds him sexually unattractive, undesirable, or in some other way unacceptable. In addition, many women find that orgasm brings about feelings of guilt, shame, and fear.

Treatment of primary and secondary orgasmic disorders involves understanding the woman's sexual value system and the reasons for her inability and/or unwillingness to achieve orgasm. Using her value system, the therapist teaches her to respond to sexual stimulation. Often, she is encouraged to focus on sexual responsiveness through masturbation or vigorous stimulation by a partner. Initially, the couple is directed to avoid intercourse but is taken through a series of treatment sessions involving an increasing amount of erotic pleasure. Orgasm is not the focus of these sessions, but ultimately it is achieved in an unhurried situation in which pressure to perform is removed from both partners.

Treatment of both male and female disorders involves teaching people not to fear failure and helping them to be free from anxiety. Both the man and woman are taught the art of giving pleasure in order to receive pleasure. They are encouraged to relax and to enjoy touching, feeling, and being sexual. The therapist may arrange desensitization experiences in real sexual encounters between the couple. Eventually, natural processes will take control and intercourse will follow in due time.

A central aspect of treatment of both male and female sexual disorders is communication. Couples must learn to communicate their sexual needs without embarrassment and misinterpretation. Such communication may be difficult. Also, for sex therapy to be successful, the sexual partners must be flexible individuals who are willing to accommodate the directive- and sometimes value-laden features of sex therapy. In addition, both partners need to develop a better understanding of male and female sexual response cues. Sex therapy may involve a specific technique, such as the squeeze technique, or an overall treatment of the couple's relationship. —*Lillian M. Range*

See also Psychology; Sexuality and sexual ethics.

BIBLIOGRAPHY

Arentewicz, Gerd, and Gunter Schmidt, eds. *The Treatment of Sexual Disorders*. New York: Basic Books, 1983.

Hyde, Janet S. *Understanding Human Sexuality*. 4th ed. New York: McGraw-Hill, 1990.

Kaplan, Helen S. *Disorders of Sexual Desire and Other New Concepts and Techniques in Sex Therapy*. New York: Simon & Schuster, 1979.

Masters, William H., and Virginia E. Johnson. *Human Sexual Inadequacy*. Boston: Little, Brown, 1970.

Wade, Carole, and Sarah Cirese. *Study Guide to Accompany Human Sexuality*. 2d ed. Chicago: Harcourt Brace Jovanovich, 1991.

Sexism

TYPE OF ETHICS: Sex and gender issues

DATE: From antiquity

ASSOCIATED WITH: The Nineteenth Amendment, which gave U.S. women the right to vote in 1920

DEFINITION: Bias toward people on the basis of their gender

SIGNIFICANCE: Sexism can influence people to treat others in ways that are based on gender rather than on personal traits or abilities

A person is sexist who believes, for example, that women cannot be competent doctors or men cannot be competent nursery school teachers. Institutions, as well as individuals, can be sexist. Sexism can be revealed in stereotypes (beliefs about people based on gender), prejudice (negatively prejudging a person solely on the basis of gender), or discrimination (acting in accordance with prejudice).

Sexism influences perceptions and behavior from birth. In one classic study, fathers described their first babies almost immediately after they were born; mothers described their babies during their first twenty-four hours. Despite objective hospital records that showed that these baby boys and girls were almost identical in color, muscle tone, reflex responses, weight, and length, parents described them differently. Baby girls were perceived as relatively softer, finer-featured, smaller, and less attentive. Fathers in particular were susceptible to this type of selective perception (Rubin, Provenzano, and Luria, 1974). Children and adults learn from these types of messages what society expects of women and men.

Sexism can be blatant, as it is when a female premedical student is told that women belong at home rather than at work or a male home economics student is told that men belong at work rather than at home. Sexism can also be subtle, as it is when people interpret the same behavior in different ways depending on whether it is exhibited by women or men. People may see a man as assertive but a woman as pushy, a man as flexible but a woman as fickle, a woman as sensitive but a man as a sissy, or a woman as polite but a man as passive. For example, in one research project, college students rated the quality of professional articles in several fields. When an article was attributed to a woman, it received lower ratings than it did when it was attributed to a man. Furthermore, women raters were as guilty as men at assuming male superiority. Therefore, sexism influences both women and men in a variety of blatant and subtle ways.

Although sexism is typically most damaging to women, men can also be victims. Even in the current era, for example, people are more willing to hire a man for a "man's job" and to hire a woman for a "woman's job."

Sexism extends to the way in which people use language. Benjamin Whorf (1956) advocated the concept of linguistic relativity, the theory that the properties of language shape perceptions of the world. His classic example compared English and Eskimo views of snow. English has only one word for snow, whereas Eskimo has many words that distinguish falling snow, slushy snow, and so forth. In recent years, the idea that language influences people's perceptions of the world has extended to the way in which sexist terms are used. Although the masculine forms are supposed to refer to both men and women, most people think of men when they are used. For this reason, some scholars substitute gender-neutral terms such as "firefighter" for gender-laden terms such as "fireman" and avoid using the terms "lady" and "girl" on the ground that they perpetuate the view of women as frivolous and childish. The American Psychological Association's *Publication Manual* contains guidelines for avoiding sexist language that include using the plural whenever appropriate, using "his and her" rather than "his," and using parallel construction (for example, "husband and wife" rather than "man and wife").

Sexist language harms people in two different ways. First, women may reach adulthood feeling inferior because of the more frequent references in language to males. For example, in an analysis of children's books published after 1972, most of the fictional characters were male, whether the stories were about children, adults, or even animals. Furthermore, boys were characterized as curious, clever, and adventurous, whereas girls were characterized as fearful and incompetent

SEXISM TIME LINE	
1500 B.C.E.	The Book of Genesis is written, blaming Eve for humans' eviction from Garden of Eden
60 C.E.	Paul's New Testament writings that women should be silent in church provide further religious foundation for sexism
1848	Women's suffrage movement begins at a convention in Seneca Falls, New York
1869	U.S. women are given the right to vote in Wyoming Territory
1875	Edward H. Clarke's *A Fair Chance for the Girls: Women in Education* states that educating women would make them sterile
1910	Freud describes penis envy
1920	The Nineteenth Amendment passes, giving all U.S. women the right to vote
1972	The U.S. Equal Rights Amendment is passed by the House and the Senate
1984	The Equal Rights Amendment fails to be ratified by a majority of states

(Tavris & Offir, 1977). Such bias takes a heavy toll on female self-esteem. Second, the use of certain terms may lead women and men to believe that certain occupations are beyond their capabilities. The harm done by this type of language can be avoided if writers and speakers are aware of the problem and motivated to change the gender-laden terms they are accustomed to using.   —*Lillian M. Range*

See also Sexual stereotypes.

BIBLIOGRAPHY

American Psychological Association. *Publication Manual of the American Psychological Association.* 3d ed. Washington, D.C.: Author, 1983.

Bem, Sandra L. "Gender Schema Theory: A Cognitive Account of Sex Typing." *Psychological Review* 88, no. 4 (July, 1981): 354-364.

Maccoby, Eleanor E., and Carol N. Jacklin. *The Psychology of Sex Differences.* Stanford, Calif.: Stanford University Press, 1974.

Matlin, Margaret W. *The Psychology of Women.* New York: Holt, Rinehart and Winston, 1987.

Rubin, Jeffrey Z., Frank J. Provenzano, and Zella Luria. "The Eye of the Beholder: Parents' Views on Sex of Newborns." *American Journal of Orthopsychiatry* 44 (July, 1974): 512-519.

Swim, Janet, Eugene Borgida, and Geoffrey Maruyama. "Joan McKay Versus John McKay: Do Gender Stereotypes Bias Evaluations?" *Psychological Bulletin* 105, no. 3 (May, 1989): 409-429.

Tavris, Carol, and Carole Offir. *The Longest War.* New York: Harcourt Brace Jovanovich, 1977.

Whorf, Benjamin L. *Language, Thought, and Reality.* Cambridge, Mass.: Technology Press of Massachusetts Institute of Technology, 1956.

Sexual abuse and harassment

TYPE OF ETHICS: Sex and gender issues
DATE: Coined 1975
DEFINITION: Any interaction between two or more individuals with sexual implications or overtones in which at least one of the individuals involved is devalued as a person and in which there is a clear distinction between the perpetrator(s) and the victim(s), the interaction is neither solicited nor wanted by the victim(s), and the interaction is rendered inappropriate by virtue of the setting in which it occurs or the relationship between the perpetrator(s) and the victim(s)
SIGNIFICANCE: This term involves such moral issues as the moral worth of a person; gender inequality; and the social distribution of power, authority, and opportunities

The above definition intentionally allows for both the perpetrator of sexual harassment and the victim of sexual harassment to be either male or female and to be either heterosexual or homosexual. It must be acknowledged, however, that in the vast majority of incidents of sexual harassment, the victim is female and the perpetrator is a male heterosexual. This is true

Anita Hill testified during the 1991 hearings on the confirmation of Clarence Thomas to the U.S. Supreme Court that she had been sexually harassed by Thomas. Her allegations helped to bring attention to the complex issue of sexual harassment. (AP/Wide World Photos)

primarily because gender inequality is systematic in virtually every culture on earth. That is, the history of the social roles of men as compared to women is such that men, owing only to an accident of birth, are granted significantly more power and authority in society and enjoy the full complement of opportunities that a particular society makes available. (Clearly, there are other factors, many of which are also accidents of birth, that might preclude some segments of a society's male population from this privileged status, such as skin color, religious affiliation, and so forth.) Women, by contrast, are granted significantly less power and authority in society (in some cases, historically, none) and suffer severe restrictions with respect to the availability of opportunities offered by the society. The result of such an institutionalized imbalance of power and opportunities between the genders is an insidious development of social expectations according to which women literally come to be viewed (even by one another) as second-class citizens.

To the extent that these traditional distinctions between the social roles of men and women come to be seen as "the norm" and to the extent that the members of society (male and female), even if only implicitly, recognize that such distinctions are attributable only to the difference in gender, a social climate is created in which any abuse of an individual who happens to be female—simply because she is female—

is taken less seriously than it would be were the same type of abuse to be directed at a male. The rationale for this difference in response is based on the abused individual's status as a member of the privileged or the nonprivileged gender.

It should come as no surprise, then, that social settings in which the imbalance of power and opportunities between the genders is most prevalent are ripe for sexual abuse or harassment; two such examples are the work environment and the educational environment.

In the typical work environment, positions of power and authority are held, for the most part, by men, while women usually hold positions of significantly less power and authority. This tradition has been maintained, in large part, because of an institutionalized lack of opportunity for women even to be considered eligible for positions of greater power and authority. Given this fact, it is not at all uncommon for women in the workplace to be the victims of sexual harassment. Such harassment typically involves a male perpetrator of sexual harassment who holds a position of authority over the female victim of sexual harassment. In the work environment, sexual harassment can also take other forms; for example, the perpetrator might be the male client of a female employee who is the victim.

The most obvious imbalance of power and authority in the educational environment is the fact that the instructor determines the grades of the students. Given this fact, there is always the potential for an instructor to abuse the educational system by sexually harassing a student. Although, in theory, the possibility is greater here for both the perpetrator and the victim to be of either gender and of either sexual orientation, in practice, more often than not, the victim is female and the perpetrator is male (heterosexual). The fact that, more often than not, the perpetrator in this environment is male and heterosexual is explained fundamentally (but not completely) by the fact that although female instructors, within the student-instructor relationship, possess the power to assign student grades, in the society at large, they are still members of the nonprivileged gender, which fact has great influence on their social behavior. Furthermore, in the society at large, there are far more heterosexual males than there are homosexual males.

Additional environments in which sexual harassment occurs are the therapeutic environment and the religious environment. Incidents of sexual harassment in the therapeutic environment are usually similar to those that take place in the educational environment, while incidents of sexual harassment in the religious environment are usually similar to those that take place in the work environment.

Having recognized some examples of specific social environments that allow for above-average potential for sexual harassment because of their very one-sided imbalance of power and opportunities between perpetrator and victim, it is important to acknowledge that any social setting is a potential stage for sexual harassment. Moreover, sexual harassment is not restricted to relationships that involve only one perpetrator and only one victim, and it is not restricted to a private setting. For example, two or more perpetrators of sexual harassment might together verbally abuse several other persons at the same time and might do so in a public forum.

Some specific types of sexual harassment are sexist comments (remarks or jokes that stereotype or disparage a single gender), unwelcome attention (uninvited flirtations), body language (fixed eye contact on specific body parts of another), physical sexual advances (pinching, fondling, and so forth), verbal sexual advances (such as nonspecific verbal expressions of sexual interest), explicit sexual propositions (unambiguous invitations for sexual encounters), and sexual coercion or bribery (unambiguous invitations for sexual encounters with the implicit or explicit promise of rewards for acceding or the threat of punishment for refusing).

What makes sexual harassment morally repugnant is that the victim is devalued as a person, in that the victim's dignity as a person is abused, and that such harassment inhibits the victim's ability to pursue whatever activities he or she was engaged in prior to the occurrence of the incident. Any defense that has ever been offered by a perpetrator of sexual harassment, after the fact, has involved the idea that the fact of harassment, or the offense that it engenders, depends upon the person; that is, what offends one person might not offend another, even another of the same gender in the same circumstances. Although it can be granted that sexual harassment is, in a sense, "in the eye of the beholder," this in no way morally excuses it. In the final analysis, the determining factor for what constitutes sexual harassment must be the interpretation of the victim as reasonably construed from the victim's perspective. —*Stephen C. Taylor*

See also Abuse; Child abuse; Children; Children's rights; Coercion; Feminism; Incest; Professional ethics; Rape; Sexism; Sexual stereotypes; Sexuality and sexual ethics.

BIBLIOGRAPHY

Dodds, Susan M., et al. "Sexual Harassment." *Social Theory and Practice* 14 (Summer, 1988): 111-130.

Hughes, John C., and Larry May. "Sexual Harassment." *Social Theory and Practice* 6 (Fall, 1980): 249-280.

MacKinnon, Catharine A. *Sexual Harassment of Working Women*. New Haven, Conn.: Yale University Press, 1979.

Wall, Edmund. "The Definition of Sexual Harassment." *Public Affairs Quarterly* 5 (October, 1991): 371-385.

Wise, Sue, and Liz Stanley. *Georgie Porgie: Sexual Harassment in Everyday Life*. London: Pandora, 1987.

Sexual revolution

TYPE OF ETHICS: Sex and gender issues

DATE: 1960's

ASSOCIATED WITH: The development of reliable contraception

DEFINITION: The increased occurrence and social acceptability of sexual behavior

SIGNIFICANCE: The sexual revolution reflected society's attitudes about what types of sexual behaviors were right (ethical) or wrong (unethical)

In the 1940's and 1950's, the United States and most other Western countries were sexually restrictive. Prepubertal sexuality was ignored or denied, marital sex was considered the only legitimate sexual outlet, and other forms of sexual expression were condemned or prohibited by law.

In the 1960's, with the development of reliable contraceptive methods, sexual activities became less restricted. Premarital intercourse became more acceptable and more frequent, the latter particularly so among women. Young people became more sexually active at younger ages, and society tolerated a wider variety of sexual behavior than had been tolerated in the past. This change, the sexual revolution, was most prominent among women.

In the 1990's, however, despite any so-called revolution, adolescent boys still reported more sexual activity than adolescent girls, with about 80 percent of boys and 70 percent of girls reporting sexual intercourse before the end of adolescence. Also, a double standard for sexual behavior existed: males were subtly encouraged to engage in sexual behavior but females were subtly discouraged from engaging in sexual activity. Additionally, the life-threatening disease AIDS made people aware that sexual activity could result in death. Finally, society in general became more conservative. The sexual revolution changed, with sexual activity and attitudes becoming more conservative, and some differences between men and women remained present.

See also Sexism; Sexuality and sexual ethics.

Sexual stereotypes

TYPE OF ETHICS: Sex and gender issues
DATE: From antiquity
DEFINITION: The assignment of emotional and ability characteristics to all men or all women, solely on the basis of physical sexual identity
SIGNIFICANCE: Sexual stereotyping encourages discrimination against and victimization of women, thus decreasing equity within society; sexual stereotyping is related to racism, ageism, and other forms of prejudice

Sexual stereotypes are based on the idea that all females are alike in personality, interests, and abilities, and that males also constitute a homogeneous group. The masculine stereotype includes the characteristics of aggressiveness, achievement orientation, dominance, rationality, independence, high sexual interest, and physical strength. The feminine stereotype emphasizes passivity, submissiveness, emotionality, nurturance, modesty, low sexual interest, and physical weakness. Although stereotypes are an easy way of categorizing people, they are extreme generalizations. They destroy individuality and lead to discriminatory behavior and the victimization of women in the forms of domestic abuse, rape, and pornography.

History. Male and female sexual stereotypes have existed in European civilization since ancient Greece and probably even earlier. Aristotle, Paul of Tarsus and other leaders of the Christian church, and civil authorities have endorsed the idea that women share typical characteristics. The concept of women as evil was an important rationale for the witch-hunts of the sixteenth and seventeenth centuries. European males typically considered women the "weaker sex," not only physically but also intellectually and morally.

Criticism of sexual stereotypes grew out of John Locke's political philosophy of natural rights. Mary Wollstonecraft's treatise *On the Subjection of Women* (1792) was an early statement about the effects of sexual stereotypes on the liberty and personal growth of women. Elizabeth Cady Stanton and other leaders of the mid-nineteenth century women's movement in the United States worked chiefly for civil liberties and intellectual parity. The negative effects of sexual stereotypes were restated by Simone de Beauvior in *The Second Sex* in 1953. They were an important concern in the women's liberation movement and in social science research during the second half of the twentieth century.

Ethical Principles. Sexual stereotypes are attitudes about a group of individuals. These attitudes are ethically significant because they often lead to discrimination. Women were denied political liberty because they were regarded as incapable of rational thinking. Thus, strongly held stereotypes typically imply an infringement on the liberty of individuals.

Furthermore, stereotypes lead to various problems in social equity, including educational and job discrimination and the denial of economic power. The stereotyped differences between men and women are assumed to be innate rather than cultural or socially acquired. Historically, women have been denied access to educational opportunities at the pre-college, college, and graduate level. Lessened opportunities are reflected in lower salaries, less prestige and influence, and fewer opportunities to advance. Job discrimination in hiring and promotions results from stereotypes about what work is appropriate for women. Accordingly, stereotypes can be used to justify denying civil and economic rights to women and granting preferential treatment to men.

Stereotypes of women as passive—even masochistic—and of men as aggressive and sexually driven contribute to the victimization of women by means of domestic abuse, rape, and pornography. These stereotypes are reflected in the psychoanalytic theories of Sigmund Freud and other psychodynamic theorists. "Natural" male aggression can be used as justification for violence; this argument removes ethical responsibility for actions from the aggressor. Stereotypes can even be used to suggest that the victim should be blamed for inappropriate conduct that led to the offense; for example, it may be suggested that a woman who enters a bar alone is inviting rape.

Ethical Issues. The controversy regarding whether to emphasize equality between the sexes, or to recognize true gender differences remains an issue. Whether women should seek equality with men by attempting to reduce stereotypes to a minimum or should challenge male domination with a different, feminine ideology is unclear. For example, Carol Gilligan has proposed that there are clear ethical differences in the kinds of reasoning that men and women use to analyze ethical dilemmas. Males usually describe their reasoning as being based on principles that are applicable to every situation. Females frequently make ethical decisions that are strongly weighted by a consideration of the particular situation and, especially, by social relationships and responsibilities. Although it is important to reduce stereotypes, it may also be important to maintain a diversity of gender perspectives.

Annette Baier proposes that a particularly feminine ethical stance is that of trust. Trust underlies cooperation and thus is significant for ethical interpersonal relations. Trust is significant in family relations, between husband and wife as well as between parent and child. Because trust is part of the feminine stereotype, however, it has been largely ignored by philosophy.

Relationship to Other Forms of Stereotyping. Sexual stereotypes; racial, ethnic, and religious stereotypes; and age stereotypes are similar. People who rigidly hold one kind of stereotype frequently espouse other stereotypes. Because such attitudes lead to discriminatory behavior, all such stereotypes tend to deny equality and opportunity to members of a stigmatized group. In Western society, elderly minority women experience a triple oppression because of stereotypes and discrimination.

Prejudice against homosexual males and lesbian women is also related to sexual stereotyping. Some prejudicial attitudes result from a perception that homosexual males and lesbians do not act in accord with commonly held stereotypes. Social stigmatization and other forms of harassment frequently result from such views.—*Mary M. Vandendorpe*

See also Abuse; Ageism; Bigotry; Determinism and freedom; *Feminine Mystique, The*; Feminism; Homophobia; Normative vs. descriptive ethics; Pornography; Racial Prejudice; Rape; *Second Sex, The*; Sexism; Sexual abuse and harassment; Social justice and responsibility; Wollstonecraft, Mary; Women's liberation movement.

BIBLIOGRAPHY

Baier, Annette. *Postures of the Mind.* Minneapolis: University of Minnesota Press, 1985.

Davis, Angela Yvonne. *Women, Race, and Class.* New York: Random House, 1981.

Faludi, Susan. *Backlash.* New York: Crown, 1991.

Gilligan, Carol. *In a Different Voice.* Cambridge, Mass.: Harvard University Press, 1982.

Jaggar, Alison M. *Feminist Politics and Human Nature.* Totowa, N.J.: Rowman & Littlefield, 1988.

Kaschak, Ellyn. *Engendered Lives.* New York: Basic Books, 1992.

Kittay, Eva Feder, and Diana T. Meyers, eds. *Women and Moral Theory.* Totowa, N.J.: Rowman & Littlefield, 1987.

Lloyd, Genevieve. *The Man of Reason: Male and Female in Western Philisophy.* Minneapolis: University of Minnesota Press, 1984.

Sexuality and sexual ethics

TYPE OF ETHICS: Sex and gender issues

ASSOCIATED WITH: Sex education and the sexual revolution

DEFINITION: Differences between males and females in psychology, anatomy, and physiology that are also augmented by social standards

SIGNIFICANCE: Sexuality is fundamental to personality and affects most human interaction; sexual behavior involves ethics at the deepest levels

Men and women have most things in common. In that sense, the biblical view that one sex comes from the middle of the other is very appropriate. The biological view that the male is a modified female also indicates this strong commonality.

Concepts of sexuality, however, focus on the differences associated with gender. Sexual assignment and the many behaviors associated with it are basic to personality. The most fundamental difference between male and female is that males produce sperm and females produce eggs, but to be classified as male or female does not involve merely the obvious differences in anatomy; sexuality has profound effects on how a person feels, thinks, communicates, and acts. Attraction between the sexes and the pleasure inherent in the sex act constitute an efficient biological design that tends to continue the species, but sex is more than reproduction, and most human sex does not involve producing babies. Sex involves the desire for a meaningful, close relationship with another, and it involves the most pleasurable short-term act of which the body is capable. The intimacy of the sex act calls for trust and commitment. The philosopher Richard Solomon has stated, "To think that one can indulge in the traditionally most powerful symbolic activity in almost every culture without its meaning anything is an extravagant self-deception."

Several biological factors are unique to human sex. First, humans are apparently the only creatures that realize that sex is linked to reproduction. Other animals do not know that intercourse may cause pregnancy. Second, human females may be sexually receptive at any time. In contrast, many mammals mate only seasonally, when the hormonal levels, especially of estrogens, cause females to signal their receptivity to males. At that time females are said to be in "heat." Some mammals have more frequent periods of heat. The sexual interest and activity of human females, however, is different. It is influenced, but not limited to, specific hormone-dependent times. Circumstances, judgments, cultural norms, mood, and emotions play larger roles than do hormones when it comes to the timing of the sex act by humans. A third factor is that humans often have sex face-to-face, which seems to be significant in that it promotes bonding and commitment for the protection of possible offspring.

Childhood experiences affect the choice of a mate. Certain characteristics come to be valued. If a person meets and gets to know another person and this person meets many of the desired characteristics, attraction occurs. At that point, the brain is affected by chemicals (especially phenylethylamine) that are similar to amphetamines. The person experiences a chemical high that can last several years, causing the feelings of being in love. The continued presence of a partner causes endorphins to be released internally, causing feelings of calmness and security. This promotes long-term attachment. Finally, another chemical, oxytocin, is released. This chemical is thought to cause cuddling and to enhance pleasure in sex.

There is much that is not known, but sexual behavior is definitely more than simply genes and chemical reactions. Human sexuality is formed by a complicated interplay and overlap of genetics, culture, experiences, and free will. The roles of these elements are difficult to define. One can always argue about the extent to which females are biologically bound to be passive, coy, and monogamous. Likewise, one can question the extent to which males are dealing with genes that compel them to be aggressive, dominating, risk-taking, and promiscuous. How much weight should people give to genetics? How free are human actions?

Genetic Determination. Genes, mainly but not exclusively, determine the production of hormones that cause the development of the sex organs and the various secondary physical differences such as body size, percentages of fat, tilt of the pelvis, muscle thickness, voice pitch, and thickness of body hair. Even the development of the brain and patterns of behavior are affected by the sex genes. Normally, two X chromosomes will basically program a female, while having both an X and a Y chromosome will produce male characteristics. In 1987, geneticist David C. Page and his colleagues found that there is a particular gene on the Y chromosome that is required to produce a male. In a study of abnormal cases, Page found that a twelve-year-old girl was XY but that the Y chromosome was not complete, apparently lacking the male gene. About one in 20,000 men is XX but also has inherited a small piece of the Y chromosome that includes the sex gene, causing him to develop as a male. Such XX males and XY females are usually infertile. The location of the sex gene on the Y chromosome (and the additional discovery of a similar sex gene on the X chromosome) indicates that genetic factors in sex determination are not completely understood. While further study is needed, questions about whether homosexuality is a matter of choice or inheritance are being raised. Preliminary investigation indicates that a gene for homosexuality may also exist. Other studies also indicate a physical difference in the structure of the brain when homosexuals and heterosexuals are compared.

Cultural Influence. Length of hair, type of dress, vocational choices, and many sexual behaviors seem to be mainly cultural values. Because every society has legitimate interests in sexual conduct, certain standards and norms of behavior are maintained. These may vary from culture to culture, but both religion and government tend to be involved, often reinforcing each other, as in the case of requiring marriage to be formalized as a way of providing family structure for the nurturing of children. Within a family, male and female children are usually raised quite differently. At times, these standards within a culture may change.

Many behaviors have more than one cause. For example, self-assertiveness, the ability to communicate openly and honestly in a functional way, appears to be related to gender. Hormones can certainly be given some credit for male aggressiveness in many activities, but women seem to be encouraged by society to be quiet, polite, and considerate of others' feelings, while men are encouraged to take charge. Change in this area can certainly be made by means of teaching and practicing communication techniques that allow both sexes to communicate openly and freely about their feelings, needs, and desires.

Only recently have many girls and women increased their participation in competitive athletics. The positive results have shown that cultures may have mistaken ideas about fixed or natural sexual limits and roles.

Free Will. One can argue that all behavior and even culture is programmed by genetics, but biological determinism is a gloomy mechanistic view of life. Are people free to choose or do they merely respond in programmed ways to various signals? Free will allows people to accept, augment, or reject both nature and nurture. Individuals may choose to modify sexual characteristics, whether they are biological or cultural. One can shave hair or allow it to grow. One can wear high-heeled shoes that accent side movement in walking. A person may consciously choose to dress and act in ways that a society may generally see as part of the role of the opposite sex. Yet perhaps what is perceived as freedom is an illusion. Perhaps such modifications are also programmed. Are humans trapped by their biology? Biology is certainly not irrelevant to social behavior; however, as biologist Richard Lewontin has argued, there is simply not enough DNA to code for all the situations that humans face. Patterns of behavior can only be very generally coded. Humans do have choices.

Areas of Concern. Sexual ethics is concerned with questions about how sexuality might influence one's behavior, how basic biology might require careful thought and control, and how the common good might be preserved. Sexuality can have many goals, but even if sex and reproduction could be completely divorced, sex and morality cannot. Sex almost always involves another person. Sex, or the choice not to have sex, involves valuing others as ends in themselves, not merely as the means to selfish pleasure. This is not a new principle, even with Immanuel Kant, but goes back to the ancient Jewish and Christian command to love one's neighbor: to be concerned for the emotional and physical welfare of others. Beyond being a means of procreation, sex is a form of communication. Sex involves much of ethics: trust, truth-telling, commitment, friendship, and fairness. There really is no special variety of sexual ethics, but ethics in the sexual realm is very special. This is because sexual behaviors reflect the core of one's personality and can allow the most intimate knowledge of one's being. At the same time, the way in which sexuality is treated profoundly affects all interactions in a society. If the most personal relationships are unethical, then all relationships are at risk.

Societies have a justifiable interest in the area of sexuality. Children need good parents to care for them. The spread of sexually transmitted diseases (STDs) should be prevented; casual sex can carry mortal risk. The education of teenagers should not be interrupted by extramarital pregnancy. Respect for persons requires that sex should never be forced on another person.

Adultery. If two people consent to have sexual intercourse outside marriage, is this immoral? If it is a private matter between consenting adults, what is the harm? Richard Wasserstrom argues that this activity involves the breaking of an important promise. First, the breaking of this promise involves deep hurt and pain to the innocent spouse. Second, such activity almost always involves deception about where a person was and about what was occurring. Third, sexual intimacy should reflect a person's real feelings for another. Western culture teaches that sexual intercourse involves the strongest feelings that one person can have for another. Therefore, the restriction of sexual intercourse to a marriage is logical. To engage in extramarital sex involves the deepest deception about true feelings, toward either the innocent spouse or the extramarital partner. Society has yet to answer various questions. Can one separate sexual activity from its deep meanings of commitment to a single person? What is sexual love? How could it be different? What price would people pay if sexual relations came to mean something else? Would the institution of marriage be lost and the nurture and protection of children suffer?

Natural or Unnatural. Sometimes in arguments about sexual matters a judgment will be made regarding whether an activity or behavior is natural. The implication is that perhaps "the laws of nature" can be violated, but the laws of nature are only descriptive and by their nature cannot be violated. They are not prescriptive for behavior, and life would be gloomy if it were so. As Sarah Blaffer Hrdy has said, people need to rise above nature in sexual ethics. Arguments that will convince the general population must be based on ethical traditions that consider the consequences of an action (teleological theories) or traditions that maintain that people have duties (deontological theories).

Sexism. False assumptions about the intrinsic worth of either females or males often cause trouble in society. Children of the "wrong sex" may be devalued and even aborted. Programs or instruction in schools should not favor one sex. Equal work and responsibility calls for equal pay and equal opportunities for promotion. To use biological differences such as sex or race, over which a person has no control, as a systematic basis for denying anyone their rights violates individual human dignity and autonomy.

A most serious danger is to describe one sex as setting the standards for the species. When this is done, the other sex is viewed as not fully developed, abnormal, and therefore is devalued. For example, during the nineteenth century, Paul Broca claimed that female brains were smaller than normal ("normal" was a European white man's brain) and therefore not capable of higher learning. Educational policies and women's aspirations were affected until this view was overcome, when people realized that general body size and many other factors must be considered. Female brains are normal for females. Female intelligence is not limited by sexuality.

Gay Rights. Although the issue of respect for privacy discourages and complicates the enforcement of laws that regulate sexual behavior, the courts are not silent regarding such matters. In 1993, a Virginia County Circuit Court found that a woman's lesbian relationship made her "an unfit parent." The judge noted that the woman admitted to engaging in oral sex, which is a felony in Virginia, concluded that her conduct was immoral, and left the woman's child in the custody of the grandmother. The grandmother testified that the child might grow up confused about sexuality. The judge cited a 1985 Virginia Supreme Court ruling that said that a parent's homosexuality is a legitimate reason for losing parental rights. Since 1985, however, about 100 gay people have gained parental rights through the courts by means of what is called coparent, second-parent, or same-gender adoption. The issue is far from settled.

Sex Sells. Advertising plays an important role in society. The device of associating a product with a beautiful or handsome model raises the issue of honesty. The ethics of using sexuality to sell products and to promote messages is questionable and is demeaning to the persons so used. Interesting cases have developed involving the hiring of women as newscasters. What is really going on when management tells a female newsperson to wear her hair differently?

Sexuality is Sold. Billions of dollars are spent annually on cosmetics, especially by women, to enhance beauty and sexuality. (The testing of cosmetic products on animals is an ethical issue in itself.) The clothing fashion industry is also keyed to promoting attractiveness. Models are selected to promote particular images of female body shape and beauty. These images may be unrealistic for most females and may lead to the development of low self-esteem or even serious illness (anorexia, bulimia). Furthermore, Cornel West (1993) has pointed out that the ideology of white female beauty even tends to permeate black thinking. "The ideal of female beauty in this country puts a premium on lightness and softness mythically associated with white women and downplays the rich stylistic manners associated with black women." Damaged self-image and lack of self-confidence can cause fundamental harm to a whole race.

How sexuality is treated in society and how individual humans act sexually involves all of ethics. Making responsible decisions in this area may be more difficult than in others because of the effects of biology and culture. Nevertheless, the effort must be made to affirm sexuality, to recognize it as fundamental to human existence. In all its uses, however, sexuality also needs to be disciplined to communicate truth. William Starr has pointed out that one can have purely casual sex. There is pleasure in it or the act would not be performed. "But what sort of pleasure is it?" Starr continues. "It is short term, transitory, lacks lasting value, lacks continuity with the rest of one's life . . . and adds nothing to the quality of one's life." Sexual relations with a person who is loved, however, represent "a part of the ongoing process of the enhancement of one's existence."

—*Paul R. Boehlke*

See also Equal Rights Amendment (ERA); Feminism; Gay rights; Homosexuality; Marriage; Personal relationships; Rape; *Second Sex, The*; Sexual revolution; Sexually transmitted diseases.

BIBLIOGRAPHY

Gould, Stephen Jay. *The Mismeasure of Man*. New York: W. W. Norton, 1981. Gould shows how society and science can impose imagined gifts and limits on people according to nature. His section on Broca's studies of women's and men's brains shows that both society and science can err.

Hrdy, Sarah Blaffer. "The Primate Origins of Human Sexuality." In *The Evolution of Sex: Nobel Conference XXIII*, edited by Robert Bellig and George Stevens. San Francisco: Harper & Row, 1988. Hrdy indicates that some aspects of human sexuality are not entirely unique, especially when primate behavior is studied. She concludes that, ethically, humans need to rise above nature.

MacKinnon, Catharine. *Feminism Unmodified*. Cambridge, Mass.: Harvard University Press, 1987. The chapter "Sex and Violence" describes the nature of rape, sexual harassment, pornography, and battery.

Solomon, Robert C. "Sex, Conception, and the Conception of Sex." In *Thirteen Questions in Ethics*, edited by G. Lee Bowie et al. Fort Worth, Tex.: Harcourt Brace Jovanovich College Publishers, 1992. Solomon concludes that sex cannot be free from morals, because it allows for the deepest interpersonal expressions.

Toufexis, Anastasia. "The Right Chemistry." *Time* 141 (February 15, 1993): 49-51. Discusses the evolutionary roots, experiences, and chemicals involved in falling in love. The experiences and people of childhood apparently lead one to select a particular person to love. Internal chemicals cause a natural high. Toufexis argues that nature's love lasts about four years and is not exclusive.

West, Cornel. *Race Matters*. Boston: Beacon, 1993. The whole book is fascinating, but the chapter on black sexuality is particularly significant regarding the effects of culture.

Sexually transmitted diseases

TYPE OF ETHICS: Bioethics

DATE: The origins of syphilis and gonorrhea are controversial; AIDS was recognized in 1981

ASSOCIATED WITH: Sex education and the sexual revolution

DEFINITION: Diseases that are generally, but not exclusively, spread by sexual intercourse

SIGNIFICANCE: Sex education must provide an ethical basis for responsible decisions regarding sexually transmitted diseases

Sexually transmitted diseases (STDs), whose incidence is rapidly increasing, are caused mainly by specific bacteria and viruses. Gonorrhea, chlamydia, and syphilis are bacterial and can be treated with antibiotics. Untreated cases of these diseases can result in sterility, infections of newborn children, and other serious problems.

Among the viral infections are herpes 2, genital warts, and acquired immunodeficiency syndrome (AIDS). Herpes 2 and AIDS have no cures. Herpes 2 causes painful sores on the sex organs that heal but reappear. A mother can infect her child with herpes 2 at birth. Genital warts may lead to cancer of the cervix and other tumors.

Although all STDs are serious, AIDS is devastating. The human immunodeficiency virus (HIV) damages the immune system by taking over and killing CD4 white blood cells. A person is said to have AIDS when his or her CD4 count falls below 200 per microliter (normal is 800-1,200 per microliter). At that point, the victim is likely to die from various opportunistic infections.

The risk of getting any STD varies with behavior. Practicing abstinence until marriage is the best safeguard against STDs. Risk increases with the number of sexual partners. Latex condoms offer some protection but are not perfect.

About 64 percent of AIDS cases in the United States involve homosexual men and correlate with high-risk anal intercourse. Another 28 percent of AIDS cases are caused by the sharing of contaminated needles during drug abuse. About 3 percent are the result of receiving transfusions of infected blood. HIV can also cross the placenta or be in a mother's milk and infect a baby. HIV transmission by heterosexual intercourse is increasing. The risk of HIV infection increases ten to one hundred times if sores from another STD are present.

Ethical Principles. In *Grounding for the Metaphysics of Morals* (1785), Immanuel Kant wrote that people must not treat others only as a means to some end. All people must be valued as ends in themselves. Respect for persons, fairness, truth-telling, and promise-keeping are vital to meaningful sexual behavior. Margaret Farley of Yale University concluded that sexual desire without interpersonal love leads to disappointment and loss of meaning. Justice must discipline sexuality so that no one is harmed and the common good is considered. Farley added that sexuality should be freed and nurtured while also being channeled and controlled. One cannot allow that "anything goes" even between consenting adults. Society has legitimate interests regarding the care of offspring, the limiting of extramarital pregnancies, and the control of disease.

Ethical Issues. To transmit disease carelessly by sexual means violates standards of love, commitment, respect, fairness, and honesty. Consider, for example, that a man might, through extramarital affairs, give his wife HIV. What are the responsibilities of any sexual partner?

In 1991, Kimberly Bergalis died at age twenty-three from a nonsexual HIV infection transmitted to her from her dentist. Other patients were also infected. Before her death, Bergalis asked that health workers be tested and their conditions be made public. Should health workers be tested? Are health workers in greater danger from their patients? Are these private matters? Often, privacy must be balanced with other concerns. Should an infected person reveal or tell all previous sexual partners? Should even the fact that a person has been tested be kept private?

In many cases, fear of AIDS has fed apathy and discrimination. The parents of the late Ryan White, who contracted HIV from a blood transfusion, had to file a discrimination suit against his school to allow him to attend. Many STD clinics fail to act sympathetically toward patients. Homosexuals are thought by some to deserve AIDS as punishment. How should people act when others carry an infectious disease? Should research monies be allocated for prevention or cure? Preventive and therapeutic HIV vaccines will need to be tested on animals and humans. What concerns will have to be met?

Legal Issues. Individuals can sue former partners for damages caused by STDs. Such civil actions are based on tort law. A tort is a wrongful act or injury that is committed either intentionally or negligently. Furthermore, many states have passed laws against STD transmission that set fines and prison terms.

In a 1979 landmark case, Margaret Housen of Washington, D.C., was awarded $1.3 million in compensatory and punitive damages for a gonorrhea infection. Also, when movie star Rock Hudson died of AIDS in 1985, his homosexual lover, Marc Christian, sued Hudson's estate. Christian was found to be HIV negative but was awarded $21.75 million for "grave emotional distress."

In sum, individuals must inform a sexual partner of possible infection. Noninfected partners are under no obligation to ask. Consenting to have sex does not imply consenting to being exposed to an STD. In a landmark legal case in 1993, it was decided that a Texas woman who was raped at knife point was not consenting to have sex merely because she asked the assailant to wear a condom. In another case, a prisoner with AIDS was convicted of attempted murder because he bit the hand of a prison guard.

Ethical Decision Making. The "sexual revolution" of the 1960's, which involved improved contraception, sexual behavioral studies, the women's movement, and trends toward openness, challenged the traditional structures of monogamous relationship: marriage and the family. Mixed messages in the popular culture often neglect birth control and concern for the partner.

Meanwhile, The Centers for Disease Control (1992) reported that 73 percent of U.S. high school seniors have experienced sex and that 4 percent of secondary students have STDs. The World Health Organization (WHO) reported in 1992 that 350,000 cases of STDs were being transmitted each day worldwide. The only current disease that is more infectious is the common cold.

A pandemic makes ethical considerations seem like a luxury. Nevertheless, some experts place hope not in medical breakthroughs but in changes in sexual behavior. As Robert Ashmore of Marquette University has stated, "we must not lose sight of the idea that the purpose of moral inquiry is practical." Can people who are "in love" be rational? Making responsible decisions in an area involving biological desires, peer pressure, society's concerns, moral standards, and individual autonomy may be a formidable task, but it is a necessary one.   —*Paul R. Boehlke*

See also Acquired immunodeficiency syndrome (AIDS); Marriage; Moral education; Self-control; Self-respect; Sexual revolution; Sexuality and sexual ethics.

BIBLIOGRAPHY

Ashmore, Robert B. *Building a Moral System*. Englewood Cliffs, N.J.: Prentice-Hall, 1987.

Farley, Margaret A. "Sexual Ethics." In *Encyclopedia of Bioethics*, edited by Warren T. Reich. New York: Free Press, 1978.

Gibbs, Nancy. "How Should We Teach Our Children About Sex?" *Time* 141 (May 24, 1993): 60-66.

Green, Richard. *Sexual Science and the Law*. Cambridge, Mass.: Harvard University Press, 1992.

Merson, Michael H. "Slowing the Spread of HIV: Agenda for the 1990s." *Science* 260 (May 28, 1993): 1266-1268.

Thielicke, Helmut. *The Ethics of Sex*. Translated by John W. Doberstein. Grand Rapids, Mich.: Baker Book House, 1975.

Shaftesbury, Earl of (Anthony Ashley Cooper; Feb. 26, 1671, London, England—Feb. 15, 1713, Naples, Italy): Philosopher

TYPE OF ETHICS: Renaissance and Restoration history

ACHIEVEMENTS: Author of the three-volume collection of philosophical essays *Characteristics of Men, Manners, Opinions, Times* (1711)

SIGNIFICANCE: Shaftesbury believed that the source of human morality was an innate "moral sense" that was allied with, and promoted, the good of society

Shaftesbury's education was placed in the hands of the philosopher John Locke by the boy's grandfather, the First Earl of Shaftesbury. He was fluent in classical Latin and Greek in his early youth, as well as in modern French; in his later youth, he spent three years on the European Continent and became thoroughly familiar there with art and music. His later writings, in fact, are of equal importance in both aesthetic and moral philosophy. In Shaftesbury's time, English moral philosophy was heavily influenced by Thomas Hobbes (1588-1679), who maintained that human nature is essentially selfish and that unless they are coerced by society, people will not cooperate to act decently. In direct contradiction of Hobbes, Shaftesbury maintained that the very existence of society demonstrates a predisposition for moral cooperation—the "moral sense" that he was the first to name. Because it was bound up with society, the moral sense found its greatest virtue in pursuing the public interest. Shaftesbury also believed that morality and religion were separable, which enhanced the status of the moral sense as an innate human attribute. Shaftesbury's views directly influenced the British philosophers Francis Hutcheson and David Hume.

See also Hobbes, Thomas; Hume, David; *Leviathan*; Locke, John; Moral-sense theories; Secular ethics; Selfishness.

Sharî'a

TYPE OF ETHICS: Religious ethics
DATE: Beginning during the revelations to Muḥammad (609-632)
ASSOCIATED WITH: Islamic law
DEFINITION: Any of the several traditions of Islamic law
SIGNIFICANCE: All of Islamic ethics is, in one of several possible ways, connected to *sharî'a*, since Islam does not separate the private, political, and religious realms of behavior

A clear distinction cannot be made in Islam between law and ethics; they are seen, instead, as facets of the single effort to build a community that is guided by the will of God. The Qur'ân (the primary source of Islamic law), for example, provides religious law ("Set not up with Allah any other God"), moral rules ("come not near unto adultery"), social regulations (on fiduciary management of the property of orphans), and guidance for the development of good character—all intermingled in *sûra* 17:22-39. In issues not addressed by the Qur'ân and its exegesis, the next recourse is usually to the traditions (*hadîth*) of the life of Muḥammad. There is a broad diversity of views about possible additional sources of law, which could include *'ijmâ* (consensus among the learned, which is important in Sunnî traditions) or the *imâm* (the leader of the faithful, who is important in Shî'a traditions). There can be no "wall of separation" (Thomas Jefferson's phrase) between church and state in Islam, since all sovereignty resides with God and human authorities administer only through his will.

See also *Hadîth*; Islamic ethics; Law.

Shî'a

TYPE OF ETHICS: Religious ethics
DATE: From 661
DEFINITION: One of the two main sects of Islam
SIGNIFICANCE: Provided a different interpretation of Islam and its tenets from that supplied by the Sunnî majority

Islamic religion is divided into two main sects: Sunnîs and Shî'ites. Shî'ites are followers of 'Alî ibn Abî Ṭâlib, a cousin and son-in-law of the Prophet Muḥammad, and 'Alî's sons, Ḥasan and Ḥusayn. Shî'ites contend that 'Alî should have succeeded Muḥammad at his death. They view the other three caliphs, Abû Bakr, 'Uthmân, and 'Umar, as usurpers. 'Alî was chosen caliph after the third caliph, 'Uthmân, was assassinated.

After 'Alî's death, Mu'awiya assumed the caliphate despite opposition from many followers of 'Alî, who considered 'Alî's sons, Ḥasan and Ḥusayn, the rightful successors. After Mu'awiya's death, his son Yazid succeeded him. 'Alî's second son, Ḥusayn, tried to claim the caliphate but was defeated and killed by Yazid's forces. The anniversary of Ḥusayn's death is commemorated by Shî'ites as a major religious event. There are two main branches of Shî'ites: the Twelvers, or Imâmis, and the Seveners, or Ismâ'îlites. The Twelvers believe that there were twelve Imâms, or leaders, after 'Alî, each chosen by his predecessor. The twelfth Imâm disappeared when he was a small child. Shî'ites believe that he will appear at an appropriate time as Mahdî, or savior, to rescue the world and restore the glory of Islam. The Ismâ'îlites believe that Ismâ'îl should have succeeded Imâm Jafar, the sixth Imâm. Ismâ'îl was Jafar's son. The Twelvers are the predominant branch of Shî'ism. Currently approximately 10 percent of the world's Muslim population is Shî'ite.

See also 'Alî ibn Abî Ṭâlib; Islamic ethics; Sunnîs.

Shinran (1173, near Kyōto, Japan—1262, Kyōto): Buddhist monk

TYPE OF ETHICS: Religious ethics
ACHIEVEMENTS: Founded the Japanese Mahāyānist Buddhist sect Jōdo Shinshū, or the True Pure Land Sect
SIGNIFICANCE: Taught that real truth (faith) refers to the gift of salvation in the next world, while common truth (morality) refers to one's duty to society in this world

A monk at Mt. Hiei from age nine to age twenty-nine, Shinran had a vision in which Kannon (Avalokiteśvara, the bodhisattva of compassion) directed him to follow the teachings of Hōnen (1133-1212). Both men taught that salvation could be achieved through reciting the nembutsu, the phrase "Hail [or 'I place . . . my faith in'], Amida Buddha." Amida was understood as a Buddha who lived in the Western Paradise and would bring there all persons who came to him in faith. While Hōnen thought that the nembutsu should be repeated over and over, Shinran thought that it was sufficient to pray sincerely to Amida once, since reciting the nembutsu was an act of gratitude for the gift of salvation, not a work by which one earned salvation. In the salvation experience, the believer experiences undoubting faith in Amida and simultaneously utters the nembutsu. Upon death, the devotee is reborn in the Western Paradise, which Shinran identified with nirvana. There the devotee would become a Buddha and return to the earth to enable others to achieve salvation. Shinran broke with his master over the celibacy of monks, married, and fathered six children.

See also Avalokiteśvara; Bodhisattva ideal; Buddhist ethics.

Shinto ethics

TYPE OF ETHICS: Religious ethics
DATE: Third century C.E. to present
DEFINITION: The religious system that played a major role in the development of the national state of Japan and that

continues to have a major influence on the conduct of the Japanese people

SIGNIFICANCE: Emphasizes that there is no one simple way of doing the right thing throughout the ages, but that the context must be thoroughly considered before a decision is made

Shinto, the "Way of the Gods," is the indigenous religion of Japan. After several centuries of development of traditions, rituals, and observances, it evolved into an organized religion between the third and sixth centuries. Shinto is best described as a religion of daily life. Love and respect for spirits and ancestors are far more important than is appeasement of deities or immortality.

History. From the beginning, Shinto was influenced by or through China. Confucianism infiltrated Japan from northern China in the third century and was followed in the sixth century by Buddhism. Buddhism, when united with Shinto, gave Japanese religion renewed vitality, universal ideals, and transcendental speculation. Confucianism, which is basically an ethical system, provided the ethical foundation for the social and political development of Japan.

In spite of the infusion of Confucianism, Western scholars have had difficulty in discovering concrete ethical principles in Shinto. Although earlier Shinto reveals very little ethical thought, Confucian contributions brought a major increase in ethical thinking.

This growing ethical consciousness experienced great change and adaptation in later centuries. One of the most serious changes was the Meiji ("enlightened government") Restoration in 1868. This event officially established Shinto as the state religion of Japan and set the nation on a path of imperialism and conquest. The ethical consequences of this path are abundant. Shinto ethics, as used by the state, helped to formulate the conduct and blind obedience of Japanese military personnel during World War II. Negative examples of such behavior include the brutal treatment of prisoners by the Japanese on the Bataan Death March and the work of the Kamikaze suicide pilots near the end of the war.

State Shinto was disestablished after the national humiliation of military defeat in 1945, but it was not eliminated as a national faith.

Ethical Principles. A careful study of Shinto ethics reveals at least eight principles that are dominant influences on the daily lives of the Japanese people. The foundational principle of Shinto ethics is embodied in the Three Sacred Treasures of Shinto. These treasures, to which are attached moral and ethical values, are displayed in all significant Shinto shrines. The mirror stands for wisdom, integrity, purity, and righteousness. The sword reflects valor and justice. The last treasure, the stone necklace, symbolizes benevolence, affection, and obedience.

The second principle is tribal ethics, or the authority of the community. In this ethic, the individual melts into unreasoning submission to communal authority. At key points in Japanese history, this has been the power that solidified the people, but it also has been used to justify aggressive national conduct. Tribal ethics fosters a tendency to refer ethical decisions to government offices. It emphasizes a contextual approach and glorifies the ethics of intention.

A strong social ethic is built on the position of the emperor as a direct descendant of the sun goddess and also as the head of a giant family. The roof over the family has often been extended to include the entire world. This ethic has established an almost unbreakable relationship between the emperor and the people, with very few attempts at revolutionary change.

Consistent with the situational nature of Shinto ethics is the concept of *makoto*, or "truth." Truth is relative, thus in Shinto there is no ultimate truth. *Makoto* involves an inner heart-searching while confronting any ethical issue.

Related to *makoto* is the principle that all evil is external. When a person is untrue to himself or herself or to others, it is only a result of a lack of awareness caused by external influences.

The Shinto ethic of guilt is better understood as shame. A person who fails to fulfill his or her proper role, as determined by the communal authority, is often consumed by an overwhelming shame, even to the point of suicide.

A unique principle of Shinto ethics is *maka-ima*, or the "middle present." *Maka-ima*, which first appeared in the imperial edicts of the eighth century, means that the present moment is the most important moment of all times. Shintoists are thus exhorted to make each moment as true and as worthy as possible.

The last ethic of Shinto is a strong concept of racial superiority. This concept became extremely important after the inauguration of State Shinto in the nineteenth century. It produced a jealous contempt for all non-Japanese culture and a major attempt to keep such influences out of Japanese life. Officially, this principle was abolished by imperial decree on January 1, 1946.

Conclusion. Japan's military defeat in 1945 unleashed long-suppressed forces of change. The embodiment of moral and ethical truth in the community headed by the emperor was forever broken. Replacing that sentiment was a feeling of individual cooperation by morally responsible citizens of the community. Although many traditional Japanese values have been retained, there is now more freedom to accept the ethical principles of other cultures.

Problems related to State Shinto did not all disappear in 1945. The ethics involved in shrine worship—particularly the Yasukuni Shrine, which honors as deities more than two million war dead—remained as a continual dilemma for many Japanese people. The basic ethical nature of State Shinto has, however, been replaced by the ethic of world peace and an attempt to contribute to the well-being and advancement of all world cultures.   —*Glenn L. Swygart*

See also Buddhist ethics; Christian ethics; Hindu ethics; Islamic ethics; Taoist ethics.

Bibliography

Anesaki, Masaharu. *History of Japanese Religion*. Rutland, Vt.: Charles E. Tuttle, 1963.

Holtom, D. C. *Modern Japan and Shinto Nationalism*. Chicago: University of Chicago Press, 1943.

Mason, J. W. T. *The Meaning of Shinto*. Port Washington, N.Y.: Kennikat Press, 1935.

Ono, Sokyo. *Shinto: The Kami Way*. Rutland, Vt.: Charles E. Tuttle, 1962.

Ross, Floyd Hiatt. *Shinto: The Way of Japan*. Boston: Beacon Press, 1965.

Sidgwick, Henry (May 31, 1838, Skipton, Yorkshire, England—Aug. 28, 1900, Cambridge, Cambridgeshire, England): Philosopher

Type of ethics: Modern history

Associated with: Utilitarianism

Achievements: Wrote *Methods of Ethics* (1874); founded the Society for Psychical Research in 1882 and served as its first president

Significance: Sidgwick attempted to discover a rational means of making ethical decisions and further developed the utilitarian ideas of John Stuart Mill by applying to them Immanuel Kant's notion of the categorical imperative; his work is considered by some scholars the most important English-language work on ethics of the nineteenth century

In *Methods of Ethics*, his greatest book, Sidgwick argues that there are no grounds for rational action in judging an act either on the basis of the happiness it brings to the actor (egoism) or on the basis of criteria other than the promotion of happiness (intuitionism). Instead, he proposes a system of "universal hedonism" in which one seeks to reconcile the conflict between one's own pleasures and those of others. His argument is similar to that of Kant and is parallel to the latter's "categorical imperative." Sidgwick's interests went beyond formal systems of ethics; he also engaged in psychic research and studied political economy. Among his works are *Principles of Political Economy* (1883), *Elements of Politics* (1891), and *The Development of European Polity* (1903), which was published after his death.

See also Egoism; Intuitionist ethics; Kant, Immanuel: Mill, John Stuart; Utilitarianism.

Sierra Club

Type of ethics: Environmental ethics

Date: Founded 1896

Associated with: Preservationism

Definition: An organization advocating wilderness preservation, natural history publication, and wilderness recreation

Significance: Promotes the wilderness ethic

Stimulated by John Muir's writings about the Sierra Nevada, 162 Californians founded the Sierra Club in 1892. Their principal incentive was protecting Yosemite and the mountain-

John Muir, founder of the Sierra Club. (Library of Congress)

ous Pacific Coast. They also sponsored wilderness recreation, including the "High Trips," annual extended mountain outings. This activity has grown to become a worldwide program of tours, outings, and excursions. Efforts to protect and enlarge Yosemite National Park generally were successful. Opposition to San Francisco's Hetch Hetchy Valley water project, however, failed in 1913, but large-scale, nationwide lobbying against it brought permanent expansion of lobbying, political action, and publicity. After World War II, Club membership expanded throughout the country, and a permanent, professional staff was employed. The campaign against Echo Park Dam in Dinosaur National Park in 1955 is a good example of the Sierra Club's postwar political action. In the 1990's, the club began to advocate the dismantling of existing dams and roads to restore wilderness. The first Sierra Club book, *Place Names of the High Sierra*, appeared in 1926. The club published about fifty books and six calendars in 1990. The Sierra Club had almost 750,000 members throughout the United States and Canada in 1990. The national staff was about 300, including lawyers, lobbyists, editors, a tour organizer, and publicists.

See also Muir, John; National Park System, U.S.

Sikh ethics

Type of ethics: Religious ethics

Date: Fifteenth century to present

Definition: A system of religious belief centered in Punjab, India, that focuses on the worship of one God and the equality of all people

Significance: Presents a challenge to the Hindu conceptions of polytheism and hierarchy that predominate in India; offers the model of the "saint-soldier" for whom spiritual insight and physical courage are complementary

The Sikhs are a religious group that constitute approximately 2 percent of the total population of India. The majority of the Sikhs live in the state of Punjab in the northwest, but followers of the Sikh faith are also in diaspora across north India and in the United States, the United Kingdom, and Canada. There are about sixteen million Sikhs in total.

Sikhism, which began in the fifteenth century, draws from elements of both Hinduism and Islam, the predominant religions of the Indian subcontinent. Persecuted by both Hindu and Muslim rulers at various points in their history, the Sikhs have developed a firm sense of themselves as a separate community and have recently begun agitating for separate nationhood. Issues concerning the use of violence in maintaining Sikh autonomy are at the forefront of ethical debates within the Sikh community.

The Development of Sikhism. Sikhism as a system of faith was initiated by Nānak, the first of a series of ten Sikh Gurus, or teachers. Guru Nānak, drawing on meditative traditions within Hinduism but rejecting its elaborate ritualism, gathered a group of disciples (*sikhs*) around him to form a community called the *Panth*. Within the Panth, caste differences were eradicated, as were inequalities between men and women. In addition, the multiple deities of Hinduism were replaced by devotion to a single God something like that of Islam.

Sikhism quickly acquired converts from the lower-caste levels of the Hindu system. In this, it followed the pattern of several other heterodox religious movements of India, notably Buddhism and Jainism. For many, however, Sikhism remained heavily intertwined with Hinduism, with many villages and even many families incorporating both Sikhs and Hindus in relative harmony.

Guru Nānak himself is venerated not only as the religion's founding figure but also as a kind of mediator between the human and the divine. He was followed by a succession of nine other Gurus who took up the leadership of the Panth. Two of these in particular left a lasting stamp on the nature of the Sikh faith. Hargobind, the Sixth Guru, donned the double-edged sword that has become symbolic of the Sikhs, representing the recognition that Sikhism must wield both spiritual and temporal power to be successful. This theme was carried further by the Tenth and last Guru, Guru Gobind Singh, who, after years of persecution, came to the conclusion that the Sikhs had to become militant in defense of their religious beliefs and social order.

Guru Gobind Singh created a brotherhood of militant Sikhs called the *khalsa*, or "pure," who were ready to die in defense of their faith. They all took on the surname of Singh ("lion") and adopted the five symbols of Sikh identity: uncut hair, comb, breeches, sword, and steel bangle. One effect of these five signs was to make Khalsa Sikhs highly visible, with the characteristic turbans into which their uncut hair was bound their outstanding feature. Probably this innovation was related to an awareness of the fate of other rebellious religious movements in Indian history, which tended to become merged into the overarching Hindu frame-

THE FIVE SIGNS OF THE SIKH (FIVE "K's" IN PUNJABI)	
1.	Uncut hair (*kesh*)
2.	Comb (*kangi*)
3.	Breeches (*kachch*)
4.	Sword (*kirpan*)
5.	Steel bangle (*kara*)

work. Guru Gobind Singh believed, however, that physical violence on the part of the Khalsa was to be used only in *defense* of the Sikh faith, and only after all other means had failed.

Sikh communities in India and abroad cluster around their *gurudwaras*, or temples (literally, "gateways to the Guru"). The communal kitchen is a key feature of the Sikh community, symbolic of the Sikhs' rejection of caste rules forbidding interdining. (The kettle and the sword are said to be representative of Sikh beliefs—the kettle for feeding the hungry and the sword for defending the weak.) Worship services at Sikh gurudwaras may involve readings from their scripture, the Guru Granth Sahib, as well as the singing of hymns, recitation of poetry, or other kinds of contributions from community members including, recently, political statements.

The holy city of the Sikhs and center of the Sikh faith is Amritsar in Punjab, India. (*Amrit* is the nectar stirred by the sword and drunk to consecrate a commitment; Amritsar is the "pool of nectar.") The so-called "Golden Temple" is the main Sikh shrine at Amritsar, and it has been the focal point of the dispute between the Sikhs and the government of India that has been developing over the past decade. In 1984, the Golden Temple complex was the scene of intense fighting between the Indian Army and Sikh insurgents agitating for an independent state of Khalistan ("Land of the Pure"). The perceived desecration of this shrine by Indian troops, and the Hindu-Sikh rioting that followed, pushed many Sikhs to take a more militant political posture. Upheaval has continued in Punjab, and it is one of the major security concerns of the Indian government. Human rights issues surrounding India's handling of the Punjab problem have become a focus of several international investigations.

Ethical Issues of Contemporary Sikhism. Sikhism is at its heart an ethical system as well as a theology and a design for living. The foundation of Sikh ethics is the principle of equality, which is better understood as an ideal than as an accomplishment. (Aspects of caste still persist in Sikh communities, and relationships between women and men remain inequitable in many ways.) Other ethical precepts followed by Sikhs include admonitions against theft, lying, and adultery, and a ban on smoking. Many Sikhs regard charity and courage as among the noblest virtues; the "saint-soldier" is the model emulated by many.

The most problematic issue for Sikhs today, given the political violence endemic in the Punjab, is that of legitimate defense of the faith. Sikhism has never advocated a policy of "turning the other cheek," but it does seek to restrain the aggressive, as opposed to the defensive, use of force. Whether actions in which noncombatants are killed fall within the realm of defensive violence, and whether the Sikh community is actually under a threat substantial enough to evoke the use of force, are deeply disturbing questions for many Sikhs. For outsiders, conditions in the Punjab are very difficult to evaluate because of extreme limitations on press coverage and travel in the region. It is clear, however, that many thousands of Sikhs have been killed in the past decade of violence and that there is a strong feeling of being a community under siege on the part of both Indian and overseas Sikhs.   —*Cynthia Keppley Mahmood*

See also Hindu ethics; Nānak, Guru.

BIBLIOGRAPHY

Cole, W. Owen. *The Sikhs: Their Religious Beliefs and Practices*. Boston: Routledge & Kegan Paul, 1978.

Fox, Richard G. *Lions of the Punjab: Culture in the Making*. Berkeley: University of California Press, 1985.

Kapur, Rajiv. *Sikh Separatism: The Politics of Faith*. London: Allen & Unwin, 1986.

McLeod, W. H. *The Sikhs: History, Religion, and Society*. New York: Columbia University Press, 1989.

Rai, Priya Muhar. *Sikhism and the Sikhs: An Annotated Bibliography*. New York: Greenwood, 1989.

Singh, Khushwant. *A History of the Sikhs*. Princeton: Princeton University Press, 1966.

Silent Spring: Book

TYPE OF ETHICS: Environmental ethics

DATE: Published 1962

AUTHOR: Rachel Carson

SIGNIFICANCE: This book popularized the problem of chemical pollution by illustrating the demise and death of organisms that had once been a part of a countryside spring

During the late 1950's, a proliferation of the manufacturing and use of chemical agents as insecticides and herbicides seemed to stimulate the agricultural industry. Initially, these chemicals provided relief to farmers who could now control and obliterate insect pests and weeds from cropland. Insufficient testing and monitoring of the use of these chemicals, however, led to widespread contamination of water and land, resulting in the destruction of a great variety of animals and plants. The popular book *Silent Spring* aroused public awareness of a sinister development in which streams and springs became silent as birds, frogs, fish, and other organisms died from the toxic chemicals used in adjacent fields. Ethically, the

Rachel Carson, the author of Silent Spring. *(AP/Wide World Photos)*

realization that humans can quickly and easily pollute and blight large regions through the careless use of chemicals illustrated the necessity for good stewardship of natural resources. As an alternative to control insect pests, Carson suggested the use of nonchemical methods that were more environmentally wholesome. Carson's landmark book led to the formation of numerous environmental groups that have committed themselves to protect natural resources.

See also Clean Water Act; Conservation; Earth, human relations to; Environmental ethics; Environmental movement; Environmental Protection Agency (EPA).

Sin

TYPE OF ETHICS: Religious ethics

DATE: From antiquity

ASSOCIATED WITH: Judaism, Christianity, Islam, and other theistic belief systems

DEFINITION: A violation of religious or moral law; a failure in one's duty to God; a state of rebellion against God

SIGNIFICANCE: In a theistic system of belief, the concept of sin deepens the significance and consequences of moral failure, since it involves a negative response not only to other human beings but also to God

The concept of sin has its origin in the prehistoric past in the magical attempt to deal with the forces of nature. Some of these forces are taboo—that is, dangerous to handle. The breaking of taboos is not essentially sinful, since the behavior is typically unavoidable. In ancient Mesopotamia a moral dimension entered the picture. The creation myth, the *Enuma elish*, explained that humans were created to serve the gods. The

Gilgamesh Epic took that thinking further. It tells of the creation of Enkidu, a savage of whom the other beasts knew no fear. Enticed to participate in civilization by a prostitute, he lost his innocence, joined with the hero Gilgamesh, put on clothing, and learned to eat and drink in proper proportions. In short, he became human and ultimately met the fate of all humans: death. The Greeks further developed the idea of moral guilt. Plato saw moral failure as a matter of error; no one who knew what is best would choose to do otherwise. It was, however, the Judeo-Christian tradition that more fully developed the notion of sin.

Sin in the Hebrew Bible. The story of the origin of sin occupies the third chapter of the Bible, and its scope, effects, and forgiveness occupy much of the remainder. Sin is introduced in Genesis 3 as a deliberate act of disobedience by Adam and Eve. Sin was experienced both as the rupture of their relationship with God and as a power that grasped them. It spread to all other humans like a contagious disease, disrupting both the natural and the social order as well as the standing of each sinner before God. Forgiveness for sin in the Hebrew Bible could involve animal sacrifice coupled with human contrition or intercession by a prophet or priest.

Biblical Hebrew employed about twenty different words for sin, but four in particular stand out. The first root (the basic form of a word from which various parts of speech can be derived) was used 457 times and originally meant to "miss" a target or "fail" to follow the proper order. Hence, sin was understood as the failure to comply with moral standards or obligations. This failure might include obligations to another person (parent, superior, spouse) or to God. Still other sins constituted a failure toward both: for example, murder, robbery, adultery, giving false testimony, and perverting justice.

The second root, which appears 136 times, originally meant "breach" and is used of sin in the sense of a breach of a covenant or "rebellion." Hence, sin carried with it the idea of persons revolting and dissolving the relationship between themselves and God. A sinner not only commits wrong acts but also lives in a state of rebellion against God.

The third and fourth roots can be dealt with more quickly. The third, used more than 254 times, originally meant "bend" and emphasized the condition of guilt as a consequence of bending the rules. The fourth, used 19 times, meant to "err" and emphasized that the sinner had gone astray and become lost.

The later idea of moral (or cardinal) sins derived from passages in the Hebrew Bible that associated death with the commission of certain sins (for example, premeditated murder, striking one's father, kidnapping, bestiality, and sorcery). Some passages associated a more general state of sinfulness with death (for example, Ezek. 18:20: "The soul that sins shall die").

Atonement for sins in the Hebrew Bible was conceived as a covering for sin. It was achieved primarily through sacrifice. The "sin offering" was made for unintentional offenses that broke a person's relationship with God and endangered the welfare of the community. The "guilt offering" atoned for offenses that required restitution along with a sacrifice. Less bloody means were also used. On the Day of Atonement, the high priest would symbolically lay the sins of the people upon the scapegoat and drive it out of the community, carrying their sins with it. Exodus 30:16 suggests that money could be given for the same purpose. Finally, the Hebrew Bible also speaks of prophets and priests interceding for sinners. For genuinely minor sins, penitents might pray for themselves.

Sin in Rabbinic Judaism. The rabbis, who led Judaism to think through its theology after the destruction of Jerusalem by the Romans in 70 C.E., used a term meaning "pass over" for sin. They spoke of two inclinations within humans. Literally, the names of these inclinations can be translated the "good inclination" and the "bad inclination," but these translations are misleading. The so-called "good" inclination consisted of characteristics humans were thought to share with the angels: They walk upright, have eyes on the fronts of their faces, reason, and speak. By contrast, the "evil" inclination consisted of characteristics humans share with animals: eating and drinking, voiding, mating, and dying. Clearly, none of these latter characteristics is "evil" in a moral sense, though several may lead to sin if not held in check. Just as clearly, Rabbinic Judaism did not derive from Genesis 3 a doctrine of original sin as Christianity did.

The rabbis also thought in terms of sins as transgressions of the individual commandments of the law. Thus, all sins constituted rebellion against God. Even so, the rabbis distinguished between light and severe sins. The most serious were murder, idolatry, adultery, and incest. They also distinguished sins of omission (in which one failed to follow a commandment) from sins of commission (in which one committed a prohibited act). Sins of commission generally were thought to be worse.

Sin in the New Testament. The New Testament employed two words for sin. The first originally indicated missing a target and was a near equivalent of the first word discussed above in connection with the Hebrew Bible. The second word designated lawlessness and usually indicated a state of hostility toward God.

The books of Matthew, Mark, Luke, and Acts did not speak of the nature of sin, but of specific wrong deeds. The angel informed Joseph that Jesus would save his people from their sins (Matt. 1:21), and Jesus said that he came to call sinners to repentance (Matt. 9:13). A person who recognized Jesus' mission through the Holy Spirit but refused to confess Jesus and the salvation he brought committed a sin that both Matthew and Mark declared unpardonable. The gospel of John conceptualized the mission of Jesus in terms of the sacrificial victim of the Hebrew Bible: The sinless lamb of God took sin upon himself and carried it away.

The apostle Paul extended further the New Testament conceptualization of sin by raising the issue of the power of sin over human nature and the world. Paul argued that sin entered the world through Adam's act of opposition of God in the Garden of Eden. This opposition arose from Adam's freedom. Sin brought death into the world with it. Indeed, Paul portrayed death as the wages paid by sin, the workmaster. For Paul, then, sin consisted of more than individual misdeeds; it was a state of self-assertive rebellion against God in which all humans lived. An act was sinful insofar as it was a rejection of God or his law. He argued (in Rom. 1-3) that Gentiles had refused to accept God as the origin of good, and Jews (who had the law and should have known better) had rejected the law. The result was that all human beings were enslaved to sin.

With such a view of sin and humankind's entanglement in it, the New Testament considered its proclamation of forgiveness for sin "good news." Furthermore, it employed a number of analogies to explain the role of Jesus in that forgiveness. Three examples follow. The first analogy has been mentioned already: sacrifice. Jesus' death was understood as atoning for sins in the same way that sacrifices did in the Hebrew Bible. The book of Hebrews carried that thought further by conceiving of Jesus as both the perfect High Priest (because he was sinless) and the perfect victim (because he was offered once only and for all sins). Another analogy was that of ransom; Jesus' death was understood as the ransom price paid to set sinners free. Third, Paul employed legal language in speaking of atonement as justification; the death of Jesus delivers the sinner from sin, finitude, and death.

Sin in Muslim Thought. Sin is also an important concept is Islam, which derives its ideas on the subject more from the Hebrew Bible and Rabbinic Judaism than from the New Testament and Christianity. Human beings are not considered inherently evil, as in Christianity. Rather, in thinking akin to the rabbinic notion of the two inclinations, Muslim doctrine holds that humans have both a lower nature to which evil spirits appeal and a higher nature to which angelic creatures appeal. People sin by disobeying God's commands and thus committing individual misdeeds.

Sin in Early and Medieval Christian Thought. The first Christian to write a systematic account of his theology was Saint Augustine. In his book *The Enchiridion on Faith, Hope and Love* (421 C.E.), he defined sin as a word, deed, or desire in opposition to the eternal law of God. Sin began with Adam's turning away from God, who was unchangeably good. The fall left Adam ignorant of his duty and lustful for what was harmful. Through Adam's fall all humans were corrupted and were born under the penalty of death. Augustine's thinking on original sin was echoed by the Roman Catholic church at the Council of Trent (1546): The transmission of sin comes by propagation, not by the imitation of others.

Augustine is well known for his ideas about concupiscence. Concupiscence is a characteristic considered unique to human beings, who—unlike either angels or animals—are a mixture of flesh and spirit. Concupiscence grows out of that mixture. It is the fruit of past sin, part of the punishment for that sin, and the seed of future sin. Concupiscence in the first two senses is the result of original sin and the sins of one's parents as well as of one's own past sins. Concupiscence in the third sense is a nondeliberate desire pitted against a person's freedom to choose. Hence, it is the seed of future sins, without itself being a sin. It is not, however, exclusively an impulse to act immorally. Even less can it simply be equated with the sexual drive, though it was that aspect of concupiscence that concerned Augustine most.

Augustine recognized that not all sins were of equal severity, but he thought that distinguishing trivial from heinous sins should be left to God. Later churchmen did not share his caution. They distinguished between mortal (or cardinal) sins, which disrupt one's relationship with God, and venial sins, which only introduce disorder into one's relationship with God. Mortal sins merit eternal punishment, while venial sins merit only temporal punishment. Mortal sins must be confessed; venial sins need not be. Cardinal sins are not the same as the mortal sins of the Hebrew Bible or Rabbinic Judaism, but are characteristics that render the sinner liable for Hell and are forgivable only through penance. Enumerated as seven as early as 604 C.E., they have typically included the following: pride, covetousness, lust, anger, gluttony, envy, and sloth.

Redemption from sin was the work of God through the death of the mediator Jesus. Furthermore, Augustine thought that God's grace was ultimately irresistible; if God chose a person to receive it, sooner or later that person would do so. Pardon for sin is offered through the church, specifically through three sacraments. Baptism was held to remove original sin and personal sins in cases other than those of infants. Confession removes sins one commits along the way. Extreme unction (now often called the sacrament for the sick) offered the opportunity for final confession or (for unconscious persons) complete final absolution.

Sin in Reformation Thought. The reformers reacted against much in Roman Catholic thinking; for example, limiting the sacraments to two (or three) and denying that baptism cleanses one from original sin. They differed little, however, on the doctrine of sin per se. Indeed, John Calvin, one of the leaders of the Swiss Reform movement, developed the thinking of Augustine to its logical conclusion. In his *Christianae religionis Institutio* (1536; *Institutes of the Christian Religion*), he too accepted the idea of original sin and the imputation of guilt to all of Adam's descendants. In speaking of total depravity, he said that everything in humanity (specifically including understanding, will, soul, and body) is polluted and engrossed by concupiscence. In short, human beings are corrupt through and through. Calvin drew from this analysis the further conclusion that everything the sinner does is accounted by God as sin.

Calvin also pushed Augustine's thinking on irresistible

grace. Both men applied the idea of omnipotence to the idea of grace, concluding that God would not be omnipotent if his grace could be rejected. Calvin carried the thinking one step further: If humans are thoroughly corrupt and incapable of turning from sin, and if God chooses those who will receive grace, by implication he also chooses those who will not receive grace.

Not all Protestants agreed with Calvin. In the Dutch Reform movement, Jacobus Arminius (d. 1609) opposed Calvin's view of predestination as too harsh in favor of what he called "conditional election," which he thought placed greater emphasis on the mercy of God. Arminius argued that God elects to eternal life those he knows will freely respond in faith to his offer of grace. His thinking was more influential in England than in Holland. Anglicans, General Baptists, and Methodists followed him instead of Calvin. American Protestantism, even within the Reform or Presbyterian tradition, generally speaking stands closer to Arminius than to Calvin, though one can still find staunch defenders of Calvin's view of original sin and the imputation of Adam's sin to his descendants.

Sin in Modern Thought. The concept of sin has continued to occupy some of the best thinkers, particularly theologians, of the modern period. One theologian deserving mention is Paul Tillich, who reinterpreted Christianity in terms of existentialist philosophy. For Tillich, humans find themselves in a state of estrangement from God, from others, and from themselves. Tillich retains the word "sin" to characterize this estrangement precisely because it includes the personal act of turning away from God. Hence, human estrangement is sin. The New Testament scholar Rudolf Bultmann also speaks of sin in existentialist terms by saying that being divided against oneself is the essence of human existence under sin.

Modern philosophers have been interested in the concept of sin because of its importance to ethics. Two examples must suffice. The first is the nineteenth century Danish philosopher of religion Søren Kierkegaard. As one of the founders of existentialism, he exercised great influence over Tillich, Bultmann, and many others. He argued that despair (in the sense of not willing to be oneself) is as much a form of sin as murder, theft, unchastity, and the like. It is sin because it constitutes a lack of faith in God not to be all that one could be. Likewise, he denied that sinfulness is inherited through biological generation; he did, however, find its presupposition in the anxiety common to all people. This anxiety is caused by the awareness of one's finitude and the threat of nonbeing. In their condition of anxiety, humans commit sinful deeds.

The second philosopher is Richard Swinburne, who defines sin as failure in one's duty toward God, the creator. He is more concerned, however, with the idea of original sin. Swinburne argues that one may not be held accountable for that over which one has no control. Original sin properly may be said to have begun with the first hominid (who

might even be called Adam), but it arose out of characteristics inherited in the process of human evolution. Adam's responsibility lay solely in initiating a historical and social process. Furthermore, sin arises within every hominid, whether descended from Adam or not; it is not a consequence of choices by one's forebears. It is also not the case that all humans who come after Adam are held accountable (guilty) for Adam's choices.

Kierkegaard and Swinburne have reinterpreted the concept of sin in the light of modern life and thought. Other thinkers, however, see less value in the concept of sin. Reacting against them, the psychologist Karl Menninger has complained about what he sees as the result of ignoring the concept of sin: a society that more and more has difficulty in finding grounds to condemn any behavior.

—Paul L. Redditt

See also Augustine, Saint; Calvin, John; Christian ethics; Guilt and shame; Jewish ethics; Taboos.

BIBLIOGRAPHY

Foster, Durwood, and Paul Mojzes, eds. *Society and Original Sin.* New York: Paragon, 1985. A collection of essays from a variety of disciplines and from Jewish, Christian, Muslim, and Unification church thinkers on the problem of sin in general and original sin in particular.

Menninger, Karl. *Whatever Became of Sin?* New York: Hawthorn, 1973. A popularly written discussion of changes in the understanding of morality in American society. Menninger argues that, increasingly, "sin" has been explained in psychological or other terms, which has led to a moral malaise in which nothing (or very little) is clearly immoral.

Ricour, Paul. *The Symbolism of Evil.* Translated by Emerson Buchanan. New York: Harper & Row, 1967. A thorough study of sin and guilt within the larger context of its presentation in mythology. The chapter on sin provides an excellent discussion of the subject within theism in general and the Bible in particular.

Smith, H. Shelton. *Changing Conceptions of Original Sin.* New York: Scribner's, 1955. A clearly written study of diverse views in American theology from 1750 to 1950 about the idea of original sin.

Swinburne, Richard. *Responsibility and Atonement.* Oxford, England: Clarendon Press, 1989. A defense of a self-proclaimed "liberal" Christian understanding of morality, sin, and atonement by a leading religious philosopher.

Singer, Peter (b. July 6, 1946, Melbourne, Victoria, Australia): Ethicist.

TYPE OF ETHICS: Animal rights

ACHIEVEMENTS: Author of *Democracy and Disobedience* (1973), *Animal Liberation* (1975), *Practical Ethics* (1979), and *The Expanding Circle: Ethics and Sociobiology* (1981)

SIGNIFICANCE: One of the leading contemporary advocates of animal rights, Singer popularized the concept of "speciesism," which attacks human-centered ethics and discrimination for or against animals based solely on their species

Since 1973, with the simultaneous publication of his essay "Animal Liberation" in the *New York Review of Books* and the *National Observer,* Peter Singer has been the leading advocate of animal rights from a rigorously argued and philosophically defined ethical perspective. In that essay, Singer popularized Richard Ruder's concept of "speciesism." Singer defined speciesism as "the belief that we are entitled to treat members of other species in a way in which it would be wrong to treat members of our own." Singer's use of the term "animal liberation" tied the liberation of animals to the other liberation movements of the early 1970's, such as the movements for the liberation of blacks and women. Singer's work can be understood as a philosophical examination of how far the human moral horizon and human ethical obligations extend. Once humans extend that horizon to include animals, then practices that were once regarded as natural and inevitable, such as using animals for food, clothing, or medical research, can no longer be simply assumed to be ethical. According to Singer, some of these practices will "now be seen as intolerable."

See also Animal rights.

Situational ethics

TYPE OF ETHICS: Theory of ethics
DATE: Popularized 1966
ASSOCIATED WITH: Philosopher Joseph Fletcher and Protestant theologians Rudolf Bultmann and Paul Tillich
DEFINITION: The position that all ethical decisions must be made in the light of individual circumstances and not according to moral rules or universal laws
SIGNIFICANCE: Repudiates all sets of rules or laws in favor of basing moral decisions on a single fundamental principle, such as love

Situational (or contextual) ethics is largely a reaction against legalism, the so-called "old morality" of reliance on laws and rules as dependable guides to conduct. Situational ethics emphasizes love rather than law; it begins with the unique elements of a specific ethical situation rather than with any set of laws or rules that are to be applied in every situation. Situational ethics thus takes an inductive rather than a deductive approach to ethical decision making.

Situational ethics was popularized in 1966 by the publication of Joseph Fletcher's *Situation Ethics: The New Morality*. In this best-selling book, Fletcher states his belief that there are only three basic approaches to ethical decision-making; legalism, antinomianism (the rejection of all laws and principles, sometimes called subjectivism), and situational ethics. He depicted situational ethics as being "in between" the other two extremes. The primary purpose of *Situation Ethics* was to oppose legalism, because Fletcher believed that almost all people in Western culture, especially Christians, are and have been legalistic.

Fletcher, along with other proponents of situational ethics, insisted that both Jesus and Paul taught this approach to ethical decision making. Other persons, however, find the roots of situational ethics in the philosophical approaches of existentialism and utilitarianism. Existentialist ethics has often emphasized the free choice of persons as the only avenue leading to authentic existence; such free choice is denied by any reliance on principles and rules in ethical decision making. Although Fletcher tended to categorize existentialist ethics as "antinomian," he readily incorporated into his approach the utilitarian principle of "the greatest good for the greatest number." He thus translated the principle of love into the principle of utility; the moral quality of actions derives directly from their consequences. The most loving thing to do in any ethical decision-making situation is determined by a kind of utilitarian calculus: What course of action will bring about the most good for the most people?

Among the many Christian theologians who influenced Fletcher and others who subscribe to situational ethics, Rudolph Bultmann and Paul Tillich stand out. Bultmann held that a Christian can, in love, perceive a neighbor's greatest need through a kind of moral intuition. Similarly, Tillich believed that moral judgments are based on an intuitive grasp of the potentialities of being. Fletcher quoted with approval Tillich's statement that "The law of love is the ultimate law because it is the negation of law. . . . The absolutism of love is its power to go into the concrete situation, to discover what is demanded by the predicament of the concrete to which it turns" (Tillich, *Systematic Theology*, 1951-1963).

The heart of situational ethics, according to Fletcher, is found in six propositions that demonstrate how the principle of love works itself out in concrete situations involving ethical decision making. These propositions are:

(1) "Only one thing is intrinsically good; namely, love: nothing else at all." No law, principle, or value is good in and of itself—not even life, truth, chastity, property, or marriage. (2) "The ruling norm of Christian decision is love: nothing else." Fletcher, using several admittedly extreme examples, attempted to demonstrate how the most loving thing to do might involve violating each of the Ten Commandments. (3) "Love and justice are the same, for justice is love distributed, nothing else." Justice is love working itself out in particular situations; it is Christian love "using its head." (4) "Love wills the neighbor's good whether we like him or not." Loving and liking are not the same thing; according to Fletcher, there is nothing sentimental about love. Love is attitudinal rather than emotional; therefore, it can be commanded. (5) "Only the end justifies the means; nothing else." Fletcher contested the classical Christian dictum that the end does not justify the means. In a world of relativities and uncertainties, one may do what would normally be considered evil if good results come from it. (6) "Love's decisions are made situationally, not prescriptively." The rightness or wrongness of an action does not reside in the act itself, but in the whole complex of all the factors in the situation.

Situational ethics has been, and remains, extremely controversial. In 1952, Pope Pius XII condemned "situation eth-ics" as an individualistic and subjective appeal to the con-crete circumstances of actions in order to justify decisions that are in opposition to natural law or God's revealed will. Fletcher and others, however, represent a serious attempt to develop a Christian ethic that is based on the principle of love yet is free from the restrictions of a moral code.

In response to his critics, Fletcher stated, "I personally would adopt nearly all the norms or action-principles ordi-narily held in Christian ethics." Yet he added, "I refuse, on the other hand, to treat their norms as idols—as divinely finalized. I can take 'em or leave 'em, depending on the situation. Norms are advisers without veto power" (Cox, 1968).   —C. Fitzhugh Spragins

See also Absolutes and absolutism; Bentham, Jeremy; Consequentialism; Existentialism; Mill, John Stuart; Subjec-tivism; Ten Commandments; Tillich, Paul; Utilitarianism.

BIBLIOGRAPHY

Bennett, John C., et al. *Storm Over Ethics.* Philadelphia: United Church Press, 1967.

Cox, Harvey, ed. *The Situation Ethics Debate.* Philadel-phia: Westminster Press, 1968.

Cunningham, Robert L. *Situationism and the New Moral-ity.* New York: Appleton-Century-Crofts, 1970.

Fletcher, Joseph. *Moral Responsibility: Situation Ethics at Work.* Philadelphia: Westminster Press, 1967.

_____. *Situation Ethics: The New Morality.* Phila-delphia: Westminster Press, 1966.

Outka, Gene H., and Paul Ramsey, eds. *Norm and Context in Christian Ethics.* New York: Charles Scribner's Sons, 1968.

Ramsey, Paul. *Deeds and Rules in Christian Ethics.* 2d ed. Lanham, Md.: University Press of America, 1983.

Robinson, J. A. T. *Christian Morals Today.* Philadelphia: Westminster Press, 1964.

Skepticism

TYPE OF ETHICS: Theory of ethics
DATE: Fifth century B.C.E. to present
DEFINITION: The ability to withhold assent to claims about nonevident realities while continuing the search for truth
SIGNIFICANCE: Seeks to avoid the exaggerations and hasty generalizations often associated with ethical views in or-der to keep ethical inquiries honest and meaningful

A society and the individuals who constitute it confront many situations that have moral significance, such as those involving abortion, euthanasia, racism, and war. Morally these situations involve decisions concerning the goodness of actions and the value of life that is reflected in those decision. A practical perspective is to view ethics as a summation of the decisions made by individuals and groups in those situations. A theoreti-cal perspective is to derive ethics from a set of first principles, such as "All pleasure is good" or "The only unconditionally good thing is a good will." Skepticism is not primarily con-cerned with the practical perspective. Ethical skepticism

mainly involves theories about the nature of goodness, and especially the status that is accorded first principles (that they be absolutely certain or necessarily true).

Classical Skepticism. The origins of Western philosophy are typically traced to Greece and Socrates in the fifth cen-tury B.C.E. Greek society at that time was undergoing many pervasive and rapid changes, in large part because of suc-cesses in commerce and trade that had been made possible by the defeat of the Persians and the advent of writing. These changes represented a challenge to accepted beliefs and values. A group of professional teachers known as Soph-ists made a living by offering Greek citizens a variety of theories concerning the ultimate nature of reality and the good life.

In Sextus Empiricus' *Outlines of Pyrrhonism* (c. 200), skeptical responses to exaggerated claims about hidden re-alities are elaborated. For Sextus, something is considered questionable and worthy of inquiry if it is not an immediate sensory presentation. Inquirers do not generally question ap-pearances. Inquirers are interested in observing something that has not been observed or in reasoning beyond appear-ances to determine underlying and unobservable phenomena in order to explain something that has been observed. Skep-tical inquirers are reluctant to exceed the evidence of the senses, and when they do, they hold those views with some degree of doubt. For example, a skeptic might claim that suspending judgment with regard to imperceptible realities leads to peace of mind but admit that this may not always hold true.

Sextus imagines three possible outcomes of an inquiry: (1) the object of the search is found; (2) the object being sought is declared inapprehensible; or (3) the search contin-ues. When the thing being sought is beyond the limits of human perception, Sextus calls the first position *dogmatic*, the second *academic*, and the third *skeptical*. Ironically, only the skeptic's position leaves room for more inquiry, yet skeptics are often accused of shutting the doors to specula-tion.

Nonevident Realities. A nonevident reality is one that does not make itself immediately manifest to the inquirer. There are several ways in which things might be nonevident. Referenced items might be temporarily hidden from view, as in this claim: "There is a pen locked in this desk drawer." Another way of being nonevident involves the need for spe-cial instruments of observation, such as an electron micro-scope or a radio telescope. Because the things being ob-served are extremely small or distant, there is still some uncertainty about what has been observed. Such uncertainty is evident in conclusions such as this: "There was something there, but what it was and where it is now are difficult to determine." Subatomic particles and distant quasars are less manifest and obvious than is the pen in the desk drawer.

Philosophical skeptics are not generally concerned with realities that could be made manifest to an inquirer. Instead, they are concerned with claims made about things that are permanently hidden from an inquirer's view. For example, no person can observe all things. Consequently, claims made about all things remain somewhat doubtful (unless these claims are meant only as definitions). It follows that claiming to know that "all pleasures are good" or that "only a good will is unconditionally good" is a form of exaggeration.

Skepticism in Ethics. Skepticism is properly elaborated in response to a particular dogmatic position. It is possible, however, to identify patterns of skeptical argumentation. One positivist challenge to absolute ethics is that ethical claims are without definite meaning. Ethical claims lack meaning because, unlike ordinary factual claims, they are neither verifiable nor refutable. At the most general level, ethics is about the value or the sense of the world, of everything. That value or sense, if it exists, is something transcendental, beyond this world. Therefore, ethics may be thought of as being about something higher, but something that remains beyond words.

The emotivist challenge to the language of an absolute ethics is that ethical claims such as "All abortions are evil" can be interpreted as an expression of the speaker's likes and dislikes. Ethical claims are not true or false; they merely communicate the speaker's attitudes.

The subjectivist attack is based on the argument that the ultimate criterion of an ethical truth is the individual. Differences in ethical beliefs have existed since recorded history and seem likely to continue far into the future. People choose, and thus create, their own individual ethics.

These patterns of skeptical argumentation are responses to a dogmatically held absolute ethics. Any of these views can be transformed from a skeptical response into a dogma. For example, the statement "the individual is the criterion of ethical truth" can become exaggerated and changed into the statement "there is no higher or transcendental reality."

—*J. Michael Spector*

See also Emotivist ethics; Epistemological ethics; Hume, David; Intrinsic good; Relativism; Socrates; Subjectivism; Wittgenstein, Ludwig.

BIBLIOGRAPHY

Brandt, Richard B. *Ethical Theory: The Problems of Normative and Critical Ethics.* Englewood Cliffs, N.J.: Prentice-Hall, 1959.

Empiricus, Sextus. *Sextus Empiricus.* 4 vols. Translated by R. G. Bury. Cambridge, Mass: Harvard University Press, 1949-1957.

Hume, David. *Enquiries Concerning the Human Understanding and Concerning the Principles of Morals.* Edited by L. A. Selby-Bigge. 2d ed. Oxford, England: Clarendon Press, 1966.

Nietzsche, Friedrich. *The Birth of Tragedy and the Genealogy of Morals.* Translated by Francis Golffing. Garden City, N.Y.: Anchor Press, 1956.

Werkmeister, W. H. *Theories of Ethics: A Study in Moral Obligation.* Lincoln, Nebr: Johnsen, 1961.

Wittgenstein, Ludwig. *Tractatus Logico-Philosophicus.* Translated by D. F. Pears and B. F. McGuinness. London: Routledge & Kegan Paul, 1974.

Slavery

TYPE OF ETHICS: Human rights
DATE: Prehistory to present
ASSOCIATED WITH: African Americans
DEFINITION: Slavery is principally a system in which one person is owned as property by another person and forced to perform labor for the owner
SIGNIFICANCE: Slavery has historically constituted a significant denial of human rights

Slavery is one of the oldest institutions of human society. Slavery was present in the earliest human civilizations, those of ancient Mesopotamia and Egypt, and continued to exist in several parts of the world through the late twentieth century.

Concepts. Despite the near universality of slavery, there is no consensus regarding what distinctive practices constitute slavery. In Western society, a slave typically was a person who was owned as property by another person and forced to perform labor for the owner. This definition, however, breaks down when applied to non-Western forms of slavery. In some African societies, slaves were not owned as property by an individual but were thought of as belonging to a kinship group. The slave could be sold, but so too could nonslave members of the kinship group. In certain African societies, slaves were exempted from labor and were used solely to bring honor to the master by demonstrating his absolute power over another person.

The sociologist Orlando Patterson suggested that slavery is best understood as an institution designed to increase the power of the master or the ruling group. Slaves can fulfill this role by laboring to make the master rich, but they can also do so by bringing honor to the master. One of the defining, universal characteristics of slavery is that the slave ceases to exist as a socially meaningful person. The slave relates to society only through the master. Slavery includes many mechanisms to remove the slave from membership in any groups, such as the family, through which the slave might derive an independent sense of identity. By placing the master in a dominant position over another individual, slavery is believed to increase the honor and power of the master. The slave's status is permanent and it is typically passed down to the slave's children.

History. The use of slavery was widespread in the ancient world, especially in Greece and Italy. During the classical ages of Greek and Roman society, slaves constituted about one-third of the population. Following the collapse of the Roman Empire in Western Europe during the fifth and sixth centuries, declining economic conditions destroyed the profitability of slavery and provided employers with large numbers of impoverished peasants who could be employed more cheaply than slaves. Over the next seven hundred years, slavery slowly gave way to serfdom. Although serfs, like slaves, were unfree laborers, serfs generally had more legal rights and a higher social standing than slaves.

Familiarity with the institution of slavery did not, however, disappear in Western Europe. A trickle of slaves from Eastern Europe and even from Africa continued to flow into England, France, and Germany. Western Europeans retained their familiarity with large-scale slave systems through contacts with southern Italy, Spain, and Portugal, and with the Byzantine Empire and the Muslim world, where slavery flourished. Western Europeans also inherited from their Roman forebears the corpus of Roman law, with its elaborate slave code. During the later Middle Ages, Europeans who were familiar with Muslim sugar plantations in the Near East sought to begin sugar production with slave labor on the islands of the Mediterranean.

Thus, as Western Europe entered the age of exploration and colonization, Europeans had an intimate knowledge of slavery and a ready-made code of laws to govern slaves. During the sixteenth century, as European nations sought to establish silver mines and sugar plantations in their new colonies in the Western Hemisphere, heavy labor demands led to efforts to enslave Native Americans. This supply of laborers was inadequate because of the rapid decline of the Indian population following the introduction of European diseases into the Western Hemisphere. The Spanish and Portuguese then turned to Africa, the next most readily available source of slave laborers. Between 1500 and 1900, European slave traders imported 9.7 million African laborers into the Western Hemisphere. Every European colony eventually used slave labor, which became the principal form of labor in the Western Hemisphere. Because the wealth of several modern nations was created by slave labor, some contemporary African Americans have claimed the right to receive reparations payments from nations such as the United States, which continue to enjoy the wealth accumulated originally by slave laborers.

Slavery and Race. The large-scale use of African slaves by European masters raised new moral issues regarding race. There is no necessary connection between slavery and race. A massive survey by Orlando Patterson of slave societies throughout history found that in three-quarters of slave societies, masters and slaves were of the same race. Slavery in the Western Hemisphere was unusual in human history because slaves were drawn almost exclusively from the Negro race.

In most colonies of the Western Hemisphere, the use of African slaves was accompanied by the rise of racism, which some scholars claim was a new, unprecedented phenomenon caused by slavery. Scholars seeking to understand contemporary race relations in the United States have been intrigued by the rise of prejudice in new slave societies. Did Europeans enslave Africans merely because they needed slaves and Africa was the most accessible source of slaves? If so, then prejudice probably originated as a learned association between race and subservience. Modern prejudice might be broken down through integration and affirmative action programs aimed at helping whites to witness the success of blacks in positions of authority. Did Europeans enslave Africans because the Europeans saw Africans as inferior persons ideally suited for slavery? If so, then contemporary racism is a deeply rooted cultural phenomenon that is not likely to disappear for generations to come. African Americans will receive justice only if the government establishes permanent compensatory programs aimed at equalizing power between the races.

Historical research has not resolved these issues. Sixteenth century Europeans apparently did view Africans as inferior beings, even before the colonization of the Western Hemisphere. These racial antipathies were minor, however, in comparison to modern racism. Emancipated slaves in recently settled colonies experienced little racial discrimination. The experience of slavery apparently increased the European settlers' sense of racial superiority over Africans.

After the slave systems of the Western Hemisphere became fully developed, racial arguments became the foundation of the proslavery argument. Supporters of slavery claimed that persons of African descent were so degraded and inferior to whites that it would be dangerous for society to release the slaves from the control of a master. In the United States, some proslavery theorists pushed the racial argument to extreme levels. In explaining the contradiction between slavery and the American ideal that all persons should be free, writers such as Josiah Nott and Samuel Cartwright claimed that blacks were not fully human and, therefore, did not deserve all the rights belonging to humanity.

A minority of proslavery writers rejected the racial argument and the effort to reconcile slavery and American egalitarian ideals. Writers such as George Fitzhugh claimed that all societies were organized hierarchically by classes and that slavery was the most benevolent system for organizing an unequal class structure. Slavery bound together masters and slaves through a system of mutual rights and obligations. Unlike the "wage slaves" of industrial society, chattel slaves had certain access to food, clothing, shelter, and medical care, all because the master's ownership of the slaves' bodies made him diligent in caring for his property. Slavery was depicted by some proslavery theorists as the ideal condition for the white working class.

The Antislavery Movement. From the dawning of human history until the middle of the eighteenth century, few persons appear to have questioned the morality of slavery as an institution. Although some persons had earlier raised moral objections to certain features of slavery, almost no one appears to have questioned the overall morality of slavery as a system before the middle of the eighteenth century. Around 1750, however, an antislavery movement began to appear in Britain, France, and America.

The sudden rise of antislavery opinion appears to be related to the rise of a humanitarian ethos during the Enlightenment that encouraged people to consider the welfare of humans beyond their kin groups. The rise of the antislavery movement was also related to the growing popularity of new forms of evangelical and pietistic religious sects such as the Baptists, Methodists, and Quakers, which tended to view slaveholding as sinful materialism and slaves as persons worthy of God's love. The rise of antislavery was encouraged by the American and French revolutions, whose democratic political philosophies promoted a belief in the equality of individuals. The rise of antislavery also coincided in time with the rise of industrial capitalism. The historian Eric Williams argued in *Capitalism and Slavery* (1944) that the economic and class interests of industrial capitalists rather than the moral scruples of humanitarians gave rise to the antislavery movement.

Antislavery activism initially focused on the abolition of the Atlantic slave trade. Reformers succeeded in prompting Britain and the United States to abolish the slave trade in 1807. Other nations followed this lead over the next half century until the Atlantic slave trade was virtually eliminated.

The campaign to abolish the slave trade achieved early success because it joined together moral concerns and self-interest. Many persons in the late eighteenth and early nineteenth centuries were prepared to accept the end of the slave trade while opposing the end of slavery itself. Even slaveholders were angered by the living conditions endured by slaves on crowded, disease-infested slave ships. Some masters, in fact, attempted to justify their ownership of slaves by claiming that the conditions on their plantations were more humane than the conditions on slave-trading ships or in allegedly primitive Africa. Some slaveholders supported the abolition of the slave trade because they realized that limiting the supply of new slaves from Africa would increase the value of the existing slave population. Finally, many persons believed that it was wrong for slave traders to deny liberty to freeborn Africans, but that it was not wrong for slave masters to exercise control over persons who were born into the status of slavery. Indeed, supporters of slavery argued that the well-being of society required masters to exercise control over persons who had no preparation for freedom and might be a threat to society if emancipated.

The campaign to eradicate slavery itself was more difficult and was accompanied by significant political upheavals and, in the case of Haiti and the United States, revolution and warfare. British reformers such as William Wilberforce, Thomas Clarkson, and Granville Sharp made, perhaps, the most significant contributions to the organization of a worldwide antislavery movement. In 1823, British activists formed the London Antislavery Committee, soon to be renamed the British and Foreign Antislavery Society. The Antislavery Society spearheaded a successful campaign to abolish slavery in the British Empire and, eventually, worldwide. The Antislavery Society remained in existence in the 1990's. Known by the name Antislavery International, the society

had the distinction of being the world's oldest human rights organization. Antislavery reformers were also active in the United States. From the 1830's through the 1860's, abolitionists such as William Lloyd Garrison, Wendell Phillips, and Frederick Douglass sought to arouse the moral anger of Americans against slavery. More effective, however, were politicians such as Abraham Lincoln, Charles Sumner, and Salmon P. Chase, whose antislavery message was a mixture of idealism, self-interest, and expedience.

Emancipation of Slaves. Beginning in the late eighteenth century and accelerating through the nineteenth century, slavery was abolished throughout the Western Hemisphere. This was followed in the late nineteenth and twentieth centuries by the legal abolition of slavery in Africa and Asia (see tables on following page).

In evaluating the success of abolition in any society, it is necessary to distinguish between legal and de facto emancipation. Changing the legal status of a slave to that of a free person is not the same thing as freeing the slave from the control of a master. Legal emancipation often has little impact on persons held as slaves if governments fail to enforce the abolition of slavery. For example, Britain in the nineteenth century outlawed slavery in its colonies in India, the Gold Coast, Kenya, and Zanzibar. Yet, fearing a disruption of economic production in these colonies, the British government simply abstained from enforcing its own abolition laws until pressure from reformers put an end to slavery. A similar situation existed in Mauritania, where slavery was prohibited by law three separate times: 1905, 1960, and 1980, yet the government of Mauritania enacted no penalties against masters who kept slaves in violation of the emancipation law, and the government waged no campaign to inform the slaves of their freedom. As a result, journalists and investigators for the International Labor Organisation found slavery still flourishing in Mauritania in the 1990's.

Even in societies that vigorously enforced their acts of abolition, legal emancipation was usually followed by a period of transition in which former slaves were held in a state resembling that of slavery. The Abolition of Slavery Act of 1833, which outlawed slavery in most colonies of the British Empire, provided that slaves would serve as apprentices to their former masters for a period of four to six years. In the American South after the Civil War, former slaves were subject for a time to Black Codes that greatly reduced the freedom of movement of African Americans and required them to work on the plantations of former slave masters. After the Civil Rights Act of 1866 and the Fourteenth Amendment outlawed such practices, southerners created the share-cropping and crop-lien systems which allowed planters to control the labor of many blacks through a form of debt bondage.

The efforts of former masters to control the labor of former slaves were a part of a larger effort by postemancipation societies to determine what rights freedpeople should exercise. In the United States, for instance, emancipation raised

DATES OF LEGAL EMANCIPATION OUTSIDE THE U.S.	
Country	Year
Angola	1875
Argentina	1813
Belgian colonies	1890
Bolivia	1831
Brazil	1888
British colonies	1833
Central America	1824
Chile	1823
China	1910
Colombia	1814
Cuba	1886
Dutch colonies	1863
Ecuador	1851
Ethiopia	1930
Gold Coast	1874
Haiti	1804
India	1843
Swedish colonies	1847
Kenya	1907
Madagascar	1877
Madeira	1775
Mexico	1829
Muscat and Oman	1970
Ontario	1793
Peru	1854
Portugal	1836
Portuguese colonies	1873
Puerto Rico	1873
Rwanda	1923
Saudi Arabia	1962
Sierra Leone	1928
Spanish colonies	1873
Tunisia	1819
Uruguay	1843
Venezuela	1854
Virgin Islands	1848
Zanzibar and Pemba	1897

DATES OF LEGAL EMANCIPATION IN THE U.S.	
State	Year
Alabama	1863-1865
Arkansas	1863-1865
California	1850
Connecticut	1784
Delaware	1865
Florida	1863-1865
Georgia	1863-1865
Illinois	1787
Indiana	1787
Iowa	1820
Kansas	1861
Kentucky	1865
Louisiana	1864
Maine	1783
Maryland	1864
Massachusetts	1783
Michigan	1787
Minnesota	1858
Mississippi	1863-1865
Missouri	1865
New Hampshire	1783
New Jersey	1804
New York	1799
North Carolina	1863-1865
Ohio	1787
Oklahoma	1866
Oregon	1846
Pennsylvania	1780
Rhode Island	1784
South Carolina	1863-1865
Tennessee	1865
Texas	1863-1865
Vermont	1777
Virginia	1863-1865
Washington, D.C.	1862
West Virginia	1863
Western Territories	1862
Wisconsin	1787

many questions regarding the general rights of citizens, the answers to which often remained elusive more than a century after the abolition of slavery. Should freedpeople be considered citizens with basic rights equal to other citizens? How far should equality of citizenship rights extend? Should equality of rights be kept at a minimum level, perhaps limited to freedom of movement, the right to own property, and the right to make contracts and enforce them in a court of law? Should citizenship rights be extended to the political realm, with guarantees of the right to vote, serve on juries, and hold political office? Should citizenship rights be extended to the social realm, with the protection for the right to live wherever one wanted, to use public spaces without discrimination, and to marry persons of another race?

Antislavery and Imperialism. Ironically, the international effort to abolish slavery raised troubling new moral issues. During the last quarter of the nineteenth century, in the name of suppressing the African slave trade at its source, Britain and other European nations demanded of African rulers certain police powers within African kingdoms. The Europeans also organized new African industries to encourage the shift from the slave trade to the "legitimate trade" in other commodities. In this manner, the humanitarian impulse of antislavery combined with less humane motives to produce the New Imperialism of the 1880's through the 1910's. During this thirty-year period, nearly all of Africa fell under European domination. Time and again, the campaign to suppress the slave trade became a cloak for the imperialist ambitions of the European powers. It is worth remembering that the two international conferences in which the European powers agreed to carve up Africa among themselves, the Berlin Conference of 1884-1885 and the Brussels Conference of 1889-1890, both devised significant agreements for ending the African slave trade.

Slavery in the Contemporary World. In the twentieth century, most Westerners believed slavery to be nothing more than a memory of the past. Major international treaties such as the Slavery Convention of the League of Nations (1926), the Universal Declaration on Human Rights (1948), and the United Nations (U.N.) Supplementary Convention on the Abolition of Slavery (1956) seemed to indicate the emergence of an international consensus that slavery in all its forms should be eradicated. In reality, throughout the twentieth century, new forms of slavery continued to appear. The U.N. Supplementary Convention defined debt bondage, serfdom, bridewealth (bride price), and child labor as modern forms of slavery. Many persons considered the use of compulsory labor by authoritarian regimes such as those of Nazi Germany and the Soviet Union to be a form of slavery.

International cooperation toward ending slavery in the twentieth century sometimes faltered because of Cold War rivalries. Communist states were often hostile to the antislavery work of the U.N. because Westerners sought to define the compulsory labor systems in several communist states as a form of slavery. The Soviets, likewise, charged that the wage system of capitalist countries constituted a type of slavery, since the wage system compelled people to work in jobs they did not like out of fear of starvation.

On the eve of the twenty-first century, investigations by international human rights organizations and by journalists found that millions of people still served as slaves in Haiti, the Dominican Republic, Brazil, Peru, Sudan, South Africa, Mauritania, Kuwait, Pakistan, India, Bangladesh, Thailand, and China. Even in countries such as the United States, where slavery had long been actively suppressed by the government, isolated cases of the enslavement of workers occasionally came to light with regard to migrant farm workers and illegal aliens. —*Harold D. Tallant*

See also Abolition; Civil rights; Emancipation Proclamation; Human rights; Racial prejudice; Racism.

BIBLIOGRAPHY

Bender, Thomas, ed. *The Antislavery Debate: Capitalism and Abolitionism as a Problem in Historical Interpretation.* Berkeley: University of California Press, 1992. A collection of essays that debate the question of whether the rise of industrial capitalism caused the emergence of the antislavery movement.

Davis, David Brion. *The Problem of Slavery in the Age of Revolution, 1770-1823.* Ithaca, N.Y.: Cornell University Press, 1975. A Pulitzer Prize-winning study of the intellectual background of the rise of the antislavery movement.

_____. *Slavery and Human Progress.* New York: Oxford University Press, 1984. An excellent introduction to many of the ethical issues regarding slavery organized around a discussion of changing concepts of progress.

Finley, Moses I. *Ancient Slavery and Modern Ideology.* New York: Viking Press, 1980. A study of the moral, intellectual, and social foundations of slavery by the leading expert on ancient slavery. The book is especially helpful in showing the relationships between ancient and modern forms of slavery.

Foner, Eric. *Nothing But Freedom: Emancipation and Its Legacy.* Baton Rouge: Louisiana State University Press, 1983. A brief but thought-provoking study of the problems associated with emancipation in several countries. The principal focus of the book is emancipation in the United States.

Patterson, Orlando. *Slavery and Social Death: A Comparative Study.* Cambridge, Mass.: Harvard University Press, 1982. The most important study of slavery in its various forms. The book is based on a massive survey of slave societies on all continents from the beginning of history to the present.

Phillips, William D. *Slavery from Roman Times to the Early Transatlantic Trade.* Minneapolis: University of Minnesota Press, 1985. A highly readable historical survey of the transition from ancient slavery to modern slavery. The book includes an excellent chapter on problems in defining slavery in different historical and cultural settings.

Smith, Adam (June 5, 1723, Kirkcaldy, Scotland—July 17, 1790, Edinburgh, Scotland): Economist

TYPE OF ETHICS: Enlightenment history

ACHIEVEMENTS: Author of *The Theory of Moral Sentiments* (1759), *An Inquiry into the Nature and Causes of the Wealth of Nations* (1776), and *Essays on Philosophical Subjects* (1795)

SIGNIFICANCE: Formulated a theory of ethics that was consistent with developing psychological theories and economic development

Born in Calvinist Scotland, bereft by the early death of his father, and extremely precocious, Adam Smith spent his life trying to reconcile Providence with the needs of the individual and the greater society. He became professor of moral philosophy at the University of Glasgow in 1752, and it was there that he completed his first important work.

The Theory of Moral Sentiments. During Smith's time, moral philosophy embraced a series of disciplines in what today would be considered the humanities and the social sciences. At that time, philosophers of the Enlightenment were developing the discrete social sciences, especially psychology and economics.

Although basically a skeptic, Smith never became completely skeptical, as did his close friend David Hume. Smith took Providence into account when formulating his theories of personal and social ethics, especially in the field of economics, in which he became most famous.

Smith sought to reconcile humankind's obvious selfish nature and self-love with its dependence on the greater society. There is in human nature, believed Smith, some principle that makes the fortune of others and their happiness agreeable, even necessary. The individual has a capacity for sympathy and the ability to put himself or herself into another's place and to observe that other as an "impartial observer." Hence individuals, while not compromising their own selfish needs, are able to approve of and to support that which makes others happy and to disapprove of measures that have a negative effect. Self-interest, however, remains dominant. For Smith, self-interest accounted for the habits of economy, industry, discretion, attention, and application of thought.

Smith's theories were well received, but had he written only *The Theory of Moral Sentiments*, he would have become no more than a footnote in the history of philosophy. A trip to France between 1764 and 1766, however, was to change both his outlook and his life. There he met many of the Physiocrats, early economists who began to challenge the prevailing theory that economic wealth was a static commodity and that one nation could grow rich only by impoverishing others. The Physiocrats were free traders who sought to end governmental control of the economy. Smith also had cause to observe the effect of a controlled economy on England's American colonies. What disturbed Smith was the emphasis the Physiocrats placed on land as the major source of wealth. Were this true, then Scotland, with its thin rocky soil, would be forever condemned to poverty. Smith also had occasion to observe the work of the skilled French artisans and to see that the export of their wares provided a major source of revenue for the French state. Smith became convinced that it is labor rather than land or commodities such as bullion that is the true source of wealth.

The Wealth of Nations. Smith's monumental and seminal work, *An Inquiry into the Nature and Causes of the Wealth of Nations*, appeared in 1776, the year of the Declaration of Independence by Britain's American colonies. In it, Smith posited three important points: that wealth is created by labor and is thus organic or growing, that the division of labor can enormously increase productivity, and that free trade among states or nations can vastly improve the welfare of humankind. By "wealth," Smith did not mean accumulated treasure, but rather the minimal amount of money needed to keep human beings decently fed, clothed, and housed.

Smith's great problem was the reconciliation of his theory of ethics with theories of economics. He reconciled these theories by emphasizing the selfish nature of man, the impulse of self-interest, the greed for material gain. He stated his position succinctly when he wrote that it was not the benevolence or sympathy of the butcher, the brewer, and the baker that put the dinner on one's table, but rather their self-interest. One speaks to them not of one's necessities, but of their advantage.

Smith would remove all bureaucratic impediments and permit individuals and nations alike to pursue what they do best economically. The result, and here Smith waxed lyrical,

again falling back on Providence, would be that a wonderful universal machine would be created and a "hidden hand" would distribute equitably the ever-increasing bounty of the earth and with it the greatest possible happiness. Adam Smith's name is inextricably linked to what came to be called laissez-faire economics, or free trade.

Implications for Ethical Conduct. It would seem that Smith condoned any individual action as long as it benefited the economy. Indeed, Smith's theories were often used to justify the most extreme kind of "rugged individualism" and the unconscionable exploitation of labor; economics was well on the way to becoming the "dismal science." Smith recognized the danger and exhorted that the laws of justice not be violated, appealing to instinctive human feelings of sympathy for others. He realized that his division of labor by concentrating on a single mindless operation could result in the brutalization of labor, and he called upon governments, through education, to ameliorate the lot of workers.

—*Nis Petersen*

See also Christian ethics; Economics; Exploitation; Free enterprise; Hume, David; Self-interest; Utilitarianism.

BIBLIOGRAPHY

Bronowski, Jacob, and Bruce Mazlish. "Adam Smith." In *The Western Intellectual Tradition from Leonardo to Hegel.* New York: Harper & Row, 1962.

Glahe, Fred R., ed. *Adam Smith and the Wealth of Nations: 1776-1975 Bicentennial Essays.* Boulder: Colorado Associated University Press, 1978.

Jones, Peter, and Andrew S. Skinner, eds. *Adam Smith Reviewed.* Edinburgh, Scotland: Edinburgh University Press, 1992.

Lux, Kenneth. *Adam Smith's Mistake: How a Moral Philosopher Invented Economics and Ended Morality.* New York: Random House, 1990.

Smith, Adam. *An Inquiry into the Nature and Causes of the Wealth of Nations.* Edited by Edwin Cannan. New York: Modern Library, 1937.

_____. *The Theory of Moral Sentiments.* Edited by D. D. Raphael and A. L. Macfie. Indianapolis: Liberty Classics, 1982.

Social contract

TYPE OF ETHICS: Politico-economic ethics

DATE: Present throughout history of philosophy; particularly influential in the seventeenth and eighteenth centuries

ASSOCIATED WITH: Individualism, natural law, the Enlightenment, and capitalism

DEFINITION: Social contract theory assumes that individuals exist prior to society and that these individuals freely and rationally contract to form civil society, giving their power to a sovereign

SIGNIFICANCE: Social contract theory, in all its forms, strongly asserts that it is the individual will, subject to reason, that is the ultimate source of morality

Social contract theory is a framework for understanding the origin and organization of human society. It begins with the basic assumption that people are autonomous rational moral agents who agree to give up some of their individual power to do as they please in order to live in cooperation with others who also agree to give up some of their individual power. This theory is discussed in the works of many philosophers but is probably given its clearest and most powerful voice in the works of Thomas Hobbes, John Locke, and Jean-Jacques Rousseau. It is a theory that underlies many aspects of modern political life; for example, the United States Constitution and Bill of Rights, the United Nations, trade agreements, and military treaties.

Hobbes. According to Thomas Hobbes, perhaps the clearest enunciator of social contract theory, people are naturally inclined to be in the society of others. In society, however, it is necessary that there exist a sovereign to protect each person against every other person. Without such protection, people are in what Hobbes identifies as the state of nature. In the state of nature, people have two basic rights: (1) the right to self-preservation and (2) the right to take anything they have the power to take. In the state of nature, there is a war of all against all as people seek to exercise these rights. Each person experiences the constant threat of violence against his or her self and property. In fact, to secure their rights, people will begin to act in anticipation of their being abrogated. They will kill those who are perceived as potential threats.

This insecurity is ever-present and makes society something to be avoided rather than enjoyed. Life in this state of nature is "solitary, poor, nasty, brutish, and short." Reason leads people to find this situation intolerable. Therefore, as rational autonomous individuals, people agree to form a contract, giving up some of their power to a sovereign in return for that sovereign's protection. They are then bound, absolutely, by that sovereign's laws. This contract is formed out of logical self-interest.

Locke. John Locke offers a kinder picture of the state of nature but reaches much the same conclusion as Hobbes. For Locke, the state of nature is a state of plenty in which each person is able to fulfill his or her needs. Each has a right to as much of anything as he or she can use, if enough is left for others. The only real limitation on how much a person should take is the fact that most goods will spoil if they are not used promptly. With the introduction of money, a nonperishable unit of exchange, the limits on consumption are removed and hoarding and competition begin.

This state of an unbounded right to property would be chaotic except that each person possesses reason. The state of nature is not necessarily synonymous with the state of war (as it is for Hobbes), because of the use of reason. Reason dictates a state in which people seek peace, a state in which the natural rights of life, liberty, and property are honored. This state requires that judgments be made concerning what threatens the life, liberty, and property of an individual. There is the danger here that if one person misjudges what is necessary for his or her own safety, or the

safety of others, and becomes preoccupied with achieving security, he or she may act in anticipation of harm and threaten the security of others.

For Locke, it is the absence of a common judge that distinguishes the state of nature and causes uncertainty and potential disharmony. To protect against misjudgment, people form a contract. This contract is to form a government that will hold the power of the people in trust. It will act as a judge, and it must act to preserve its citizens. The purpose of civil society is to provide each person with security.

Rousseau. Jean-Jacques Rousseau offers an approach that differs significantly from those of Hobbes and Locke. Rousseau idealizes the state of nature. People are pure and innocent in the state of nature, whose typical inhabitant is the noble savage. It is civil society itself that has corrupted people and led to strife. In the state of nature, people's wants and needs are simple and easily satisfied. Furthermore, Rousseau's goal is not so much to show the legitimate power of the individual (though he does intend to do this as well) to achieve the collective good—the general will.

Rousseau begins with the assumption that nature is good and that those things that have gone wrong are the result of the wrong actions of human society. He seeks not to explain the origins of civil society, but to create a state in which people can retain their original freedom. One should not be dependent on the opinion or will of others; one should also not be dependent on possessing power over and above one's needs or at another's expense. The general will requires that each person be free from these particular dependencies. One should not come to believe, however, that this freedom entails being independent in the sense of being free from influence or obligation.

Rousseau's individual has a duty to be aware of the general well-being, act in accord with it, and make sure that others do so as well. There is no greater sense of social obligation. Each individual feels an obligation to society through the realization of individual interdependence and equality. Rousseau thinks that as a result of showing individuals that ultimately there is no difference in vulnerability among people—that they are equal—rationality and feeling will then direct such people to form a community that is in the interest of all. Provided that they have been instilled with the correct sentiments, reason will lead to the formation of a general will in which each is bound only by his or her own will and therefore is not enslaved.

Critique. The social contract tradition has its critics. Some challenge the notion that it is possible for free, autonomous, rational people to form a contract at all. Such challengers argue that no one is free from pressure and coercion; therefore, how is it possible to tell if the contract is valid or for whom it is valid.

One particular example of this problem is the place of women in the contract. In the writings of the main proponents of the social contract theory, it is made clear that it is free, autonomous, rational men who form the primary contract, though women, children, and slaves are somehow to be bound by it as well. Carole Pateman offers an interesting reading of this issue in her book *The Sexual Contract* (1988).   —*Erin McKenna*

See also Civil rights; Enlightenment ethics; Human rights.

BIBLIOGRAPHY

Hobbes, Thomas. *Leviathan*. Edited by Michael Oakeshott. New York: Collier Books, 1962.

Locke, John. *Two Treatises of Government*. Edited and introduced by Peter Laslett. Cambridge, England: Cambridge University Press, 1988.

Macpherson, C. B. *The Political Theory of Possessive Individualism: Hobbes to Locke*. Oxford, England: Oxford University Press, 1988.

Pateman, Carole. *The Sexual Contract*. Stanford, Calif.: Stanford University Press, 1988.

Rousseau, Jean-Jacques. *On the Social Contract*. Edited by Roger D. Masters. Translated by Judith R. Masters. New York: St. Martin's Press, 1978.

Social Darwinism

TYPE OF ETHICS: Modern history
DATE: Coined late nineteenth century
ASSOCIATED WITH: Herbert Spencer, William G. Sumner, and Western colonialism and capitalism during the Industrial Revolution
DEFINITION: The misapplication of Charles Darwin's theory of biological evolution by means of natural selection to the development of society and human social behavior
SIGNIFICANCE: The application of Darwin's ideas on biological evolution to human society helped to justify the mistreatment of non-Western peoples and also those defined as lower-class in the West

Western colonialism and imperialism and the Industrial Revolution of the late nineteenth century did little to benefit all people equally. Disparity in access to resources, wealth, and social status was nothing new, but as non-Western peoples and their natural resources were exploited by those in the West, a justification for such behavior was sought. Western governments were motivated to expand their political and economic power and influence, while industrialists sought to fulfill their desires for wealth and fame. The Western clergy, in turn, saw colonial expansion as an opportunity to consummate their mission of spreading the gospel.

In 1857, Herbert Spencer (1820-1903), a British social philosopher, published "Progress: Its Laws and Causes," in which he expressed his early ideas on social evolution. Later, after Charles Darwin (1809-1882) had published *On the Origin of Species* (1859), Spencer sought to apply the ideas outlined by Darwin to human society. Spencer's ideas then were used to perpetuate the conservative status quo of the unequal distribution of wealth associated with the changing capitalist environment. Indeed, it was Spencer and not Darwin who coined the metaphors "struggle for existence" and "survival of the fittest," which Darwin later incorporated

into his fifth edition of *On the Origin of Species* (1869). Darwin's ideas on natural selection were employed to account for biological evolution. Specifically, Darwin demonstrated to the world that evolution took place and that its requirements were variation, inheritance, natural selection, and time. Since Darwin's ideas preceded those of the pioneering geneticist Gregor Mendel (1822-1884) by six years, Darwin believed that the environment was critical to explaining variation and that biological success was measured by the frequency with which one reproduced. Successful reproduction in turn was influenced by various environmental forces. For Darwin, the term "struggle" was illustrated by the subtleties of environmental influence. Simply stated, although animals and plants attempted to survive heat, cold, wind, rain, and competition with other species, they were not involved in within-species warfare and bloodshed, as was implied by those who later promoted Social Darwinism as a natural and expected precondition of human social evolution.

When Spencer introduced the groundwork for what became known as Social Darwinism, he failed to recognize the importance of Darwin's subtleties. Spencer included various value and moral judgments in his suggestion that the struggle for existence within society or between societies was a natural condition for cultural evolution. He believed that societies were comparable to biological organisms, slowly evolving from simple to complex by means of competition for resources, and that such competition was natural and to be expected within and between societies. Social Darwinists believed that those individuals, institutions, and societies that attained the greatest political and economic

A cartoonist's view of Social Darwinism. (Library of Congress)

power were by definition more fit, while those that did not were by their nature less fit.

William Graham Sumner (1840-1910), an American sociologist and economist, became a strong advocate of Spencer's ideas. He was a supporter of laissez-faire economic policy, arguing that people were not born equal and that millionaires were a product of natural selection. Typical of the industrialists who accepted Social Darwinism was John D. Rockefeller, Sr. (1839-1937), the rugged individualist and successful capitalist who founded the Standard Oil Corporation. Rockefeller is quoted in Hofstadter (1959) as having said, "The growth of a large business is merely a survival of the fittest. . . . It is merely the working-out of a law of nature and a law of God." His statements express the attitude of many Social Darwinists. Indeed, Spencer and Sumner opposed social and economic planning and any attempts to offer social assistance to the poor, because of their belief that such practices interfered with the natural process of social evolution.

Sumner argued in his book *Folkways* (1906) that customs and morals were instinctive responses to drives such as fear, sex, and hunger. Thus, Social Darwinists sought scientific justification from nature to promote individual competition and the exploitation of the poor by the rich classes. Because the concept and its followers supposed that social progress demanded that competitive struggle occur between nations, states, and races, Social Darwinism was used to justify Western ethnocentrism, racism, and eugenics. Such ideas were carried to a horrifying extreme by Nazis in Germany during World War II. Under Adolf Hitler (1889-1945), the Nazi belief in a master race and the inferiority of gypsies and Jews led to the genocide of millions of people who were believed to be inferior. It was partly because of the world's revulsion toward the acts of the Nazis that the popularity of Social Darwinism and racism began its decline.

—Turhon A. Murad

See also Anthropological ethics; Capitalism; Colonialism and imperialism; Communism; Darwin, Charles Robert; Discrimination; Ethnic cleansing; Ethnocentrism; Eugenics; Evolution, theory of; Genocide; Human rights; Humanism; Marxism; Nazism; Racism.

BIBLIOGRAPHY

Garbarino, Merwyn S. *Sociocultural Theory in Anthropology: A Short History.* New York: Holt, Rinehart and Winston, 1977.

Hofstadter, Richard. *Social Darwinism in American Thought.* New York: George Braziller, 1959.

Spencer, Herbert. *The Evolution of Society: Selections from Herbert Spencer's Principles of Sociology.* Edited by Robert L. Carneiro. Chicago: University of Chicago Press, 1967.

Sumner, William G. *Folkways: A Study of the Sociological Importance of Usages, Manners, Customs, Mores, and Morals.* Boston: Ginn, 1940.

Social justice and responsibility

TYPE OF ETHICS: Personal and social ethics

DATE: From antiquity

ASSOCIATED WITH: Plato, G. W. F. Hegel, Jean-Jacques Rousseau, John Stuart Mill

DEFINITION: Social justice refers to fair distribution of social goods and equal respect before the law; responsibility refers to duties and obligations

SIGNIFICANCE: Social justice and responsibility determine what rights individuals enjoy and what duties individuals have toward one another and toward society

Questions about justice and responsibility arise because there exist different needs, conflicting interests, and scarce resources in human society. There are conflicting demands upon society's scarce resources and there is uncertainty about who has the responsibility to meet those needs. How is it possible to adjudicate among competing claims to determine the just distribution of resources? Is it right to tax the rich to provide for the poor? Does society have an obligation to take care of the needy? These questions deal mainly with a form of justice called distributive justice.

Responsibility, too, can be interpreted in different ways. First, responsibility can refer to the character of a person. To say that a person is responsible in this sense means that the person has uprightness of character, can be trusted, and has a sense of duty. Second, responsibility means the same thing as the ability and capacity to perform some task. Third, responsibility also refers to the issues of praise and blame. Fourth, responsibility refers to position or office in accordance with which a person is entrusted with the performance of a particular task. The latter is closely tied to the question of social justice, because the concept of justice implies that someone is responsible for being just.

Distributive justice deals with the fair allotment of society's goods and services and presupposes the complementary issues of responsibility, equality, and the good society. A theory of distributive justice should determine what needs should be met and what goods individuals should give up for the common good. These issues can also be encompassed in the questions of entitlement, desert or merit, and equality.

Plato who was not an egalitarian, developed a vision of a just society along lines of unequal status. In the *Republic*, Plato attempted to define the *dikaios*, the "just person," and the *kallipolis*, the "good city." The just person is one who possesses the virtues of wisdom, moderation, and courage. The just city is divided into three classes: the working class, the warriors, and the philosopher-rulers. The city is just if it is based on an aristocratic constitution and the three social classes embody their respective virtues. The aristocratic class is wisdom-loving, the warriors are courageous lovers of honor, and the artisans exercise moderation in their pleasure seeking. Each individual and each class, by responsibly fulfilling its duty, contributes to the existence of a just society.

Another approach to social justice and responsibility has

been offered by social contract theory, which holds that justice and society are produced by a general agreement—a social contract. People are obligated to obey rules and the government because they have agreed to do so. They have made a contract to live by certain rules because it suits their self-interest. The general will of the people creates rules, laws, and government. Individuals give up certain rights and privileges for the protections and mutual advantages of the state.

Jean-Jacques Rousseau, (1712-1778) wrote an essay called "On the Social Contract" whose purpose was to explain the nature of authority. It was based on an optimistic view of human nature but a negative view about society. For Rousseau, human beings are born good, but they are corrupted by society. Social contract theory argues that human beings give up or alienate their rights by transferring them to society. The state becomes the sole possessor of political authority. The state is a legitimate power and guarantees the freedom and autonomy of its citizens through a social contract—a voluntary, unanimous agreement of all people of a society to form a united political community. Popular sovereignty is called general will.

Immanuel Kant (1724-1804) formulated, in *The Groundwork of the Metaphysics of Morals*, the categorical imperative, which holds that one should act only on that maxim that one can will to become a universal law. Kant presupposes that persons are rational creatures; that they have an infinite worth of dignity—that is, that they are ends in themselves; and that they are authors of moral law, or are autonomous. In short, human beings are ends in themselves. Therefore, Kant envisions society as a kingdom of ends.

Utilitarianism adheres to the rule that one should always try to make as many people happy as possible. This "great happiness principle" states that one ought to act so as to maximize pleasure and minimize pain. The principle of utility, which is derived from the happiness principle, is a rule that determines moral norms and actions according their ability to maximize or minimize happiness. Rule utilitarianism means that governments are to use this rule in establishing general laws and are to treat individuals according to existing rules. In his essay *On Liberty*, John Stuart Mill stated that society could progress to a higher state of civilization on the basis of what he called the basic principle—that individuals, groups of individuals, and the mass of people must refrain from interfering with the thoughts, expressions, and actions of any individual. The second principle, which is known as the "harm to others principle," holds that government may not interfere in private life except to prevent harm to others. These principles function as regulative criteria for developing public policy that preserves individual rights, limits government intervention, and fosters general well-being.   —*Michael Candelaria*

See also Hegel, Georg Wilhelm Friedrich; Justice; Mill, John Stuart; Responsibility; Rousseau, Jean-Jacques; Utilitarianism.

BIBLIOGRAPHY

Marx, Karl. *The Marx-Engels Reader*. Edited by Robert C. Tucker. New York: W. W. Norton, 1972.

Mill, John Stuart. *On Liberty*. Edited by Currin V. Shields. Indianapolis: Bobbs-Merrill, 1980.

_____. "Utilitarianism." In *Great Books of the Western World*. Vol. 43. Chicago: Encyclopaedia Britannica, 1952.

Plato. *The Dialogues of Plato*. Translated by Benjamin Jowett. In *Great Books of the Western World*. Vol. 7. Chicago: Encyclopaedia Britannica, 1952.

Rousseau, Jean-Jacques. "The Social Contract. In *Great Books of the Western World*. Vol. 38. Chicago: Encyclopaedia Britannica, 1952.

Socialism

TYPE OF ETHICS: Politico-economic ethics

DATE: Nineteenth century to present

ASSOCIATED WITH: The utopian socialism of Robert Owen and Henri Saint-Simon and the revolutionary socialism of Karl Marx and Friedrich Engels

DEFINITION: A political and economic system in which the ethical pursuit of social equality constitutes the basis for full human freedom

SIGNIFICANCE: Socialism represents an alternative vision for social ethics in which justice is realized through material equality and the eradication of exploitation, leaving all members of society free to associate in common productive efforts aimed at satisfying social needs

Socialism is a politico-economic system in which the struggle to eradicate social inequality is the highest ethical pursuit. Socialist morality generally extols the collective pursuits of the larger community and advocates that the vast potential latent in the human species can only be fully realized through freely associated, nonexploitative social relations. Throughout history, socialism has developed from its origins in the romantic visions of intellectuals and philosophers to an alternative social system that has been struggled for by exploited classes in virtually all corners of the globe. The legacy of socialism persists in the contemporary world, both as an ethical critique of capitalist values and as an alternative prescription for social justice.

Utopian Socialism. Although some of the key ethical elements within socialism can be traced back to ancient times, their consolidation into a unified vision occurred at the beginning of the nineteenth century in what has since become referred to as utopian socialism. Claude Henri Saint-Simon, Charles Fourier, and Robert Owen, among others, created a comprehensive critique of early capitalist society as it entered its industrial phase. Although the socialist visions of each thinker differed, all the utopian socialists shared a preoccupation with the morally bankrupt character of early industrial capitalism and saw the need for a more communal and egalitarian society in which an ethic of cooperation would prevail over individual greed.

Equally representative of utopian socialism was the notion that a socialist world could somehow be achieved through enlightened choice. Later socialists, such as Marx and Engels, argued that this idea amounted to a lack of a revolutionary strategy for realizing the utopian vision. Utopian socialists generally saw political violence as the historical baggage of presocialist society and believed that it would be unnecessary in a world that was being gradually civilized by means of emerging socialist values. In short, their moral critique of bourgeois society was not accompanied by an analysis of the way in which capitalist domination could be decisively broken.

Emile Durkheim, one of the founders of modern sociology, argued in his posthumously published work *Socialism* (1928) that Saint-Simon conceptually linked the ethical failures of the social era born of the Enlightenment with the urgent call for a consciously managed society—one in which production is cooperatively organized and the interests of the exploited classes are advanced through the socialization of industry. Saint-Simon's call for a "New Christianity" that would emphasize public concerns rather than the pursuit of individual self-interest made his utopian vision a complete one from Durkheim's perspective.

Robert Owen likewise espoused the notion that once socialist principles became enacted and shared, socialism's intrinsic desirability would automatically lead to its promulgation. Owen's contributions to socialism were vast, because of his agitation for reforms on behalf of the English proletariat as well as his sponsoring of experimental socialist communes that were based on socialist morality and cooperative business ventures. Charles Fourier added to the utopian socialist vision with his critique of the family and his agitation for sexual liberation. He became famous for his expression that the best measure of social freedom is the existing degree of women's freedom. Fourier argued that industrial bourgeois society repressed the human passion for love. Liberation could be gained only through smashing the prohibitions against human sexual expression, according to Fourier, and the larger community needed to guarantee all of its members the support necessary for "basic" sexual and well as economic satisfaction.

Revolutionary Socialism. Utopian visions of socialism ultimately became overshadowed by the emergence of the revolutionary socialism pioneered by Karl Marx and Friedrich Engels. Marx, a German thinker, transformed socialism into a practical program for struggle out of which organized social classes within industrial capitalist societies could create a socialist society through revolution. Marx and Engels' point of departure is their social class analysis, which argues that only the exploited working class is capable of successfully carrying out a socialist revolution. The ethical basis of what later became known as Marxian socialism is to be found in revolutionary "praxis," or practical activity, designed to overthrow bourgeois domination. The moral basis for revolutionary activity, including armed strug-

gle, was to be found in the larger historical mission of the working class, which was the ending of class exploitation.

An important distinction of Marxian socialism is its dialectical conception of ethics, which views all systems of morality as historically situated and dynamic insofar as morality changes in accordance with the ongoing struggle of social classes. The "contradictory" nature of morality thus rests in the notion that what is ethical at one stage of history becomes outmoded as human social relations continue to change and develop. The ethical basis of revolutionary armed struggle, for example, becomes transformed once new social circumstances become achieved and the need for violence has been surpassed. As Engels argued in *Anti-Duhring* (1878), a fully humanized morality can be achieved only after a socialist revolution has overcome social class inequalities and after the former system of morality has vanished from the collective memory.

Contemporary Socialism. The twentieth century can be largely characterized by the struggle between the competing systems of capitalism and socialism. Even the fall of the Socialist Bloc countries in the late 1980's and early 1990's can be related to an ethical crisis of particular political regimes and their relative inability to realize socialist goals. Most modern nations continue to experience political tensions between the status quo and powerful critics who argue for socialistic reforms and/or the need for a socialist revolution. The socialist critique of race, gender-based, and social class exploitation remains relevant in the contemporary era, and its advocates remain influential in world affairs.

—*Richard A. Dello Buono*

See also Capitalism; Communism; Lenin; Marx, Karl; Marxism.

BIBLIOGRAPHY

Berki, R. N. *Socialism.* New York: St. Martin's Press, 1975.

Bottomore, T. B., and Maximilien Rubel, eds. *Karl Marx: Selected Writings in Sociology and Social Philosophy.* New York: McGraw-Hill, 1964.

Durkheim, Emile. *Socialism.* New York: Collier Books, 1962.

Fromm, Erich, ed. *Socialist Humanism: An International Symposium.* Garden City, N.Y.: Doubleday, 1965.

McLellan, David. *The Thought of Karl Marx: An Introduction.* New York: Harper & Row, 1971.

Selsam, Howard, and Harry Martel, eds. *Reader in Marxist Philosophy: From the Writings of Marx, Engels and Lenin.* New York: International, 1963.

Tucker, Robert C. *The Marx-Engels Reader.* 2d ed. New York: W. W. Norton, 1978.

Society for the Prevention of Cruelty to Animals (SPCA)

TYPE OF ETHICS: Animal rights
DATE: Founded 1824
ASSOCIATED WITH: Broader nineteenth century British re-

form movements including abolitionism and women's rights

DEFINITION: An organization created by humanitarian activists to oppose the mistreatment of animals

SIGNIFICANCE: As the first animal welfare organization in England or Continental Europe, the SPCA influenced all future western humane organizations

According to the seventeenth century philosopher René Descartes, animals were soulless, God-created automatons lacking consciousness and the ability to feel pain. Any human use of animals was therefore justifiable. By the late eighteenth century, other philosophers challenged humanity's right to absolute dominion over animals, thus heralding the birth of the anticruelty movement. These new convictions were best summarized by the utilitarian philosopher Jeremy Bentham, who wrote in 1789, "The question is not, can they *Reason*? Nor can they *Talk*? But can they *Suffer*?" Reflecting increasing concern over animal welfare, M. P. Richard "Humanity Dick" Martin in 1822 submitted and successfully promoted the passage of a bill protecting domestic farm animals from cruelty. Meanwhile, encouraged by the Martin Act, humane activists formed the SPCA, which began policing slaughterhouses, markets and private citizens for animal abuse. With the bestowal of royal patronage in 1835, the organization became the Royal Society for the Prevention of Cruelty to Animals (RSPCA). In the late twentieth century, the United Kingdom remains a principal center of advocacy of animal rights.

See also Animal rights; Cruelty to animals.

Society for the Prevention of Cruelty to Children, American (ASPCC)

TYPE OF ETHICS: Children's rights

DATE: Founded 1895

DEFINITION: The ASPCC was formed to expose the abuse and exploitation of children, and to work for legislation prohibiting such practices

SIGNIFICANCE: The ASPCC was among the first organizations founded to prevent the neglect and abuse of children in the home, and their exploitation in the workplace

For working-class people (and working animals), nineteenth-century Britain and America were not always pleasant. Industrial towns were grimy and unsanitary, wages low, hours long, and work conditions often intolerable. Small wonder that both children and animals were the targets of unfocused anger, begrudged food and other necessities. Children were often sent out to earn a wage by the age of seven. Such children grew up unschooled and, frequently, mentally or physically impaired, and they usually passed these problems on to their own offspring. Reformers in Britain and America addressed these problems at much the same time: Child welfare laws were passed in New York City, and the New York Society for the Prevention of Cruelty to Children (NYSPCC) was founded in 1875; the National (English) SPCC began in 1884 with legislation from Parliament; and the ASPCC was founded in 1895. (Interestingly, animal welfare was dealt with nearly two gen-

erations earlier.) Most U.S. states quickly followed New York's lead and made child abuse a criminal offense, but child labor was not prohibited by federal legislation until 1938. Much action against physical and sexual abuse of children is now carried out by state and local governmental agencies.

See also Child abuse; Child labor legislation; Children; Children's Bureau, U.S.; Children's rights; Society for the Prevention of Cruelty to Animals (SPCA).

Sociobiology

TYPE OF ETHICS: Scientific ethics

DATE: From 1975

ASSOCIATED WITH: E. O. Wilson, W. D. Hamilton, Robert Trivers, Richard Dawkins, Richard Alexander, and The Human Behavior and Evolution Society

DEFINITION: Sociobiologists study the evolutionary basis of social behavior, including human behavior

SIGNIFICANCE: Because sociobiologists make the same assumptions about human behavior as about the behavior of other animals, they are often accused of promoting a biological determinist philosophy

In 1975, E. O. Wilson, a Harvard professor and world-renowned expert on ants, published a massive book in which he tied together decades of empirical research by animal behaviorists with decades of theoretical work by geneticists and evolutionary biologists. In so doing, he defined a new academic discipline, "sociobiology," the name of which is taken from the title of his book, *Sociobiology: The New Synthesis*.

The thesis of Wilson's book was that behavior, like any other attribute of an animal, has some of its basis in genetics, and therefore scientists should study behavior in the same way they do anatomy, physiology, or any other observable feature of an animal; that is, they should not only describe it but also try to figure out its function and the reasons why it evolved. Most biologists found no fault with this logic, and the discipline grew very rapidly, spawning hundreds of books and thousands of articles. Many predictions generated from this new perspective were corroborated, and many previously unexplained behaviors started to make sense.

The majority of biologists were rapidly convinced that this new approach was both useful and valid. Other scientists, however, as well as many sociopolitical organizations and representatives, immediately took a stand against it. In his book, Wilson had included a closing chapter on the sociobiology of human behavior, and his critics believed that the principles and methods used to study nonhuman animals simply could not be applied to humans. Academic critics tended to be psychologists, sociologists, anthropologists, and political scientists who believed that learning and culture, not evolution and genetics, determines most human behavior. Nonacademic critics tended to be either philosophers and theologians who believed that the human spirit makes people qualitatively different from other animals or left-leaning political organizations who believed that violent, discriminatory, and oppressive human behaviors might somehow be justified by calling attention to the existence of similar behaviors in other animals.

The first, and perhaps most significant, debate over sociobiology as it applied to humans involved explanations for altruism. Altruism, by definition, is behavior that helps another individual or group at some cost to the altruist. Since altruistic behavior would appear to help nonaltruistic recipients of altruism to survive and pass on their genes but not help altruists themselves, any genetic tendency toward altruism should rapidly die out; which would imply that altruistic behavior must be nonevolved; that is, either culturally learned or spiritually motivated, as the critics claimed.

Biologists, however, had documented altruistic behavior in a wide variety of nonhuman animals, suggesting either that other animals must also have cultural or spiritual motives (suggestions not accepted by most of the critics) or that altruism really must, somehow, increase the altruist's ability to survive and pass on genes, not merely help the nonaltruistic recipient. Two theoreticians provided explanations for how this might have occurred.

W. D. Hamilton proposed an evolutionary model based on the concept of "kin selection"; according to this model, altruistic behavior does not have to increase the altruist's chances of survival and reproduction, as long as it increases the survival and reproduction of the altruist's relatives. Since relatives share genes, even though an altruist may decrease his or her own chances of survival and reproduction, the genetic tendency for altruism can be passed on to subsequent generations because the altruist has increased the total number of his or her genes in the next generation by increasing the number of collateral, or nondirect, descendants.

Later, Robert Trivers proposed a model based on the concept of "reciprocal altruism"; according to this model, altruists do increase their own chances of survival and reproduction, because the recipients of their altruism remember them and help them out when the tables are turned. (This is often referred to colloquially as the "You scratch my back and I'll scratch yours" model.)

Largely on the basis of these two models of altruism, sociobiologists argued that even the most complex and seemingly spiritually motivated behaviors of humans could be explained solely by evolutionary biology. This notion was widely publicized in Richard Dawkins' book *The Selfish Gene* (1976), E. O. Wilson's subsequent book *On Human Nature* (1978), and Richard Alexander's *The Biology of Moral Systems* (1987).

Although many anthropologists and psychologists have converted to the evolutionary perspective and found it fruitful, many remain antagonistic to it, and sociologists, philosophers, and theologians, in particular, remain highly critical. Their argument continues to be that human behavior is qualitatively different from that of other animals because of the complexity of human culture and spirituality. They argue that a reductionist approach to human behavior will inevitably miss the most important features of human nature and social interactions.

In addition, many individuals and political groups remain hostile to sociobiology because of the widespread belief that if something is genetic it is inevitable and justifiable. Although these conclusions are not logically valid, there is legitimate concern that some people might use sociobiological arguments to try to undermine moral teaching or to promote or rationalize nepotism, aggression, racism, or sexism. To the extent that sociobiology is perceived as an ideological tool rather than a scientific enterprise, it has been argued that sociobiological research should not be funded or otherwise promoted by public institutions (such as universities). The debate has thus become one of politics and social goals as well as one of scientific philosophy and method.

—Linda Mealey

See also Academic freedom; Altruism; Evolution, theory of; Ideology; Political correctness; Social Darwinism.

BIBLIOGRAPHY

Alexander, Richard D. *The Biology of Moral Systems.* Hawthorne, N.Y.: Aldine De Gruyter, 1987.

Caplan, Arthur L., ed. *The Sociobiology Debate: Readings on Ethical and Scientific Issues.* New York: Harper & Row, 1978.

Dawkins, Richard. *The Selfish Gene.* New York: Oxford University Press, 1989.

Kitcher, Phillip. *Vaulting Ambition: Sociobiology and the Quest for Human Nature.* Cambridge, Mass.: MIT Press, 1985.

Montagu, Ashley, ed. *Sociobiology Examined.* New York: Oxford University Press, 1980.

Ruse, Michael. *Sociobiology: Sense or Nonsense?* Boston: D. Reidel, 1979.

Wilson, E. O. *On Human Nature.* Cambridge, Mass.: Harvard University Press, 1978.

_____. *Sociobiology: The New Synthesis.* Cambridge, Mass.: Belknap/Harvard University Press, 1975.

Socrates (c. 470 B.C.E., Athens, Greece—399 B.C.E., Athens, Greece): Philosopher

TYPE OF ETHICS: Classical history

ACHIEVEMENTS: Embodied an important turning point in philosophy; taught the Greek philosopher Plato

SIGNIFICANCE: Shifted the focus of Greek philosophy from external nature to knowledge of the self and ethics; argued that moral goodness is based on objective knowledge

Socrates' views on ethics must be understood against the background of his main opponents, the Sophists. They were moral relativists who believed that ethical beliefs could never be more than convention and subjective human opinions. In contrast, Socrates thought that ethical truths were universal and objective and concerned the way in which humans should best live. He said that the goal in human life was not simply living but "living well." To make an excellent ship, one must understand the purpose of ships and what constitutes the standard of excellence for a ship. Similarly, to live life well, one must understand what constitutes human excellence. For this reason, Socrates said that "the unexamined life is not worth living."

For Socrates, the goal of ethics was not obedience to some set of abstract duties. The whole purpose of ethics was to flourish as a human being, to fulfill one's true function, to achieve happiness. Hence, "Why should I be moral?" was a foolish question, for it was like asking, "Why should I live a happy, fulfilled life?" The problem is, Socrates said, that people tend to identify themselves with their bodies, and this gives them a false picture of what is the true goal in life. The body is, however, merely the outward shell, or instrument, of the soul. The immortal, nonphysical soul within one is the real person. The proper goal in life, therefore, is to "care for one's soul," to make it as good as possible, and this is achieved by striving to achieve wisdom.

Socrates' position is sometimes called "ethical intellectualism," because he believed that ethics is a matter of the intellect and that the moral person is one who has correct moral knowledge. Socrates' ethical conclusions are often called the "Socratic paradoxes" because they seem to contradict normal moral intuitions. Two of the key Socratic teachings are that virtue is knowledge and that no one knowingly does what is wrong.

Virtue is Knowledge. In the Greek language, the word for "virtue" has a much broader meaning than does its English counterpart. For anything to have "virtue" meant that it was excellent at its task or fulfilled its function well. Hence, the virtue of a shipbuilder is the skill of making high-quality ships. Human beings engage in many different and specific tasks (making music, playing sports, practicing medicine), and each activity has its appropriate goal and requires a certain sort of knowledge. Socrates believed, however, that people are all engaged in the more general task of living human life, and this is something that can be done poorly or well, depending on how well one understands this task. Hence, being a moral person requires having knowledge of what is genuinely valuable.

For Socrates, there is a difference between genuine knowledge and correct belief. Someone can be told the correct answer to a mathematics problem without really knowing why it is the correct answer. Similarly, simply having the correct moral beliefs is not enough. To truly have moral knowledge of the right way to live requires that one understand why that way is best. Socrates claimed that the end of human life is the achieving of wisdom; only wisdom will make one a morally excellent person.

No One Knowingly Does What Is Wrong. Since moral goodness is knowledge of how to live well and flourish, it was inconceivable to Socrates that anyone could have this knowledge and not follow it. Since doing what is wrong will harm the soul, however, those who do evil do so through error, thinking that they are pursuing what is good for them. For example, a thief steals because he or she believes that money is the ultimate value. By starting out with this false assumption about what is important in life, the thief logically concludes that it is good to obtain money in any way possible. What is wrong with the thief, Socrates would say, is that he or she lacks a correct understanding of what is genuinely valuable. Still, it may seem that sometimes people knowingly do what is wrong. Socrates would say, however, that when one performs an action that is morally wrong and harmful to one's soul, one does so because one's mind is blinded by desire. In that moment, one actually believes that the pleasure of the moment is a better goal to pursue than one's long-range satisfaction. For the person who has wisdom and the true vision of life, reason will guide the emotions in the right direction in the same way that a chariot driver guides his horses.

Implications for Ethical Conduct. For Socrates, being a moral person was more than simply doing the right thing. It also did not mean simply following a list of rules or duties. Instead, morality was a matter of making one's inner self as excellent as possible. This required an understanding of what is of enduring value in life as opposed to what is merely transitory and peripheral. One can gain this understanding by means of a process of self-examination in which one critiques the values by which one lives, abandoning those values that prove to be worthless, and getting a clear understanding of those values that lead to human excellence. Once one's soul has a vision of what is truly good, one will have no reason to do anything else but to steer one's life in that direction.
—*William F. Lawhead*

See also *Apology*; Plato; Platonic ethics; *Republic*; Sophists; Virtue ethics.

BIBLIOGRAPHY
Guthrie, W. K. C. *Socrates*. London: Cambridge University Press, 1971.
Plato. *The Collected Dialogues of Plato*. Edited by Edith Hamilton and Huntington Cairns. New York: Pantheon Books, 1961.
Santas, G. X. *Socrates: Philosophy in Plato's Early Dialogues*. London: Routledge & Kegan Paul, 1979.
Taylor, A. E. *Socrates*. Garden City, N.Y.: Anchor Books, 1953.
Vlastos, Gregory, ed. *The Philosophy of Socrates: A Collection of Critical Essays*. Garden City, N.Y.: Anchor Books, 1971.
_____. *Socrates, Ironist and Moral Philosopher*. Ithaca, N.Y.: Cornell University Press, 1991.

Solzhenitsyn, Aleksandr (b. Dec. 11, 1918, Kislovodsk, Russia): Novelist and historian

TYPE OF ETHICS: Modern history

ACHIEVEMENTS: Author of *Odin den' Ivana Denisovicha* (1962; *One Day in the Life of Ivan Denisovich*, 1963), *V kruge pervom* (1968; *The First Circle*, 1968), *Rakovy Korpus* (1968; *Cancer Ward*, 1968), and *Arkhipelag GULag, 1918-1956: Opyt Khudozhestvennogo issledovaniya* (1973-1975; *The Gulag Archipelago, 1918-1956: An Ex-*

Aleksandr Solzhenitsyn (The Nobel Foundation)

periment in Literary Investigation, 1974-1978), among other works; recipient of the Nobel Prize in Literature in 1970

SIGNIFICANCE: In both his literary and his historical works, Solzhenitsyn advanced the idea of the mutuality of communal and individual ethics within the context of the Russian Christian tradition

While confronted with mounting censorship from Soviet authorities during the 1960's and his eventual arrest and forced exile in 1974, Solzhenitsyn maintained an ethical identity with his homeland and his image of its historical traditions. Solzhenitsyn's ethical base was predicated on a renewal of traditional Russian Christian values; he was not attracted to the individualism or democratic institutions of the West. Solzhenitsyn condemned the oppression of the Soviet (and especially the Stalinist) phase in Russian history and described the ethical and moral bankruptcy of the Soviet regime and its institutions. In particular, he condemned the depersonalization of Russian life under the Soviets. He advanced the cause of the individual living within a free but ethically based and directed society. Although all the Solzhenitsyn canon is worthy of study, his most significant works from the standpoint of

ethics are *One Day in the Life of Ivan Denisovich* and *The Gulag Archipelago*.

See also Christian ethics; Stalin, Joseph.

Song lyrics

TYPE OF ETHICS: Arts and censorship
DATE: From antiquity
DEFINITION: The expression of views on a wide range of subjects by means of words set to music
SIGNIFICANCE: Contemporary song lyrics are central to the debate over limits to free expression

Bawdy and subversive lyrics are as old as music, and the impulse to suppress them is as old as social hierarchy. There is an ancient underground tradition of songs that defy the prevailing order, satirize the ruling class, and challenge commonly accepted precepts. Anthems such as the "Marseillaise" and the "Internationale" began as often-banned incitements to revolution. In nineteenth century Italy, the politics of the *risorgimento* circumscribed the texts of Verdi operas. Richard Strauss's *Salome* was shut down after one performance in New York in 1908, in part because of its "indecent" German libretto based on Oscar Wilde's play *Salomé*.

Modern Popular Culture. With the invention of sound recording and the advent of broadcast media, arguments favoring limits to the content of commercially distributed songs gained currency in the United States. Before the 1950's, most censorship incidents involved the proscription or laundering of Harlem Renaissance blues lyrics or Broadway show tunes such as Cole Porter's "Let's Do It." On occasion, records such as the Andrews Sisters' "Rum and Coca-Cola" (1942), whose unexpurgated lyrics refer to a mother-and-daughter team of Trinidadian prostitutes "working for the Yankee dollar," would be banned from the radio. During the McCarthy era, the socially conscious lyrics of leftist folksingers such as Woody Guthrie were widely suppressed as "communist" propaganda.

With the rise of rock and roll, the verbal content of popular music began to ignite moral panic. Rock, which evolved from African American rhythm-and-blues in the early 1950's, was considered "jungle music," a destructive combination of primitive rhythms and lewd lyrics. Early anti-rock campaigns were sometimes unapologetically racist and always maintained that the music spread violence and promiscuity. The lyrics of some songs, such as the Kingsmen's "Louie Louie," did not even have to be decipherable to be deemed obscene by the FBI and the Federal Communications Commission.

Although the sexual frankness that crept into pop lyrics as the 1960's progressed became increasingly overt, 1960's rock songs were most commonly censored or banned because of real or imagined references to drugs. The Beatles' "Lucy in the Sky with Diamonds" (1967), for example, was reviled in some quarters because it was assumed to describe the effects of LSD. More overt allusions to drug use, such as the Jefferson Airplane's "White Rabbit" (1967), with its

SONG LYRIC CENSORSHIP, ROCK TO RAP: 1954-1992	
1954	In the infancy of rock and roll, *Billboard* magazine advises radio stations to weed out "distasteful disks." Broadcasters begin banning "off-color" records and blacklisting certain artists.
1955	Parental anxiety, aroused by what *Variety* calls rock "leerics," becomes a full-scale moral panic.
1956	Segregationist Asa Carter, leader of the North Alabama White Citizens Council, launches a campaign to ban rock and roll from jukeboxes, claiming that its "sexualistic" beat and "immoral" lyrics constitute a plot to bring white teenagers "down to the level of the Negro."
1958	The Catholic Youth Center (CYC) helps to instigate efforts to ban songs that are sexually suggestive, especially ones alluding to "going steady."
1964	The FBI begins investigating the Kingsmen's hit song "Louie Louie," playing the record at various speeds and attempting to transcribe its incomprehensible lyrics, while the FCC begins threatening radio stations that give the song air time. Efforts to prove "Louie Louie" obscene drag on for two and a half years.
1965	Christian crusader David Noebel publishes "Communism, Hypnotism, and the Beatles," which seeks to prove that capitalism is being undermined by hidden messages in rock songs.
1966	The Rolling Stones' LP *Between the Buttons* features the song "Let's Spend the Night Together," an instant classic that is banned from broadcast in some areas.
1967	The Beatles' *Sergeant Pepper's Lonely Hearts Club Band* and other popular albums are attacked because of real or imagined references to drug abuse.
1969	Profanity begins entering mainstream rock lyrics. Such songs as Jefferson Airplane's "We Can Be Together" are denied airplay.
1976	The Reverend Jesse Jackson, acting as president of Operation PUSH (People United to Save Humanity), campaigns to remove "sex rock"—songs such as "Shake Your Booty"—from the airwaves.
1983	Cincinnati businessman Rick Alley, moved to action by Prince's *1999* album, starts a crusade against "porn rock." Addressing a convention of the Parent Teachers Association (PTA), Alley inspires the 5.4-million-member organization to demand a rating system from the Recording Industry of America (RIAA), which refuses to comply.
1985	Singer/songwriter Eric Boucher—better known as Jello Biafra, leader of the Dead Kennedys—is arrested on obscenity charges, ostensibly for an explicit poster enclosed in the album *Frankenchrist*. The ensuing court case destroys a group whose lyrics are on the cutting edge of iconoclastic satire.
1985	Tipper Gore, wife of Albert Gore, the Democratic senator from Tennessee and future vice president, joins other Washington wives in founding the Parents Music Resource Center (PMRC), an organization dedicated to opposing "violent and pornographic" content in pop music. Congressional hearings are held at PMRC's insistence.
1986	British heavy metal artist Ozzy Osbourne is unsuccessfully sued by parents who allege that their son's suicide was caused by the song "Suicide Solution" on Osbourne's *Blizzard of Ozz* album.
1990	The British heavy metal band Judas Priest is unsuccessfully sued for $6.2 million by the parents of two teenage boys whose suicide pact was allegedly inspired by the group's *Stained Class* album.
1990	Faced with the threat of legislation pending in eighteen states to label records or restrict their sales, the RIAA announces a voluntary labeling system that will brand some album covers with a parental-advisory logo.
1990	The rap group 2 Live Crew is arrested in Florida on obscenity charges following a live performance. Its three members are later acquitted. Meanwhile, however, record store owner Charles Freeman is convicted of obscenity for selling the group's *Nasty as They Wanna Be* album.
1992	In March, the Washington State Legislature passes an "erotic music" law that would ban sales of sexually explicit records (records with RIAA advisory labels) to minors. The law is later ruled unconstitutional.
1992	Rapper Ice-T releases the heavy metal album *Body Count*, which includes the song "Cop Killer." Right-wing political activists, especially Oliver North and his fund-raising entity Freedom Alliance, urge police associations to oppose anti-police lyrics by Ice-T and others with boycotts, lawsuits, and prosecution. The *Body Count* album is eventually recalled by Time Warner and rereleased with "Cop Killer" excised from it.

exhortations to "feed your head," often caused a song to be denied radio play. Drug-culture jargon and four-letter words at times provided authorities with convenient excuses to keep antiwar and social protest songs off the air.

In America, organized efforts to clean up rock lyrics have historically come from across the political spectrum. Leaders of such campaigns have ranged from right-wing ideologue David Noebel to civil rights activist Jesse Jackson. In the late 1970's, the messages of punk bands such as the Sex Pistols, along with the continuing popularity of "heavy metal" music among young teenagers, created concern that "morbid" and "occult" lyrics were causing a rise in teenage suicide. In the late 1980's, artists were threatened with legal action by bereaved parents and in some cases sued. Evangelists and radio personalities such as Bob Larson popularized the idea that satanic messages were encoded in rock lyrics or subliminally injected into certain albums through sound engineering.

In 1985, upset by masturbation references in Prince's song "Darling Nikki," Tipper Gore, the spouse of future vice president Albert Gore, cofounded the Parents Music Resource Center (PMRC), an organization aimed at curbing the excess of popular music. Congressional hearings held at PMRC's request resulted immediately in censorship activity at the state level. By 1990, the Recording Industry Association of America (RIAA) was pressured into instituting a voluntary warning-label system whereby some records would carry stickers with the label "Parental Advisory/Explicit Lyrics." The labeling scheme created a climate of censorship within the music industry and provided a foundation for efforts to restrict sales and criminalize certain lyrics in Louisiana, Washington State, and elsewhere.

The Demonization of Rap. In the late 1980's, Florida attorney Jack Thompson began enlisting allies in a campaign against rap, an African American art form that he considered an affront to "traditional values." Thompson helped to inspire the arrest and obscenity conviction of a record-store owner who was guilty of selling the Miami rap group 2 Live Crew's album *Nasty as They Wanna Be* (1990); the band itself was arrested in Fort Lauderdale following a live performance of such songs as "Me So Horny." Though 2 Live Crew was acquitted, Thompson continued to hound them and other outspoken rap musicians—especially NWA (Niggas With Attitude)—across the country and as far as the United Kingdom, where 22,000 copies of an NWA album were impounded.

Hysteria over "gangsta" rap reached fever pitch in 1992 with the release of Ice-T's *Body Count* album (technically a heavy metal record), an outpouring of rage over forms of racism. Its climactic song, "Cop Killer," was condemned for its venom:

> I got my twelve gauge sawed off.
> I got my headlights turned off.
> I'm 'bout to bust some shots off.
> I'm 'bout to dust some cops off.
> COP KILLER, it's better you than me.
> COP KILLER, f— police brutality!

Iran-contra figure Oliver North retained Jack Thompson as counsel in July, 1992, for the express purpose of mobilizing his lobbying operation, Freedom Alliance, against musicians. North's strategy included encouraging police organizations to use various means to eliminate the sale, broadcast, or commercial release of "seditious" music. Ice-T and his distributor, Time Warner, were finally driven to excise "Cop Killer" from future pressings of the *Body Count* album. Other artists who were legally threatened or economically pressured included Ice Cube, Tupac Shakur, Almighty RSO, and Paris, whose song "Bush Killa" vented rage at the White House.

Song-lyric censorship in the early 1990's was opposed by such advocacy groups as Rock Out Censorship and the National Campaign for Freedom of Expression. The ACLU Arts Censorship Project, led by Marjorie Heins, worked to provide legal aid to embattled musicians, producers, and retailers, helping to overturn an "erotic music" law in Washington State and to defend record stores across the country. Citing federal court rulings on speech, the ACLU maintained that song lyrics, even if they extolled armed rebellion, did not constitute a direct and imminent threat—and that First Amendment protections did indeed apply to such works as "Cop Killer." The irreconcilable disagreements in this controversy illustrated a growing rift between opposing visions of American democracy.   —*James D'Entremont*

See also Book banning; Censorship; Freedom of expression.

BIBLIOGRAPHY

Gore, Tipper. *Raising PG Kids in an X-Rated Society.* Nashville: Abingdon Press, 1987.

Heins, Marjorie. *Sex, Sin, and Blasphemy: A Guide to America's Censorship Wars.* New York: New Press, 1993.

Marsh, Dave. *Louie Louie.* New York: Hyperion, 1993.

Martin, Linda, and Kerry Segrave. *Anti-Rock: The Opposition to Rock 'n' Roll.* Hamden, Conn.: Archon Books, 1988.

Stanley, Lawrence A., ed. *Rap: The Lyrics.* New York: Penguin Books, 1992.

Victor, Jeffrey S. *Satanic Panic: The Creation of a Contemporary Legend.* Chicago: Open Court, 1993.

Sophists

TYPE OF ETHICS: Classical history

DATE: Fifth and fourth centuries B.C.E.

ASSOCIATED WITH: Protagoras, Gorgias of Leontini, Prodicus of Ceos, Thrasymachus of Chalcedon, Isocrates, and Hippias of Elis

DEFINITION: Calling themselves "the wise," Sophists were paid educators; usually based in Athens, they taught subjects ranging from cosmology to rhetoric and prepared students for public careers

SIGNIFICANCE: Sophists subjected existing values and attitudes to rational criticism; they saw social, political, and religious relationships as arbitrary constructs and promoted situational ethics

First appearing in Greece during the period of Athenian empire-building (the *Pentekontaetia*), the Sophists established a general intellectual climate rather than a well-defined school of thought. The Sophists furthered the *Pentekontaetia*'s process of dynamic change by declaring that traditions were based on optional arrangements. In an era of sharpened competition, they also claimed that the value of actions varied according to circumstances, that knowledge was necessarily imperfect, and that truth was relative. Their relativistic, individualistic, and skeptical outlook was epitomized by their foremost representative, Protagoras of Abdera, who declared that "man is the measure of all things." The Sophists' ethical relativism was sharply attacked by a new philosophical movement, led by Socrates, reaffirming absolute values. Socrates and his followers, however, adopted the Sophists' critical spirit and concern with ethical issues; by further exploring Sophist topics such as the nature of truth and the justification of values, the Socratics built upon and partially perpetuated their work.

See also Aristotelian ethics; Situational ethics; Socrates.

Sources of information

TYPE OF ETHICS: Media ethics
DATE: Early 1970's
ASSOCIATED WITH: Watchdog journalism
DEFINITION: Individuals who provide information to reporters for mass media dissemination
SIGNIFICANCE: Represents the possibilities for abuse of communication networks by journalists or by their sources through sloppy or unscrupulous reporting tactics

The information conveyed through the mass media is of fundamental importance to American society. On the basis of this information, public opinion is formed, votes are cast, and democracy is enacted. Media professionals, therefore, are obligated to seek out and make use of information sources that are reliable, credible, and well-intentioned. Too often, however, such exemplary sources do not exist, and journalists are left to struggle with questions of conduct and concerns about the ethical treatment of their sources.

The National Society of Professional Journalists attempts to address the issue by assessing both the journalist's principles and the consequences of his or her actions. Truth-telling is a fundamental governor in a free society and becomes, therefore, an activity that journalists are both morally and socially obligated to pursue. Developing and maintaining reliable news sources is an essential part of this journalistic mission, for without credible sources, reporters may never gain access to the type of information that their "watchdog" role requires. The United States Constitution, through the broad protections offered by the First Amendment, recognizes the unique nature of the press's responsibilities and grants generous latitude in the cultivation and protection of source-reporter relationships. Strict, absolute rules of conduct are incompatible with this intentionally unrestricted domain, leaving questions of ethics up for examination on a case-by-case basis.

The three main ethical considerations regarding sources of information are anonymity, confidentiality, and the source-reporter relationship. The use of anonymous sources is a fairly common media practice despite industry concerns about both its practical and ethical value. Practically, media professionals agree that the custom detracts from the press's integrity and engenders suspicion about the veracity of the report. Ethically, related considerations range from the erosion of the public trust to the publication of stolen or purchased information and the potential for furthering someone else's purpose by disseminating information that is politically or financially expedient to the source. Anonymity also undermines the journalistic mission of truth-telling because the source is an important part of the story. Failure to disclose the name of the source results in an incomplete or distorted version of truth. Once an anonymous source has been used, the issue of confidentiality arises. Various ethical questions surround this issue. How far is a news organization obligated to go in order to protect the identity of its source? How binding is a reporter's promise of anonymity? When do moral principles outweigh legal action? A 1991 Supreme Court decision ruled that the Minneapolis *Star Tribune* violated an implied contract created by the promise of anonymity when the paper publicly revealed a source's identity. The decision reinforced the mutually dependent nature of the source-reporter relationship, one that has long been the subject of controversy. While general opinion agrees that the relationship is frequently characterized by betrayal and manipulation, industry members differ regarding whether it is the reporter or the source who is guilty of malevolence. The debate sparks the question of intention and the ethical implications of using people as a means to further an individual's purpose, journalistic or otherwise.

In general, a liberalized deontological approach is employed to resolve these ethical quandaries. That is, media professionals are expected to adhere to general industry guidelines unless there is a compelling reason not to do so. For example, most news organizations have policies that reflect a cautionary stance regarding the granting of anonymity. Reporters are encouraged to try to get the source to agree to attribution and/or to find alternative ways to verify the information. Many news organizations require that journalists receive authorization from a superior before quoting from anonymous sources. Typically, editorial approval for anonymity is granted when that anonymity is supported by duty-based principles: when the information is of vital public interest and consistent with the truth-telling ethic; when the justification of minimizing grievous harm is clearly served, such as in the protection of a whistleblower or the victim of abuse; or when a concern for social justice is at stake, as in governmental corruption cases. In addition, industry guidelines seek to mitigate further the negative effects of anonymous sources by requiring identification as fully as possible, such as by position or title, and by explaining the reason for the use of anonymity.

Because anonymity is zealously guarded, once granted, the promise of confidentiality becomes supreme. The reputation of the press rests on the integrity with which sources are protected, and even the threat of legal action is not justification for exposing a confidential source. Confidentiality may be broken, however, if the news organization discovers that the source has provided false or misleading information. Malicious intent by a source, as was the case in the Minneapolis *Star Tribune* case, is not an acceptable reason to breach the confidential relationship. Rather, the responsibility lies with journalists not only to examine their own motives for publishing certain information but also to explore the possible motives of their sources. These actions act as safeguards against the likelihood that media professionals will fall prey to sources who are using the press in an effort to damage another's reputation, and reinforces a basic Judeo-Christian principle: Reporters should not treat others, nor should they allow themselves to be treated, as a means to someone else's end.

The use of anonymous sources raises a number of ethical considerations in itself, as well as the potential for confidentiality and source-reporter relationship abuses. Therefore, journalists should pursue such a course of action only after thoughtful and deliberate consideration.

—*Regina Howard Yaroch*

See also Confidentiality; Journalistic ethics.

BIBLIOGRAPHY

Black, Jay, Bob Steele, and Ralph Barney. *Doing Ethics in Journalism: A Handbook with Case Studies.* Greencastle, Ind.: The Sigma Delta Chi Foundation and The Society of Professional Journalists, 1993.

Boeyink, David E. "Anonymous Sources in News Stories: Justifying Exceptions and Limiting Abuses." *Journal of Mass Media Ethics* 5, no. 4 (1990): 233-246.

Christians, Clifford G., Kim B. Rotzoll, and Mark Fackler. *Media Ethics: Cases and Moral Reasoning.* 3d ed. New York: Longman, 1991.

Day, Louis A. *Ethics in Media Communications: Cases and Controversies.* Belmont, Calif.: Wadsworth, 1991.

Meyer, Philip. *Ethical Journalism.* New York: Longman, 1987.

Sovereignty

TYPE OF ETHICS: International relations
DATE: Entered English language fourteenth century
DEFINITION: Sovereignty is the exclusive right to rule over a particular territory based upon either legal title or effective control
SIGNIFICANCE: The claim of a right to rule necessarily raises the moral questions of when and why one ought to obey the sovereign

Sovereignty is a central concept in domestic and international law as well as in political theory, and its ethical implications are enormous.

To be sovereign in international law, a nation must be completely self-governing—recognizing no exterior legal authority to have the right to control its actions. The form of a national government is not an issue in determining sovereignty; a democracy, an absolute monarchy, a military junta, or a communist dictatorship may be sovereign if it submits to no higher, external legal authority.

In international affairs, one often contrasts de jure with de facto sovereignty, sovereignty in law versus sovereignty in fact. Some nations have been officially self-governing, but have been, in fact, controlled by another. In the 1930's and 1940's, for example, Egypt was officially an independent nation but was, in fact, ruled by the British Empire in an arrangement that some historians have called an "informal empire."

Alternatively, some nations are nominally under foreign control but do, in fact, govern themselves. Such was clearly the case between the Balfour Declaration of 1926, wherein the British Government promised not to interfere in the self-government of the dominions, and the Statute of Westminster (1931), which granted the dominions de jure independence.

During civil wars and wars of independence, questions of sovereignty are often blurred. The American colonies declared their independence from the British Crown on July 4, 1776, but the Crown did not recognize that independence until the Treaty of Paris (1783). When did sovereignty pass from the King in Parliament to the Continental Congress (or, more exactly, to the several states)?

Legally, of course, such issues of sovereignty in international law are often solved by resort to competing interpretations by domestic law. American law views the date of the Declaration of Independence as the effective date of American sovereignty for all legal purposes, while in British law, the Treaty of Paris marks the end of British sovereignty in the thirteen American colonies.

In international law, land without a sovereignty over it is called *terra nullius* (or *territorium nullius*)—empty land—even though it may have a substantial human population. *Terra nullius* is open for annexation by existing sovereignties under international law on the theory that land without a sovereign is dangerously susceptible of producing lawlessness, such as piracy or terrorism, or armed conflicts between existing nations. Given the new dispensation in international affairs under the United Nations charter, it is likely that an area of *terra nullius* that contained a large population but had not developed (or had lost) a governmental structure capable of asserting an "international legal personality" would be put in a trusteeship relationship with an established nation until such time as it might be capable of asserting sovereignty. By this means, the aura of direct colonialism might be averted.

The concept of sovereignty has application in political philosophy as well as in international law. Sovereignty is not only a claim of a right to rule made vis-à-vis other sovereignties but also one made domestically in regard to those subject to a governmental authority.

Political philosophers as divergent as Thomas Hobbes and Jean-Jacques Rousseau have recognized the essential truth that sovereignty is illimitable and indivisible.

In recent years, these observations have fallen into general disuse, perhaps in the aftermath of the rise of the American Republic. In the British system, whatever Parliament passed and the King signed was law, without question and without limitation. Political theorists spoke of the legal omnipotence of the King-in-Parliament.

With the development of the U.S. Constitution, with its division of powers and its system of checks and balances between the executive, legislative, and judicial branches, it may, perhaps, have seemed that sovereignty could be divided and limited. Writing in the *Federalist Papers*, Alexander Hamilton, James Madison, and John Jay propounded the new sovereignty, which was tamed not only by the relationships of the branches of the national government but also by a federalism that preserved a sphere for the power of states and a system of enumerated rights that protected the citizen from governmental abuse.

In fact, in the U.S. Constitution, as in all political systems, sovereignty remains undivided and without limitation. Within the constitutional order, an ordinary sovereignty operates with divisions and limitations of power, but an extraordinary sovereignty resides also. The process of constitutional amendment could create a monarchy, establish an official church, authorize torture, eliminate elections, abolish the Supreme Court, and so forth. Seeming limitations, such as the prohibition upon depriving a state of its equal suffrage in the Senate, prove to be only procedural variants, because an amendment reducing the senatorial representation of a particular state would need ratification by that state, and an amendment to abolish the Senate would require unanimous ratification by the states.

In all approaches to sovereignty, of course, there are underlying implications of a moral right to rule, in addition to a legal right and a practical power to rule. Even with legal positivism, in which moral questions are not directly injected into the pure theory of law—in which law is seen as merely "the command of the sovereign"—morality reenters through the questions of why, when, and whether the subject ought to obey the sovereign.

Also concerned in the ethical issues surrounding sovereignty has been its origin: Is sovereignty natural, or is it the construct of a social contract arising out of a state of nature? Anarchists, furthermore, including theoretical anarchists, such as Robert Paul Wolff, have viewed sovereignty as a morally dangerous illusion.   —*Patrick M. O'Neil*

See also Anarchy; Colonialism and imperialism; Constitution, U.S.; Hobbes, Thomas; International law; Intervention; *Leviathan*; Montesquieu, Charles-Louis; Nationalism; Revolution; Sedition; Social contract; Treason; *Two Treatises of Government*.

BIBLIOGRAPHY

Austin, John. *The Province of Jurisprudence Determined and the Uses of the Study of Jurisprudence.* London: Weidenfeld & Nicolson, 1954.

Bryce, James. *Studies in History and Jurisprudence.* Vol. 2. Oxford, England: Clarendon Press, 1901.

Marshall, Geoffrey. *Constitutional Theory.* Oxford, England: Clarendon Press, 1971.

Soviet psychiatry

TYPE OF ETHICS: Psychological ethics

DATE: Approximately 1862 to the 1990's

ASSOCIATED WITH: Involuntary confinement and the use of psychiatry for the suppression of political or religious dissent

DEFINITION: For many years, organizations such as the World Psychiatric Association have documented widespread human rights violations by psychiatrists in the Soviet Union

SIGNIFICANCE: The confinement of religious and political dissidents by Soviet psychiatrists has been a vivid reminder of the ways in which a profession can function unethically as an agent of social control

The persecution of both political and religious dissidents by mental health authorities in the former Soviet Union was long a source of great concern to organizations that monitor human rights violations. Extensive evidence exists that hundreds if not thousands of mentally healthy dissidents were involuntarily committed to Soviet psychiatric hospitals. These individuals were committed in order to remove them from society and thus suppress their dissenting ideas and opinions.

History. Although psychiatric facilities in the Soviet Union practiced this type of abusive social control for many years, soviet psychiatry was not always an ethically compromised profession. The field of psychiatry was founded in the Soviet Union by Ivan Belinski, a Russian physician, who formed the first Russian psychiatric society in 1862. Belinski promoted psychiatric training and worked to establish outpatient treatment for the mentally ill. Under his leadership, the profession of psychiatry grew rapidly. In 1887, the first Congress of Russian Psychiatrists met in Moscow and endorsed the humane, scientifically informed treatment of mental patients as well as the notion that, if possible, psychiatric patients should be cared for in their home environments. Such ideas put Russian psychiatrists on an equal plane with their fellow practitioners in the rest of the world.

Positive developments continued to take place in the field of Soviet psychiatry after the Communist Revolution of 1917. At the time of the revolution, a People's Commissariat of Health was formed, with a special division devoted to psychiatry. Under the Commissariat's leadership, many types of services were offered free of charge to the mentally ill, such as crisis intervention, sheltered workshops, and home care programs. Many Soviet psychiatrists also began to develop an interest in the young field of psychoanalysis, and the major works of Sigmund Freud were widely distributed.

The Advent of Abuse. Problems began to develop in the late 1920's, as Joseph Stalin consolidated his hold on the government of the Soviet Union. Stalin had little concern for the rights of the mentally ill, and he viewed involuntary psychiatric commitments as an effective way to control his ideological opponents. Although psychiatric hospitals continued to treat individuals who suffered from genuine forms of mental illness, they also became a place of involuntary confinement for individuals who openly disagreed with the political or religious doctrine of the government. Labor organizers and artists who advocated creative freedom were favorite targets of the psychiatric establishment. Placing such dissidents in psychiatric facilities served both to remove them from society and to discredit their ideas by allowing the government to label them as insane.

A special diagnostic category, known as "sluggish schizophrenia," was developed. Anatoly Snezhnevsky, a notorious Russian psychiatrist who rose to a position of high authority under the Stalinist regime, defined sluggish schizophrenia as delusions of reforming the country's social system in the mind of an otherwise normal individual. This type of false diagnosis enabled psychiatrists such as Snezhnevsky to label mentally stable individuals as insane and have them involuntarily committed to psychiatric facilities. Even if such an individual was eventually fortunate enough to be discharged, his or her name was maintained on a national list of mental patients. This registry was distributed to prospective employers and schools, ensuring that the individual would suffer from life-long discrimination. Doctors who refused to follow the unethical practices of this system were routinely disciplined or even imprisoned. Over time, Soviet psychiatrists became virtual servants of the state, with no professional autonomy and little room for ethical judgment.

The Use of Torture. Psychiatric treatment in the Soviet Union eventually became so abusive that some dissidents were actually tortured during their hospitalization. A convincing account of such treatment has been provided by Anatoly Koryagin, a Soviet psychiatrist who was himself hospitalized involuntarily because he refused to carry out government policy. Throughout his fifteen-month hospitalization, Koryagin was kept on a virtual starvation diet, so that he was severely emaciated and in a constant state of hunger. He was forced to take various psychiatric medications and also reports having had a probe smeared with salytic acid placed in his stomach in order to induce excruciating pain. This type of torture was apparently designed to force Koryagin and other dissidents to renounce their ideological beliefs. Because of such extreme violations of human rights, the World Psychiatric Association (WPA) condemned Soviet psychiatry in 1977. Six years later, the All-Union Society of Soviet Psychiatrists resigned from the WPA rather than face certain expulsion.

Such international condemnation, however, did little to change the field of psychiatry in the Soviet Union. Peter Reddaway, a political scientist who has written extensively about Soviet psychiatric abuse, has noted that only Glasnost and the reorganization of Soviet society has brought about genuine reform. In what was once the Soviet Union, the reorganized profession of psychiatry appears to be returning to its humanitarian roots.   —*Steven C. Abell*

See also Psychology; Stalin, Joseph.

BIBLIOGRAPHY

Amnesty International, USA. *Political Abuse of Psychiatry in the USSR: An Amnesty International Briefing.* New York: Author, 1983.

Bloch, Sidney, and Peter Reddaway. *Psychiatric Terror: How Soviet Psychiatry Is Used to Suppress Dissent.* New York: Basic Books, 1977.

_____. *Soviet Psychiatric Abuse: The Shadow over World Psychiatry.* Boulder, Colo.: Westview Press, 1985.

Fireside, Harvey. *Soviet Psychoprisons.* New York: W. W. Norton, 1979.

Kanas, Nick. "Contemporary Psychiatry: Psychiatry in Leningrad." *Psychiatric Annals* 22 (April, 1992): 212-220.

Koryagin, Anatoly. "The Involvement of Soviet Psychiatry in the Persecution of Dissenters." *British Journal of Psychiatry* 154 (March, 1989): 336-340.

Sperm banks

TYPE OF ETHICS: Modern history
DATE: Established late twentieth century
ASSOCIATED WITH: Artificial insemination and in vitro fertilization
DEFINITION: Places where sperm are frozen and stored for later use in artificial insemination and in vitro fertilization techniques
SIGNIFICANCE: The process of choosing sperm donors raises various issues of genetic manipulation

The freezing of tissue, or cryopreservation, is a procedure that is used to delay the normal degenerative processes that occur when a tissue is removed from the body. Sperm banks acquire sperm from male donors and then deep freeze the sperm in liquid nitrogen, where they can be preserved for more than a decade. When needed, the sperm can be thawed out and used in processes such as artificial insemination and in vitro fertilization. Some sperm donors are husbands who cannot have children with their wives by ordinary means. Others are men who face sterilization through vasectomies or as the result of chemotherapy drugs for cancer. Still others are healthy men who donate their sperm for the money. Those interested in obtaining donor sperm can often choose the sperm based on the physical characteristics, hobbies, and/or intellectual capacities of the donor. This technology tends to tempt persons to manipulate the gene pool so as to create a superior class of persons, avoid individuals with undesirable traits, and attempt to create the "perfect child." One problem involves determining the true father of the child—the biological donor or the parent who raises the child but did not donate the sperm. Additionally, some people believe that the commercialism inherent in the business of sperm banking tends to lessen the value of procreation.

See also Bioethics; Eugenics; In vitro fertilization.

Spinoza, Baruch (Nov. 24, 1632, Amsterdam, United Provinces—Feb. 21, 1677, The Hague, United Provinces): Philosopher

TYPE OF ETHICS: Renaissance and Restoration history
ACHIEVEMENTS: Author of *Renati des Cartes principiorum philosophiae pars I et II, more geometrico demonstratae, per Benedictum de Spinoza* (1663; *Descartes' Principles of Philosophy Geometrically Demonstrated by Benedict Spinoza*), *Tractatus Theologico-politicus,* (1670; *A Theologico-Political Treatise,* 1862) and *Ethica* (1677; *Ethics,* 1870), among other works

SIGNIFICANCE: Constructed a monistic philosophy of God and nature in which ethical behavior would follow naturally from understanding the unified whole

In the seventeenth century, academic scholasticism, with its syllogistic reasoning and its Aristotelian epistemology, was withering away after a millennium of dominance. The empirical scientific methods of Copernicus, Kepler, and Galileo showed a new direction of philosophical understanding, and a rising interest in mathematics suggested new types of philosophical proof based on the methods of Euclidian geometry. Spinoza played a part in the movement that resulted, together with such notable thinkers as Francis Bacon, Thomas Hobbes, René Descartes, and Gottfried Leibniz.

Life. Spinoza was born into a family of prosperous Jewish merchants in Amsterdam, an area with a tolerance for religious practice and dissent in advance of its time. His education was in the Hebraic tradition of his community, with studies of the Old Testament and the Talmud, as well as of scholastic philosophy and theology. Preparing to become a rabbi, he continued his studies after finishing school, becoming acquainted with the Kabbala and the thinking of medieval Jewish philosophers. His own views, fueled by a determination to think everything through ab initio, diverged from orthodoxy to the point that he was expelled from the Jewish community (by civil, not religious, authority) in 1656. He renounced his Hebrew name, Baruch, and was thenceforward known as Benedict (de) Spinoza. He continued in Amsterdam for a time, studying Latin, Greek, physics, geometry, and the philosophy of Descartes, and associating with members of a number of free-thinking Christian sects such as the Mennonites, the Collegiants, and the Remonstrants. In 1660, he left Amsterdam to live successively in Rijnsburg, Voorburg, and finally The Hague (all on an axis of approximately thirty miles between Amsterdam and The Hague). In these places, he supported himself as an expert lens grinder and met for discussion with groups of philosophically minded friends. This activity led to his early writings, in which he set forth his views on God, humanity, and the universe, and produced an account of Descartes' philosophy. These were original and powerful enough that his reputation quickly spread beyond his immediate circle, and within a few years he was in correspondence with major philosophers in Europe and England, including Leibniz and the physicist Christiaan Huygens on the Continent, and in England Henry Oldenburg, secretary of the Royal Society of London, and the scientist Robert Boyle. *A Theologico-Political Treatise* was published anonymously in 1670 and was widely condemned for its religious skepticism. All of Spinoza's other works, including his major production, the *Ethics*, were published posthumously by his friends. In 1672, the French general Condé (Prince Louis II of Bourbon) invited Spinoza to visit, possibly with a position in mind, but no position was forthcoming. In the following year, he was offered a position at Heidelberg University, but he declined it. Spinoza's last years were spent virtually as an invalid, and at the age of forty-four he died of consumption, probably aggravated by the silica dust from his lens-grinding activities.

Early Thought and Work. The *Short Treatise* of 1660 and the exposition of Descartes' philosophy were written when Spinoza's thinking was developing into the mature expression of the *Ethics*. The Descartes work, written for a group of students, was expressly not his own thinking. Nevertheless, he derived valuable ideas from it through reaction, notably his rejection of the dualism of mind and body (or spirit and matter) and his affirmation that the individual must form his own judgments in political and religious matters, free from the pressures alike of church and state. It was this conviction, as expressed in the *A Theologico-Political Treatise*, that first aroused opposition that later became virulent. Spinoza's notion of freedom of thought and action is absolute, a position that does not sit well with religious or political authority.

Ethics. The reason for this absolute freedom becomes evident in the *Ethics*. Laid out in Euclidian fashion with definitions and axioms, and propositions deduced from them, the *Ethics* first deals with God and nature, which are one. God/nature is its own cause, requiring no prior cause and encompassing all that is, including humankind. Properly understood, this eternally existing unity admits of no internal contradictions. It also admits of no free will and is absolutely impersonal about the fate of humankind. These last conclusions led to Spinoza's condemnation as a dangerous atheist, although his God informs his entire system of morality and ethics. In his deterministic universe, the ethical imperative is unending rational inquiry to learn the true nature of things. The free individual perceives what he or she must do and acts accordingly. Those with confused ideas about their universe are in some degree not free, and they act not through understanding but because they cannot help themselves.

Significance and Influence. Morality and ethics are individual matters for Spinoza, and they lead to political and religious consensus only when enough people, made free by rational and empirical inquiry, act on the understanding they have gained. Spinoza's philosophical system is remarkably complete and self-contained, which has led to much misunderstanding by later thinkers who tried to extract and develop portions of it. This misunderstanding, together with the charge of atheism, produced an almost total lack of influence of Spinoza's work for more than a century. Only in the nineteenth century, in the time of rejection of monarchy and despotism, were his ideas taken up by the German and English romantics and idealists. No school of thought has grown from his writings, and his influence on philosophy has been more catalytic than structural.

—*Robert M. Hawthorne, Jr.*

See also Descartes, René; *Ethics*.

BIBLIOGRAPHY

Allison, Henry E. *Benedict de Spinoza: An Introduction.* Rev. ed. New Haven, Conn.: Yale University Press, 1987.

Donagan, Alan. *Spinoza*. Chicago: University of Chicago Press, 1989.

Hampshire, Stuart. *Spinoza*. New York: Penguin Books, 1987.

Harris, Errol E. *Spinoza's Philosophy: An Outline*. Atlantic Highlands, N.J.: Humanities Press International, 1992.

MacIntyre, Alasdair. "Spinoza, Benedict (Baruch)." In *The Encyclopedia of Philosophy*, edited by Paul Edwards. Vol. 7. New York: Macmillan, 1972.

Spinoza, Benedictus de. *The Chief Works of Benedict de Spinoza*. Translated by R. H. M. Elwes. New York: Dover Publications, 1955.

Stalin, Joseph (Joseph Vissarionovich Dzhugashvili; Dec. 21, 1879, Gori, Georgia, Russian Empire—Mar. 5, 1953, Moscow, U.S.S.R.): Political leader

Type of ethics: Modern history

Achievements: Leader of the Communist Party of the Soviet Union and the Union of Soviet Socialist Republics, 1928-1953

Significance: Directed the transformation of the Soviet Union into a totalitarian state and led the country in the Great Patriotic War against Nazi Germany

Joseph Vissarionovich Dzhugashvili Stalin was one of the most powerful leaders of the twentieth century. His rule would have a permanent impact upon not only the Soviet Union but also the entire international system. Stalin governed his political behavior according to the Marxist-Leninist tenet that the ends—the transformation of society along the lines anticipated by Marx and Lenin toward socialism, under the undisputed leadership of the Communist Party of the Soviet Union (CPSU)—justified whatever means were deemed to be appropriate by the Party leadership. In addition, Stalin accelerated and eventually fully implemented many of the policies and trends initiated during the period of Lenin's active rule in the Soviet Union (1917-1922). These included the complete consolidation of CPSU totalitarian intrusion into all social, economic, cultural, political, and even personal aspects of life in the Soviet Union, as well as the acceleration and eventually the institutionalization of the centralizing, bureaucratic, authoritarian trends within the Party itself. Finally, Stalin directed the industrialization of the Soviet Union, led the USSR's tenacious defense during World War II, and significantly buttressed Soviet security in the war's aftermath. In doing so, however, Stalin applied a degree of mass coercion and terror rarely equaled in human history.

Stalin and Totalitarian Rule. Following the 1917 Revolution, Stalin rose rapidly to power largely as a result of his early institutional control over the CPSU Apparat via his position as general secretary of the Party's Central Committee, as well as his membership in the Party's top decision-making organs. As a result of these institutional positions, particularly that of general secretary, Stalin was able to assign personal allies and protégés to strategic leadership positions not only within the CPSU organization itself but also throughout the Soviet state bureaucracy. Since that development was framed against the rapid expansion of CPSU and Soviet state totalitarian control over all aspects of Soviet public and even private life, by 1928, Stalin had successfully placed his lieutenants in virtually all key positions of power throughout the Soviet Union. Simultaneously, by the end of the 1920's, he had isolated and effectively eliminated or rendered politically powerless all of his political rivals from the early post-Revolutionary period.

Between 1928 and his death in 1953, Stalin was unquestionably the most powerful single individual within the Soviet leadership. As power increasingly concentrated at the highest level of the Party hierarchy, Stalin continuously, but with extreme skill and perception, coalesced a sufficiently powerful, though ever-changing, body of allies and supporters to enable him to remain the dominant Soviet leader, despite periodic challenges to his ruling position from within the Party elite. Conversely, within this dynamic but largely shrouded framework of coalitions and counter-coalitions that characterized Soviet politics at the political center, Stalin aggressively purged real or imagined policy dissidents and individuals who appeared to threaten his personal leadership from positions of power and authority. Although Stalin's practice of purging the ranks of the Party can be traced to the precedent of Lenin's theory and practices regarding the enforcement of Party discipline, the massive scope and degree of Stalin's use of terror, imprisonment, and physical liquidation within the CPSU were both qualitatively and quantitatively unprecedented in Party annals prior to the 1930's. Although the precise or even approximate number of Party members and affiliated individuals purged during the Stalin period will never be known, it has been estimated that during the period of the 1930's alone, approximately one million perished. Furthermore, in addition to the physical decimation of the Party's ranks caused by the purges of the Stalin era, the terror engendered within the Party created a tone of fear, denunciation, and paralysis of individual initiative and willingness to assume personal responsibility that permanently influenced the character of the CPSU and the attitudes of its members.

Stalin's use of arbitrary arrest, imprisonment, torture, execution, and terror were not confined to the ranks of the Party, but were extended on a much larger scale throughout the entirety of Soviet society. Indeed, as the tentacles of Party control and the domain of its self-assigned responsibilities extended throughout the whole of the Soviet public and private sectors, and, further, as the Stalin-led Party leadership moved to reshape the entire character of the Soviet Union, those who individually or collectively offered actual or perceived resistance to the Party's policies or who could be utilized by the Party as scapegoats for the CPSU's failures to fulfill promises in return for societal sacrifices felt the harsh, cold, bureaucratic, deadly wrath of the authorities. Hence, tens of millions of Soviet citizens were killed, imprisoned, or simply disappeared during the two and a half

STALIN TIME LINE	
1879	Stalin born (December 21)
1914	World War I begins
1917	Overthrow of the Tsarist government Bolshevik Revolution
1918	Treaty of Brest Litovsk—War with Germany ends Civil War begins War Communism begins
1920	War with Poland Defeat of counterrevolutionary armies in Crimea
1921	Tenth CPSU Congress Kronstadt Rebellion New Economic Policy adopted
1922	Stalin elected general secretary of the CPSU Central Committee Lenin suffers first stroke
1924	Lenin dies
1926	Zinoviev, Kamenev, and Trotsky expelled from the CPSU Politburo
1928	First Five Year Plan Adopted
1929	Collectivization of Agriculture Bukharin and Tomsky expelled from the CPSU Politburo
1934	Seventeenth CPSU Congress Kirov assassinated
1935	Great purges begin
1939	Great purges draw down Eighteenth CPSU Congress Nazi-Soviet Non-Aggression Pact Germany invades Poland USSR occupies Eastern Poland Winter War with Finland begins
1940	Winter War ends USSR annexes Estonia
1941	Soviet-Japanese Pact Germany invades USSR Battle of Moscow
1942	Battle of Stalingrad begins
1943	German forces surrender at Stalingrad Battle of Kursk Kiev liberated
1944	Siege of Leningrad lifted Soviet troops enter Poland and Rumania
1945	Red Army captures Berlin Germany surrenders United States drops atomic bomb on Hiroshima USSR declares war on Japan United States drops atomic bomb on Nagasaki Japan surrenders
1946	Zhdanov launches ideological campaign
1948	Zhadanov dies Leningrad affair
1949	People's Republic of China established USSR tests atomic bomb
1950	Korean War begins
1952	Nineteenth CPSU Congress
1953	Doctor's Plot Stalin dies (March 5)

decades of Stalin's rule. Between ten and fifteen million perished during the 1930's alone, not including the victims of the famine associated with the collectivization of agriculture.

Stalin and the Transformation of the Soviet Union. As the CPSU increasingly established totalitarian control over the entire Soviet Union, the tone, direction, and specific policies adopted in every sector of Soviet life were increasingly determined by Stalin and the Party leadership. One of the aspects of Soviet life most transformed during the Stalin era was the Soviet economy. Stalin inaugurated and directed the collectivization of Soviet agriculture, which, though enormously costly in both human life and material resources, was designed to break permanently the politico-economic power of the Russian peasantry and to secure the agricultural resources necessary to sustain the accompanying industrialization effort. The industrialization of the Soviet Union under the rubric of a series of centrally formulated and administered "Five Year Plans," which were inaugurated in the late 1920's, rapidly expanded the Soviet Union's heavy industrial and defense output. As with the agrarian sector, the dramatic expansion of Soviet capital output was accomplished at a very high human, material, and environmental cost. Overall, the Stalinist economy left a legacy of overcentralization of economic direction; imbalances between sectors of the economy, with most resources dedicated to the priority heavy industrial and defense components of the economy at the expense of consumer industries and agriculture; and a resultant lack of material incentives for Soviet workers. Notwithstanding these human, material, and long-term systemic and environmental costs, however, in 1928 Stalin inherited an economy in the early stages of industrialization and transformed it into a major heavy industrial and defense production power by the time of his death in 1953.

In addition to directing the transformation of the Soviet economy and virtually every other aspect of Soviet domestic life, Stalin also orchestrated the successful defense of the Soviet Union in the 1941-1945 war against Nazi Germany— "The Great Patriotic War." Notwithstanding the initial successes enjoyed by the Germans following their massive surprise attack upon the Soviet Union on June 22, 1941, a combination of German politico-strategic-operational errors, combined with the tenacious resistance of the Soviets themselves, enabled the Red Army to halt and drive the Germans back at the gates of Moscow in December, 1941, and on the banks of the Volga River, at Stalingrad, in late 1942 and early 1943. Following the Soviet victory at the Battle of Kursk in July, 1943, the offensive capability of the German Army on the Eastern Front was permanently broken and the Soviet forces surged relentlessly westward. By mid-1944, when the Western allies successfully landed their armies on the beaches of Normandy, the Soviets had successfully liberated most of the pre-1939 Soviet territory. Finally, throughout the remainder of 1944 and into 1945, the Red

Army fiercely fought across Poland and into the eastern portion of Germany, as well as up the Danube River Valley into Austria and Czechoslovakia. The war, the largest land conflict in human history, left a tremendous wake of devastation throughout most of the western portion of the Soviet Union. Within the Soviet Union alone, between twenty-five and forty million Soviet citizens had died, tens of millions more were wounded in body or spirit, and massive urban, industrial, and agrarian destruction extended throughout the European half of the country.

By the conclusion of hostilities in Europe, the Red Army dominated eastern and much of central Europe. Capitalizing upon this unprecedented level of military power, combined with the inability of the United States and Great Britain to counter effectively Soviet postwar designs on the areas it dominated, Stalin not only successfully secured de facto Western acknowledgment of the Soviet annexation of Estonia, Latvia, and Lithuania, as well as portions of Finland, Poland, Czechoslovakia, and Rumania, but also imposed Soviet satellite regimes in Poland, Czechoslovakia, Hungary, Albania, Rumania, and Bulgaria. These measures, combined with the establishment of a Soviet zone of occupation within prewar German territory, significantly enhanced Soviet security against the threat of future overland invasion from the West and extended Soviet influence over a large portion of Europe. Similarly, in the Far East, in return for the Soviet Union's entry into the war against Japan in August, 1945, Stalin obtained direct Soviet control over the Kurile Islands and the southern half of Sakhalin Island. In addition, he oversaw the erection of satellite regimes in North Korea and, in 1949, over the entirety of mainland China. Finally, Stalin encouraged the prompt development and acquisition of atomic and thermonuclear weapons. In short, by the time of his death in 1953, Stalin had not only greatly enhanced the geo-strategic security of the Soviet Union but also had expanded Soviet influence to engulf a significant portion of the Eurasian landmass. Indeed, the entire character of the post-World War II international system was shaped, in large measure, by the policies of Stalin.

On March 5, 1953, Joseph Stalin died in circumstances that remain shrouded in mystery. True to the ethics of Marxism-Leninism, Stalin used any and all means necessary to reshape the Soviet Union in accord with his plan for the advancement of the historical process toward his vision of socialism. Ultimately, however, after two and a half decades of Stalinist rule, the means had clearly consumed the ends, thereby permanently marring the achievements of the Stalin era.
— *Howard M. Hensel*

See also Lenin.

BIBLIOGRAPHY

Conquest, Robert. *The Great Terror*. New York: Oxford University Press, 1990.

Medvedev, Roy. *Let History Judge*. Rev. ed. Edited and translated by George Shriver. New York: Columbia University Press, 1989.

Tucker, Robert C. *Stalin as Revolutionary: 1879-1929*. New York: W. W. Norton, 1973.

_____. *Stalin in Power*. New York: W. W. Norton, 1990.

Ulam, Adam B. *Stalin*. New York: Viking Press, 1973.

Volkogonov, Dmitrii. *Stalin: Triumph and Tragedy*. Edited and translated by Harold Shukman. New York: Grove Weidenfeld, 1991.

State of nature

TYPE OF ETHICS: Politico-economic ethics
DATE: Seventeenth and eighteenth centuries
ASSOCIATED WITH: Thomas Hobbes, John Locke, and Jean-Jacques Rousseau
DEFINITION: A concept used as part of the social contract theory of society or government to explain how and why societies and governments come into existence; it is the condition of individuals prior to the existence of society or government
SIGNIFICANCE: The concept is used by those who subscribe to the social contract theory to help explain, among other things, the function and purpose of ethics

The state of nature describes those conditions in which individuals find themselves prior to the existence of any society or government. To envision the state of nature, try to imagine what conditions would be like if there were no law, no society, no government. The resulting image captures what is meant by the state of nature.

Thomas Hobbes, John Locke, and Jean-Jacques Rousseau make extensive use of the concept in their political writings to explain the origin of society and government. The resulting theory is known as the social contract theory. One goal of the social contract theory is to explain how and why individuals moved from the state of nature to form society and government. Their explanations, though they have the common thread of the social contract, vary as a result of their differing conceptions of the state of nature.

Thomas Hobbes. Thomas Hobbes, in *Leviathan* (1651), spells out his account of the state of nature. Since there is no society, there is no right or wrong. There are no constraints, whatsoever, except for physical limitations, on human actions. Human beings, then, are completely free. In addition, human beings are essentially equal. There is an equality of need. All humans need more or less the same things; for example, food, clothing, and shelter. There is, however, a scarcity of the things that are needed. Resources are limited. All human beings have an equality of power. Though one individual may be physically stronger than another, no one person is so strong that he or she cannot be conquered, through cunning, intelligence, conspiracy, or other means, by another. Finally, there is limited altruism. In this state of nature, people will think and act for themselves first and rarely act for others.

According to this view, the state of nature is bleak and intolerable. Nothing productive could be done for fear that what one produced would be taken. Commerce and trading could not take place because there would be no guarantees that people would be fair in their dealings with one another. In short, people would live in constant fear. Hobbes labels these conditions a state of war, and life in such a state would be unbearable.

It is no wonder, then, that individuals want out of the state of nature. Hobbes shows that the way to escape the state of nature is for individuals to cooperate with one another. The way to ensure cooperation is to have a strong government that will guarantee that individuals will coexist peaceably in society.

John Locke. In his *Second Treatise on Civil Government* (1690), John Locke also makes use of the state of nature to explain the origin of society and government, but his account is far different from that of Hobbes. In fact, one could make the case that the *Second Treatise* was written in response to and as a criticism of Hobbes's account. Locke disputes Hobbes's claim that the state of nature is identified with the state of war. Locke believes the state of nature to be peaceful, because he thinks that human beings by nature are rational and that there is a natural moral law that reason can discover. In Hobbes's account, there are absolutely no laws that bind individuals in the state of nature, while Locke contends that there are natural laws that individuals as rational agents will discover and follow. Such laws hold that one should not infringe on another's life, liberty, or property. The state of war comes about only when individuals fail to heed the dictates of the natural moral laws.

There is, then, for Locke, less of a motivation to escape the state of nature and form society. For Hobbes, conditions were quite intolerable. Locke can imagine, however, that conditions would be quite comfortable if everyone followed the natural laws. Unfortunately, what individuals ought to do and what they actually do are two different things. The individuals in Locke's state of nature get together to form society to ensure that those individuals who do not obey the natural law because it is a rational thing to do so will obey it because they will be punished if they do not.

Jean-Jacques Rousseau. In *A Discourse upon the Origin and Foundation of the Inequality among Men* (1758), Jean-Jacques Rousseau spells out his version of the state of nature. It has elements in common with the thought of both Hobbes and Locke but also is different in significant ways. Like Hobbes, Rousseau claims that individuals in the state of nature are motivated by self-interest and are not bound by laws of any kind. Unlike Hobbes, however, Rousseau does not believe that this will lead to intolerable conditions. Rousseau believes that humans are naturally good and will feel compassion for, not animosity toward, their fellow humans. This compassion is a by-product of an individual's self-interest. Unlike Hobbes, Rousseau acknowledges that natural inequalities of physical strength and talent exist, but he does not think that this will lead to problems, because of the existence of compassion. Hence, the state of nature

is not tantamount to the state of war but is an idyllic state that is to be sought and envied.

Like Locke, Rousseau believes that individuals possess a special quality that makes them noble and their situation tolerable. For Locke, that quality is rationality. For him, the individual is a noble thinker. For Rousseau, that quality is the sense of freedom. For him, the individual is a noble savage. Rousseau thinks that individuals in the state of nature live off the land, coming and going as they please, enjoying their freedom and self-indulgence while having natural compassion for all other individuals.

Why, then, would individuals give up this life and choose to live in society? For Hobbes and Locke, the formation of society was a positive step. For Rousseau, it entailed mixed blessings at best. Individuals in the state of nature noticed that their freedoms were secured and sometimes enhanced by engaging in social behavior. They entered naively into the social contract to form society without seeing the dangers to freedom that would result. In particular, they failed to recognize that the political, economic, and moral inequalities that forming a society generate would ultimately curtail rather than expand their freedom. Rousseau thought that the state of war that both Hobbes and Locke claimed arose in the state of nature could exist only after the formation of society. —*John H. Serembus*

See also Hobbes, Thomas; *Leviathan*; Locke, John; Rousseau, Jean-Jacques; Social contract; *Two Treatises of Government*.

BIBLIOGRAPHY

Edwards, Paul, ed. *The Encyclopedia of Philosophy*. New York: Macmillan, 1967.

Hobbes, Thomas. *Leviathan: Or the Matter, Forme and Power of a Commonwealth Ecclesiastical and Civil*. Edited by Michael Oakeshott. New York: Collier Books, 1962.

Locke, John. *The Second Treatise on Civil Government*. Buffalo, N.Y.: Prometheus Books, 1986.

Rousseau, Jean-Jacques. *A Discourse upon the Origin and Foundation of the Inequality among Men*. New York: Dutton, 1950.

Solomon, Robert. *A Passion for Justice: Emotions and the Origins of the Social Contract*. Reading, Mass.: Addison-Wesley, 1990.

Stoic ethics

TYPE OF ETHICS: Classical history

DATE: Fourth century B.C.E. to third century C.E.

ASSOCIATED WITH: Stoic philosophers of the ancient Mediterranean world

DEFINITION: An ancient Greek philosophy of living that arose from humanity's search for happiness; the Stoics believed that happiness was defined as the result of making wise moral choices

SIGNIFICANCE: An understanding of Stoic ethics helps to set a historical foundation for some of the implicit principles and values that underlie contemporary human behavior

Background and Goals. Stoicism was one of the most significant philosophical movements of the Hellenistic Age. The founder of Stoicism was the Greek Zeno (335-263 B.C.E.), who lived and taught in Athens. He taught his disciples in the *stoa poikilē*, the painted colonnade of the market place, from which the name of this movement was derived. Stoicism, like most philosophies in the ancient world, was concerned not only with abstract concepts but also with how an individual behaved in society. Therefore, the teachings and writings of Zeno and his later followers had a major ethical component.

The basic goal that undergirds Stoic ethics is humanity's search for happiness. Happiness is not defined in the sense of emotional well-being, but is a description of living with what is good and moral. In the Stoic system, this goal of happiness is ultimately achieved by making wise choices that are based upon nature. For the Stoics, the ultimate virtue was to live harmoniously with nature, which would result in a lifestyle that would guarantee happiness.

Basic Beliefs. The Stoics believed that a person was constantly engaged by his or her passions. These passions were generated by outside images that would entice a person's internal impulses to choose that which was undesirable. The goal for the wise person in Stoicism was to allow the logos (the reason or intellect within a person) to rule. When the logos ruled, then one could choose what was best and be free of the passions. This freedom does not mean that one is not feeling or is unpassionate, but that a person does not let these areas interfere with making the right and logical judgments in the ethical realms of life.

This decision-making process can be taught to a certain extent. There are those things in the world that can be classified as good, evil, and indifferent. The indifferent would be those areas such as death, life, fame, scandal, hardship, lust, wealth, poverty, sickness, and health. If one considers these areas as indifferent to one's life, these areas have no bearing upon the experience of happiness. Because of their indifference to such areas of life, the Stoics were often incorrectly labeled as passionless and perhaps unfeeling individuals. This perception has carried over into the contemporary usage of the word "stoic," when it is applied to a person who, in the face of what appears to be a traumatic and emotional event, does not express feelings.

The process of choosing between good and evil is more difficult and more intuitive in the Stoic system. This intuitive decision making of right judgments is assisted, however, when the wise person uses nature as a guide or criterion. The good is that which is in harmony with nature; the bad or evil is that which is against or in tension with nature. For the Stoics, nature becomes the all-encompassing norm that enables one to evaluate situations and make decisions. In observing nature, a Stoic could make some rational deduction regarding what is natural in relationship to plants, animals, and humanity. For example, it is not inherent in nature for a person to starve; it is unnatural. Therefore, the

Stoics would render the logical action of feeding starving people. When one attempts to live according to nature, one practices a strong social ethic. Therefore, a Stoic individual honors the kinship networks and his or her native land.

When events or situations occur within nature that do appear as natural, these only help to reinforce what is the norm. For example, the birth of a six-legged cat is an anomaly that helps illustrate that in nature cats have four legs. The Stoic system illustrates that one considers the whole on the basis of its parts. When nature is considered as a whole, it becomes clear that it is perfect. It is humanity's task to strive for that perfection and to live in harmony with nature. The founder of Stoicism, Zeno, used a metaphor to illustrate the choice that humanity could make regarding living in this harmonious relationship with nature. He compared the situation of humanity to that of a dog tied behind a cart. The dog has the choice to run freely with the cart or to be dragged along. The choice is the dog's to make. To freely follow along behind is to live in harmony with nature and to ensure one's happiness. To be dragged is to live contrary to nature and to ensure one's misery.

To live in harmony with nature was the ultimate goal for a Stoic because it culimated in happiness. Yet followers of the Stoic tradition lived with the realization that they could never truly attain this goal. The ideal toward which to strive was to become a sage who, when faced with a choice, would invariably choose the good. In the Stoic system, one always attempted to reach the level of sage, but it was a rare feat. One of the later Stoic teachers, Seneca, remarked that a good man (a sage) appeared only once every five hundred years.

Conclusion. While Stoicism as a movement no longer exists, its influence is evident in many areas of ethics and human behavior. The Stoics placed a great deal of emphasis upon those things that are indifferent, and one natural outcome of this emphasis is a form of asceticism. Groups that practice forms of abstinence or austerities often employ some of the ideological framework of Stoicism. Also, one can see traces of Stoicism in Immanuel Kant's categorical imperative: "Always act in such a manner that your actions can be taken as a universal maxim." Kant's emphasis is upon reason, which Stoics valued in all decision making.

—David M. May

See also Cynicism; Epictetus; Marcus Aurelius; Natural law; Reason and rationality.

BIBLIOGRAPHY

Colish, Marcia L. *The Stoic Tradition from Antiquity to the Early Middle Ages.* 2 vols. Leiden: E. J. Brill, 1985.

Long, A. A. *Hellenistic Philosophy: Stoics, Epicureans, Sceptics.* New York: Charles Scribner's Sons, 1974.

_____, ed. *Problems in Stoicism.* London: Athlone Press, 1971.

Rist, John M. *Stoic Philosophy.* Cambridge, England: Cambridge University Press, 1977.

Wenley, Robert. *Stoicism and Its Influence.* New York: Cooper Square, 1963.

Stonewall Inn riots

TYPE OF ETHICS: Sex and gender issues

DATE: Began June 28, 1969

DEFINITION: The Stonewall Inn riots occurred when members of the gay and lesbian community in New York City reacted violently to a routine raid on the Stonewall Inn bar in Greenwich Village

SIGNIFICANCE: The Stonewall Inn riots signaled the beginning of the gay and lesbian community's organized response to harassment and its drive to achieve social equality for its members

There are moments in history when conditions come together to create the impetus for great social change. Though the roots of the social movement for gay, lesbian, and bisexual equality date back to mid-nineteenth century Germany, many historians and activists place the beginning of the modern movement at the Stonewall Inn, a small bar in New York City's Greenwich Village that was frequented by drag queens, gay and lesbian street people, students, and others.

At approximately 1:20 A.M. on June 28, 1969, Deputy Inspector Seymour Pine, along with seven other officers from the Public Morals Section of the First Division of the New York City Police Department, conducted a routine raid on the bar on the basis of the trumped-up charge that the owners had been selling alcohol without a license.

Police raids on gay and lesbian bars were a frequent occurrence in New York City; for example, laws were enacted for the express purpose of closing establishments that catered to a gay and lesbian clientele. Statutes forbade more than "three homosexuals at a bar at any given time"; behavior that was considered "campy"; and same-sex dancing, touching, and kissing. It was also required that bar patrons wear at least three "gender-appropriate" garments.

Although small pockets of resistance to police raids on gay and lesbian bars had occurred before June 28, 1969, bar patrons usually accommodated officials. This time, however, was different. Believing that they had been harassed for far too long, bar patrons and others challenged police officers with varying degrees of intensity for the next five days, flinging bottles, rocks, bricks, and trash cans, and using parking meters as battering rams.

The Stonewall Inn riots occurred in a larger social and political context of enormous upheaval and change. It is also probably no coincidence that the riot began only a few hours after the funeral of Judy Garland, a longtime cultural icon to gay and lesbian people.

The events that occurred at the Stonewall Inn would lead to the development of a number of both militant and mainstream groups that jointly would constitute a new, highly visible movement. In commemoration of the riots, June is designated each year as "Gay, Lesbian, and Bisexual Pride (or History) Month," and marches and various celebrations are held during that month.

See also Gay rights; Homophobia; Homosexuality; Sexual stereotypes.

Subjectivism

TYPE OF ETHICS: Theory of ethics

DATE: From antiquity

ASSOCIATED WITH: Emotivism, Sophists, hedonism, subjective idealism, and phenomenology

DEFINITION: The view that knowledge of the external world of objects is dependent upon the perspective and disposition of the knowing subject

SIGNIFICANCE: Subjectivism maintains that ethical judgments and moral norms are relative to the standpoint and disposition of the moral actor

Epistemological subjectivism is the belief that the objects of knowledge are constituted by consciousness. In this doctrine, reality, truth, knowledge, meaning, and understanding are limited to the subjective states of the subject of knowledge. Metaphysical subjectivism leads directly to solipsism, the idea that the world exists only for the self, or to subjective idealism which reduces the world to the realm of ideas found in an individual consciousness.

In epistemology, the "subject" is the agent or apprehender of the knowing process. The "subject" may be understood as a conscious ego, a transcendental ego, mind, the cognitive state, the self, and so forth. "Object" refers to that which is being apprehended, known, or being attended to by an act of perception, cognition, or understanding. Simply put, the subject is the perceiver and the object is what is perceived. "Objective" means possessing the character of a real object existing independently of the knowing mind.

Ethical Subjectivism. Ethical subjectivism holds that ethical judgments refer directly to certain feelings, attitudes, and beliefs of individuals or groups; namely, feelings of approval or disapproval with regard to some person or action or quality. Ethical judgments are regarded either as meaningless or as relative to the individual who holds them. Bertrand Russell maintained that differences about values are really differences about tastes. Ethical judgments really express feelings of approval or disapproval. This is the doctrine called emotivism. Ethical judgments are neither true nor false, but are simply expressions of feelings of approval or disapproval.

Ancient Greek Thought. The Sophists believed that the senses were the only source of knowledge about the world and that reality was in a constant process of change. Everything that exists is only a matter of appearance. Therefore, the Sophists believed in the relativity of knowledge and were skeptical regarding truth. They questioned the validity of ethical principles and claimed that morality was a matter of social convention. Protagoras of Abdera (481-411 B.C.E.) said, "Man is the measure of all things, of things that are, that they are, of things that are not, that they are not." This philosophy relativizes truth and morality. Interestingly, it ends up justifying democracy and equal rights, because it holds that each individual must decide for himself or herself.

Epicurus held that pleasure is the sole good. This doctrine is known as hedonism. The view that people value pleasure above all else is known as psychological hedonism. Ethical hedonism goes a step further and holds that people not only seek pleasure but ought to seek pleasure. Since pleasure is relative to an individual's experience, feelings, and tastes, however, hedonism amounts to ethical subjectivism.

Ethical Subjectivism. Bishop George Berkeley believed in the doctrine called immaterialism, which denied the existence of the immaterial world. Whatever exists, exists in the mind—*esse est percipe* ("to be is to be perceived"). This doctrine amounts to solipsism, the idea that nothing exists but one's mind and its ideas.

Immanuel Kant held to a motivistic theory of ethics. According to this doctrine, the rightness or wrongness of an act depends upon the motives and intentions of the moral agent, not upon the intrinsic character of the act or the consequences of an act.

Johann Gottlieb Fichte (1762-1814) believed that the ego, which is pure creative activity, makes possible not only the awareness of self but also that of the nonego (whatever is not regarded as self). According to Fichte, the conscious mind creates the objects of the world because they exist only in the mind's knowledge of those objects. Therefore, both subject and object are generated by a creative ego. It is the ego that makes the world intelligible.

Existentialism. Søren Kierkegaard (1813-1855) adhered to the doctrine that truth is subjectivity. Truth involves passion. There is no objective absolute truth. Truth is that on which the individual acts, a way of existence. Truth does not consist in what is said but in how it is said. Because there is no absolute truth, uncertainty accompanies subjectivity, calling for a leap of faith.

Jean-Paul Sartre claimed that humanity is condemned to freedom. People are absolutely free and morality is relative. One creates one's own values.

Phenomenology. Edmund Husserl employed a philosophical method called phenomenological reduction that considered only the pure phenomena of consciousness—that is, self-evident, certain, and intuitive thoughts and ideas of consciousness. Phenomenological reduction revealed three elements of knowledge: the phenomenological ego, which is identical to the stream of consciousness; thinking activities; and the objects of thought. Husserl's doctrine of intentionality claimed that every act of consciousness was a consciousness of something, and that something was a mental entity. Therefore, knowledge of the world is purely subjective.

Ethical Problems. If moral standards are merely subjective, there seems to be no objective way of settling ethical disputes and disagreements regarding moral behavior. Mistakes about values are impossible to make. What becomes of the sense of duty in this scenario? Sometimes, the sense of acting out of duty to others means acting against one's own inclinations. Finally, subjectivism seems to contradict ordinary language and common sense, in which it is assumed that "good," "bad," "right," and "wrong" have the same meanings for everyone.   —*Michael R. Candelaria*

See also Epistemological ethics; Existentialism; Hedonism; Kant, Immanuel; Kierkegaard, Søren Aabye; Sartre, Jean-Paul; Sophists.

BIBLIOGRAPHY

Ayer, Alfred Jules. *Language, Truth, and Logic.* New York: Dover Publications, 1952.

Behler, Ernst, ed. *Philosophy of German Idealism.* New York: Continuum, 1987.

Husserl, Edmund. *Cartesian Meditations: An Introduction to Phenomenology.* Translated by Dorion Cairns. The Hague: Martinus Nijhoff, 1988.

Kant, Immanuel. *Critique of Pure Reason.* Translated by Norman Kemp Smith. New York: Humanities Press, 1929.

Smith, Thomas Vernon. *Berkeley, Hume, and Kant.* Edited by T. V. Smith and Marjorie Grene. Chicago: University of Chicago Press, 1967.

Suffrage

TYPE OF ETHICS: Sex and gender issues

DATE: Seveneenth century to present

DEFINITION: The right to vote in elections at various levels of government

SIGNIFICANCE: Suffragists seek the full participation of women in the political process

Woman suffrage is the basis of political power for women. From the nineteenth and early twentieth century campaigns for woman suffrage in the United States and Great Britain, the issue of suffrage spread worldwide. By the late twentieth century, women could vote in most countries.

History. Participation in the political process through voting was either nonexistent or limited to a small elite until the nineteenth and twentieth centuries (the United States removed all property qualifications for voting in the 1830's). Suffrage in the colonial United States was limited to white, male property owners, and women did not vote or, if married, even exist legally.

Because of the eighteenth century revolutionary movements that were active in America and parts of Europe, the question arose whether the rights of man should not also apply to women. In England, Mary Wollstonecraft, in *A Vindication of the Rights of Woman* (1792), asserted that women could be good citizens of the state if men would let them participate. The state constitutions in the new United States of America, however, prohibited women from voting except in New Jersey, which allowed all property owners to vote. Spinsters and widows who owned property voted until 1807 when New Jersey restricted suffrage to white male property owners. By the 1830's, however, there was universal adult white male suffrage throughout the United States, while women and racial minorities remained disfranchised.

In the early nineteenth century, many women in the northern states embraced reform movements, including the antislavery movement. The antislavery movement split in the 1830's over the proper role for women within its organi-

A demonstration for women's voting rights in New York City in 1912. (Library of Congress)

zations and within society as a whole. In 1840, American women delegates to the World Anti-Slavery Convention in London, England, were excluded from the convention and relegated to a curtained gallery to observe deliberations. As a result, Elizabeth Cady Stanton and Lucretia Mott decided that women needed to work for their own rights.

They organized a women's rights convention on July 19 and 20, 1848, in Seneca Falls, New York. Cady Stanton wrote the document that was adopted by the convention, the most controversial resolution of which was a demand for woman suffrage. Other women's rights conventions followed. Susan B. Anthony and Lucy Stone joined the cause in 1851, with Anthony doing most of the work before the Civil War.

The women's rights movement interrupted its activities during the war, but its members felt betrayed when their antislavery male allies proved to be more interested in securing rights for freedmen than for women. When the Fourteenth Amendment (1869) introduced the term "male inhabitants" into the Constitution, suffragists were alarmed, and the proposed Fifteenth Amendment, extending suffrage to black men but not to women, divided the woman suffrage movement. In 1869, Cady Stanton and Anthony formed the National Woman Suffrage Association, which advocated a wide range of women's rights and advocated a federal amendment to achieve woman suffrage. The American Woman Suffrage Association, headed by Lucy Stone, focused on suffrage and worked on campaigns at the state and local level.

Suffragists campaigned for woman suffrage between 1867 (Kansas referendum) and the 1920 ratification of the Nineteenth Amendment. They participated in state referenda campaigns (mostly unsuccessfully) and petitioned and lobbied legislatures and state constitutional conventions, while con-

tinuing to advocate a federal amendment. In the western United States some women were voting, beginning in the Wyoming (1870-1890) and Utah (1870-1887) territories. By 1900, women had the vote in four Rocky Mountain states: Wyoming (statehood, 1890), Colorado (referendum, 1893), Utah (statehood, 1896) and Idaho (state constitutional amendment, 1896). In some areas, women had limited suffrage (school board or municipal or presidential elections). In 1890, the rival suffrage organizations merged, becoming the National American Woman Suffrage Association (NAWSA).

In 1903, Emmeline Pankhurst organized the Women's Social and Political Union to demand woman suffrage in England. The group quickly adopted militant tactics, resulting in arrests of the Suffragettes. In January, 1918, Parliament passed a law granting suffrage to women thirty years of age or older who met specified property qualifications (in 1928 suffrage was extended to all women older than twenty-one). By 1918, women also had the right to vote in New Zealand (1893), Australia (1902), Finland (1906), Mexico (1917), and Russia (1917), and suffrage was extended in 1918 to Austria, Canada, Czechoslovakia, Germany, Hungary, Ireland, Poland, Scotland, and Wales.

Carrie Chapman Catt, president of NAWSA (1900-1904 and 1916-1920), designed the "Winning Plan." This plan involved state campaigns that would continue until women were able to vote in thirty-six states (the number needed to ratify a federal amendment), after which there would be a campaign to pass the "Anthony Amendment" for woman suffrage. Suffragists became more visible, adopting some of the tactics of the English Suffragettes. Catt believed that, although it was important that women support the involvement of the United States in World War I (1917-1918), they should continue working for suffrage during the war. The radical National Woman's Party, headed by Alice Paul and Lucy Burns, opposed the war, and its members picketed the White House for suffrage, with some of them being arrested. Catt secured the support of President Woodrow Wilson for the "Anthony Amendment" in 1918. Congress passed the Amendment in June, 1919. On August 24, 1920, Tennessee became the thirty-sixth state to ratify the Nineteenth Amendment, thereby enfranchising women in the United States.

In the twentieth century, woman suffrage extended throughout the world. In 1954, the United Nations Convention on Equal Political Rights affirmed women's right to suffrage and political activity. By 1985, only in Saudi Arabia and the Gulf States were women still completely disfranchised. —*Judith A. Parsons*

See also Civil rights; Equality; Mill, John Stuart; Political liberty; Wollstonecraft, Mary.

BIBLIOGRAPHY

Flexner, Eleanor. *Century of Struggle: The Woman's Rights Movement in the United States.* New York: Atheneum, 1968.

Frost, Elizabeth, and Kathryn Cullen-DuPont. *Women's*

Suffrage in America: An Eyewitness History. New York: Facts on File, 1992.

Giele, Janet Zollinger, and Audrey Chapman Smock, eds. *Women: Roles and Status in Eight Countries*. New York: John Wiley & Sons, 1977.

Mackenzie, Midge, ed. *Shoulder to Shoulder*. New York: Alfred A. Knopf, 1975.

Rhoodie, Eschel M. *Discrimination Against Women: A Global Survey of the Economic, Educational, Social, and Political Status of Women*. Jefferson, N.C.: McFarland, 1989.

Sufism

TYPE OF ETHICS: Religious ethics
DATE: Beginning early in the Islamic era through the present
ASSOCIATED WITH: Numerous mystics, poets, and mystical movements in the Islamic world
DEFINITION: Mystical practices and traditions associated with Islam
SIGNIFICANCE: "Sufism" includes many important paths of spiritual and ethical discipline, and has been important in the dissemination of Islam

Sufism embraces so many mystical traditions that many scholars debate whether there is one referent to "Sufism" and whether some Sufi traditions are Islamic. Sufi mystics emphasize the importance of extreme, ascetic adherence to *sharî'a* (Islamic law), or ecstatic union with God (sometimes associated with antinomianism), or a middle ground between those extremes. Some Sufis believe legalistic and antinomian traditions to be mutually exclusive. Others view them as aspects of a single, larger truth, as did Sanâ'î in his famous claim that "the veils are many, but the Bride is One."

Most often, Sufis abjure worldly goods and follow a "path" (*tarîqa*) of exercises for spiritual discipline and purification. Along the path, the Sufi attains "stations" (*maqâmat*) or plateaus of spiritual development, to each of which there is a proper "state" (*hâl*). The ultimate state to which Sufis aspire is variously indicated as "love" (*mahabbat*), "gnosis" (*ma'rifat*), "annihilation" (*fanâ'*), or "union" (*ittihâd* or *tauhîd*). These goals sometimes have attracted the condemnation of Islamic legists who have argued that these states imply pantheism or, at least, a denial of the absolute transcendence of God.

In its early history, Sufism was the private spiritual effort of individual Sufis. In the eighth century, groups of students or disciples began to assemble informally around prominent Sufis. In the eleventh century, these informal associations began to formalize as clearly defined Sufi orders, with distinctive sets of spiritual practices, and these orders often were housed in a compound at the tomb of an important Sufi whose spiritual power (*barakat*) remains at the tomb.

Sufism provides popular ethical guidance in several ways. The keepers of Sufi tombs, to which many turn (for practical needs) in order to avail themselves of *barakat*, are a source of popular religious and ethical guidance. Reverence for individual Sufis such as Râbi'a serves as a frequent reminder of the importance of detachment from worldly goods and of love of God. Sufi poetry and hagiography have been extremely popular and have been important in transmitting Islam and Sufi spiritualism in vernacular languages. Sufism's devotionalism and instrumental religion associated with *barakat* often have been more accessible than the sometimes-austere Islamic legalism, and often have served to gradually assimilate popular culture to Islam.

Philosophical treatises are not prevalent in Sufism, but some Sufis (notably al-Ghazâlî and Ibn 'Arabî) have made significant contributions to ethical theory, especially through analyses of moral psychology and the epistemic status of direct apprehension of God.

See also al-Ghazâlî, Abû Hâmid; al-Hallâj, al-Husayn ibn Mansûr; Ibn al-'Arabî, Muhyî al-Dîn Muhammad; Islamic ethics; Râbi'a al-'Adawiyya; al-Rûmî al-Balkhî, Maulânâ Jalâl al-Dîn.

Suicide

TYPE OF ETHICS: Personal and social ethics
ASSOCIATED WITH: Right to die, euthanasia, and mental illness
DEFINITION: Suicide is a self-initiated intentional act directed toward, and resulting in, the ending of one's own life
SIGNIFICANCE: Most religions condemn suicide as immoral; however, humanitarian organizations argue that persons have a right to choose death rather than suffer

Albert Camus (1913-1960), in *The Myth of Sisyphus*, asserts that the core philosophical question is whether or not to choose suicide. Existential suicide is founded on the idea that as a person comes to the insight that life is an empty absurdity, he or she must confront suicide as an option.

Deaths by suicide are notoriously underreported, even in countries that do not strongly condemn the act. In countries where there are adverse sanctions related to suicide, powerful pressures exist to coverup suicidal deaths. Therefore, caution must be used in interpreting officially recorded suicide statistics.

In 1985, conservative estimates held that, worldwide, more than 400,000 persons committed suicide. Although suicide is a major problem in the United States, which had more than 30,000 documented suicides in 1988, the suicide rate in the United States is notably lower than are those of many developed countries. According to the World Health Organization, many countries have suicide rates that are double that of the United States (Hungary, Denmark, Finland, and others), and many others have rates, which, although not double, are substantially higher (Japan, Czechoslovakia, China, Sweden, Switzerland, and others). Of particular concern in the United States was the near tripling of the suicide rates of adolescents and young adults between the 1950's and the 1980's. As of 1990, suicide was the second leading cause of death of adolescents and the third leading cause of death among adults aged 20 to 24 in the United States.

Western opinions concerning the morality of suicide have been heavily influenced by the teachings of Judaism and Christianity. Although the Old Testament of the Bible provides no condemnation as it records the suicides of several important persons (Abimelech, Saul, Samson, and others), rabbis and theologians have rebuked suicide as a violation

SUICIDE RATES BY COUNTRY AND YEAR			
Country	**Year**		
	1952[1]	1970[2]	1988[3]
Australia	10.6	12.4	13.0
Austria	23.4	24.2	25.0
Belgium	13.1	16.5	21.0
Canada	7.3	11.2	13.3
Chile	4.3	5.5	5.6
China	na	na	17.3
Columbia	1.6	2.7	3.7
Czechoslovakia	na	25.3	17.6
Denmark	22.9	21.5	25.9
Egypt	0.3	0.0	0.1
Finland	17.6	21.3	28.2
France	15.5	15.4	20.6
German Democratic Republic	na	30.5	25.8
German Federal Republic	17.7	21.5	16.5
Greece	na	3.2	4.0
Hungary	17.8	34.9	41.5
Iceland	2.2	1.8	7.4
Israel	na	5.3	6.1
Italy	6.6	5.7	7.6
Japan	18.5	15.3	17.3
Mexico	0.9	1.1	2.5
New Zealand	10.1	9.6	13.8
The Netherlands	6.3	8.1	10.2
Norway	6.9	8.4	16.6
Poland	5.7	11.3	11.2
Portugal	na	8.4	7.2
Singapore	na	8.9	14.9
Spain	5.9	4.2	7.1
Sri Lanka	na	16.6	35.0
Sweden	16.7	22.3	17.3
Switzerland	21.5	18.6	22.6
Union of Soviet Socialist Republics	na	na	19.7
Union of Soviet Socialist Republics: Byelorussian SSR	na	na	18.8
Union of Soviet Socialist Republics: Ukrainian SSR	na	na	19.5
United Kingdom: England and Wales	9.9	8.1	7.3
United Kingdom: Northern Ireland	3.0	3.9	7.3
United Kingdom: Scotland	5.5	7.6	10.3
United States of America	10.0	11.5	12.2
Venezuela	na	6.4	4.4

[1]*Source: Demographic Yearbook, 1957.* New York: Economic and Social Affairs, Statistical Office, United Nations, 1958. Most figures are from 1952; a few come from 1953 or 1954.

[2]*Source: Demographic Yearbook, 1974.* New York: Economic and Social Affairs, Statistical Office, United Nations, 1975. All figures are from 1970.

[3]*Source: World Health Statistics Annual, 1990.* Geneva, Switzerland: World Health Organization, 1991. Most figures are from 1988; some are from 1986, 1987, and 1989.

na = not available

of the sixth commandment: Thou shalt not kill. According to the fifth century Christian theologian Saint Augustine, no degree of torment, no physical injury or disease, no threat to personal safety, no amount of personal suffering can justify suicide.

Although many of the world's other major religions condemn suicide, some do not. Islam damns the person who commits suicide, although exceptions are made for suicides that are part of a holy war or for a female to protect her virginity. For the Baha'i, suicide is forbidden, and anyone who commits suicide will suffer spiritually in the afterlife. Buddhism rejects suicide on the principle that all life is sacred. Still, there have been cases in which Buddhist priests have used self-immolation as a method to draw attention to morally intolerable situations. While Hindus and Sikhs reject most suicides because they interfere with reincarnations, both religions concede special circumstances in which suicide is either allowed or encouraged. For example, in the Hindu rite of suttee, a widow is encouraged to die in her husband's funeral pyre. Although honoring a person who commits suttee is illegal in India, instances of the practice continue to be reported.

Any discussion of suicide becomes confused when the practice of euthanasia is brought into the deliberation. Euthanasia has been variously defined as the good death, death with dignity, mercy killing, and the deliberate putting to death of a person suffering intolerable life circumstances. The two most commonly discussed forms of euthanasia are passive euthanasia and active euthanasia.

Initially, passive euthanasia was defined as including the refusal of life-sustaining medications, requests that resuscitation not be provided, and other solicitations related to not being subjected to unwanted medical procedures. Later, the concept of passive euthanasia was broadened to include a variety of alterations or abatements of medical treatments that might hasten death. Therefore, disconnecting a patient from a respirator, provision of adequate dosages of pain-relieving narcotics, and the termination of forced feeding were included as examples of passive euthanasia. Most religions accept all but the last practice (termination of feeding) as acceptable choices. These practices are not viewed as murder or suicide because a natural course of events is being allowed to unfold. Active euthanasia, however, the administration of a lethal agent or the initiation of a process that will prove fatal, is condemned by most religions. Furthermore, if a second person aids in the commission of active euthanasia, the second person may be charged with homicide or held responsible under a statute that makes aiding suicide illegal.

During the 1980's, many states broadened patients' rights in regard to living wills and the right to refuse unwanted treatments. Despite the fact that most states either allow or are mute regarding the right of a competent person to terminate his or her life, they all permit the involuntary commitment and forced treatment of suicidal persons deemed to be suffering mental diseases. According to the American psychiatrist Thomas Szasz, "in treating desires as disease, we only end up treating man as a slave." Although he does not oppose treating the person who voluntarily seeks psychiatric assistance, Szasz concludes, "if the prevention of death by any means necessary is the physician's therapeutic mandate, then the proper remedy for suicide is indeed liberticide."

—Bruce E. Bailey

See also Bushido; Camus, Albert; Durkheim, Émile; Euthanasia; Existentialism; Kevorkian, Jack; Life and death; Mental illness; Nihilism; Right to die; Sartre, Jean-Paul.

BIBLIOGRAPHY

Berger, Arthur, S., and Joyce Berger, eds. *To Die or Not to Die? Cross-Disciplinary, Cultural, and Legal Perspectives on the Right to Choose Death.* New York: Praeger, 1990.

Larue, Gerald A. *Euthanasia and Religion: A Survey of the Attitudes of World Religions to the Right to Die.* Los Angeles: The Hemlock Society, 1985.

Lester, David. *Why People Kill Themselves: A 1990's Summary of Research Findings on Suicidal Behavior.* 3d ed. Springfield, Ill.: Charles C Thomas, 1992.

Pohier, Jacques, and Dietmar Mieth, eds. *Suicide and the Right to Die.* Edinburgh: T & T Clark, 1985.

Rachels, James. *The End of Life: Euthanasia and Morality.* New York: Oxford University Press, 1986.

Summa Theologica: Book

TYPE OF ETHICS: Medieval history

DATE: Written c. 1265-1273

AUTHOR: Thomas Aquinas

SIGNIFICANCE: Encompassed, modified, and extended the ethics of Aristotle within a Christian framework; advanced the view that Christian morality was rationally defensible

Purpose. Thomas Aquinas intended the *Summa Theologica* to provide instruction to students in Catholic theological schools who not only studied the Old and New Testaments of the Bible but also participated in oral disputations concerning controversial theological questions. The *Summa* is a written, if condensed, version of these theological debates.

The work was also intended to reform the teaching of sacred doctrine, which for Aquinas involved not only the exposition of those religious tenets known through revelation—such as the nature of salvation—but also the aspects of the Christian faith that are accessible to reason—such as the question of God's existence. Reducing the confusing number of topics, arguments, and distinctions that were often arbitrarily arranged in the standard theological texts, the *Summa* argues its way point by point through questions concerning first the nature of God, then "the rational creature's movement towards God," and finally Jesus Christ (a person's way to God). Aquinas died before finishing the third part; a supplement, drawn from his earlier writings, completes the plan of the work. Part 1 is divided into three parts (the divine essence, the persons of the Trinity, and creation, and part 2 into two parts (part 2-1, the general treatment of virtues of vices, and part 2-2, their specific treatment). Part 3 deals with Jesus Christ, the sacraments of the Church, and with resurrection and eternity.

The Nature of True Happiness. For Aquinas, and for Aristotle (whom the *Summa* calls "the Philosopher"), everything in the universe has a purpose, an "end," a teleology. The purpose of a saw is to cut; the purpose of the acorn is to grow into a tree. Since human beings can reason and act, they are able to choose what they think will fulfill their desire for the perfect good; human moral choices, by their nature, are oriented toward this "last end." Happiness is the fulfillment of human desire for the perfect good, but as both Aquinas and Aristotle point out, happiness is not equivalent to wealth, honor, power, or pleasure. Instead, since human beings share a common human nature, happiness involves a life full of all the things that all human beings really need, in the right order and the right proportion. For Aquinas, the perfect happiness is in the life to come and consists of the contemplation of God's essence. In this life, however, happiness involves not only (imperfect) contemplation but also the development of practical reason to direct human actions and feelings into a life of choosing what is truly—not apparently—good, and learning to enjoy those choices.

In Aquinas' Aristotelian view, morality touches all of life; everyday choices tend to develop in the individual either virtue (human excellence) or vice. "Right reasons" must direct human activity to acquire that which is objectively good for human beings (such as knowledge). These goods are intrinsically to be desired, but their acquisition is also a means of building the kind of stable character with which God is pleased. Without courage, for example, a person would be unable to act in accordance with right reason.

Aquinas took Aristotle's view to be complementary to his own, not competitive. Unaided by supernatural grace, Aquinas said, reason could discern the kind of character that a human being ought to have, but a complete picture of an individual required God's grace, which would provide the theological direction that human beings could not discover through philosophic reflection alone. Already in this life God was suffusing human beings with faith, hope, and charity (love), the three theological virtues, which were given not by human action but by the Holy Spirit. They prepared a believer for the vision of God in the life to come.

Central to the *Summa*'s discussion of true happiness and the final end is the concept of law. A law is made by reason for the common good by those in charge of a community, and persons cannot become truly virtuous independent of society. God's eternal law—His divine plan—governs the universe; the natural moral law, which is made up of those precepts that human beings discern through the use of right reason, reflects the eternal law. Actions that oppose the natural moral law are forbidden not because God arbitrarily says they are wrong, but because they are contrary to the development of full human potential. In addition, there is positive divine law, in which God wills that individuals receive grace through the sacraments, and those are positive human laws, in which communities or states restrain actions that are detrimental to society and promote obedience to the natural moral law; unjust laws do not have to be obeyed. Governments exist not only to provide peace and protection but also to nurture the common good. In times of need, the resources of a community become "common property," and thus it is not sinful for someone to take bread to feed a starving child. People may resist tyrannies and overthrow them, unless there is good reason to believe rebellion would make matters worse.

The *Summa* presents a synthesis of faith and reason that was declared to be of permanent value to the Catholic church by Pope Leo XIII in 1879.

Divisions of the Work. The three parts of the *Summa* (as well as the supplement to the third part) are divided into questions dealing with the main subtopics of each part; in turn, every question is divided into several articles. Each of the 3,112 articles in the *Summa* is a stylized disputation beginning with an assertion of the position contrary to the one that Aquinas will take and a presentation of several objections to Aquinas' position. Aquinas answers by supplying a relevant quotation from the Bible or a Church father (such as Saint Augustine), followed by his own argument. The point here is to show that reason (that is, Aquinas' reply) is in harmony with sacred Scripture and the theologians of the Church. Finally, there are specific replies to each objection.

—*Dan Barnett*

See also Aristotelian ethics; Christian ethics; Natural law; Thomas Aquinas.

BIBLIOGRAPHY

Coplestan, F. C. *Aquinas*. Harmondsworth, England: Penguin Books, 1955.

Glenn, Paul J. *A Tour of the Summa*. St. Paul; Minn.: B. Herder, 1960.

Kreeft, Peter, ed. *Summas of the Summa: The Essential Philosophical Passages of St. Thomas Aquinas' "Summa Theologica" Edited and Explained for Beginners*. San Francisco: Ignatius Press, 1990.

McInerny, Ralph. *A First Glance at St. Thomas Aquinas: A Handbook for Peeping Thomists*. Notre Dame, Ind.: University of Notre Dame Press, 1990.

Sigmund, Paul E., ed. *St. Thomas Aquinas on Politics and Ethics*. New York: W. W. Norton, 1988.

Sunnîs

TYPE OF ETHICS: Religious ethics

DATE: From the sixth century

DEFINITION: One of the two main sects of Islam

SIGNIFICANCE: The majority of Muslims belong to the Sunnî sect of Islam

Islamic religion is divided into two main sects: Sunnîs and Shî'ites. Sunnî Islam developed over many centuries. An important distinction between the two sects is that the Shî'ites relied on Imâms to provide spiritual guidance, while the Sunnîs emphasize the Qur'ân; the Sunna, or examples, from Muhammad's life and his practice of Islam; and interpretations of these sources by eminent religious scholars. The interpretation of Islamic concepts by these scholars led to the emergence of several schools of thought. Four of the most important of these schools were led by Imâm Abû-Hanîfa, Mâlik ibn-Anas, al-Shafi'i, and Ahmad ibn-Hanbal. With the passage of time and expansion of the newly emerging Muslim empire, numerous issues relating to the meaning of the various religious concepts emerged. One such issue that ultimately helped to define the Sunnîs was the definition of a Muslim. A group of people known as Khârijites believed that only those who strictly adhered to the teachings of the Qur'ân and Sunna could be called Muslims, and those who did not should be declared non-Muslims and expelled from the community of Muslims. Others thought that even sinners should be considered Muslims, and that the punishment for their sins should be left to God. People belonging to the later school were ultimately defined as Sunnîs.

See also Islamic ethics; Qur'ân; Shî'a.

Supererogation

TYPE OF ETHICS: Theory of ethics
DATE: First century
ASSOCIATED WITH: The Latin Vulgate version of the New Testament
DEFINITION: Doing what is morally praiseworthy beyond what is required by duty or what is required to be free of moral blame
SIGNIFICANCE: If supererogation is possible in human life, then moral goodness is not entirely swallowed up by moral duty; it is possible to go above and beyond the call of duty

The term "supererogation" derives from the Latin verb *supererogare*, which means "to overspend" or "to spend in addition." The first known appearance of this verb is in the Latin Vulgate biblical account of the good Samaritan (the tenth chapter of the Book of Luke). The modern notion of supererogation is based upon the idea of making an expenditure of one's goods or energy over and above what is required of one by moral duty. More precisely, the modern notion requires that an act satisfy three conditions to qualify as an act of supererogation. First, the performance of the act must be morally praiseworthy. Second, the performance of the act must not fulfill moral duty. Third, the omission of the act must not be morally blameworthy.

Although the idea of rising above and beyond the call of duty is familiar to most people, there has for centuries been great opposition to this idea. The major figures of the Protestant Reformation associated the idea of supererogation with the detested practice in the Catholic Church of selling indulgences, which was based upon the idea that the good actions of the saints create a treasury of merit. The Protestants Martin Luther, John Calvin, and Philipp Melanchthon taught, on the contrary, that God requires all people to do what is good or praiseworthy; hence, it is impossible to do good over and above the requirements of duty. No matter how saintly or heroic one's behavior is, even to the point of sacrificing one's life, one is simply doing what God requires as a matter of duty.

The Protestant Reformers were also bitterly opposed to the scholastic distinction between the commandments of God and the counsels of God. According to Thomas Aquinas and other scholastics, the commandments of God are obligatory to obey, but the counsels of God are optional recommendations. Although Christians are not required to obey the counsels of God, such as renouncing riches and carnal pleasures, following them is recommended to those who wish to lead more perfect lives. Clearly, this distinction opens the door to the possibility of supererogation, and the Reformers refused to acknowledge that there are any counsels of God apart from what God demands as obligatory. If it is good to renounce wealth or carnal pleasure, that is exactly what one is required to do.

Opposition to the idea that supererogation is possible has more recently come from two of the major modern traditions in ethics: Kantian ethics and act utilitarianism. According to Kantian ethics, an act can be a moral act only if it is performed in obedience to moral duty. Thus, if an act is performed that goes beyond the requirements of duty, Kantians dismiss it as an act that falls outside the sphere of ethics or morality. One cannot, according to their view, act morally in a way that transcends duty.

Act utilitarianism is based roughly upon the idea that persons ought at a given time to perform whatever act produces the greatest benefits for the greatest number of persons. In this view, duty requires one to choose the alternative that maximizes benefits. If a person chooses this alternative and acts accordingly, the person has fulfilled his or her duty. If the person chooses another alternative and acts accordingly, the person has violated his or her duty. In both cases, however there is no possibility of doing what is praiseworthy without fulfilling duty. Either one's act fulfills duty or it does not, but if it does not fulfill duty it is the violation of duty and hence cannot be praiseworthy.

In spite of all the opposition to the idea that acts of supererogation are possible in human life, there is also much support for the idea. An article by J. O. Urmson entitled "Saints and Heroes," published in 1958, has been particularly significant in restoring popularity to the notion of supererogation. Urmson, a philosophical ethicist, presents several persuasive arguments to show that saintly and heroic behavior cannot plausibly be regarded as the fulfillment of duty. In one example, Urmson describes a soldier who throws himself upon a live grenade to save the lives of his comrades. Surely it would be wrong to judge that the soldier has a duty to perform this act, and surely it would be wrong to blame him for deciding not to perform it. Yet it is clearly a morally praiseworthy act, and hence it qualifies as an act of supererogation.

Urmson admits that saints and heroes often regard their own behavior as the fulfillment of duty. People frequently reply that they were only doing their duty when congratulated for performing acts of saintliness or heroism, and this is a phenomenon that has led many people to conclude that there really are no acts of supererogation in human life. Urmson argues, however, that people who react to their own saintly or heroic acts in this manner are simply mistaken. They have subjected themselves to a standard of duty that is unrealistically rigorous, and they have in reality gone beyond the call of duty.

David Heyd has argued that, in addition to heroism and saintliness, there are five other categories of acts that are capable of qualifying as supererogatory. First, there are acts of beneficence, such as acts of charity, generosity, and gift giving; second, doing favors for others; third, volunteering or promising something; fourth, forbearing to do what is within one's rights; and fifth, forgiving, pardoning, and showing mercy. In each of these categories there is room for performing acts of supererogation.

Although acts of supererogation are almost always portrayed in dramatic fashion, it is important to realize that small acts of generosity, courtesy, or kindness can satisfy the three conditions required of being supererogatory. Thus, it can be supererogatory to buy lunch for a coworker who has arrived at work without any money, to put in a good word about someone else to a person in authority, or to offer to cover the office phone while everyone else is downstairs at the office Christmas party. —*Gregory Mellema*

See also Duty.

BIBLIOGRAPHY

Attfield, Robin. *A Theory of Value and Obligation*. London: Croom Helm, 1987.

Heyd, David. *Supererogation*. Cambridge, England: Cambridge University Press, 1982.

Mellema, Gregory. *Beyond the Call of Duty*. Albany: State University of New York Press, 1991.

Urmson, J. O. "Saints and Heroes." In *Moral Concepts*, edited by Joel Feinberg. London: Oxford University Press, 1969.

Supreme Court

TYPE OF ETHICS: Legal and judicial ethics
DATE: Established 1789
ASSOCIATED WITH: U.S. federal government
DEFINITION: As the highest appellate court in the U.S. federal judicial system and final arbiter of disputes involving interpretation of legislation, the Supreme Court has the power to decide what laws are constitutional
SIGNIFICANCE: The Supreme Court is the ultimate authority regarding whether laws created by the executive and legislative branches of government conform to the principles on which the nation was founded

The most significant decision ever rendered by the Supreme Court came in 1803, when it handed down its opinion in the case of *Marbury v. Madison*, which established the principle of judicial review. With *Marbury*, the Court consolidated its authority by at once claiming and exercising the power to review and abrogate acts of the administration and of Congress that it found to be in conflict with the Constitution, declaring that it is "the province and the duty of the judicial department to say what the law is."

History. The idea of a federal judiciary—including one supreme court—is set out in Article III of the U.S. Constitution. It was not until President George Washington signed the first Judiciary Act into law in 1789, however, that the Court began to take shape. The Judiciary Act of 1789 specified that the Supreme Court should consist of one chief justice and five associate justices. Accordingly, at the same time that he signed the Act into law, Washington forwarded his six nominations to the Senate for confirmation—all were among the founders of the new nation. The first Supreme Court—known as the Jay Court, because it was headed by Chief Justice John Jay—opened its first session on February 1, 1790 in the Royal Exchange Building in New York City.

The Jay Court lasted until 1795. Since that time, the size of the Court has increased to nine justices, the seat of the Court has moved twice (first to Philadelphia, then to Washington, D.C.), and there have been fifteen more "Courts" headed by fifteen more chief justices.

Supreme Court justices are political appointees, who are appointed for life. Although some early courts, such as the uniformly Federalist Ellsworth Court, have been notorious for their partisanship, and some later courts, such as the Warren Court, have been notable for their political orientation, the justices' lifelong tenure and the Court's tradition of secrecy contribute to the even-handedness with which it customarily dispenses justice.

Jurisdiction. The Court began to define its jurisdiction—its power to hear and decide cases—early in its history. When asked by President George Washington to rule on certain questions of foreign policy, the Jay Court declined, establishing the Court's still extant policy not to issue purely advisory opinions. Instead, the court of last resort (like all other United States appellate courts) rules on questions of law only in the context of reviewing real cases and controversies.

Today, although the Court has original jurisdiction in all cases concerning ambassadors and other public ministers, and in all cases in which a state is a party, the Court's work consists almost entirely of reviewing appeals from lower federal court decisions and from cases involving questions of federal law decided by state courts. Because of this appellate jurisdiction, the Supreme Court rarely reviews questions of fact raised at the trial level, focusing instead on the constitutionality of the legislation at issue in a given case.

Appeals are almost always heard on a discretionary basis and reach the Court only if at least four of the nine justices vote in favor of one of the parties' appeal or petition for a writ of *certiorari*, whereby the Court orders the lower court to forward a record of the parties' case.

Opinions. The Court does not always issue a written opinion in conjunction with its decisions, but opinions explaining how the justices reached their determinations almost always accompany important cases affecting many Americans. The job of writing the majority opinion is assigned to one justice, but any justice who wishes to do so may write his or her own opinion, which might be concurring (agreeing with the outcome of the vote but disagreeing with the majority's reasoning) or dissenting (dissenters sometimes merely go on record with their status rather than write an opinion).

The way in which the Court votes determines the effect of any given decision. So important was the issue in *Brown v. Board of Education* (1954), school desegregation, that the Warren Court felt obligated to issue a unanimous decision. The unity and authority with which the Court spoke in this case arguably resulted in the most profound changes in the social fabric that the United States has ever experienced.

—Lisa Paddock

See also Adversary system; *Brown v. Board of Education of Topeka*; International justice; Jurisprudence; Supreme Court justices, selection of.

BIBLIOGRAPHY

Baum, Lawrence. *The Supreme Court.* 4th ed. Washington, D.C.: CQ Press, 1992.

Lankevich, George J., ed. *The Supreme Court in American Life Series.* Millwood, N.Y.: Associated Faculty Press, Inc., 1986-1987.

Steamer, Robert J. *Chief Justice: Leadership and the Supreme Court.* Columbia, S.C.: University of South Carolina Press, 1986.

Wagman, Robert J. *The Supreme Court: A Citizen's Guide.* New York: Pharos Books, 1993.

Witt, Elder. *Congressional Quarterly's Guide to the U.S. Supreme Court.* 2d ed. Washington, D.C.: Congressional Quarterly, 1990.

Supreme Court Justices, selection of

TYPE OF ETHICS: Legal and judicial ethics
ASSOCIATED WITH: U.S. Supreme Court
DEFINITION: The processes by means of which Supreme Court justices are chosen
SIGNIFICANCE: The ethical considerations involved in the selection and nomination of justices to the United States Supreme Court have a substantial relationship to the morals, values, and ethics in American society; the Supreme Court resolves many of the most important and controversial issues in the United States, and in doing so, it shapes government policy in areas as diverse as civil rights and environmental protection; through its interpretation of the law, established in the case of *Marbury v. Madison*, the Supreme Court plays a critical role in the policy making system of the federal government

Article II, Section 2 {2}, of the United States Constitution states that the president of the United States shall have the power, with the advice and consent of the Senate, to nominate and appoint justices of the Supreme Court of the United States. Supreme Court justices are appointed for life by the president of the United States and confirmed by the Senate. The nomi-

JUSTICES OF THE UNITED STATES SUPREME COURT CHIEF JUSTICES		
Name	**Term on Supreme Court**	**Appointing President**
John Jay	1789-1795	George Washington
John Rutledge	1795-1795	George Washington
Oliver Ellsworth	1796-1800	George Washington
John Marshall	1801-1835	John Adams
Roger Brooke Taney	1836-1864	Andrew Jackson
Salmon Portland Chase	1864-1873	Abraham Lincoln
Morrison R. Waite	1874-1888	Ulysses S. Grant
Melville Weston Fuller	1888-1910	Grover Cleveland
Edward Douglass White	1910-1921	William Howard Taft
William Howard Taft	1921-1930	Warren G. Harding
Charles Evans Hughes	1930-1941	Herbert Hoover
Harlan Fiske Stone	1941-1946	Franklin D. Roosevelt
Fred M. Vinson	1946-1953	Harry S Truman
Earl Warren	1953-1969	Dwight D. Eisenhower
Warren Burger	1969-1986	Richard M. Nixon
William H. Rehnquist	1986-present	Ronald Reagan

JUSTICES OF THE UNITED STATES SUPREME COURT
ASSOCIATE JUSTICES

Name	Term	Appointing President	Name	Term	Appointing President
James Wilson	1789-1798	George Washington	Rufus Peckham	1896-1909	Grover Cleveland
William Cushing	1790-1810	George Washington	Joseph McKenna	1898-1925	William McKinley
John Blair, Jr.	1790-1795	George Washington	Oliver Wendell Holmes, Jr.	1902-1932	Theodore Roosevelt
John Rutledge	1790-1791	George Washington	William R. Day	1903-1922	Theodore Roosevelt
James Iredell	1790-1799	George Washington	William H. Moody	1906-1910	Theodore Roosevelt
Thomas Johnson	1792-1793	George Washington	Horace H. Lurton	1910-1914	William Howard Taft
William Paterson	1793-1806	George Washington	Charles Evans Hughes	1910-1916	William Howard Taft
Samuel Chase	1796-1811	George Washington	Willis van Devanter	1911-1937	William Howard Taft
Bushrod Washington	1799-1829	John Adams	Joseph Rucker Lamar	1911-1916	William Howard Taft
Alfred Moore	1800-1804	John Adams	Mahlon Pitney	1912-1922	William Howard Taft
William Johnson	1804-1834	Thomas Jefferson	James Clark McReynolds	1914-1941	Woodrow Wilson
Brockholst Livingston	1807-1823	Thomas Jefferson	Louis D. Brandeis	1916-1939	Woodrow Wilson
Thomas Todd	1807-1826	Thomas Jefferson	John H. Clarke	1916-1922	Woodrow Wilson
Gabriel Duvall	1811-1835	James Madison	George Sutherland	1922-1938	Warren G. Harding
Joseph Story	1812-1845	James Madison	Pierce Butler	1923-1939	Warren G. Harding
Smith Thompson	1823-1843	James Monroe	Edward T. Sanford	1923-1930	Warren G. Harding
Robert Trimble	1826-1828	John Quincy Adams	Harlan Fiske Stone	1925-1941	Calvin Coolidge
John McLean	1830-1861	Andrew Jackson	Owen J. Roberts	1930-1945	Herbert Hoover
Henry Baldwin	1830-1844	Andrew Jackson	Benjamin Nathan Cardozo	1932-1938	Herbert Hoover
James M. Wayne	1835-1867	Andrew Jackson	Hugo L. Black	1937-1971	Franklin D. Roosevelt
Philip Barbour	1836-1841	Andrew Jackson	Stanley F. Reed	1938-1957	Franklin D. Roosevelt
John Catron	1837-1865	Andrew Jackson	Felix Frankfurter	1939-1962	Franklin D. Roosevelt
John McKinley	1838-1852	Martin Van Buren	William O. Douglas	1939-1975	Franklin D. Roosevelt
Peter V. Daniel	1842-1860	Martin Van Buren	Frank Murphy	1940-1949	Franklin D. Roosevelt
Samuel Nelson	1845-1872	John Tyler	James F. Byrnes	1941-1942	Franklin D. Roosevelt
Levi Woodbury	1845-1851	James K. Polk	Robert H. Jackson	1941-1954	Franklin D. Roosevelt
Robert C. Grier	1846-1870	James K. Polk	Wiley B. Rutledge	1943-1949	Franklin D. Roosevelt
Benjamin Curtis	1851-1857	Millard Fillmore	Harold H. Burton	1945-1958	Harry S Truman
John A. Campbell	1853-1861	Franklin Pierce	Tom C. Clark	1949-1967	Harry S Truman
Nathan Clifford	1858-1881	James Buchanan	Sherman Minton	1949-1956	Harry S Truman
Noah H. Swayne	1862-1881	Abraham Lincoln	John M. Harlan II	1955-1971	Dwight D. Eisenhower
Samuel F. Miller	1862-1890	Abraham Lincoln	William Brennan, Jr.	1956-1990	Dwight D. Eisenhower
David Davis	1862-1877	Abraham Lincoln	Charles E. Whittaker	1957-1962	Dwight D. Eisenhower
Stephen Field	1863-1897	Abraham Lincoln	Potter Stewart	1958-1981	Dwight D. Eisenhower
William Strong	1870-1880	Ulysses S. Grant	Byron R. White	1962-1993	John F. Kennedy
Joseph Bradley	1870-1892	Ulysses S. Grant	Arthur J. Goldberg	1962-1965	John F. Kennedy
Ward Hunt	1873-1882	Ulysses S. Grant	Abe Fortas	1965-1969	Lyndon B. Johnson
John Marshall Harlan	1877-1911	Rutherford B. Hayes	Thurgood Marshall	1967-1991	Lyndon B. Johnson
William B. Woods	1881-1887	Rutherford B. Hayes	Harry A. Blackmun	1970-present	Richard M. Nixon
Stanley Matthews	1881-1889	James A. Garfield	Lewis Powell, Jr.	1972-1987	Richard M. Nixon
Horace Gray	1882-1902	Chester A. Arthur	William H. Rehnquist	1972-1986	Richard M. Nixon
Samuel Blatchford	1882-1893	Chester A. Arthur	John Paul Stevens	1975-present	Gerald Ford
Lucius Q. C. Lamar	1888-1893	Grover Cleveland	Sandra Day O'Connor	1981-present	Ronald Reagan
David J. Brewer	1890-1910	Benjamin Harrison	Antonin Scalia	1986-present	Ronald Reagan
Henry B. Brown	1891-1906	Benjamin Harrison	Anthony M. Kennedy	1988-present	Ronald Reagan
George Shiras, Jr.	1892-1903	Benjamin Harrison	David H. Souter	1990-present	George Bush
Howell E. Jackson	1893-1895	Benjamin Harrison	Clarence Thomas	1991-present	George Bush
Edward D. White	1894-1910	Grover Cleveland	Ruth Bader Ginsburg	1993-present	Bill Clinton

nation process has become very publicized in recent years, because the decision making of the Court has had an increasing effect on the lives of all American citizens and has become an important factor in presidential politics. People are more aware now more than ever that an elected president will nominate Supreme Court justices who generally (though not always) support his political views and will make their decisions based on these views, often for a long period of time after the president has left office. Although most judges make their decisions based on facts as opposed to ideological precepts, their own ideological precepts are often used in guiding them in interpreting facts.

The selection of judges to the United States Supreme Court is one of the most important responsibilities of the republic. Their decisions are very rarely, if ever, overturned, and the policies that are set by them have a profound effect on the entire nation, collectively and individually.

There are no set qualifications to be a judge or justice on the federal bench. The courts were set up by the Constitution as the third branch of the government in order to ensure the separation of powers. They were to be an independent, impartial branch of government that would serve, as Alexander Hamilton wrote in *The Federalist* "as bulwarks of a limited Constitution, as an intermediate body between the people and the legislature, in order, among other things, to keep the latter within the limits assigned to their authority." This principle was embraced by Chief Justice John Marshall, who established the power of judicial review in the case *Marbury v. Madison*, giving the Supreme Court the power to declare legislative acts and laws unconstitutional.

Although the Court is an impartial judicial branch, its members have all been nominated by a president who is a political figure. Any president will try to select Supreme Court justices who share his outlook. To demand minute particulars, however, would make impossible the president's real task: to find men and women of learning, character, and wisdom. The most important factor shaping the Court's policies at any given time is the identity of its members, which is why the nomination process so clearly reflects the potential justice's views on the direction that the laws need to take in order to reflect the values and priorities of the society that he or she serves. The Supreme Court makes policy through the interpretation of the law, but the way in which this goal is achieved raises an ethical dilemma. Issues of public policy come to the Court through legal questions that the court is asked to resolve. Two parties bring a dispute before the Court and ask the Court to review it. The Court reviews it and makes a judgment about the specific dispute brought to it, gives an interpretation of the legal issues involved in that dispute, and takes a position on the policy questions that are connected to the legal issues. Although the function of the Supreme Court is not that of a legislative body, should the Court be free to overturn and thwart legislatures because of what the justices perceive to be unjust or unfair results of a case as applied to the existing laws

and precedents? That is the main question that is posed in discussions of the ethics of selecting Supreme Court justices.

The extent to which judges should be bound by statutes and case precedents as against their own ethical ideas and concepts of social, political, and economic policy involves the question of which should prevail when justice and the law appear to the judges to be out of alignment with one another. Some judicial lawmaking is inevitable, but to what extent? Should the ideological agenda of a judge or a group of people be imposed through judicial decree rather than through directly elected officials? Should the Senate and the president of the United States ask a particular nominee how he or she would rule on a controversial issue of law, such as abortion, prior to appointment and should his or her answer be grounds for disqualification? Should judges be more concerned with granting new civil liberties that they perceive to be fair or with interpreting the Constitution? Does interpreting the Constitution mean relying upon the original intent of the Founding Fathers for guidance, or does the Constitution change as society changes and becomes more open and permissive? Is the job of the judge to adhere to the law or to do justice? If there is an injustice in society and Congress and the states have failed to act, should the Supreme Court fill the void? What is the main source of societal change: judges or the people? How far should the Supreme Court go in using its substantial power of the citizens?

These are all questions that are answered many different ways by many different judicial nominees, based on their philosophy of law and their experiences. Although there is no denying that judicial nominees to the Supreme Court must adhere to the highest standards of personal conduct, there are vast differences in judicial philosophy and interpretations of the role of the Court that present ethical dilemmas that will always be with the United States in the nomination of justices to the highest Court in the land.

—*Amy Bloom*

See also Jurisprudence; Supreme Court.

BIBLIOGRAPHY

Abraham, Henry J. *Justices and Presidents: A Political History of Appointments to the Supreme Court.* 3d ed. New York: Oxford University Press, 1992.

Chase, Harold W. *Federal Judges: The Appointing Process.* Minneapolis: University of Minnesota Press, 1972.

Danelski, David J. *A Supreme Court Justice Is Appointed.* New York: Random House, 1964.

King, Gary. "Presidential Appointments to the Supreme Court: Adding Systematic Explanation of Probabilistic Description." *American Politics Quarterly* 15 (July, 1987): 373-386.

Perry, Barbara A. *A Representative Supreme Court? The Impact of Race, Religion, and Gender on Appointments.* New York: Greenwood Press, 1991.

Stewardt, Alva W. *U.S. Supreme Court Appointments, 1961-1986: A Brief Bibliography.* Monticello, Ill.: Vance Bibliographies, 1987.

Surrogate motherhood

TYPE OF ETHICS: Bioethics

DATE: Coined 1976

ASSOCIATED WITH: Custody battle for Baby M, a baby born to surrogate Mary Beth Whitehead in 1986

DEFINITION: The bearing of a child by one person for another person

SIGNIFICANCE: Surrogacy involves many moral issues, including adultery; exploitation of infertile couples, surrogate mothers, and children by baby brokers; buying and selling of babies; dehumanization of reproduction; rights to privacy; medical need for use of the procedure; and custody and identity problems

Infertile couples and others may seek the services of a surrogate if other reproductive procedures such as artificial insemination, in vitro fertilization, or adoption are not options for them.

There are three forms of surrogacy. The first occurs when sexual intercourse is used by the husband of an infertile woman to impregnate another woman for the purpose of bearing a child for the couple. A second method involves using artificial insemination of the surrogate with sperm provided by the prospective father. A third method, in vitro fertilization, uses sperm and eggs provided by the genetic parents to produce an embryo (a test-tube baby) that is then implanted into the surrogate. Artificial insemination is used most often.

In modern society, the first form of surrogacy is normally not used because it reqires that sexual intercourse occur between the prospective father and the surrogate. This is considered to be an adulterous act and is usually unacceptable to the infertile couple. This type of surrogacy also places the burden of prostitution and possibly unwed motherhood on the surrogate and illegitimacy on the resulting child. Arguments in favor of this form of surrogacy include precedent of the biblical story of Abram and Serai, who engaged their maid-servant Hagar to bear them a son, Ishmael (Gen. 6). Other arguments in favor include the use of wet nurses to provide milk for infants and organ donors, which also may be considered types of surrogates.

The second type of surrogacy, which is now called traditional surrogacy, is also objectionable to some people because it removes procreation from marriage, replaces natural processes with artificial ones, and introduces a third party, which can damage personal relationships within the family. Proponents argue that artificial insemination obviates the adultery problem and that artificial processes are often medical necessities for those who are infertile.

Similar ethical arguments can be made for and against the third type of surrogacy, involving in vitro fertilization and embryo transfer, which is called gestational surrogacy. In such a case, the surrogate is a carrier or incubator and does not contribute genetic material to the resulting child. Those who object to it say that this procedure is immoral because it removes the act of reproduction from marriage by using artificial means and enlists the services of a third-party surrogate. In addition, the in vitro technique requires that the embryos be cultured and evaluated for a few days. Defective embryos are discarded, some may be frozen for future use and others are implanted into the host. Opponents say that this places human life in peril and allows medical professionals to make God-like decisions concerning life and death. Those who support this type of surrogacy say that the parent's natural desire to have children outweighs the ethical arguments against it and that progess in medical science eventually will free humans from all the constraints of infertility.

The legalization and widespread use of surrogacy may raise other ethical and social questions. One concern is the right to privacy. Do the infertile parents have the right to meet the surrogate? Can they interview her to determine her suitability or should this be done by an intermediary? Another concern is allocation of responsibility. Who is responsible for medical costs during the pregnancy? Will there be joint responsibility for decisions regarding the health of the unborn baby? Will the surrogate agree to prenatal tests such as amniocentesis? If prenatal tests indicate the presence of fetal defects, who will determine the action to be taken, such as terminating the pregnancy? What about the behavior of the surrogate during pregnancy? Will she be allowed to drink alcohol, smoke, or engage in other activities that may harm the baby? The prospective parents will certainly insist that such behavior be curtailed during the contract period with the surrogate. Will the popularization of surrogacy lead to the exploitation of poor women? Opponents argue that surrogacy could become another low-paying, high-risk job for the underprivileged and that it degrades women by commercializing pregnancy and childbirth. Advocates argue that women of various socioeconomic backgrounds become surrogates of their own will and often do so without compensation out of a sense of sympathy for the infertile couple. Will surrogacy be regulated so that only those in dire need of the procedure will be provided access to it or will anyone with the money, infertile or not, be allowed to use it? Should surrogacy be deemed appropriate in some situations but not others? What about the interests of the child? Some have argued that hiring a surrogate can be equated to purchasing a baby. They say that the legalization of surrogacy will encourage the development of an industry of baby brokering. Those opposed to surrogacy say that treating human babies as a commodity to be bought and sold constitutes a type of dehumanization that is similar to slavery. Advocates say that surrogacy should be viewed in the same light as foster care or adoption and that the exchange of money is purely for the time and inconvenience of the surrogate, not the child. Another issue is identity. Who is the child's legal mother, its gestational mother or its care-giving mother? This creates identity problems similar to those experienced by adopted children.

Another unforeseen problem that has come to the forefront is custody. In some instances surrogate mothers have

SURROGATE MOTHERHOOD TIME LINE	
1975	First publicized artificial insemination of a surrogate under contract is performed by Harris F. Simonds, M.D., of San Rafael, California.
1981	In *Doe v. Kelly*, 307 N.W. 2d 483, the Michigan Appellate Court rules that surrogate motherhood is legal but that a state statute prohibits monetary compensation for such purposes.
1986	In *Surrogate Parenting Associates, Inc., v. Kentucky,* 704 S.W. 2d 209, the Supreme Court of Kentucky rules that the state attorney general could not revoke the corporate charter of the defendant since the state legislature had not yet addressed the legality of surrogate motherhood contracts.
1986	In *Adoption of Baby Girl, L.J.*, 132 N.Y. Misc. 2d 972, 505 N.Y.S. 2d 813, a New York state court rules that the adoption of a surrogate-borne child by the contracting parents is legal and allows the payment of a fee to the surrogate. Later, a New York law is enacted that prohibits payments to surrogates and brokers.
1987	Louisiana passes the first state law to prohibit surrogacy. In the five years following, eighteen states pass legislation prohibiting or restricting commercial surrogate births.
1988	In *Mary Beth Whitehead v. William and Elizabeth Stern* (Baby M case), the New Jersey Supreme Court rules that surrogate contracts are invalid and against public policy when the payment of a fee is involved and when the surrogate is bound to give up the child.
1993	In *Anna L. Johnson v. Mark and Crispina Calvert*, the California Supreme Court becomes the first state judicial body to validate a gestational surrogacy agreement in a case where the surrogate refuses to surrender a test tube conceived baby. The California court places a high value on the preconception intent of individuals entering into a surrogacy contract; that is, the woman who intends to bring about the birth and raise a child is considered to be the natural mother, not the surrogate.

become so emotionally attached to the babies they have carried that they have refused to give them up to the contractual parents. The best-known is that of Baby M. In 1985, William and Elizabeth Stern contracted with Mary Beth Whitehead (all of New Jersey) to bear them a child using William Stern's semen by means of artificial insemination. When the child was born in 1986 (named Melissa by the Sterns) a custody battle ensued in the New Jersey courts that, ultimately resulted in the termination of parental rights (but not visitation rights) for Mary Beth Whitehead.

—Rodney C. Mowbray

See also Bioethics; In vitro fertilization.

BIBLIOGRAPHY

Bach, Julie S., ed. *Biomedical Ethics*. St. Paul, Minn.: Greenhaven Press, 1987.

Keane, Noel P., and Dennis L. Breo. *The Surrogate Mother*. New York: Everest House, 1981.

Landau, Elaine. *Surrogate Mothers*. Edited by Iris Rosoff. New York: Franklin Watts, 1988.

Overvold, Amy Zuckerman. *Surrogate Parenting*. New York: Pharos Books, 1988.

Sloan, Irving J., ed. *The Law of Adoption and Surrogate Parenting*. New York: Oceana, 1988.

Taboos

TYPE OF ETHICS: Beliefs and practices

DATE: The term began to appear in anthropological inquiries into the origins of religion toward the end of the eighteenth century

ASSOCIATED WITH: Classic works in cultural anthropology, such as Sir James Frazer's *Golden Bough* (1911-1915), and psychology, such as Sigmund Freud's *Totem and Taboo* (1913)

DEFINITION: Practices proscribed by the moral or religious codes of a tribe, race, or nation

SIGNIFICANCE: Taboos are often the foundation stones of ethical systems and moral codes built on proscriptive principles of tradition or religious belief as opposed to rational inquiry

Two Senses of Taboo. There are two senses, two related concepts, that are signified by the term "taboo." The older sense, derived from the Polynesian *tapu* and its applied meaning, refers to that which is paradoxically both sacred but potentially harmful and pure but subject to defilement. In the second, more generic and familiar sense, a taboo is a practice or behavior that is forbidden by the mores of a particular culture.

In the first sense, "taboo" is used, for example, to refer to the former untouchables of the Hindu caste system. It can also be used to refer to religious or quasi-religious objects with alleged magical powers, such as the Holy Grail of medieval legend, or sacred places, such as tribal burial grounds.

In general, the term applies to objects of primal power that have an ambiguous potential to harm or destroy and to heal or empower and therefore to things both feared and venerated. The concept thus relates to the dual religious potential both to injure and heal, punish and reward.

In the second sense, most directly relating to applied ethics codified as law, the term is applied to any practice beyond a society's moral pale. In this sense, common taboos are incest and cannibalism, which are nearly universal examples; thus, the term relates more to an act than an object or place.

There is an inherent relationship between the two meanings derived from the attitude toward taboos in primitive cultures. In the Polynesian culture, a taboo object was so powerful that it was sacrosanct and could be approached only by priest or shaman. If the taboo were violated—touched by an uninitiated intruder, for example—it could require purification through a ritual that could include the death of the offender.

Totem and Taboo. In many primitive cultures, taboos are revealed as part of a rite of passage through significant stages of life, such as birth, marriage, and death, and are recorded on a tribal or clan totem as formulas or symbols, frequently depicted as animals or plants. Thus, the term "totem" is often linked to "taboo" and is sometimes used to refer to folk customs, such as rules of courtship and mourning, as opposed to taboos or moral prohibitions of a specific culture.

Some taboo objects in primitive societies were anathema, or cursed and therefore feared, which relates to the revulsion experienced in the violation of a taboo in the second meaning of the word. In many cultures, moral repugnancy is associated with such acts as cannibalism or incest, or even with violations of strict dietary laws or sexual practices.

Ethical Implications. Many taboos are so deeply and strongly rooted in the beliefs and practices of a folk as to be a priori foundation stones that preclude the need for their iteration in ethical coda, a prime example being the Judaic-Christian Decalogue, which carries no prohibitions against either cannibalism or incest, both of which are fundamental taboos in Western culture.

Canonical, civil, and criminal laws have all addressed taboo issues, often in vague terms such as "crimes against nature" that reflect a historical unwillingness to be explicit in legal formulations dealing with them, in part because the graphic language necessary for describing taboo acts may itself be taboo. Statutes written in indefinite language have increasingly come under judicial review and have been revised, particularly in those cases in which human behavior has denuded a taboo of its inhibitive power.

Although some taboos, such as those against cannibalism and incest, have in many cultures been rigidly observed for centuries, others, such as those against sodomy and miscegenation, have been modified if not completely abandoned. Law, of course, is always slow to reflect changing mores; therefore, much condoned social behavior remains technically condemned by law.

In societies where personal freedom has evolved and the right to privacy has been ensured, many taboos have been gradually depleted of their force. Even the most permissive societies, however, have some taboos and impose legal or social penalties for their violation. Moreover, scientific and technological advances have greatly muddied the ethical waters by introducing new imponderables that must be resolved in philosophical thought before being distilled into viable legal codes. For example, scientific evidence revealing that sexual preference is not a matter of choice but of inherited, genetic makeup has had profound ethical implications and has forced the liberalization of laws against sodomy based on principles of scriptural sanctions, moral choice, or "natural" behavior.

The modification or abandonment of a traditional taboo may result from a war that is waged on a moral battleground between forces deeply committed to inherited values, often based in religious convictions, and those embracing new attitudes supported by modern science and medicine. Two notable examples are the practices of abortion and euthanasia, which were almost universally condemned in the past but now have been condoned by many people as both appropriate and ethical in at least some instances.

—John W. Fiero

See also Abortion; Bioethics; Euthanasia; Homosexuality; Incest.

BIBLIOGRAPHY

Brain, James Lewton. *The Last Taboo: Sex and the Fear of Death.* Garden City, N.Y.: Anchor Press, 1979.

Browne, Ray Broadus, ed. *Forbidden Fruits: Taboos and Tabooism in Culture.* Bowling Green, Ohio: Bowling Green University Popular Press, 1984.

Douglas, Mary. *Purity and Danger: An Analysis of the Concepts of Pollution and Taboo.* London: Ark, 1984.

Fryer, Peter. *Mrs. Grundy: Studies in English Prudery.* New York: London House & Maxwell, 1964.

Hardin, Garrett James. *Stalking the Wild Taboo.* Los Altos, Calif.: W. Kaufmann, 1973.

Webster, Hutton. *Taboo: A Sociological Study.* Stanford, Calif: Stanford University Press, 1942.

Taft-Hartley Act. *See* Labor-Management Relations Act.

Tagore, Rabindranath (May 7, 1861, Calcutta, India—August 7, 1941, Calcutta, India): Poet and philosopher

TYPE OF ETHICS: Modern history

Rabindranath Tagore (The Nobel Foundation)

ACHIEVEMENTS: One of the most famous Indian (Bengali) poets of the twentieth century and recipient of the Nobel Prize in Literature in 1913 for *Gitánjali* (1910, *Gitanjali* (Song offerings), 1912); founded Vishvabharati University in Shantiniketan, India in 1921

SIGNIFICANCE: Worked to promote mutual understanding between India and the West

Tagore began to write poetry as a child. His first book was published when he was seventeen years old. After returning to India from a trip to England in 1878 to study law, he became the most popular author of the colonial era. Through the short stories, novels, and plays that he wrote, he conveyed his belief that truth lies in seeing the harmony of apparently contrary forces. He was not interested in building a philosophical system; instead he wanted to deepen mutual Indian and Western cultural understanding. He was very much influenced by the Upaniṣads but interpreted them theistically. His artistic nature made him more of a follower of the way of *bhakti*, or "devotion," than of the way of jñāna, or "knowledge," of Advaita Vedānta. Because he believed in the harmony of complementary forces, however, he did not reject the Advaita, or monistic, view of Vedānta. In Tagore's view, both the one and the many are real. The doctrine of *māyā*, or illusion, points to the false belief that the world is independently real. God, humanity, and the world are interrelated. Tagore viewed life in a positive way, as the discovery of the divine nature of humanity.

See also Upaniṣads; Vedānta.

Talmud: Book

TYPE OF ETHICS: Religious ethics

DATE: Earlier part of the second century B.C.E. to circa 500 C.E.

SIGNIFICANCE: A repository of ideas and wisdom reflecting Jewish religious and cultural activity as interpreted by centuries of sages who lived in Eretz Israel and Babylonia (today part of Iraq) from before the common era to the beginning of the Middle Ages; the primary source for post-biblical Jewish law and lore, the Talmud is second to the Bible in authority

If the Bible (*TaNaK*) is the cornerstone of Judaism, then the Talmud is its magnificent edifice. Its bricks and mortar are shaped by the revelation of the written Torah as represented, understood, and lived by the sages who molded Israel's salvific apparatus from the ruins of the Second Temple (destroyed by the Romans in 70 C.E.) until the beginning of the Middle Ages. Their accomplishment, the Mishnah, and its commentary, the Gemarah, which together form the Talmud, became the dominant structure of Judaism.

The Talmud is not easily classified in any literary genre. This is because of its encyclopedic range of topics, including law, legend, philosophy, science, and some history; its pragmatic treatment of everyday life issues alongside flights into abstract and ethereal problems; its multiple and varied methodologies, equally logical and fanciful; its terse writing style, which is reminiscent of note taking; and the meticulous final editing of pedantic redactions, themselves based on free-flowing ideas composed centuries earlier.

More a library than a single book, the Talmud is an anthology of national expression responding to the Roman catastrophe of the first and second centuries, and it is more meaningful when it is learned and studied than it is when it is read. The association between one idea and another, a rabbi in Galilee and another in Babylon, the first century and the fifth century, is tenuous at first, but persistent study connects the diverse pieces of knowledge in a way that is reminiscent of the links of a chain—the chain of tradition. The thought of the sages is like a winding stream of consciousness that flows into the "sea of the Talmud" and nurtures the religious and national life of a people. Accordingly, though not surprising, forces hostile to Israel as "a light unto the nations" have maligned the Talmud, prohibited its study, and consigned its pages to flames countless times during the Middle Ages, in fin de siècle Europe, and during the Nazi era. From such horrendous acts, a *talmud* (in a limited sense, the word means "instruction") has been revealed: Strip the Talmud from the "people of the Book," and chances for Israel's spiritual and, ultimately, physical survival are almost nonexistent.

Mishnah. The Mishnah is the core document of the rabbinic system of philosophy and legalism traditionally called *Torah shehbe'al peh* (oral Torah). The quintessential "tradition of the elders," it represents a Pharisian application of the written Torah in the life of the people. Inevitably, as a living interpretation, reflecting changing times and events, it added, subtracted, and modified the written teaching of God. Humility (many teachings are given anonymously), respect for sanctity of the teaching of Moses, and concern that the rabbinic spirit might replace the letter of the Torah in the eyes of the people (for example, *mamon tahat ayin* ["monetary compensation for bodily injury"] in place of *ayin tahat ayin* ["eye for eye"]; near abolishment of the death penalty, introduction of a court administered *prosbul* to overcome the cancellation of debts during the year of release, and so forth) inhibited individual schools of rabbis from writing down their decisions.

Ultimately, successful dissension within greater Judaism (for example, Jewish Christianity) and greater Roman oppressiveness in response to ill-fated Jewish wars led to conditions of exile and set the stage for the redaction of the Mishnah. Rabbi Judah the Prince collated the unwritten rules, customs, interpretations, and traditions of multiple masters, pre-70 and post-70, into a written guide. The Mishnah ("repetition" or "recapitulation" of the revelation at Sinai) claimed an authoritative affinity to Sinai ("everything which a sage will ask in the future is already known to Moses at Sinai") and also claimed to be its living successor ("We teach more Torah [than . . .] received at Sinai"). Therefore, the Mishnah designates the transition from Israelite religion to the system now called Judaism in the same manner that the New Testament points the way from Israelite religion to Christianity.

The Mishnah is divided into six orders (*sedarim*), which are divided into sixty-three topical sections (*massekhtot*), with each *massekhet* containing multiple chapters (*perakim*). The Mishnah, also known as *SHaS*, an acronym for the six orders (*shishah sedarim*), covers a range of Pentateuchal legislative topics:

1. "Seeds" (*Zeraim*): agricultural rulings (gleanings, tithes, the Sabbatical year, and so forth), though the first *massekhet* is a discussion on "Benedictions" (*Berakhot*).

2. "Appointed Festivals" (*Mo'ed*): regulations governing holy time, such as the Sabbath, the holidays, and their respective festival offerings.

3. "Women" (*Nashim*): ordinances on marriage, divorce, and vows, and related exceptional cases, such as Levirate marriage, suspected adulteresses, and the Nazarite vow.

4. "Damages" (*Nezikim*): civil and criminal decrees, and the conduct of and conduct before an ecclesiastical court of law. Includes the tractate *Avot* ("Founders"), a selection of maxims and ethical statements given in the names of sixty *tannaim* (Aramaic for "repeaters," or teachers) of the oral Torah; its five chapters (and a sixth one, added centuries later) are traditionally studied on the six Sabbath afternoons between Passover and Pentecost.

5. "Sacred Things" (*Kodashim*): the holy things of the Temple, pertaining mainly to animal, fowl, and meal offerings.

6. "Purifications" (*Tohorot*): conduct dealing with cultic and domestic purity and defilement.

In sum, the Mishnah is an enigmatic corpus. It claims the authority of revelation but it was not admitted by the Rabbis into the canon of Holy Scriptures. Written in Hebrew, it departs from the style and syntax of biblical Hebrew. It does not speak of an eschatological future (stable material in the holy writings of world religions), and it fuses a cultic past (the Temple), regarding which it has no direct access, into a present that is dubious and fanciful. Its many *halakhot* (laws) regulate an "existing" priesthood, Jewish government, and courts, totally oblivious to the ruin of these institutions during the first and second centuries. Other *halakhot* relate to religious practices that have no bearing on the Judaism of the day. It purports to be a code of law, but it is actually a compilation of unresolved legal disputations together with biblical exegesis (*midrash*) and nonlegal material (*aggadot*). Despite these facts, however, the Mishnah's paradoxical complexity is justified by its objective: the restoration of the peoplehood of Israel when all signs, internal and external, pointed to its disintegration. In the end, the Mishnah represents a beginning: the initiation of a salvation grounded more in polity survival than in personal salvation.

Gemarah. In the generation following its appearance, the Mishnah proved to be the focus of increasingly involved discussions by groups of rabbis and their students. The first generation (early third century) clarified obscure passages, and the succeeding generations developed and expanded principles and rules of conduct from the extant mishnaic material as they applied to situations arising in their own societal setting. In due time, new tributaries of oral Torah called *gemarah* ("completion," "learning tradition") in Aramaic and *talmud* ("learning") in Hebrew gushed forth from academies in Galilee and in Babylonia.

Decades of *gemarah* expansion became a virtual reservoir of oral Torah, and the need arose to legitimate the process by editing inconsistencies, curtailing new interpretations, and showing coherent linkage between *gemarah* and Mishnah. In addition, the abrupt Roman closure of Galileean schools of learning in the mid-fourth century and the exile of Jewish communities from Babylonia hastened the pace of selection and collation. The informed result was the creation of two Talmuds, each named after the place of redaction: Yerushalmi (a product of the land of Israel, not Jerusalem, as the name would suggest), circa 400 C.E., and Bavli (Babylonia), circa 500 C.E.

The Talmuds share the same Mishnah (for the most part), but their *gemarah* are written in different dialects of Aramaic (Yerushalmi in Western Aramaic, with a considerable mixture of Greek words; Bavli in Eastern Aramaic, with many Hebrew loan words). They differ in length (Bavli is about twice the length of Yerushalmi), style, syntax, and methodological principles. Their diverse emphasis and *halakhot* may be explained by their places of composition. For example, the Yerushalmi, serving Palestinian Jewry, has *gemarah* for all tractates dealing with agriculture in the Order *Zeraim*, but this is lacking in the Bavli, a product of diaspora *amoraim* (Aramaic for "interpreters" of the Mishnah). Similarly, the Bavli records that the fourth century Amora, Mar Samuel of Nehardea, laid down the principle *Dina deMalkhuta Dina*, which holds that, in civil matters, the law of the land (Jews were a minority in Babylonia) is as binding on Jews as are the commandments of the written Torah.

A dwindling Jewish community in Eretz Israel, stunted in its growth in oral Torah, and a growing diaspora Jewry, which drew succor and moral support from the Babylonian sages, combined to make the Bavli the Talmud of authority during the past 1,500 years of Jewish life and learning, and conceivably for the future as well. For all practical purposes, the Yerushalmi has become a closed book; its many obscure passages have become the objects of antiquarian research. The reclamation of the Temple Mount by the Israelis in the Six Day War (June, 1967), however, has renewed interest in the Yerushalmi by groups of religious nationalists, who believe that the Talmud of the land of Israel holds the key for the rebuilding of the Third Temple and proper worship therein.

Temple building and its complementary idea, Israel's messiah, however, were conceived by the framers of the Talmud in an ahistorical framework. The main purpose of the oral Torah is to emphasize the holiness of everyday acts and thoughts, which are the way to achieve individual and group happiness and survival. The Talmud successfully preserved the teachings of earlier generations so that later generations could continue them. Its directive "Go forth and study!" is heard to this day.   *—Zev Garber*

See also Jewish ethics; Torah.

BIBLIOGRAPHY
Danby, Herbert, ed. *The Mishnah.* Oxford: Clarendon Press, 1933.

Maccoby, Hyam. *Early Rabbinic Writings.* New York: Cambridge University Press, 1988.

Montefiore, Claude G., and Herbert M. Loewe, eds. *A Rabbinic Anthology.* New York: Meridian Books, 1960.

Neusner, Jacob. *Judaism: The Classical Statement: The Evidence of the Bavli.* Chicago: University of Chicago Press, 1986.

_____. *Judaism: The Evidence of the Mishnah.* Chicago: University of Chicago Press, 1981.

_____. *Judaism in Society: The Evidence of the Yerushalmi.* Chicago: University of Chicago Press, 1983.

Urbach, Efraim E. *The Sages: Their Concepts and Beliefs.* Jerusalem: Magnes Press, Hebrew University, 1975.

Taoist ethics

TYPE OF ETHICS: Classical history

DATE: Sixth to fourth century B.C.E.

ASSOCIATED WITH: Chinese classics *Tao Te Ching* and *Chuang Tzu*

DEFINITION: A theory of ethics that rejects conventional moral codes in favor of a natural, simple, spontaneous life

SIGNIFICANCE: Provided insightful thought concerning the value of simplicity and spontaneity; functioned as a major rival to Confucianism in Chinese mentality; strongly influenced the ethics of Zen Buddhism and neo-Confucianism

Taoism is one of the great classical philosophies of China. It is named after its central concept, *Tao* (pronounced *Dao*), which literally means "path" in Chinese. The philosophy is mainly represented by the books of Lao Tzu (the author of *Tao Te Ching*) and Chuang Chou (the author of *Chuang Tzu*).

Morality Indicates the Decline of the Tao. Taoists use the concept Tao to name both the way of the natural world of reality and the proper way of life, including the way of government and the way of the right social order. To the Taoist, the best way of life is to live in harmony with nature. It is a life of simplicity and spontaneity. According to the Taoists, this is how ancient people used to live. As skill and conventional knowledge developed, however, people came to have more and more desires; the increase of desires led to conflicts among people and conflicts between humans and their natural environment, which made life more difficult. Morality was introduced to cope with the problems, but morality does not remove the causes of these problems; it creates new problems because it imposes rules on people, thus making them constrained and mentally crippled. Morality should therefore be cast away in favor of a better solution. Thus, Lao Tzu wrote:

The influence of Taoist ethics is still strong in the Chinese martial arts. (Asian American Studies Library, University of California, Berkeley)

Banish wisdom, discard knowledge,
And the people will be benefitted a hundredfold.
Banish kindness, discard morality,
And the people will be dutiful and compassionate.
Banish skill, discard profit,
And thieves and robbers will disappear.
As these three touch the externals and are inadequate,
The people have need of what they can depend upon:
To see the simplicity,
To embrace one's uncarved nature,
To cast off selfishness,
And to have few desires.

Superior *Te* and Inferior *Te*. In saying "discard morality," the Taoist is not encouraging immoral acts. As Chuang Chou puts it, it is better for fish to live in water and be able to forget about each other than to be on a dry road and have to moisten each other with their spit. The *Te* (virtue) of helping each other with spit is inferior to the *Te* of living in accordance with the Tao. Taoist ethics contains teachings that resemble those of other normative ethics. For example, from the *Tao Te Ching*: "In dealing with others, be gentle and kind. In speech, be true. In ruling, get peace. In business, be capable. In action, watch the timing." "I am good to people who are good. I am also good to people who are not good. Virtue is goodness. I have faith in people who are faithful. I also have faith in people who are not faithful. Virtue is faithfulness." Here, however, virtue (*Te*) is not to be understood as moral virtue. The Taoist uses *Te* in the sense of the power or proper function of something. Thus, for example, mercy is considered virtue, because it brings courage, strength, and victory.

The Tao of Going Forward Is Like Retreat. "The superior *Te* let go of (the inferior, moral) *Te*, and therefore has (the superior) *Te*." Taoism values freedom, but freedom is to be achieved by having no "self" (desires and expectations) rather than by fighting against restrictions. "Only if you do not fight, no one can fight against you." "This is known as the virtue of not striving." Taoism values happiness, but "the highest happiness has no happiness." It does not come from active searching for happiness. Taoism values true wisdom, but true wisdom does not mean the wisdom of obtaining profits. It is the wisdom of seeing the value of simplicity and spontaneity. To the Taoist, a truly mature person is like a little child who has few desires and less knowledge. Such a person is simple-minded and even looks like a fool, because great knowledge is like ignorance. The Taoist teaches being calm, soft, female-like, desireless, nonaggressive, and content. The Taoist likes the image of water: It is soft, yet there is nothing it cannot penetrate.

The Ethics of Religious Taoism. Philosophic Taoism (*Tao chia*) is the origin of, yet must not be confused with, religious Taoism (*Tao chiao*). Religious Taoism turned respect for nature into the worship of numerous deities, such as the gods of wealth, war, and longevity. It turned the Te of living a simple and spontaneous life into the principles of serenity and calmness in therapeutic techniques and martial arts that could be used to achieve personal advantages (mainly immortality). Misfortunes were no longer considered the result of having excessive desires, but instead were considered mainly the result of magic trespasses.

—Peimin Ni

See also Chuang Chou; Lao Tzu.

BIBLIOGRAPHY

Chan, Wing-tsit. *A Source Book in Chinese Philosophy*. Princeton, N.J.: Princeton University Press, 1963.

Chuang Tzu. *Basic Writings*. Translated by Burton Watson. New York: Columbia University Press, 1964.

Fung Yu-lan. *A History of Chinese Philosophy*. Vol. 1. Translated by Derk Bodde. Princeton, N.J.: Princeton University Press, 1953.

Graham, Angus C. *Disputers of the Tao*. La Salle, Ill.: Open Court, 1989.

Lao Tzu. *Tao Te Ching*. Translated by Gia-Fu Feng and Jane English. New York: Vintage Books, 1972.

_____. *The Way and Its Power: A Study of Tao Te Ching and Its Place in Chinese Thought*. Edited and translated by Arthur Waley. New York: Grove Press, 1958.

Welch, Holmes. *The Parting of the Way: Lao Tzu and the Taoist Movement*. Boston: Beacon Press, 1957.

Technology

TYPE OF ETHICS: Scientific ethics

DATE: Twentieth century to present

ASSOCIATED WITH: Mid-twentieth century critics of technology and the debate of autonomy versus mastery

DEFINITION: An emerging discipline that assesses both the process of technology and its moral consequences on the individual and on the human race

SIGNIFICANCE: Involves a reconsideration of personal and social values to ensure the wise use of technology and to prevent dehumanization and environmental destruction

Through technology, humans have developed the means to transcend certain physical and mental limitations of their bodies. In the process, they have modified materials and their environment to better satisfy their needs and wants. Technological change has, however, resulted in an expanded range of choices and new ethical dilemmas that necessitate a reconsideration of personal and social values. Ethical analysis of technology involves reviewing whether the social and personal impact, economic costs, environmental damage, and potential dangers associated with technology are worth its benefits. Are humans still in control of technology or have they become enslaved by it? Such analysis is used in combination with scientific knowledge to formulate goals and policies to help ensure the responsible development and utilization of technology.

History. Despite its profound influences on humanity and the environment, technology has seldom been a subject of ethical inquiry. Philosophical concerns about technological impact on humans were voiced by William F. Ogburn, Leslie White, Lewis Mumford, and C. P. Snow from 1920 to 1959, but their writings had relatively little impact on the widely held view that science and technology were value-neutral. The use of the atomic bomb during World War II raised the level of consciousness of responsibility among scientists. Not until the 1960's, however, did a combination of continuing military applications of technology, biomedical advances, and environmental issues begin to alter society's affection for technology. Philosophers of the technological age (for example, Herbert Marcuse, Jacques Ellul, Victor Ferkiss, and Jacob Bronowski) emerged and began to formulate the foundations of a new ethic. A review of how the cultural context of science and technology has changed with time is useful in understanding why technology eventually came under the scrutiny of ethical analysis during the second half of the twentieth century.

Although technology is often thought of as the application of scientific knowledge, it actually preceded science. Humankind's first use of tools and the development of agriculture were early forms of technology. The word "technology" originates from the Greek *technè*, which means "art," "craft," or "skill." In contrast, science, in ancient times, was equated with the search for truth and understanding of the world and of human life. Greek philosophers such as Plato and Aristotle were the first to formulate ideas about matter, although they never experimentally tested their ideas. Their discourse focused on determining what was real and unique about humans relative to other forms of matter.

A relationship between science and technology began in the Middle Ages with the practice of alchemy—a sort of mystical chemistry practiced by people with an interest in human health and the quality of life. Alchemists prepared elixirs in efforts to remedy ailments as well as to confer immortality. It was Francis Bacon (1561-1626), however, who first perpetuated the belief that knowledge obtained through science could be utilized to enrich human life through new inventions.

Bacon, who was concerned about a lack of progress in science, sought ways in which the human mind might be opened to the full image of the world. He lived in an age when people first used instruments to collect information about nature and the universe but also considered the influence of the stars upon their destinies and believed in witchcraft. As an alternative, Bacon outlined what was to become the modern scientific method—a process characterized by induction, experiment, and the empirical study of data.

In the next hundred years, René Descartes, Thomas Hobbes, Robert Boyle, and Sir Isaac Newton further contributed to the philosophical basis of the scientific revolution. Science was viewed as one of humanity's noblest enterprises and one of the best means for gaining an understanding of nature.

Of relevance to ethics was the fact that this new image of science differed from previous philosophical thought on at least two major points. Classical ethics assumed that there were limits on humanity's power over natural phenomena; nature and the future were controlled by fate, chance, or some divine power. According to Bacon, however, the power obtained through knowledge would enable humans to control nature and their own destiny. Also, scientific knowledge was considered objective and tangible. Scientific judgments could be tested by observation of facts and logical analysis; one could provide clear evidence of truth. In contrast, moral judgments were seen as subjective, abstract, and incapable of being empirically tested. Ethical analysis provided information only about the attitudes of the persons involved.

Bacon could not have fully imagined the extent to which his predictions would come true as a result of technological innovations beginning with the Industrial Revolution. By the mid-twentieth century, numerous dreaded diseases had been virtually eliminated with the discovery of antibiotics and vaccines; fertilizers, pesticides, and scientific animal breeding had increased and enriched the world's food supply; new materials such as plastics and fibers had brought new products into homes; industrial automation had increased leisure time; advances in transportation and communications had linked remote regions of the world; and humanity had begun to look toward outer space as a new frontier.

The public was content to leave the details of scientific concepts to the experts, having something of a blind acceptance of science and technology. Science was practiced by an elite group working in what have been called "ivory towers." Technology, the practical result of this work, was the means to improve the quality of life for the "average person."

During this same period, however, specific events contributed to changing attitudes. The development of the assembly line in 1913 was initially hailed as a means of providing affordable products for everyone. During the Great Depression, however, the assembly line was blamed for the loss of jobs. Despite this development, mechanization propagated as the industrial robot and other forms of automation were introduced. Philosophers questioned whether the machine was an amplifier of human power that challenged human productive abilities or something that placed humans into a new serfdom. After World War II, some scientists began to challenge policies that were related to military applications of technology. In the 1950's and 1960's, they protested nuclear weapons testing, the antiballistic missile, and

military research being done within university settings.

Despite a move in the United States to isolate scientific research from political control, the opposite situation occurred. Scientists and engineers were consulted by the government for advice on technology—especially that related to atomic energy. Federal government involvement in science expanded during the 1950's and early 1960's, with the formation of funding agencies such as the National Science Foundation and the National Institutes of Health.

Changing economic and political situations in the 1960's, however, led to decreased federal appropriations for research. There was a new emphasis on accountability; scientists were expected to be productive and research was expected to lead to practical applications. Phrases such as "applied science" and "publish or perish" became popular, further diminishing the distinction between science and technology. The increased involvement of government in research and technology and the increased dependence of science on public funding severely challenged the previously held ideal that these were ethically neutral areas. Value judgments, social attitudes, and political and economic pressures clearly played a major role in structuring science and technology.

In the 1960's, people such as Rachel Carson pointed out that science and technology had the potential to destroy the world, not only through warfare but also by irreversibly damaging the environment. This development led to an overall increased social awareness of environmental hazards resulting from some technology. The public began to question whether technology was good after all.

Several books emerged during the 1960's and 1970's in which the authors questioned the value of technology. The evils of technology were often emphasized, and it was pointed out that technology had altered the image of humankind. New methods of analysis emerged; one example was Norbert Wiener's notion of cybernetics, which was introduced in 1965 as the science of communication and control processes in both animate and inanimate systems. This process stressed goals and feedback and became a basis for some ethical analyses of technology. Science fiction writers portrayed the horrors of technology gone awry, and Alvin Toffler's *Future Shock* (1970) detailed the impact of technological change on the human psyche.

Since the 1970's, private institutes such as the Hastings Center in New York and government advisory groups such as the Office of Technology Assessment and the National Academy of Sciences have initiated discussions and studies of ethical issues in technology. They emphasize the personal and social impact and regulation of technology and ways in which the public can become better informed about technology. International gatherings of scientists, most notably the meeting on recombinant DNA technology held at Asilomar, California, in 1975, focused on ethical dilemmas related to the safe application of new and controversial technology in scientific research, industry, and agriculture.

Public concern about science and technology persisted into the 1990's; nuclear energy, resource availability, biomedical technologies, genetic engineering, animal welfare, the value of "big science" (space exploration, strategic defense initiatives, superconductors, the Human Genome Project, and so forth), and the economic and environmental impact of technology were among the main topics of concern. Ethical dilemmas related to the distribution of wealth and technological knowledge became a major focus of foreign policy.

Ethical Principles. Traditional ethics were anthropocentric, and the fundamental nature of the human entity was presumed to be constant. Classical theories such as Immanuel Kant's theory on the universalizability of moral judgments focused on similarities between kinds of situations and people. Questions of good or evil actions toward fellow humans were confined to the foreseeable future and to individuals to whom a person was either related or was close in the sense of time or physical location. Actions toward nonhuman objects were considered to be outside the realm of ethical consideration.

Modern technology has altered these premises of classical ethics by changing the nature and the realm of human actions. The image of humanity has changed and may be changed even further through genetic engineering. Individualism and uniqueness, rather than similarities, are valued; society is pluralistic. Innovations in communication and transportation have altered perceptions of time and space. Humans must think globally in terms of their actions, since they can affect not only living relatives and neighbors but also unknown people living thousands of miles away or someone who might be born several generations later. Nature is critically vulnerable to technological intervention, and the realm of moral consideration is being expanded to include nonhuman living organisms, or even all components of the planet.

Contemporary ethics, which emerged in the twentieth century, is usually divided into three components. Through descriptive ethics, one seeks an accurate, objective account of moral behavior or beliefs. Metaethics involves examining the meanings and uses of moral terms such as "good" or "right" and studying moral reasoning and foundations for moral judgments. In normative ethics, moral arguments about what types of conduct are right or wrong, or good or bad, are analyzed. Normative ethics is also concerned with how human beings might best lead their lives and which states of affairs ought to be furthered in society. It is this latter branch of contemporary ethics on which discussions about technology focus.

The fundamental ethical question of whether technology is good or evil is frequently debated. Goodness is, however, a function of either a personal or a societal set of values, and there is no absolute set of standards from either classical or contemporary ethics that can be used in this area. Such analysis is further complicated by divided views as to whether technology is mechanical or autonomous (organic).

In the mechanical view, or instrumental theory, technology is seen as a tool with which to accomplish a humanly defined goal. As such, it has instrumental value depending on its usefulness to humans, and ethical judgments can only be made regarding the goals for which the tools are used. Humans are responsible for the use of technology, which can be misused. In the autonomous view, or substantive theory, technology has a life of its own and may no longer even be under human control. Technology is viewed as an end rather than a means; thus, it has intrinsic value. Ethical concerns center on whether to control technology and on the moral impact of technology.

If technological change is considered inevitable, attempts are made to evaluate its outcomes. This has been difficult, since society cannot agree on what ends should be served or how conflicting values should be prioritized. There is a general consensus that technology should be regulated, but the development of public policy has been hampered by the unanswered question of who should decide what the moral boundaries for technology should be. Values of freedom (respect for autonomy) and of individual choice conflict with ideas on what is right for society as a whole (the utilitarian perspective). It is typical of Western philosophy that there is conflict between self-interest and profit on one side and the sense of obligation for the common good on the other.

In applying ethics to technology, a series of unanswered questions remain. What are the foundations of an ethic that is applicable to this new technological age? How should new moral principles be devised? How should the new image or images of humans be defined in a technological age? How can the survival of humanity, which many people claim is permanently threatened by automation, computers, and genetic engineering, be ensured? How does a pluralistic society reach a consensus regarding values and priorities?

Ethical Issues. Most ethical considerations of technology are issue- or case-oriented (applied ethics). Such assessments draw on traditional ethical theory and principles when possible, but analysis also relies on scientific evidence as well as on psychological, political, economic, and historical factors.

The New Ethics. Humans have never before dealt with the types of ethical implications to which technology has given birth. For example, gene therapy, an application of genetic engineering, became possible in the 1980's, resulting in several new ethical questions related to medicine. Now that such genetic manipulation has become a reality, humans should determine acceptable limits for this technology. Should humans genetically modify themselves or other animals? Are scientists tinkering with evolution and natural selection? The U.S. Supreme Court decision in *Diamond v. Chakrabarty* (June 16, 1980) ruled that oil-eating bacteria produced by genetic engineering were living inventions and thus were patentable. This decision has sparked ethical debate over whether life forms should be engineered, much less patented.

New technology raises questions of priorities, especially when resources are limited. Should ending world hunger be a higher priority than having humans walk on Mars? Proponents argue that technology stimulates human intellect, national prestige, and pride. Of what value are these? When a nation has a large national debt, how much technology is needed for security (whether to serve as a deterrent or for defense)? What would be the social price of not using technology?

Ethical dilemmas also arise as side-effects of technology. Innovations in agriculture enhanced the world's food supply, but now overpopulation threatens the planet. Should birth control (via technological products) be mandated? Should technologically advanced countries continue to use resources obtained from less-developed countries? If so, what constitutes a fair compensation?

Technology is blamed for the depletion of many natural resources. Can limited resources be shared or conserved? If technology cannot provide alternatives to scarce resources, what valued material goods and comforts would humans be willing to sacrifice? What alternative energy sources are acceptable substitutes when traditional ones are depleted?

David Hume stated that a system of justice was necessary because of human passions, selfishness, and limits of resources. Ethical discussions of technology often refer to the tragedy of commons. The commons are those provisions of the earth that humans must share; the tragedy is that human nature compels people continually to increase their well-being—often at the expense of fellow humans. Can a spirit of cooperation prevail if competition is instinctual?

Most countries realize that their welfare is dependent in part on scientific and technological capacity. In the past, the poor (including those in technological countries) have benefited least from technology. How is it possible to distribute justly the benefits of technology? Should everyone enjoy some equitable level of quality of life before further technological advances are permitted?

Countries may be obligated to share not only the benefits of technology but also certain kinds of knowledge, such as that related to the eradication of disease. For poor countries, the information may be useless unless financial assistance for implementation is also provided. Who becomes responsible for such financial support? Other technical information, such as that linked to national security, may require protection. Who decides which information is to be shared?

Other new ethical questions relate to responsibilities toward future generations and the environment. What impact will continued technological development have on the future of humanity and Earth's ecosystem? Are these even within the realm of human responsibility?

Has Technology Altered Humans? An early ethical concern about technology was whether it was a threat to the dignity of humans; were they becoming slaves to the machine without realizing it? Some people argue that the machine has freed humans from demoralizing and tedious physical labor, allowing them to more fully develop their intellectual capacities.

Computers and artificial intelligence are now blamed for diminished communication skills and a loss of imagination. Are impersonal interactions and loss of privacy worth the ability to augment intellectual power? Good or bad, the world has become highly dependent on communications networks and computers.

Through technology, scientists have revealed the "secret of life" (DNA structure), and it is theoretically possible to modify humans through genetic engineering. Scientists are identifying the chemical reactions that are responsible for learning, memory, and the perceptions of pleasure and pain. What impact does such knowledge have on human beings and their spirituality? What will humans do with this knowledge?

Individual value systems are influenced by a person's experiences and environment. One's sense of self and decision-making abilities are, in turn, determined by these values. What happens to human values when the factors that influence them are in constant flux? Values are known to change more slowly than the reality of human experience; what sort of crisis does this present?

That the rate of technological change is increasing is well documented, as is the explosion of knowledge in the world. Humans are confronted with more choices than ever. With shifting values and no set of common societal values, how can decisions be made?

Responsibility for Technological Decisions. If technological change is inevitable, consideration must be given to how it should be controlled and assessed and how progress should be defined. Is continued evidence of technological progress a sufficient measure of the healthful state of our culture? Is it possible to identify common values and consider objectives for technology that different cultures within a society can accept? The responsible use of technology can be directed through wise public policy making. Ironically, modern decision making is dependent on the collection and analysis of data and the use of technological devices for this process. Technology is used to assess and make decisions about technology. Where does ethical analysis fit into the process?

The increased social consciousness of the risks associated with technology and the need for public policy has led to a new dilemma. Scientific and technological information has expanded at such a staggering rate that even highly trained experts have difficulty keeping up with developments in their own specialized areas. The public is typically scientifically illiterate. How then, in a democratic society, can citizens participate in wise decision making relative to technology?

If the public is to play a role in the future of technology, what responsibility do people have to educate themselves, to gain some scientific and technological knowledge? How does the public gain access to the relevant information?

What are the obligations of scientists and technologists in disseminating complex information to the public?

Technological Risk. Technology provides numerous benefits to society, but it also entails risk. One particular problem is that not all potential dangers resulting from technology can be foreseen, since predictive knowledge falls behind the technical knowledge and humankind's power to act. On what basis, then, are choices about technology made?

Risk-benefit analysis (a utilitarian approach) is not relevant in all cases. Choices must be made regarding things that humans have not yet experienced. In addition, perceptions of the nature, magnitude, and acceptability of the risk differ tremendously among people. How should people address risk in a way that accommodates the perceptions and values of those who bear it? What is an acceptable level of risk?

What is the obligation of scientists to use their expertise to call public attention to the dangers of new technology? How do scientists and technologists balance loyalties to their employers, their profession, and the public in calling attention to potential risks arising from their work?

Even when intelligent decisions are made, errors can occur. Who becomes responsible for undesirable consequences of technology? The unpredictable nature of humans and the complexity of political and economic factors make it impossible to foresee all consequences. How can people know the truth about the future conditions of humankind and the earth? How can people know what might possibly be at stake? How important does trust become when regulating the power that humankind obtains through technology?

—Diane W. Husic

See also Artificial intelligence; Atom bomb; Computer crime; Computer technology; Manhattan Project; Research, industrial; Science, ethics of; *Silent Spring*; Union of Concerned Scientists; Virtual reality.

BIBLIOGRAPHY

Ballard, Edward Goodwin. *Man and Technology: Toward the Measurement of a Culture.* Pittsburgh: Duquesne University Press, 1978. Provides an in-depth analysis of the nature of self, interactions between humans and technology, and ways in which to measure the quality of people and their machines. A very readable book.

Burke, John G., and Marshall C. Eakin, eds. *Technology and Change.* San Francisco: Boyd & Fraser, 1979. An anthology of essays dealing with ethics, attitudes toward technology, and policy issues. Includes classic excerpts from philosophers of the technological age.

Burkhardt, Jeffrey. "On the Ethics of Technological Change: The Case of bST." In *Technology in Society* 14, no. 2 (1992): 221-243. Includes a discussion of the basic ethical concepts applied to technological change. Illustrates the specific example of bovine somatotropin, a growth hormone that can be genetically engineered and given to cows to increase milk production. This journal, like *Science, Technology, and Human Values* and *Bulletin of Science, Technology, and Society*, frequently contains articles related to applied ethics.

Jonas, Hans. *The Imperative of Responsibility: In Search of an Ethics for the Technological Age.* Chicago: University of Chicago Press, 1984. Although this volume is not easy to read, the author provides an excellent presentation of ethical principles and theories relevant to technology and responsibility.

Ophuls, William, and A. Stephen Boyan, Jr. *Ecology and the Politics of Scarcity Revisited: The Unraveling of the American Dream.* New York: W. H. Freeman, 1992. A broad look at the interweavings of ethics, science, and politics as they are used in analyzing technology. Although the book is case-study oriented, the authors make frequent references to classical philosophers and illustrate how their philosophies are relevant to modern technological issues.

Teich, Albert H., ed. *Technology and Man's Future.* 3d ed. New York: St. Martin's Press, 1981. Contains a series of articles that examine the impact of technology on society and values, the assessment and control of technology, and the assumptions underlying mainstream technology.

Watkins, Bruce O., and Roy Meador. *Technology and Human Values: Collision and Solution.* Ann Arbor, Mich.: Ann Arbor Science, 1977. Cowritten by an engineer and a science writer, this concise book presents several ethical arguments for and against technology. The authors critically analyze each side of the debate, providing a very balanced perspective.

Teleological ethics

TYPE OF ETHICS: Theory of ethics

DATE: Fourth century B.C.E. to present

ASSOCIATED WITH: Utilitarianism, ethical egoism, and other goal-based or consequentialist ethical theories

DEFINITION: Theories that give a central place to goals and ends in determining the moral quality of conduct and character

SIGNIFICANCE: One of the two major types of theories of ethics; the other is deontological ethics

The term "teleological" is derived in part from the Greek word *telos*, which means end or goal. Teleological ethics refers to ethical theories that base the rightness of actions or the moral value of character traits on the ends or goals that they promote or bring about. A teleological perspective was typical in ancient and medieval ethical thought. Its classic expression is found in Aristotle's *Nicomachean Ethics*, particularly in the opening lines of chapter 2 of book 1: "Now if there is an end which as moral agents we seek for its own sake, and which is the cause of our seeking all the other ends . . . it is clear that this must be the good, that is the absolutely good. May we not then argue from this that a knowledge of the good is a great advantage to us in the conduct of our lives?" Aristotle, like most ancient and medieval thinkers, used ends and goals to justify virtues and other character traits as well as actions. Until the recent revival of virtue-based ethics, most modern teleological ethical theorists were concerned with theories of obligation; that is, of right and wrong action.

The English philosopher C. D. Broad, writing in the early part of the twentieth century, was the first to use the term "teleological" more narrowly to refer to theories of obligation. According to Broad, "Teleological theories hold that the rightness or wrongness of an action is always determined by its tendency to produce certain consequences which are intrinsically good or bad." In Broad's classification scheme, which has become standard, teleological theories are contrasted with deontological theories. The latter judge at least some actions to be right in certain circumstances, regardless of what their consequences might be. Leading deontological ethical theorists include Immanuel Kant, W. D. Ross, and John Rawls. No standard or standards of right action are agreed on by all deontologists; instead, what is common to such theorists is a denial of the teleologists' claim that the goodness of consequences is the sole right-making feature of actions or rules of action. For example, Ross insisted that some acts, such as keeping a promise, are right even if doing something else would result in a slight gain in the value of the total consequences. Ross's criticism is of a familiar type directed specifically at the aspect of teleological theories that is sometimes referred to as their "consequentialism"; that is, their requirement that right actions are those having the best consequences. The English philosopher G. E. M. Anscombe first used the term "consequentialism" in a 1958 paper to classify moral theories of obligation. She objected to such theories because of their moral laxity, in that they justified violating rules if the consequences of observing the rules were sufficiently bad.

Another way of expressing the contrast between teleological theories and deontological theories is that suggested by William Frankena and John Rawls. This approach begins with the idea that the two basic moral concepts are the right (the rightness or obligatoriness of actions) and the good (the intrinsic goodness or value of things or states of affairs). Teleological theories give priority to the good over the right in that they define the good independently of the right and then define the right as that which maximizes the good. It is possible to identify what is good or has value independent of any idea of what is right. By contrast, deontological theories define the right independently of what is good, thus allowing that a right action may not necessarily maximize the good.

Looked at this way, one of the questions that teleological theories must address is: "What is good in itself, or has intrinsic value?" The theory of value that is adopted by a teleologist may judge a single kind of thing, such as pleasure, to be good, or it may hold a plurality of things to be good. Jeremy Bentham, the famous English utilitarian, was a defender of the former view, called "hedonism," while the early twentieth century English philosopher G. E. Moore subscribed to the latter, pluralist view. Another conception of value is a "perfectionist" one, according to which some

ideal of human excellence is seen as valuable and worthy of pursuit. Aristotle maintained that the human good consisted of the active exercise of the distinctively human faculty of reason.

Teleological theories also provide different answers to the question of whose good it is that should be promoted. Egoistic theories contend that the relevant good is the good of the agent, the person acting, while universalistic theories hold that agents must consider the good of all those who are affected by an action. The best-known of all teleological theories is the universalistic one: utilitarianism. Developed by Jeremy Bentham in the early nineteenth century, utilitarianism has been one of the dominant ethical theories and social philosophies in the English-speaking world. Classical utilitarians such as Bentham, John Stuart Mill, and Henry Sidgwick were hedonistic utilitarians who asserted that actions, policies, and institutions are to be judged on the basis of the amount of pleasure (as opposed to pain) they produce, considering all those affected. Other utilitarians have departed from the classical view in several ways: Some "ideal" utilitarians, such as G. E. Moore, took the position that things other than pleasure were intrinsically good, while other "rule-utilitarians" stated that rules, not actions, should be judged on the basis of goodness of consequences. While utilitarianism in its various forms remains an important system of moral thought, its once dominant position has been eclipsed in the late twentieth century by other types of teleological theories—especially by deontological theories, which have regarded utilitarianism as being open to the charge of insufficiently respecting the value of individuals and allowing too easily the sacrifice of one individual for the greater good of others. —*Mario Morelli*

See also Consequentialism; Deontological ethics; Egoism; Utilitarianism.

BIBLIOGRAPHY

Aristotle. *The Nicomachean Ethics.* Translated by W. David Ross. New York: Oxford University Press, 1980.

Broad, C. D. *Five Types of Ethical Theory.* London: Routledge & Kegan Paul, 1930.

Frankena, William. *Ethics.* Englewood Cliffs, N.J.: Prentice-Hall, 1963.

Mill, John Stuart. *Utilitarianism.* Edited by Samuel Gorovitz. New York: Bobbs-Merrill, 1971.

Rawls, John. *A Theory of Justice.* Cambridge, Mass.: Belknap Press of Harvard University Press, 1971.

Ross, W. D. *The Right and the Good.* Oxford: Clarendon Press, 1930.

Temperance

TYPE OF ETHICS: Personal and social ethics

DATE: 1800 to present

DEFINITION: In a general sense, temperance is the quality of moderation and self-restraint; in a specific sense, it is the practice of not drinking alcohol

SIGNIFICANCE: Temperance serves to provide restraint that guards against self-indulgence; prohibition was a failure because it was an attempt to impose temperance from without, when in fact it must come from within

The term "temperance" is used to refer to moderation in all activities, especially those of eating and drinking. Aristotle advised that "moderation in all things is a virtue." Temperance can also refer to the practice of not drinking alcohol at all, and that is how the term will be used in this essay.

In the United States, the Prohibition Era lasted from 1920 to 1933. The violence of the underworld gangs that supplied illegal liquor and the wild activities of the men and women who defied the law and drank at illegal bars called "speak-easies" earned the decade the nickname "the Roaring Twenties."

Early Prohibition Efforts. In the early 1800's, the temperance movement began to urge Americans to avoid alcoholic beverages of all kinds. The term "temperance" as it related to this movement was a misnomer, since the members of the movement actually advocated total abstinence from alcohol. The supporters of the temperance movement were known as the "drys." They believed that alcohol endangered people's physical and mental health as well as encouraged crime and violent behavior. In 1846, Maine passed the first prohibition law, and by 1860, twelve more states had adopted prohibition. Throughout the Civil War the issue of temperance was ignored. The Women's Temperance Union and the Anti-Saloon League picked up the battle from 1875 to 1900. In 1872, the Prohibition Party was formed, and it nominated candidates for president and vice-president. The zenith of the party's influence was reached in 1892, when it won 271,000 votes for its candidates. After that time, the party steadily lost ground.

By 1900, prohibitionists had lost so much ground that only five states still had prohibition laws. As a result, advocates of prohibition decided to make it a national issue, and they succeeded. In 1913, Congress passed the Webb-Kenyon Act, which forbade the shipment of alcohol from a wet to a dry state. During World War I, prohibitionists argued that using grain needed to feed soldiers to make alcohol was unpatriotic. A strong puritan strain in American culture served to support the prohibitionists' claims. In 1917, the Eighteenth Amendment to the U.S. Constitution was passed, which prohibited the import, manufacture, sale, and transport of alcoholic beverages. Congress provided enforcement power by passing the Volstead Act, which penalized violations of the Eighteenth Amendment.

Life Without Legal Alcohol. Hundreds of thousands of U.S. citizens disobeyed prohibition laws, claiming that they had the right to live by their own standards. They believed that the laws were unjust and violated their rights, and were thus to be ignored.

As has been the case with illegal drugs, the demand for alcohol drove prices up, and the huge profits that could be realized attracted organized crime to the alcohol trade. The most notorious profiteer was Al Capone of Chicago, who made millions of dollars selling beer and liquor. The wealth and power of the crime gangs made it possible for them to bribe police and government officials. Those who could not be bribed were threatened or even killed. Gangs controlled the governments of several U.S. cities and were difficult to oppose.

Gangs not only made alcohol themselves but also found ways of controlling alcohol made by others. It was legal to make "near beer" by brewing beer of regular strength and then weakening it. Bootleggers simply bought or stole the strong beer and sold it to the public at exorbitant prices. The government allowed industries to make alcohol for medical purposes and research. Again, the gangs either bought or stole this alcohol and converted it into beverages. The gangs also imported alcohol illegally by smuggling it into the United States from Europe, the Caribbean, or Canada. In 1924, this smuggled alcohol had an estimated worth of $40 million, a huge sum of money at the time.

The outlawing of alcohol brought about great changes in American life. In the same way that some people produce drugs in home laboratories today, some people during the Prohibition Era made liquor at home, calling it by such names as "white lightning" and "bathtub gin." Such liquor was strong and of poor quality, but it served to get people drunk. Prior to 1920, few women drank alcohol in public, but both sexes drank together in the crowded speakeasies. This made it acceptable for women to drink in bars with men. Many people carried liquor in concealed hip flasks or in purses. Because the government never had enough agents to enforce prohibition, people found it easy and relatively safe to defy the prohibition laws. Since these laws were so unpopular with the public, many officers were reluctant to enforce them.

Legalization. Many Americans concluded that prohibition created more harm than good. It criminalized behavior that people were determined to pursue, thereby increasing crime and making a mockery of law enforcement. In addition, the 1929 stock market crash led to the Great Depression, and Americans had problems larger than alcohol consumption to worry about. Many people wanted to end prohibition, and they argued that legalizing alcohol would help the government recover from the Depression by allowing it to tax the manufacture and sale of liquor. Consequently, in 1933, the Twenty-first Amendment to the Constitution repealed the Eighteenth Amendment and ended the Prohibition Era. In 1966, the state of Mississippi became the last state to repeal its prohibition laws. Less than 2 percent of Americans live in areas that have prohibition laws. In most cases, such laws reflect the influence of churches, not prohibition or temperance groups.

By 1976, only 16,000 Americans voted for the Prohibition Party's candidate for president. In 1977, the Prohibition Party changed its name to the National Statesman Party. It works closely with the American Council on Alcohol Problems and the Anti-Saloon League. Since the repeal of the

One view of the temperance movement. (Library of Congress)

Eighteenth Amendment, such groups have been relatively ineffective in promoting the prohibition of intoxicants.

Conclusions. For most people, the subjects of intemperance, alcoholism, and addiction conjure up mental images of individuals who are out of control, who are belligerent, argumentative, and violent. Many Americans associate substance abuse with spouse and child battering, frequent fighting, crimes against persons and property, and fetal alcohol syndrome. Once it was believed that alcoholics and other addicts could overcome their addiction through heroic acts of will. Nowadays, however, many physicians believe that a predisposition to alcoholism may be hereditary. Today, society views addiction as a disease rather than as a character flaw. Medical models have replaced social models, and addicts are now seen as people who need twelve-step programs and support groups such as Alcoholics Anonymous, and medical treatment rather than criticism, incarceration, and condemnation. Addiction is a complex issue that involves physiology as much as morality. —*Dallas Browne*

See also Christian ethics; Morality; Self-control; Virtue.

BIBLIOGRAPHY

Aristotle. *Nicomachean Ethics*. Translated by Martin Ostwald. New York: Macmillan, 1986.

Carter, Paul. *Another Part of the Twenties*. New York: Columbia University Press, 1977.

Cashman, Sean. *Prohibition: The Lie of the Land*. New York: Free Press, 1981.

Clark, Norman. *Deliver Us from Evil: An Interpretation of American Prohibition*. New York: W. W. Norton, 1976.

Thornton, Mark. *The Economics of Prohibition*. Salt Lake City: University of Utah Press, 1991.

Wallace, James. *Virtue and Vices*. Ithaca, N.Y.: Cornell University Press, 1978.

Temptation

TYPE OF ETHICS: Personal and social ethics

DATE: Coined 1340

DEFINITION: Feeling inclined to act in some unethical or questionable way, or trying to make another person feel so inclined

SIGNIFICANCE: Many people argue that the central task of ethics is to lead people to resist temptation to perform unethical acts

Oscar Wilde's witty descriptions of temptation help to demonstrate the tremendous power of temptation over the human will. He said: "I can resist everything except temptation" and "The only way to get rid of a temptation is to yield to it."

Temptation is closely linked conceptually to the phenomenon of the weakness of human will. Paradoxically, although stories of weakness of will are found as early as in the biblical story of Adam and Eve, many philosophers have insisted that weakness of will does not exist. Weakness of will is usually defined as action that is contrary to one's better judgment. Some people have argued that it is impossible for a rational agent to act voluntarily while simultaneously re-

alizing that his or her best judgment condemns that very act. Others have argued that since the acts in question are voluntary, the best evidence of what an agent wanted most strongly is the act itself. Therefore, they argue, it is impossible to know that weakness of will has been involved in any observed act.

Such arguments fly in the face of ordinary human experience, but the plausibility of the arguments does make the temptation involved in weakness of will seem paradoxical. Some thinkers (such as Sterling Harwood and David McNaughton) suggest that weakness of will should be defined not as action contrary to one's better judgment but as a disposition to act against one's higher-order desires. Lower-order desires include hunger, thirst, and lust. Higher-order desires are desires that have to do with desires such as a dieter's desire for a suppressed appetite. This is one possible way to resolve the paradox, for it allows one to define the temptation in weakness of will as an unusually strong disposition to do the tempting act, whether or not one in fact succumbs to the temptation by performing that act. This conception of temptation seems to fit the hard data of human experience, which show (Fingarette, 1988) that even those who are professionally treated for alcoholism indulge their craving for drink about as often as those who are left untreated, and also show that smoking tobacco is roughly as addictive as heroin. —*Sterling Harwood*

See also Self-control; Will.

BIBLIOGRAPHY

Fingarette, Herbert. *Heavy Drinking: The Myth of Alcoholism as a Disease*. Berkeley: University of California Press, 1988.

Harwood, Sterling. "For An Amoral, Dispositional Account of Weakness of Will." *Auslegung* 18 (1992): 27-38.

Kruschwitz, Robert B., and Robert C. Roberts, eds. *The Virtues: Contemporary Essays on Moral Character*. Belmont, Calif.: Wadsworth, 1987.

McNaughton, David. *Moral Vision: An Introduction to Ethics*. New York: Basil Blackwell, 1988.

Mele, Alfred R. *Irrationality: An Essay on Akrasia, Self-deception, and Self-control*. New York: Oxford University Press, 1987.

Mortimore, Geoffrey. *Weakness of Will*. New York: St. Martin's Press, 1971.

Plato. *Protagoras*. Translated by C. C. W. Taylor. Oxford, England: Clarendon Press, 1976.

Ten Commandments

TYPE OF ETHICS: Religious ethics

DATE: Proclaimed c. 1290 B.C.E.

ASSOCIATED WITH: Moses, ancient Israel, and the Judeo-Christian tradition

DEFINITION: Ten absolute ethical principles; according to the Hebrew Bible, they were given by divine revelation to Moses at Mount Sinai

SIGNIFICANCE: The Ten Commandments summarize the

moral demands of Judaism and Christianity; also adopted by Islam, they remain the ethical foundation of half the world's population

The Ten Commandments, or the Decalogue, appear twice in the Hebrew Bible (Christianity's Old Testament)—in Exodus 20:1-17 and Deuteronomy 5:6-21—with only slight variations in the wording.

Origins and Context. The Decalogue was given within the context of Israel's deliverance from slavery and selection as the chosen nation of God. "I am the Lord thy God, which have brought thee out of the land of Egypt, out of the house of bondage" (Exod. 20:2; all biblical quotations in this article are from the King James Version). Following God's liberation of the Israelites from Egyptian servitude, God entered into a covenant relationship with them at Mount Sinai. The Lord (Yahweh) pledged to protect the Israelites and make them prosper, and they in turn vowed to honor Yahweh as their sovereign and to obey his commandments. The motivation for obedience was to be gratitude for the gracious actions of the Lord.

Contents. The first four commandments deal with humanity's duties toward God; the concern of the last six is people's obligations to others. Biblical scholars generally agree that the commandments were stated originally in a concise fashion, probably as follows:

1. *"Thou shalt have no other gods before me."* Allegiance to other deities is prohibited. Unlike Israel's polytheistic neighbors, the nation of Yahweh must worship only the Lord. The first commandment establishes a practical—and perhaps a theoretical—monotheism, thus making Israel's faith unparalleled in the ancient world.

2. *"Thou shalt not make unto thee any graven image."* A graven image is an idol, a visual representation of Yahweh for use in worship. Imageless worship was another unique feature of Israel's religion. The second commandment implies that Yahweh is so awesome that nothing in the physical world can represent him.

3. *"Thou shalt not take the name of the Lord thy God in vain."* The term "in vain" means for an empty or worthless purpose. Forbidden here are frivolous, deceitful, and manipulative uses of the divine name. Examples of irreverent speech include profanity, magical incantations, and false oath-taking in Yahweh's name. In the Bible, the Lord's name is equivalent to his very person; therefore, the misuse of the divine name makes God himself to appear empty and worthless.

4. *"Remember the sabbath day, to keep it holy."* The sabbath is the seventh day, or Saturday. To keep it holy means to observe it as a day that is different from the other days on which ordinary work is performed. Labor must cease on the sabbath; the sabbath is to be a day of rest and worship. Interestingly, this is the only commandment that is not repeated in the New Testament for Christians to observe. In commemoration of Christ's resurrection, the early church changed the day of worship from Saturday to Sunday.

5. *"Honour thy father and thy mother."* Children of any age are to respect, obey, and cherish their parents. The admonition refers especially to supporting helpless elderly parents. They are not to be abandoned when they can no longer provide for themselves. Old and weak dependents must be cared for by their adult children.

6. *"Thou shalt not kill."* Prohibited here is the unlawful killing of a human being; that is, murder. The Old Testament condemns murder as particularly heinous because it assaults the very image of God in man, a feature that makes human life unique and especially precious in the eyes of the Lord. The sixth commandment does not, however, outlaw warfare, capital punishment, or the killing of animals. All these are clearly sanctioned elsewhere in the Hebrew Bible.

7. *"Thou shalt not commit adultery."* This injunction aims to protect the sanctity of marriage and also reflects the importance that Yahweh places upon faithfulness in relationships. By implication, the seventh commandment relates to the entire range of sexual ethics. Adultery is singled out as the most pernicious sexual sin because it involves infidelity to a covenanted partner and undermines the stability of the home.

8. *"Thou shalt not steal."* Theft covers all attempts to deprive an individual of his livelihood and property. In the Old Testament, property is viewed as a gift of God and necessary for earning a living. Hence, the eighth commandment implicitly upholds a person's right to own property. By extension, it also attempts to preserve human freedom, since the worst kind of theft involves kidnapping a human being and selling him or her into slavery.

9. *"Thou shalt not bear false witness against thy neighbour."* To bear false witness is to lie. This commandment primarily forbids perjured testimony in a lawsuit involving a neighbor. Its application may be broadened, however, to cover any false statements that could damage a neighbor's reputation. This prohibition underscores the value that Yahweh places upon truthfulness.

10. *"Thou shalt not covet any thing that is thy neighbour's."* The word "covet" refers to strong desire or craving for personal gain at the expense of one's neighbor. An Israelite was to be content with what the Lord provided. This final precept takes Yahweh's absolute ethical standard into an individual's inner life. By implication, all evil desires are prohibited. The tenth commandment reflects the teaching of the Hebrew prophets and Jesus that the source of almost all sinful behavior lies within the human heart.

—Ronald W. Long

See also Christian ethics; Divine command theory; Ethical monotheism; God; Jesus; Jewish ethics; Moses; Religion; Revelation; Sin.

BIBLIOGRAPHY

Barclay, William. *The Ten Commandments for Today.* Grand Rapids, Mich.: Wm. B. Eerdmans, 1977.

Craigie, Peter C. "The Ten Commandments." In *Evangelical Dictionary of Theology*, edited by Walter A. Elwell.

Grand Rapids, Mich.: Baker Book House, 1984.

Harrelson, Walter J. "Ten Commandments." In *The Interpreter's Dictionary of the Bible*. Vol. 4. New York: Abingdon Press, 1962.

Kaiser, Walter C., Jr. *Toward Old Testament Ethics*. Grand Rapids, Mich.: Zondervan, 1983.

Kaye, Bruce, and Gordon Wenham, eds. *Law, Morality, and the Bible*. Downers Grove, Ill.: Inter-Varsity Press, 1978.

Sampey, John R. "The Ten Commandments." In *The International Standard Bible Encyclopaedia*, edited by Geoffrey W. Bromiley. Rev. ed. 4 vols. Grand Rapids, Mich.: Wm. B. Eerdmans, 1979-1988.

Theory and practice

TYPE OF ETHICS: Beliefs and practices

DATE: Late nineteenth century to present

DEFINITION: The application of theories developed through the use of the scientific method to practical problems in various areas

SIGNIFICANCE: When knowledge generated by a theory is translated into technology and put to practical use, it becomes part of other human purposes and therefore can be used or misused

According to George F. Kneller (1978), science is the pursuit of knowledge about nature. Science seeks facts; that is, events or states or things that happen. In the service of that pursuit, science has developed a powerful method of inquiry that distinguishes it from other areas of inquiry, such as philosophy, literature, art, or religion. Kneller divides this scientific method into four successive steps: observation, classification, laws, and theories.

Observations. By using their senses and sophisticated instruments, scientists make systematic and detailed observations about the universe, which yield facts.

Classification. As facts accumulate, classification serves the purpose of discovering commonalities among a set of facts and thus making general statements about those facts. For example, Dmitry Mendeleyev proposed in 1869 that if the various elements were arranged in order of atomic weight, they would arrange themselves into groups that have similar chemical properties.

Laws. Classification leads to laws, which are statements that describe regularities. Laws summarize a number of separate facts and enable predictions to be made. Isaac Newton's second law of thermodynamics (which states that heat cannot by itself pass from a colder to a hotter body) and Galileo's law of freely falling bodies are well-known examples of laws.

Theories. Theories stand at the pinnacle of the scientific method and are the most important part of the process. Theories organize and explain a number of known laws and also generate new predictions that can be tested. If the predictions are confirmed, new knowledge is obtained and the process begins anew. If the predictions are not confirmed, the theory will have to be revised or abandoned. Einstein's theory of relativity is a famous example of a theory that has stood the test of time and has greatly advanced our understanding of the universe.

Theory into Practice: Ethical Considerations. Ethical issues enter into theory construction and testing in two ways. First, the knowledge that the theory generates by incorporating bodies of existing knowledge and by uncovering new knowledge can often be translated into technology and put into practice at a practical level. Technological applicability means that scientific knowledge is not necessarily neutral. It becomes part of other human purposes and endeavors and therefore can be used or misused. As long as scientific knowledge could not be applied via technology, unhampered search for the truth was a laudable goal. In the late nineteenth century, however, technology began to make significant use of scientific theory. The chemical industry, for example, used scientific theory to alter natural substances and, eventually, to synthesize new ones.

The great English scientist Francis Bacon said in the seventeenth century that science must be responsible to humanity. Since knowledge confers power, knowledge that benefits humankind should be sought. Science thus has a specific ethical, moral, and social responsibility to regulate itself that is more important than professional responsibility, personal ambition, or the advancement of science. Kneller argues that scientists should not conduct research that may pose a danger to the public or may have technological uses that are potentially more harmful than useful.

Other scientists, however, have argued that the goal of science and theory building is to seek knowledge. It is axiomatic that knowledge is good, and it is the responsibility of the scientist to seek that knowledge without concern for its consequences or practical applications. As long as ethical guidelines are followed in conducting research and constructing and testing theories, then the pursuit of knowledge should be unregulated. A potential for abuse exists in any area of research. Through vigilance and external review boards, however, this problem can be managed.

The second issue is that, in the words of Norwood Russell Hanson (1958) "observations are infused with the concept; they are loaded with the theories." That is, theories define a phenomenon in a particular way and influence the perception of that phenomenon. For example, as Hanson observed, Tycho Brahe and Johann Kepler may both have seen the same sun, but each saw it differently. Brahe's geocentric theory caused him to see the sun rise over the earth. Kepler's heliocentric theory led him to see the earth's horizon fall away from the sun.

To take but one example of these two issues, the reigning theory of human sexuality has for a long time stated that sexual orientation is learned. Furthermore, it was held that heterosexuality was the normal sexual orientation and homosexuality was abnormal. Because homosexuality was both abnormal and learned, homosexuality was to be treated and undone. Male and female homosexuals were subjected to a variety of therapies that were derived from this particular theory of sexuality, some that were appalling. None proved to be in the least effective, but many were continued because of the theoretical orientation regarding homosexuality.

Recent research suggests that sexuality is strongly influenced by biology. Sexuality is therefore not learned and normally occurs as heterosexual and homosexual. Rather than reassuring the homosexual community, this new theory has aroused considerable anxiety in some quarters. Such knowledge could be used by homophobic individuals or agencies to once again seek a "cure" for homosexuality, this time through chemical or surgical treatment of the nervous system.

Scientists working in this field, however, reply that the potential for abuse exists in every area of biomedical research. To discontinue such work would stop efforts to construct a theory of sexual orientation, thus simultaneously forgoing the acqusition of new knowledge and the benefits that such a theory could provide.

The ethical issues involved in putting theories into practice thus constitute a dilemma. Two ethically defensible responses can be justified. The most common approach seems to be to let research and theory building progress in as unfettered a way as possible, while scrutinizing them carefully and watching for potential abuses. *—Laurence Miller*

See also Bioethics; Science, ethics of; Technology.

BIBLIOGRAPHY

Burr, Chandler. "Homosexuality and Biology." *The Atlantic* 271 (March, 1993): 47-65.

Hanson, Norwood Russell. *Patterns of Discovery.* Cambridge, England: Cambridge University Press, 1958.

Kneller, George F. *Science as a Human Endeavor.* New York: Columbia University Press, 1978.

Matson, Floyd W. *The Broken Image.* New York: George Braziller, 1964.

Strewer, Nancy S. *Theory as Practice.* Chicago: University of Chicago Press, 1992.

Therapist-patient relationship

TYPE OF ETHICS: Psychological ethics

DATE: Began c. 1892

ASSOCIATED WITH: Psychoanalysis, cognitive and behavior therapies, and existential therapies

DEFINITION: The relationship between a psychotherapist and a patient

SIGNIFICANCE: Psychotherapeutic services require high standards of competence, integrity, professional responsibility, and respect for the dignity and concern for the welfare of others; all these qualities involve adherence to ethical standards

Therapy Techniques. There are often disagreements among therapists regarding what constitutes the best treatment for a given individual. At last count, almost three hundred different forms of treatment had been described for the alleviation of emotional disorders. Samuel Perry, Allen Frances, and John Clarkin group treatments into three broad categories in their book *A DSM-III Casebook of Differential Therapeutics* (1985). These categories are exploratory, directive, and experiential. Exploratory techniques include psychoanalysis and treatments that are not as lengthy or as frequent as psychoanalysis but utilize at least some psychoanalytic techniques. Proponents of these psychodynamic treatments argue that their treatments are useful for many patients and can be adapted to the requirements of individual patents better than can traditional psychoanalysis, which requires the patient to come to therapy four to five days a week.

Directive techniques include the use of principles derived from the study of how people learn and may utilize reward, punishment, advice giving, or other methods designed to change maladaptive behaviors. For example, some directive therapists argue that patients have learned misconceptions about themselves or others that must be unlearned. Other therapists attempt to reduce patient anxieties by gradually exposing them to frightening situations in order to reduce and eliminate the impact of the anxiety-provoking situation.

Experiential techniques utilize a different perspective. Advocates of these techniques emphasize the expression of feelings. They see little, if any, value in diagnosis or psychiatric classifications. They also object to the power differential found in most therapist-patient relationships. Instead, experiential therapy is viewed as an encounter between two equal individuals who care for each other as real people. Experiential therapists tend to focus on the present and believe that personal growth is an important aspect of therapy. Thus, it is not necessary to be emotionally disturbed to benefit from experiential treatment.

It should be pointed out that these descriptions are necessarily brief and are designed to give the reader an overview rather than a detailed understanding of techniques used in therapist-patient relationships. They are helpful, however, for providing a foundation for understanding some of the ethical issues involved in such relationships.

Informed Consent and Confidentiality. The American Psychological Association's "Ethical Principles and Code of Conduct" (1992) discusses a number of topics relevant to therapist-patient relationships. The code of conduct requires therapists to discuss with patients such topics as the nature and anticipated course of therapy, fees, and confidentiality. Thus, the beginning of a therapist-patient relationship involves the informed consent of the patient. Daniel R. Somberg, Gerald L. Stone, and Charles D. Claiborn (1993) suggest that this includes discussion of the potential risks of therapy, the length of treatment, the procedures to be used, alternatives to therapy, and the limits of confidentiality. Therapists need to be sure that the patient has given consent freely, and if the patient is unable to give consent legally (for example, if he or she is a young child), permission must be obtained from those who are able to give legal consent. Even with individuals who are not capable of giving informed consent, however, psychologists have an obligation to explain the proposed intervention and to seek cooperation and agreement. In addition, the therapist must take into account that person's best interest.

With regard to confidentiality, the limits of confidentiality must be discussed. In many jurisdictions, for example, there are limitations on confidentiality when treatment is done in a group or family setting. There may also be limitations on confidentiality whenever more than one therapist and one patient are present, as in marital therapy, for example. Disclosures of confidential information are not permitted without the consent of the individual unless permitted by law. Usually, disclosures are limited in order to obtain professional consultations and to provide needed professional services. In addition, disclosures can be made in order to protect a patient or others from harm. Such disclosures are discussed further under the duty to warn.

Duty to Warn. This requirement arose out of a suit brought by the parents of Tatiana Tarasoff around 1976. Tatiana had been killed by an individual who had been in treatment at the student health facility at the University of California at Berkeley. The patient had revealed to the therapist that he was extremely attached to Tatiana and that he planned to purchase a gun. The therapist, after consulting with colleagues, concluded that the patient was both mentally ill and dangerous and should be hospitalized. Police interviewed the patient and decided there was no need for hospitalization after the patient agreed not to contact Tatiana. The parents of Tatiana sued, and their attorney eventually came before the California Supreme Court, arguing that the treating therapist should have warned Tatiana Tarasoff or her family and that the patient should have been committed involuntarily to an inpatient facility. Initially, the court decided that not only did the therapist have a duty to warn because of the special relationship between therapist and patient but also that the police might be liable, since their questioning of the patient probably resulted in the patient's decision to terminate treatment.

In a later opinion, the same court broadened the duty of the therapist to protect others form dangerous actions of patients but no longer held the police liable. Since that time, a number of states have passed laws requiring therapists to breach confidentiality in the face of patient threats to harm others. Alan Stone, in his book *Law, Psychiatry, and Morality* (1984), argues that therapists are not effective in consistently evaluating the dangerousness of their patients. Nevertheless, he believes that when a therapist is convinced of the dangerousness of a patient, the special relationship between patient and therapist does justify the legal duty to protect both the patient and the public. Thus, therapists are called upon to balance the interests of society against the interests of patient-therapist relationship. —*Norman Abeles*

See also Institutionalization of patients; *Principles of*

Medical Ethics with Annotations Especially Applicable to Psychiatry; Professional ethics; Psychology.

BIBLIOGRAPHY
American Psychological Association. "Ethical Principles of Psychologists and Code of Conduct." *American Psychologist* 47 (December, 1992): 1597-1611.

Crits-Christoph, Paul, and Jacques P. Barber, eds. *Handbook of Short-Term Dynamic Psychotherapy*. New York: Basic Books, 1991.

Perry, Samuel, Allen Frances, and John A. Clarkin. *A DSM-III Casebook of Differential Therapeutics*. New York: Brunner/Mazel, 1985.

Somberg, Daniel R., Gerald L. Stone, Charles D. Claiborn. "Informed Consent: Therapists' Beliefs and Practices." *Professional Psychology: Research and Practice* 24 (May, 1993): 153-159.

Stone, Alan A. *Law, Psychiatry, and Morality*. Washington, D.C.: American Psychiatric Press, 1984.

Thomas Aquinas (1224 or 1225, Roccasecca, Italy— Mar. 7, 1274, Fossanova, Italy): Theologian

TYPE OF ETHICS: Medieval history

ACHIEVEMENTS: Author of *Summa theologica* (c. 1273; *Summa Theologica*, 1911-1921) and *Summa contra gentiles* (c. 1258-1264; *Summa Contra Gentiles*, 1923), among other works

SIGNIFICANCE: Synthesized Aristotle's philosophical ethics based on happiness and virtue with the Christian understanding of law, grace, and love of God

The moral life, for Thomas Aquinas, consists in each person achieving human fulfillment through freely chosen actions. Presupposed is a human nature with a given, determinate structure and a corresponding determinate fulfillment or perfection. Actions are morally good if they promote this fulfillment and bad if they hinder it. In this sense, Aquinas' ethics are teleological and eudaimonistic, but unlike classical utilitarianism, the end of good action is not simply pleasure, but the perfection of the human being. Being naturally social, persons cannot attain their perfection alone, but only in community. Consequently, although the ethical life is ordered to promote personal fulfillment, it is not individualistic. Every aspect of Aquinas' ethics (good action, virtue, law, and so forth) is understood in the light of achieving one's fulfillment.

Happiness and Beatitude. Aquinas recognized two levels of human fulfillment or happiness. First is the perfection of human nature simply on the natural level, which is the object of philosophical ethics. Second is the Christian understanding of human nature as raised by divine grace and destined to a supernatural end. Theological ethics treats the latter and was Aquinas' major concern. At both levels, happiness lies primarily in intellectual activity, that of knowing God. The natural end consists in knowing God by philosophical investigation, while the supernatural end consists in a direct vision of God, which is possible only after death.

Good and Evil Actions. Actions such as studying, educating, praying and temperate eating are good because they are intrinsic to true human fulfillment, while acts like murder, stealing, or adultery hinder it and therefore are evil. Besides choosing and performing a good act, a person must intend a good end; friendship in itself is good, but it would not be morally good if it were chosen for the sake of vanity or ambition. Morally good action requires a good act, the right circumstances, and a good intention.

Virtue and Vice. An integral part of Aquinas' ethics is his theory of virtue and vice. Both virtue and vice are "habits," steady inner dispositions inclining an agent to a certain mode of action. The virtue of courage inclines one to face dangers when reason judges that good action requires it; under the influence of the vice of cowardice, one would tend to commit evil action rather than face danger. Hence, all habitual tendencies toward perfective activities are virtues and their opposites are vices. There are many different moral virtues and vices corresponding to the many different spheres of moral action: the virtue of religion is a disposition to be properly related to God, liberality is the virtue of being generous with one's wealth, truthfulness concerns speaking the truth, and so on. The chief moral virtues are the four cardinal virtues: temperance, the right disposition toward pleasures (opposed vices: gluttony, drunkenness, sexual promiscuity); courage, the right disposition toward fearful dangers (opposed vices: cowardice, recklessness); justice, the disposition to respect the rights of others and to treat them fairly (opposed vice: injustice); and prudence, the disposition to deliberate well about moral action. Since all good action requires a good judgment about what should be done, every other virtue depends upon prudence. These moral virtues are acquired by repeatedly performing appropriate virtuous actions.

The theological virtues are infused by God and are dispositions toward actions directed to the supernatural end. By means of the three theological virtues, faith, hope, and charity (love), a person believes, hopes in, and loves God. These virtues, for Aquinas, are higher than the moral virtues, and among them charity is the highest. Ultimately, every virtuous action is done for the love of God and therefore depends upon the virtue of charity.

Moral Law. Moral law is a rational principle that directs actions toward their proper ends. Lacking animal instinct, free, rational, moral agents direct themselves toward an end according to a rational conception. This is supplied by the law, which commands good acts and prohibits bad acts. Since action always occurs in singular, concrete circumstances, however, law alone is an insufficient rule. Every particular action requires a prudential judgment as its proximate rule.

There are several kinds of law. First is the divine law, the explicit commands of God, such as the Ten Commandments or the Beatitudes, which direct persons to their supernatural end. Second is the natural law, consisting of general principles of right action that are discovered by reason, which reflects on human experience and learns over time what leads to fulfillment and what does not. Because human nature is determinate and is shared by all, the general principles of the natural law are valid for everyone and for all times. Finally, there are human positive laws, the civil laws enacted by society. These are part of the moral law in that they direct moral actions, especially those related to life in society. If, however, a civil law contradicts the natural law or the divine law, it is not a true law and has no binding force. All law, Aquinas said, is ultimately part of the eternal law, the ordering wisdom of God by which he governs the whole of creation. —*David M. Gallagher*

See also Aristotle; Christian ethics; *Summa Theologica*; Teleological ethics.

BIBLIOGRAPHY

Bourke, Vernon J. *Ethics: A Textbook in Moral Philosophy.* New York: Macmillan, 1966.

Klubertanz, George. *Habits and Virtues: A Philosophical Analysis.* New York: Appleton-Century-Crofts, 1965.

McInerny, Ralph. *Ethica Thomistica: The Moral Philosophy of Thomas Aquinas.* Washington, D.C.: Catholic University of America Press, 1982.

Pieper, Josef. *The Four Cardinal Virtues.* Notre Dame, Ind.: University of Notre Dame Press, 1966.

Simon, Yves. *The Tradition of Natural Law.* Edited by Vukan Kuic. New York: Fordham University Press, 1992.

Thomas Aquinas. *Summa Contra Gentiles.* Translated by Anton Pegis et al. 5 vols. Notre Dame, Ind.: University of Notre Dame Press, 1975.

_____. *Summa Theologica.* Translated by Fathers of the English Dominican Province. 5 vols. Westminster, Md.: Christian Classics, 1981.

Weisheipl, James. *Friar Thomas d'Aquino: His Life, Thought and Work.* Washington, D.C.: Catholic University of America Press, 1983.

Thoreau, Henry David (July 12, 1817, Concord, Mass.—May 6, 1862, Concord, Mass.): Writer and philosopher

TYPE OF ETHICS: Modern history

ACHIEVEMENTS: Author of "Resistance to Civil Government" (1849), *Walden: Or, Life in the Woods* (1854), "Slavery in Massachusetts" (1854), "A Plea for Captain John Brown" (1860), "Wild Apples" (1862), and "Life Without Principle" (1863)

SIGNIFICANCE: The most influential practitioner of New England Transcendentalism, Thoreau believed that the self-reliant person could, by using nature as a guide, live a moral and productive life without the excessive use of material goods

Whether the words of *Walden* and "Resistance to Civil Government" ("Civil Disobedience") or the actions on which they are based have had greater influence, it is clear that Thoreau's life refutes the notion that the Transcendentalists spent their time in the clouds rather than on earth. A skilled observer of nature as well as a citizen who spoke his mind on current ethical questions, Thoreau made the idealism of Transcendental philosophy a part of his daily life. At Walden Pond, he put into practice Ralph Waldo Emerson's advice to be self-reliant and self-directed. He built his own house, planted his own garden, and lived without a conventional job for more than two years quite contentedly and, as he goes into great detail to show, quite economically. He believed that to mire oneself in materialism and then to sacrifice one's principles for fear of losing those material things was to sink into evil. This point is established in "Resistance to Civil Government," in which Thoreau chas-

tises his fellow citizens for grumbling about the government's war in Mexico while continuing to pay the taxes that supported it. His own refusal to pay was based not only on his moral judgment of the war but also on the questionable ethicality of a private individual's being forced to support any activity of the larger society. In "Resistance" and other essays—"A Plea for Captain John Brown," "Slavery in Massachusetts," "Life Without Principle"—Thoreau chides his fellow citizens for the disparity between their actions and their principles.

See also Emerson, Ralph Waldo; Transcendentalism; *Walden.*

Henry David Thoreau (Library of Congress)

Tillich, Paul (Aug. 20, 1886, Starzeddel, Brandenburg, Germany—Oct. 22, 1965, Chicago, Ill.): Theologian

TYPE OF ETHICS: Modern history

ACHIEVEMENTS: Author of *Systematic Theology* (1951-1963), *Dynamics of Faith* (1956), and *The Protestant Era* (1948)

SIGNIFICANCE: One of the leading Christian theologians of the twentieth century, Tillich proposed a new conduit of Christian systematic theology that helped to facilitate essential dialogue between Protestant and Catholic Christianity, and enabled the Christian faith to relate to other world religions and to the world of secularism

Tillich was a professor of theology and philosophy at a number of German universities before he was expelled by the Nazi regime for his ties with the Religious Socialists and his vehement anti-Nazi stand. He emigrated to the United States in 1933 and taught at Union Theological Seminary in New York (1933-1955), Harvard University (1955-1962), and the University of Chicago (1962-1965).

Tillich's major teaching in *Dynamics of Faith* (1957), the classic introduction to his thought, is the significance of faith as ultimate concern, which means that the unpredictable, and often forceful, penetration of the abstract ("ultimate") into one's consciousness elicits a concrete response ("concern"), making the revelationary manageable in one's own *Weltanschauung* (worldview). The experience of ultimate concern is a continual process of unconditional correlation of opposite but related elements (subject/object, particular/universal; law/freedom, and so forth), which Tillich views as the essential-existential ground of being, intellectually and emotionally. A true ultimacy, such as God-centrism, is worthy of human commitment, and such an ultimacy is reached by means of an assemblage of rites and symbols that point to and participate in but never replace the sacredness of an ultimate concern. A false ultimacy is an ultimate commitment to that which is not ultimate (idolatry) and opens the way to the demonic. Thus, for Tillich, the absolutization of Jesus, in opposition to orthodox Christology, is a form of heresy (Christolatry).

Though Tillich's categories of thought are not easily classified, this quintessential liberal Protestant thinker always wrote in the spirit of *Ecclesia Semper Reformanda*, as his complete works and supplementary volumes (Stuttgart, 1959-1981) show clearly. In his last public address (at the Divinity School of the University of Chicago, on October 12, 1965), "The Significance of the History of Religions for the Systematic Theologian" (*The Future of Religions*, 1966), he expressed limitations both in the supersessionist view of traditional Christian theology and the contemporary views of neo-orthodoxy and the "God is dead" movement, and he proposed that future Christian systematic theology needs to consider the basic insights of other world religions. He taught as he lived—"on the boundary."

See also Christian ethics.

Tolerance

TYPE OF ETHICS: Personal and social ethics

DATE: Eighteenth century to present

DEFINITION: Sympathy or indulgence for beliefs or practices that differ from or conflict with one's own

SIGNIFICANCE: Over the past two centuries, the centuries-old habit of actively opposing convictions and practices contrary to those regarded as right has been increasingly challenged

History of Concept. The history of tolerance is shorter than are those of most of the concepts pertaining to personal and social ethics that are included in this work. The word itself has a long history, deriving from Latin and Greek words meaning "to bear" or "to put up with," but for centuries it referred to circumstances of physical conditions. In the sense of putting up with practices regarded as contrary to one's own, the word is not found before 1765. Although the word "toleration" was used in this general sense two centuries earlier, that term invariably referred to civil or religious bodies that were regarded as authoritative and capable of restricting the exercise of nonconforming thought. To tolerate dissident views implies the power not to tolerate them. The idea of tolerance as a personal ethical principle or general social attitude has developed much more slowly.

The Paradox of Tolerance: Early Advocates. Why should one have any sympathy for beliefs or practices that one believes to be wrong or wrongheaded? Throughout most of human history, the right to differ, especially in religious matters, has simply been denied. A historical survey of human behavior in such matters might raise the question of whether powerful convictions and tolerance can ever coexist.

Michel de Montaigne was a man of remarkable tolerance for his time. He first published his *Essays* in 1580, and the title of one essay, "It Is Folly to Measure the True and the False by Our Own Capacity," suggests his disinclination to pass moral judgments. Although Montaigne did not preach nonconformity, the whole tenor of his work is individualistic and nonjudgmental. A corollary of the Renaissance spirit of individualism exemplified by Montaigne is respect for others as worthwhile individuals in their own right.

An early advocate of religious tolerance was the Jewish philosopher Moses Mendelssohn (grandfather of the composer Felix Mendelssohn-Bartholdy), whose friendship with Gotthold Ephraim Lessing, a noted writer of German Protestant origin, in the mid-eighteenth century shocked most of his coreligionists. He went on to defy Mosaic law by denouncing excommunication—certainly ironic behavior for a man named Moses. He saw excommunication as the attempt to control thought, which in his view neither church nor state had the right to do.

In the nineteenth century, Harriet Taylor identified the idea of conformity as "the root of all intolerance." John Stuart Mill, much influenced by Taylor (who became his wife), made individuality the subject of the third chapter of his *On Liberty* (1859). "In proportion to the development of his individuality, each person becomes more valuable to himself, and is therefore capable of being more valuable to others," he writes. Thus, Mill would allow the widest latitude in people's ideas and behavior as long as they do no unjustifiable harm to others. One should not oppress the individuality of another, Mill argues, although one has a right to exercise one's own individuality in opposition in various ways; for example, by avoiding the society of, or cautioning others against, a person whose views one regards as wrong or dangerous.

Organized Religion and Tolerance. Liberal Protestant thought has tended to minimize doctrine or at least find room for considerable differences within the confines of doctrine. Like orthodox Judaism, Roman Catholicism was slower to countenance deviation from official doctrine, but since the Second Vatican Council (1962-1965) Catholicism too has shown more of an inclination to tolerate views formerly regarded as dangerous. The ecumenical movement among Christians of various denominations has subsequently fostered tolerance as a positive and spiritually enriching value.

Tolerance as a Modern Challenge. Increasingly in the modern world, liberal ethical thought has condemned the attitude of intolerance on the part of those who do not or cannot actively interfere with nonconforming individualists, the point being that people can hardly be expected to act tolerantly in the social sphere if they harbor intolerant attitudes. Certainly, many people without the disposition or capacity to interfere significantly with others' liberties express their intolerance in small ways that nevertheless work hardships on nonconformists and contribute to a general milieu of intolerance.

The limits of tolerance are often manifest in the public arena. For example, abortion, though morally acceptable to millions of people, remains for other millions a horrid evil not to be tolerated. It is unlikely that the fierce opposition to abortion clinics throughout the United States can be explained merely by the objection to the expenditure of public funds on a practice believed by its opponents to be evil. Abortion is, to many of its opponents, intolerable in itself despite its acceptance by others whose ethical standards generally appear to be above reproach. Some normally law-abiding people are quite willing to break the law to prevent what they regard as the murder of innocents; others are appalled by what they regard as the blatant infringement on a woman's right not to bear unwanted children who in many cases would impose a burden on society.

It may well be that the soundest ethical basis for tolerance is to be found not in organized religion but in humanistic respect for others and their right to express themselves freely so long as their expression does not harm other individuals or society. Because it is so difficult to achieve a consensus regarding what constitutes serious and unjustifiable harm, however, the ethical value of tolerance remains controversial.

—*Robert P. Ellis*

See also Civil rights; Freedom of expression; Mill, John Stuart; Private vs. public morality.

BIBLIOGRAPHY
Katz, Jacob. *Exclusiveness and Tolerance*. Westport, Conn.: Greenwood Press, 1980.

Mendus, Susan, ed. *Justifying Toleration: Conceptual and Historical Perspectives*. Cambridge, England: Cambridge University Press, 1988.

Mill, John Stuart. *On Liberty*. Edited by Gertrude Himmelfarb. New York: Penguin Books, 1982.

Newman, Jay. *Foundations of Religious Tolerance*. Toronto: University of Toronto Press, 1982.

Wolff, R. P., et al. *A Critique of Pure Tolerance*. Boston: Beacon Press, 1969.

Torah

TYPE OF ETHICS: Religious ethics
DATE: From the biblical period
DEFINITION: The Pentateuch (the five books of Moses: Genesis, Exodus, Leviticus, Numbers, and Deuteronomy); in a broader sense, the Hebrew Scriptures; in common religious usage, the unity of total revelation, the written Scriptures, and related authoritative rabbinical commentary
SIGNIFICANCE: Torah is a system derived from contact between the human and the divine that instructs by means of narratives, aphorisms, laws, commandments, and statutes, providing rules of life for individuals, nature, and society; the goal provided by Torah is to achieve spiritual and temporal happiness in the full realization of the divine will

The Term. Torah is a feminine noun formation of the verbal root *yrh* ("to instruct") in its causative conjugational form; the root may be semantically related to the Arabic *rawa(y)* ("to hand down") or to the Akkadian *(w)aru* ("to guide"). The renderings of the biblical Hebrew word *torah* as *nomos* in the Greek Septuagint (first half of the third century B.C.E.) and as *lex* in the early Latin Bible translations have historically and theologically given rise to the misunderstanding that *torah* means legalism and that Torah means "Law." In essence, Torah is not supernatural revelation, religious dogma, or general self-evident propositions. It is the cumulative record of moral truths formed by the divine, and codified by humanity. In addition, modern Hebrew uses the word *torah* to designate the thinking system of a savant (for example, the *torah* of Plato, Maimonides, or Einstein) or a body of knowledge (the *torah* of mechanics).

Dual Torah. Various biblical verses point to the Pentateuch as Torah distinct from the rest of the Scriptures. The verse "Moses charged us with the Teaching (Torah) as the heritage of the congregation of Jacob" (Deut. 33:44) suggests the inalienable importance of Torah to Israel: It is to be transmitted from age to age, and this transmission has become the major factor for the unity of the Jewish people throughout their wanderings.

The rabbis of the Talmud kept the Torah alive and made its message relevant in different regions and times. This has been done by means of the rabbinic hermeneutic of a dual Torah that has been read into verses from the book of Exodus. Regarding God's words to Moses regarding the covenantal relationship between Himself and Israel, it is said in Exodus, "Write down (*ktav*) these words, for in accordance (*'al pi*; literally, 'by the mouth') with these words I have made a covenant with you and with Israel" (Exod.

will not be changed, and that there never will be any other Torah from the Creator, blessed be His Name." It is clear from Maimonides' philosophical magnum opus *The Guide for the Perplexed* (c. 1200) that the written Torah is not to be taken in a literal fashion. For example, Genesis 1:26a says, "And God said, Let us make man in our image, after our likeness." If Judaism expresses strict monotheism, then what is to be made of the plural cohortative "us" and the notion that humanity and God share a "likeness"? For Mai-

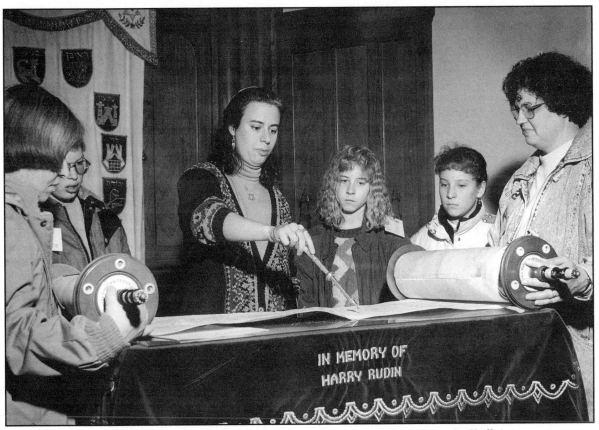

An Ashkenazic rabbi explains the Torah to Jewish schoolchildren. (James L. Shaffer)

34:27), and, "I will give you the stone tablets with the teachings (*torah*) and commandments which I have inscribed (*ktav-ti*) to instruct (by word of mouth) them" (Exod. 24:12). The sages saw the words "write," and "accordance" and "instruct" as the legitimate warrant for the written Torah (*Torah shehbiktav*) and the oral Torah (*Torah shehb'al peh*). In their view, the written Torah, the teaching of Moses, is eternal. The oral Torah is the application of the written Torah to forever changing historic situations, which continues to uncover new levels of depth and meaning and thus makes new facets of Judaism visible and meaningful in each generation.

The Process of Torah: Revelation and Reason. The ninth principle of the Creed of Maimonides (1134-1204) states, "I believe with perfect faith that this (written) Torah

monides, revelation teaches that God is incorporeal and ineffable, while reason imparts that humanity is finite, thus rending a nonliteral reading (that the plural is that of majesty, anthropomorphic language, figurative speech). Not only in narrative but also in legislation are revelation and reason the primary forces in understanding Torah. Take *lex talionis*, for example.

Three times the Pentateuch mentions the legislation of *lex talionis* (the law of retaliation, of an "eye for an eye"): regarding the penalty for causing a pregnant bystander to miscarry when two individuals fight (Exod. 21:23-25), the case of one who maims another (Lev. 24:19-20), and the punishment meted out to one who gives false testimony (Deut. 19:18-21).

Though the law of "measure for measure" existed in the ancient Near East and persists today in parts of the Muslim Middle East, there is little evidence that the Torah meant that this legislation should be fulfilled literally except in the case of willful murder. "Life for life" is taken literally in cases of homicidal intention, and fair compensation is appropriate when physical injuries are not fatal. Equitable monetary compensation is deemed appropriate by the oral Torah in the case of a pregnant woman whose unborn child's life is lost and when animal life is forfeited. Indeed, the written Torah casts aside all doubts regarding the intent of the biblical *lex talionis* injunction: "And he that kills a beast shall make it good; and he that kills a man shall be put to death" (Lev. 24:21).

Rejecting the literal application of *lex talionis* puts an end to the mean-spirited charge that Judaism is "strict justice." Instead, Judaism advocates remedial justice for the guilty and concern for the injured. The wisdom of *mamon tahat 'ayin*, the "value of an eye," is not arbitrary, but a principle that is central in any democratic system of torts. The modern Jew who carefully probes for the reasons behind the commandments inculcated by the Torah will see their importance not in faith alone but also in association with logic and practicality.

Nevertheless, the severe language of the written Torah's "eye for an eye" sends forth a strong reminder. There is no remuneration in the world that can properly compensate serious injury, death, or any act of serious victimization.

The Eternal Torah. The doctrine of the eternity of the Torah is implicit in verses that speak of individual teachings of the Torah in phrases such as the following: "A perpetual statute throughout your generations in all your (lands of) dwellings" (Lev. 3:17) and "throughout the ages as a covenant for all time" (Exod. 3:16). Biblical (Proverbs, in which Torah equals wisdom), Apocryphal (the wisdom of Ben Sira), and Aggadic (Genesis Rabbah) traditions speak of the preexistence of Torah in Heaven. Though the Talmud acknowledges the prerevelation existence of Torah in Heaven, which was later revealed to Moses at Sinai, it concentrates more on Torah's eternal values.

Jewish thinkers from the first century to the nineteenth century have proclaimed the Torah eternal, some in terms of metaphysics, others in terms of theology, and most in defense of Judaism against the political polemics of Christianity and Islam, which taught that aspects of Torah are temporal or have been superseded. In the first century, Philo Judaeus spoke metaphysically of the Torah as the word (*logos*) of God, the beginning of creation. In the tenth century, Saadia Gaon proclaimed that the Jews were unique only by virtue of Torah; if the Jewish nation will endure as long as the heaven and earth, then Torah must also be eternal. In the twelfth century, Maimonides extolled the perfection (eternity) of Torah, regarding which there is neither addition or deletion. After Maimonides, the issue of the eternity of the Torah became routine; the Torah's eternity became an undisputed article of belief. The schools of Kabbala, however, declared that the preexistent form of Torah is eternal but that the words and message of the Torah are recycled every 7,000 years.

In the nineteenth century, the *Wissenschaft des Judentums* (Scientific Study of Judaism) movement, inspired by the scholarship of biblical critics, presented a historical-critical approach to Torah study. As a result, the traditional concept of the eternity of the Torah became a non sequitur and the idea of the Torah as a human book prevailed. By the mid-twentieth century, however, responding to negative trends in higher literary criticism, which was affected by classical Christian bias and "higher" anti-Semitism, objective and critical studies by Jewish loyalists helped to reaffirm the Jewishness of the Bible's origins. No matter how a Jew views the nature of Torah—as a kind of "mythicizing history" or as a product of the people for the people or as written (inspired) by God—Torah as ultimate authority is an indisputable article of faith.

The Way of Torah: Three Paths. Whether the Torah is defined as the result of an exclusive encounter at Sinai or of an evolving journey from Sinai, this national treasure is traditionally understood by the response of *na'aseh ve-nishma'* ("We shall do and we shall hear [reason]"). Accordingly, the way of Torah presents three paths for the contemporary Jew:

1. One should believe that God's Torah given at Sinai is all knowledge. (*Na'aseh* alone.)

2. The Torah-at-Sinai tradition should be abandoned, and Torah should be explained in purely rationalist terms. Torah is made in the image of the Jewish people. (*Nishma'* alone.)

3. One should accept the existential position that God's teaching was shared at Sinai, face to face, with all of Israel, present and future. "Present" implies that God's revelation occurred and that Torah is the memory of this unusual theophany; "future" hints that Israel's dialogue with God is an ongoing process. This view holds that people know only a part of divine truth and that each generation seeks, makes distinctions, categorizes, and strives to discover more. (*Na'aseh ve-nishma'*.)

Na'aseh alone permits no ultimate questions; *nishma'* alone provides no ultimate answers. *Na'aseh* and *nishma'* together ask questions and attempt answers but leave many uncertainties unanswered. Yet uncertainty is truth in the making and the inevitable price for intellectual freedom.

—*Zev Garber*

See also Israel; Jewish ethics; Moses; Philo Judaeus; Talmud.

BIBLIOGRAPHY

Buber, Martin. *Moses: The Revelation and the Covenant.* New York: Harper, 1958.

Cassuto, Umberto. *The Documentary Hypothesis and the Composition of the Pentateuch.* Jerusalem: Magnes Press, Hebrew University, 1961.

Hertz, Joseph H., ed. *The Pentateuch and Haftorahs.* London: Soncino Press, 1952.

Heschel, Abraham Joshua. *Torah Min Hashamayim* [Theology of Ancient Judaism]. New York: Soncino Press, 1962.

Plaut, W. Gunther. *The Torah: A Modern Commentary.* New York: Union of American Hebrew Congregations, 1974.

Segal, Moses Hirsch. *The Pentateuch: Its Composition and Its Authorship and Other Biblical Studies.* Jerusalem: Magnes Press, Hebrew University, 1967.

Torture

TYPE OF ETHICS: Beliefs and practices

DATE: Until the Enlightenment, in the 1700's, torture was legally condoned in Western culture

ASSOCIATED WITH: Once openly sanctioned for forcing confessions, torture is now considered a covert, aberrant practice of rogue nations or sociopathic groups and individuals

DEFINITION: The deliberate, systematic inflicting of physical or mental pain, either as a means of coercing information or confession or as a form of punishment

SIGNIFICANCE: Framers of relevant ethical imperatives, such as judicial and penal codes, have been enjoined by human rights organizations to make torture illegal and to declare it a moral evil

The darker chapters in human history, including those of the modern era, have all involved torture. In fact, modern torture on a large scale, as practiced in Hitler's death camps and Stalin's gulags, has eclipsed even the horrors of the notorious Spanish Inquisition. Yet there are no places where torture is still legally sanctioned, and it is viewed as morally repugnant, if not universally, at least in more highly developed countries. That, however, has not always been the case.

Judicial Torture. In Europe after 1300, when the Roman canon law of evidence replaced ordeal as the basis for determining criminal guilt, legal torture became widespread. Ironically, the new law, in attempting to protect the accused against capricious justice, fostered judicial torture, because the death penalty, imposed for a variety of crimes, required "full proof" (the evidence of two eyewitnesses) or "half proof" (sufficient circumstantial evidence) plus a confession. Because many crimes were not witnessed, magistrates were empowered to torture suspects to exact confessions, and they had at their disposal the infamous devices that haunt even the modern imagination—thumb and leg screws, pressing weights, rack, iron maiden, and strappado.

Although barbaric, torture was allowed because almost all criminal offenses carried blood sanctions, from death and maiming to branding and whipping. Capital punishment, which was exacted for crimes as minor as burglary, was meted out through such gruesome means as hanging, drawing and quartering, burning at the stake, pressing, gibbeting, beheading, and impaling. Knowing what the accused faced, magistrates demanded that suspects bear witness against themselves, and they usually resorted to torture only when the suspects remained uncooperative. Torture was seldom employed in full-proof cases or when the penalties faced were less severe than execution, and its use for punishment was not widely condoned.

Abolishment of Legal Torture. The practice of judicial torture was gradually abandoned, partly because alternatives to death as punishment for serious criminal offenses made it less necessary. Transportation and indentured servitude, imprisonment, and conveyance to the galleys were options for judges in capital cases in which conviction was based on strong circumstantial evidence rather than incontrovertible proof. Furthermore, the validity of confessions exacted through torture had always been in doubt, and during the Enlightenment, circa 1750, that doubt was joined to the moral arguments promulgated against torture by such thinkers as Voltaire (1694-1778). By the end of the nineteenth century, legal torture had become an anomaly, and protections against it, as provided by the "cruel and unusual punishment" injunction of the Eighth Amendment to the U.S. Constitution, were almost universally in place.

Modern Torture. It is, however, one thing to abolish a practice on paper, to make it illegal, and another to curtail completely its practice. As late as 1984, when the United Nations adopted the Convention against Torture and Other Cruel, Inhuman, or Degrading Treatment or Punishment, dozens of nations, in violation of their own laws, were secretly sanctioning its use. In recent history, it has been a particularly invidious practice during war, despite Geneva Conference protocols, and during civil unrest and insurrection, when it has been used as an instrument of persecution and suppression, as in internally troubled states such as Chile, El Salvador, South Africa, Cambodia, and the former Yugoslavian state of Bosnia-Herzegovina.

It is unlikely that torture can ever be completely eradicated. It only takes two, persecutor and victim, to dance torture's grim dance, and the potential for torture exists in any interpersonal relationship in which one party exercises physical or psychological control over another, as in, for example, familial relationships between parent and child or husband and wife.

The crude instruments of the *ancien régime* are now museum pieces, but they have been replaced by such things as psychoactive "brain washing" drugs and electroshock, courtesy of modern science. The crude methods have not disappeared, even in the United States, as the burned, scarred, and starved bodies of abused children have testified.

Although organizations such as Amnesty International can bring before the United Nations evidence of the torture of citizens by governments, exposure of its practice under private circumstances—for example, within the family—has depended largely on the willingness of victims to complain. In the last few decades, victims have been more inclined to seek help and legal remedy, encouraged by civil rights legislation, counseling, and an awareness, fostered by media coverage of abuse, that their situation is not unique.

Tragically, tortured children are often too young to know that redress is even possible.

The belief that the modern era is more humane and more morally astute than were previous eras is partly illusory. Although modern efforts to rectify human abuse and cruelty may be unprecedented, extending even to animals, modern events have repeatedly revealed and psychological studies have often documented that the sadomasochistic impulses that lie behind torture frequently accompany such fundamental human feelings as frustration, rage, guilt, and shame. The best hope for ending torture lies in legal recourse made possible by public awareness and ethical vigilance.

—John W. Fiero

See also Abuse; Animal rights; Coercion; Cruelty; Holocaust; Oppression; Punishment; Voltaire.

BIBLIOGRAPHY

Amnesty International. *Report of an Amnesty International Mission to Israel and the Syrian Arab Republic to Investigate Allegations of Ill-treatment and Torture, 10-24 October 1974.* London: Amnesty International Publications, 1975.

_____. *Torture in the Eighties.* London: Amnesty International Publications, 1984.

Langbein, John H. *Torture and the Law of Proof: Europe and England in the Ancien Régime.* Chicago: University of Chicago Press, 1977.

Peters, Edward. *Torture.* New York: Blackwell Publishers, 1985.

Stover, Eric, and Elena O. Nightingale, eds. *The Breaking of Bodies and Minds.* New York: W. H. Freeman, 1985.

Tragedy

TYPE OF ETHICS: Theory of ethics

DATE: 500 B.C.E. to present

ASSOCIATED WITH: Aristotle, Plato, G. W. F. Hegel, Friedrich Nietzsche, Arthur Schopenhauer, and Miguel de Unamuno y Jugo

DEFINITION: A form of literary drama and a topic of philosophical investigation that involves the extremes of human behavior in the face of life's great misfortunes

SIGNIFICANCE: Both tragedy and ethics focus on the moral value of human conduct in the face of life's conflicts and extremities

The term "tragedy" has been used in at least two distinct senses. First, tragedy refers to a genre of literary and dramatic works originally developed in ancient Greece. Aristotle (384-322 B.C.E.) defined tragedy, in this first sense, as an imitation (a theatrical play) of an action by, typically, a noble person whose character is flawed by a single weakness (such as pride, or envy) that causes him to make an error in judgment resulting in his downfall. The hero moves from a state of ignorance to one of insight generally at the cost of personal misery. Aristotle believed the spectator of a tragic drama underwent a catharsis, or cleansing, of his own emotions. In the second sense, tragedy has been used to refer to a subject of philosophical theorizing

involving the meaning of tragic literature as well as the possible existence of tragic events in the world that must be philosophically reckoned with in any worldview. This article will focus on the latter meaning of tragedy, since therein lies the primary ethical import. It is unlikely, however, that the two senses can or should be completely disentangled, since presumably literature and drama often mirror something significant about human existence.

Plato (430-347 B.C.E.), unlike Aristotle, believed that there were several ethically undesirable consequences of Greek tragedy and drama. Plato condemned tragic poetry for making men too emotional. Tragic drama, Plato argued, implies that a good person may be undone by an accidental reversal of fortune. Tragedies thus teach the young that their well-being is contingent upon the whims and vagaries of appearance. For Plato, the world of appearance and consequently what generally passes for "tragedy" is ultimately unreal. Even one's physical death is tragic only as long as one is in ignorance. For example, Socrates, Plato's teacher, understood the immortality and superiority of the real; hence, he did not fear the hemlock poison that the Athenian town counsel required him to drink. What appeared to be a tragedy was in actuality a great victory for the good. Tragedies, however, encourage the audience to think that a hero can be undone by an accidental reversal of fortune. Consequently, for Plato, tragedies teach falsely and inspire fear of unrealities.

G. W. F. Hegel (1770-1831) held that, in the first sense noted above, Aristotle's definition of tragedy was definitive. In the second sense, however, tragedy is motivated by a conflict of two great moral forces, both justified and both embodying the good. For example, in the Greek play *Antigone,* one protagonist—Antigone—is motivated by justifiable family values to provide a proper burial for her brother, while King Creon is equally justified by public values to prevent her from doing so. The task of the tragic hero is to attain a "synthesis" in which the claims of each side are reconciled. Antigone and Creon are both right but not right enough. Consequently, their destruction is just and reveals the absolute rule of the divine principle. Hence, in Hegel, the ethical dilemma of tragedy consists in the conflict between two goods that can be resolved only through a higher synthesis of good. In one-sidedness, the tragic hero fails to comprehend this synthesis and is justifiably overruled and destroyed by the might of absolute justice.

Arthur Schopenhauer (1788-1860), taking a consistently pessimistic view of human life, argued that all existence is tragic. Quoting an ancient Greek source, he notes that the greatest thing that one could ever hope for was to have never been born. A quick death would be the next most desirable event. Thus, tragic art reveals the terrible side of life, which relentlessly destroys and annihilates anything that the human spirit might cherish. For Schopenhauer, tragedy teaches that the only resolution to the arbitrary cruelties of life is total renunciation of the will.

Friedrich Nietzsche (1844-1900), a student of Schopen-hauer's, believed that Greek tragedy answered a fundamental need of human life. Greek tragedy gave the Greeks the ability to face the horrors and arbitrariness of life and yet find a basis for self-affirmation. Nietzsche, while acknowledging the reality of human suffering, rejected the excessive rationalism of Plato and the excessive pessimism of Schopenhauer. In the two Greek gods Dionysus and Apollo, Nietzsche discovered two basic elements of human nature. Dionysus embodies excess, vitality, and passion, while Apollo represents reason, order, and balance. In the time of the ancient Greeks, the tragic art form accomplished a unification of these tendencies and enabled the Greek culture to grow strong and noble. In Nietzsche's later work, he showed that perception of the tragic realities of life could lead in two directions: to nihilism or to the superman. The superman is an individual who declares, "Joy is deeper than woe!" He affirms life and self in full light of the ambiguities and tragic qualities to which human flesh is heir. These elite and noble "Yea-Sayers" of Nietzsche represent his answer to the ethical challenge given by the tragic aspect of life.

In the latter half of the twentieth century, there has been general concern that the tragic sense of life has been lost, to the detriment of humanity's self-image. Tragedy has generally depicted a sometimes horrifying but heroic picture of the human condition. Although in tragedy there have been great "reversals of fortune," there has also been the implication that humanity has fallen from a great height. The twentieth century has not sustained a vision of human nature that is sufficient for great tragedy. For example, in Samuel Beckett's *Waiting for Godot* and Arthur Miller's *Death of a Salesman*, tragedy has been superseded by the "Theater of the Absurd." The protagonists of these tragicomedies minimize the horror and terror of life but also fail even to hint at its possible greatness. These antiheroes exit the stage with a "whimper" not a bang.

Some recent developments, however, have followed the ennobling promises of modernity. Miguel de Unamuno y Jugo (1864-1936), author of *The Tragic Sense of Life*, argued that humanity thirsts for a status in life that reason cannot support. People live in the tragic sense of life when they refuse to abandon either the heart or the intellect. Humanity is neither God nor worm, but something in between. Unamuno suggests that this tension is unresolvable, yet people may live authentically by refusing to deny either aspect of life. Thus, a form of "tragic optimism" appears to be emerging in the late twentieth century. By following the guidelines of Nietzsche, Unamuno, and other twentieth century philosophers, it is possible to recapture the nobility of humanity at the expense of illusions about absolutes. In the recognition that life is a mystery to be heroically lived and not a problem to be intellectually solved, the birth pain of a new postmodern form of tragedy may be heard.

—*Paul Rentz*

See also Aristotle; Hegel, Georg Wilhelm Friedrich; Nietzsche, Friedrich; Plato; Schopenhauer, Arthur; Unamuno y Jugo, Miguel de.

BIBLIOGRAPHY

Kaufmann, Walter A. *Tragedy and Philosophy.* Garden City, New York: Doubleday, 1968.

Nietzsche, Friedrich. *The Birth of Tragedy.* Translated by William A. Haussman. New York: Russell & Russell, 1964.

Nussbaum, Martha C. *The Fragility of Goodness: Luck and Ethics in Greek Tragedy and Rome.* New York: Cambridge University Press, 1986.

Unamuno, Miguel de. *The Tragic Sense of Life in Men and Nations.* Princeton, N.J.: Princeton University Press, 1972.

Weitz, Morris. "Tragedy." In *The Encyclopedia of Philosophy*, edited by Paul Edwards. Vol. 8. New York: Macmillan, 1972.

Transcendentalism

TYPE OF ETHICS: Theory of ethics

DATES: 1781; 1830-1855

ASSOCIATED WITH: Immanuel Kant and the German idealists; Ralph Waldo Emerson and members of the Boston Transcendental Club

DEFINITION: Belief in a class of ideas that do not originate in sensory experience; an American social movement that emphasized the spiritual life over the material one

SIGNIFICANCE: Since the mind is the source of ethical conduct, remaining true to it is an individual's most important ethical duty

Transcendentalism was an idealistic revolt against materialist philosophies such as John Locke's empiricism, Sir Isaac Newton's mechanism, and William Paley's utilitarianism. In those materialist theories, one's code of behavior derived from a compilation of sensory experiences by means of which one determined what was good or useful. The transcendentalist, however, believed that one's code of behavior preceded his experiences, that the structure of ideas inherent in the mind itself molded ethical conduct.

Origins. Although the term "transcendental" had been employed by medieval philosophers, the Prussian philosopher Immanuel Kant first used the term in its modern meaning in the late eighteenth century. His *Critique of Pure Reason* (1781) addressed a fundamental philosophical question: Does all knowledge come from the senses' interactions with the world or is some knowledge embedded in the mind prior to sensory experiences? He concluded that there were ideas that "transcended" experience and that ethical conduct was a matter of the mind's inherent desire to act consistently with itself.

Philosophers and literary figures in Germany, France, Great Britain, and the United States who were seeking a liberating idealism believed that they had found it in Immanuel Kant's work. His idea that the mind contained a set of moral ideas that helped mold a person's relationship to the universe made his theories a welcome alternative to materialistically based ones. His idea that one's primary ethical duty was to remain faithful to the ethical laws dictated by one's own mind appealed to those who were hungry for a more spiritually and individually based set of ethics. Many strongly believed that this set of transcendent ideas was humankind's connection to God, in which its highest and noblest aspirations could be found.

American Transcendentalism. Among those who were influenced by Kant were the American Transcendentalists, although they received his philosophy secondhand through the works of the British authors Samuel Taylor Coleridge and Thomas Carlyle. This group consisted generally of New Englanders, many of them Unitarian ministers or ex-ministers, who were most influential from the first meeting of the Transcendental Club in 1836 until the American Civil War. Prominent members of the movement were Bronson Alcott, George Ripley, Theodore Parker, William H. Channing, Margaret Fuller, Henry David Thoreau, and Ralph Waldo Emerson, most of whom also contributed to the literary journal *The Dial*.

A popular idea among the group was Coleridge's simplified version of Kant's theory that the mind was divided into a higher faculty, called "reason," that sought to systematize and unify the various impressions collected and analyzed by the lower faculty, termed the "understanding." The work of Emerson and Thoreau both emphasize reason. "Higher laws" or "spiritual laws," as they called them, ranked above the mechanical rules of cause and effect in the material world and gave unity and ethical purpose to human activities. The permanence of the higher laws appealed to these thinkers, who deplored the utilitarian values and relative ethics that seemed to have replaced principled behavior. They also liked Kant's idea that the source of morals, and thus the closest link to God, was found in one's own mind. From this premise, they developed their influential concept of self-reliance.

Many of the major works of American Transcendentalism appropriated Kant's idea that morality exists in the mind and fused it with a mystical belief that a divine spirit was prevalent in nature. In *Nature* (1836), Emerson argued that ethics and the natural world were inextricably linked: "the moral law lies at the centre of nature. . . . All things with which we deal, preach to us. What is a farm but a mute gospel?" Thoreau expressed similar thoughts in *Walden* (1854). He spent two years at Walden Pond, where he built his own house, planted and harvested his own food, and yet reserved ample time for reflection. He consistently linked the simple acts of his daily life, such as hoeing a bean field or plumbing the depths of the pond, to the immanence of a universal spirit.

Although they resisted the trendiness of social movements, the American Transcendentalists were attracted to the moral issues raised by those movements. Margaret Fuller, in *Woman in the Nineteenth Century* (1845), argued the case for women's rights. Thoreau went to jail rather than pay taxes that supported an immoral war, an experience that he chronicled in "Resistance to Civil Government" (1849), and in "Slavery in Massachusetts" (1854), Thoreau opposed slavery and the moral irresponsibility of those who allowed themselves to become accomplices to its evil.

Aside from the major political events of their time, the Transcendentalists were also concerned with the ethical content of their own day-to-day lives and those of their fellow citizens. In "The Transcendentalist" (1842), Emerson seemed almost to plead with his audience that it "tolerate one or two solitary voices in the land, speaking for thoughts and principles not marketable or perishable." Thoreau, in "Life Without Principle" (1863), makes a similar case for the role of principles in the too often materialistic lives of the populace.

After several centuries of empirically based philosophy, Transcendentalism provided strong evidence that humankind still recognized a spiritual element in its personality. The Transcendentalists believed that innate spiritual insights were essential in directing ethical judgments.

—William L. Howard

See also Emerson, Ralph Waldo; Kant, Immanuel; Kantian ethics; Thoreau, Henry David.

BIBLIOGRAPHY

Boller, Paul F. *American Transcendentalism, 1830-1860: An Intellectual Inquiry*. New York: Putnam, 1974.

Emerson, Ralph Waldo. *Essays and Lectures*. New York: Viking Press, 1983.

Frothingham, Octavius Brooks. *Transcendentalism in New England: A History*. New York: Harper, 1959.

Kant, Immanuel. *Critique of Pure Reason*. Translated by Norman Kemp Smith. New York: Modern Library, 1958.

Koster, Donald N. *Transcendentalism in America*. Boston: Twayne, 1975.

Liddell, Brendan E. A. *Kant on the Foundation of Morality: A Modern Version of the "Grundlegung."* Bloomington: Indiana University Press, 1970.

Thoreau, Henry David. *Walden and Civil Disobedience*. Edited by Owen Thomas. New York: W. W. Norton, 1966.

Transplants and organ substitutions

TYPE OF ETHICS: Bioethics

DATE: 1900 to the present

DEFINITION: The replacement of worn-out, diseased, or injured organs and tissues with healthy substitutes

SIGNIFICANCE: Raises problems of the definition of death, the equitable distribution of scarce resources, and the quality of life of the transplanted patient

For centuries, humans have longed to be able to replace the diseased or injured parts of the body with healthy organs. Stories abound from ancient civilizations of attempts at organ and tissue transplantation, but until recently these seem to have been mostly dreams. Finally, in the early nineteenth century, there were successful skin grafts. These were autografts in which a patient's own tissue was used, and thus there was little danger of rejection. When material was taken from one member of a species and placed in another (an allograft), however, it was rejected by the recipient.

This was not the only problem faced by these early medical pioneers. Before organ transplantation could be done on a routine basis, it was necessary to develop better methods of tying up weakened arteries, aseptic surgery, anesthesia, and tissue typing. By 1913, the French physician Alexis Carrel transplanted a kidney from one cat to another and later developed a profusion machine that drenched a removed organ in blood, thus sustaining its life.

Yet a major obstacle remained; namely, the rejection of the transplanted organ. The mechanics of this little-understood process were discovered by Peter Medawar at the University of Oxford during the 1940's. He found that this process was caused by the immune rejection of the body's lymphoid organs. Thus, the recipient's system recognized the donor tissue as foreign and responded by destroying the transplant. The amount of genetic disparity of the two individuals determines the degree and speed of this rejection. Attempts to limit the activity of the immune system eventually led to the use of a combination of a corticosteroid (prednisone) with the antileukemia drug (azathioprine). A third medicine, cyclosporine, discovered in 1972, was particularly important because it took less of a scattergun approach than the others. Rather than suppressing the entire immune response, cyclosporine targets the T cells, the particular parts of the system that attack alien tissues. The most effective treatment of transplant patients includes daily doses of these three drugs.

There are twenty-one different transplantable organs and tissues in the human body, including the heart, liver, kidneys, lungs, pancreas, cornea, bone marrow, and blood vessels. In 1954, a team of Boston physicians led by Joseph E. Murray successfully transplanted a kidney from one twin brother to another. Cardiac transplantation began in 1967, when Christian Barnard performed a human-to-human operation, but the first fully successful heart transplant was done by Norman Shumway in the United States. Although lung transplants were attempted as early as 1964, because of problems with infection that are peculiar to this organ it was not until the 1980's that John D. Cooper of Toronto made the process feasible. The work of Thomas E. Starzl led in 1967 to successful transplanting of the liver. Also during the decade of the 1960's, the pancreas, bone marrow, cornea, and blood vessels were transplanted with increasing frequency.

Presently, more than 16,000 kidney, liver, pancreas, heart, heart-lung, and lung transplants are performed each year in the United States. These operations seem to be the only treatment that can transform individuals from a near-death condition to a relatively normal life in a matter of days. Such procedures raise a number of ethical and moral problems. Those that concern organ donation often result from worry that individuals will not receive adequate

treatment if they sign donor agreements.

An understanding of the modern definition of death can deal with much of this confusion. Until the 1960's, cessation of brain function inevitably followed cessation of cardiopulmonary function. Individuals did not live for extended periods with the heart and other organs functioning after the brain activity ceased. New medical techniques such as the use of respirators made this condition possible. Machines could maintain blood and oxygen circulation even when the body could never again operate on its own. The notion of "brain death" was therefore proposed. In 1966, Pope Pius XII defined death as the departure of the spirit from the body through the cessation of brain function rather than the loss of pumping action of the heart. The United States and other countries have passed laws that have given legal sanction to this definition. Patients who are brain dead may be kept alive for a few days, but not permanently. A physician can confirm this situation beyond a doubt through neurological examination. Public support for this position has gained wide acceptance, and currently very few people oppose organ donation.

More difficult problems remain that involve the recipient. Some of these concern the selection of those who are to receive transplants. Despite the thousands of operations performed in 1991, there were still more than 30,000 individuals listed by the United Network for Organ Sharing (UNOS) who needed one or more of the major organs. In an attempt to alleviate this shortage, UNOS, an organization of transplant centers, was founded. It has established a national waiting list to ensure equitable organ allocation according to policies that forbid favoritism based on race, sex, financial status, or political influence. The only considerations are the medically determined conditions of the patients. This organization has been quite successful in raising awareness of the need for donor organs.

Even if a person receives a transplant, there is a continuing need for a more healthy lifestyle and the constant cost and bother of daily medication. Finally, the entire situation of the expense and availability of transplants is a microcosm of the macrocosm of health care for everyone. How can scarce resources be allocated? Who is wise or caring enough to decide who will die and who will have a chance at a new life? Such questions must be addressed by the general field of medical ethics.   —*Robert G. Clouse*

See also Health care allocation; Life and death; Medical ethics; *Principles of Medical Ethics*.

BIBLIOGRAPHY

Fox, Renee, and Judith P. Swazey. *The Courage to Fail: A Social View of Organ Transplants and Dialysis.* 2d ed. rev. Chicago: University of Chicago Press, 1978.

Sabiston, David C., Jr., ed. *Textbook of Surgery, The Biological Basis of Modern Surgical Practice.* 13th ed. Philadelphia: W. B. Saunders, 1986.

Sheil, A. G., and Felix T. Rapapport. *World Transplantation.* 3 vols. East Norwalk, Conn.: Appleton & Lange, 1989.

Starzl, Thomas E. *The Puzzle People: Memoirs of a Transplant Surgeon.* Pittsburgh: University of Pittsburgh Press, 1992.

Warshofsky, Fred. *The Rebuilt Man.* New York: Thomas Y. Crowell, 1965.

Treason

TYPE OF ETHICS: Politico-economic ethics

DATE: In the English language, the word "treason" goes back into Old English; in English law, it was first defined in the Statute of 1340 during the reign of Edward III

ASSOCIATED WITH: Radical political ideologies, ethnic and religious dissension, civil wars, and foreign occupations

DEFINITION: The betrayal of one's nation or one's nation's government, without sufficient moral justification, to its enemies, either foreign or domestic

SIGNIFICANCE: Questions of treasonable behavior always raise issues of the degree of loyalty owed to one's country versus duties to self, family, ethnic group, religion, ideology, and so forth

The U.S. Constitution defines treason as "giving aid and

FAMOUS TRAITORS	
Name	**Treasonous act**
Alcibiades (450-404 B.C.E.)	Defected from Athenian army to fight for Sparta in Peloponnesian War (fifth century B.C.E.)
Cataline (ca. 108-62 B.C.E.)	Plotted to overthrow Roman Republic (65-62 B.C.E.)
Guy Fawkes (1570-1606)	Plotted to blow up James I and the English Parliament in 1605
James Scott, Duke of Monmouth (1649-1685)	Rose against James II in 1685
Benedict Arnold (1741-1801)	U.S. general who plotted to surrender West Point to British forces in Revolutionary War in 1780
Aaron Burr (1756-1836)	Allegedly conspired to take over Western territories of U.S. during Jefferson Administration
Sir Roger Casement (1864-1916)	Plotted with Germans during World War I to obtain arms for Irish rebels
Mildred Gillars ["Axis Sally"] (1900-1988)	U.S. citizen who broadcasted for the Nazis during World War II
Iva Toguri ["Tokyo Rose"] (1916-)	U.S. citizen who broadcasted for Japan during World War II
Ezra Loomis Pound (1885-1972)	U.S. citizen who broadcasted for Italy during World War II
William Joyce ["Lord Haw-Haw"] (1906-1946)	British subject who broadcasted for Germany during World War II
Henri Petain (1856-1951) and Pierre Laval (1883-1945)	French leaders who collaborated with German occupation during World War II
Vidkun Quisling (1887-1945)	Norwegian officer who collaborated with German occupation during World War II
Alger Hiss (1904-)	Allegedly spied for the Soviet Union against United States during 1930's and 1940's
Julius Rosenberg (1918-1953) and Ethel Rosenberg (1916-1953)	Allegedly they spied for the Soviet Union against U.S. atom bomb project during the 1940's
Klaus Emil J. Fuchs (1911-)	Stole British and U.S. atomic secrets for the Soviet Union during the 1940's
Guy Burgess (1911-1963), Kim Philby (1912-), and Donald Maclean (1915-)	Spied on British intelligence operations for the Soviet Union during the 1940's and 1950's
Sir Anthony Blunt (1907-1983)	Spied on Britain for the Soviet Union from the 1930's to the 1950's
John Anthony Walker (1937-)	Spied for the Soviet Union against the U.S. military during the 1970's and 1980's

comfort to the enemies of the United States." In most legal systems, however, treason consists also in attempting to overthrow the legal government within the state, and it may be supplemented by crimes such as espionage and sedition. Most ethical systems see one as having moral obligations, including loyalty, to one's nation and to its rulers. Treason, therefore, is ordinarily a seriously blameworthy act, and the attendant horrors of foreign military conquest or revolutionary upheaval add to its inherent evils.

An anarchist could scarcely acknowledge the legitimacy of the concept of treason, but supporters of natural law and Kantian ethics, for example, would advocate a strong degree of deference owed to the sovereign but would also acknowledge that the sovereign may be defied, overthrown, or even assassinated if he or she commands or commits great evil.

Although there is almost universal opprobrium attached to treason done for profit or advancement, other cases of treason are muddied by the contrast of the objective evaluation of the ideology, religion, or philosophy prompting the act with the subjective element of the traitor's personal commitment to that belief.

The "judgment of history" often seems particularly amoral. To cite one example, Adolf Hitler is never labeled a traitor despite his having tried unsuccessfully to overthrow the Bavarian state government in the Munich "Beerhall Putsch," because his eventual capture of the German government a decade later seems to have extinguished the guilt of treason in that view.

See also Citizenship; Duty; Espionage; Nationalism; Politics; Revolution; Sedition; Sovereignty.

Treaty of Versailles

TYPE OF ETHICS: International relations
DATE: June 28, 1919
ASSOCIATED WITH: The 1919 Peace of Paris, the weakness of the Weimar Republic, and the rise of Adolf Hitler
DEFINITION: The treaty that formally ended the state of war between Germany and the Entente powers, and imposed punitive conditions aimed at permanently reducing German power
SIGNIFICANCE: The harsh, economically disruptive terms of the Treaty of Versailles undermined democracy in Germany and fostered the nationalistic excesses that produced totalitarianism, state terrorism, and renewed global warfare

The Treaty of Versailles encouraged the rise of German Fascism and was an underlying cause of World War II. The German surrender in 1918 was based on a general acceptance of President Woodrow Wilson's Fourteen Points. In formulating the peace terms, the British and French ignored most of those points. The treaty stripped Germany of human and material resources, in violation of its avowed goals of national self-determination and respect for territorial integrity, and reduced the German armed forces to a level that was incompatible with national defense. It also imposed crushing indemnities upon Germany and forced Germans to accept sole war guilt. The treaty's blatant unfairness and economically destabilizing consequences, further aggravated by the onset of the Great Depression in 1931, aided the success of Adolf Hitler's revanchist, extremist National Socialist (Nazi) Party. Hitler's sustained efforts to reverse the Versailles treaty provoked World War II, the most devastating conflict in history.

See also Fascism; Hitler, Adolf; League of Nations; Nationalism; War and peace.

Triage

TYPE OF ETHICS: Bioethics
DATE: Coined fourteenth century
DEFINITION: The process of sorting victims of war, accident, or disaster to determine priority of medical treatment
SIGNIFICANCE: Sets priorities in emergency situations in which the persons requiring help far outnumber the time and/or the resources available to help them

Triage employs a utilitarian calculation concerning how to do the most good with whatever resources are available, determining which patients will be helped at all, and in which order those to be helped will be treated. Triage may be employed in any situation in which all the injured, sick, or wounded cannot be treated: on the battlefield, at the site of a natural disaster, in the first moments of a traffic accident, in the emergency room of a large hospital, or in a country suffering from mass starvation. Triage is more easily defended than are some other types of utilitarian calculations, since there is no intent to sacrifice the innocent for the greater good of the majority. Since triage does require that one make a "quality of life" judgment before one decides which victims will be helped, however, it may be an ethically objectionable practice. If it is wrong to judge who is worth helping and who is not, then it is arguable that triage should be replaced with a "first-come-first-helped" principle.

See also Medical ethics; Military ethics.

Truman Doctrine

TYPE OF ETHICS: International relations
DATE: March, 1947
ASSOCIATED WITH: U.S. president Harry S Truman
DEFINITION: A foreign policy initiative undertaken by the Truman Administration to prevent the spread of Soviet Communism into Greece and Turkey
SIGNIFICANCE: This initiative signaled a shift in American foreign policy; it acknowledged a sphere of influence in the Middle East, which had never been a traditional interest of the United States

The Truman Doctrine was prompted by the British government's announcement that it would withdraw from Greece after the British had liberated the country from the Nazis in 1944. After World War II, the Soviet Union was a threat to the Balkan Peninsula, and the Eastern European communist regimes were aiding the Greek communists in their civil war

Harry S Truman (White House Historical Association)

against the Greek government. To offset this communist threat, Truman asked the Congress for $400 million for military and economic aid to Greece and Turkey.

See also International justice; International law.

Trustworthiness

TYPE OF ETHICS: Personal and social ethics

DATE: The term "trustworthiness" was first used in the nineteenth century, but the concept of trust is ancient

ASSOCIATED WITH: Feminism, in which trustworthiness in personal relations sometimes has been regarded as especially important; financial businesses, in which a reputation for trustworthiness is essential; and professions, which need to be founded on trust

DEFINITION: Trustworthiness is a disposition of character that leads people to do reliably what others have a right to expect them to do

SIGNIFICANCE: Trustworthiness is a crucial virtue for people living together in a community, where personal, commercial, and professional relationships depend on it

Trustworthiness involves both words and conduct. A trustworthy person speaks truthfully to others, and therefore the words of such a person are to be trusted. Also, a trustworthy person is willing to make commitments concerning future behavior, and can and will keep whatever commitments have been entered into; therefore, the conduct of such a person is to be relied upon. A trustworthy mechanic, for example, can be counted on both to tell one truthfully what repairs one's automobile needs and to fulfill the terms of any contract that he or she enters into to do the work.

Trustworthiness is an admirable trait of character because it is socially useful. Hence, it is appropriate to classify it as a moral virtue, even though it has been little discussed by traditional ethical theorists, the word "trustworthy" having entered English only in the nineteenth century.

The term "trustworthy" is ambiguous because it does not specify whether it refers to trustworthiness in some specific respect or trustworthiness as a pervasive disposition of a person's character. When one calls a mechanic trustworthy, one is usually speaking only of trustworthiness regarding automotive repairs, though one could mean to say that the person is trustworthy in all aspects of life. Marital fidelity and honesty in paying income tax will count as evidence of trustworthiness in a mechanic only when the second, broader meaning is intended.

Trustworthiness is akin to and overlaps such other virtues as truthfulness, honesty, and fidelity, but it is distinguishable from each of these. Trustworthiness differs from truthfulness in that the latter pertains only to communication, while the former can relate to a much wider range of behavior. Trustworthiness differs from honesty in that it can concern the keeping of commitments of any kind, not merely those the breach of which would be dishonest. It differs from fidelity in that trustworthiness requires greater effectiveness in the carrying out of commitments than is needed for fidelity; thus, a loyal but incompetent person can be faithful without being trustworthy.

Trustworthiness must also be distinguished from trustfulness (which is not, in general, a virtue) and from the appropriate degrees of trust that ought to pervade various relationships (these degrees of trust often arise only in proportion as the participants are properly trustworthy, yet this proportionality is merely contingent).

Within the family and in personal relationships generally, trustworthiness is required if all is to go well. When a husband is worthy of his wife's trust and she of his, this makes it likelier that they will indeed trust each other and that their affections will remain firm and their responsibilities will be effectively shared. Lovers, friends, neighbors, and acquaintances all will find that their relationships tend to be strengthened when there are appropriate degrees of trustworthiness on each side.

Some feminist thinkers have particularly focused on the importance of trustworthiness. Sara Ruddick, for example, writes of trustworthiness as one of the virtues especially needed by a mother who is to have a sound relationship with her child. She stresses that the child must be able to rely on the mother to stand up for it against the father, against intrusive government, and against the archaic mores of society. Ruddick's emphasis is controversial, and one might wish to add that children also need to find their fathers trustworthy and need to be taught to be trustworthy themselves. In any case, trustworthiness on all sides seems to be indispensable for good family relationships.

Is trustworthiness more prized in men by women than it is in women by men? There may be some truth in Schopenhauer's view that women prize stability (and hence trustworthiness) in their liaisons, while men tend to seek variety. Yet such sweeping generalizations carry little weight.

It is in the world of business, however, that trustworthiness finds its most distinctive place in modern life, especially in connection with the provision of financial services. Banking activities of a recognizable kind seem to have had their origin during the Renaissance in the dealings of merchant families, among whom the Medici and the Fuggers were leaders. Initially, these families had merely bought and sold on their own account, but then gradually they began to provide financial services to others, transferring money from one city to another, holding deposits, making commercial loans, and insuring against the loss of ships and shipments. The availability of these services became enormously helpful to commerce and set the stage for the rise of capitalism.

It was essential that the providers of such services should develop strong reputations for trustworthiness, since no merchant wanted to deposit funds except with a banker who could be relied upon to handle them as promised. The concept of trust (Latin, *fiducia*) has been central to the activities of banking and insurance from the start. Members of these businesses always have sought to cultivate favorable reputations and have found that the most reliable way of doing so is by actually being trustworthy. Since the eighteenth century, the fiduciary trustworthiness of corporate entities has come to be even more important than that of individuals and families (some corporate entities even came to be called "trusts"). Without fiduciary trust, the economic world as it is known could not exist.

In the professions, such as medicine and law, trustworthiness also has come to play a central role. The patient or client is not equipped to make independent judgments about the complex technicalities of medicine or law and therefore must rely on the knowledge and technical skill of the professional, as well as on the professional's motivation to serve well. Only professionals who acquire reputations for trustworthiness are likely to be successful in the long run. Part of the role of professional organizations has been to promote trustworthy behavior by members of the professions and to encourage potential patients and clients to trust them.

—*Stephen F. Barker*

See also Honesty; Loyalty; Professional ethics; Promises; Truth; Virtue.

BIBLIOGRAPHY

Baier, Annette. "Trust and Antitrust." *Ethics* 96, no. 2 (January; 1986): 231-260.

Bok, Sissela. *Lying: Moral Choice in Public and Private Life.* New York: Pantheon Books, 1978.

Murphy, Kevin R. *Honesty in the Workplace.* Pacific Grove, Calif.: Brooks/Cole, 1993.

Pellegrino, Edmund D., et al., eds. *Ethics, Trust, and the Professions.* Washington, D.C.: Georgetown University Press, 1991.

Ruddick, Sara. *Maternal Thinking: Toward a Politics of Peace.* Boston: Beacon Press, 1989.

Truth

TYPE OF ETHICS: Theory of ethics

DATE: From antiquity

DEFINITION: A transcendent fundamental or spiritual reality; the body of real things, events, and facts; true statements that are in accord with reality; the object of the search for knowledge; the opposite of "falsehood"

SIGNIFICANCE: Truth is indispensable to ethics, since without truth there could be no reasonable system of ethics; if there were no truth, there would be no reality upon which to base a theory of ethics

Truth is a feature of propositions—assertions, statements, and claims. If one claims that one's notebook is on a desk, and it is, one's claim is true. The desk is not true and the notebook is not true: They simply exist. If one removes the notebook but makes the same assertion as before, the assertion is false, but falseness would still not be a characteristic of the desk or the notebook. Equally, the number nine is neither true or false, but the equation $9 + 5 = 14$ is true, while $9 + 15 = 23$ is false.

Truthful statements or assertions represent "things" as they are—reality. False assertions do not depict things as they are. Truthful statements and falsehoods depend on those things as they are, not on a person's (or a society's) beliefs, desires, wishes, or prejudices. Furthermore, at the elemental level of logic, the "law of the excluded middle" is operative. According to that law, it is assumed that statements or claims have only two possible conditions: A claim is either true or false.

Throughout history, philosophers have attempted to develop sweeping theories to explain the nature of truth and its opposite, falsehood.

Coherence Theory. Several philosophical theories of truth are extant, one being the coherence theory. Its groundbreakers include such thinkers as Baruch Spinoza, G. W. F. Hegel, and Gottfried Leibniz, and it is associated with the great rationalist system-making metaphysicians. In coherence theory, when one says that a statement or judgment is true or false, one means that the statement coheres or does not cohere with other statements, which, taken together, create a "system" that is held together either by logic or by pure mathematics. To be called "true," a statement must fit into a comprehensive account of the universe and its reality. In everyday language, people often reject outlandish assertions (such as someone claiming that he or she sees ghosts or claiming that God visits him or her every day), because the assertions do not cohere with other scientific views or even with common sense.

Believers in the coherence theory justify their position, in part, on the basis of their view of the theory of knowledge and also, in part, on the basis of a priori reasoning such as that found in such fields as mathematics and logic. They believe that all knowledge is a vastly organized and logically expressed interlocking series of statements or judgments.

Critics who reject the coherence theory point out that a priori statements that are typical of mathematics and physics are unlike empirical statements about observations of everyday life, and thus they give priority to empirical evidence rather than a priori judgments. For example, scientists may have determined by observation that water boils at 100 degrees Celsius but may, after further observation, learn that the statement is true of water at sea level but is not true of water at higher altitudes; either way, empirical evidence is the key to "the truth."

Correspondence Theory. Influenced by Bertrand Russell, many modern philosophers embrace the correspondence theory of truth, which holds that the truth corresponds to reality. As Russell defined the term, truth exists in some form of correspondence between belief and fact (reality). Actually, the lineage of this belief can be traced back to Aristotle, who held that "A" is always "A" and non-"A" is never "A." By the "facts" of a case, the case is true if the "facts" are true or is false if the "facts" are untrue. The "liar's paradox," however, bedevils those who embrace this theory. Eubulides, a Megarian philosopher, a near contemporary of Aristotle, first formulated the paradox: "I am a liar, and what I'm now saying is false." Correspondence theorists would have to reason that the statement is true if the man is a liar; that is, it is true if it itself is false, but false if it is true.

Writing after the turn of the twentieth century, G. E. Moore justified the correspondence theory on the grounds that statements that reflect reality are true and those which do not reflect reality are false. Moore held that truth is agreement between belief and fact. If the former is true, there is a "fact" in the universe to which the belief corresponds; if the belief were false, there would be no "fact" to which it could correspond. Bertrand Russell added that there can be no incompatibility among "real" facts, but there are many incompatibilities among falsehoods.

Pragmatic Theory. Pragmatic theory holds that the truth is the satisfactory solution to a problematic situation. This theory developed, in part, as a reaction against Cartesian logic. René Descartes considered matters individually and subjectively, believing that an idea was clear and true if it seemed to him to be clear and true, never considering that an idea might seem clear and true even though it was false. Pragmatists such as Charles S. Peirce, who wrote in the late nineteenth and early twentieth centuries, argued that truth had a public rather than an individual character and that it should never be severed from the practicality and reality of human life or from the human pursuit of knowledge. Peirce then defined scientific truth as a learned judgment ultimately agreed upon by all who investigate a certain statement, issue, or problem.

John Dewey's definition of pragmatic theory differed

from that of Peirce; Dewey held that truth originates with doubt, which in turn prompts an investigation. First, relevant "facts" are gathered and applied; they mark off what seems safe and secure (true). Investigation then begins, lasting until "reality" (truth) is verified. Russell disagreed with Dewey, however, holding that truth is still truth even if it is not verified by an investigator. Another critic formed an example of what Russell meant: Smith committed a crime on Monday that was not discovered until Friday. The truth (the crime), "happened" on Monday and became reality then even if the authorities did not verify that truth until later.

Another pragmatist, William James, developed his own views of truth, holding that truth was expedient—it was whatever put one in a satisfactory position with the world. James came under attack from others who objected to his amoral approach, for if truth was only an expedient and a satisfactory position then lies might become truth, good might become bad, and all definitions of truth would be torn asunder.

Many pragmatists are also empiricists. For example, Isaac Newton's theory of gravitation is true because Newton's ideas lead to computations that agree with observations. The old corpuscular theory of light was eventually rejected because certain of its ideas did not agree with experience and observation.

Early Evolution of the Philosophical Concern for the Truth. From the beginnings, many early philosophers, in addition to those mentioned above, decided that objective truth existed. Plato's ideas included elements of both the correspondence and coherence theories, and, as mentioned above, Aristotle also developed the correspondence model. Challenges and criticisms of this idea were made by the early Sophists, who held that the truth was relative, and early skeptics, who argued that the real truth is not knowable by humans and that people should therefore live in a state of suspension of judgment.

During the Middle Ages, the doctrine of double truth was in vogue, largely because it appeared to save theology from philosophy. Those who stressed double truth claimed that what might be true in philosophy might be false for religion. Thomas Aquinas contributed to the debate by modifying the correspondence theory. He held that truth was the "adequation" of thought to things, and added that since truth is a transcendental concept, the highest truth was that of God. In the modern era, the double truth doctrine remains in vogue, as would-be religionists allow science and theology to coexist.

Later philosophers added depth to the search for truth. Baruch Spinoza, for example, argued that truth was the standard literally of itself and of the false as well. Leibniz drew a distinction between truths of reason and truths of facts (today's analytic-synthetic distinction). The former relied on the principle of identity and the latter simply on "sufficient" reason. John Locke joined the debate by drawing distinctions between truths of thought and truths of words; the former rested on the agreement of ideas with things, the latter on the agreement of ideas. Hegel explored what he called the "historical truth" versus formal truth, with the former relating to concrete existence and the latter to mathematics.

Truth, Error, Logic, and Morality. Formal logic holds that a proposition or a fact is true if it reports, portrays, or describes "things" as they are (reality). A true idea corresponds in structure to reality. Formal logic, however, cannot account for certain types of falsehoods or errors, especially those that have moral or ethical overtones. Out of prejudice, ignorance, willfulness, or "feelings," people may embrace error. Many, for example, are superstitious; some deny certain scientific "truths" because they are not in accord with feelings or beliefs. Others embrace patently false philosophies and doubtful theological heresies because such heresies make them "feel" better. Worse, humans who are ignorant of "facts" experience a certain type of a void or a vacuum, and they often fill in their void or vacuum with errors.

Volitional untruth often leads to immorality and/or unethical behavior. Many a liar, for example, justifies his or her falsehoods with the phrase "everyone does it." Many a politician justifies the courting and the accepting of bribes because "everyone does it." Many a priest, preacher, or rabbi professes goodness while leading a private life that no "good" God could condone. Unfortunately, religion provides fertile ground for volitional untruth. Religionists believe in doctrines and ideas that are impossible to prove true. Yet many religionists still persecute and discriminate against those who do not embrace their unprovable assertions.

Prejudice appears to be a major source of volitional untruth that causes great harm. Historical examples could include the Holocaust, the German slaughter of at least six million Jews; Joseph Stalin's mass murders before and during World War II; and Serbia's "ethnic cleansing," a euphemism for attacks (that led to much destruction and many deaths) on other ethnic groups in what used to be Yugoslavia. It is clear that, worldwide, much racism and rabid ethnocentrism still exists.

Truth as Common Sense. When "common" people, living in the real world, use the term "common sense," they generally contrast the term with its opposite, nonsense, for what is opposed to common sense is nonsensical. Generally, people who have common sense tend to trust their five senses of perception and therefore to trust the observations about reality that their senses record. Common sense as a form of truth is usually opposed to "high" and obvious paradox, and it offers people protection from gross absurdity. For example, a person with common sense probably will not give much consideration to the following question: "if a tree falls in the forest, does it make a noise if no one is there to hear it?" Common sense dictates that one should disregard that question, because it involves only mental gymnastics. Likewise, most people do not attempt to determine how many angels can stand on the head of a pin.

In terms of the truth (or philosophy) of common sense, Aristotle was one of the first to stress "A" and "non-A" and to argue that the reality of the world was for the most part exactly what it seemed to be. Some modern philosophers echo Aristotle's dictum. For example, G. E. Moore, developed "truisms" that implied the correctness of common sense: Earth has existed many years in time and in space; human beings have also existed for many years and have related to the material Earth and to each other. Thus, Moore condemned philosophers who tried to deny the existence of material things, of space, and of time. Some woebegone philosophers, Moore complained, had even denied the existence of minds other than their own; thus, they had to convince their listeners or their readers that they—the listeners and readers—did not exist, but if they did not exist, how could they hear of or read about the philosopher's opinions in the first place?

Common sense observations do, of course, have limitations. Common sense can produce error. Primitive humans probably could not have believed the modern "view" that the earth is always revolving in a orbit around the sun. Trusting their powers of observation, primitives would likely laugh at such a statement because, the earth under their feet was not moving. Philosophers who stress common sense, however, argue that such error is always temporary because common sense evolves as more is learned about the world and reality.

Truth and Untruth in the World of Politics and Economics. In the real world in which people live, falsehoods and unethical behavior abound (caused by, for example, personal character flaws or someone's drive for power). Nowhere is this more evident than in the United States' political system and economic system. In politics, for example, in recent decades Americans have witnessed something of a public circus. The Watergate scandal of the early 1970's disgusted many people, especially after certain tapes revealed that President Richard Nixon, in speaking to aides, acted much like a Mafia chieftain who plotted the destruction of his political enemies (real or imagined). The tapes also proved that Nixon was deeply involved in the scandal, not blameless as he had earlier maintained.

The 1980's and early 1990's witnessed such episodes as the "Iran-Contra," affair which tainted President Ronald Reagan, and various congressional scandals involving the House of Representatives' "bank," its "post office," and its restaurant. Concerning economics, people witnessed such developments as the Savings and Loan scandal, a scandal that cost billions of dollars, most of which the people ultimately will have to pay.

If one multiplied the examples above by one hundred, one might begin to approach the number of scandals that have occurred in modern America. The root cause has to do with unethical behavior, with falsehood rather than truth, with "bad" rather than "good." So wrong have things gone that many people have despaired and become apathetic, not knowing whom to trust. Furthermore, many analysts from different academic fields now talk about the decline of American civilization.

Conclusion. After considering the foregoing analyses, at least one thing seems clear: Truth has a direct relationship with reality as humans know it and experience it. One supposes, however, that truth will continue to elude many people who, for one reason or another, refuse to recognize reality and refuse to adopt ideas that are consistent with that reality.   —*James Smallwood*

See also Aristotle; Descartes, René; Dewey, John; Hegel, Georg Wilhelm Friedrich; James, William; Leibniz, Gottfried; Locke, John; Moore, G. E.; Peirce, Charles Sanders; Plato; Platonic ethics; Russell, Bertrand; Spinoza, Baruch; Thomas Aquinas.

BIBLIOGRAPHY

Binion, Rudolph. *After Christianity: Christian Survivals in Post-Christian Culture*. Durango, Colo.: Logbridge-Rhodes, 1986. Binion advances the thesis that Christianity, one of the bedrocks of Western civilization and ethics, has undergone a tremendous decline, so much so that the author believes that the Western world has entered the post-Christian era.

Broad, William. *Betrayers of the Truth*. New York: Simon & Schuster, 1983. Broad's work examines various fields of science and finds so many examples of fraud that it leads one to question many aspects of those sciences.

Engel, Pascal. *The Norm of Truth: An Introduction to the Philosophy of Logic*. Buffalo, N.Y.: University of Toronto Press, 1991. Engel analyzes truth from the vantage points of philosophy and logic.

Goleman, Daniel. *Vital Lies, Simple Truths: The Psychology of Self-Deception*. New York: Simon & Schuster, 1985. This study examines the nature of cognition and of "social" truths, "psychological" truths, and psychological defense mechanisms for denying truth.

Munitz, Milton Karl. *The Question of Reality*. Princeton, N.J.: Princeton University Press, 1990. Wide in scope, Munitz's volume considers events and ideas relevant to creation, to reality, and to the theory of knowledge.

Quine, W. V. *Pursuit of Truth*. Cambridge, Mass.: Harvard University Press, 1990. A well-written book of much breadth, this volume examines "truth" from the standpoint of meaning and semantics and also considers the theory of Knowledge.

Rorty, Richard. *Objectivity, Relativism, and Truth*. New York: Cambridge University Press, 1991. Rorty's work examines the relationships among truth, "representation" (in philosophy), relativity, objectivity, and postmodernism.

Sartre, Jean-Paul. *Truth and Existence*. Chicago: University of Chicago Press, 1992. The existentialist philosopher focuses on the relationships among reality, knowledge, and existentialism.

Two Treatises of Government: Book

TYPE OF ETHICS: Enlightenment history
DATE: Published 1690
AUTHOR: John Locke
SIGNIFICANCE: This political philosophical work of classical liberalism articulated a rational moral justification of natural rights, private property ownership, limited government, and the construction of a legitimate government on the basis of consent and a social contract

The *Two Treatises of Government* was supportive of the political agenda of the Whigs and articulated a revolutionary sophisticated political theory of classical liberalism. John Locke's political theory and political ethical arguments were derived from his interpretation of the natural and rational human self-interests to survive and to acquire private property. The moral premises of universal natural rights and government's ethical obligation to protect such rights underpinned Locke's interpretation of natural law.

The law of nature was a source of rational moral political principles and a universal code of ethics. It was morally obligatory for all individuals to consult and comply with these moral precepts. Because of partiality, self-interest, and the personal pursuit of private property, however, humans often misunderstood the law of nature. The law of nature required all individuals to preserve their own lives and property, and "no one ought to harm another in his life, health, liberty, or possessions." Locke asserted a moral objectivist perspective, based on his assumption that the law of nature had universal applicability and transcended any particular historical or social context. In the state of nature, because of the lack of public authority each individual was responsible for the interpretation and implementation of the law of nature as well as for the punishment of transgressors. Although individuals were relatively equal, free, and independent rational moral agents who pursued property in the state of nature, inconveniences and disputes regarding property transactions prompted individuals to unite by means of a social contract to institute a civil society.

The concept of a state of nature was viewed by Locke as a fictional contrivance that served to demonstrate the normative basis of legitimate political authority. Unlike Thomas Hobbes's political ethical theory that humans were primarily motivated by fear of violent death to fulfill their moral obligations to the state, Locke's moral political philosophy held that individuals were guided by reason in the creation of their social and political institutions. Locke interpreted the political authority relationship as being derived from the consent of citizens to government. Governments were entrusted specifically to protect the natural rights (particularly of private property) of individuals. The *First Treatise* rejected the political theory of royal absolutism, monarchical prerogative, patriarchalism, and divine right of kings advocated by Sir Robert Filmer's *Patriarcha*. In contrast to Hobbes's theory of political absolutism, which was based upon the passive obedience of citizens, Locke's political

No twentieth century tyrant was more brutal than Joseph Stalin, who ruled the Soviet Union from 1924 to 1953. (Library of Congress)

theory of classical liberalism was grounded in the normative principles of limited government, governmental accountability, and the active moral assessment by citizens of public authority. Locke justified rebellion against an arbitrary, tyrannical sovereign who ruled by absolute power and existed in a state of war with the people. In addition to simply being a moral justification of an individual's natural right to mix his or her labor with material objects and thereby claim exclusive property ownership, Locke's labor theory of value and concept of property were broadly identified with the ethical principle of individual moral autonomy.

See also Hobbes, Thomas; *Leviathan*; Locke, John; Natural law; Social contract.

Tyranny

TYPE OF ETHICS: Politico-economic ethics

DATE: First used seventh century B.C.E.

ASSOCIATED WITH: Rulers who obtain power without the consent of the people and rule through fear

DEFINITION: Oppressive and unjust rule by a strong leader whose power is absolute

SIGNIFICANCE: Tyranny involves the rejection of sovereignty of law in favor of rule by force

In seventh century Greece, aristocrats ruled city-states called *poleis*, whose citizens obeyed the laws made by kings and governing councils, called *archons* in Athens. The first tyrant was Cypseleus, who took power by force in Corinth in 657 B.C.E. Pisistratus overthrew the political leadership in Athens with his army and ruled as a tyrant from 546 B.C.E. to his death in 528 B.C.E. A Greek tyrant was not necessarily feared or hated.

Pisistratus, for example, built temples, sponsored festivals, and was admired, if not loved, by many Athenians. Tyranny, however was established through extralegal means, and even if the tyrant later obtained popular approval, he still imposed his will on the people. It is this aspect of tyranny that has been emphasized in criticisms of rulers from George III of England by the Americans to Czar Nicholas II by the Russian revolutionaries. Tyranny implies the use of force by a powerful leader to control the people. It results in the denial of freedom and the imposition of the will of the ruler.

See also *Leviathan*; Machiavelli, Niccolò; *Two Treatises of Government*.

Tzaddik

TYPE OF ETHICS: Religious ethics

DATE: From the biblical era

ASSOCIATED WITH: The Bible, the Kabbala, and Hasidism

DEFINITION: An individual who is just, righteous, pious, and virtuous or an action that is morally correct; in Hasidism, synonymous with the *rebbe*, the leader of a Hasidic court

SIGNIFICANCE: The concept of the *tzaddik* provides Jews with an ideal model of moral and ethical behavior

The Bible considers the *tzaddik*, who lives by faith, to be an abomination to the wicked and holds that the actions of the tzaddik can influence others to be righteous. Several of the prophets, however, along with the books of Ecclesiastes and Job, suggest a dilemma: The tzaddik is rewarded with material prosperity and divine blessings but suffers tribulations; his merit may endure forever, but he may perish in his righteousness. For the rationalist rabbis, the concept of absolute righteousness is unattainable. In their opinion, however, the tzaddik

is to be praised more than are the ministering angels; his creative acts are coequal with those of God, and he is capable of canceling or at least minimizing the stern decrees of heaven and earth. Indeed, it is because of the sustaining merit of the tzaddikim, rather than psychological determinism and mechanics, that the world exists. The Kabbala teaches that the soul of the tzaddik exhibits a harmonious relationship between the hidden aspect of the divine and the divine as it is manifested. The tzaddik's life, therefore, suggests that the inner turmoil of one's soul is not a problem that defies solution but a mystery that can be resolved if, following the tzaddik's narrow path to otherworldliness, one loves and fears God in joy. In the words of one talmudist-kabbalist, "The justification of [man's] life is that, at every moment, he burns in the consuming fire of the Lord, for his soul is the candle of God." A central concept in the Kabbala is the symbiotic interaction of God and humanity, in which the actions of the lower world have an impact on the higher world. In the Hasidic world, this developed into the complementary roles of the rebbe/tzaddik and the *hasid* ("pious"). During the Shoah (the Holocaust), for example, the cadres of rebbeim/tzaddikim were a source of *hithazqut* ("encouragement"), which served to diminish despair (*ye'ush*) among the Hasidim. The rebbeim/tzaddikim acted as a kind of sponge for misery, absorbing pain and cruelty before they spilled out and overcame all else. They taught that multiple acts of holiness in the service of God and humanity help to restore dignity and self-respect, and can bring sanity to a shattered world. This view provides a marked contrast to the "theology of suffering," which views sainthood in terms of martyrdom.

See also Hasidism; Jewish ethics; Kabbala; Talmud; Torah.

U.N. Covenant on Civil and Political Rights

Type of ethics: Civil rights

Date: 1966

Associated with: United Nations Commission on Human Rights

Definition: The Covenant is a legally binding agreement by which countries promise to ensure civil and political rights

Significance: Following the Universal Declaration on Human Rights, which established standards for civil and political rights, this Covenant binds nations to meet those standards

For years after the 1948 Universal Declaration of Human Rights, the United Nations struggled to prepare treaties that would oblige nations to guarantee the rights and freedoms described in the Declaration. In 1966, two covenants were presented: the International Covenant on Civil and Political Rights, and the International Covenant on Economic, Social, and Cultural Rights. Those nations who are party to the Covenant on Civil and Political Rights have agreed to guarantee to all individuals under their jurisdiction certain basic rights. No distinctions are made because of race, color, sex, language, national origin, and so on. The rights and freedoms guaranteed under this Covenant include the right to life and liberty, freedom from slavery, freedom from torture or inhuman punishment, freedom from arbitrary detention, the right to travel freely, and the freedom of thought and religion. Furthermore, the Covenant guarantees protection for ethnic, religious, and linguistic minorities, and guarantees that no one may be forced to testify against himself or herself. Signatory nations found to be in violation of this Covenant may be held accountable by the United Nations.

See also International law; Universal Declaration of Human Rights.

U.N. Declaration of the Rights of the Child

Type of ethics: Children's rights

Date: 1959

Associated with: The United Nations

Definition: The U.N. Declaration laid out ten principles according to which individuals, organizations, and governments should aid and protect children

Significance: The United Nations Declaration of the Rights of the Child stated that children worldwide have value and rights

The United Nations Declaration of the Rights of the Child grew out of earlier international accords: the 1924 League of Nations Declaration of the Rights of the Child, and the 1948 Universal Declaration of Human Rights. The 1959 Declaration reiterates that all people—regardless of race, color, religion, sex, and so on—have rights and freedoms simply because they are human. Children are often neglected or abused, however, because they cannot stand up and claim their basic human rights. Therefore, it is the duty of every person and every government to take extra steps to guarantee the rights of children. The Declaration spells out principles to guide this effort. All children are entitled to a name, a nationality, medical care, nutrition, housing, education, and recreation. Handicapped children have rights to special care. Governments should assist families in caring for children, and children without families are entitled to care. Children should not be subject to discrimination or taught to discriminate. In 1989, a U.N. Convention on the Rights of the Child listed thirty-eight rights of children that ratifying nations must respect.

See also Children's rights; Universal Declaration of Human Rights.

U.N. Declaration on the Rights of Disabled Persons

Type of ethics: Disability rights

Date: 1975

Associated with: The disabled persons' movement

Definition: A Declaration that proclaims that the physically disabled person has the same rights that other human beings have

Significance: This Declaration was the first of several attempts by the United Nations to address the specific rights and needs of physically disabled persons

Adopted in 1975, the U.N. Declaration on the Rights of Disabled Persons confirmed and expanded the 1971 Declaration on the Rights of Mentally Retarded Persons. Although the preferred terminology has changed since these declarations were made, their intention was to recognize the humanity of mentally and physically challenged people. The 1975 Declaration defines "disabled person" as anyone who is prevented, because of a physical or mental deficiency, from pursuing a normal life. The Declaration promises the same rights to disabled persons that other human beings share and recognizes that delivering on these promises may mean providing special programs. Disabled people are entitled to proper medical care, physical therapy, education, and training. They have a right to economic security. They have a right to guardians and advisers, when needed, and the right to be protected from abuse and exploitation. The adoption of the Declaration led to further study and action by the United Nations, which sponsored an International Year of the Disabled (1981) and a U.N. Decade of Disabled Persons (1983-1992).

See also Disability rights; Universal Declaration of Human Rights.

U.S. National Commission for the Protection of Human Subjects of Biomedical and Behavioral Research

Type of ethics: Bioethics

Date: Established July, 1974

Associated with: U.S. Department of Health, Education, and Welfare (DHEW)

Definition: An interdisciplinary body that formulated guidelines governing the treatment of human subjects in federally funded research

SIGNIFICANCE: The earliest and most successful government effort to establish basic ethical guidelines regulating science

From 1966 through 1972, several revelations that reputable scientists had routinely risked the health and well-being of subjects without their knowledge eroded public confidence in science. Many incidents involved poor, institutionalized, elderly, military, or prison populations. Most notorious were the 1972 Tuskegee Syphilis Study revelations. For forty years, Public Health Service researchers had studied the natural course of syphilis in poor African American men from Tuskegee, Alabama; the researchers kept the man unaware of the study's purpose, failed to treat them, even when penicillin became available, and actively prevented outside treatment. In 1974, Congress established the Commission and provided that its recommendations were to be accepted by the U.S. Department of Health, Education, and Welfare unless the reasons for rejecting them were made public.

The Commission issued several reports, including the *Belmont Report: Ethical Principles and Guidelines for the Protection of Human Subjects of Research* (1978), which led to the establishment of comprehensive regulations. The basic regulations require that most federally funded researchers obtain informed consent, protect confidentiality, and minimize risks to subjects. Additional safeguards were implemented from other reports to govern research on children, pregnant women, prisoners, and other special populations. The Commission's impact extends beyond directly funded research. Since institutions receiving federal funds must ensure that all research is conducted ethically, most institutions review all research under the same guidelines, which have become the accepted standard for ethical research.

See also Bioethics; Experimentation, ethics of; Medical research.

Unamuno y Jugo, Miguel de (Sept. 29, 1864, Bilbao, Spain—Dec. 31, 1936, Salamanca, Spain): Philosopher

TYPE OF ETHICS: Modern history

ACHIEVEMENTS: Author of *Del sentimiento trágico de la vida en los hombres y en los pueblos* (1913; *The Tragic Sense of Life in Men and Peoples*, 1921), *L'Agonie du christianisme* (1925; *The Agony of Christianity*, 1928), and *La Vida de Don Quijote y Sancho* (1905; *The Life of Don Quixote and Sancho*, 1927), among other works

SIGNIFICANCE: Passionately independent, Unamuno explored his own soul in an attempt to understand humankind's quest for immortality; he believed that the emotions and faith were the best tools with which to explore the tragedy of life

Subjectivity, individualism, an acknowledgment of the role of irrationality, and a sense of life's anguish and tragedy were among the existential values that Miguel de Unamuno y Jugo shared with Søren Kierkegaard, Martin Heidegger, and Friedrich Nietzsche. Although he gave his own distinctive accent to their concept of the tragic sense of life, Unamuno rejected their idea that life was nothingness. He found meaning in his own passionate desire to escape annihilation by questing for the immortality of body and soul, and he concluded that this quest was common to all people. This perception was not derived from the principal philosophical systems of the day. Those systems were too abstract for Unamuno because they yielded only dehumanized ideas about human nature and human beings themselves: "thinking man," "economic man," or "freedom-seeking man."

Having devoted his intellect to exploring his inner self, Unamuno viewed humanity as a creature of flesh and bones, not as a philosophical object or an academic construct. Real humans were driven by passions and by faith. Since reason could explain neither the human search for immortality nor its own existence, Unamuno viewed humanity as being caught in a tragic struggle between reason and faith—faith being simply the hope that death does not bring annihilation. Unamuno's faith had, as Catholic theologians say, a "vital" religious base that also provided a foundation for his subjectivity and his intense individualism. Regarding most political systems as, at best, cloaks for civil privateering or masks for tyranny, and remaining innately suspicious of ethical and scientific ideals, he was a lifelong champion of the divine rights of individuals and of the battle for the human spirit.

See also *Being and Nothingness*; *Beyond Good and Evil*; Heidegger, Martin; Ortega y Gasset, José; Tillich, Paul.

Uncle Tom's Cabin: Book

TYPE OF ETHICS: Race and ethnicity

DATE: Published 1852

AUTHOR: Harriet Beecher Stowe (1811-1896)

SIGNIFICANCE: Appealing to Christian ethics, Stowe attacked slavery as immoral and aroused popular sentiment against it

Harriet Beecher Stowe's bestselling novel was the most influential antislavery work published in the years just prior to the American Civil War. It was a direct response to the moral concessions in the Compromise of 1850, and particularly the Fugitive Slave Law, which required Northerners to return runaway slaves to their Southern owners. The novel also refuted some contemporary religious arguments that attempted to justify slavery through biblical evidence. Stowe was determined to expose slavery as antifamily and atheistic. She believed that the materialistic values of mid-nineteenth century commerce had numbed Americans' moral sense and blinded them to the tragic consequences of the slave trade. Stowe believed that the Christian, domestic values embodied by wives and mothers were the best antidote for this evil, and her book makes numerous appeals to American women to use their humanizing influence to end slavery. Another ethical issue raised by the novel is the appropriate response of slaves to oppression. Although some modern readers question the docility of the titular hero, Stowe's purpose was to create a Christ-like figure who embodied superior character traits, such as humility, goodness, and submission to God's will, that were essential in Stowe's Christian value system.

See also Abolition; Racism; Slavery.

Harriet Beecher Stowe, the author of Uncle Tom's Cabin. (Library of Congress)

Unconditional surrender

TYPE OF ETHICS: Military ethics

DEFINITION: A surrender in which the surrendering entity or entities have no power to negotiate and must accept any conditions that are imposed upon them by the victor or victors in the conflict

SIGNIFICANCE: Raises various questions regarding the morality of unlimited warfare

During some of the most critical days of World War II, American president Franklin D. Roosevelt and British prime minister Winston S. Churchill met in January, 1943, in Casablanca, Morocco. Their intent was to plan future Allied operations and to reassure their hard-pressed Soviet ally that they would make no diplomatic deals with the common Axis enemy. Concluding this Allied North African Conference (ANFA), Roosevelt publicly announced that the war against Nazi Germany, Japan, and

Italy would end only with the "unconditional surrender" of those countries. Roosevelt made it clear that the Allies were conducting war not against the peoples of these enemy nations but against their governments and military machines. Enunciated after Great Britain had been at war for nearly four years and the United States had been at war for two, the doctrine of unconditional surrender signaled the Allied resolve to fight the war to the finish. Roosevelt's announcement surprised some of his own military chiefs, as well as Churchill, and it subsequently proved to be a source of confusion and controversy.

The Doctrine's Origins. Just as the French Revolution introduced Europeans to the realities of the beginnings of total war, so too did the Civil War introduce Americans to them. In February, 1862, the previously little-known Brigadier General Ulysses S. Grant gained recognition by demanding the "unconditional surrender" of Confederate Fort Donelson. One year later, in January, 1863, he gained fame for demanding unconditional surrender at Vicksburg, when the commander of Confederate forces holding the town, Simon Bolivar Buckner, requested terms of surrender from Grant. Buckner had reason to expect generosity, for he and Grant had been friends at West Point. Grant's reply, however, was "unconditional surrender." In making this reply, Grant expressed his, and the Union's, acceptance of a grinding, bloody total war. In terms of doctrine, it hardly mattered that Grant later allowed his exhausted and starving Confederate prisoners to go home on parole or that the terms that Grant offered to Confederate general Robert E. Lee, which ended the war at Appomattox, were extremely generous.

The Doctrine's Evolution. The diplomacy preceding and during warfare was something with which Americans had little experience between the Civil War and the nation's participation in the last years of World War I. The issuance of President Woodrow Wilson's Fourteen Points in January, 1918, marked a fresh and controversial approach to settling with the enemy, chiefly Wilhelminian Germany. An armistice was predicated on the overthrow of Kaiser Wilhelm and his government and the installation of a government that represented the German people—one that thereby became acceptable to Wilson. On November 9, 1918, the Kaiser abdicated and a new government was formed; on November 11, an armistice ended the fighting. Subsequently, Wilson's detailed peace plans were compromised and the planned American participation in a League of Nations failed to materialize. Supporters of Wilson believed that Wilson's Fourteen Points and armistice terms, by separating the German people from the policies of the Kaiser's government, had helped to shorten the war. Many people believed, however, that Germany should have been crushed, that Berlin and most of Germany should have been occupied by the United States and its allies. By the mid-1930's, American disappointment over its wartime experience, combined with the new presence of a rearmed and militant Hitlerian Germany, led to the conclusion that Germany had profited from too much leniency in 1918. The unlimited warfare unleashed by Germany, Japan, and their allies in World War II provided ample grounds for reviving Grant's concept of unconditional surrender.

The Doctrine in World War II. President Roosevelt's reassertion of unconditional surrender at Casablanca was aimed at attaining several immediate objectives. A global war had reached a critical stage. A long string of unbroken Allied defeats had just been ended. The Battle of the Atlantic was still being lost. Mistrust persisted between Britain and the United States, on the one hand, and their invaluable ally the Soviet Union, on the other. Thus, the doctrine was intended to raise Allied morale, reassure the Russians, and signal Allied resolve to the enemy. Scholars later noted that of all the Allied statements, this was the only one that Adolf Hitler believed completely.

In 1943, Roosevelt's military chieftains apparently had little or no prior knowledge of the unconditional surrender doctrine. Initially, therefore, the doctrine did not represent a military initiative. Roosevelt probably drew upon the recommendations of a 1942 State Department Advisory Committee on Postwar Policy that had been passed on to him by Committee Chairman Norman Davis. The recommendation was that "nothing short of unconditional surrender by the principal enemies, Germany and Japan, could be accepted" (Pogue, 1963-1987). (The way was left open for a "negotiated peace" with Italy.) Amid the drama of Casablanca, Roosevelt apparently recalled the Committee's recommendation.

After the Allies won a number of victories in 1944, Roosevelt and his military commanders decided that German resistance had been stiffened by the doctrine, thus prolonging the war, but Winston Churchill adamantly refused to abandon the doctrine. Consequently, in order to preserve harmony within the Grand Alliance, unconditional surrender was retained.

Ethical Implications. The questions of whether the doctrine of unconditional surrender lengthened the war, whether it was necessary for military victory, and whether it was morally justifiable continued to be controversial after the war's end. Did the ruthless acts of the Axis nations make it ethically permissible to match total war and terror with more total war and terror? No conclusive answers to this question have been found. American Cold War doctrine (1946 to 1986) in reaction to Soviet policy indicated, however, that if war came, the United States and its allies were prepared for a nuclear war of mutually assured destruction (MAD). Logically, the doctrine of unconditional surrender meant annihilation. —*Clifton K. Yearley*

See also Hiroshima and Nagasaki, bombing of; Limited war; Military ethics; War and peace.

BIBLIOGRAPHY
Armstrong, Anne. *Unconditional Surrender*. New Brunswick, N.J.: Rutgers University Press, 1961.

Eisenhower, David. *Eisenhower At War: 1943-1945*. New York: Random House, 1986.

Grob, Gerald N., ed. *Statesmen and Statecraft of the Modern West*. Barre, Mass.: Barre, 1967.

Matloff, Maurice. *Strategic Planning for Coalition Warfare: 1943-1944*. Washington, D.C.: Office of the Chief Military History Department of the Army, 1959.

Pogue, Forrest. *George C. Marshall*. New York: Viking Press, 1963-1987.

Union of Concerned Scientists

TYPE OF ETHICS: Scientific ethics
DATE: Founded 1969
ASSOCIATED WITH: Post-World War II nuclear activism
DEFINITION: An organization originally established to examine the uses and hazards of nuclear energy
SIGNIFICANCE: The Union of Concerned Scientists pursues a vigorous program of education and public advocacy concerning the effects of advanced technology on society and public policy

At the end of the 1960's, the testing of nuclear weapons had been suspended by the United States, the Soviet Union, and other nations with nuclear arms, but the Strategic Arms Limitation Treaty (SALT) talks that would halt the construction of weapons had not yet begun. In addition, the first nuclear power plants were either on the drawing boards or actually under construction. The Union of Concerned Scientists (USC) was founded at this time to gather information on the nuclear arms race, arms control, nuclear reactor safety, energy policy, and other related matters. (Although the membership of the USC is not made up exclusively of scientists, a core of technically competent professionals makes its studies definitive and disinterested.) The USC's findings are made available in its own periodicals, in conferences, in public presentations in the media, in speaking engagements, and in educational packets provided for school use. The USC also provides court testimony and appearances at hearings such as those conducted by the Nuclear Regulatory Commission (NRC) regarding the relicensing of atomic power plants. More recently, the USC has broadened its scope to deal with the impact of advanced technology in general on society and has organized scientists on a worldwide basis out of concern for the earth's ecology.

See also Atom bomb; Atomic Energy Commission (AEC); Earth, human relations to; Mutually Assured Destruction (MAD); Nuclear energy; Nuclear Regulatory Commission, U.S.; SALT treaties; Science, ethics of.

Universal Declaration of Human Rights

TYPE OF ETHICS: Human rights
DATE: December 10, 1948
ASSOCIATED WITH: United Nations Commission on Human Rights
DEFINITION: A declaration of fundamental principles of human rights to which all nations could aspire
SIGNIFICANCE: The Universal Declaration of Human Rights, as an unbinding statement of basic principles, provided common standards of rights; later, binding agree-

Albert Einstein was deeply concerned about the ethics of science and technology. (AP/Wide World Photos)

ments would measure how well nations adhered to these standards

In its Charter, the United Nations affirmed its faith "in fundamental human rights" and its commitment to promote and encourage "respect for human rights." To fulfill that responsibility, the U.N. formed a Commission on Human Rights in 1946 to begin drafting an international bill of rights. On December 10, 1948, the General Assembly of the United Nations adopted the Universal Declaration of Human Rights. This Declaration was not legally binding on member nations, but it established the fundamental principles upon which legally binding treaties would be based. The Declaration proclaimed several principles of civil and political rights that were already found in many declarations and constitutions: that all human beings are free and equally valuable; that everyone is entitled to freedom regardless of race, color, nationality, political opinion, and so on; that humans have rights to life, liberty, and security; and that all people are entitled to freedom from torture, freedom to travel, and freedom to own property. The Declaration was unusual in also proclaiming several principles of economic, social, and cultural rights. These two sets

of principles were regulated in 1966 by U.N. Covenants, which are legal treaties.

See also Human rights; International law.

Universalizability

TYPE OF ETHICS: Theory of ethics
DATE: Coined 1788
ASSOCIATED WITH: German philosopher Immanuel Kant
DEFINITION: The idea that, in making a moral decision, one should be able to will that others should make the same decision
SIGNIFICANCE: According to the concept of universalizability, because ethics is based on reason, a particular right action should be right not only for an individual but also for all people

Immanuel Kant's ethical theory is called a deontological or nonconsequential or duty-based ethical theory. According to Kant, an action is right if it follows from duty; that is, an action should be done not because of its consequences but because it is the right thing to do. The principle that one follows must be universalizable; in other words, it should be possible to argue that everyone ought to act the same way in a similar situation. For example, the rules that promises should not be broken by anyone, that no one should kill others, and that no one should cheat should be followed by everyone always. There are certain moral rights that everyone possesses. Kant uses the example of making a false promise to make his point. In a particular situation, making a false promise might suit one's purpose, yet one cannot make the principle of making a false promise into a universal law, because then the concept of promising would have no meaning.

See also Deontological ethics; Kant, Immanuel.

Upaniṣads: Hindu Scriptures

Type of ethics: Religious ethics
Date: 800-400 B.C.E.
Author: Unknown
Significance: The Upaniṣads stress the importance of the practice of physical, mental, ethical, and spiritual disciplines as the prerequisites for the realization of the knowledge of Brahman, or ultimate reality

The Upaniṣads, literally meaning "to sit near someone," constitute the concluding portion of the Vedas, the first original Hindu scripture, which has four sections: Samhitās or collections—hymns, prayers, and formulas of sacrifice; Brāhmaṇas—prose treatises discussing the significance of sacrificial rites and ceremonies; Āraṇyakas, or forest texts; and the Upaniṣads, or later Vedas. The Upaniṣads are the main basis for the Vedānta school of philosophy. The doctrines of the Upaniṣads were imparted orally. Groups of students sat near the teacher to learn from him the truths by which ignorance could be destroyed. The authors of the Upaniṣads, of which there are more than two hundred are not known. The principal Upaniṣads are the *Īśa, Kena, Katha, Praśna, Muṇḍaka, Māṇḍūkya, Taittirīya, Aitareya, Chāndogya,* and *Bṛhadāraṇyaka* Upaniṣads. Śaṅkara, the Vedānta philosopher, wrote commentaries on the above ten and on the *Śvetāśvatara Upaniṣad*. In addition, the *Kauṣitaki, Mahānārāyana* and the *Maitri* are also considered principal Upaniṣads. These Upaniṣads were written partly in prose and partly in verse.

The Upaniṣads are concerned with the meaning of the sacrificial rites, and in the process of discussing them, they introduce some profound metaphysical and religious ideas. With the Upaniṣads began the period of speculative research into human nature and the individual's position in the universe. The practical result of the Upaniṣads was to depersonalize the universe and to minimize the importance of earlier Vedic gods. The Upaniṣads were not philosophical treatises, but they contained certain fundamental ideas that form the basis of a philosophical system out of which the orthodox schools of Indian philosophy—Sāṃkhya, Yoga, Nyāya, Vaíśeṣika, Mīmāṃsā, and Vedānta—developed their systems.

The Upaniṣads have for their ideal the realization of Brahman, becoming one with God. The world is not an end in itself. It comes from God, through his mysterious power, and it ends in God. Everything in the phenomenal world, including the individual, must realize the infinite, must strive to reclaim the highest. The Absolute is the highest and most desirable ideal. The performance of duty is necessary if one is to achieve the highest perfection. Morality is valuable because it leads one toward this highest perfection. Inner purity is more important than outer conformity. The ethics of the Upaniṣads insist on the transformation of the whole person. In the process of this transformation, one knows that one's liberation from the phenomenal appearance depends on oneself and not upon the grace of transcendent deity. The idea of rebirth, the idea that the individual who has not gained the ultimate reality will be subject to the cycle of birth and death, is also presented for the first time in the Upaniṣads.

See also Hindu ethics; Śaṅkara; Vedānta.

Utilitarianism

Type of ethics: Theory of ethics
Date: Eighteenth century to present
Associated with: Jeremy Bentham, John Stuart Mill, The Philosophic Radicals, and hedonism
Definition: Utilitarianism is a decision procedure that is intended to promote the general welfare; the classical version of utilitarianism combines hedonism, consequentialism, and universalism, defining right action as that which results in the greatest happiness for the greatest number
Significance: Utilitarianism marks an early attempt to devise a secular, rational, scientific moral system; its influence can be attributed to its simplicity, its adaptability, and the talent of its defenders

Utilitarianism is a decision procedure for normative ethics that holds that the rightness (or wrongness) of human actions, policies, or rules is determined by their effects on the general welfare. Since the late eighteenth century, it has been one of the most prominent moral theories. In addition, utilitarian principles have become major factors in shaping social policy and have given rise to numerous applications, ranging from behaviorist psychology to cost benefit analysis. Utilitarianism has undergone many changes, and it exists in many forms. Consequently, there are many versions of utilitarianism, which makes it difficult to discuss in general terms.

The dominant version was developed and articulated by Jeremy Bentham (1748-1832), who applied it to the reformation of the legal, political, social, educational, penal, and economic institutions of Britain and other countries. His principle of utility formed the standard by which actions are judged: "It is the greatest happiness of the greatest number that is the measure of right and wrong." Classical utilitarianism is based on a hedonistic theory of value. Happiness (that is, pleasure and the absence of pain) is the only thing that is intrinsically good. Other things are valuable only to the extent that they bring happiness. Thus, moral actions result in producing the greatest balance of pleasure over pain. Bentham held that pleasure and pain (in the basic, feeling sense) are quantifiable, and he devised a "felicific calculus" to measure the utility of acts numerically and to make comparisons among them. Utilitarianism is consequentialist, not deontological: Actions are evaluated by their outcomes and not by the agent's intentions or motives. This is consistent with Bentham's desire to devise a system that would be objective and scientific. Although one can empirically ascertain the results of people's actions, one can only guess regarding their intentions. Utilitarianism is universalist rather than egoistic. One should seek to maximize the pleasure of all, not act selfishly to maximize one's own pleasure at the expense of others. Hence, utilitarianism is egalitarian, since each person's happiness is of equal value. Even the feelings of animals can be taken into account. Bentham claims that the principle of utility is not susceptible to direct proof, because it is the principle that is used to prove everything else.

Bentham's moral system drew storms of protest. Many critics complained that an ethics based on hedonism legitimized crass self-indulgence and base animal pleasures. Christians were troubled by utilitarianism's secularism. Critics also complained that utilitarianism reduced ethics to cold, impersonal calculations; that it was too difficult and demanding; that it was too simplistic and easy, and that it could easily lead to rights violations and injustices. The history of utilitarianism since Bentham consists of the ways in which its advocates have reacted to critics by reshaping and improving the theory.

Bentham's chosen successor was his godson John Stuart Mill. In his major ethical work, *Utilitarianism*, Mill responded to the aforementioned charges. He defended utilitarianism (to varying degrees of success), but he also changed Bentham's hedonism in significant ways. Responding to Thomas Carlyle, whose distaste for ethical hedonism led him to denounce utilitarianism as a "sordid pig-philosophy," Mill argued that pleasures differed qualitatively and that some pleasures are superior to others. Another significant change came forty years later, when G. E. Moore articulated his "ideal utilitarianism," which allows for the intrinsic goodness and desirability of other values besides happiness.

Charges that utilitarianism could lead to injustice have persisted despite the explanations of Bentham, Mill, and a host of others. The strong claim that one should always do whatever results in the greatest utility has prompted critics to imagine scenarios in which utilitarianism is construed to endorse such detestable actions as gladiator fights (if the aggregate pleasure of the multitudinous spectators outweighs the pain of the participants); the punishing of innocents (if convicting someone of committing a sensational crime appeases the masses, staves off riots, and restores faith in the system); torture (if torture could force a captured terrorist to confess where a bomb has been planted); and even murder (if surgeons harvest an individual's organs for transplant in other patients, thus improving and saving several lives). Such problems have led to the distinction between act- and

rule-utilitarianism and the view that utilitarianism is more effective as a formula for developing basic rules than as a method for rationalizing the best action in a particular case. John Rawls has argued that utilitarianism neglects basic principles of justice and fairness by ignoring the distinction between persons and the distribution of goods. He believes that emphasizing the sum total of happiness or average utility not only leads to inequalities but also legitimizes them. Utilitarians maintain that there is a natural dynamic that favors egalitarianism, in that a given sum of money will likely have greater utility value for a poor person than for a wealthy person. Moreover, utilitarians claim that it is unlikely that an extremely inegalitarian distribution of resources or benefits would bring about the greatest possible amount of happiness.

The success of utilitarianism is remarkable. Few persons regard themselves as utilitarians, yet utilitarianism remains among the dominant schools of ethical theory. Its influence extends beyond ethics into social sciences and formal decision theory. Thanks to its able advocates, its appeal to basic rational principles, and its flexibility, utilitarianism has adjusted to the challenges of critics and maintained its prominence.   —*Don A. Habibi*

See also Bentham, Jeremy; Consequentialism; Epicurus; Hedonism; Mill, John Stuart; Moore, G. E.; Sidgwick, Henry; Universalizability.

BIBLIOGRAPHY

Allison, Lincoln, ed. *The Utilitarian Response: The Contemporary Viability of Utilitarian Political Philosophy*. London: Sage, 1990.

Bentham, Jeremy. *An Introduction to the Principles of Morals and Legislation*. Oxford, England: Clarendon Press, 1879.

Glover, Jonathan, ed. *Utilitarianism and its Critics*. New York: Macmillan, 1990.

Lyons, David. *The Forms and Limits of Utilitarianism*. Oxford, England: Clarendon Press, 1965.

Mill, John Stuart. *Utilitarianism*. Edited by George Sher. Indianapolis: Hackett, 1979.

Utopia: Book

TYPE OF ETHICS: Medieval history
DATE: Published 1516 in Latin
AUTHOR: Sir Thomas More
SIGNIFICANCE: Revitalized ethical thinking on ideal societies and social planning, prompting a flood of utopian literature in the following centuries

More coined the word "utopia" for this book and simultaneously provided a noun to describe an ideal society and an adjective—utopian—to signify a hopelessly impractical approach to living. The word "utopia" derives from the Greek for "no place," but it is also a pun on "good place." With this play on words, More sowed the seeds of argument regarding his book: Was he serious? Was he a communist, a liberal, an autocrat? Was he an advocate of euthanasia and divorce?

Background. *Utopia* shows many influences. More was a classical scholar of high standing—a product of the Renaissance. He also pursued a career in law with great success. Amerigo Vespucci's writings on America inspired him with references to paradisiacal lands and the communal ownership of property. The Catholic Church was the dominant influence of his boyhood, and perhaps of his whole life. Interestingly, More wrote *Utopia* in a lull before the Reformation; one year after its publication, Martin Luther defied the Church by nailing his ninety-five theses to the door of All Saints Church in Wittenberg.

Utopian Practices and Ethics. In book 1, More describes meeting a man called Hythloday, who first castigates European society and then proceeds in book 2 to describe Utopia with heartfelt admiration. Hythloday condemns the idle of Europe, including noblemen and their servants. He asserts that rulers wage war, not peace, and that ministers at court do not listen to arguments, but indulge in politics for their own gain. His remedies for economic ills include stopping the enclosure and monopoly of land by the rich. With strong words, he condemns the execution of thieves as unfair and ineffective, stating that it incites men to kill, since murder, carries the same penalty.

Book 2 describes More's fictional state in detail. The Utopians live a regulated, standardized life. All the cities are beautiful and identical. All citizens wear the same simple clothes, with some modifications for gender. They live together in families of specific size and work six hours a day, spending their leisure time reading and attending lectures. Women may marry at the age of eighteen, men at twenty-two. Adultery is strongly condemned and can result in slavery or even execution. In extreme circumstances of recurrent adultery or perversion, however, divorce is permitted.

Utopia is a state founded on compassion and altruism. No one wants for material goods. Health care is universal, though few get sick. Society gently encourages euthanasia when a mortally ill person suffers from great pain. All property is owned communally. Every ten years, a family exchanges its house, which is supposed to encourage people to take proper care for the next tenant. Even their eating takes place in a large hall that holds as many as thirty households.

Ultimately, authoritarianism is a strong feature of this model state. No one has the freedom to remain idle. Everyone needs permission to travel. Any discussion of government matters outside official meeting-places is punishable by death. Utopia also has rigid hierarchies: children defer to adults, women to men, younger to older, and families to their elected representatives. Paradoxically, however, Utopia has strong democratic elements, including voting for all key political posts, though people are barred from canvassing votes, to minimize corruption. Slavery replaces hanging as the deterrent for deviant behavior. Serious criminal behavior leads to slavery, which entails working constantly in chains, performing the meanest labor.

Citizens may practice any religion, but strong proselytizing is barred for fear that it may lead to argument. Certain tenets must be held by all: belief in a wise Providence and an afterlife. Utopians pursue pleasure as natural and logical, but they abhor vanity and pomp and place no value on gold and silver, even while storing it for economic advantage and for trade. They avoid war whenever possible but conduct military training for both sexes. When threatened by another nation, they offer rewards to kill the ruler of the opposing nation. Failing that, they sow contention in that nation and, as a last resort, hire mercenaries to fight alongside their own soldiers.

Discussion. More uses this book to debate opposing viewpoints for intellectual stimulation. For example, when Hythloday says that as long as there is property there will be no justice, More counters that in a communist society people would not work or have any incentive to better themselves. Hythloday contrasts the greed and selfishness of Europe with Utopia's communism based on a harmony of purpose, with the family unit at its core. Utopia also, however, has internal contradictions. The residents' humanistic values—respecting individual inquiry and religious freedom—contrast with the total conformity of their lives and the fact that certain basic beliefs must be held by all.

Utopia is a commentary on More's own society, a combination of monasticism and feudalism, but Utopia is founded on reason, not Christianity. More is pleading: If they can do so well without divine revelation, why can Europe not do better with it? It is impossible to believe that More meant *Utopia* as a blueprint for an ideal society. Elements that support this conclusion include the deadpan humor (Anider, a river, means "no water"; Utopians use gold in making chamber pots) and the contrast with More's own religious convictions (he persecuted heretics and chose execution rather than compromise his opposition to divorce). Ultimately, *Utopia* is not so much interesting or original in itself as it is noteworthy because it stimulated discussion regarding "social engineering" as a remedy for society's ills.

—*Philip Magnier*

See also Capital punishment; Communism; Communitarianism; Criminal punishment; Democracy; Economics; Euthanasia; Family values; Humanism; Luther, Martin; *Republic*.

BIBLIOGRAPHY

More, Thomas, Sir. *More's Utopia and Its Critics*. Edited by Ligeia Gallagher. Chicago, Ill.: Scott, Foresman, 1964.

Negley, Glenn, and J. Max Patrick. *The Quest for Utopia*. College Park, Md.: McGrath, 1971.

Nelson, William. *Twentieth Century Interpretations of Utopia*. Englewood Cliffs, N.J.: Prentice-Hall, 1968.

Time-Life Books. *Utopian Visions*. Alexandria, Va.: Time-Life, 1990.

Tod, Ian, and Michael Wheeler. *Utopia*. New York: Harmony Books, 1978.

Value

TYPE OF ETHICS: Theory of ethics
DATE: Third century B.C.E. to present
ASSOCIATED WITH: All major philosophers of ethics
DEFINITION: Value is what makes actions, character traits, and objects good or bad
SIGNIFICANCE: Examining the moral qualities of people or actions and their nonmoral properties inevitably raises the question of the nature or source of those values

Values are of signal importance; without them, human life would be drained of significance, a bland and textureless existence without differentiation. Academic disciplines focus on value in a variety of ways: The arts explore expressions of value; sociology, anthropology, and history all examine the ways in which values are embedded in society's structures; and psychology, including the work of philosophical psychologists such as Friedrich Nietzsche, looks at the ways in which individuals acquire their beliefs about values and the roles these beliefs play in their psyches. The philosophical study of value, axiology, tries to step back from these particular inquiries and look instead at the question "What is value?" Axiology has been a central focus of philosophical inquiry throughout the history of the discipline. For all that, however, little consensus has emerged, although certain positions tend to run as threads throughout the discussion.

Answers to the question "What is value?" take two possible forms. The first and simplest provides a list of values, such as courage, honesty, beauty, and compassion. The second attempts to answer the question "What is value in general?" It may seem relatively simple to compile a list of values, but history and anthropology reveal that such lists vary considerably at different times and in different cultures. Homeric heroes were applauded for their ability to lie and dissimulate, and classical Japanese samurai were expected to test a new sword by slicing through an unlucky wayfarer from the shoulder to the opposite flank. The honor of both the samurai and the swordmaker depended on a clean bisection.

Assuming that a list of values can be compiled, the inevitable next question is "What exactly is meant by 'courage' or 'beauty' or 'friendship'?" Plato focused on questions of this "What is X?" form in his early dialogues. The *Laches* seeks the definition of courage, the *Euthyphro* that of piety, and the *Lysis* that of friendship. Although these dialogues are notorious for providing few answers and for clearly showing how quickly simplistic answers become tangled in their own contradictions, one important implication becomes clear: One cannot know what particular values are unless one knows the nature of value in general.

Subjectivism/Objectivism. Plato begins to address the question "What is value in general?" in the *Meno*, and it is a central theme in many of his other dialogues. One view to which he is clearly attracted is that personal excellence is knowledge; that view, however, is replaced in later dialogues, notably his *Republic*, by the view that there is a source of excellence, for both people and objects, that can

be known. He argues that, since all instances of a certain value—for example, beauty or courage—share some property, there must be something, the "form" of that excellence, that they make manifest. Forms for Plato are separable essences with an independent existence that infuse the objects or people who display them. Objects or people are excellent or have value insofar as they make manifest the form of a particular value. There are, therefore, forms of all excellences, and the highest of these is the form of the good. One's own particular excellence or excellences are produced by one's knowledge of the good, and it is this knowledge that is the ultimate goal of all philosophical inquiry. This emphasis on an external source of value is one of the threads that runs through all discussions of value.

The second thread arises from the indubitable fact that people have emotional responses to instances of value. Humans are moved by compassion and repulsed by wanton cruelty; they admire bravery and appreciate beauty. This raises the following question. Do people have these responses to these actions and objects because they have the value they do or do they have the value they do because people have these responses to them? In this article, "subjectivism" is taken to be the position that human emotional responses to actions, character traits, or objects are what endow them with value. "Objectivism" is taken to be the position that there is some source or standard of value that is separate from the emotions; emotional responses to actions, character traits, or objects are prompted by, but in no way contribute to, their having value. Both negative and positive values are included in these analyses. Plato clearly took the objectivist path, and in this he was followed by many other great thinkers: Saint Thomas Aquinas, echoing Aristotle, said in his *In Divinis Nominibus* (1265), "It is not that a thing is beautiful because we love it, but we love it because it is beautiful and good." Other philosophers, however, have argued powerfully that what makes something valuable is the act of valuing it; perhaps the greatest of these thinkers is David Hume.

Hume drew an important distinction between matters of fact and matters of value. In a famous passage from his *Treatise of Human Nature* (1739-1740), he said, "In every system of morality . . . I have always remark'd, that the author proceeds for some time in the ordinary way of reasoning . . . when of a sudden I am surpriz'd to find, that instead of the usual copulations of propositions, *is*, and *is not*, I meet with no proposition that is not connected with an *ought*, or an *ought not*. This change is imperceptible; but is, however, of the last consequence. For as this *ought*, or *ought not*, expresses some new relation or affirmation, 'tis necessary . . . a reason should be given, for what seems altogether inconceivable, how this new relation can be a deduction from others which are entirely different from it." The illegitimacy of deriving value (ought) statements from factual (is) propositions alone was later labeled the "naturalistic fallacy" by G. E. Moore.

Hume's views on human psychology are an integral part of his answer to how one moves from matters of fact to matters of value. He identifies two distinct psychological processes: reason and sentiment. Reason establishes matters of fact, while sentiment, or the passions, provide a motive for action. For example, one's reason may tell one that one is standing on a railway line, that a train is coming, and that if one does not move one will be crushed, but it is only one's desire not to be crushed that provides the motive force to move. Given that moral judgments provide motives for action, Hume reasoned that they must be the result of sentiment "gilding and staining all natural objects with [its] colours."

Distinguishing between matters of fact and matters of value and locating the source of value in human sentiment—usually some form of happiness or pleasure—are integral parts of the subjectivist position. People value, and ascribe value to, those things that make them happy or sad, or that cause them pleasure or pain. Although the notion of what constitutes happiness or pleasure can be somewhat crude (Aristippus opted for immediate physical pleasures, whereas Epicurus advocated philosophical reflection and a diet of bread, cheese, and milk), in the hands of someone like David Hume, it is a subtle and many-layered aspect of the psyche.

Although subjectivism holds that all positive value has its source in positive human sentiment, the corollary does not hold; not everything in which people find happiness or pleasure is good. Pulling the wings off flies is not good simply because generations of small children have relished it; there are better and worse pleasures. John Stuart Mill recognized this distinction in the quality of pleasures, and in *Utilitarianism* (1863) he wrote that "Few human creatures would consent to be changed into any of the lower animals, for a promise of the fullest allowance of that beast's pleasures; no intelligent human being would consent to be a fool, no instructed person would be an ignoramus, no person of feeling and conscience would be base, even though they should be persuaded that the fool, the dunce or the rascal is better satisfied with his lot than they are with theirs." For Mill, the good life was founded on the refined pleasures of the higher faculties. The pleasures of a life of intelligent understanding, fine feeling, and elevated conscience are better than the pleasures of a life of ignorance, selfishness, and lack of restraint. His evidence for this is the fact that those who have had a chance to experience both types of life overwhelmingly prefer the more refined variety.

Objections and Replies. Locating the source of value in refined human sentiments brings with it three serious problems. The first is that, as G. E. Moore pointed out in an application of the naturalistic fallacy, simply because people *do* seek and value what provides them with pleasure does not mean that they *ought* to seek it. Subjectivists, including Mill and Hume, have tried to get around this objection by asserting that happiness is the only good in itself and that all else is sought as a means of obtaining it, but this fails to answer the thrust of Moore's objection. Even if everything else is sought as a means to happiness, it still does not mean that happiness is that which people ought to seek. The second problem is the parochialism of the idea of refined sentiment. While everyone can recognize what is wrong with the sadist who relishes inflicting pain, it is harder to say with any credibility that someone whose life is dedicated to a sybaritic wallow in the pleasures of the flesh is doing something *wrong*. (There is, of course, the issue of harm to others caused by this indulgence, but that is a separate question.) With this parochialism comes a potentially disturbing paternalism; if the refined pleasures are somehow better, then I may have some moral grounds for forcing unenlightened others to enjoy them. There are undertones of this view in Mill's *On Liberty* (1859).

Finally, there is the problem that if the source of value lies within the sentiments, then the value of an individual to others depends on their, the others', sentiments. X's value to Y depends on Y's feelings about X, not on some source of value possessed by X, and this does not seem to capture what philosophers mean when they talk about the moral value of persons. People, as Immanuel Kant pointed out, are valuable as ends in themselves, not simply as means to another's ends (in this case, the enjoyment of certain individual or social passions). These considerations have led many thinkers to reject the subjectivist source for value and to seek instead a source external to the human psyche. Plato identified the form of the good as this source, and generations of theistic writers including Aquinas and Saint Augustine of Hippo have taken a similar line by identifying God as the source of all value. Immanuel Kant saw the dictates of pure practical reason as the test for what was good and bad, and Moore argued that the good was an unanalyzable nonnatural property that one came to know by means of ethical intuition.

Although there is a problem of relativism with this position similar to that of subjectivism (Which religion or religious person has heard God's word correctly? Whose intuition has apprehended the good?), objectivism at least has a ready reply: Although humans may have an imperfect understanding of the good, there is nevertheless one right answer that they must find. A second difficulty is what J. L. Mackie in *Ethics* (1977) called the problem of "queerness." If there is an external, objective value, what would it look like; what kind of existence would it have? Clearly, it would have to be unlike anything else anyone has ever come across. The third and more serious problem comes by way, once again, of the naturalistic fallacy. Even supposing that there is a standard of right and wrong, a source of objective value, why should it necessarily be the case that we should accede to it? Assuming that God decrees compassion to be a valuable character trait, one still must decide, presumably by some separate standard, whether one ought to follow God's word. As Hume would say, the fact that God approves of compassion has no power over one's action unless one already wants to, or feels one ought to, obey God. Kant tries to argue that duty, one's motive force for obeying the dictates of pure practical reason, is not a sentiment, because it is produced by internal reason and not by fear or desire of external conditions, but this answer is extremely thin.

Other Alternatives. Faced with the seeming failure of both objectivism and subjectivism to provide an unequivocal and palatable answer to the question "What is value?" philosophers have tried other approaches. Existentialists such as Søren Kierkegaard, Jean-Paul Sartre, and Albert Camus focused on the fundamental choices and commitments by which people create value in the face of an absurd world. In the analytic school in the mid-twentieth century, axiology waned as the focus switched to analyzing the meaningfulness of value-language. Sir Alfred Jules Ayer and Leslie Stevenson both argued that value language had no literal meaning, it described no real property or object, and that it was rather an expression of emotion. Saying "Justice is good" was semantically equivalent to saying "Justice—hooray," and the theory quickly became known as the "boo hooray" theory.

The problem at the heart of this issue is that both the factual aspects of actions or character traits and human emotional responses to them are important elements in valuation. The sharp division in Western philosophy between reason and emotion means that the issue has usually been framed as a dichotomy: The source of value is either in the emotions or in some objective standard. One way around this disjunction is to deny the dichotomy and to see value as an emergent property arising from the interaction between factual characteristics and beliefs about, and emotional responses to, those characteristics. Emergent properties are those properties that exist as part of a dynamic system and are not reducible to any part or additive combination of parts of that system. Therefore, people appreciate a beautiful object or a noble deed because it exhibits certain characteristics, and it is those characteristics that make it beautiful or noble. What isolates those characteristics from the total description of the action or object, groups them together, and endows them with significance, however, are one's beliefs about and emotional responses to them. These responses, in turn, are shaped and guided by the characteristics that one perceives as significant.

In observing a bullfight, for example, one can isolate and describe many of the natural features of the event: the size and color of the bull, the number of people in the crowd, the blood of the bull on the sand, the color of the matador's trousers, the pleasure experienced by the crowd, the day of the week, the pain experienced by the bull, the color of the sky, and so on. Only some of these features will be relevant to an ethical assessment of the value of a bullfight, and the network of beliefs and emotions through which we perceive them will group some of those features together and endow them with significance. For most observers, the pain of the

bull will be relevant, while the color of the sky will not. The way in which that pain is interpreted, however, will vary depending on the beliefs of the observer; it may be seen as evidence of the nobility of the bull and the bullfight or as evidence of the cruelty both of the event and the matador. It is not that the source of the value lies solely in the beliefs and emotions of the observers or solely in the natural features of the bullfight that one groups together, but rather in the interaction between the two. Such a process will, as Hume says, "raise, in a manner, a new creation." Out of the vast array of features, beliefs, and emotions will rise a morally significant event, an odious or noble bullfight.

—*Robert Halliday*

See also Absurd, The; Objectivism; Relativism; Subjectivism.

BIBLIOGRAPHY

Hume, David. *An Enquiry Concerning the Principles of Morals*. Edited by J. B. Schneewind. Indianapolis: Hackett, 1983. The standard edition of this seminal work in which Hume develops the ideas postulated in his *Treatise of Human Nature*.

MacIntyre, Alasdair. *After Virtue*. 2nd ed. Notre Dame, Ind.: University of Notre Dame Press, 1984. An extremely influential book that argues that virtues can be understood only in the context of a social practice.

Mill, John Stuart. *Utilitarianism*. Edited by George Sher. Indianapolis: Hackett, 1979. Mill's classic discussion of happiness as the source of all values and his distinction between higher and lower happiness. This edition includes his equally influential *On Liberty*.

Plato. *Plato's Republic*. Edited by Lewis Campbell and Benjamin Jowett. New York: Garland, 1987. A mature Platonic dialogue in which the idea of the good is explicated and defended. One of the great classics in moral and political philosophy.

Sartre, Jean-Paul. *Existentialism and Humanism*. Edited and translated by Phillip Mairet. Brooklyn: Haskell House, 1977. A short lecture in which Sartre addresses the foundations of existentialism. Provides a more accessible introduction to existential commitment than does his giant *Being and Nothingness* (1956).

Values clarification

TYPE OF ETHICS: Theory of ethics

DATE: Mid-1960's

ASSOCIATED WITH: Humanistic and moral education

DEFINITION: A series of strategies designed to help individuals process their personally held values when those values collide

SIGNIFICANCE: Provides a means of reconciling value conflicts within the individual through a "valuing process" so that a workable ethical framework of personal conduct may emerge

Traditionally, educators have taught values development through such strategies as didactic moralizing, prescriptive modeling, inspiring, and appealing to conscience. Yet these traditional strategies have not noticeably produced the desired results—at least, so believe the proponents of values clarification, who advocate a different set of strategies to develop effective values consciousness.

Background. Values clarification evolved in the mid-1960's, when American activists challenged the war in Vietnam along with the political system and promoted civil rights for minorities. Concurrently, critics attacked the schools for ignoring the teaching of values in a time of crises. Noting that parents and religious institutions had little impact, critics believed that the media, particularly television, adversely affected the values of the young. Hence, they argued that education should teach the young how to develop appropriate values.

The first major book on values clarification, Louis Rath's *Values and Teaching* (1966), argued that Western pluralistic society made it impossible to inculcate a uniform set of values. Instead, Rath wanted to teach individuals the processes through which values emerge and may be acted upon. Rath and his associates proceeded to devise the theoretical construct of values clarification and create appropriate strategies.

How Values Clarification Works. Values clarification involves three stages: (1) identifying and analyzing values, (2) clarifying them, and (3) internalizing or acting upon those reconstituted values.

The clarifying stage is most crucial because clarification cannot occur unless values collide with competing values. Suppose that one strongly believes in the importance of sustaining life. Place that value in a particular situation, such as that of an elder suffering unbearable pain caused by an incurable disease. Two values thus conflict: the importance of sustaining life and the importance of lessening or eliminating pain.

To clarify and then resolve the conflict of what to do, one must proceed through Rath's seven-question framework: (1) What are the alternatives, given the choices? (2) What are the consequences of each alternative? (3) Can one's choices be made independently? (4) What are one's value preferences? (5) Can one declare one's preferences publicly? (6) Once decisions are made, can one act upon one's choices? (7) Can one develop a values stance that is consistent with a long-term framework of personal conduct?

The goals of values clarification are to help individuals select and reflect on the values chosen that best suit a particular situation. Borrowing from John Dewey the basic tenet that values are not fixed but change as life situations change, advocates of values clarification perceive all values as relative.

To engage in values clarification, its advocates recommend the workshop, with small informal groups providing an interchange of ideas. The leader-teacher stimulates the moral reasoning within the group, often providing some subject for the values discussion; for example, a story, poem,

cartoon, game, or news event. After recapping the subject's content, the leader-teacher and the group probe both the intrinsic values of the material itself and the values of the group.

The Impact of Values Clarification on Ethics. Values clarification was initially regarded as an exciting era in education, filled with potential. Later, values clarification became an explosive educational issue.

Initial Reactions. Protest activists of the mid-1960's brought values-clarification techniques to the attention of the public through media events. Suddenly values clarification was "in." Teachers, too, reported that it stimulated students because of its wide applications to everyday experiences. Students not only learned to deal with their feelings but also practiced communication and decision making skills and articulated their value judgments.

Values clarification advocates such as Sidney Simon, Howard Kirschenbaum, and Jack Fraenkel created innovative strategies. Both teachers and students delighted in using value ladders, role playing, value grids, rank-order and forced-choice dilemmas, time diaries, and so forth.

Later Reactions. Once the novelty of values clarification lessened, some educators raised warning flags. For example, hard research data on its effectiveness was nonexistent. Because values clarification deals with feelings and emotions, some critics equated it with "touchy-feely" activities found in sensitivity training. Others questioned the idea that values-clarification strategies are value free, noting that the valuing process itself, the seven-step criteria, held hidden values.

Likewise, inexperienced teachers allowed values discussions to drift and, on occasion, because of cultural differences, provoked unsettling confrontations among participants. Peer pressures among youngsters often discouraged the open, free exchange of ideas, while teachers were uncertain as to how far they should go in accepting all values. Were all values equal?

Parents, once aware that their children were engaging in values clarification, complained the children were not mature enough to participate in such complex processes. Moreover, if all values were viewed as equal, children were not learning right from wrong.

Pressure groups increasingly charged that values clarification practices confused children because schools and teachers lacked standards of conduct. They also claimed that the schools brainwashed the children, insisting that teachers cannot remain ethically neutral and that they manipulate student values—inadvertently or by design.

When pressure groups offered values clarification activities as evidence that schools were practicing "secular humanism," many school boards banned books and workshops on values clarification. The real conflict was over whose values should be taught and how.

Since the late 1970's, educators have sought compromise, attempting to balance the clarification of personal values with the transmission of lawful societal values. In sum, the major contribution of values clarification to the field of ethics has been the development of innovative exercises and strategies designed to allow individuals to clarify their values. —*Richard Whitworth*

See also Dewey, John; Moral education; Value.

BIBLIOGRAPHY

Fraenkel, Jack. *How to Teach About Values: An Analytic Approach.* Englewood Cliffs, N.J.: Prentice-Hall, 1977.

Kirschenbaum, Howard, and Sidney Simon. *Readings in Values Clarification.* Minneapolis, Minn.: Winston Press, 1973.

Rath, Louis, et al. *Values and Teaching.* 2d ed. Columbus, Ohio: Charles E. Merrill, 1978.

Simon, Sidney, et al. *Values and Teaching: Working with Values in the Classroom.* Sunderland, Mass.: Values Press, 1991.

_____. *Values Clarification: A Handbook of Practical Strategies for Teachers and Students.* Sunderland, Mass.: Values Press, 1991.

Vardhamāna (known as Mahāvīra, or the "Great Hero"; c. 599 B.C.E., Kundagrama, Bihar, India—527 B.C.E., Papa, Bihar, India): Religious reformer

TYPE OF ETHICS: Religious ethics

ACHIEVEMENTS: Founded the Jain religion

SIGNIFICANCE: As the humanitarian Albert Schweitzer said, the nonviolent message of Vardhamāna was a supreme event in spiritual history that showed that ethics is unlimited

Once, when he was attacked by a powerful man, Mahāvīra responded not with violence, anger, or fear but with love. This approach conquered his assailant, and thus Mahāvīra discovered the power of nonviolence. A new religion in India, Jainism arose from the flames of Mahāvīra's love. In a world of destructive force, Mahāvīra bequeathed a great weapon to those seeking peace and justice: moral force. This moral force influenced the peace, civil rights, and animal rights movements.

Salvation for All. In the sixth century B.C.E., India was dominated by Hinduism and the caste system. Mahāvīra rebelled against this system, and at age thirty he renounced wealth, position, and his own family to seek spiritual fulfillment. Practicing an extreme asceticism, in twelve years he became a perfected soul, a *jina*, or "conqueror," of passions.

The focus of his teaching was love of *all* life. To Mahāvīra, true justice meant to cause no suffering for any life, and thus required the practice of vegetarianism.

Three Jewels. Salvation required the three jewels of the soul: right knowledge, right conviction, and right conduct. Mahāvīra regarded right conduct as the most precious jewel of the three. It consists of five vows: no killing of any living creature, no lying, no stealing, no sexual pleasure or alcohol, and no desire or attachments.

Mahāvīra believed that no harm could ever befall a good man. Ritual, prayer, sacrifice, and social power could not make one worthy. The only value is the good life, which must be realized by right conduct.

Implications for Ethical Conduct. Mahāvīra and the Jains so loved life that they would not even harm insects. At a time when life has become cheap, perhaps nothing is more ethically relevant than the reverence for all life that Mahāvīra so fervently practiced. —*T. E. Katen*

See also Ahiṁsā; Animal rights; Environmental ethics; Hindu ethics; Jain ethics; Vegetarianism.

BIBLIOGRAPHY

Gerber, William. *The Mind of India.* New York: Macmillan, 1967.

Jaini, Jagomandar Lal. *Outlines of Jainism.* Westport, Conn.: Hyperion Press, 1982.

Prabhavananda, Swami. *The Spiritual Heritage of India.* Garden City, N.Y.: Doubleday, 1963.

Schweitzer, Albert. *Indian Thought and Its Development.* Translated by Mrs. Charles E. B. Russell. Boston: Beacon Press, 1954.

Stevenson, Mrs. Sinclair. *The Heart of Jainism.* New York: Oxford University Press, 1915.

Zimmer, Heinrich. *Philosophies of India.* New York: Meridian Books, 1956.

Vedānta

TYPE OF ETHICS: Religious ethics

DATE: Sixth century to present

DEFINITION: Major school of Indian philosophy

SIGNIFICANCE: The goal of Vedānta is to achieve the ultimate reality, or Brahman, by breaking the cycle of birth and rebirth in three different ways: the way of knowledge, or *jñāna*; the way of devotion, or *bhakti*; and the way of action, or *karma*

Vedānta, literally meaning the "end of the Vedas," is a school of Indian philosophy. The Upaniṣads, Bhagavad Gītā, and Brahma Sūtra, together with their commentaries, form the essence of the Vedānta philosophy.

Advaita, or Nondualistic, Vedānta. Śaṅkara (788-850) is considered the most powerful advocate of pure monism, or Advaita. Śaṅkara advocates the way of knowledge, or *jñāna*, as the only way to attain liberation, or *mokṣa*. The basic question of Advaita is the nature of Brahman, or ultimate reality. Brahman is pure consciousness, devoid of attributes. Brahman is nondual (*advaita*) and transcends the distinction between the knower, knowledge, and the known. The world is not real, it is an illusion, or *māyā*. It appears to be real because of ignorance, or *avidyā*, but when one comes to the realization of Brahman, one realizes the illusoriness of the world. In understanding Indian philosophy, one must realize that it believes in different levels of being. Therefore, one who comes to the realization of Brahman, becomes identical with Brahman and is, therefore, at the highest level of being and has the highest reality. Every individual has a phenomenal self, which is empirically real, since it is a part of his or her experience, and a real self, or *ātman*, which is transcendentally real and is one with Brahman.

Viśiṣṭadvaita, or Qualified Monism. Ramanuja (1070-1137) refutes the absolute monism of Śaṅkara and denies that the world is illusory, or *māyā*, and emphasizes *bhakti*, or worship, as a means of liberation. He advocated the way of devotion as opposed to the way of knowledge advocated by Advaita Vedāntins. For Ramanuja, Brahman, or ultimate reality, is spirit but has attributes. Brahman has self-consciousness and has a conscious will to create the world and bestow salvation. For Ramanuja, Brahman is a whole consisting of interrelated elements. There is no pure, undifferentiated consciousness. Brahman, for Ramanuja, is not a formless entity but a supreme person qualified by matter and souls. Matter *(achit)*, soul *(chit)*, and God (Iśvara) are real, but matter and soul are dependent on God. God (Iśvara) is Brahman, and he manifests himself in various forms for his devotees. Souls are in bondage because of ignorance. Liberation can be achieved, according to Ramanuja, by the intuitive realization that the soul is a mode of God. The soul that is liberated is not identical with Brahman because soul is always finite and God is infinite. That is why Ramanuja believes that liberation can be achieved only after death, when the soul is separated from the body. Ramanuja's view opened the way for theism, especially Vaiṣnavism, within Vedānta.

Dvaita, or Dualistic, Vedānta. During the thirteenth century, Mādhava developed the philosophical view called Dvaita, or dualistic, Vedānta, and he was outspoken against Advaita Vedānta philosophy. Mādhava was considered an incarnation of the God Viṣṇu. He stressed duality and, like Ramanuja, advocated the way of devotion, or *bhakti*. For Mādhava, God is distinct from individual souls and matter, an individual soul is distinct from another individual soul, the individual soul is distinct from matter, and when matter is divided, each part of that matter is distinct from each other. According to Mādhava, souls can be classified into three groups: those who are devoted to God alone and are bound to achieve liberation, those who will never attain liberation and are destined to perpetual rebirth, and those who revile Viṣṇu and are subject to damnation. Mādhava believed that there are different degrees of knowledge and enjoyment of bliss in liberated souls. The worship of Viṣṇu in thought, word, and deed was for him the way to liberation.

Modern Vedānta. In the twentieth century, Sri Aurobindo (1872-1950) has made a unique contribution to Vedānta philosophy. His view is popularly called the Philosophy of Integralism, or Integral Nondualism. His teaching is that the Absolute, God, world, and souls are One. His philosophy is a reinterpretation of traditional Vedānta that applies it to the social context. According to Aurobindo, human life can be transformed into the highest form of spiritual reality by practicing yoga. If one searches for the divine force that is within one and accordingly transforms all dimensions of life, one will be able to live in the highest possible divine way. So-

ciety should also be reshaped in such a way that is helpful to this transformation of life.

Vivekānanda (1862-1902), a disciple of Ramakrishna, organized the Ramakrishna Mission (it is also called the Vedānta Society in the United States). Vivekānanda considered himself an advaitin, but his Advaita viewpoint did not lead to inactive meditation; it was instead a call to action. He viewed knowledge, devotion, and action as three paths leading in different directions but reinforcing each other. He stressed practical work to achieve liberation. Since a person is identical with God, one should seek to abolish the indignities of the world.

Sarvepalli Radhakrishnan (1888-1975), a philosopher and the second president of India (1962-1967), contributed to Advaita Vedānta philosophy by providing a positive approach to Brahman in which human values were preserved. He argued that the phenomenal world is temporal, which does not mean that it is unreal and does not have any meaning and significance. Karma should not be interpreted pessimistically. It is true that the past cannot be changed, but the past does not determine the future. An individual is still free to act within the limits of the past. He emphasized that one can lead a meaningful life here and now. His view constitutes a spiritual democracy that allows everyone to work side by side. He stressed unity rather than diversity. He conveyed his teaching to the West by stating that each religion is valid to the extent that it helps one to achieve spiritual realization.   —*Krishna Mallick*

See also Hindu ethics; Śaṅkara; Upaniṣads.

BIBLIOGRAPHY

Isherwood, Christopher. *Vedanta for the Western World.* Hollywood, Calif.: Marcel Rodd, 1945.

Reyna, Ruth. *The Concept of Maya from the Vedas to the Twentieth Century.* Bombay, India: Asia, 1962.

Zaehner, R. C. *Hinduism.* London: Oxford University Press, 1962.

Vegetarianism

TYPE OF ETHICS: Animal rights
DATE: From antiquity
ASSOCIATED WITH: Famine relief and the animal rights and environmental movements
DEFINITION: The dietary practice of subsisting primarily or entirely without foods of animal origin, especially red meat and poultry
SIGNIFICANCE: Vegetarian diets have been advocated on ethical grounds because they are believed to promote human health and/or to prevent animal suffering, famine, and environmental degradation

Although vegetarian diets have been advocated for ethical reasons since ancient times, the English term "vegetarian" came into general use upon the founding of the Vegetarian Society at Ramsgate, England, in 1847.

Types of Vegetarians. Modern nutritionists recognize several categories of vegetarians. *Vegans* are strict vegetarians who consume neither meat nor meat "by-products" (animal-based foods, such as dairy products and eggs, that can be obtained without slaughtering the animal). Among less strict vegetarians, *lactovegetarians* eat no meat but do eat dairy products, *ovovegetarians* eat no meat but do eat eggs, and *lacto-ovovegetarians* eat no meat, but do eat both dairy products and eggs. *Pescovegetarians* eat fish but neither poultry nor red meat (from mammals), and *semi-vegetarians* eat dairy products and eggs, and some poultry and fish, but no red meat.

Ethical Arguments for Vegetarianism. Several kinds of ethical arguments have been given for adopting vegetarian diets. These arguments differ in terms of the entities for which they express concern (human beings versus nonhuman animals and/or ecosystems) and which kind(s) of vegetarianism they support (semi-vegetarianism or lacto-ovovegetarianism versus veganism, for example).

Arguments from human health are based on scientific studies of the effects of vegetarian diets on human health. During the 1970's and 1980's, evidence accumulated that diets high in saturated fats contribute to cardiovascular disease and that diets emphasizing vegetables might help to prevent certain cancers. Jeremy Rifkin and John Robbins emphasized these concerns in popular books which combined this human health argument with concerns about famine, ecology, and animal welfare related to diets heavy in meat and animal by-products.

Although a broad consensus emerged that Americans were eating too much red meat for their own good, arguments from human health do not decisively support veganism so much as semi-vegetarian, pescovegetarian, or lacto-ovovegetarian diets, for two reasons.

First, even lacto-ovovegetarian diets can be high in saturated fats (if one eats a lot of cheese and eggs, for example), and saturated fat can be reduced significantly without eliminating meat. As beef consumption dropped in the 1980's, consumption of poultry and fish (which are lower in fat) increased, butchers began removing more fat from cuts of meat, and farmers experimented with leaner breeds of pigs and cattle.

Second, some nutritionists believe that vegan diets are inordinately risky, especially for women and young children. Vegans commonly are cautioned to plan their diets carefully in order to avoid deficiencies of nutrients such as iron and calcium, which are either less prevalent in or less efficiently absorbed from nonanimal sources, and vitamin B_{12}, which is present only in animal products. Nutrition researchers have tended, however, to identify vegans with members of religions and cults who eat extremely simplified diets and eschew medical supervision and nutritionally fortified foods, and research on these individuals may not accurately portray the risks and benefits of a vegan diet.

Two other arguments support limited vegetarianism. The argument from famine, popularized by Frances Moore Lappé, stresses that vegetarian diets are a particularly efficient way to feed the hungry. More people could live by virtue of grains and vegetables that could be produced on the good farm land that is now used to raise feed grains supporting only feedlot cattle. Related ecological arguments oppose the consumption of meat, especially beef, produced by razing third world rain forests or in other ecologically unsustainable ways. Both arguments, however, support only semi-vegetarian or pescovegetarian diets. Two alternative ways to help alleviate hunger would be to harvest fish from the oceans and to raise livestock on rangelands unsuitable for row crop production, and neither of these practices is necessarily ecologically unsustainable.

Ethical support for stricter vegetarian diets comes from animal rights and animal welfare arguments, such as those popularized by Peter Singer and Tom Regan, whose arguments were criticized in detail by Raymond Frey. Many in the animal rights movement became vegetarians because they believed either that intensive, "factory" farming is inhumane (an animal welfare perspective) or that it is inherently wrong to slaughter animals for food, no matter how humanely they may have been treated (a true animal rights perspective).

Although primarily concerned with slaughter, the animal rights movement also targeted egg production as a particularly inhumane form of animal agriculture. Following World War II, economies of scale were achieved by confining laying hens in crowded "battery" cages in highly mechanized operations, in which the entire flock is slaughtered and replaced when average egg production drops below a certain level (approximately every twelve to fifteen months). Consequently, more than 90 percent of American laying hens were caged by 1990.

Dairy products also came under fire from some in the animal rights movement, because of intensification (epitomized by the development of bovine growth hormone in the 1980's and 1990's) and because of ties between the dairy industry and the veal and beef industries. Male offspring of dairy cattle are sold as veal calves, and dairy cows themselves spend only three to four years (on average) in production, after which they are slaughtered as low-grade beef. On these grounds, animal rights and animal welfare arguments are used to support not only lacto-ovovegetarianism but also veganism. —*Gary E. Varner*

See also Ahiṁsā; Animal rights; Cruelty to animals; Environmental ethics; Hunger; Singer, Peter; Vivisection.

BIBLIOGRAPHY

Frey, Raymond G. *Rights, Killing, and Suffering: Moral Vegetarianism and Applied Ethics.* Oxford, England: Basil Blackwell, 1983.

Lappé, Frances Moore. *Diet for a Small Planet.* 10th ed. New York: Ballantine Books, 1982.

Regan, Tom. *The Case for Animal Rights.* Berkeley: University of California Press, 1983.

Rifkin, Jeremy. *Beyond Beef.* New York: Dutton, 1992.

Robbins, John. *Diet for a New America.* Walpole, N.H.: Stillpoint, 1987.

Singer, Peter. *Animal Liberation*. 2d ed. London: Jonathan Cape, 1990.

Vice

Type of ethics: Personal and social ethics
Date: From antiquity
Associated with: Organized religion and the criminal justice system
Definition: Vice is the tendency toward habitual immoral or harmful conduct
Significance: The conflict between social mores and personal self-interest is central to legal and ethical systems, and to issues of personal liberty versus social control

Introduction. The term "vice," from the Latin word for "flaw," originally meant any defect of the will predisposing an individual toward socially unacceptable behavior. The opposite term, "virtue," also refers to habitual behavior. The so-called "Seven Deadly Sins" of medieval moralists—pride, envy, anger, sloth, avarice, gluttony, and lust—are more properly termed cardinal vices, because they are habitual character defects that affect large numbers of people

The general concept of vice can be derived from observation and is not culture-specific, but the list of vices and the gravity ascribed to each vary markedly from culture to culture and historically within a culture. For example, masturbation, which was regarded as an exceedingly grave vice in early twentieth century European and American society, is ignored by many traditional cultures and has become acceptable in Western culture in recent years; attitudes toward homosexuality similarly range from acceptance to extreme condemnation.

Vice can involve any habitual act or attitude, but the vices that plague society are the common ones—those that tempt the average person and that the perpetrator may recognize as unwise, illegal, and potentially damaging, but not as heinous or depraved.

Vice and Criminal Justice. In modern U.S. law enforcement, "vice" has come to be roughly synonymous with "victimless" crimes, including alcohol and drug abuse, prostitution, gambling, pornography, and sexually deviant behavior between consenting adults. This catalog of modern vices includes behavior that is damaging to the perpetrator, to society as a whole, and to indirect targets (notably, the family of the perpetrator), rather than to a specific intended victim. Such vices are typically psychologically if not physically addictive. Indeed, the medieval concept of vice and the modern concept of psychological addition are surprisingly close.

Efforts to combat vice through the criminal justice system have a poor record of success and a tendency to coopt the machinery of justice. Strong psychological, physiological, and financial motivations to persist in exercising proscribed vices have created a powerful underground subculture capable of corrupting and intimidating police and government officials. The collapse of communism in Russia has demonstrated that even a regimented totalitarian regime is more effective at hiding than at suppressing vice, which blossomed with amazing rapidity once controls were loosened.

Vice and Biology. The question of the origin of vice has long been a subject of debate and speculation, and, like most complex questions of human nature, probably has no single answer. The concept is not simply an artifact created by human prejudice; it is a product of long experience identifying what is harmful in a particular social context. Prejudice and changing conditions, however, can and often do cause harmless actions to be labeled as vices.

The prevalent medieval view of vice (exemplified by Thomas Aquinas) stated that human beings, having free will, are free to choose evil, and they acquire vices by repeatedly performing evil acts. Since people are also free to choose virtue, vices can be overcome through grace, the exercise of virtue, knowledge, and prayer. Restated in modern terms, vice is learned, self-reinforcing behavior that can be overcome by education and behavior modification.

The alternative view, that vice is an innate, congenital quality, possibly suppressible but ultimately incurable, is in its earliest formulation a corollary of predestination: The qualities that damn the sinner are preordained by God, and neither petition nor the exercise of virtuous acts can change the underlying reality.

In the early part of the twentieth century, the popularization of Charles Darwin's theory of evolution and especially of Social Darwinism, the application of Darwinian biological models to society and psychology, led to a revival of the idea of vice as an innate quality. The Italian criminologist Cesare Lombroso proposed the theory of atavism, which gained wide currency. According to this theory, vices are relics of a lower state of evolution, are inherited, and are correlated with apelike physiognomy. Such a model readily lends itself to the labeling of non-European physical characteristics as atavistic, citing them as proof of the moral inferiority of other ethnic groups, and atavism was accepted as scientific dogma in Nazi Germany. Sociobiology also hypothesizes that certain types of habitual antisocial behavior (such as lust and aggression) may be a legacy from primitive hominid ancestors, but it does not postulate that atavism is more pronounced in any race or social group.

There is also some recent evidence that specific genetic factors may predispose individuals to vice. A large Danish study of children of criminal parents adopted at birth showed a high incidence of crime in this population, and a study of men with a doubled y chromosome suggested that this group was prone to violence. Homosexuality and alcoholism commonly affect both individuals in a pair of homozygous twins and occur in family clusters with frequencies resembling those of known recessive genetic traits. The precise physiologic mechanisms for the above-mentioned "vices" are unknown, not all studies concur, and the whole issue is so emotionally and politically charged that unbiased studies are virtually impossible to conduct. Human personality is complex and malleable, and a genetic predisposition toward particular behavior is not a mandate. —*Martha Sherwood-Pike*

See also Censorship; Evolution, theory of; Private vs. public morality; Sexuality and sexual ethics; Social Darwinism; Virtue.

BIBLIOGRAPHY

Bloomfield, Morton W. *The Seven Deadly Sins: An Introduction to the History of a Religious Concept, With Special Reference to Medieval English Literature.* East Lansing: Michigan State College Press, 1952.

Cook, Philip J. "An Introduction to Vice." *Law and Contemporary Problems* 51 (Winter, 1988): 1-7.

McCracken, Robert J. *What Is Sin? What Is Virtue?* New York: Harper & Row, 1966.

Pick, Daniel. *Faces of Degeneration: A European Disorder, c. 1848-c. 1918.* New York: Cambridge University Press, 1989.

Vietnam War

TYPE OF ETHICS: Military ethics

DATE: 1965-1975

ASSOCIATED WITH: The U.S. presidency

DEFINITION: This late twentieth century war bitterly divided public opinion in the United States until it ended in an American defeat

SIGNIFICANCE: The war stands as a landmark in the long debate over how, and whether, war can be waged justly

The question of when a powerful nation should intervene militarily in the affairs of a small country is not susceptible to a simple answer. Failure to intervene can mean that a small country will be subjected to tyranny, anarchy, or even genocide. Yet a military intervention that is bloody and inconclusive can also wreak havoc on a small country; furthermore, sending troops into a combat situation abroad means that some people will be killed or wounded. The unsuccessful end of the costly and controversial American intervention in Vietnam by no means ensured that policy makers would be spared similar dilemmas in the future.

History. The United States had been involved in the affairs of Vietnam ever since that country was divided, in 1954, into a communist North and an anticommunist South. As long as the American military mission in South Vietnam was small-scale, it aroused little opposition in the United States. Between 1965 and 1968, however, the number of American combat troops in Vietnam rose from 50,000 to 500,000; the casualties suffered by the troops, and the monthly draft calls, soared, and the loud debate at home reached an unprecedented level.

Religious Opposition to the War. Although at least one theologian (R. Paul Ramsey) did support the American military intervention in Vietnam, members of the clergy and theologians were conspicuous in the movement against such intervention. In 1966, the organization Clergy and Laymen Concerned About Vietnam was formed. Vocal opponents of the American war effort included the Protestant theologian Robert McAfee Brown; Yale University's Protestant chaplain, William Sloane Coffin; and two Roman Catholic priests, Daniel Berrigan and Philip Berrigan.

Ethical Principles: The Just War Tradition. The just war tradition was first elaborated by the theologians of Christian Europe in the late Middle Ages. After centuries of indifference by peoples and governments, this tradition was revived by the Nuremberg War Crimes Trials of 1946, which followed the defeat of Nazi Germany in World War II (1939-1945).

The just war tradition sets forth six criteria for determining whether a particular war is just. The war must be waged for a just cause; it must be waged as a last resort; the intent behind the war must be right; there must be a reasonable hope of success; the war must be waged by a legitimate, duly constituted authority; and the harm inflicted by the war must not be disproportionate to the good that one hopes to achieve. During the Vietnam War, America's clergy, theologians, and laypersons questioned whether American military intervention in Vietnam met all or even most of these criteria for a just war.

The Issue of Legality. The American Constitution, while making the president commander-in-chief of the Armed Forces, gives Congress the right to declare war. Yet the massive war effort in Vietnam, dissenters pointed out, had come about through presidential orders alone. The first substantial increase in troop levels in Vietnam had been announced on July 28, 1965, at a little-publicized presidential news conference. The dissenters did not have an airtight case, however: The Korean War (1950-1953) had also started without a Congressional declaration.

The Question of the Identity of the Aggressor. The official justification for the war, given by presidents Lyndon Baines Johnson (1963-1969) and Richard M. Nixon (1969-1974), was that the American military was in South Vietnam to repel aggression launched from communist North Vietnam. Defenders of the war viewed the conflict through an ideological lens, as an assault by international communism against those who loved freedom. The moral and material support that the world's major communist states, Communist China and the Soviet Union, gave to North Vietnam was cited as evidence for this interpretation.

The opponents of the war, by contrast, stressed the facts that both sides of the conflict were ethnic Vietnamese and that Vietnam had been a single country until 1954. Dissenters viewed the United States as meddling in another country's civil war and thus committing aggression itself, rather than nobly defending a victim of unprovoked aggression; hence, the war did not meet the "just cause" criterion.

The Question of Necessity. The dissenters' localized view of the Vietnam conflict led them to scorn the notion that defeating the Communists in South Vietnam was necessary to protect the United States itself. The dissenters saw the Vietnamese Communists as nationalist defenders of Vietnamese independence, not as the Southeast Asian arm of a worldwide conspiracy against American democracy.

Hence, the war, dissenters believed, did not meet the "last resort" criterion.

The Conduct of the War: The Question of War Crimes. Until the early 1970's, the spearhead of the Communist assault on the South Vietnamese government was not the North Vietnamese Army, but the so-called National Liberation Front, or Viet Cong. The Viet Cong, drawn from Communist sympathizers in the South, were not regular troops in uniform; instead, they were guerrillas who wore peasant clothing and blended in with the villagers after conducting hit-and-run raids against American or South Vietnamese troops.

It was nearly impossible for American troops to fight such an enemy without hurting some innocent civilians. The American military attacked villages whence sniper fire had come (one officer declared that he had had to destroy a village in order to save it) and decreed whole areas to be free-fire zones, where anybody who moved was assumed to be the enemy. The chemical Agent Orange was used to defoliate certain areas, in order to deprive the Viet Cong of food. Napalm, a burning jelly, was dropped on centers of enemy fire; inevitably, some children were hurt. In the My Lai massacre of March, 1968 (made public in 1969), all the people in a village were killed by American troops under the command of Lieutenant William Calley.

Such suffering led all dissenters to question whether the war met the "proportionality" criterion; some dissenters even condemned the war as genocidal. Defenders of the war effort pointed out that the Viet Cong also committed atrocities and that the perpetrators of My Lai were finally subjected to American military justice.

Continuation of the Debate After the War's End. In April, 1975, the North Vietnamese, having signed a peace agreement with the United States in January, 1973, overran and conquered South Vietnam. As a result, the United States admitted, by airlift, a wave of refugees. Contrary to the fears of earlier American administrations, the loss of South Vietnam did not lead to a communist advance to Hawaii or even to the fall of all of eastern Asia; the only other Asian countries to become communist were Vietnam's neighbors, Laos

Secretary of State Henry Kissinger (left) and President Richard Nixon, who engineered the pullout of U.S. troops from Vietnam. (Library of Congress)

and Cambodia. By 1979, however, the repressiveness of the Communist regime led to another massive flight of refugees, this time by boat; ironically, at least a few of the new refugees were former Viet Cong. The results of defeat started a new debate in America.

In 1978, historian Guenter Lewy published a history of the Vietnam War, defending American intervention in that conflict; in 1982, magazine editor Norman Podhoretz did the same thing. Both looked back on the Vietnam War as a noble effort to defend a free people against communism; so also did the president of the United States in the 1980's, Ronald Reagan. Political philosopher Michael Walzer, in a 1978 book on just war theory, condemned the means used in the Vietnam War without thoroughly discussing the issue of the war's rationale. In 1985, former President Richard M. Nixon published a book defending his administration's Vietnam policy. Podhoretz's view, that post-1975 Communist repression provided a retrospective justification for the American war effort of 1965 to 1973, never won a great following among academics or the general public. By the end of the 1980's, as the Cold War ended, the question of the morality of the war was still controversial among historians and journalists. —*Paul D. Mageli*

See also Cold War; Conscientious objection; International law; Military ethics; Pacifism.

BIBLIOGRAPHY

Brown, Robert McAfee, Abraham Heschel, and Michael Novak. *Vietnam: Crisis of Conscience.* New York: Association Press, 1967.

Capps, Walter H. *The Unfinished War: Vietnam and the American Conscience.* Boston: Beacon Press, 1982.

Casey, William Van Etten, and Philip Nobile, eds. *The Berrigans.* New York: Praeger, 1971.

Hall, Mitchell D. *Because of Their Faith: CALCAV and Religious Opposition to the Vietnam War.* New York: Columbia University Press, 1990.

Knoll, Erwin, and Judith Nies McFadden, eds. *War Crimes and the American Conscience.* New York: Holt, Rinehart and Winston, 1970.

Levy, David W. *The Debate over Vietnam.* Baltimore, Md.: The Johns Hopkins University Press, 1991.

Lewy, Guenter. *America in Vietnam.* New York: Oxford University Press, 1978.

Nixon, Richard M. *No More Vietnams.* New York: Arbor House, 1985.

Podhoretz, Norman. *Why We Were in Vietnam.* New York: Simon & Schuster, 1982.

Ramsey, Paul. *The Just War.* New York: Scribner, 1968.

Walzer, Michael. *Just and Unjust Wars: A Moral Argument with Historical Illustrations.* New York: Basic Books, 1977.

Violence

TYPE OF ETHICS: Personal and social ethics
ASSOCIATED WITH: The just war tradition, Marxism, and liberation theology

DEFINITION: Violence consists of a violation of another person's or a group of people's freedom, dignity, integrity, sense of self-worth, or well-being; it may be physical, psychological, or emotional
SIGNIFICANCE: It is a matter of debate whether violence is ever justified in, for example, a just war or the revolutionary overthrow of a tyrannical regime

When people think about violence, they tend to think most often of a person being physically assaulted, raped, or murdered. As Robert McAfee Brown has noted in his book, *Religion and Violence,* however, violence may be either personal or institutional, either overt or covert. Thus, personal overt violence may be physical assault. Personal covert violence could be psychological or emotional abuse of another person. Institutional overt violence may take the form of war or revolution. Covert institutional violence may take the forms of repression, racism, or the denial of human rights. This article will be primarily concerned with issues of institutional violence—just war theory, violence and the civil rights movement, violence and revolution in liberation theology and Marxism.

It is not clear whether violence or aggression is a natural part of the human species or a learned behavior. Thomas Hobbes, the author of *Leviathan,* advocated a strong authoritarian government, partly using arguments based on a naturalistic concept of aggression. Chapter 13 of *Leviathan,* the famous passage on the "Natural Condition of Mankind," claims that because of a kind of natural equality, human beings are, in their natural condition, always in a state of war, a *Bellum omnium contra omnes,* a "war of all against all." He characterized the life of man as "solitary, poore, nasty, brutish and short." He held to a dim view of human nature. Behavior arises because of "aversions" from fear and want and the desires for security and gain. A commonwealth becomes a necessary antidote to the horrors of human nature.

From a psychoanalytic point of view, Sigmund Freud argued that aggression was a natural human instinct. In his early writings, he developed the idea of instinctual conflict within the human psyche between two principles: the pleasure principle and the reality principle. The pleasure principle is the most impulsive instinct in driving the organism toward immediate gratification. The reality principle, however, operates as a rational mechanism that allows the organism to defer gratification and to sublimate potentially destructive wishes by means of a redirection of energy toward work. Both principles operate to reduce stress. Freud also discovered a compulsion on the part of neurotics to repeat past negative experiences as a defensive measure that often turned self-destructive. This led Freud to postulate the death instinct, or Thanatos. The death instinct preserves the organism from threats of death. When it confronts such threats, aggression results. Directed at the self, aggression becomes self-destructive.

Konrad Lorenz worked out a theory of aggression based on Darwin's theory that struggle is pervasive in nature and in evolution. It appears in the struggle for survival, the defense of offspring, and the improvement of the species. The question therefore arises, "Does aggression play a positive and necessary role in furthering the organization of the human species?" That aggression can be destructive and harmful is indisputable, but can aggression be directed rightfully for the just pursuit of good and beneficial consequences? Can violence be a force for good?

Just War Theory. Saint Augustine, in *City of God*, argues that not all homicide is murder. Even God, the supreme authority, makes exceptions to the law against killing. The law against killing, says Augustine, is not broken by those who wage war by the authority of God or impose the death penalty by the authority of the state. Thus, Augustine sets up the state and God as authoritative and just sources of power. Here, then, is one of the criteria for waging a just war—it must be declared by a legitimate authority.

Aggression may also be justified on account of the wickedness of a neighboring nation. In Augustine's opinion, honest people do not go to war against peaceful neighbors. Thus, the cause must be just. It is not enough to wage war to increase one's borders. The increase of the empire may be justified, however, by the wickedness of those against whom war is waged.

The increase of empire was assisted by the wickedness of those against whom just wars were waged. In Augustine's words, "For it is the injustice of the opposing side that lays on the wise man the duty of waging wars; and this injustice is assuredly to be deplored by a human being."

In the thirteenth century, Thomas Aquinas gave fuller exposition to the just war theory. In answer to the question "Is it always sinful to wage war?" Aquinas set forth criteria for a just war. First, there must be a declaration on the part of a legitimate authority—the ruler of the state, for example. War may not be declared by a private individual. It is not the business of the private individual. Second, a just cause is required. Those who are attacked should be attacked because they deserve it, on account of some fault. Third, war should be waged with the right intention so that either good is advanced or evil is avoided. Fourth, the outcome of war must be peace. Fifth, a just war must avoid inordinate and perilous arms.

Martin Luther, in his political tract "Temporal Authority: to What Extent It Should be Obeyed" (1523), formulates the two-kingdoms theory, a theory obviously acquired from Augustine's *City of God—civitas Dei* (spiritual authority) and *civitas mundi* (earthly authority). Luther attempts to answer questions concerning the division of powers between Church and state. Is the Church an earthly power? Can secular rulers claim spiritual authority? Luther recognized the secular authority of the state and the spiritual authority of the Church. Each has its own realm. Each realm is a tool of the *Regnum Dei* (Kingdom of God) to fight the *Regnum diaboli* (Kingdom of the Devil). The state's weapons are law, power, force, and authority. The Church's weapons are

faith and the Gospel. In effect, the individual becomes bifurcated into a public person and a private person. As a private person the individual abides by the gospel of love, but as a public person the individual may serve the state with the sword to inflict punishment on wrongdoers. The two-kingdoms theory was used by the Lutheran State churches in Germany to remain neutral in the face of Nazism (Ansbach Decree, 1935).

Violence and the Civil Rights Movement. Martin Luther King, Jr. (1929-1968) embodied a nonviolent philosophy of social change. He was catapulted to public attention by the bus boycott in Montgomery, Alabama, in 1955. He led voter registration drives and a desegregation campaign. His famous March on Washington eventually led to the signing of the Civil Rights act in 1963, and, in 1964, he won the Nobel Peace Prize. His influence waned after the Watts riots in 1965. He came to his philosophy of nonviolent resistance through reading Thoreau's "Civil Disobedience." He also studied W. Rauschenbusch's *Christianity and the Social Crisis* which laid the theological foundations for Christian social action and connected socioeconomic conditions to spiritual welfare. Karl Marx sharpened King's consciousness of the gap between superfluous wealth and abject poverty. King was also influenced by Gandhi's concept of satyagraha— "truth force" or "love force"—which advanced a love ethic as a powerful instrument of social and collective transformation. Gandhi presented the method of nonviolent resistance as the only moral way out for oppressed people. Reinhold Niebuhr refuted the false optimism of liberalism, and his work helped King to see the destructive power of sin not only at the level of personal life but also at the social, national, and international levels. E. S. Brightman and L. Harold Dewolf, King's Boston University professors, insisted, in their philosophy of personal idealism, that personality is ultimately and cosmically real. This idea laid the ground for conceiving a personal God and the concept of cosmic backing for justice and the dignity of human beings.

King was convinced that love is an instrument of social transformation and that suffering is to be accepted without retaliation because unearned suffering is redemptive. Hate destroys, but love builds up. Martin Luther King, Jr., set forth his method of nonviolence in the following principles: ascertain the situation of justice, attempt revolution by dialogue, undergo personal purification and accept violence, use direct nonviolent action. In his famous "Letter from a Birmingham Jail," King also delineated several principles of nonviolent direct action: do not be cowardly; do not seek to defeat the opponent, but seek friendship and understanding; defeat the forces of evil, not people; accept suffering without retaliation; reject inward violence; have faith that justice has a cosmic backing.

Malcolm X, King's contemporary in the leadership of the African American civil rights movement, rejected King's nonviolent philosophy and advocated his own brand of social revolution, which made room for violence. Malcolm X

This "Stop the Madness" rally opposing gang violence received the support of entertainers such as Arsenio Hall (center). (Lester Sloan)

believed that when the law failed to protect African Americans, African Americans were justified in using arms to protect themselves from harm at the hands of whites. He believed that it was criminal to remain passive in the face of being attacked. He not only encouraged self-defense but also mandated it. In his own words, "I am for violence if nonviolence means we continue postponing a solution to the American black man's problem—just to avoid violence. I don't go for non-violence if it also means a delayed solution."

Violence and Liberation Theology. As has been shown, Christian thinkers have concerned themselves with the ethics of violence. Attitudes toward institutional forms of violence have included just war, holy crusades, pacifism, and civil disobedience. With liberation theology, Christian thinkers took seriously the question of a just revolution. Dom Helder Camara, a bishop from Recife, Brazil, believed that a repressive state starts a spiral of violence through institutional injustice that leads the oppressed to revolt. In his eyes, people had a right to revolt against an unjust government. Yet he cautioned that revolt would only lead to more repressive measures on the part of the government. Because of the fear of brutal retaliatory measures on the part of the state, Dom Helder Camara advocated a nonviolent approach. A Colom-

bian cleric, Camilio Torres, was exasperated by the brutality of the repressive state and believed in the people's right to revolt. Unlike Dom Helder Camara, however, Torres did not turn to passivism out of fear of the military and police apparatuses of the state. Instead, Torres left the church and joined guerrilla forces in the mountains to overthrow the unjust government. He believed that the essence of Christianity consisted in the love of one's neighbor. He also concluded that the welfare of the majority could only be attained through a revolution. Taking state power was necessary to complete the teaching of Christ to love one's neighbor. According to Torres, love must be embodied in social structures and the concern for well-being must be translated into a program for change. If those in power will not willingly share power, then the only other effective means of change is revolt. Revolution becomes obligatory for Christians in order to realize their love of humanity. In the viewpoint of Torres, there can there be a just revolution.

Hugo Assmann, a Brazilian philosopher and theologian, argues for a Third World anti-imperialistic revolution for a universal and equitable share of the world's goods and for antioligarchic revolutions for political freedom. Assmann defines the world as a world in conflict. He argues for a language of liberation denouncing domination, articulating the mechanics of dependence, opposing capitalist economic systems, and breaking with unjust political governments.

Gustavo Gutierrez, a Peruvian priest, points out that the unjust violence of the oppressor is not to be equated with the just violence of the oppressed. Thus, he makes a distinction between just violence and unjust violence. Repression is unjust, but revolt against tyranny is just. For Gutierrez, the goal of the struggle against institutional injustice is the creation of a new kind of human being. The Exodus of the Hebrew slaves from Egypt serves as the paradigm for active participation in the building of a new society. Christian brotherhood, according to Gutierrez, must be understood within the context of class struggle. Class struggle, in his opinion, is a fact; therefore, neutrality is impossible. Universal love cannot be achieved except by resolutely opting for the oppressed, that is, by opposing the oppressive class.

In the view of José Miguez Bonino, from Argentina, history is a dialectic that implies a certain violence for the emergence of the new. Hence, violence will be accepted in the struggle for justice or rejected in the state's attempt to create law and order at all costs. Miguez Bonino agrees with Gutierrez and Assmann that class struggle is a fact. On the one side, the dominant class tries to maintain the status quo; on the other, the oppressed classes struggle for a new society.

Violence and Marxism. The question of violence, in liberation theology, had to do with making Christian love effective in a situation of oppression. The issue of violence for Marxism has to do with the relationship between means and end in the struggle for social transformation. That Karl Marx was a passionate and ardent revolutionary goes without saying. His advocacy of violence must be carefully regarded in the context of his writings. In his "Introduction" to *Towards a Critique of Hegel's Philosophy of Right* (1844), Marx claims that the weapon of criticism cannot supplant the criticism of weapons and that material force must be overthrown by material force.

In the famous *Communist Manifesto*, written on the eve of the 1848 revolutions, Marx clearly regarded the takeover of state power as the aim of the Communist Party: "The immediate aim of the Communists is the same as that of all the other proletarian parties: formation of the proletariat into a class, overthrow of the bourgeois supremacy, conquest of political power by the proletariat."

Speaking in Amsterdam in 1872, Marx made it perfectly clear that the use of violence varies from circumstance to circumstance. In his own words, "there are countries like America, England . . . and Holland where the workers can achieve their aims by peaceful means. . . . [I]n most of the countries . . . it is force that must be the lever of our revolutions."

Marx believed that violence may be necessary to effect a socialist revolution, but he was not dogmatic and absolute about the use of violence. He also was not adamant about the velocity of the transformation to socialism. For Marx,

violence was a means, not an end.

What Marx was unbending about was the fact that class struggle involves violence, coercion, and repression. Workers are exploited and alienated. Because of propertylessness, workers are coerced into selling their labor power for means of subsistence. If they try to organize themselves, mobilize, and politicize their interests, they are met with repression. Violence breeds violence. The workers' revolution may require violence.

Mikhail Bakunin, an erstwhile companion of Marx, believed that destruction was a necessary tool of social change. Georges Sorel (1847-1922) was a syndicalist Marxist who denied the then-popular theory that capitalism would collapse because of its own contradictions. He espoused a radical brand of revolutionary syndicalism. In 1906, in *Reflections on Violence*, he set up class war as the very essence of socialism. Acts of violence, he believed, would create a workers' morality, destroy the bourgeoisie, and lay the foundations for socialism.

Vladimir Ilich Lenin believed that the Marxist doctrine of the dictatorship of the proletariat meant the seizing and holding of state power by the use of violence. Karl Kautsky argued in *Terrorism and Communism* (1919) that Lenin's concept of the dictatorship of the proletariat was leading away from the essence of socialism. Leon Trotsky replied, in his own Terrorism and Communism (1920), that a violent revolution was necessary because parliamentary means were ineffective. The revolutionary class should attain its end by any means at its disposal—even terrorism. György Lukács decried Kautsky's peaceful transistion to socialism and denied the validity of the question of the legality or illegality of means. For him, what counted was what would be most successful in achieving social transformation. A sense of world history and the sense of the world mission of the proletariat would determine the question of tactics and ethics.

—*Michael R. Candelaria*

See also Aggression; Augustine, Saint; Communism; Freud, Sigmund; Hobbes, Thomas; King, Martin Luther, Jr.; Lenin; Luther, Martin; Malcolm X; Marx, Karl; Socialism; Thomas Aquinas.

BIBLIOGRAPHY

Augustine, Saint, Bishop of Hippo. *Concerning the City of God Against the Pagans*. Translated by Henry Bettenson. Harmondsworth, England: Penguin Books, 1972. Augustine originally wrote this book as a response to criticism leveled against Christians after the sacking of Rome.

Brown, Robert McAfee. *Religion and Violence: A Primer for White Americans*. Philadelphia: Westminster Press, 1973. This text nicely summarizes the just war theory and offers a stimulating criticism of it. The author also argues that the criteria justifying war could be used to justify revolution.

Freud, Sigmund. *The Ego and the Id*. Translated by Joan Rivier. Edited by James Strachey. New York: W. W. Norton, 1962. Here Freud introduces the instincts he calls "Eros" and "Thanatos."

Gutierrez, Gustavo. *The Theology of Liberation.* Maryknoll, N.Y.: Orbis Books, 1973. This is the classic text of liberation theology. Here were laid down the major lines of thought that are central themes in liberation theology.

Thomas Aquinas, Saint. *On Law, Morality, and Politics.* Edited by William P. Baumgarth and Richard J. Regan. Indianapolis: Hackett, 1988. Aquinas expounds on the just war theory more systematically and clearly than does Augustine.

Virtual reality

TYPE OF ETHICS: Scientific ethics

DATE: Late twentieth century

DEFINITION: Interactive computer and video simulation of objective reality

SIGNIFICANCE: Virtual reality has many positive applications but can also be abused in a number of ways; sorting the good from the bad requires an application of ethical principles

Virtual reality (VR) is a computerized system of data presentation that allows the user to project himself or herself into a simulated three-dimensional space and move about in that space, introduce other objects into it, change the positions and shapes of objects already there, and interact with animate objects in the space. VR was made possible by the enormous increase in computer memory and data-processing capacity, even in personal computers (PCs), and by the development of miniaturized video and audio devices and motion sensors that give the illusion of motion and of touching and manipulating material objects. Other descriptive names for this technology are artificial reality, virtual environment, telepresence, and immersive simulation, but VR is the preferred term.

Equipment: Software and Presentation Devices. The memory software of VR consists of many, many points of a three-dimensional grid, built from either an actual scene or a computer-generated space. The array of coordinates must be complete enough to allow the space to be rotated on three axes and the viewpoint to be moved similarly. In addition, other objects, animate and inanimate, must be held in memory with complete manipulability (including the tactile sensing of shape, inertia, texture, and so forth); and provision must be made for the creation of new objects with equal flexibility. Clearly, this technology calls for enormous memory capacity and complex programs to accomplish the apparent motion. VR presentations can be very simple, such as viewing a scene on a PC monitor, or very complex, such as donning a helmet containing a miniature television screen for each eye, to give stereoscopic vision, headphones for directional sound, motion sensors to slew the scene left or right, up or down as the viewer's head moves, and a so-called Dataglove both to accept motion commands from the hand and to give back pressure information to define objects, motion, and so forth. Presentations between the simple and the complex seem to be missing; at the upper end, a whole-body sensing suit is expected to be available in the future. This very brief description of equipment may suggest why

VR had to wait until microchip technology made the necessary memory available within reasonably sized computers.

Positive Applications of VR. Many uses of VR raise few if any ethical questions. It is used, for example, to train surgical students on a "virtual" patient before they actually perform an operation. Experienced surgeons can practice a complex new procedure before using it in the operating room. Operators of heavy construction equipment can train on VR devices, and in some cases controls have been redesigned for greater simplicity and efficiency on the basis of such experience. Physiological chemists can manipulate molecules in VR to see—or feel—how they fit together in three dimensions. Attractions and repulsions of functional groups in the molecules are programmed into memory, and the user can actually feel, through the Dataglove, when a drug molecule fits or fails to fit in a cellular structure, or a when virus clicks into place on a cell receptor. Pilots can be trained in VR simulations so lifelike that an hour of training is considered as effective as an hour of actual flying time. In fact, the Air Force was an early major developer of VR presentations. Architects and their clients can stroll through a building that has yet to be built, to get the feel of it and to identify where the design needs to be changed for greater comfort. These are all fairly unexceptionable applications.

Possible Ethically Negative Aspects. One of the most frequently voiced criticisms of VR is that it makes possible what might be called participatory pornography—not simply reading, television viewing, or telephone talk, but all these combined but together with the tactile feedback of a whole body suit that will allow virtual sexual experience of all varieties. Some designers and marketers of VR equipment speak enthusiastically of such pornography as an exciting prospect for the future. Critics view it as a real moral menace in a society that is already awash in casual sexuality. Others believe that it is merely an extension of the pornography that has always existed. One commentator spoke sourly of "the myth that sex and pornography are the keys to understanding the growth of all new technologies." Perhaps the real menace here is that VR can be a powerful new device for furthering the alienation of individuals by making artificial experience easier and more exciting than actual human contact. This is true not only of VR sex but also potentially of all VR experience except training applications. Another aspect of this ethical concern lies in the enormous amount of time and attention that could be wasted because of VR. In a society that already spends a tenth of its time in front of television, imagine what the effect would be if every household had its own VR. Other questions arise with VR that are perhaps medical rather than ethical but are worth mentioning: Can the tactile feedback become vigorous enough to cause physical damage? VR causes physical reactions for some users (such as nausea and actual vomiting in flight simulations); can it cause mental damage as well? Is this a technology that should be kept away from the undeveloped psyches of children and restricted to adults? All these ethical questions have yet to be addressed.

Conclusion. In sum, VR appears to be simply another new technology that can be used well or badly. Its capacities for good and evil seem not much greater than those of electric power, the automobile, or the telephone. The decisions lie, as always, in human hands.

—*Robert M. Hawthorne, Jr.*

See also Computer technology; Science, ethics of; Technology.

BIBLIOGRAPHY

Churbuck, David C. "Applied Reality." *Forbes* 150 (September 14, 1992): 486-489.

Dvorak, John C. "America, Are You Ready for Simulated Sex and Virtual Reality?" *PC Computing* 5 (May, 1992): 78.

Earnshaw, Rae, Huw Jones, and Mike Gigante. *Virtual Reality Systems.* San Diego: Academic Press, 1993.

Hsu, Jeffrey, "Virtual Reality." *Compute* 15 (February, 1993): 101-104.

McLellan, Hilary. *Virtual Reality: A Selected Bibliography.* Englewood Cliffs, N.J.: Educational Technology, 1992.

Rheingold, Howard. *Virtual Reality.* New York: Summit Books, 1991.

Woolley, Benjamin. "Being and Believing: Ethics of Virtual Reality." *The Lancet* 338 (August 3, 1991): 283-284.

_____. *Virtual Worlds: A Journey in Hype and Hyperreality.* Cambridge, Mass.: Blackwell Scientific, 1992.

Virtue

TYPE OF ETHICS: Personal and social ethics

DATE: From antiquity

ASSOCIATED WITH: Greek philosophers Plato and Aristotle; Christian writers Paul, Saint Augustine, and Thomas Aquinas

DEFINITION: Principles of goodness and rightness in character and conduct that lead a person toward moral excellence and away from moral depravity

SIGNIFICANCE: Elaborated lists of virtuous principles such as the "cardinal" and "theological" virtues provide diverse cultures with criteria for judging moral goodness

Each thought and act a person takes sets in motion two tendencies: a greater likelihood to engage in similar thoughts and acts, and a change in the character of the person. Thinking and action that lead a person away from life, goodness, and perfection of inner nature create *vice*—evil or wicked behavior and character. Conversely, those thoughts and acts that are life-promoting, aim for goodness, and work to perfect the inner nature lead to *virtue*—moral excellence of behavior and character. When people choose vice, their inner natures change and it becomes easier for them to choose the bad and more difficult for them to choose the good. In contrast, choosing virtue changes the inner nature so that it becomes easier, and more natural, to choose good rather than evil. Furthermore, this same

principle appears to be operative with groups of individuals. For example, it seems quite logical that if a society wishes to prosper and to promote the well-being of its members, it should teach and encourage those people to pursue that which is virtuous. After all, is it possible to have a good society without good people? It is, therefore, in the best interests of both the individual and society to identify, promote, and practice those principles that work toward the ultimate good.

Numerous lists of virtuous principles have been put forth by diverse cultures over thousands of years to serve as moral guidelines for those particular cultures. One such list, the Seven Virtues, which includes the cardinal and the theological virtues, has been particularly influential in Western thought. Although the Seven Virtues deserve special attention, it is important to consider conceptions arising from other cultures. Only by doing so can the attempt be made to identify virtues that are both universal and, perhaps, eternal.

Confucian Virtue. Confucius, who lived in the sixth century B.C.E., was the most influential person in the shaping of Chinese ethics. In *The Confucian Analects*, he describes himself as a transmitter of ancient wisdom, particularly in regard to distinctions between right and wrong and the characteristics of a virtuous character. In *The Doctrine of the Mean*, Confucius considers virtue to be a mean between the extremes of excess and deficiency. In the short treatise known as *The Great Learning*, steps for promoting personal and governmental virtue are described.

Confucianists believe that there are five primary virtues: charity, righteousness, propriety, wisdom, and sincerity. All these virtues are described in detail in *The Confucian Analects*. Charity is the virtue of human relations, the practice of benevolence and respect to others. Confucius believed that this virtue was summed up in the most important principle guiding a person's life: the Golden Rule (Do unto others as you would have them do unto you). Righteousness is the virtue of public affairs: duty, responsibility, the following of just principles. Propriety is concerned with fitting and proper behavior in human affairs. Confucius taught that propriety must always be accompanied by charity to keep a person from pride. Wisdom about humans, divine commands, and language is extolled by Confucius as the virtue of personal growth that comes only from study and practice. The final virtue, sincerity, is concerned with truthfulness and faithfulness in interactions with others.

Buddhistic Virtue. Siddhārtha Gautama, who lived in India in the sixth century B.C.E., taught that right thinking and self-denial would enable a person to reach true wisdom and, ultimately, nirvana—a state free of all suffering and sorrow. Gautama was given the title of Buddha—one who embodies the divine characteristics of virtue and wisdom. The Eightfold Path, consisting of rightness of views, speech, thoughts, actions, living, recall, exertion, and meditation, was taught by the Buddha as the way to nirvana. In the Dhammapada, a collection of proverbs and moral principles, it is said that a person can rightly be called a *brāhmin*—a Hindu of the priestly class—if that individual leads a life that expresses such virtues as patience, self-restraint, contentment, sympathy, and mildness. As precepts for all Buddhists, the Buddha set forth five commandments: Abstain from killing, stealing, adultery, lying, and strong drink. An interesting feature of Buddha's teaching was that these moral principles were interpreted particularly stringently for those aspiring to be monks or nuns. Thus, while the ordinary person was enjoined to simply refrain from adultery, absolute abstinence from all sexual activity was required of monks and nuns.

The closest Buddhist teaching to a list of virtues is contained in the six *pāramitās*—perfections of character. The pāramitās are virtues of love, morality, patience, courage, meditation, and knowledge. Followers of the Buddha are enjoined to exercise these virtues perfectly.

Muḥammad and Islam. The Arabian prophet Muḥammad, who lived from 570 to 632, wrote in the Qur'ân (the sacred book of the Moslems) that it is the duty of all people to believe in Allah (the Moslem name for God) and to live a life of high moral standards. Although the Qur'ân presents numerous moral principles such as kindness to parents, kin, and strangers, the sum of Muḥammad's teaching consists of believing in Allah and living a virtuous life according to the Five Pillars of Moslem law: the creed, the prayer ritual, beneficence (loving acts to others), fasting, and the pilgrimage. The Golden Rule was also taught by Muḥammad and could plausibly be considered a sixth primary moral duty.

Teutonic Virtues. Tacitus, the Roman historian of the first and second centuries C.E., describes in his book *Germania* the social and moral lives of the Teutonic peoples—inhabitants of northern Europe. The Teutonic virtues identified by Tacitus in the first century have been greatly influential in the shaping of Western ideals in the succeeding centuries. Eight of these virtues have particular relevance to nobility of character: endurance (of purpose), loyalty, generosity, hospitality, truthfulness, modesty, marital purity (abstinence from adultery), and courage—considered the most important virtue by the Teutons.

Virtue in Classical Greek Philosophy. The great Greek philosophers of the fifth and fourth centuries B.C.E., Socrates, Plato, and Aristotle, devoted much attention to the subject of virtue. Their teachings on virtue have a timeless quality, shaping and stimulating modern thinking on moral matters. The ideas of Aristotle will be discussed first; Socrates and Plato will be dealt with in the discourse on the Seven Virtues.

In the *Nicomachean Ethics*, Aristotle distinguished between theoretical and practical virtues. The three theoretical virtues included wisdom—the ability to order knowledge into an ultimate system of truth, science (the ability to draw knowledge from demonstrations), and understanding (the ability to apprehend the truths that lie at the roots of knowledge). The two practical virtues were art (the ability to know how to produce or create things) and prudence (the ability to know how to act well in life's affairs). Prudence is con-

sidered to be the virtue most applicable to living a good moral life.

Like Confucius, Aristotle also proposed a doctrine of the mean, arguing that the essence of virtue is a middle ground between the vices of excess and deficiency. Thus, the virtue of courage can be considered the middle ground between cowardice on the one hand and impulsiveness on the other. Aristotle did not intend to convey the notion that people should therefore look for the middle ground between leading a moral versus an immoral life. On the contrary, he said that people should find virtue and live it to the fullest. For example, the soldier should not settle for a middle ground between rashness and cowardice, but instead should serve as courageously as possible.

The Seven Virtues in Western Thinking. Socrates, according to Plato in the *Republic* (book 4), contends that the ideal state would exemplify and promote four main qualities: wisdom, courage, temperance, and justice. Although the implication in the *Republic* is that these virtues were known and taught by the predecessors of Socrates, it is Plato who first identifies these as the core components of the noble moral character. The four qualities are called the cardinal virtues (from the Latin word *cardo*, meaning "hinge,") because all other virtues are seen to hinge, or be dependent, on them. These four virtues, according to Plato, promote health and harmony of the soul—Plato's definition of virtue. These virtues also correspond to Plato's conception of the soul: Wisdom is the virtue of the intellect; courage that of the will; temperance that of feelings; and justice that of the soul's relation to others—that is, society.

The acceptance of the four cardinal virtues as primary qualities of the moral life can be seen in the writings of subsequent Greek and Christian philosophers. Aristotle centered his *Nicomachean Ethics* on them although he opposed the Platonic idea of innate virtue, arguing instead that they are acquired through experience. The Stoic school, opposing the Epicureans, who were promoting pleasure as the ultimate good, contended that virtue is the only good. The Stoic philosopher Zeno of Citum (333-262 B.C.E.) taught that people should live their lives in accordance with the divine plan of nature and that virtue alone was important in living the good life. Among the early Christian writers, Origen, born in 185, taught that science and philosophy could be in accord with Christian teachings, and was among the first Christian writers to argue that the four cardinal virtues were essential to the Christian moral character. The crucial step in Christianizing the cardinal virtues was taken by Saint Augustine (354-430), who interpreted the cardinal virtues in light of the love of God: prudence is love's discernment; courage, love's endurance; temperance, love's purity; and justice is the service of God's love. It is in the teachings of Saint Augustine that the cardinal virtues are placed alongside the theological virtues of the New Testament (I Corinthians 13): faith, hope, and love. Among later Christian philosophers, Saint Thomas Aquinas in the thirteenth century, preeminent as a champion of the virtuous life, presents in works such as *Summa Theologica* the seven virtues as the chief signs of the Christian moral character. More recently, the great Christian author of the twentieth century, C. S. Lewis, in his classic defense of the Christian faith, *Mere Christianity* (1943), writes that proper Christian behavior manifests the qualities of the seven virtues.

The Seven Virtues Described. Prudence means exercising common sense and sound judgment in practical matters, carefully considering the consequences of one's actions. It involves forethought, caution, discretion, discernment, and circumspection. It is not the same thing as intelligence; Great geniuses may act imprudently. The prudent person can speak the "fitting" word at the proper time, knows when and how to promote the interests of both self and others, and knows how to arrange his or her affairs for the greatest benefit.

Temperance refers to moderation and self-restraint in the pursuit and expression of all pleasures. The essence of temperance is self-control, not, generally speaking, complete abstinence. It involves moderation with food, chastity with sexuality, and humility with great success. A person lacking in temperance would be given to gluttony, promiscuity, and arrogance. Conversely, too much restraint would leave a person with austere eating habits, excessive prudishness in sexual behavior, and a self-deprecating personality.

Justice demands that affairs among people be guided by fairness, impartiality, and equality. Aristotle divided justice into general and particular categories. General justice can be construed as a social justice in which societies are organized in such a way that all members contribute to and benefit from the common good. Particular justice is subdivided into corrective justice, the fulfilling of contracts between people, and distributive justice, fairness and impartiality in the distribution of goods and burdens. The just person is honest, truthful, stands for what is right, and keeps his or her word.

Courage is the ability to face danger and distress with endurance and purpose of heart. Courage involves not only withstanding evil but also attacking it and working to overcome it. The courageous person will stand for the moral right and persevere in it no matter how unpopular that may be. Bravery, determination, sturdiness, and tenacity are the characteristics of those who are courageous. Courageous people are not those who lack fear. Courageous people act in spite of fear, work to overcome their fears, and triumph in the face of fear.

Faith, according to the New Testament writer Paul (Heb. 11:1), is "the substance of things hoped for, the evidence of things not seen." Faith, in the theological sense, involves apprehending, trusting, and holding on to spiritual truth. Although the context of faith in the writings of the apostle Paul certainly emphasizes the divine dimension, the importance of faith in the human condition cannot be ignored. The faithful person demonstrates the traits of loyalty, steadfastness, dependability, and trustworthiness. Faith works to bring and keep people together in marriage, politics, and religion (with God). It is the glue that binds one human heart to another. Infidelities of all sorts serve to separate even the closest of human relationships.

Hope is the expectation that one's desires will be realized. Hope is forward-looking, giving direction, purpose, and energy to life. The apostle Paul (Heb. 6:19) describes hope as the "anchor of the soul, both sure and steadfast." The person who hopes is stimulated to greater personal growth, works toward a better society, and believes in something better to come. Lack of hope—apathy, helplessness, and pessimism—saps life from individuals, brings stagnation to civilizations, and empties religion of its meaning.

Love is a transcending devotion to another. In his great discourse on love in I Corinthians 13:4-8, the apostle Paul describes love as "always patient and kind; it is never jealous; love is never boastful or conceited; it is never rude or selfish; it does not take offense, and is not resentful. Love takes no pleasure in other people's sins but delights in the truth; it is always ready to excuse, to trust, to hope, and to endure whatever comes. Love does not come to an end." Love is affective; it involves feelings of closeness, tenderness, and passion. Love is behavioral; it has to do with how one person acts and intends to act toward another. Love is cognitive; it involves knowing another, wishing for and thinking of another's best. The loving person cares for others, is benevolent, and stands against hatred and malice wherever it appears. In I Corinthians 13:13, love is considered to be preeminent over faith and hope. Indeed, many have called love the greatest of the seven virtues.

It is notable that in religiously inspired lists of virtues, love is almost always included and occupies a prominent position. In many secular lists, such as the cardinal virtues, love is often absent or is only indirectly mentioned. Perhaps to consider the greatest good, God, necessitates the consideration of the greatest virtue, love.

—*Paul J. Chara, Jr.*

See also Aristotelian ethics; Aristotle; Augustine, Saint; Buddhist ethics; Christian ethics; Confucian ethics; Islamic ethics; Plato; Platonic ethics; Socrates; Thomas Aquinas.

BIBLIOGRAPHY

Aristotle. *On Man in the Universe.* Introduced and edited by Louise Ropes Loomis. New York: W. L. Black, 1943. English translations of five of Aristotle's greatest works are presented: *Metaphysics*, *Parts of Animals*, *Nicomachean Ethics*, *Politics*, and *Poetics*. The first seven books of *Nicomachean Ethics* are particularly concerned with virtue and closely related issues.

Erikson, Erik H., ed. *Adulthood.* New York: W. W. Norton, 1978. Erikson's theory of personality development is one of the few modern psychological theories to integrate the notion of virtue into psychological growth. Erikson's description of the virtues attainable in each development stage is presented in the first chapter of the book, "Dr. Borg's life cycle."

Fagothey, Austin. *Fagothey's Right and Reason: Ethics in Theory and Practice*. 9th ed. Columbus, Ohio: Merrill, 1989. A general introduction to the study of ethics written in a style accessible to the novice reader. Many of the chapters are relevant to the topic of virtue; however, the sixteenth chapter, "Habit," specifically goes into detail regarding the cardinal virtues.

Lewis, C. S. *Mere Christianity*. Rev. and enl. ed. New York: Macmillan, 1967. This book, written by a Cambridge scholar, is a lucid exposition of the Christian faith and is considered to be among the greatest Christian works ever penned. Book 3, "Christian Behavior," relates each of the seven virtues to Christian living.

Plato. *The Collected Dialogues of Plato*. Edited by Edith Hamilton and Huntington Cairnes. Princeton, N.J.: Princeton University Press, 1969. English translations of five of Plato's greatest works are presented: *Apology, Crito, Phaedo, Symposium*, and *Republic*. Book 4 of the *Republic* deals specifically with the cardinal virtues. It is here that these virtues are first accepted as the standard virtues of the ancient world.

Virtue ethics

TYPE OF ETHICS: Theory of ethics
DATE: 1950
DEFINITION: An approach to both understanding and living the good life that is based on virtue; virtue is a predisposition toward action for good that is shaped by moral judgment and daily discipline
SIGNIFICANCE: Much current ethical thought deals with rules, principles, obligation, and consequences; virtue ethics focuses on what is important to both the individual and society: being a good person

Everyday life and the actions that constitute it involve patterns of interaction. People do good and perform right actions not so much as a consequence of individual acts of moral reasoning but as a consequence of inherited patterns of right and wrong, good and bad. It is in taking responsibility for these inherited patterns that meaningful ethical life takes place, not in esoteric discussions and tentative moral actions related to new technologies, fads, and lifestyles that seek ethical justification. Certainly, discussions of new ethical challenges must take place, but support for and recognition of the importance of character, values, and virtues in everyday life must be recognized as imperative.

Virtue Ethics: Providing Primacy. One's point of view is expressed in one's thoughts and actions. These actions manifest one's values, commitment, and character. Good character is not an accident. It requires discipline, reflection, and responsibility. A virtue is a reflection of good character because it is a pattern of action. It should not be suggested, however, that one's ethical life is isolated and is developed apart from other people. One's virtues depend on others for their origin and sustenance—for their origin, because one usually inherits the virtues of parents, peers, and significant others; for their sustenance, because to sustain a pattern of action over a prolonged period of time, one needs encouragement and positive reinforcement.

Virtue Ethics: Focusing on Human Life Rather than Human Rules. Much of contemporary ethics focuses on specific acts that are justified by rules or consequences. Virtue ethics focuses on good judgment as a consequence of good character. Beliefs, sensitivity, and experience are of more importance than are rules and consequences for determining one's ethical life.

Because its focus is on human life rather than on human rules, virtue ethics becomes involved with various psychologies of ethics as well as with the ways in which gender, race, ethnicity, economics, and power shape character and thus the experience of virtue.

How is one fulfilled as a human being? Does fulfillment vary on the basis of gender, race, ethnicity, and economic position? The answer to these questions is of vital importance to virtue ethics.

Difficulties. Since virtue ethics gives a significant role to feelings in the ethical life, many wonder where the consistency necessary for ethical living, independent of the subjectivity of daily life and transitory human feelings, exists. If feeling is central to virtue, then the ethical life is built on the shifting sands of human emotion. Those who practice virtue ethics recognize this difficulty and agree with the thrust of the critique. Yet it must be recognized that one reason for the growth of virtue ethics is that "rules and consequences ethics" leaves out an essential part of human life—feelings. All ethical theories and practice must deal with the whole person: mind and feelings, rules and consequences.

Virtue ethics presuppose that one will be drawn to the personally perceived good. Christians suggest, however, based on the doctrine of original sin, that humans are more attracted to the bad than to the good. The increase in the prison population as well as daily experience may cause many non-Christians to fear an ethic based on human perfectibility. One cannot say, "I will be good someday, but not today," they claim. One must see one's duty and do it. These individual acts are important and cannot wait to become part of some overall pattern of living.

Virtue ethics, while reaffirming that people readily deceive themselves when searching for the good, prefers to speak about development. Human perfectibility is the base principle. Vice will always be part of that journey of perfectibility. Virtue is gained only in dealing with vices, but it is gained, say virtue ethicists, only because virtue is seen as better than vice.

Some virtues are part of any listing of virtues: justice, prudence, generosity, courage, temperance, magnanimity, gentleness, magnificence, wisdom. Yet there is no agreed-upon list of virtues. Some authors point out that there may be conflicts between some virtues—gentleness and justice, for example, that cannot be resolved. These authors suggest that the only way to resolve such conflicts is to give primacy to "rule and consequences ethics" rather than virtue ethics. Yet the challenge of human living is to deal with conflict in a constructive way, and virtue ethics holds that dealing with such conflicts will lead to growth in a person's ethical character. —*Nathan R. Kollar*

See also Morality; Sin; Vice; Virtue.

BIBLIOGRAPHY

Carr, David. *Educating the Virtues: An Essay on the Philosophical Psychology of Moral Development and Education.* New York: Routledge, 1991.

Donahue, James A. "The Use of Virtue and Character in Applied Ethics." *Horizons* 17 (Fall, 1990): 228-243.

Kruschwitz, Robert B., and Robert C. Roberts, comps. *The Virtues: Contemporary Essays on Moral Character.* Belmont, Calif.: Wadsworth, 1987.

MacIntyre, Alasdair. *After Virtue.* Notre Dame, Ind.: University of Notre Dame Press, 1981.

_____. *Whose Justice? Which Rationality?* Notre Dame, Ind.: University of Notre Dame Press, 1988.

Yearley, Lee H. "Recent Work on Virtue." *Religious Studies Review* 16 (January, 1990): 1-9.

Vivisection

TYPE OF ETHICS: Animal rights
DATE: Coined early eighteenth century
ASSOCIATED WITH: Animal rights groups such as the National Anti-Vivisection Society)
DEFINITION: Performing an operation on a living animal, especially if done without anesthesia or for trivial reasons
SIGNIFICANCE: Animal rights activists oppose vivisection on moral grounds

Formed from the Latin words *vīvi* (living) and *sectio* (cutting), the word "vivisection" was used as early as 1707 to refer to an operation performed on a living animal. In both the nineteenth and twentieth centuries, people opposed to research on animals organized under the heading of "anti-vivisection" (for example, the National Anti-Vivisection Society). Since animal rightists do not necessarily oppose all animal experimentation, however, "vivisection" usually is taken to refer specifically to operations performed without anesthesia or for trivial reasons. Many or most scientists (and some animal rights advocates) assume that if the animals involved feel no pain or distress (for example, they are anesthetized), then no moral issues are raised by their use. The development of paralytic drugs in modern medicine created a problem. These strong muscle relaxants thoroughly immobilize the subject, allowing very delicate operations (like open heart surgery) to be performed, but when used alone (a practice called "chemical restraint"), they do not deaden sensations of pain. Chemical restraint is sometimes practiced on animals and human infants.

See also Animal consciousness; Animal research; Animal rights; Cruelty to animals; National Anti-Vivisection Society; Sentience.

Voltaire (François-Marie Arouet; November 21, 1694, Paris, France—May 30, 1778, Paris, France): Writer and philosopher
TYPE OF ETHICS: Enlightenment history
ACHIEVEMENTS: Author of *Candide: Ou, L'Optimisme* (1759; *Candide: Or, All for the Best*, 1759)
SIGNIFICANCE: Viewed morality as a commitment to justice and humanity, which was based on the universal ethical precepts of natural law

Voltaire (Library of Congress)

Voltaire, one of France's greatest writers, distinguished himself as a historian, novelist, dramatist, poet, philosopher, and crusader against religious intolerance. As a rationalist and Deist, he rejected the traditional Christian view of God and belief in the immortality of the soul. He adhered to a natural religion, believing in an impersonal, remote deity whose attributes were beyond human understanding but who inspired a great sense of awe. Voltaire shared the belief of fellow Deists who considered the essence of religion to be morality, a commitment to justice and humanity. He strongly believed that universal ethical principles were inherent in natural law and that the merit of human laws was determined by the extent to which they reflected such just and humane standards. Even though all religions derived from a universal rational source, the teachings of theologians and priests distorted the common truth, divided humanity, and perpetuated intolerance. Only under the guidance of enlightened thinkers who rose above superstition and prejudice could a rational morality be cultivated that would bring about human brotherhood. In practice, Voltaire promoted a social ethic that was conducive to the harmonious interest of the entire society. In pursuing this goal, he was quite willing to accept socially useful beliefs that he personally rejected. Thus, he held that, even though the deity probably did not concern himself with human affairs, it was good for the people to believe that there are rewards and punishments for human actions. Among his deepest concerns was the happiness of the individual in society. In *Candide*, he satirized the view that this is the best of all possible worlds, but he nevertheless imagined that in time reason and enlightenment would lessen superstition and fanaticism and bring about a more harmonious social order. To this end, Voltaire remained a passionate advocate of individuals who had been denied justice, especially by the power of the Church, and of judicial reform.

See also Deism; God; Humanism; Leibniz, Gottfried; Locke, John; Montesquieu, Charles-Louis; Natural law; Rousseau, Jean-Jacques; Social justice and responsibility.

Wage discrimination

TYPE OF ETHICS: Sex and gender issues
DATE: Became prominent as a topic in the 1960's
ASSOCIATED WITH: Theories of marketplace behavior
DEFINITION: Payment of different wages to different identifiable groups for reasons unconnected with job performance
SIGNIFICANCE: Wage discrimination takes away the right of each person to be paid what he or she is worth

During the 1960's, various disadvantaged groups asserted their rights in the job market. The Equal Employment Opportunity Commission and various laws provided for equal access to jobs in the United States, but little was said about the compensation for those jobs. Studies quickly established that white men in the United States earned more than people of any other race-and-sex combination.

Business advocates quickly postulated reasons for the discrepancies, including differences in experience, intelligence, education, on-the-job training, occupational choice, and attachment to the labor force. Many studies focused on women, who, it was argued, are more prone to periodic absences resulting from child care responsibilities and also are more likely to leave their jobs for long periods, or permanently, to have children. These propensities make them less valuable in the long run, even if their daily performance while on the job is identical to that of men. Employers defended their right to invest less in workers who were less likely to stay around and pay back the investment. One argument thus became circular: Women were paid less because they had less training, and they were given less training because they were women. Defenses of lower wages for minority workers rested primarily on lack of experience and lower levels of education and training.

Various studies explored these reasons for wage differences. They typically found about half of the differences between men's and women's wages to be explained by objective factors, leaving the other half of the difference unexplained, possibly a result of discrimination.

See also Affirmative action; Equal pay for equal work; Hiring practices.

Wagner Act. *See* National Labor Relations Act.

Walden: Book

TYPE OF ETHICS: Environmental ethics
DATE: Published 1854 as *Walden: Or, Life in the Woods*
AUTHOR: Henry David Thoreau
SIGNIFICANCE: *Walden* provides a model of the ethical uses of nature and serves almost as a handbook for an environmental ethics

Thoreau's two-year experiment of living at Walden Pond was on one level an effort to determine whether a person really needed the material possessions that were considered essential in mid-nineteenth century America. His book demonstrated that one could attain the good life by living in harmony with nature supplied only with the bare necessities. The first chapter, entitled "Economy," demonstrates that human needs are few; thus, there is no need to exploit nature to attain them. Much of the rest of the book attacks the acquisitive spirit. At bottom, Thoreau argues, materialistic values indicate not enterprise but a basic lack of spiritual self-reliance. In Thoreau's ethic, ownership of the land is invalid. Humans should act as stewards rather than squires.

Thoreau's own love of nature is illustrated in the intricate detail with which he describes the seasons, flora and fauna, natural processes, and Walden Pond itself. If he measures and documents, plumbs the depths of the lake, scrupulously counts every penny spent in the building of his house, and ponders his profit after selling produce from his garden, it is to show that empirical science does have a use, but that it should be subordinate to a guiding spirit that respects and loves the natural environment rather than exploits it. *Walden* continually demonstrates "correspondences"; that is, clear relationships between the ethical life of humankind and nature, an interconnectedness that Thoreau believed deserved more acknowledgment and respect.

See also Earth, human relations to; Nature, rights of; Thoreau, Henry David.

Wang Yang-ming (Nov. 30, 1472, Yu-yao, Chekiang, China—Jan. 9, 1529, Nan-en, Kiangsi, China): Philosopher

TYPE OF ETHICS: Medieval history
ACHIEVEMENTS: Author of *Ch'uan-hsi lu* (1572; *Instructions for Practical Living*, 1963)

COMPARISON OF MEDIAN ANNUAL INCOMES OVER TIME FOR FULL-TIME WORKERS			
Time Period	**Percentage of Income of White Men**		
	Caucasian Women	All Other Women	Non-Caucasian Men
1955-1959	63.2	36.4	60.6
1960-1964	59.5	38.8	63.0
1965-1969	57.8	42.8	65.8
1970-1974	57.1	50.4	70.7
1975-1978	58.6	55.8	75.3
Source: Data provided by the U.S. Bureau of the Census in Series P-60 of the Current Population Reports.			

SIGNIFICANCE: In his search for the source of human life and morality, Wang rejected what he considered the duality of principle and material force, insisting instead on the unity of knowledge and action in human affairs

At the time that Wang developed his ideas, Confucianism had been a major religion in China for more than 1,700 years, from the time when the ideas of Confucius were gathered, along with commentaries, during the Han dynasty (256 B.C.E.-220 C.E.). Confucianism was a secular religion emphasizing proper conduct and relationships learned by observation of exemplary individuals. The eclectic writings of Confucianism were codified in the twelfth century C.E. by Chu Hsi, who clarified the notion of principle (*li*, somewhat like the Platonic "idea"), which acted through the mind and material things to create the world, physical and moral, that people perceive. Wang regarded this as an unacceptable dualism, insisting that principle and mind are one, that knowledge and action are inseparable and are related to principle and mind, and that the way to understand these things is not through study of canonic writings, as Chu Hsi taught, but by direct investigation of one's own mind to find the knowledge of the good that resides there. These ideas led to the practice of a Zen-like form of meditation. Wang's ideas were influential in Chinese Confucianism well into the eighteenth century, and even later in Japan.

See also Chu Hsi; Confucian ethics; Confucius; Secular ethics.

War and peace

TYPE OF ETHICS: Politico-economic ethics
DATE: From antiquity
ASSOCIATED WITH: All eras of human history
DEFINITION: War is an organized attempt by a group of people (most often a state or nation) to dominate another group by means of violence and mass killing; peace is a state in which diverse groups of people live together without resorting to organized force, resolving political (particularly national), economic, social, and ideological differences in a nonviolent manner made possible by an attitude of tolerance
SIGNIFICANCE: Raises many questions regarding the ethics of violence, killing, and the destruction of property

Benjamin Franklin said, "There never was a good war or a bad peace." Studying history reveals past mistakes, making it possible to avoid war in the future.

The Just War Theory. The ethics of Jesus Christ, Buddha, Confucius, and Mohandas K. Gandhi generally condemn war. The Christian "just war" theory was developed by Saint Augustine and Thomas Aquinas and Protestants Martin Luther and John Calvin. The "just war" theory holds that certain evils and injustices in the world justify the use of arms to stamp them out. Yet who defines evil and injustice? In the 1640's, the Quakers developed a pacifistic religion that still influences institutionalized Christianity. The Quakers argue that nothing justifies the taking of a human life.

The problem with the doctrine of just war is that a politician can quote the Bible or a bishop to excuse almost anything. Politicians can employ clerics to create war propaganda that manipulates naïve believers.

During the American Civil War, Northern churches could argue that Saint Paul believed in the equality of souls and that free men or slaves resulted from military and political accident. Jesus did not promote slavery; thus, the slaves should be free. Southern churches could quote the Bible to argue that the early Church did not outlaw slavery, while ancient Rome and Greece used slaves out of economic necessity. Each side assumed that God was on its side.

In the past two hundred years, Christianity has become an ideology that must compete with secular ideologies. Conservatism, liberalism, socialism, communism, and anarchism also claim to be universal. They have their own pacifistic and just war theorists.

The growth of a global economy has brought Buddhism, Confucianism, Hinduism, and Islam into dialogue with Christianity. The traditional Asian religions are now undergoing internal reform and moving toward secularism, following the pattern of the Western European transformation of Christianity. Ideology, a term invented in the eighteenth century, refers to popular philosophy or secularized religion. It assumes the existence of a continuing system of group ethics and beliefs.

The results of World War I called the just war theory into doubt. The Anglican church backed England, the Catholic church backed the Austrian state, and the Orthodox church backed Russia. Clerics for the most part justified the belligerent ambitions of their national leaders and did little to shorten or limit the war. It was socialists such as Vladimir Lenin and liberals such as Woodrow Wilson who brought the stalemate to an end while planting the seeds of a new war.

Mohandas K. Gandhi, a Hindu, and Albert Einstein, Erich Fromm, Martin Buber, and Elie Wiesel, four Jews moved by the Nazi Holocaust, led many Christians to rediscover the early Christ, the Quaker Jesus, and the nineteenth century peace prophets Leo Tolstoy and Henry Thoreau. More and more, pacifist Christians rejected medieval just war theories.

After World War II, Christians such as Albert Camus adopted existentialist ethics. Vatican II (1962-1965) repudiated earlier Catholic doctrines that had promoted dualistic, Manichaean attitudes—anti-Semitism, anticommunism, antiliberalism and anti-Protestantism. U.S. church leaders more often protested the Indochinese wars and the American-Soviet nuclear arms race that lasted from 1955 to 1985, in alliance with secularists such as British philosopher Bertrand Russell. The nuclear arms race, in which devices were built that could not actually be used, was largely irrational. It weakened the economies and the ecologies of the nations that poured money and resources into it.

Types of War. Modern war takes three forms: first, the determination of the balance of power between or interstate conflict of near equals (such as Germany and the United States from 1941 to 1945); second, the imperial war of the strong against the weak; and third, the civil war or domestic revolution.

National Wars to Determine the Balance of Power. The bloodiest wars of the twentieth century, World War I and World War II, were caused basically by a breakdown of international law. In the 1914 crisis, the European great powers blundered into an unlimited war without clear aims. The peace treaties of 1919 to 1923 were largely truces, and a stable balance of power was not created. Only Britain and France put much faith in the newly established League of Nations.

Coming to power in 1933, Adolf Hitler pursued vengeance for the 1919 Versailles Treaty. He withdrew the Third Reich from the League of Nations. Then he carried out a campaign of aggression, first by intimidation and then by invasion, from 1936 to 1939. As he outlined in *Mein Kampf* (1925), Hitler wanted to expand into the Soviet Union and set up an empire based on that country's raw materials and cheap labor. It took until 1941 for three great rival powers to ally to fight Hitler. Within four years Britain, the Soviet Union, and the United States defeated the Nazi dictator on the battlefield along with his fascist allies, Japan and Italy.

The German Führer, who was an ideologue, used anticommunism from 1933 to 1939 to help him acquire his allies, but his 1939 deal with Joseph Stalin allowed them to divide Poland. Then, in June, 1941, Hitler invaded the Soviet Union. His unlimited imperial ambitions in Western and Eastern Europe made it impossible to negotiate with him. The morally repulsive Holocaust against the Jews stemmed from his racist theories and his association of Judaism with communism.

The rise and fall of Nazi Germany raised profound ethical questions about the meaning of Christianity, democracy, socialism, and Judaism. The Nazis killed the idea of exclusive biological racism. Chauvinistic nationalism, however, still exists.

The Nuremberg and Tokyo Tribunals broke new ethical ground by trying defeated Axis leaders and holding them personally responsible for violating international treaties.

The joint victory of the United States and the Soviet Union over Hitler's Germany left the United States and the Soviet Union as major rivals for the next forty years. In 1945, Harry Truman launched an American anticommunist crusade that used some propaganda tactics that had been perfected by Benito Mussolini and Hitler. American presidents from the 1950's, through Ronald Reagan's first term, followed in Truman's footsteps. The Americans and Soviets mistakenly did not seize the opportunity provided by Stalin's death in March, 1953. Intolerant anticommunism and anticapitalism fueled a costly and unnecessary nuclear arms race in the United States and in the Soviet Union. When communism came to be considered bankrupt as an ideology, anticommunism was similarly finished. Despite their mutual ideological denunciations, Moscow and Washington managed to keep peace in Europe until the Bosnian civil war of the 1990's, when they tried to cooperate in the United Nations to shorten that conflict.

Imperial Wars. Over the centuries, great powers have not only gone to war with one another in Europe in order to maintain a favorable balance of power but also have fought imperial wars. The direct or indirect taking of land, labor, capital, or culture by a great power from a small power is imperialism. Imperialistic actions may be broader and more indirect than the more limited activities of colonialists who occupy another's land. The United States has historically manipulated Honduras in an imperial way, while the British Crown Colony of the Falklands exemplifies direct political colonialism.

Imperialists act on four levels: military, political, economic, and ideological. From 1415 to 1763, Portugal, Spain, and France saw their empires rise and fall. Britain became the primary imperial power from the end of the Seven Years War in 1763 until World War I.

From the point of view of Asia, Africa, North America, and South America, the European nations gradually forced territories around the world into the developing global economic system after 1415. Politicians, missionaries, and soldiers followed the traders, exporting culture (later called Western civilization). This process gradually subverted local traditional cultures, including those of long-term empires such as Turkey, India, and China.

After more than a century of capitalist penetration, Mao Tse-tung's revolution in 1949 brought a form of Marxism to China. After Mao's death in 1976, international capitalists and their culture renewed their influence in China.

Compared with British imperialism, the Germans made a late bid for colonies, economic concessions, and spheres of influence in the era of Kaiser Wilhelm, from 1890. Politically, the United States did not understand the implications of its military action in 1917 and 1918, and it withdrew, practicing isolationism until 1941, when, for a second time, it was drawn into the European process. German and Japanese imperialism during World War II later led the American empire to make its own claims. Since 1945, the United States has been the prime expansionist power, and Japan and part of Germany were occupied militarily by the United States.

Growing from European colonies, U.S. culture, itself mainly imported from Europe, justified joining the European great powers in the race for spheres of influence overseas. Therefore, the United States already had an imperial tradition before World War II. Like the British, the U.S. imperialists of 1812 (failing to gain Canada), 1848 (annexing more than half of Mexico), and 1898 (taking over Spanish colonies) ultimately succeeded by disguising their military and economic expansion with democratic-sounding ideology. Various secretaries of state, based on nineteenth century traditions, took it for granted that their global mission included protecting American property in Europe, Latin America, and Asia.

Remnants of the British, French, Dutch, Belgian, Portuguese, and Spanish empires were dismantled politically and militarily after World War II, but Western culture and corporations continue to exert influence in the Southern Hemisphere.

After 1945, democracy was weakened in America by the growth of the military-industrial complex. Democratic institutes declined and "strategic" think thanks were established. "Strategic" is a useful word in military thinking. Stalin assumed that Poland was strategic to his needs, whereas the Poles assumed that Soviet strategic actions were imperialist. German generals in 1914 viewed Belgium as of strategic value to them, while the Belgians viewed the German invasion as imperialistic. The American military assumed in 1965 that Hanoi and Cam Ranh Bay were of strategic value against China. The French military and the Japanese military had assumed this years before. The North Vietnamese leader Ho Chi Minh, like the Poles and Belgians, regarded his enemies' strategic interests as victimizing Vietnam.

The clever metaphor "cold war" was invented by American financier Bernard Baruch, in April, 1947. The complex rivalries between the Soviet Union and the United States, between capitalism and communism as economies, between democracy and totalitarianism, were lumped together within this slogan. Propaganda battles of the "cold war" fueled two real wars: the Korean War and U.S. military intervention in the Indochinese wars (1961 to 1975).

The Soviet Union also tried to destroy "capitalism and imperialism" but did not fight the United States directly. Instead, its leaders encouraged socialist revolutionaries to overthrow capitalism in the Third World. In addition, Soviet armies in 1945 occupied Eastern European nations against their will.

Korea serves as a natural buffer between three historic empires: the Chinese, the Japanese, and the Russian. In 1945, having knocked out the Japanese empire, American and Soviet imperialists split the land at the thirty-eighth parallel. The United States and China blundered into the Korean War, which lasted from 1950 to 1953. U.N. flag use was authorized by the General Assembly during a Soviet boycott, but 90 percent of U.N. troops were American, and hundreds of thousands of Red Chinese intervened. The Security Council was not involved militarily, as was originally envisaged by the U.N. Charter, because of the hostility among its permanent, veto-wielding members: the United States, Britain, France, and Taiwan versus the Soviet Union and Mainland China. North Korea wound up tilting more toward China than toward the Soviet Union, but the United States preserved an independent Japan. The divided Koreans could see themselves only as victims of imperialism.

Fortunately, despite mutual denunciations from 1945 to 1985, the American and Soviet governments did stay in the United Nations. The Korean War underlined their dispute about how the U.N. Charter should operate. Washington and Moscow accused each other at the United Nations of illegal usurpations of power. Unlike the United States, however, the Soviet Union did not fight openly in Korea, Indochina, or Iraq.

The American war in Indochina (1961 to 1975) dragged on because the United States ignored the U.N. Charter. Military intervention by the United States against the Indochinese communists, begun quasi-secretly in 1949, became by 1961 open warfare. No nation was strong enough to condemn the United States at the U.N. Assembly, Security Council, or International Court. The Indochina war was a disaster, politically, legally, ethically, intellectually, and economically. Hundreds of thousands of Indochinese and tens of thousands of Americans died before domestic opposition based on democracy and anti-imperialist ideals forced the U.S. government to withdraw.

The gains of Joseph Stalin's military imperialism, which undermined the idealism of Vladimir Lenin's crusade against economic imperialism, were dramatically reduced by Michail Gorbachev between 1985 and 1991. Having exhausted itself in a conflict in Afghanistan, the Soviet empire collapsed rather suddenly in 1991.

During the Gulf War, the United States used U.N. machinery to isolate Iraq; Iraq's Middle Eastern neighbors were divided, and the battle over Kuwait ended quickly. This was the kind of limited war the League of Nations Covenant and U.N. Charter had anticipated. The five great powers at the Security Council unanimously opposed Iraq.

The 1991 war protected the Organization of Petroleum Exporting Countries (OPEC) and maintained cheap oil prices. The war was conducted by a powerful U.N. coalition that had been cleverly constructed by the United States. Still, Japan and Germany profited by remaining neutral. Paradoxically, the American military empire maintained its number-one status because of the Gulf War, despite economic decline at home as Japanese and European banks took over much of American industry. American sovereignty and empire were being challenged by a new phenomenon of multinational corporations. Was the age of traditional imperialism coming to an end?

Revolutionary War. Successful revolutionary and civil wars lead to independence and sovereignty or to modification of a state's constitution. In unsuccessful riots and rebellions, subordinate communities fail to overthrow the dominant group. In a revolutionary war, military dictators often emerge. George Washington, Oliver Cromwell in England from 1640 to 1660, the French Jacobins from 1789 to 1815, and Lenin in Russia were revolutionary leaders who saw themselves as liberators of their people.

During the civil war in Russia, Lenin's victory over the Whites, who had foreign imperial support, was achieved under the flag of communism. Nationalists rallied behind the revolutionary leader.

Joseph Stalin, who ruled the Soviet Union from 1924 to

1953, was both a counterrevolutionary and an imperialist, even though he often denounced colonialism. At home, the Soviet dictator was more autocratic than most czars had been.

Combining the techniques of Lenin and Stalin, Mao Tse-tung imposed communism in China, the oldest empire in the world. In both major communist revolutionary wars, entrenched autocracy has meant that democracy is still struggling to emerge decades after a revolutionary war.

Ethical Principles. Moral belief systems—Buddhism, Christianity, Islam, Judaism, and secular humanism, among others—generally condemn social violence. The mass murder of war may be adopted by zealous politicians, however, to eliminate people of differing nationality, class, race, or ideology. Tolerance and the peaceful values of almost all philosophies may be swept aside by intolerant religious and ideological zealots proclaiming "holy war."

Ideally, a pacifist is absolutely opposed to war. Existential pacifists, peacemakers, and pacifistic groups would like to live up to this ideal, but for political or ideological reasons, people may abandon pacifism for the just war doctrine. Many veteran pacifists from World War I defected from pacifism in the face of the acts of tyrants such as Adolf Hitler and Joseph Stalin.

All war is illegal according to the U.N. Charter. Article 51, however, allows nations to go to war in self-defined "self-defense." This defect in the Charter is one reason that the United Nations cannot be called a world government. The United Nations is a quasi or incipient government that over time could evolve into a world government.

In principle, acts of aggression can legally be declared only by the United Nations and are determined by international law. In fact, however, many nations have unilaterally declared a mere threat to their presumed national interests as an "act of aggression."

A national police force is established by the laws of a sovereign state. The police force has an overwhelming, quasi-monopoly on the use of weapons mobilized against scattered, recalcitrant individuals. When two organized police forces fight one another, the result is war. In the Korean War (1950 to 1953), the United States misused the concept of the police force. The American, British, French, and Soviet armies in occupied Germany (1945 to 1948) did true international police work.

Experimental U.N. armies of "volunteers" were used in Bosnia, Cambodia, Croatia, Cyprus, Egypt, Kuwait, Lebanon, El Salvador, Somalia, and Zaire. These operations required sovereign states to furnish the peacekeepers.

Ethical Issues. Such desirable American goals as freedom, justice, democracy, equality, and self-determination may contribute to starting wars but are not necessary to establish international peace. Latin American states might be repressive at home, but they have avoided international war better than have the countries of Europe, Asia, and North America.

Despite much public interest in military history, the military's role as an instrument of politics is often overlooked. Old men declare most wars, while young men sacrifice their lives in battle. Especially in modern wars, women and children are the primary victims and refugees.

Connections among war, taxes, deficits, and modern military technology are seldom made. Instead of explaining how taxes and expanded debts are used to fight a war, politicians ignore the fact that war must be paid for.

Ethical Decision Making. In a democracy, each individual should consider how politicians, corporations, and the press contribute to create a peaceful or a warlike atmosphere. Informed voters, politicians, and pressure groups can influence a government to move toward peace.

A peacemaker can work in four basic fields: politics and law; education in philosophy, literature, and the social sciences; economics and business; and police work.

First, in the United States, Congress theoretically has the power to declare war and to build up or scale back military expenditures. Congress debates which national interests are worth the risk of war. Judges decide international cases that can dampen nationalist egotism or raise national tension. Second, teachers may encourage students to look for peaceful resolutions of conflicts or they may teach that war is an inevitable and even healthy process. Third, the seeking of profits can lead to calls for national forces to save a firm's property abroad. The fourth category, police work, is most controversial internationally.

Peacemaking assumes that there is a legal framework for peace. Anarchists and pacifists say that, in the long run, force does not succeed. Because force generates feelings of revenge, it encourages the next generation of opponents to a regime in power.

Public Policy. The U.S. Constitution is based on the law of nations. The adherence of the United States to the U.N. Charter obligates the U.S. government and citizens to work for peace. Theoretically, Congress has the power to declare war, but in practice the president determines when a clear and present danger necessitates war. Presidents from Harry Truman to George Bush have abused this power in Korea, Indochina, Cuba, Nicaragua, and Iraq. In fact, the issues that cause a particular war are often ambiguous and debatable. Every war in history could have been avoided or shortened if politicians and moral leaders had acted more wisely.

If nations would follow the U.N. Charter, war would be impossible. Acts of aggression would be defined by the United Nations, and no nation could attack another for any reason. By subscribing to the Charter, a nation-state supposedly gives up the right to decide on war to an international committee. In practice, however, this principle has not been followed.

—Robert Whealey

See also Biological warfare; Bushido; Chemical warfare; Dresden, bombing of; Hiroshima and Nagasaki, bombing of; Holocaust; Limited war; Military ethics; Neutron bomb; Scorched-earth policies.

BIBLIOGRAPHY

Angell, Norman. *The Great Illusion.* Edited by S. J. Stearns. New York: Garland, 1972. Written by a liberal Anglo-American journalist who tried to head off World War I with an appeal to economic rationality. He rejected Social Darwinism as an excuse for war.

Arendt, Hannah. *Eichmann in Jerusalem: A Report on the Banality of Evil.* Rev. ed. New York: Penguin Books, 1987. Supports the need for international law to prosecute war criminals.

Bainton, Roland. *Christian Attitudes Toward War and Peace: A Historical Survey and Critical Re-evaluation.* New York: Abingdon, 1960. A clearly written history of the topic by a Protestant at Yale.

Best, Geoffrey. *Humanity in Warfare.* New York: Columbia University Press, 1980. A British historian of the nineteenth century argues the "just war" doctrine.

Bondurant, Joan V. *Conquest of Violence: The Gandhian Philosophy of Conflict.* Rev. ed. Berkeley: University of California Press, 1965. Written by an American Gandhi scholar.

Brinton, Crane. *The Anatomy of Revolution.* Rev. ed. New York: Vintage Books, 1965. Compares the French Revolution with the English Revolution (1640-1660), the American Revolution, and the Russian Revolution (1917-1941). Brinton's pendulum theory might be applied to the Chinese Revolution.

Falk, Richard A. *The Vietnam War and International Law.* 4 vols. Princeton, N.J.: Princeton University Press, 1968-1976. Collected legal essays and judicial decisions intended to demonstrate that the American war in Indochina was illegal under international law. Veteran legalist Quincy Wright and Telford Taylor, the chief U.S. prosecutor at Nuremberg, are included.

Hobson, J. A. *Imperialism: A Study.* 3d ed. London: Unwin Hyman, 1988. A classic liberal criticism of imperialism.

Kennedy, Paul. *The Rise and Fall of the Great Powers.* New York: Random House, 1987. The British-born Kennedy is now a historian at Yale. Like A. J. P. Taylor, he takes a classic view of balance of power politics since 1500 but adds the importance of economic factors.

Miller, Richard. *Interpretations of Conflict: Ethics, Pacifism and the Just-War Tradition.* Chicago: University of Chicago Press, 1991. A critique of contemporary Christian liberation as well as classic and Catholic theologians.

Staley, Eugene. *War and the Private Investor: A Study in the Relations of International Politics and International Private Investments.* New York: H. Fertig, 1967. Treats systematically the imperialism problem; written before the United States became the number-one world power.

Taylor, A. J. P. *The Struggle for Mastery in Europe: 1848-1918.* London: Oxford University Press, 1971. Employs multinational archives to outline the nationality question and operation of the balance of power system while downplaying the importance of ideology in explaining political behavior.

Teichman, Jenny. *Pacifism and the Just War.* New York: Basil Blackwell, 1986. A simple yet comprehensive volume that draws on the work of the more scholarly Peter Brock.

Wank, Solomon, ed. *Doves and Diplomats: Foreign Offices and Peace Movements in Europe and America in the Twentieth Century.* Westport, Conn.: Greenwood Press, 1978. Thirteen chapters by historians that concentrate on Germany and Austria before 1914, on British socialists during World War I, and on the anti-nuclear movement after World War II.

Wright, Quincy. *A Study of War.* 2d ed. Chicago: University of Chicago Press, 1983. A well-balanced account by an idealist with a peace slant.

Warranties and guarantees

TYPE OF ETHICS: Business and labor ethics

DATE: Middle Ages to present

DEFINITION: Assurances to consumers that their purchases will meet certain standards

SIGNIFICANCE: In the absence of enforceable warranties and guarantees, some sellers would choose to lie about the quality of their products

The terms "guarantee" and "warranty" are virtually synonymous in their marketplace meanings. Laws in the United States generally use the term "warranty," while "guarantee" is perhaps more common in everyday speech. Both terms imply some sort of assurance of quality or standards to the buyer of a product or service. Sellers of products have probably always offered some form of guarantee, if nothing more than their reputation. During the Middle Ages, guilds for various professions set standards for the training and qualifications of their members. This could be considered to be the first formal type of guarantee.

Forms of Warranties. Warranties can take the form of written or oral statements. Some warranties are implied and are in force even though they are not directly communicated from seller to buyer. Sellers have some protection, in that they can specify that products are warrantied only for "reasonable use" or can attach warnings that products are not suited for particular uses. Many product liability lawsuits hinge on the meaning of "reasonable use" and whether a product is as safe as could reasonably have been expected.

In the United States, written warranties are covered by the Magnuson-Moss Warranty Act (1975). According to the provisions of that act, a warranty must describe the specific coverage offered and what the purchaser of a product has to do to obtain it, as well as what the warrantor must do to remedy a problem. Prior to passage of the act, a warranty could be used to limit the seller's responsibility to what was stated on the warranty, thus breaking some reasonable expectations on the part of the buyer. The act states that warranties must be available in writing and must be available for purchasers to read before a purchase is made.

The Magnuson-Moss Warranty Act specifies two types of

implied warranties that almost always are in force even though they are not stated in a seller's written warranty. In most cases, sellers are not able to release themselves from these implied warranties. The implied warranty of merchantability states that the product or service is suited for ordinary use. The implied warranty of fitness for a particular purpose states that sellers are responsible for providing correct information regarding particular uses to which a buyer might put a product. Sellers in this case represent themselves as experts whom consumers can trust for advice. For example, a consumer might tell a vacuum-cleaner salesperson what types of carpets the vacuum cleaner is being purchased to clean. The salesperson then would make a recommendation based on this information. The consumer has a right to expect that the vacuum cleaner will perform, even if the use to which it is put is not ordinary.

Warranties can be either full or limited. The Magnuson-Moss Warranty Act states conditions that must be met for a warranty to be labeled as "full." Limited warranties restrict the promises made by sellers. They can include clauses calling for payment of labor charges by the purchaser, reinstallation charges, or pro-rata refunds based on how long the product had been in use.

Many warranties apply only to new products. Consumers have less protection when they buy used goods, particularly if the goods are specifically sold "as is." Implied warranties most often do not apply to such sales.

Ethical Implications. Warranties and guarantees protect consumers both from unscrupulous behavior and from unanticipated consequences. An honest seller may unintentionally sell a defective product. His or her guarantee to the purchaser may be a simple oral statement that the product can be returned if it is defective. It may also take a formal contractual form. In either case, buyers face little risk when dealing with honest sellers.

Written warranties protect consumers from sellers who misrepresent their products, perhaps lying about the characteristics or expected performance of the product or about what the sellers will do to remedy defects or other consumer dissatisfaction. In the absence of enforceable warranties, sellers would be able to make any claims about their products, and consumers would have no way of making judgments other than the reputation of the seller. Unscrupulous sellers could then make sales based on exaggerated claims, then refuse to back those claims. The marketplace might even offer an incentive for such behavior, since consumers would be drawn to products for which exaggerated claims had been made, at least until the sellers' dishonesty had been established.

Warranties thus provide protection against dishonest marketplace behavior. They serve to make marketplaces more efficient, because consumers can be more certain of the information provided to them rather than having to rely on reputation. Warranties also increase the rewards to honest sellers, who are not faced with dishonest competitors who can make sales through false claims about their products. Warranties thus serve to enforce and reward ethical behavior.

—*A. J. Sobczak*

See also Business ethics; Consumerism; Sales, ethics of.

BIBLIOGRAPHY
Eiler, Andrew. *The Consumer Protection Manual.* New York: Facts on File, 1984.

Eisenberger, Kenneth. *The Expert Consumer: A Complete Handbook.* Englewood Cliffs, N.J.: Prentice-Hall, 1977.

Maynes, E. Scott. *Decision-Making for Consumers: An Introduction to Consumer Economics.* New York: Macmillan, 1976.

Sapolsky, Harvey M., ed. *Consuming Fears: The Politics of Product Risks.* New York: Basic Books, 1986.

Weinstein, Alvin S., et al. *Products Liability and the Reasonably Safe Product: A Guide for Management, Design, and Marketing.* New York: John Wiley & Sons, 1978.

Washington, Booker T. (Apr. 5, 1856, Hale's Ford, Va.—Nov. 14, 1915, Tuskegee, Ala.): Educator

TYPE OF ETHICS: Race and ethnicity

ACHIEVEMENTS: Founder and principal of Tuskegee Normal and Industrial Institute and author of *Up from Slavery* (1901)

SIGNIFICANCE: Interpreted human actions by utilitarian and pragmatic principles; evaluated behavior on the basis of the results achieved

Booker T. Washington's ethical position is set against the cultural, political, and societal forces of the late nineteenth and early twentieth centuries. His life corresponded with the Reconstruction years and its aftermath, when the South was adjusting to the post-Civil War trauma. The United States was emerging as a powerful industrial nation, and few restraints had been placed on economic competition. The era was dominated by industrialists who amassed great wealth through hard work and shrewd business practices. Some of the wealth, however, was diverted to select philanthropic causes.

By 1881, when Washington became principal of the Tuskegee Normal and Industrial Institute, the status of African Americans, particularly in the South, had eroded. Jim Crow laws, supporting racially discriminatory practices, proliferated. There was growing support in all sections of the country for disenfranchisement. The U.S. Supreme Court, in 1883, overturned that portion of the 1875 Civil Rights Act that had prohibited racial discrimination in the public sector. In 1896, the Court held in *Plessy v. Ferguson* that "separate but equal" public facilities were constitutional. In this context, Washington lived and developed his ethical and social views.

Cotton States and International Exposition Address. The Atlanta Address on September 18, 1895, established Washington as a spokesperson for many African Americans, those he called the "masses of my race." The speech summarized his position on race relations, and it found an enthusiastic audience, especially among white listeners. Thereafter, he was in great demand as a speaker and a national symbol for his race, being publicly recognized by presidents William McKinley, Theodore Roosevelt, and William Howard Taft as well as Queen Victoria of England.

In the Address, he proposed a compromise through which demands for full political and civil rights of African Americans would be exchanged for a share in the economic benefits that were expected to arise out of industrial development in the South. Instead of appealing for political power and recognition, he urged African Americans to establish respect by developing marketable vocational skills. He asserted that prosperity would come "in proportion as we learn to dignify and glorify common labor and put brains and skills into the common occupations of life." Without confrontation and with practical skills, African Americans could present themselves as law abiding and nonoffensive citizens so that the social standards of the South would not be challenged. In a separate-but-equal appeal he found a willing audience when he said, "In all things purely social we can be as separate as the fingers, yet one as the hand in all things essential to mutual progress." Social equality was rejected in exchange for "material prosperity [which] will bring into our beloved South a new heaven and a new earth." Later, when he proposed greater economic cooperation between the races, he was reminded by the white establishment that even business relationships were social and therefore should be treated as separate. His correspondence, however, reveals that Washington was secretly working to combat disenfranchisement and segregation.

Although the Address brought praise and fame to Washington as a nonthreatening voice for African Americans, he was never able to move significantly from the compromise position he had so convincingly established in the speech. Strong opposition to his philosophy of accommodation was vocalized by W. E. B. Du Bois, founder of the Niagara Movement, and, later, executive secretary of the National Association for the Advancement of Colored People. Du Bois was a staunch advocate of full social, civil, political, and economic opportunities and recognition for all African Americans.

Up from Slavery. Since there was widespread interest in Washington's life, his 1901 autobiography presented the story of his rise from slavery, his diligent effort to receive an education, particularly at Hampton Institute, and his ensuing dedication to the development of Tuskegee and his race.

His story became a sacred text for many of his readers, and he was regarded as a hero, even a messiah-like figure. The autobiography was widely translated and was read in Africa, Asia, and Europe. Some regarded his story as an inspirational example of success against great odds, but others saw it as a safe statement intended for a white audience. Washington saw himself, however, as a moral leader who was capable of guiding both races to a new level of racial justice. He verbalized the traditional views of American so-

ciety toward nonwhites, presenting an uncomplicated and childlike image of African Americans.

Ethical Implications. Washington's strategy was both utilitarian and pragmatic. His prevailing view was that economic success was the key to success in other areas of life. He was convinced that manual labor brought dignity and self-esteem. He wanted to send each of his graduates into society "feeling and knowing that labor is dignified and beautiful." Success came as a result of using practical principles to meet racial goals. Although some of his critics insisted that he was perpetuating a caste system, he insisted that industrial, vocational, and agricultural education were morally valuable. He strongly believed that it was the duty of an African American "to deport himself modestly in regard to political claims, depending upon the slow but sure influences that proceed from the possession of property, intelligence, and high character for the full recognition of his political rights." Washington's pragmatic approach deemphasized claims to inherent rights.

Booker T. Washington (Associated Publishers)

At the conclusion of his autobiography, although he was optimistic about the future, he recognized that there was an ongoing struggle "in the hearts of both Southern white people and their former slaves to free themselves from racial prejudice." Washington left no successor to guide the Tuskegee enterprise, and because his dreams were rooted in the past, his influence on the resolution of twentieth century racial complexities was marginal. —*Coleman C. Markham*

See also Civil rights; Discrimination; Du Bois, William Edward Burghardt; National Association for the Advancement of Colored People (NAACP); Pragmatism; Segregation; Utilitarianism.

BIBLIOGRAPHY

Evans, James H., Jr. *Spiritual Empowerment in Afro-American Literature*. Lewiston, N.Y.: Edwin Mellen, 1987.

Harlan, Louis R. *Booker T. Washington: The Making of A Black Leader, 1856-1901*. New York: Oxford University Press, 1972.

_____. *Booker T. Washington: The Wizard of Tuskegee, 1901-1915*. New York: Oxford University Press, 1983.

_____. *Booker T. Washington in Perspective: Essays of Louis R. Harlan*. Edited by Raymond W. Smock. Jackson: University Press of Mississippi, 1988.

Meier, August. *Negro Thought in America, 1880-1915: Racial Ideologies in the Age of Booker T. Washington*. Ann Arbor: University of Michigan Press, 1963.

Washington, Booker T. *The Booker T. Washington Papers*. 14 vols. Edited by Louis R. Harlan. Urbana: University of Illinois Press, 1972-1989.

_____. *Story of My Life & Work*. Irvine, Calif.: Reprint Services Corporation, 1991.

_____. *Up from Slavery*. New York: Penguin Books, 1986.

Watergate break-in

TYPE OF ETHICS: Politico-economic ethics

DATE: 1972

ASSOCIATED WITH: The Republican presidential campaign of 1972

DEFINITION: Illegal campaign tactics

SIGNIFICANCE: The break-in cast a pall over political campaigning, and the public's trust in politicians reached an all-time low; indeed, many people came to believe that politicians had no ethics

In early 1972, on behalf of President Richard M. Nixon's reelection campaign, a group of so-called "plumbers" broke into the Democratic national headquarters, which was located in the Watergate complex in Washington. They photographed various documents and "bugged," or tapped, the phone lines. Later, the plumbers broke in again to photograph more material, but the second time they were caught by an observant security guard.

Although the Watergate crisis seemed to drag on forever, eventually some of the truth finally came out in the courts and in the U.S. Senate Watergate hearings; the crusading newspapermen Bob Woodward and Carl Bernstein managed to learn some of the truth because they would not give up on the story. Eventually, investigators learned that President Nixon had approved of the Watergate break-in.

Many people who were linked to the break-in served terms in prison, including several high-ranking Nixon associates. After Nixon was pardoned by Gerald Ford, the public's esteem for politicians (most of them lawyers) fell to an all-time low.

See also Corruption; Political realism; Politics.

President Richard Nixon was forced to resign after his connection with the Watergate break-in became public. (National Archives/Nixon Project)

Weber, Max (Apr. 21, 1864, Erfurt, Prussia—June 14, 1920, Munich, Germany): Sociologist

TYPE OF ETHICS: Modern history

ACHIEVEMENTS: Author of *Die protestantische Ethik und des Kapitalismus* (1904-1905; *The Protestant Ethic and the Spirit of Capitalism*, 1930)

SIGNIFICANCE: One of the prominent social scientists of the twentieth century, Weber explored the ways in which Protestant religious and ethical beliefs influenced the development of modern capitalism

Weber is considered to be one of the founders of modern social science. His intellectual achievement reflected extraordinary breadth, including original studies of economy and law, social structure, comparative civilizations, and methods of the social sciences. He is best known for *The Protestant Ethic and the Spirit of Capitalism*, in which he analyzed human motives—that is, beliefs and values determining action—in the development of capitalism and concluded that certain religious beliefs could be linked to economic trends. The Calvinist doctrine of predestination held that God had singled out humans before their births either to be saved by grace or to be damned. The uncertainty of not knowing whether believers were saved or damned prompted them to exhibit controlled and methodical conduct in the pursuit of their worldly calling, which Weber called "inner-worldly asceticism." Many Calvinists came to regard economic success, including the accumulation of capital, as a possible sign of God's grace and salvation, which often had been achieved by abstinence from "unnecessary" consumption, leading to savings and reinvestment in economic growth. Weber did not deny that other material and psychological factors were conducive to the development of capitalism, but he pointed out that never before the advent of capitalism had religious beliefs viewed economic success as a sign of God's grace. In studies of world religions, he attempted to explain how religious beliefs shaped a people's social and political institutions and economic activities. He argued, for example, that in Confucianism and Hinduism particular doctrines inhibited economic advance under conditions that were otherwise favorable to economic pursuit. Such a finding, he hoped, would make more convincing the uniqueness of religious and ethical factors in the development of western European capitalism.

See also Calvin, John; Capitalism; Economics; Luther, Martin; Marxism.

Welfare programs

TYPE OF ETHICS: Human rights

DATE: Mid-nineteenth century to present

DEFINITION: Programs intended to ensure a minimum standard of living

SIGNIFICANCE: Raises the issue of the responsibilities of societies to their less fortunate members

One of the first compulsory national programs of social insurance was instituted in Austria in 1854, but societies have always recognized responsibilities to less fortunate members. Welfare programs simply institutionalize society's responses to the various problems that individuals face.

Private Versus Public. Many of the tasks of national or state welfare programs have been, and still are, performed by smaller groups. Many families care for their sick, elderly, or unemployed members. In other cases, individuals form voluntary organizations to protect their standards of living. Insurance companies and mutual aid societies are examples of individuals agreeing to provide for others in exchange for a guarantee that they will be provided for if necessary. Governments step in when families or other larger groups are unwilling to or cannot provide what is deemed to be an adequate standard of living.

Private systems of contracting sometimes break down, or the scale of programs becomes so large that government provision becomes the least costly means of delivery. In other cases, society may declare that a condition is desirable, in opposition to individuals. One example concerns child labor and education. Poor families may decide that having a child work and provide an income is preferable to having the child become educated. Society as a whole may enforce education and prohibit child labor, both for the children's immediate good and to break a cycle of poverty in which uneducated children grow up unable to earn a living.

Types of Welfare. The most basic welfare programs provide cash grants so that recipients can buy what they need. Concerned that welfare recipients may make poor choices, welfare providers sometimes provide goods "in kind"; for example, food stamps and housing vouchers that can be used only for those specific goods or services. These restrictions on welfare are sometimes justified on the basis of the argument that the adult direct recipients of welfare may not, in the absence of restrictions, pass on benefits to indirect recipients such as children.

Welfare programs correct a variety of individual problems. People may be unable to work because of illness or injury, or simply because they cannot find jobs. They may have the responsibility of caring for someone else. Perhaps society deems that people above a certain age should not have to work. In any of these cases, welfare programs may provide income to take the place of wages or salaries.

Programs can also provide particular goods and services. Provision of food, housing, health care, and education is common. Health care and education programs have become so institutionalized that many people do not consider them to be welfare. In many cases, however, these services are provided to consumers at a price lower than would exist in a free, competitive market.

International Comparisons. Typically, the countries of Western Europe have the most extensive welfare systems. Great Britain, for example, has a national health care system. Several Western European countries provide widespread housing allowances. Switzerland went so far as to provide that local governments would plant rosebushes on graves if the friends or relatives of the deceased were unwilling or unable to do so. Clearly, different governments have differing definitions of an adequate standard of living and how far government should go to provide it. It is not uncommon for a Western European government to spend 20 percent or more of its gross national product on welfare programs. Much of this spending takes the place of private spending, as in the case of housing allowances, but the figure still illustrates a deep commitment to social welfare.

In less developed countries, an adequate standard of living may mean simply having enough food to avoid starvation. These countries cannot afford to set higher standards, even though such standards obviously are desirable. Some of the wealthier countries therefore have extended welfare programs to encompass foreign aid.

Ethical Issues. Ethical issues arise regarding both the acceptance and the provision of welfare. Acceptance of welfare implies a moral choice. Numerous cases exist in which people have abused welfare systems by claiming benefits for which they have no true need, perhaps choosing not to work when they are able and when jobs exist. Some programs insist that able-bodied welfare recipients either work or enroll in training programs to enhance their job skills.

Welfare providers must make choices. Money spent to achieve one standard of living cannot be spent on another goal, and money spent on one family cannot be spent on another. Some system of priorities therefore is necessary. A further tradeoff is that money spent on welfare programs cannot be spent on other types of programs such as national defense or research. Finally, money given to one person must be taken from someone else. Governments must decide how much redistribution is equitable and must be concerned that taking money from those who work discourages them from working.

A different set of issues concerns the goals of welfare programs. An obvious goal is ensuring that individuals achieve a minimum standard of living. Means of achieving that goal, however, differ in their consequences. Providing aid to someone, for example, may destroy private initiative. People may become dependent on welfare. Rules of welfare programs may also instigate a "cycle of poverty" in which children raised on welfare learn the rules of that system but do not learn how to earn a living on their own. Welfare rules that provide extra payments to families may encourage women to have children, thus locking them in to child care and dependence on the welfare system. Welfare planners must consider such unintended consequences.

—*A. J. Sobczak*

See also Altruism; Generosity; Hunger; Utilitarianism; Welfare rights.

BIBLIOGRAPHY

Davis, Kenneth S., ed. *The Paradox of Poverty in America.* New York: H. W. Wilson, 1969.

Glazer, Nathan. *The Limits of Social Policy.* Cambridge, Mass.: Harvard University Press, 1988.

Gregg, Pauline. *The Welfare State: An Economic and Social History of Great Britain from 1945 to the Present Day.* Amherst: University of Massachusetts Press, 1969.

Levitan, Sar A., and Clifford M. Johnson. *Beyond the Safety Net: Reviving the Promise of Opportunity in America.* Cambridge, Mass.: Ballinger, 1984.

Lutz, Mark A., and Kenneth Lux. *The Challenge of Humanistic Economics.* Menlo Park, Calif.: Benjamin/Cummings, 1979.

Moynihan, Daniel P. *The Politics of a Guaranteed Income: The Nixon Administration and the Family Assistance Plan.* New York: Random House, 1973.

Welfare rights

TYPE OF ETHICS: Human rights; Politico-economic ethics; Religious ethics

DATE: 1940's

ASSOCIATED WITH: Industrial capitalism, socialism, and human rights

DEFINITION: The belief that all persons, regardless of status, have a right to the basic economic resources needed to maintain well-being

SIGNIFICANCE: Central to arguments pertaining to definitions of justice and the nature and scope of human rights

In traditional (precapitalist) societies, persons recognized a mutual obligation to meet the essential economic needs of all other members of the community. This obligation is asserted in Judaism, Christianity, Islam, Hinduism, Buddhism, Taoism, and Confucianism. In African and Native American traditions, moral development was demonstrated by giving away personal wealth during festivals. All these various traditions operated with a kinship model of ethics (in which all members of the community are to be treated as family). As these traditions developed, their morality was universalized so that all humanity was to be regarded as family. Based on these religious foundations, peasants in feudal societies retained certain economic rights (subsistence rights) vis-à-vis the nobility. The contemporary concept of welfare rights draws on this earlier, highly developed concept of community obligation.

Modern History. The rise of industrial capitalism in the nineteenth century destroyed the earlier model. Modern individualism and laissez-faire economics separated the individual from the community and made survival dependent upon individual employment, effort, opportunity, and reward. In the process, poverty was reconceptualized as being self-caused and the poor were denigrated as being lazy and immoral. Consequently, society renounced any moral obligation to help the poor. A distinction was drawn between the deserving poor (disabled and orphans) and the undeserving, but programs to help the poor became a matter of optional private charity, not of justice and social policy. The right to accumulate unlimited personal wealth by almost any means, regardless of social cost, was given moral priority over meeting the needs of all persons in the community. In response, protest against the widespread harsh forms of poverty generated by capitalism developed. Recognizing that the primary causes of poverty were economic cycles of depression and unemployment, exploitation of workers, low wages, and lack of educational opportunity, socialist movements reasserted the right of all to basic economic security. Karl Marx proposed an economic system based on the following principle: "From each according to ability, to each according to need." Frightened by threats of socialist revolution and labor unrest, models of capitalism were proposed that included welfare rights, a guaranteed level of subsistence for all. A rudimentary welfare state was implemented in Germany in 1871.

This model gained influence in the 1930's in response to the Great Depression. U.S. president Franklin D. Roosevelt's New Deal incorporated many of the elements of the welfare state. The actual term "welfare state" was first employed in 1941 by British archbishop William Temple. Following World War II, most European nations adopted systems based on a recognition of welfare rights, which included health care, adequate diet and housing, and guaranteed employment or a guaranteed minimum annual income for all. Such policies were endorsed by the United Nations' Declaration on Human Rights (1948). The United States was one of the few developed nations to reject such rights.

The 1960's recognized the emergence of a new period of social activism on behalf of welfare rights. Socialist revolutions erupted in numerous Third World nations. In the United States, George Wiley formed the National Welfare Rights Organization (NWRO) and Lyndon Johnson initiated the War on Poverty, expanding welfare programs. In 1966, the United Nations ratified the Covenant on Economic, Social, and Cultural Rights, giving universal validation to the concept of welfare rights. Welfare rights, however, continue to conflict with the basic premises of American individualism and laissez-faire economics. The United States did not endorse the United Nations' Covenant and in the 1980's began a conservative attack on welfare programs and welfare rights. Nineteenth century arguments against helping the poor and distinctions between the deserving and the undeserving were resurrected and used to shape social policy. The number of the poor and severity of their conditions increased dramatically. This attack was resisted by liberal religious groups that instituted programs to feed and house the poor. They also reaffirmed the centrality of the moral obligation to meet the needs of the poor. Third World liberation theologians and the U.S. Catholic Bishops' pastoral, *Economic Justice for All* (1986) cite a "preferential option for the poor" that should inform all social policy. A similar concept is articulated by philosopher John Rawls in his earlier work *A Theory of Justice* (1971). The central issue remains the relative rights and obligations of persons in a community to one another.

Ethical Arguments Employed. (1) Basic economic needs (food, shelter, education, health care) must be met, since they are necessary for survival and development. (2) All persons have equal worth. (For religious persons, all are created equal.) (3) Greed and personal pleasure are not sufficient reasons for depriving others of resources needed for human survival. (For religious persons, God created the world to benefit all.) (4) The primary causes of poverty are a function of chance (place of birth, social location, innate capabilities, economic cycles). Therefore, there exists a moral obligation to meet the basic needs of others. (5) For religious persons, the primary moral requirement "Love your neighbor" obligates persons to meet others' needs. (6) As part of a community that provides myriad benefits, members of the community have a moral obligation to assure the economic subsistence of all other members. (7) Fulfilling welfare rights improves the quality of life for all by reducing crime, reducing class antagonisms and conflicts, and providing a healthy, well-educated work force.

—*Charles L. Kammer III*

See also Capitalism; Economics; Human rights; Socialism; Universal Declaration of Human Rights; Welfare programs.

BIBLIOGRAPHY

Brown, Robert McAfee, and Sydney Thomson Brown, eds. *A Cry for Justice: The Churches and Synagogues Speak.* New York: Paulist Press, 1989.

Moon, J. Donald, ed. *Responsibility, Rights and Welfare: The Theory of the Welfare State.* Boulder, Colo.: Westview Press, 1988.

Piven, Frances Fox, and Richard A. Cloward. *The New Class War: Reagan's Attack on the Welfare State and Its Consequences.* New York: Pantheon Books, 1982.

Schorr, Alvin. *Common Decency: Domestic Policies after Reagan.* New Haven, Conn.: Yale University Press, 1986.

Winston, Morton E., ed. *The Philosophy of Human Rights.* Belmont, Calif.: Wadsworth, 1989.

Whistleblowing

TYPE OF ETHICS: Business and labor ethics
DATE: Coined mid-twentieth century
ASSOCIATED WITH: Corporate responsibility and standards of conduct for business and professional people
DEFINITION: The act of reporting by an employee any corporate or professional misconduct that is likely to result in significant harm to others
SIGNIFICANCE: Presents a moral conflict between loyalty to one's employer and/or colleagues and the prevention of harm to third parties

Blowing the whistle on a person or activity is intended to bring to a halt some activity that will cause harm to the public. Since it is generally recognized that one should prevent harm to others if one can do so without causing great harm to oneself, whistleblowing would seem to be morally required. It is also generally recognized, however, that one should be loyal to one's employers and professional colleagues. Since whistleblowing by an employee appears to breach this loyalty by reporting the harmful activity to those outside the corporation, the employee who discovers misconduct is faced with a moral dilemma. Some writers argue that such "ratting" on one's employer is always wrong. Others argue that those who are willing to risk their futures to expose wrongdoing are heroes. Still others assess individual acts of whistleblowing by asking various questions: Have all the internal reporting channels been exhausted without results? Is the harm to the public without a report significantly greater than the harm to the corporation with a report? What is the likelihood that the report will actually prevent the harm; that is, is the report believable and substantiatable?

See also Business ethics; Corporate responsibility; Loyalty; Obedience; Professional ethics.

White-collar crime

TYPE OF ETHICS: Business and labor ethics
DATE: Became prominent as a topic in the 1970's
DEFINITION: Criminal activity in the corporate, commercial, professional, and political arenas
SIGNIFICANCE: Brought about discussion of standards of professional behavior

White-collar crimes are distinguished by the fact that they most commonly take place at the workplace and involve activities related to otherwise legitimate occupations. In addition, white-collar criminals rarely use violence or weapons.

The lowest level of white-collar crime, and the one easiest to identify and prosecute, is employee theft, ranging from taking office supplies for nonwork use to the theft of products intended for sale. Higher levels of white-collar crime typically involve manipulations of bookkeeping accounts or legal documents. These crimes are more difficult to trace, particularly as more records are kept in electronic form, with fewer "paper trails" to identify wrongdoing. A variation of this type of crime involves violating the terms of a business contract or law with the intent of earning a profit in a way not intended by the other contracting parties or by society. An example is insider trading, in which stock, bond, or commodity traders use information they have learned earlier than other traders in order to make a profit in their trading. This example points out a difficulty in prosecuting some white-collar crime: It is difficult to say what information is illegal to use, since financial markets are designed to reward those who make effective use of information. The lines of ethical and legal behavior are also difficult to draw in cases of political corruption; "constituent service" to one person might be considered to be political favoritism or graft to another.

See also Business ethics; Corporate responsibility; Corruption; Insider trading.

Whitehead, Alfred North (Feb. 15, 1861, Ramsgate, Isle of Thanet, Kent, England—Dec. 30, 1947, Cambridge, Mass.): Mathematician and philosopher

TYPE OF ETHICS: Modern history
ACHIEVEMENTS: Author of *Science and the Modern World* (1925), *Religion in the Making* (1926), *Process and Reality: An Essay in Cosmology* (1929), *Symbolism: Its Meaning and Effect* (1927), and *Adventures of Ideas* (1933)
SIGNIFICANCE: Contributed significantly to the application of mathematical and scientific processes in the formulation of relevant ethics for twentieth century society

In 1924, at the age of 63 and nearing compulsory retirement at the Imperial College, London, Whitehead accepted an appointment to teach philosophy at Harvard University in Cambridge, Massachusetts. For the next thirteen years, he lectured and developed his metaphysics. Influenced by the thought of Henri Bergson and, at the same time, an erstwhile Platonist, Whitehead considered the requirements for an ethical society through an analysis of religion (*Religion in the Making*) and the fundamental requirements for a dynamic society (*Adventures in Ideas*). He argued that religion—realized only through profound human reflection—contributed to an ethical understanding of the relationship of the individual in society and the universe. After earlier affiliations with Anglicanism and Roman Catholicism, Whitehead did not identify with any organized religion; he did not consider religion as a societal institution to be very meaningful. *Adventures of Ideas* constituted Whitehead's most comprehensive statement of his philosophy and has been his most widely acclaimed and read book. Individual freedom required an ordered society; Whitehead was not sympathetic to anarchism, which frequently advanced values similar to his. Whitehead was concerned with the nature of beauty, art, and peace, predicated upon an ethics that recognized the fundamental primacy of the individual within the context of Western civilization.

See also Bergson, Henri; Plato; Platonic ethics.

Wickedness

TYPE OF ETHICS: Theory of ethics
DATE: Eighteenth century to present
DEFINITION: Acting not for the sake of self-interest or for what is perceived as good but for the sake of evil as evil
SIGNIFICANCE: Wickedness poses a challenge to ethical theories that state that one does not willfully or knowingly do evil unless it is in some way seen to be good

The problem of evil is an ancient problem in philosophy and religion. In religion, the problem consists in explaining why God, who is all good, can allow for evil in the world; in philosophy, the problem entails accounting for the motives that lead people to do evil things. Socrates, for example, denies that people are motivated to do evil; he claims that people are motivated to do what is good and that it is only from ignorance of what is good that people do evil. Thus, people do not knowingly do wrong. Others have taken a similar stance with respect to God, arguing that God does not allow for evil and that it is only the inadequate and finite human knowledge of God that leads people to think that evil exists. Both these responses to the problem of evil, therefore, simply deny the existence of evil. In the philosophical discussion that has surrounded the topic of wickedness, however, there has been an acceptance of the fact that evil does indeed exist; because of this acceptance, the problem of why people are wicked (the problem of evil) reappears with all its force.

In Immanuel Kant's article "Of the Indwelling of the Bad Principle Along with the Good" (1927), he argues that evil results when people are not properly motivated. By being properly motivated, Kant means that one should be motivated to act out of respect for the moral law (that is, universal moral principles), not from self-interest. It is when one's moral principles follow from one's self-interest, and not the other way around as it should be, that one can be wicked and evil. Despite this account of why people do evil, Kant nevertheless believes that evil actions are to be understood in the light of the good that motivates them—that is, the good as perceived in terms of self-interest rather than of the universal moral law. Kant consequently does not believe that people are ever wicked or do evil for the sake of wickedness or evil, and thus he is part of the tradition that denies the existence of evil as such.

Arthur Schopenhauer, in his book *The World as Will and Representation* (1818), denies the traditional rejection of evil and sets forth the notion of "pure wickedness" as an act done solely for the sake of evil. Citing the character Iago from William Shakespeare's play *Othello*, Schopenhauer claims that people can be wicked because they derive disinterested pleasure from the suffering of others or because they are motivated to act by evil.

S. I. Benn has set forth a more detailed typology and discussion of wickedness in his article "Wickedness" (1985). Benn cites two ways in which one can be wicked: either one is wicked in pursuing what one perceives to be good, or one is wicked in acting for the sake of evil. Benn further divides the first class of wickedness into "self-centered," "conscientious," and "heteronomous" wickedness. With self-centered wickedness, one acts in order to promote the interests of oneself or one's family, company, or nation, but does so with a ruthless disregard for others. With conscientious wickedness, one believes that the good that one pursues is universally valid, not only valid for oneself, and pursues this good ruthlessly while excluding others. A Nazi, for example, may act according to a good that he or she believes to be universally valid, but will exclude others to the point of genocide. Heteronomous wickedness entails choosing to act according to another's principles—principles that can be seen to be evil.

The second class of wickedness that Benn discusses, acting for the sake of evil, corresponds to Schopenhauer's idea of "pure wickedness"; Benn labels it "malignity" or "unalloyed wickedness." In discussing this class of wickedness, Benn turns to the problem of evil: Why are people wicked if they are not motivated by self-interest or by something that is thought of as good? Benn's answer to this question consists largely of showing the inadequacy of attempts to subsume all evil actions under a motivation to do good; when it comes to stating why one would be motivated to

do evil because it is evil, however, Benn for the most part avoids the issue.

The problem of why people are wicked, or why evil is pursued as an evil and not as a good, is the central theme of Mary Midgley's book *Wickedness: A Philosophical Essay* (1984). Midgley argues that wickedness cannot be explained by referring it to external, social causes or by denying it exists. Wickedness, she argues, is a real potential that all people have. This potential results from what Midgley takes to be a perversion of natural hostilities and conflicts with others. Midgley claims that this perversion is not the same thing as Sigmund Freud's concept of the "death-instinct" (which is an instinct that serves to bring about death and destruction). People have motives that aim toward negative, destructive ends (such as eliminating enemies and threats), and the perversion of such motives leads to the pursuit of negative ends for their own sake. In short, this perversion entails doing something evil simply because it is evil; it is, as Midgley and others have understood it, wickedness.

—*Jeff Bell*

See also Cruelty; Evil, problem of; Fascism; Kant, Immanuel; Kantian ethics; Schopenhauer, Arthur.

BIBLIOGRAPHY
Benn, S. I. "Wickedness." In *Ethics and Personality: Essays in Moral Psychology*, edited by John Deigh. Chicago: University of Chicago Press, 1992.

Fromm, Erich. *The Anatomy of Human Destructiveness.* New York: Holt, Rinehart and Winston, 1973.

Kant, Immanuel. "Of the Indwelling of the Bad Principle Along with the Good." In *Kant's Theory of Ethics*, translated by T. K. Abbot. London: Longman, Green, 1927.

Midgley, Mary. *Wickedness: A Philosophical Essay.* Boston: Routledge & Kegan Paul, 1984.

Schopenhauer, Arthur. *The World as Will and Representation.* Translated by E. F. J. Payne. 2 vols. New York: Dover, 1966.

Wiesel, Elie (b. Sept. 30, 1928, Sighet, Transylvania): Writer

TYPE OF ETHICS: Modern history

ACHIEVEMENTS: Winner of the 1986 Nobel Peace Prize; author of *Un die Velt Hot Geshvign* (1956; *Night*, 1960), among many other works

SIGNIFICANCE: An outstanding defender of human rights and a pioneer interpreter of the Shoah (Holocaust), Wiesel utilizes his experiences in various concentration camps to explore ways in which the faith of Holocaust survivors can be used to help heal the post-Holocaust world

Wiesel's writings have made him the messenger of the Jewish Holocaust dead and the prophetic muse of the post-Auschwitz age. This fact may explain why he wrote his first published memoir, *Night*, in Yiddish, the *lingua franca* of the murdered Jewish people, rather than in French, the language in which he wrote all of his other works. Wiesel writes masterfully, with a Kafkaesque pen, and his themes include pogroms, the destruc-

Elie Wiesel (The Nobel Foundation)

tion of the *shtetls* (Jewish villages), songs of mourning and exile, the madness of the Messiah, divine love and silence, and the guilt and obligation of survival, all of which are interwoven with threads of Hasidic tales, Kabbalistic mysticism, talmudic wisdom, and pietistic folklore. Theologically, Wiesel's testimony is a continuous *Din Torah* (a disputation based on the judgment of the Torah) with God, who allowed Auschwitz to occur, and with radical dehumanization, the existence of which raises the possibility that the world is either not listening to or does not care about the lessons that can be learned from the Shoah. Wiesel has done more than anyone to establish "Holocaust" (a word that invokes images of fire and burnt offerings) as the accepted term for the Judeocide that occurred during World War II. Because the term is associated with the *akedah*, or "binding," of Isaac in the biblical story in which Abraham is tested and Isaac is victimized (Gen. 22), the use of the term permits Wiesel to question the intentions of God. This act of questioning does not diminish the paradox of the Shoah, but serves to make the issue more significant and more troubling, and therefore also more full of hope. Wiesel has strongly advocated that the specific lessons of the Shoah should never be lost. His eyewitness approach to the issue, which is rooted in the redemptive quality of memory, carries the message that one can survive with morality, a message that will appeal to all those who have suffered or will suffer.

See also Anti-Semitism; Holocaust.

Wilderness Act of 1964

TYPE OF ETHICS: Environmental ethics
DATE: September, 1964
ASSOCIATED WITH: U.S. Congress, the environmental movement, and the Sierra Club
DEFINITION: A federal law that ensures that future generations will have the benefit of an enduring resource of wilderness by setting aside tracts of land in their pristine state and managing them so that the natural conditions of the wilderness ecosystem are not altered
SIGNIFICANCE: Although the Wilderness Act acknowledged the need to allow multiple uses of land, it also, for the first time, brought into federal law the idea that nature is valuable for its own sake, not only for the uses to which humans can put it

A Wilderness bill was first introduced in the U.S. Senate in 1956, but because of conflicts between economic interests and conservationists regarding the appropriate uses of land in areas set aside for wilderness, it was not until 1964 that the Wilderness Act was finally made law. The Wilderness Act of 1964 defines wilderness as "an area where the earth and community of life are untrammeled by man, where man himself is a visitor who does not remain." The Act does allow prospecting for minerals and protects mining interests that existed as of January 1, 1964, but it does not allow any new mineral patents after that date. This was a compromise that was difficult to effect. No motorized equipment, motor vehicles, motorboats, or commercial enterprises are allowed in wilderness areas. Supporters of the Act stated that these exclusions did not violate the multiple-use principle, which calls for public lands to be used for their highest and best use, but indeed applied the principle by reserving some lands for the whole of the community to enjoy. The Act embodies the principle that nature should not be managed, in these wilderness areas, merely to suit people, but so as to preserve and protect the land in its natural condition in accordance with wilderness values.

See also Conservation; Leopold, Aldo; Muir, John; National Park System, U.S.

Will

TYPE OF ETHICS: Theory of ethics
DATE: Fifth century B.C.E. to present
ASSOCIATED WITH: Plato, Aristotle, Saint Augustine, Thomas Aquinas, and René Descartes
DEFINITION: The mental faculty by means of which conscious beings are able to intitiate autonomous action
SIGNIFICANCE: The will is posited to account for the fact that human beings can initiate actions for which they are morally responsible

One of the presuppositions of morality is the belief that a human being is a special kind of agent that is to be held morally responsible for its actions. A boulder that tumbles from a precipice and crushes the leg of a climber is an agent, because the energy that it has acquired is a source of change, the crushing of the climber's leg. Nevertheless, the boulder is not held responsible for its actions, since it is not deemed a moral agent. Although there have been periods when animals other than human beings have been treated as moral agents, it is generally true that human beings alone are held morally responsible for their actions and thus are taken to be the only moral agents within the natural order. (This remark must be confined to the natural order, since many theists believe that God and other spiritual beings—angels, demons, and so forth—are moral agents.) The convictions that a human being is an agent in this special way is often explained by claiming that a human being has a will, a capacity to initiate action through the formation of mental events (volitions) that prompt the desired action.

The Will's Nature. Although philosophers who believe in the will are in agreement concerning its importance to moral responsibility, there is considerable disagreement over what kind of thing it is.

Some philosophers (for example, Plato, Augustine, and Thomas Aquinas) maintain that the will is a faculty that is literally a part of the soul. The will, according to this view, is distinct from other mental faculties such as the intellect and also distinct from its volitions.

Other philosophers (such as Baruch Spinoza and David Hume) reject the notion that the will is literally a part of the soul. These thinkers maintain that the attribution of a will to human beings is simply a shorthand way of saying that the human soul can form volitions and that these volitions can initiate action. In this view, there is no distinct faculty or part of the soul that stands behind its volitions; rather, the will is simply the sum-total of all the soul's volitions.

Regardless of the stand that one takes on the precise nature of the will, one still must deal with the two most difficult issues confronting any adequate theory of the will. The first issue is that of explaining the mechanism whereby volitions exert their influence. This issue is one aspect of the larger philosophical problem of explaining how the mind and the body interact—the so-called "problem of interaction." The second issue is that of specifying what it is about the will's agency that distinguishes it from other agents in a morally significant way. This second issue is that of the will's freedom or autonomy.

Problem of Interaction. Experience seems to indicate that bodily events can cause mental events and that mental events can cause bodily events. The unfortunate climber mentioned at the beginning of this essay experienced the bodily event of a broken leg and then experienced the pain, a mental event, caused by this physical trauma. In fact, all sensations, all cases of tasting, touching, seeing, smelling, and hearing, seem, at least uncritically, to involve bodily events (in which the physical environment acts upon one's sensory organs) that cause mental events (the actual sensory experiences). By the same token, experience indicates that mental events cause bodily events. The mental event of willing to raise one's hand does, under normal circumstances, lead to the bodily event of one's hand raising. The problem of interaction refers to the challenge of explaining this apparent causal interplay between the mind and the body. With regard to the will, the problem of interaction arises in terms of the need to explain how the mind's volitions can give rise to bodily actions.

Though the problem of interaction was explicitly formulated at least as early as the fourth century B.C.E. in Aristotle's *De anima*, attention to it intensified dramatically in the seventeenth century in response to René Descartes' promulgation of substance dualism. Substance dualism is a theory of human nature that holds that human beings are composed of two radically different kinds of substances: mind and body. Descartes conceived of the mind as an immaterial (spatially unextended) substance and the body as a material (spatially extended) substance. In addition, he maintained that the mind and the body can exist apart from each other.

Although the Cartesian philosophy grew in popularity in the late seventeenth and early eighteenth centuries, concern over the problem of interaction grew as well. The radical heterogeneity of the mind and the body upheld by Cartesian dualism led thinkers to wonder how such radically different substances could interact. Descartes himself never fully came to grips with this issue; however, a number of solutions were developed by those who were either avowed Cartesians or were at least heavily influenced by Descartes' philosophy.

Nicholas Malebranche (1638-1715) attempted to solve the problem by conceding that the mind and the body do not really interact. The reason that mental events appear to cause bodily events is that God creates these events so that they exhibit the correlation that people experience. Thus, the connections between willing to raise one's arm and the subsequent act of arm raising must be explained in terms of God's causing the arm to raise on the occasion of the volition that it be raised. Insofar as it implies that mental events and bodily events are not true causes but are only occasions upon which God acts as a cause, this view is known as occasionalism.

The German philosopher Gottfried Wilhelm Leibniz (1646-1716) worried that the occasionalists' supposition of God's ongoing intervention in the world was an unjustifiably complex assumption that would destroy the possibility of there being laws of nature. He preferred his own view of pre-established harmony. Like occasionalism, pre-established harmony conceded that the mind and the body do not really interact. Unlike the occasionalists, however, Leibniz explained the correlation between mental and bodily events by supposing that the events occurring within a substance result from an internal principle of development that God placed in the substance from the outset and designed so that the events unfolding in the mind would be in harmony with the events unfolding in the body.

A third response to the problem of interaction was that of rejecting the dualism that gave rise to the problem. In the seventeenth century, this solution was attempted in two very different theories. First, the British philosopher Thomas Hobbes (1588-1679) maintained that the very concept of an immaterial substance was a contradiction in terms, for substance could only mean body. According to this materialism, then, mental events are nothing other than internal bodily events; thus, the interaction of the mind with the body is always nothing more than matter acting upon matter.

Also rejecting the dualism of Descartes was Baruch Spinoza (1632-1677). Spinoza, like Hobbes, maintained that there is only one substance in the universe. Unlike Hobbes, however, he maintained that this substance should not be characterized exclusively as material, for spatial extension and thought are both attributes of the single substance constituting the universe. In keeping with this dual-aspect theory, Spinoza maintained that correlated mental and bodily events are really the same event viewed from different standpoints: the standpoints of thought and extension. Insofar as there is, at bottom, only one event behind any given mind-body correlation, the problem of explaining the interaction of distinct events dissolves in Spinoza's system.

Regardless of which of these avenues one chooses to explain the efficacy of volitions, one still must undertake the task of explaining why the agency manifested by the will is of a special type that can support the attribution of moral responsibility. Although recognition of the will's special agency is commonly made by referring to it as free and autonomous, there is considerable disagreement concerning the nature of this freedom and autonomy.

Freedom and Autonomy. Numerous theories of human freedom have been defended throughout the history of philosophy; however, it does not do excessive violence to the subtleties of these theories to classify them all in one of the two following categories: voluntarism and compatibilism.

Advocates of voluntarism note that people normally do not punish others for actions that they could not have altered, and they thus maintain that the agency underpinning moral responsibility cannot be one that is governed by causal necessity. With this in mind, voluntarists (also known as incompatibilists and indeterminists) maintain that the will's freedom entails that its volition not be necessitated by antecedent causes or conditions. According to the voluntarist, if one could reproduce the external and internal conditions immediately preceding an individual's choice, the individual would still be free to choose otherwise than he or she actually did. Thus it is that voluntarists such as John Duns Scotus (c. 1265-1308) and William of Ockham (c. 1280-1347) explain the will's freedom in terms of its complete independence of causally determining factors.

In direct opposition to voluntarism, compatibilism maintains that it is possible for certain human actions to be both free and causally determined. Also known as soft determinism and necessitarianism, compatibilism admits that all human actions are causally determined; it maintains, however, that certain human actions are still free insofar as they are free from external constraint and compulsion. One's walking to the corner to mail a letter is, in this view, free, even though it is causally determined by one's beliefs, desires, and character traits. Were another individual to force one to post the letter and drop it in the box, however, one's action would be compelled and hence not free. Freedom thus does not consist in an absence of all causes; rather, it consists in being caused by the right kind of causes: beliefs, desires, and character traits.

Fully aware that their attempt to reconcile freedom with causal determinism seems to amount to nothing more than inventing a new meaning for the term "free," the compatibilists are quick to point out that it is their definition of "free," not that of the voluntarists, that makes sense of moral responsibility. According to the compatibilist, voluntarism makes free choice a random affair, since it implies that no sufficient explanation can be given for an individual's choices. This is problematic, according to the compatibilist, because people do not hold others morally accountable for actions that happen randomly or by chance. People do not think that the lottery official who randomly pulls the ticket of a destitute mother is more charitable than is the official who randomly draws the name of a tycoon. These events happen by chance and are thus to neither official's moral credit or discredit. For this reason, the compatibilist charges the voluntarist with having reduced human freedom to a kind of internal lottery, a lottery that undermines the very

moral responsibility that freedom is supposed to explain.

In defense of their own definition of "free," compatibilists point out that people do think it appropriate to punish those whose actions flowed from wicked wants or a wicked character and to praise those whose actions flowed from virtuous wants or a virtuous character. This fact shows, they argue, that people do not hesitate to hold people responsible for actions that are caused, provided they are caused by the appropriate internal states.

The debate is not thus decided in favor of the compatibilist, however, for the voluntarist will note that the compatibilists' attempt to uphold freedom only succeeds while one focuses upon the immediate causes of free action, the agent's beliefs, desires, and character traits. When one considers the causes of these internal states, one quickly sees that compatibilism implies that they are ultimately caused by factors that are wholly external to the individual in question, factors that obtained even before the individual was born. The voluntarist therefore notes that the causal determinism that is part of compatibilism undermines its attempt to redefine freedom. Since determinism implies that all of an agent's actions are ultimately the results of wholly external causes, it turns out that no actions are free even according to the compatibilists' definition of "free."

Convinced of the inability of both voluntarism and compatibilism to offer a satisfactory account of moral responsibility, some philosophers have resisted the call to offer a theory of freedom. Such hard determinists as Joseph Priestley (1733-1804) resist the call by simply denying that there is any such thing as free agency. Freedom, they insist, is merely an illusion created by one's ignorance of those causal factors that have determined the way that one will act on a given occasion. Other philosophers, such as Immanuel Kant (1724-1804), see freedom as a necessary condition of moral responsibility and thus are not willing to dismiss it; nevertheless, they resist the call to supply a theory of freedom by maintaining that the nature of free agency is a mystery that cannot be penetrated by human reason.

Though philosophical discussion of the will's freedom and autonomy normally focuses on the degree to which the will must be immune from determining factors, an interesting sidelight to this debate concerns the possibility that an individual can, freely and knowingly, choose evil.

Weakness of Will. Acting in a way that is contrary to one's moral obligation while one is fully aware of that obligation constitutes weakness of will. Sometimes called moral weakness or incontinence, weakness of will seems to be a part of most individuals' experience. What is philosophically interesting about incontinence is that some philosophers have been unconvinced by the abundance of experiential evidence for its occurrence and have insisted that it never actually happens.

Probably the best-known advocate of the impossibility of incontinence is Socrates. He rejected incontinence on the grounds that no person wants to be miserable and that the surest way to make oneself miserable is by disregarding the demands of morality. Having accepted these points, Socrates was led to explain those who do choose lives of vice by supposing that they must be ignorant of the true nature of a virtuous life.

Other philosophers (such as R. M. Hare) have rejected incontinence on the grounds that it is impossible to act contrary to the moral principles that one holds insofar as the only true indicator of one's moral principles are the actions that one performs. According to this view, it is what a person does and not what he or she says that reveals his or her actual moral principles. It is only because people delude themselves into thinking that they hold certain moral principles that the illusion of incontinence is so prevalent.

—*James M. Petrik*

See also Accountability; Autonomy; Descartes, René; Freedom and liberty; Political liberty.

BIBLIOGRAPHY

Bergson, Henri. *Time and Free Will*. New York: Macmillan, 1959. This work contains an influential defense of voluntarism.

Bourke, Vernon. *Will in Western Thought*. New York: Sheed & Ward, 1964. Arguably the best introduction to philosophical thought on the will, Bourke's book identifies and analyzes eight distinct conceptions of the will that have been prevalent in the history of Western philosophy.

Edwards, Paul, and Arthur Pap, eds. *A Modern Introduction to Philosophy: Readings from Classical and Contemporary Sources*. 3d ed. New York: Free Press, 1973. The chapter "Determinism, Freedom and Moral Responsibility" contains an extensive, annotated bibliography.

Evans, E. P. *The Criminal Prosecution and Capital Punishment of Animals: The Lost History of Europe's Animal Trials*. London: Faber & Faber, 1987. A fascinating account of periods in European history in which nonhuman animals were treated as moral agents.

Kenny, Anthony. *Will, Freedom, and Power*. New York: Barnes & Noble Books, 1976. Provides a clearly argued defense of an Aristotelian/Thomistic conception of freedom.

Mortimore, Geoffrey, ed. *Weakness of Will*. London: Macmillan, 1971. This anthology includes selections from a broad historical spectrum and is a helpful introduction to the issue of moral weakness.

New York University Institute of Philosophy. *Determinism and Freedom in the Age of Modern Science*. Edited by Sidney Hook. New York: Collier, 1961. This work offers an understanding of the dialectical interplay among the theories of hard determinism, soft determinism, and voluntarism.

O'Shaughnessy, Brian. *The Will: A Dual Aspect Theory*. 2 vols. Cambridge, England: Cambridge University Press, 1980. Perhaps the most sustained treatment of the will offered in the twentieth century, O'Shaughnessy's book is a development and defense of a dual-aspect theory. Though very difficult, this work will repay a careful reading.

Ryle, Gilbert. *The Concept of Mind*. New York: Barnes & Noble, 1949. Considered by many to be the definitive critique of Cartesian dualism and its theory of volitions, it is also an excellent example of ordinary-language philosophy that was one of the dominant philosophical schools of the twentieth century.

Stevenson, Leslie, et al, eds. *Mind, Causation, and Action*. Oxford, England: Basil Blackwell, 1986. The essays in this volume are fairly technical treatments of the status of causation in the mental activity of human beings.

Thorp, John. *Free Will: A Defence Against Neurophysiological Determinism*. London: Routledge & Kegan Paul, 1980. A clearly written attack on neurophysiological determinism that includes an interesting attempt to delineate between incompatibilist freedom and randomness.

Wittgenstein, Ludwig (April 26, 1889, Vienna, Austro-Hungarian Empire—April 29, 1951, Cambridge, England): Philosopher

TYPE OF ETHICS: Modern history

ACHIEVEMENTS: Author of *Tractatus Logico-Philosophicus* (1922), *Philosophical Investigations* (1953), *Notebooks 1914-1916* (1961), "A Lecture on Ethics" (1968), *Lectures and Conversations on Aesthetics, Psychology, and Religious Belief* (1978), *Remarks on Frazer's Golden Bough* (1979), and *Culture and Value* (1980), among other works

SIGNIFICANCE: Wittgenstein argues that moral value falls outside the purview of philosophy, which he views as an activity that is primarily concerned with the explanation and delimitation of meaning in the purely factual description of the world

Wittgenstein's philosophy is divided into early and later periods. The early period is marked by his interest in the formal semantics for possible languages. Wittgenstein believed that language could only be meaningful if sentences are analyzable into ultimate atomic constituents that, in a one-one correspondence, exactly mirror possible facts, thereby providing a picture of the world. The sentence that describes a fact about the world is a concatenation of names for simple objects that corresponds to a juxtaposition of the named objects. The implication is that language is meaningful only if it describes contingent empirical states of affairs. This means that sentences that purport to express moral judgments and values are literally meaningless. Wittgenstein regards this conclusion as showing that ethics must be transcendent, by which he means that value—right and wrong, good and evil—is neither part of the world nor a truth about the world. From this it follows that there simply is no matter of fact about whether it is right or wrong to do something; instead, moral value is a function of subjective attitude, aesthetic taste, or emotional response to the facts of the world. It is in this sense that Wittgenstein, in the *Tractatus* (6.421), enigmatically declares: "It is clear that ethics cannot be expressed. Ethics is transcendental. (Ethics and aesthetics are one.)" Wittgenstein sees the mind's transcendent moral stance toward the world of facts as vitally important to philosophy and the conduct of life, despite the claims that value statements are literally meaningless and that value judgments cannot be stated, but only *shown*. In his later development, Wittgenstein rejected the picture theory of meaning but continued to regard ethics as being deeply rooted in common social practices, or *forms of life*. There can be no adequate reductive philosophical theory of forms of life, because they are too basic, and they constitute the foundation in Wittgenstein's later work for the philosophical explanation of the meaningfulness of discourse. After rejecting the semantic theory of the *Tractatus*, Wittgenstein, in the *Philosophical Investigations* and other posthumously published writings, continued to regard philosophy as a kind of therapy for eliminating philosophical problems that arise through the misunderstanding of language. It is not the function of philosophy to offer a positive doctrine of right and wrong, of good and evil, but only to explain what Wittgenstein calls the *philosophical grammar* of these terms as they can permissibly be used in the language of ethics. The business of philosophy is to arrive at a correct understanding of meaning, not to formulate and defend substantive commitments to particular doctrines of morally justified action or the good.

See also Art; Language; Right and wrong; Transcendentalism; Truth; Values.

Wollstonecraft, Mary (Apr. 27, 1759, London, England—Sept. 10, 1797, London, England): Journalist and educator

TYPE OF ETHICS: Modern history

ACHIEVEMENTS: Author of *A Vindication of the Rights of Woman* (1792)

SIGNIFICANCE: Brought together her interests in women's education and democratic human rights to argue that women deserve an education equal to that of men

Wollstonecraft's significant public activities included running a girls' school and working with radical political groups that supported the French Revolution. She wrote many articles that were published in left-wing periodicals as well as eight books, including novels, educational manuals, and partisan political treatises. In her most famous work, *A Vindication of the Rights of Woman*, Wollstonecraft criticized the view that women should learn only how to keep house and be attractive. Being admired for one's beauty and vocational skills, she said, is demeaning to a human being. Human beings, both male and female, are distinguished from animals in that they were created by God with the ability to shape their emotions and morals through reason. All human beings deserve an education that cultivates their reason. If all people had such an education, they would be able to respect one another as self-controlled, independent, moral, and rational beings. Mutual respect of this sort between husbands and wives is the only route to a happy marriage. In her second most famous work, *A Vindication of the Rights of Men* (1790), Wollstonecraft argued that mutual respect of this sort between social classes is the route to a just society.

See also Equal pay for equal work; Equal Rights Amendment (ERA); Feminism; Suffrage.

Women's ethics

TYPE OF ETHICS: Sex and gender issues

DATE: Began to emerge as separate area in the mid- to late 1970's

ASSOCIATED WITH: Feminism, the women's movement, and liberation theory

DEFINITION: An area of philosophy that examines women's experiences and values in comparison with traditional ethical theories and proposes a revised ethical position

SIGNIFICANCE: Women's ethics has challenged the traditional emphasis on reason, impartiality, autonomy, and universal principles, thus opening up many areas of criticism not thoroughly considered before in ethics, epistemology, metaphysics, and logic

The inclusion of women's experience and the increasing number of women philosophers have had an impact on ethical theory and practice. This impact has been enormous and varied. It is difficult to identify "women's experience." Women are not only women alone, but also belong to socioeconomic classes, racial groups, religions, geographical areas, and cultures. What is common to women's ethics is that experience matters. Just as women's experience is varied, so is women's ethical theory and practice varied.

The common classifications of women's ethical theory are maternal, psychoanalytic, liberal, socialist, Marxist, radical, and lesbian. Each of these views can be divided further among those who extol some aspect of the "feminine" as the highest virtue, those who accept the traditional "masculine" values but seek to redefine them as human, and those who propose a challenge to the idea of feminine and masculine virtues and seek to generate new concepts of morality.

Women's ethics, of any variety, recognizes "traditional" ethical theories as male centered. These theories either intentionally exclude women (and people of certain races and classes) from moral experience or unintentionally use certain male moral experience as the standard for all moral experience, thus effectively excluding women (and people of certain races and classes). The result of such exclusion is a tradition that generally favors reason over emotion, impartiality over partiality, autonomy over interdependence or dependence, the abstract over the concrete, the universal over the particular, and justice over caring. In response to this exclusion, and the resulting tradition, women's ethics consciously considers women's experiences.

Maternal Ethics. Maternal ethics, also referred to as the ethic of care, holds that women's unique experiences as mothers (biological or social) lead to an ethic that focuses on relationships and interdependence, and includes self-sacrifice and care for others as primary moral qualities. Whether they believe women are specially suited for such moral action by biology or by socialization, proponents of such theories

WINNERS OF THE WOMEN OF CONSCIENCE AWARD PRESENTED BY THE NATIONAL COUNCIL OF WOMEN OF THE UNITED STATES	
Year	Winner
1963	Rachel Carson
1964	Hazel Brannon Smith
1965	Virginia Senders
1966	Judge Florence M. Kelley
1967	Ellen Jackson
1969	Annie Mae Bankhead
1970	Ellen Sulzberger Straus
1972	Sister Ruth Dowd
1973	Patricia Smith
1974	Frances Pauley
1975	Margaret Mead
1976	Barbara Jordan
1977	Nancy Hanks
1978	Frances Lehman Loeb
1979	Mary Allen Engle
1980	Elise Boulding
1981	Anne Carlsen
1982	Ethlyn Christensen
1983	Sarah McClendon
1984	Julia E. Robinson
1985	Betty Bumpers
1986	Daisy Screven George
	Anne Morrow Lindbergh
	Mildred Robbins Leet
1987	Suzan D. Johnson
1989	Margaret C. Snyder
1990	Julia Hines Mabus

believe that it is these moral characteristics that women should be recognized as having. Celebrating women's differences from men leads some theorists to suggest that women's morality is different from but complementary to the more male voice of justice. Others suggest that the feminine voice is superior and should be the model for all humanity.

Psychoanalytic Ethics. Psychoanalytic feminists see the family arrangement, in which it is primarily the woman who stays with and cares for the children, as problematic. They believe that it is this arrangement that leads to sharp gender distinctions and inequalities. Because girls stay attached to the same-sex parent and never learn to define themselves as selves, they remain dependent. Boys, however, must define themselves in opposition to the mother and therefore become excessively autonomous. These differences have played out in power struggles in which boys learn to break away and be independent and girls learn to compromise and save relationships. These gender distinctions could be minimized, such feminists believe, by increasing dual parenting. This approach challenges the tradition by questioning the moral superiority of autonomy over interdependence.

Liberal Ethics. The liberal feminist generally calls for the equal education of women and equal opportunity to pursue traditionally male occupations. It is at times summarized as fighting for the opportunity for women to become men. Liberal feminism does not go too far in challenging the traditional approach to ethics; instead, it asks that women be included as human under the same definition as men—as rational, autonomous moral agents.

Marxist and Socialist Ethics. Marxist feminists see the power imbalance as primarily economic. If the marketplace is changed, women will no longer be available to be possessions of men and equality will emerge. Socialist feminists share this concern about the need to change the market but also believe that it will be necessary to change education, the home, media, and women's self-images if equality is to emerge. These approaches also accept much of the tradition and ask that conditions be changed so that women too can be rational autonomous actors.

Radical and Lesbian Ethics. Radical and lesbian feminists call for women to separate from men (the length and extent of the called-for separation vary). They claim that women cannot know who they are or what they believe unless they define themselves in terms of relationships with other women rather than relationships with men. If they are to avoid copying the oppression and power inequalities of patriarchy, they must first break out of it. This approach seeks to challenge the tradition at its very foundation, by rejecting it and calling women to build a separate tradition for themselves that is based on their own rich and varied experiences.

Conclusion. Despite the varied theories of women's ethics, they do pose some common challenges to the tradition. These theories bring to the forefront the dynamics of power that are present in almost any given situation. The solutions that they offer to address the power imbalance between men and women vary, but they all suggest a reevaluation of the assumption that moral decisions are faced by, or made by, people with real or perceived power. They ask people to evaluate traditional "universal values" from the point of view of the disempowered and ask if they still appear to be universal values. They force people to see that being inclusive of many different viewpoints requires a willingness to be critical of the canon of traditional ethics in ways not previously attempted. It would be a mistake to remove the word "man" and replace it with "human." The differences between men and women must be addressed.

Some of these possible differences include seeing relationships and interdependence as the moral starting point and questioning the ideals of impartiality and autonomy as absolute moral values. Women's ethics forces people to rethink the concept of the moral agent and the moral act. It is necessary to see the connectedness of feeling and thinking and to broaden the notion of what counts as moral.

—*Erin McKenna*

See also Environmental ethics; Feminism; Human rights; Personal relationships.

BIBLIOGRAPHY

Gilligan, Carol. *In a Different Voice.* Cambridge, Mass: Harvard University Press, 1982.

Jaggar, Alison M. *Feminist Politics and Human Nature.* Totowa, N.J.: Rowman & Littlefield, 1988.

Kittay, Eva Feder, and Diana T. Meyers, eds. *Women and Moral Theory.* Totowa, N.J.: Rowman & Littlefield, 1987.

Pearsall, Marilyn, ed. *Women and Values: Readings in Recent Feminist Philosophy.* Belmont, Calif.: Wadsworth, 1986.

Tong, Rosemarie. *Feminine and Feminist Ethics.* Belmont, Calif.: Wadsworth, 1993.

SELECTED ARTICLES FROM THE UNITED NATIONS DECLARATION OF THE RIGHTS OF WOMEN

Article 1. Discrimination against women, denying or limiting as it does their equality or rights with men, is fundamentally unjust and constitutes an offence against human dignity.

Article 2. All appropriate measures shall be taken to abolish existing laws, customs, regulations, and practices which are discriminatory against women, and to establish adequate legal protection for equal rights of men and women. . . .

Article 4. All appropriate measures shall be taken to ensure to women on equal terms with, without discrimination:
   (a) the right to vote in elections and be eligible for election to all publicly elected bodies;
   (b) the right to vote in all public referenda;
   (c) the right to hold public office and to exercise all public functions.
   Such rights should be guaranteed by legislation.

Women's liberation movement

TYPE OF ETHICS: Sex and gender issues

DATE: 1960's to present

DEFINITION: An organized movement whose goal is to obtain basic rights and equality for women (First Wave); an ideology that stresses the differences between men and women (Second Wave)

SIGNIFICANCE: Seeks to raise women's consciousness and to obtain basic rights for women that have so far been denied them by society

First Wave Women's Liberation. Women's liberation is the dominant version of feminism in contemporary Western society. Women's liberation emerged in the political context of the American New Left in the 1960's. Prior to this time, the earlier feminist movement, often called the "Old Wave" or "First Wave," referred to the formation of the suffrage movement in the United States and in Britain between about 1840 and 1920. The suffrage movement stressed reforms for women in family law, economic opportunity, and obtaining the right to vote. First Wave feminists of the 1960's carried on the suffrage movement tradition by promoting a vision of equality between men and women. They spoke and thought in terms of equality of rights, nondiscrimination, equity, and fair treatment for everyone, and they worked for constitutional changes to guarantee equal opportunity, especially in politics and education. For example, a prominent First Wave advocate, Supreme Court Justice Ruth Bader Ginsburg, championed a vision of women's liberation in the 1970's that rejected the traditional belief that men and women lived in separate and different spheres. Laws based on this distinction were designed to seemingly protect the "weaker sex" by, for example, limiting work hours or acceptable occupations. These laws created the perception that women could not take care of themselves and needed special legal protection. Ginsburg and other feminists, however, argued that such laws only justified legal subordination. They attacked laws that treated men and women differently and demanded that men and women be given equal rather than special treatment. The accomplishments of this contemporary First Wave women's liberation constitute a great and significant American success story.

Second Wave Women's Liberation. In the 1960's and 1970's, a different and more radical women's liberation movement evolved. Self-examination in consciousness-raising groups caused the unifying theme to emerge that women were systematically and thoroughly dominated, controlled, victimized, and oppressed legally, economically, and culturally by a male-dominated social structure ("androcentricity," "hetero-patriarchy," or "sex-gender system"). As part of consciousness-raising, women would come to realize that this oppression and victimization on an individual level could from the basis for collective action, activism, and political change at a group level. This shift from stressing equity and fair treatment for everyone to stressing the oppression and victimization of women by men and the differences between men and women characterizes the "Second Wave" of women's liberation, a term coined by Marsha Weinman Lear in 1968.

ing the position of women in society. Certainly, both waves have had a profound effect on American politics and society, American consciousness, and awareness of gender roles and

MILESTONES IN WOMEN'S LIBERATION		
Year	Event	Significance
1848	Declaration of Sentiments	Crucial document of nineteenth century feminism
1848	Geneva Falls Convention of Women	First women's rights convention
1869	American and National Suffrage Associations	Early Old Wave feminist organizations founded
1920	Nineteenth Amendment ratified	Women given the right to vote
1963	*The Feminine Mystique*	Pioneering First Wave book by Betty Friedan
1963	President's Commission on the Status of Women	Recommends appointment of women to important political positions
1966	National Organization of Women (NOW) founded	Influential contemporary women's organization
1970	*The Female Eunuch*	Important Second Wave book by Germaine Greer which focused media attention on women's oppression
1972	Equal Rights Amendment (ERA) ratified by Congress	Takes an important step toward guaranteeing equal rights to all women
1972	National Women's Political Caucus organized	Pioneering group for involving women in the political process
1972	Title IX passed by Congress	Prohibits discrimination based on sex in schools receiving federal monies
1973	*Roe v. Wade*	Affirms woman's right to abortion via her right to privacy
1975	*Signs: Journal of Women, Culture and Society* founded	Groundbreaking forum for publication of feminist scholarship and theory
1976	Democratic National Convention	A rule is made that women must make up half of all delegates
1980-1988	Reagan Administration	The administration's antifeminist tone bias causes many setbacks for women's movement
1981	Greenham	All-women's peace camp is set up at an Air Force base; positive use of feminist theory
1982	Sandra Day O'Connor appointed to U.S. Supreme Court	First woman Supreme Court Justice
1982	ERA defeated	Not ratified by enough states
1991	Anita Hill-Clarence Thomas hearings	Catalyzed the women's movement; key event in consciousness-raising
1992	*Casey v. Planned Parenthood*	Abortion rights somewhat limited
1992-1993	"Year of the Woman"	Historic number of women run for and are elected to Congress
1992-	Clinton Administration	Many women appointed to important positions
1993	Ruth Bader Ginsburg appointed to U.S. Supreme Court	Second woman Supreme Court Justice
1993	Violence Against Women Act	Enhances penalties for crimes motivated by gender

The Two Waves Compared. The First and Second Waves of women's liberation are similar in that they both believe that sexual politics is central in the struggle for women's rights. Many of their goals are the same in terms of improv-

the relationship between men and women. The fundamental difference between the First and Second Waves is that the Second Wave is, as Maggie Humm pointed out, an ideology whose purpose is to create an environment for women that transcends social equity. That is, the Second Wave stresses the separateness of and differences between women and men and the communality between women and seeks to provide for the emancipation of women from their yoke of male oppression, victimization, and dominance. A major goal is to challenge and change the relevant social institutions and their practices, which have created and perpetuated these oppressive systems. These goals can be accomplished only by developing "gynaesthesia," a term coined by Mary Daley in 1978 to describe the radically new and altered perception and understanding that occur in women when they become Second Wave feminists. Christina Hoff Sommers describes this situation as a "gyncentric prism"; that is, a sharing among women of certain women-centered beliefs and social organizations. Rather than viewing men and women as equals, Second Wave feminists generally believe that equality is impossible to achieve given the patriarchical structure and orientation of American society. To adhere to equality between men and women would be like sleeping with the enemy. Men are the enemies of women, and there is a gender war in progress. The difference between the First and Second Waves is starkly defined in three statements, two by First Wave feminists Betty Friedan and Iris Murdoch, and one by Germaine Greer, a Second Wave feminist. According to Betty Friedan, "We must not let feminism be co-opted as a mask for cynical corruption by women or by men. We must resist that polarization of us against them (women against other women, even women against men) with our new vision of community that puts first the real needs of people in life." Iris Murdoch says, "to lay claim to [Second Wave feminism] . . . is to set up a new female ghetto. . . . It is a dead end in danger of simply separating women from the mainstream thinking of the human race." According to Germaine Greer, however, "male hostility to women is a constant; all men hate all women some of the time; some men hate all women all of the time; some men hate some women all of the time. . . . What is remarkable, given the implacability of male hostility to uppity women, is that we have survived."   —*Laurence Miller*

See also Equal Rights Amendment (ERA); Feminism; Women's ethics.

BIBLIOGRAPHY

Hole, Judith, and Ellen Levine. *Rebirth of Feminism*. New York: Quadrangle Books, 1971.

Humm, Maggie. *The Dictionary of Feminist Theory*. Columbus: Ohio State University Press, 1990.

McGlen, Nancy E., and Karen O'Connor. *Women's Rights*. New York: Praeger, 1983.

Rosen, Jeffrey. "The Book of Ruth." *The New Republic* 209, no. 5 (August 2, 1993): 19-31.

Work

TYPE OF ETHICS: Beliefs and practices

DEFINITION: Work is human life-activity whose purposes are the production of goods necessary for human subsistence and the realization of human abilities and capacities

SIGNIFICANCE: Personal and social attitudes toward work determine the meaningfulness of work in society

Ambivalent Attitudes Toward Work. The Hebrew Bible, known to Christians as the Old Testament, in the mythology of creation in Genesis and in the pessimistic poetry of Ecclesiastes, evinces both a positive and a negative attitude toward work. According to the Genesis myth, God commanded the first human pair to subdue and have dominion over the earth (Gen. 1:28). God placed Adam in the Garden of Eden "to dress it and keep it" (Gen. 2:5). Thus, work was considered a necessary and integral part of human life in this world.

According to the Genesis myth, however, because of the sin of Adam and Eve, work would be filled with hardship and toil:

> Cursed is the ground for thy sake; in sorrow shalt thou eat of it all the days of thy life. Thorns also and thistles shalt it bring forth to thee; and thou shalt eat the herb of it all the days of thy life; In the sweat of thy face shalt thou eat bread, till thou return unto the ground; for out of it was thou taken; for dust thou art, and unto dust shalt thou return. . . . Therefore, the Lord God sent him forth from the garden of Eden to till the ground from whence he was taken (Gen. 3:17-19, 23).

This ambivalent attitude toward work also appears in Hebrew wisdom literature. The author of Ecclesiastes, an anonymous Hebrew poet, rhetorically asks with a pessimistic tone, "What profit hath a man of all his labour which he taketh under the Sun?" (Eccles. 1:3). Human labor appears to be empty and futile. "Then I looked on all the works that my hands had wrought, and on the labour that I had laboured to do: and behold, all was vanity and vexation of spirit, and there was no profit under the sun." The poet, who is traditionally held to be Solomon, also expresses a positive attitude, and, in the end, seems to be as ambivalent as are the Genesis myths. "There is nothing better for a man, than that he should make his soul enjoy good in his labour. This also I saw, that it was from the hand of God."

The ancient Greeks were just as ambivalent toward work as were the Hebrews, although, overall, the Greek attitude toward work, especially manual labor, was pessimistic. Plato, writing in the *Statesman*, depicts primordial life in the mythical time of Chronos as idyllic. Work was not necessary in those days because the earth, unaided by human cultivation, brought forth fruits from trees that no human had planted. The seasons were mild, the air was fresh, and the people were naked and lounged on couches of grass. In the *Laws* (book 4), Plato called the time of Chronos a "blessed rule" in which humans were happy and provisions were abundant and spontaneously generated.

Not only the ancients but also the moderns were unsure about the role of work in early human life. Jean-Jacques Rousseau postulated an early state of nature in which the needs of human beings were provided for by a generous, benevolent world: "The produce of the earth furnished him with all he needed, and instinct told him how to use it" (*A Discourse upon the Origin and Foundation of Inequality Among Mankind*, 1761). Hegel, even though he castigated early human beings as lazy, regarded toil as a universal feature of human activity intended to satisfy need (*Philosophy of Right*, 1875).

Work as Necessity. Even the fanciful and speculative Greeks realized that labor was necessary in order to make leisure and happiness possible. Plato, in *Critias*, stated that mythology and intellectual inquiry were possible only after the necessities of life had been provided for. In the *Metaphysics*, Aristotle claimed that the arts of recreation, which were more esteemed than the arts of life's necessities, could be practiced only in an environment of leisure. In book 10 of the *Ethics*, Aristotle opined that happiness depended upon leisure and that people occupied themselves in work in order to have leisure. In book 1 of the *Politics*, he made the commonsense claim that one cannot live well until the necessities of life are provided for. Hegel, in the *Philosophy of History*, held that the worker, in diligently providing for his or her needs, created his or her dignity. Montesquieu, in the *Spirit of the Laws*, wrote that the activity of an "industrious" people was the source of their "blessing." Adam Smith held that the industriousness of even the lowest type of worker made possible the necessities and conveniences of life.

The Nature and End of Work. Usually, a distinction has been made between types of work. One distinction was between honorable and dishonorable types of work. In *Charmides*, Plato quoted Hesiod, who held that work is no disgrace. In fact, Plato made reference to things nobly and usefully made as works, although he explicitly excluded such ignominious activities as shoemaking and pickle selling. Plato's distinction seems to be based on the belief that things that serve a utilitarian purpose are mundane and therefore ignoble. Plato, in *Republic* and *Timaeus*, separated the class of husbandmen and artisans from the class of guardians. In *Laws*, Plato strictly forbade artisans from participating in politics and citizens from occupying themselves in the handicraft arts. The craft of citizenship requires much study and knowledge, and no individual could occupy himself well with two different arts. In the *Politics*, Aristotle agreed with Plato and insisted that the citizen refrain from the trades and crafts; otherwise, there would be no distinction between master and slave. According to Aristotle, the food-producing class and the artisans provide for the necessities of life and thus are necessary elements of the life of the state, but the state has a higher end: providing for the greater good. Aristotle also deemed the mastercraftsman more honorable and wiser than the manual laborer because the former has thorough knowledge about his activity, whereas the latter works in ignorance. In *Politics*, Aristotle wrote that some duties are necessary but others are more honorable.

In the *Critique of Judgment*, Kant made a similar distinction between artistic production and manual labor. Artistic production is distinguished from labor in that the former is free and the latter is drudgery.

Hegel, however, was not so pessimistic about the nature of labor. He believed that adults, in working, devoted their lives to labor for definite intelligent and objective aims. Adam Smith echoed the ancient Greeks in his claim that people who pursue trades for a livelihood that others pursue merely as diversions are inferior people. Smith also made a distinction between productive and nonproductive labor that would figure prominently in the thought of classical political economy. Labor that adds value to the product is productive labor, and labor that merely renders a service but fails to add value to a product is nonproductive labor. This distinction yielded ethical advantages for the advocates of capitalism, who wanted to justify the social utility and ethical value of wage labor.

Hobbes's attitude toward work was practical and utilitarian. He advocated the creation of laws that would force those with strong bodies to be employed in useful arts and manufacture. Rousseau, with his negative attitude toward the stultifying and dehumanizing aspects of modern civilization, deplored the unhealthy trades because they shortened human life and destroyed human bodies.

Work and Property. Jesus said that "The workman is worthy of his hire" (Matt. 10:10). The social philosophy embedded in this pithy epigram simply sets forth the ethical principle that the worker deserves just compensation, in some form, for his or her labor. Each deserves what is proper. Property means what properly belongs to a person. Views on property have ranged from the communitarianism of Plato and Marx to the concepts of private ownership found in John Locke.

In *Laws*, Plato advocated communal ownership of property and cited the old saying that "Friends have all things in common." The communal state, according to Plato, is the ideal state. Plato argued that in the ideal state there should exist neither the extreme of poverty nor that of wealth, for they produce social evils. Aristotle modified Plato's concept of property ownership. Property should be common but private. In other words, the production of property should be social but ownership should be private. Aristotle presumes that individuals will be more industrious if they look out for their own property and attend to their own business. Yet extreme poverty should not be allowed, because it lowers the character of democracy. People should be given the opportunity to start a farm or learn a trade. As Hobbes saw it, accident and fortune may make it impossible for some to sustain themselves by means of their labor; therefore, the state must force the physically fit to work, thereby creating social resources to be distributed to the unfortunate. Rousseau, like Plato and Aristotle, believed that government should prevent inequality by denying individuals the ability and opportunity to accumulate wealth. Rousseau believed that society enslaved the poor and empowered the rich, thereby destroying natural human liberty. Property laws and inequality worked for the advantage of the few and subjected the many. Rousseau claimed that he could not conceive how property could come about except for manual labor.

John Locke appears to agree with Rousseau, but in the end Locke took a decidedly opposing stand. In the *Second Treatise of Government*, Locke began the section on property by ostensibly arguing for limited appropriation on the basis that an object that was created by means of one's labor was one's property. Yet, as he saw it, the introduction of money allowed the unlimited appropriation of property. According to Hegel, what makes an object the property of a person is that the person stamps his or her will into the thing. Hegel believed that property could be alienated only because it was external to the essential being of the worker. An individual may alienate—give up, sell, set aside, yield, or abandon—any possession, because it is external to the personality of the individual. Personality, ethical character, morality, and faith are essential characteristics of the self and therefore may not be alienated. Hegel believed that an individual could alienate his or her abilities to another person for a restricted period but not for a whole lifetime, because that would amount to making the essence of the self into a thing.

Even Adam Smith conceded that the entire product of labor does not belong to the laborer. According to Smith, in the original state of nature the entire product belonged to the producer; he deplored the condition in modern society in which, all the lands having been converted into private property, the landlords reaped where they did not sow.

Marxism and Work. Karl Marx condemned capitalism because it ripped away the meaningfulness of work from the worker and, through the imposition of alienated labor, dehumanized the worker. For Marx, the question of work is central to the social question, because the mode of production of material life determines the social, political, and cultural aspects of life. Work is essential to human nature, first of all, because it provides for the physical existence of human life. Work is not, however, only a means for physical existence; work is valuable for its own sake. Work is human life-activity itself. It is the realization and the fulfillment of human capacities and drives.

By means of work, human beings objectify themselves and create a human world, an environment that is conducive to the full development and flowering of all human potentials and capacities. The object of labor is not only to create a product but also to build the objective social world. The construction of the human world is the primary end of work.

Under capitalism, however, human work becomes alienated labor. Alienated labor dehumanizes the worker by enslaving the worker to an activity in which the worker becomes a passive object rather than an active agent. The worker becomes a slave of work because work is given by the capitalist and because work becomes necessary in order to maintain existence as a physical organism. The alienation of labor stems from the fact that the human being is not realized or fulfilled in work; such work does not affirm the humanity of the worker but denies it. Work is not freely entered into but is coerced. In the modern industrial world, the worker becomes a commodity, because the worker not only produces commodities but also is a commodity.

Alienated labor presupposes private property. Therefore, the emancipation from alienation, the process of dealienation, entails the abolition of private property. Dealienated labor becomes the foundation for the formulation of just political institutions and social arrangements and must be included in any conception of justice. Work is essential to human nature, a necessary expression of human life-activity and the form of human self-realization. Finally, work is the foundation of culture. By means of their work, human beings shape and construct a human world in all its aspects: culture, politics, society, and so forth.

Herbert Marcuse, in *Eros and Civilization* (1955), viewed emancipation in terms of the play impulse. The character of work itself could be changed in accord with the nondistorted needs of the life instincts. The very character of production could change as a result of instinctual transformation entering into the relations of production. The character of the working day would change, causing the elimination of the distinction between necessary time and leisure time. Human production and self-creation would lose their antithetical character. Technological advancement would allow labor to be transformed into a realm of freedom within the realm of necessity. Rationality of gratification would inform new science and new technology. It would require a new worker and a new sensibility that would abolish the distinction between productive utilitarian labor and the creative aspects of work. The new sensibility would unite work and play. Such a unity can only come about, however, if it becomes a basic need of human nature.

In *An Essay on Liberation* (1965), Marcuse stated that aim-inhibited sexuality develops in individuals a sense of what is permissible and what is not—the reality principle. Repression is heightened in advanced capitalism to prevent human beings from enjoying emancipatory possibilities; it keeps them in productive gear. In socialism, a properly repressed libido will emerge in new human relations and in culture-building activities. The prospect of automation suggests the elimination of the distinction between labor and leisure.

Christianity and the Social Question of Work. Saint Paul enjoined Christians to work and not be idle. The Cistercians' *ora et labora* cautioned the faithful to pray and work. Martin Luther interpreted the call to salvation as being inextricably tied to the position that one held in society. One's call to salvation was also a call to accept work as vocation. John Calvin interpreted work as enterprise and held that success justifies work. Max Weber demonstrated that, for Calvinist Protestants, successful work proved God's election. This idea found fertile soil in the Puritan ethos, where frugality and hard work were believed to be the keys to success. Weber called this Protestant ethic the "spirit of capitalism." Jürgen Moltmann interprets work as participation in God's history. Work is not only self-supporting but also self-realizing. Work affirms existence; therefore, work is a right that presupposes freedom. Work must allow for self-formation. Work requiring cooperation helps in the socialization of the individual. Therefore, work should be understood as part of the socialization process. Through work, people participate in creating or destroying the world. Thus, work has eschatological significance.

In *Laborem exercens*, Pope John Paul II strongly emphasizes the central role that work plays in solving social ills. Making life more human presupposes making work more human. Men and women participate with God in creation by carrying out the mandate given in Genesis to subdue and dominate the earth. Men and women are created in the image of the Creator. Therefore, human beings are creative subjects and agents who are capable of planning and rationally deciding about the future. Men and women are not only workers but also the subjects of work. They are persons apart from their work. Thus, work should realize their humanity. From this idea is derived the ethical idea of work. Work is ethical because in it, and by means of it, human beings realize their humanity and rationally decide to bring about their future. The dignity of work therefore is based on the subjectivity of the person who works. Accordingly, John Paul stresses the primacy of work over capital, the priority of human beings over things. Work is also considered to be a means toward self-realization, as is expressed in the Vatican II documents *Mater et Magistra* and *Gaudium et Spes*. The Church views the commodification of the worker, the treatment of the worker as a mere means of production, as a denial of human dignity.

John Paul also affirms the world-shaping power of work. It is the foundation of the family and society. It is foundational for the family because it provides for the subsistence of the family. Work, combined with the virtue of industriousness, influences the process of family education. In the Church's social teaching, work has been considered as a fundamental force shaping the world of culture and society in a human and rational manner. —*Michael R. Candelaria*

See also Capitalism; Communism; Marx, Karl; Socialism.

BIBLIOGRAPHY
Catholic Church. Pope John Paul II. *Laborem exercens*. Boston: St. Paul Editions, 1981. *Laborem exercens* sums up centuries of Catholic social teaching on work and characteristically takes up a middle position between capitalism and socialism. It is crystal clear in its call for the right to meaningful work.

Marcuse, Herbert. *Eros and Civilization: A Philosophical Inquiry into Freud*. Boston: Beacon Press, 1955. Using Freudian categories, Marcuse argues that advanced capitalism represses the fundamental creative powers of human beings. He sets forth the idea that the very nature of work should change and that work and leisure should not be so radically distinguished.

_____. *An Essay on Liberation*. Boston: Beacon Press, 1969. Written in the turbulent late 1960's, *An Essay on Liberation* offers a new vision of socialism in which unchained aesthetic sensibilities would unleash creative productive powers that would make possible an environment of freedom. Work is interpreted as being playful.

Marx, Karl. *Selected Writings*. Edited by David McLellan. Oxford, England: Oxford University Press, 1977. In particular, one should read the economic and philosophical manuscripts to fully appreciate Marx's theory of the nature of work. In these manuscripts, Marx also develops his fullest expression of alienated labor.

Plato. *Republic*. Translated by G. M. A. Grube. Indianapolis: Hackett, 1992. This book captures Plato's vision of the good city, which is divided into three classes with three varieties of duty.

Weber, Max. *The Protestant Ethic and the Spirit of Capitalism*. Translated by Talcott Parsons. New York: Charles Scribner's Sons, 1958. This classic text successfully demonstrates the power of ideas to influence social and economic structures. It does not quite refute Marx's materialist concept of history but does a convincing job of linking the origins of capitalism with the Calvinistic-Puritan work ethic.

World Health Organization

TYPE OF ETHICS: Environmental ethics
DATE: Founded 1948
ASSOCIATED WITH: The United Nations
DEFINITION: An organization that initiates and coordinates efforts to solve international health problems
SIGNIFICANCE: Only an organization of supranational scope can address medical and health problems that cross national boundaries and affect regions, continents, or the entire earth; the World Health Organization (WHO) is that organization

International health organizations have existed from the first decade of the twentieth century, but WHO's scale is far larger than that of anything that existed earlier. It admits and provides services to all states, regardless of whether they are U.N. members. Its tasks fall by their nature into three categories. The first, carried out mainly at headquarters in Geneva, might be called "minding the store": maintaining international drug standards and sanitary and quarantine regulations, and disseminating information regarding epidemics, drug addiction, chemical residues, radiation hazards, and so forth. The second involves providing education and technical assistance for member nations, experts to help plan and set up local health centers, teachers, temporary medical personnel, and so forth. The third is mobilization to deal with specific diseases, including services provided by the central organization, national health bodies, medical laboratories, and other entities. The list of targets is striking: smallpox (eradicated in 1980), polio and leprosy (target date 2000), AIDS, tuberculosis, malaria, yellow fever, cholera, diphtheria. In the nondisease category, goals include the providing of new contraceptives, chemical and mechanical, male and female; the promotion of health practices for mothers and children in Third World countries; and even antismoking campaigns. As its charter states, WHO aims for "the highest possible level of health" for all people.

See also Bioethics; Geneva conventions; League of Nations.

World Society for the Protection of Animals

TYPE OF ETHICS: Animal rights
DATE: Founded 1981
ASSOCIATED WITH: More than two hundred national humane organizations worldwide
DEFINITION: A world surveillance association dedicated to the protection and the alleviation of suffering of domestic and wild animals; also promotes conservation of animals and the environment
SIGNIFICANCE: The WSPA, which has chapters in sixty countries, monitors and intervenes in cases of animal cruelty and detrimental ecological practices

Formed by the merger of two international organizations, the World Federation for the Protection of Animals (founded in 1950) and the International Society for the Protection of Animals (founded in 1959), and by absorbing the International Council Against Bullfighting in 1984, the World Society for the Protection of Animals (WSPA) has more than 100,000 international members. The Society studies international animal welfare laws and intervenes in a diverse variety of cases involving cruelty. In 1990, for example, WSPA activities included a campaign against the annual Texas rattlesnake round-up, which was condemned because of the suffering of the snakes and because of adverse ecological effects. The Society also operates an emergency rescue service for individual distressed animals, which took action, for example, in 1989, when Colombian peasants discovered and aided a wounded Andean condor. The WSPA engineered the condor's removal to a Bogotá zoo and found a sponsor to pay for its extensive medical treatment.

See also Animal rights; Conservation; Ecology; Humane Society of the United States.

Wretched of the Earth, The: Book
TYPE OF ETHICS: International relations
DATE: Published 1961 as *Les Damnés de la terre*
AUTHOR: Frantz Fanon
SIGNIFICANCE: Focusing on Africa, Fanon condemned colonialism and neocolonialism from a Marxist perspective and called for natives to rise in violence against the settlers

Fanon indicted colonialist countries for using force to exploit raw materials and labor from colonized countries. Attempting to justify their actions, colonialists stereotyped natives as savages and referred to natives' "precolonial barbarism." Colonialists proclaimed that European culture was the ideal for natives to emulate and used violence and divide-and-conquer strategies to keep the natives down. Fanon advocated violence against the settlers as the way for colonized people to regain their sense of self-respect. Although he was a psychiatrist, Fanon did not show that such violence would be psychologically liberating. Instead, he cited cases in which such violence led to psychological degeneration. Even if anticolonial violence were the only way to regain a sense of self-respect, however, such violence would not be automatically justifiable. Rape is not justifiable even if it appears to be the only way for a person to gain a feeling of self-respect. Thus, it is a mistake to think that Fanon has adequately justified terrorist attacks on the innocent. Fanon encouraged the colonized to reject the dehumanizing domination of Western culture. He claimed that Western culture corrupted the leaders of the decolonized state, making them put their own interests above the interests of the people. He urged ex-colonial powers to compensate their former colonies instead of continuing to exploit them.

See also Colonialism and imperialism.

Zen

TYPE OF ETHICS: Religious ethics
DATE: Late fifth century to present
ASSOCIATED WITH: Mahāyāna Buddhism
DEFINITION: A Buddhist school whose adherents seek an experiential perception of reality through meditation
SIGNIFICANCE: The mindsets and actions of millions of the world's people are influenced by Zen

Zen, or Zen Buddhism, is a major religion of China and Japan. The name (*Ch'an* in Chinese, *Zen* in Japanese) means "meditation." Zen is one branch of the Mahāyāna School of Buddhism.

Background. Buddhism originated in India before 500 B.C.E. The historical Buddha ("Enlightened Being")—whose sculpted image is familiar worldwide—taught followers to meditate to gain understanding of the true self, or Buddhanature. Bodhidharma, the legendary founder of Zen in China, came from India in the late fifth century C.E. Great teachers and Taoist doctrine helped shape Zen, and two Chinese schools developed, with different methods of seeking enlightenment and using meditation; these had entered Japan by the fourteenth century as Rinzai and Sōtō. Temples and monasteries arose, and Zen influenced Japanese military life, poetry, art, and landscape gardening. In the twentieth century, writings by Daisetz Teitaro Suzuki and Alan Watts helped to popularize Zen in the West.

Ethical Implications. A compassionate realist, Buddha hoped to control suffering and eliminate possessiveness, greed, and self-centeredness. Nirvana, freedom from all earthly ties, was a spiritual goal. Although Buddha avoided specific ethical rules, his Eightfold Path sought to cure humanity's "dislocation" with right views, right aspiration, right speech, right conduct, right vocation, right effort, right mind control, and right meditation. Still central to Zen, these steps encourage careful, truthful thought and speech; respect for basic moral laws; useful work that hurts no one; and suppression of physical appetites and materialism. Though Zenists have sometimes been stereotyped as "happy have-nothings," one traditional Zen precept has been daily work.

Zen stresses inwardness over altruism or social interaction, assuming that people who are at peace with themselves will harmonize with the world and others. Zen tries to eliminate selfishness by curbing ego, teaching that the intuitively wise person is compassionate and humane. It encourages restraint, humility, patience, and quietness. It emphasizes the symbiotic continuity of life and the connectedness of thought and action. —*Roy Neil Graves*

See also Bodhidharma; Buddha; Buddhist ethics; Dōgen; Five precepts; Hui-neng.

BIBLIOGRAPHY
Abe, Masao. *Zen and Western Thought.* Edited by William R. LaFleur. Honolulu: University of Hawaii Press, 1985.

Ross, Nancy Wilson. *Three Ways of Asian Wisdom: Hinduism, Buddhism, Zen, and Their Significance for the West.* New York: Simon & Schuster, 1966.

Suzuki, Daisetz Teitaro. *Zen Buddhism: Selected Writings.* Edited by William Barrett. Garden City, N.Y.: Doubleday, 1956.

Suzuki, Shunryu. *Zen Mind, Beginner's Mind.* Edited by Trudy Dixon. New York: Weatherhill, 1970.

Watts, Alan W. *The Way of Zen.* New York: Pantheon, 1957.

Zero-base ethics

TYPE OF ETHICS: Legal and judicial ethics
DEFINITION: The idea that one person's gain is balanced by another's loss
SIGNIFICANCE: Entails the idea that ethics involves deciding who should suffer and who should benefit

The zero-base concept is an economic concept that is often illustrated by means of the "fixed pie" analogy: The pie is of a fixed size, so if one person gets a larger piece, another person must get a smaller piece; if one person gets a piece at all, someone else must get none.

Zero-base economics has two major implications for ethics. First, zero-base ethics primarily involves the distribution of resources, not their production. Second, the question of distribution becomes the problem of deciding whose interests must be sacrificed so that others' may be satisfied.

Those who accept zero-base economics often use "life-boat" scenarios to illustrate the essence of ethics. If eight people are on a lifeboat that contains provisions only for six, then the task is to decide which two must be sacrificed, voluntarily or not, so that the other six can live.

Zero-base economics is contrasted to the "expanding pie," or "win/win," model of production and distribution. Advocates of the expanding pie model argue that the production of wealth can be a dynamic, ever-increasing process, and therefore that ethics is fundamentally about production, not distribution. They point out, for example, that between the years 1750 and 2000, the world's population increased by roughly a factor of 6, yet during that time the world's production increased roughly by a factor of 1,600.

Zero Population Growth (ZPG)

TYPE OF ETHICS: Environmental ethics
DATE: Founded 1968
ASSOCIATED WITH: Contraception and abortion issues
DEFINITION: ZPG was established to fight for social and economic stability through balancing the earth's population with the available resources that support human life and development
SIGNIFICANCE: ZPG not only focuses on encouraging individuals to do their part to improve living conditions for all peoples of the world but also mounts political campaigns intended to change policies in order to limit population growth and destruction of the environment

With a 1991 membership of more than 40,000 and an income of more than $2,000,000, ZPG promotes protection of the environment through reduction of population growth. Because

1990 figures reflect an increase of 95 million people per year worldwide, scientists fear that the ability of the earth's resources to support the population will be seriously undermined. ZPG works in several ways, both within the United States and internationally, to educate legislators, organizations, teachers, and individuals regarding the massive negative impact of the burgeoning population and its consequent demands upon the earth's resources because of increasing food and energy demands, as well as lifestyle choices that result in the wasting of resources and pollution. Among the organization's activities are political action to ensure reproductive rights, including making available safe, reliable family planning information and services and legal abortion when contraception fails; enhancing the economic and social status of women worldwide through both governmental and private efforts; and, most important, educating people regarding the crucial link between continued population growth and environmental degradation, pollution, poverty, and political and social unrest.

See also Conservation; Ecology; Malthus, Thomas; Population control.

Zionism

TYPE OF ETHICS: Race and ethnicity
DATE: Formally established 1897
ASSOCIATED WITH: Jewish Hungarian journalist Theodor Herzl and modern Jewish nationalism
DEFINITION: A movement whose goal was to establish a national Jewish state in Palestine, the ancient homeland of the Jews
SIGNIFICANCE: Zionists believed that the reestablishment of a Jewish state was the only remedy for escaping virulent anti-Semitism and the only way that Jews could fully implement Judaism as a way of life

In 1882, after a series of pogroms (organized persecutions of Jews) in Russia, Jewish youths formed a group called the *Hovevei Ziyyon* ("Lovers of Zion") to promote immigration to Palestine. "Zion" is the ancient Hebrew poetic term for the abode of the faithful; specifically, Jerusalem and the Holy Land. The *Hovevei Ziyyon* began what was called "practical Zionism."

In 1896, after witnessing anti-Semitic demonstrations in Paris resulting from the Dreyfus Affair, Theodor Herzl wrote *The Jewish State*, in which he reasoned that if an army officer (Alfred Dreyfus) could be falsely convicted of treason in as supposedly enlightened and ethical a country as France, simply because he was Jewish, there was no hope for Jews to live in peace anywhere except in an independent Jewish national state. Subsequently, Herzl organized "political Zionism" on a worldwide scale at the First Zionist Congress in Basel, Switzerland, in 1897.

After Herzl's death in 1904, Zionist leaders worked tirelessly in the face of Arab hostility and the horrors of the Holocaust to bring about the founding of the State of Israel on May 14, 1948. By the 1980's, practically all Jews of the Diaspora had become committed to Zionism, or at least to its mission of supporting Israel and human rights for Jews.

See also Anti-Semitism; Bigotry; Hitler, Adolf; Holocaust; Israel; Nazism; Oppression; Pogrom; Racism.

Zoroastrian ethics

TYPE OF ETHICS: Religious ethics
DATE: c. 1700 B.C.E. to present
DEFINITION: The principles of right human conduct defined by Zoroastrian religion emphasize personal free choice and responsibility for good or evil behavior and its effect on the world and on the individual
SIGNIFICANCE: Has heavily influenced the ethical doctrines of Judaism, Christianity, Islam, and Buddhism

Zoroastrian doctrine teaches that human beings freely choose right or wrong behavior and are personally responsible for their conduct. To achieve lasting happiness, people should recognize and engage in right conduct as it is defined in Zoroastrian teachings. At death, the good and evil thoughts, words, and actions of each person are judged by God; the good souls are rewarded in Paradise, while the bad are punished in Hell. Right and wrong conduct, which are clearly defined in Zoroastrian texts, encompass thoughts, words, and actions.

History. The basic doctrines of Zoroastrianism were first expressed in the *Gathas* (inspired poems, or *manthra*), which were composed from approximately 1500 to 1700 B.C.E. Their author, Zoroaster (Zarathushtra), was a priest in a preliterate society probably in eastern Iran, where he experienced a series of divine visions and a call to teach all people a new spiritual way that would become the first divinely revealed world religion.

This way emphasizes right conduct and teaches a cosmic duality of two opposing divine spirits: the All-Wise and Good God (Ahura Mazda) and the All-Ignorant and Evil Adversary (Angra Mainyu). During Zoroaster's life, a system of rituals and customs developed as part of the new religion, many of them adapted from the older polytheistic religion that he had practiced. These rituals and customs are strikingly similar to early Hindu religious observances, suggesting a common origin of Hinduism and Zoroastrianism.

By 600 B.C.E., Zoroastrianism had become the state religion of the widespread Persian empire and eventually was adapted by peoples from the borders of Greece in the West to those of India and China in the East. It remained the official state religion of Persia until 700 C.E., when Islam replaced it. In the 1,200 years that followed, it gradually lost both prestige and membership. It continues to be practiced in small communities, chiefly in Iran and India.

Ethical Doctrine. Human conduct plays a crucial role in the fate of the world, according to Zoroastrian teachings. By choosing the right conduct defined by Zoroaster, humans join the All-Wise God and the accompanying six holy immortal ones and other divinities (*yazatas*), including Mithra, in an ongoing cosmic battle against the Adversary and his followers, the race of evil ones.

This battle, which began when the Adversary attacked the

newly created world, will continue to rage until righteousness finally overcomes evil, the savior of the world appears, and the day of final judgment arrives. Therefore, the personal choices in daily human life are a battleground of good and evil forces. When individuals choose good thoughts, words, and actions, they support the All-Wise One and strengthen the world's prosperity, growth, and natural order: the power of the just (*asha*). When individuals choose evil thoughts, words, and actions, they support the Adversary and increase distortion, decay, and conflict in the world: the power of the evil force (*drug*). Followers of this teaching must, therefore, recognize and follow right conduct, resist the temptations of wrong conduct, and purify themselves when they think, say, or do evil.

Human conduct not only influences the outcome of the cosmic battle of good and evil but also is the sole basis of individual reward or punishment in life after death. After death, humans continue to exist in a spiritual state and are judged by the All-Wise God regarding their right or wrong conduct; good and evil conduct are placed on the scale of justice to determine reward or punishment in an afterlife of paradise or hell, with a shadowy place for the indeterminate ones.

Thus, good conduct leads to a place of joy and peace, while evil conduct leads to a place of suffering and conflict. Another judgment and a permanent assignment occur on the day of resurrection and judgment, when all living and dead people meet and are finally judged based on their conduct to be sent to either eternal life in a perfect material Paradise or final destruction.

Right Conduct. Since both individual and world salvation depend on the sum of an individual's own thoughts, words, and actions, the precepts of right conduct are paramount. They are the means of both fighting evil and supporting good in daily life. Good thoughts include intention and effort to preserve good and oppose evil. Good words include prayers, agreements, and promises. Good actions include protection of the natural world, a perfect creation of the All-Wise God.

These precepts entail many rituals that are found in other religions: daily prayer, careful preparation of food, caring for the poor and sick. Other, less common practices include marrying next of kin (brother-sister, father-daughter), conserving land and vegetation, protecting water and fire from pollution, and treating carefully dead bodies and waste material. Conserving the purity found in nature (vegetation, lakes, and so forth) and purifying unclean pollutants (decaying flesh, sewage, and so forth) become the basis of personal and world salvation.

Influence of Ethics. Although Zoroastrian ethics have insignificant direct influence today, they have indirectly influenced modern societies through other religions, including Judaism, Christianity, and Buddhism, which adapted and preserved these teachings. This influence occurred when these religions came into prolonged contact with Zoroastrianism and Zoroastrian ideas gained recognition and respect.

Chief among the adapted teachings are these: the individual is solely responsible for his or her spiritual destiny; the individual freely chooses good or evil conduct; the individual can learn to support good and oppose evil conduct; conduct has permanent moral consequences; salvation is based on the sum of thoughts, words, and actions. These ethical ideas survive today in religions practiced by millions of people.
                                                    —*Patricia H. Fulbright*

See also Buddhist ethics; Christian ethics; Hindu ethics; Islamic ethics; Jewish ethics.

BIBLIOGRAPHY

Boyce, Mary. *Zoroastrians, Their Religious Beliefs and Practices.* London: Routledge & Kegan Paul, 1979.

Duchesne-Guillemin, Jacques. *Symbols and Values in Zoroastrianism, Their Survival and Renewal.* New York: Harper & Row, 1966.

Frye, Richard N. *The Heritage of Persia.* Cleveland, Ohio: World Publishing, 1963.

ORGANIZATIONS, SOCIETIES, AND INSTITUTES

Listed below are various significant organizations, societies, and institutes that conduct research, distribute information, sponsor education, and, in some cases, advocate policies focused on the ethical topics and concerns discussed herein.

American Academy of Religion
Atlanta, Georgia
The Academy is the major professional organization for American scholars in the field of religious studies. Its conferences and publications often feature work in ethics.

American Catholic Philosophical Association
Washington, D.C.
Largely composed of college and university teachers of philosophy, the Association's membership conducts research and holds conferences that often focus on basic issues in ethics.

American Enterprise Institute for Public Policy
Washington, D.C.
The Institute's aims include preserving and improving cultural and political values in the United States. It conducts and publishes research on moral issues as well as on domestic and international economic policy.

American Philosophical Association
Newark, Delaware
The APA is the major professional society for professors and scholars of philosophy in the United States. Ethical issues are a major concern of its membership, the Association's conferences, and the many affiliated organizations that the APA helps to support. The APA publishes newsletters that are important sources of information about ethics. The newsletters emphasize ethical issues raised by computer use, feminism, law, medicine, and race. The teaching of ethics is also frequently addressed.

American Society for the Prevention of Cruelty to Animals
New York, New York
Founded in 1866, the Society seeks to promote appreciation for and humane treatment of animals. It conducts educational programs and circulates animal-related information for children and adults.

Amnesty International
London, England
This human rights movement was organized in 1961 to conduct research and organize worldwide action against human rights abuses. It sends delegates to observe trials, to visit countries to interview prisoners, and to meet with government officials.

Anti-Defamation League
New York, New York
Established in 1913, the ADL publishes monographs, articles, and teaching materials. Its work includes stopping the defamation of Jewish people and attempting to secure justice and fair treatment for all citizens.

Association for Practical and Professional Ethics
Bloomington, Indiana
The Association encourages high-quality interdisciplinary scholarship and teaching in ethics. It supports efforts to develop curricula and fosters communication and joint ventures among centers, schools, colleges, and individual scholars.

Association for the Prevention of Torture
Geneva, Switzerland
The Association seeks to abolish the torture of prisoners worldwide. It conducts and promotes visitations to places of detention to ensure that prisoners are not being tortured or treated inhumanely.

Brookings Institution
Washington, D.C.
The Institution, an independent organization created in 1916, is devoted to nonpartisan research, education, and publication in the fields of economics, government, and foreign policy. It conducts numerous conferences, forums, and seminars each year.

Center for Science in the Public Interest
Washington, D.C.
Concerned with the effects of science and technology on society, the Center has concentrated on food safety and nutrition problems in the United States. It produces educational materials and attempts to influence policy decisions about American health.

Council on Foreign Relations
New York, New York
Founded in 1921, the Council studies the international aspects of American political, economic, and strategic problems. Its publications include *Foreign Affairs*, an influential journal in the field.

The Elie Wiesel Foundation for Humanity
New York, New York
The Foundation sponsors international conferences focused on human rights and ways to curtail hatred and prejudice. It also conducts an annual ethics essay contest that is open to full-time senior undergraduates at accredited colleges and universities in the United States.

Ethics and Public Policy Center
Washington, D.C.
The Center conducts a program of research, writing, publication, and conferences to encourage reflective debate on major domestic and foreign policy programs. Its work emphasizes the role of religion in the public policy arena.

Ethics in Public Service Network

Washington, D.C.

The Network keeps its members informed about key ethical questions that deserve attention in the professions and in public policy.

Ethics Resource Center

Washington, D.C.

The Center develops educational materials and training programs for use in business, government, and public schools. It aims to increase public trust in American institutions by strengthening their ethical foundations.

Facing History and Ourselves

Brookline, Massachusetts

This educational organization conducts research, prepares curricula for schools, and sponsors workshops for teachers. It aims to combat prejudice and racism, to promote human rights, and to support such efforts by teaching about the Holocaust.

Greenpeace International

Amsterdam, The Netherlands

Greenpeace International began its work in 1971. It tries to stop and to reverse environmental destruction. Its areas of interest include the protection of marine animals and their habitats; the prevention of land, air, and water pollution; and the creation of restrictions on the dumping of toxic waste.

Human Rights Information and Documentation Systems, International

Oslo, Norway

This network of human rights organizations aims to improve access to and distribution of public information on human rights. It coordinates documentation systems and studies problems and techniques of information handling in this area.

Human Rights Watch

New York, New York

This organization evaluates the human rights practices of governments in accordance with standards recognized by international laws and agreements, including the United Nations Declaration of Human Rights and the Helsinki Accords.

Humane Society of the United States

Washington, D.C.

Founded in 1954, the Humane Society promotes public education to eliminate the abuse of animals and to safeguard endangered species.

Institute for Philosophy and Public Policy

College Park, Maryland

This educational and research institute investigates the conceptual and ethical aspects of public policy formulation and debate. It focuses attention on issues such as equality of opportunity, the teaching of ethics, and mass media and democratic values.

Intercollegiate Studies Institute

Bryn Mawr, Pennsylvania

A nonpartisan educational organization directed primarily at the college campus, the Institute promotes scholarship on issues pertaining to individual liberty, limited government, free-market economics, and private property.

Internet: International Human Rights Documentation Network

Ottawa, Canada

The Network's goals are to encourage communication among scholars, activists, and policy makers in the human rights area and to function as an information clearinghouse by responding to questions about current research, publications, teaching resources, and activities of human rights organizations.

The Josephson Institute of Ethics

Marina del Rey, California

The Institute is devoted to encouraging the teaching of ethics in schools and colleges, businesses, and workplaces. Its focus is on applied ethics.

The Media Institute

Washington, D.C.

Encouraging and promoting the development of knowledge and understanding of American media and communications, the Institute conducts research into the legal, economic, political, and ethical aspects of the media and communications industry and its role in American society.

National Association for the Advancement of Colored People

Baltimore, Maryland

Established in 1909, the NAACP is a civil rights organization that strives to achieve equal rights through the democratic process and to eliminate racial prejudice by removing racial discrimination in housing, employment, voting, schools, the courts, transportation, and business.

National Endowment for the Humanities

Washington, D.C.

Through its public programs and support of individual research projects, the Endowment promotes awareness and understanding of a wide range of issues and traditions that are central to moral reflection.

National Institute Against Prejudice and Violence

Baltimore, Maryland

The Institute studies and responds to the problem of violence and intimidation motivated by racial, religious, ethnic, or anti-gay prejudice. It conducts research into the causes and prevalence of prejudice and violence and their effects on victims and society.

National Organization for Women

Washington, D.C.

NOW works to end prejudice and discrimination against women in government, industry, the professions, religious groups, political parties, medicine, law, and other areas. It also strives to increase the number of women elected to public office in the United States.

North American Society for Social Philosophy

Highlands, North Carolina

The Society sponsors conferences and supports research focusing on contemporary moral and political issues. Its major publication is the *Journal of Social Philosophy*.

People for the Ethical Treatment of Animals

Washington, D.C.

This educational and activist group opposes all forms of animal exploitation. It addresses the abuse of animals in experimentation, the manufacture of fur apparel, and the slaughter of animals for human consumption.

Philosophy Documentation Center

Bowling Green, Ohio

The Center acts as a clearinghouse for bibliographic and other information regarding philosophy, including ethics, and philosophers. Its helpful publications include the *Directory of American Philosophers* and *The Philosopher's Index: An International Index to Philosophical Periodicals and Books*.

Society for the Advancement of American Philosophy

Seattle, Washington

The Society promotes research and interest in the history of American philosophy, often emphasizing issues of ethical concern.

Society for Asian and Comparative Philosophy

Oneonta, New York

The Society advances the development of Asian and comparative philosophies and brings Asian and Western philosophers together for a mutually beneficial exchange of ideas.

Society of Christian Philosophers

Grand Rapids, Michigan

The Society fosters discussion about issues in the philosophy of religion and ethics. Its journal, *Faith and Philosophy*, is important in the field.

Society for Values in Higher Education

Washington, D.C.

The Society brings together scholars and teachers who share the conviction that questions about moral and religious values should be central to higher education. It holds conferences and supports research.

Southern Poverty Law Center

Montgomery, Alabama

The Center seeks to protect and advance the legal and civil rights of poor people, regardless of race, through education and litigation. Often, its work has concentrated on helping individuals injured or threatened by the activities of the Ku Klux Klan and related groups.

United Nations

New York, New York

The U.N. and its many suborganizations seek to identify and solve international disputes that threaten world peace and security. Advocating human rights, they work to create conditions in which justice and respect for treaties and international law can be maintained.

United Nations Centre for Human Rights

Geneva, Switzerland

The Centre carries out research and prepares reports on the implementation of human rights programs. In addition to collecting and sharing information, it sponsors training programs for government officials who deal with human rights issues.

United States Holocaust Memorial Museum

Washington, D.C.

Through its exhibits, educational outreach, and research programs, the Museum concentrates on teaching about the Holocaust in ways that underscore the moral implications and lessons of that genocidal event.

Women's Legal Defense Fund

Washington, D.C.

The purpose of this organization is to secure equal rights for women through litigation, advocacy, and public education. It publishes handbooks, manuals, and brochures on discrimination in employment, domestic relations law, and other areas.

World Health Organization

Geneva, Switzerland

This international health agency of the United Nations affirms that good health is a fundamental right of every human being, regardless of race, religion, political belief, economic situation, or social condition. Its commitment is to support health services that help all people to lead socially and economically productive lives.

TIME LINE

Listed below are the dates of significant events that relate to the ethical topics and concerns discussed herein.

c. 3100 B.C.E.	Pharaoh Menes unites Lower and Upper Egypt.
c. 3000 B.C.E.	Cuneiform writings of the Sumerians begin the recorded history of the Middle East.
c. 2500 B.C.E.	The Indus Valley civilization begins at sites such as Harappa and Mohenjo-daro in present-day Pakistan.
c. 2350 B.C.E.	Sargon of Akkad conquers the Sumerians and unites their city-states under his rule.
c. 2100 B.C.E.	Minoan palace construction begins on the Mediterranean island of Crete.
c. 1750 B.C.E.	Hammurabi conquers Sumer and establishes the Babylonian empire. Hammurabi's code dates from this era.
c. 1600-c. 1400 B.C.E.	The high point of Minoan civilization is reached.
c. 1500 B.C.E.	The Aryans of central Asia invade India.
c. 1400 B.C.E.	The Phoenicians develop a phonetic alphabet.
c. 1369-c. 1353 B.C.E.	Pharaoh Akhenaton introduces monotheistic reforms in Egyptian religion.
c. 1290 B.C.E.	Moses leads the Hebrew tribes out of Egyptian captivity.
c. 1200 B.C.E.	Olmec civilization flourishes in the Western Hemisphere.
c. 1000 B.C.E.	The Chou dynasty begins to control China, Latin tribes settle south of the Tiber River, and Etruscans settle in the west central region of the Italian peninsula.
c. 750-c. 338 B.C.E.	Athens, Corinth, Sparta, and Thebes emerge as the chief city-states of Greece during the Hellenic Age. Socrates (470-399 B.C.E.), Plato (427-347 B.C.E.), Aristotle (384-322 B.C.E.), and Epicurus (c. 342-c. 270 B.C.E.) make their major contributions to moral philosophy. Athens and Sparta fight the Peloponnesian War (431-404 B.C.E.), which ends with a Spartan victory.
c. 600-c. 200 B.C.E.	Composition of Hinduism's Upaniṣads occurs. Nebuchadnezzar destroys Jerusalem (586 B.C.E.) and sends the Jews into Babylonian exile. The life and teachings of Buddha (c. 566-c. 486 B.C.E.) begin to exert their influence. Confucius (c. 551-c. 479 B.C.E.), Mencius (c. 372-c. 289 B.C.E.), and Chuang Tzu (c. 370-c. 285 B.C.E.) make their major contributions to Chinese philosophy.
c. 200 B.C.E.	The Han dynasty begins its four-hundred-year rule of China. The development of Hīnayāna and Mahāyāna Buddhism is under way.
146 B.C.E.	The Romans destroy Corinth and conquer Greece.
c. 100 B.C.E.	The Bhagavad Gītā is composed.
55-54 B.C.E.	Julius Caesar leads the Roman invasion of Britain.
27 B.C.E.	Augustus becomes the first Roman emperor.
c. 4 B.C.E.-c. 30 C.E.	The life and death of Jesus of Nazareth leads to the development of Christianity.
70	Roman forces under Titus capture and destroy Jerusalem.
313	Constantine grants the Christians of the Roman Empire freedom of religion in the Edict of Milan, an act that leads to Christianity's becoming the dominant religion of the Western world. Augustine (354-430) writes his *Confessions* and *The City of God*.
320	India begins a golden age under the Gupta dynasty.
395	The Roman Empire splits into the East Roman Empire and the West Roman Empire.
455	The Vandals sack Rome.

476	The Western Roman Empire comes to an end.
c. 570-632	The life and death of Muḥammad leads to the development of Islam.
700-1230	The empire of Ghana flourishes in Africa.
711	The Muslims invade Spain and begin an occupation that lasts for about seven hundred years.
800	Pope Leo III crowns Charlemagne Emperor of the Romans. The Tendai and Shingon schools of Buddhism are founded in Japan (c. 800).
1066	The Normans conquer England.
1099	Christian forces capture Jerusalem, ending the First Crusade.
1187	Muslim troops under Saladin recapture Jerusalem.
1192	Yoritomo becomes the first shogun to rule Japan.
c. 1200	The Mali empire rises in Africa. Islam begins to exert a strong influence in India.
1215	English barons force King John to grant the Magna Carta. Thomas Aquinas (c. 1225-1274) makes his major contributions to philosophy and theology.
1337	Hundred Years War begins.
1348-1350	The Black Plague ravages Europe.
1368	The Ming dynasty establishes its three-hundred-year rule of China.
c. 1440	Johannes Gutenberg, a German printer, invents movable type.
1453	The Ottoman Turks capture Constantinople and overthrow the Byzantine Empire.
1476-1534	The Inca empire dominates much of present-day South America.
1492	Columbus reaches America and claims it for Spain.
1517	The Protestant Reformation begins in Germany.
1519-1522	Magellan circumnavigates the globe.
1558-1603	Queen Elizabeth I reigns in England.
1618	Thirty Years' War begins.
1650-1800	The European Enlightenment includes significant scientific and philosophical works by Thomas Hobbes (1588-1679), Baruch Spinoza (1632-1677), John Locke (1632-1704), Isaac Newton (1642-1727), David Hume (1711-1776), Adam Smith (1723-1790), and Immanuel Kant (1724-1804).
1776	The American Declaration of Independence is proclaimed.
1789	The French Revolution begins.
1807-1815	Britain and France abolish the slave trade.
1815	Napoleon's armies defeated at Waterloo.
1815-1900	Vast industrialization of Europe and North America occurs.
1824	The armies of Simón Bolívar and Antonio José de Sucre defeat the Spaniards at Ayacucho, ending the Latin-American wars of independence.
1848	Revolutions occur in France, Italy, Germany, and Austria. Karl Marx and Friedrich Engels write *The Communist Manifesto*.
1853-1854	Commodore Matthew Perry visits Japan and opens two ports to U.S. trade, ending Japan's isolation.
1859	Charles Darwin publishes *On the Origin of Species*.
1865	Union forces defeat the Confederates in the American Civil War after four years of fighting.
1868	The Meiji restoration introduces Westernizing influences into Japan.

1869	The Suez Canal opens.
1871	Germany becomes united under the Prussian king, who rules the new empire as Kaiser Wilhelm I.
1880-1900	Much of Africa is colonized by European nations.
1914	The assassination of Archduke Francis Ferdinand of Austria-Hungary starts World War I (1914-1918).
1917	Revolutionaries overthrow Czar Nicholas II, and the Bolsheviks seize power in Russia.
1920	The League of Nations is established. The Panama Canal opens.
1921	Chinese Communist Party is founded.
1922	Fascist leader Benito Mussolini becomes dictator of Italy. The Union of Soviet Socialist Republics is established.
1929	The Great Depression begins.
1933	Adolf Hitler becomes the dictator of Nazi Germany.
1939	World War II (1939-1945) begins with Germany's invasion of Poland. During this period, the Holocaust is unleashed by the Nazis, destroying millions of European Jews.
1941	The Japanese attack Pearl Harbor, and the United States enters World War II.
1945	The United Nations is established. The first atomic bombs used in warfare are dropped by U.S. planes on Hiroshima and Nagasaki.
1946-1948	Communist regimes take over much of Eastern Europe.
1947	Britain grants independence to India and Pakistan.
1948	The state of Israel achieves independence.
1949	The Chinese Communists conquer China.
1950	The Korean War (1950-1953) begins.
1957	Russia opens the space age by launching Sputnik I, the first artificial satellite to circle the earth.
1961	The Berlin Wall divides East and West Germany.
1965	The Vietnam War expands.
1968	Martin Luther King, Jr., is assassinated.
1969	Two American astronauts become the first humans to walk on the moon.
1972	The United States withdraws from the Vietnam War, which ends in 1975.
1989	The Berlin Wall comes down, and the Soviet empire disintegrates, bringing an end to the Cold War.
1990-1994	Nationalistic, ethnic, and racial strife, particularly in the former Yugoslavia, erupts around the world.

BIBLIOGRAPHY

The works listed below constitute a representative sample of important books that deal with the ethical topics and concerns discussed herein.

Introductions to Ethics: Textbooks, Anthologies, Encyclopedias, Bibliographies, and Histories of Ethics

Albert, Ethel M., Theodore C. Dennis, and Sheldon P. Peterfreund, eds. *Great Traditions in Ethics*. 7th ed. Belmont, Calif.: Wadsworth, 1992.

Arthur, John. *Morality and Moral Controversies*. 3d ed. Englewood Cliffs, N.J.: Prentice-Hall, 1993.

Becker, Lawrence C., and Charlotte B. Becker, eds. *Encyclopedia of Ethics*. 2 vols. New York: Garland, 1992; London: St. James Press, 1992.

_____. *A History of Western Ethics*. New York: Garland, 1992.

Bourke, Vernon J. *History of Ethics*. 2 vols. Garden City, N.Y.: Doubleday, 1968.

Christian, James L. *Philosophy: An Introduction to the Art of Wondering*. 5th ed. New York: Holt, Rinehart and Winston, 1990.

Copleston, Frederick. *A History of Philosophy*. 9 vols. London: Burns Oates and Washbourne, 1946-75; Garden City, N.Y.: Doubleday, 1962-1977.

Edwards, Paul, ed. *The Encyclopedia of Philosophy*, 8 vols. New York: Macmillan, 1972.

Feinberg, Joel, ed. *Reason and Responsibility*. 7th ed. Belmont, Calif.: Wadsworth, 1989.

Frankena, William K. *Ethics*, 2d ed. Englewood Cliffs, N.J.: Prentice-Hall, 1973.

Heilbroner, Robert L. *The Worldly Philosophers*. 5th ed. New York: Simon & Schuster, 1980.

Jones, W.T. *A History of Western Philosophy*. 2d ed. 5 vols. New York: Harcourt Brace Jovanovich, 1975.

Jones, W.T., et al., eds. *Approaches to Ethics*. 2d ed. New York: McGraw-Hill, 1969.

MacIntyre, Alasdair. *A Short History of Ethics*. New York: Macmillan, 1966; London: Routledge and Kegan Paul, 1967.

Magill, Frank N., and Ian P. McGreal, eds. *World Philosophy: Essay-Reviews of 225 Major Works*. 5 vols. Englewood Cliffs, N.J.: Salem Press, 1982; London: Bowker, 1982.

Magill, Frank N., and John K. Roth, eds. *Masterpieces of World Philosophy*. New York: HarperCollins, 1990.

May, Larry, and Shari Collins Sharratt. *Applied Ethics: A Multicultural Approach*. Englewood Cliffs, N.J.: Prentice-Hall, 1994.

Nagel, Thomas. *What Does It All Mean?* New York and Oxford: Oxford University Press, 1987.

Nolan, Richard T., et al. *Living Issues in Ethics*. Belmont, Calif: Wadsworth, 1982.

Pojman, Louis P. *Ethics: Discovering Right and Wrong*. Belmont, Calif: Wadsworth, 1990.

Rachels, James, ed. *The Right Thing to Do: Basic Readings in Moral Philosophy*. New York: Random House, 1989.

Reese, W.L., ed. *Dictionary of Philosophy and Religion*. 3d ed. Atlantic Highlands, N.J.: Humanities Press International, 1988.

Roth, John K. *Ethics: An Annotated Bibliography*. Pasadena, Calif.: Salem Press, 1991.

Roth, John K., and Frederick Sontag. *The Questions of Philosophy*. Belmont, Calif.: Wadsworth, 1988.

Solomon, Robert C. *Ethics: A Brief Introduction*. New York: McGraw-Hill, 1984.

Stewart, Robert M., ed. *Readings in Social and Political Philosophy*. New York and Oxford: Oxford University Press, 1986.

Strauss, Leo, and Joseph Cropsey, eds. *History of Political Philosophy*. 3d ed. Chicago: University of Chicago Press, 1987.

Wagner, Michael F. *An Historical Introduction to Moral Philosophy*. Englewood Cliffs, N.J.: Prentice-Hall, 1991; London: Prentice-Hall International, 1991.

Some Major Primary Sources in Philosophical Ethics

This section lists works chronologically instead of alphabetically by author. That arrangement makes it easier to see when these significant philosophical contributions to ethics were made. Although dates for the authors and their works' first appearance are provided, these primary sources are often available in so many editions that specific references to particular places or dates of publication are omitted.

Confucius (c. 551-c. 479 B.C.E.). *The Analects of Confucius* (exact date uncertain).

Bhagavad Gītā (exact author and dates unknown).

Plato (427-347 B.C.E.). *Dialogues* (exact dates uncertain).

Aristotle (384-322 B.C.E.). *Nicomachean Ethics and Politics* (exact dates uncertain).

Mencius (c. 372-c. 289 B.C.E.). *Meng Tzu* (exact date uncertain).

Chuang Tzu (c. 370-c. 285 B.C.E.). *Chuang Tzu* (exact date uncertain).

Epicurus (c. 342-c. 270 B.C.E.). *Principal Doctrines* and *Letter to Menoeceus* (exact dates uncertain).

Tao Te Ching (author unknown and exact date uncertain).

Epictetus (c. 65-c. 135). *The Enchiridion* (c. 120).

Marcus Aurelius (121-180). *Meditations* (exact date uncertain).

Plotinus (c. 204-270). *Enneads* (c. 256).

Augustine (354-430). *Confessions* (c. 397) and *The City of God* (413-426).

Hui-neng (638-713). *The Platform Scripture of the Sixth Patriarch* (c. 677).

Śaṅkara (c. 788-c. 820). *Crest Jewel of Wisdom* (exact date unknown).

Avicenna (980-1037). *The Book of Salvation* (exact date uncertain).

Averroës (1126-1198). *The Incoherence of the Incoherence* (exact date uncertain).

Maimonides (1135-1204). *Guide of the Perplexed* (1190).

Thomas Aquinas (c. 1225-1274). *Summa Theologica* (c. 1265-1274).

More, Thomas (1478-1535). *Utopia* (1516).

Machiavelli, Niccolò (1469-1527). *The Prince* (1532).

Hobbes, Thomas (1588-1679). *Leviathan* (1651).

Spinoza, Baruch (1632-1677). *Ethics* (1677).

Locke, John (1632-1704). *The Second Treatise of Government* (1690).

Montesquieu, Baron de (1689-1755). *The Spirit of the Laws* (1748).

Hume, David (1711-1776). *An Enquiry Concerning the Principles of Morals* (1751).

Rousseau, Jean-Jacques (1712-1778). *The Social Contract* (1762).

Smith, Adam (1723-1790). *An Inquiry into the Nature and Causes of the Wealth of Nations* (1776).

Kant, Immanuel (1724-1804). *Foundations of the Metaphysics of Morals* (1785).

Bentham, Jeremy (1748-1832). *An Introduction to the Principles of Morals and Legislation* (1789).

Hegel, Georg Wilhelm Friedrich (1770-1831). *Philosophy of Right* (1821).

Malthus, Thomas Robert (1766-1834). *An Essay on the Principle of Population* (1826).

Marx, Karl (1818-1883). *Selected Writings* (1837-1883).

Emerson, Ralph Waldo (1803-1882). *Essays* (1841-1844).

Kierkegaard, Søren (1813-1855). *Either/Or* (1843).

Darwin, Charles (1809-1882). *On the Origin of Species* (1859).

Mill, John Stuart (1806-1873). *Essay on Liberty* (1859) and *Utilitarianism* (1863).

Nietzsche, Friedrich (1844-1900). *Beyond Good and Evil* (1886).

Moore, George Edward (1873-1958). *Principia Ethica* (1903).

Weber, Max (1864-1920). *The Protestant Ethic and the Spirit of Capitalism* (1904-1905).

Santayana, George (1863-1952). *The Life of Reason* (1905-1906).

James, William (1842-1910). *Pragmatism* (1907).

Royce, Josiah (1855-1916). *The Philosophy of Loyalty* (1908).

Dewey, John (1859-1952). *Human Nature and Conduct* (1922).

Buber, Martin (1878-1965). *I and Thou* (1923).

Whitehead, Alfred North (1861-1947). *Process and Reality* (1929).

Freud, Sigmund (1856-1939). *Civilization and Its Discontents* (1930).

Bergson, Henri (1859-1941). *The Two Sources of Morality and Religion* (1932).

Niebuhr, Reinhold (1892-1971). *Moral Man and Immoral Society* (1932) and *The Children of Light and the Children of Darkness* (1944).

Sartre, Jean-Paul. *Being and Nothingness* (1943).

Ayer, Alfred Jules (1910-1988). *Language, Truth, and Logic* (1946).

Camus, Albert (1913-1960). *The Rebel* (1951).

Tillich, Paul (1886-1965). *The Courage to Be* (1952).

Wittgenstein, Ludwig (1889-1951). *Philosophical Investigations* (1953).

Rawls, John (1921-   ). *A Theory of Justice* (1971).

MacIntyre, Alasdair (1929-   ). *After Virtue* (1981).

Theoretical Issues in Ethics

Bernstein, Richard J. *Beyond Objectivism and Relativism: Science, Hermeneutics, and Praxis*. Oxford: Blackwell, 1983; Philadelphia: University of Pennsylvania Press, 1985.

Bowie, Norman, ed. *Ethical Theory in the Last Quarter of the Twentieth Century*. Indianapolis: Hackett, 1983.

Byrne, Peter. *The Philosophical and Theological Foundations of Ethics*. New York: St. Martin's Press, 1992; London: Macmillan, 1992.

Carr, David. *Educating the Virtues: An Essay on the Philosophical Psychology of Moral Development and Education*. London and New York: Routledge, 1991.

Cooper, Neil. *The Diversity of Moral Thinking*. New York: Oxford University Press, 1981.

Dworkin, Ronald. *Taking Rights Seriously*. Cambridge, Mass.: Harvard University Press, 1977; London: Duckworth, 1977.

George, Robert P., ed. *Natural Law Theory*. Oxford: Clarendon Press, 1992; New York: Oxford University Press, 1992.

Gert, Bernard. *Morality: A New Justification of the Moral Rules*. New York and Oxford: Oxford University Press, 1988.

Gewirth, Alan. *Reason and Morality*. Chicago and London: University of Chicago Press, 1978.

Gibbard, Alan. *Wise Choices, Apt Feelings: A Theory of Normative Judgment*. Cambridge, Mass.: Harvard University Press, 1990; Oxford: Clarendon Press, 1990.

Goldman, Alan H. *Moral Knowledge*. London and New York: Routledge, 1988.

Harman, Gilbert. *The Nature of Morality*. New York: Oxford University Press, 1977.

Ignatieff, Michael. *The Needs of Strangers*. London: Chatto and Windus, 1984; New York: Penguin Books, 1986.

Keown, Damien. *The Nature of Buddhist Ethics*. New York: St. Martin's Press, 1992; London: Macmillan, 1992.

Kohlberg, Lawrence. *The Philosophy of Moral Development*. San Francisco and London: Harper & Row, 1981.

Kupperman, Joel. *Character*. New York and Oxford: Oxford University Press, 1991.

McShea, Robert J. *Morality and Human Nature*. Philadelphia: Temple University Press, 1990.

Midgley, Mary. *Can't We Make Moral Judgments?* Bristol: Bristol Press, 1991; New York: St. Martin's Press, 1993.

Nozick, Robert. *The Nature of Rationality*. Princeton, N.J.: Princeton University Press, 1993.

_____. *Philosophical Explanations*. Cambridge, Mass.: Harvard University Press, 1981; Oxford: Clarendon Press, 1984.

Outka, Gene, and John P. Reeder, eds. *Prospects for a Common Morality*. Princeton, N.J.: Princeton University Press, 1993.

Rawls, John. *Political Liberalism*. New York: Columbia University Press, 1993.

Singer, Peter. *Practical Ethics*. 2d ed. Cambridge: Cambridge University Press, 1993.

Sprigge, Timothy. *The Rational Foundations of Ethics*. London and New York: Routledge, 1988.

Stout, Jeffrey. *Ethics after Babel: The Languages of Morals and Their Discontents*. Boston: Beacon Press, 1988; Cambridge: James Clarke, 1989.

Williams, Bernard. *Ethics and the Limits of Philosophy*. Cambridge, Mass.: Harvard University Press, 1985; London: Fontana, 1985.

Applied Ethics

Economics and Business

Applebaum, David, and Sarah V. Lawton, *Ethics and the Professions*. Englewood Cliffs, N.J. Prentice-Hall, 1990.

Bayles, Michael D. *Professional Ethics*. 2d ed. Belmont, Calif.: Wadsworth, 1989.

Beauchamp, Tom L., and Norman E. Bowie, eds. *Ethical Theory and Business*. 4th ed. Englewood Cliffs, N.J. and London: Prentice-Hall, 1993.

Benson, George C. S. *Business Ethics in America*. Lexington, Mass.: Lexington Books, 1982; Aldershot, Hampshire: Gower, 1982.

Blanchard, Kenneth, and Norman Vincent Peale. *The Power of Ethical Management*. New York: Morrow, 1988; London: Heinemann Kingswood, 1988.

Cederblom, Jerry, and Charles J. Dougherty. *Ethics at Work*. Belmont, Calif.: Wadsworth, 1990.

Chappell, Tom. *The Soul of a Business: Managing for Profit and the Common Good*. New York: Bantam Books, 1993.

De George, Richard T. *Business Ethics*. New York: Macmillan, 1982.

_____. *Competing with Integrity in International Business*. New York: Oxford University Press, 1993.

Des Jardins, Joseph R., and John J. McCall, eds. *Contemporary Issues in Business Ethics*. 2d ed. Belmont, Calif.: Wadsworth, 1990.

Donaldson, Thomas. *The Ethics of International Business*. New York and Oxford: Oxford University Press, 1989.

Freeman, R. Edward, ed. *Business Ethics: The State of the Art*. New York and Oxford: Oxford University Press, 1991.

Jacobs, Jane. *Systems of Survival: A Dialogue on the Moral Foundations of Commerce and Politics*. New York: Random House, 1992; London: Hodder and Stoughton, 1993.

Kuhn, James W. and Donald W. Shriver. *Beyond Success: Corporations and Their Critics in the 1990s*. New York and Oxford: Oxford University Press, 1991.

Novak, Michael. *The Spirit of Democratic Capitalism*. New York: Simon & Schuster, 1982.

Solomon, Robert C. *Ethics and Excellence: Cooperation and Integrity in Business*. New York: Oxford University Press, 1992.

Velasquez, Manuel G. *Business Ethics: Concepts and Cases*. 3d ed. Englewood Cliffs, N.J.: Prentice-Hall, 1992; London: Prentice-Hall International, 1992.

The Environment

Attfield, Robin. *The Ethics of Environmental Concern*. New York: Columbia University Press, 1983; Oxford: Blackwell, 1983.

Cranor, Carl F. *Regulating Toxic Substances: Philosophy of Science and the Law*. New York: Oxford University Press, 1993.

Ehrlich, Paul R., and Anne H. Ehrlich. *The Population Explosion*. New York: Simon & Schuster, 1990; London: Hutchinston, 1990.

Freyfogle, Eric T. *Justice and the Earth*. New York: Free Press, 1993.

Gore, Albert. *Earth in the Balance: Ecology and the Human Spirit*. Boston: Houghton Mifflin, 1992; London: Earthscan, 1992.

Leopold, Aldo. *A Sand County Almanac*. London and New York: Oxford University Press, 1987.

Nash, Roderick Frazier. *The Rights of Nature: A History of Environmental Ethics*. Madison and London: University of Wisconsin Press, 1989.

Orr, David W. *Ecological Literacy*. Albany: State University of New York Press, 1992.

Regan, Tom. *All That Dwell Therein: Essays on Animal*

Rights and Environmental Ethics. Berkeley: University of California Press, 1982.

Reisner, Marc. *Cadillac Desert: The American West and Its Disappearing Water*. New York: Viking, 1986; London: Secker and Warburg, 1990.

Rolston, Holmes, III. *Environmental Ethics: Duties to and Values in the Natural World*. Philadelphia: Temple University Press, 1988.

———. *Philosophy Gone Wild: Environmental Ethics*. Buffalo, N.Y.: Prometheus Books, 1989.

Singer, Peter. *Animal Liberation: A New Ethics for Our Treatment of Animals*. 2d ed. New York: Random House, 1990; London: Cape, 1990.

Stegner, Wallace. *Where the Bluebird Sings to the Lemonade Springs*. New York: Penguin Books, 1992.

Zimmerman, Michael E., et al., *Environmental Philosophy: From Animal Rights to Radical Ecology*. Englewood Cliffs, N.J.: Prentice-Hall, 1993.

Public Policy

Beauchamp, Tom L., and Terry P. Pinkard, eds. *Ethics and Public Policy*. 2nd ed. Englewood Cliffs, N.J. and London: Prentice-Hall, 1983.

Bellah, Robert N., et al. *The Good Society*. New York: Knopf, 1991.

Bok, Sissela. *Lying: Moral Choice in Public and Private Life*. New York: Random House, 1978; Brighton: Harvester Press, 1978.

———. *Secrets: On the Ethics of Concealment and Revelation*. New York: Pantheon Books, 1982; Oxford: Oxford University Press, 1984.

Callahan, Joan, ed. *Ethical Issues in Professional Life*. New York and Oxford: Oxford University Press, 1988.

Christopher, Paul. *The Ethics of War and Peace: An Introduction to Legal and Moral Issues*. Englewood Cliffs, N.J. and London: Prentice-Hall, 1994.

Jarrett, James L. *The Teaching of Values: Caring and Appreciation*. London and New York: Routledge, 1991.

Johnson, Deborah G. *Computer Ethics*. 2d ed. Englewood Cliffs, N.J. and London: Prentice-Hall, 1994.

Lappe, Francis Moore. *Rediscovering America's Values*. New York: Ballantine Books, 1989.

Olen Jeffrey. *Ethics in Journalism*. Englewood Cliffs, N.J.: Prentice-Hall, 1988.

Sichel, Betty A. *Moral Education: Character, Community, and Ideals*. Philadelphia: Temple University Press, 1988.

Singer, Peter, ed. *Applied Ethics*. Oxford and New York: Oxford University Press, 1986.

Gender and Sexuality

Bishop, Sharon, and Marjorie Winzweig, eds. *Philosophy and Women*. Belmont, Calif.: Wadsworth, 1986.

Frazer, Elizabeth, Jennifer Hornsby, and Sabina Lovibond, eds. *Ethics: A Feminist Reader*. New York: Oxford University Press, 1992; Oxford: Blackwell, 1992.

Gilligan, Carol. *In a Different Voice*. Cambridge, Mass. and London: Harvard University Press, 1982.

Grimshaw, Jean. *Philosophy and Feminist Thinking*. Minneapolis. University of Minnesota Press, 1986.

Held, Virginia. *Feminist Morality*. Chicago: University of Chicago Press, 1993.

Jaggar, Alison M. *Feminist Politics and Human Nature*. Savage, Md.: Rowman & Littlefield, 1983; Brighton: Harvester, 1983.

Kittay, Eva Feder, and Diana T. Meyers, eds. *Women and Moral Theory*. Savage, Md.: Rowman & Littlefield, 1987.

Mahowald, Mary B., ed. *Philosophy of Woman*. 2d ed. Indianapolis: Hackett, 1983.

Noddings, Nel. *Caring: A Feminine Approach to Ethics and Moral Education*. Berkeley and London: University of California Press, 1984.

Pearsall, Marilyn, ed. *Women and Values: Readings in Recent Feminist Philosophy,* 2nd ed. Belmont, Calif.: Wadsworth, 1993.

Tong, Rosemarie. *Feminine and Feminist Ethics*. Belmont, Calif.: Wadsworth, 1993.

———. *Feminist Thought: A Comprehensive Introduction*. Boulder, Colo.: Westview Press, 1989; London: Unwin Hyman, 1989.

Race and Ethnicity

Bell, Derrick. *Faces at the Bottom of the Well: The Permanence of Racism*. New York: Basic Books, 1992.

Du Bois, W. E. B. *The Souls of Black Folk*. New York: New American Library, 1969; London: Constable, 1994.

Ezorsky, Gertrude. *Racism and Justice: The Case for Affirmative Action*. Ithaca, N.Y. and London: Cornell University Press, 1991.

King, Martin Luther, Jr. *Why We Can't Wait*. New York: Harper & Row, 1963.

Malcolm X, with Alex Haley. *The Autobiography of Malcolm X*. New York: Grove Press, 1966; London: Hutchinson, 1966.

Rosen, Philip. *The Neglected Dimension: Ethnicity in American Life*. Notre Dame, Ind. and London: University of Notre Dame Press, 1980.

Stone, John. *Racial Conflict in Contemporary Society*. Cambridge, Mass.: Harvard University Press, 1985; London: Fontana, 1985.

Wacker, F. Fred. *Ethnicity, Pluralism, and Race*. Westport, Conn.: Greenwood Press, 1983.

West, Cornel. *Race Matters*. Boston: Beacon Press, 1993.

Zack, Naomi. *Mixed-Race and Anti-Race*. Philadelphia: Temple University Press, 1993.

Medicine and Health, Life and Death

Ackerman, Terrence F., and Carson Strong. *A Casebook of Medical Ethics*. New York and Oxford: Oxford University Press, 1989.

Alpern, Kenneth D. *The Ethics of Reproductive Technology*. New York and Oxford: Oxford University Press, 1992.

Annas, George J., and Sherman Elias, eds. *Gene Mapping: Using Law and Ethics as Guides*. New York: Oxford University Press, 1992.

Beauchamp, Tom L., and James F. Childress. *Principles of Biomedical Ethics*. 4th ed. New York and London: Oxford University Press, 1994.

Beauchamp, Tom L., and LeRoy Walters, eds. *Contemporary Issues in Bioethics*. 4th ed. Belmont, Calif.: Wadsworth, 1994.

Cassell, Eric J. *The Nature of Suffering and the Goals of Medicine*. New York: Oxford University Press, 1991.

Grodin, Michael A., and Leonard E. Glantz, eds. *Children as Research Subjects: Science, Ethics, and Law*. New York: Oxford University Press, 1994.

Lockwood, Michael, ed. *Moral Dilemmas in Modern Medicine*. London: Oxford University Press, 1985; New York: Oxford University Press, 1986.

McNeill, Paul M. *The Ethics and Politics of Human Experimentation*. Cambridge, England: Cambridge University Press, 1993.

Pierce, Christine, and Donald Van de Veer, eds. *AIDS: Ethics and Public Policy*. Belmont, Calif.: Wadsworth, 1988.

Rachels, James. *The End of Life: Euthanasia and Morality*. Oxford and New York: Oxford University Press, 1986.

Wicclair, Mark R. *Ethics and the Elderly*. New York and London: Oxford University Press, 1993.

Genocide and the Holocaust

Bauman, Zygmunt. *Modernity and the Holocaust*. Ithaca, N.Y.: Cornell University Press, 1989; Cambridge, Polity, 1989.

Berenbaum, Michael. *The World Must Know: The History of the Holocaust as Told in the United States Holocaust Memorial Museum*. Boston: Little, Brown, 1993.

Chalk, Frank, and Kurt Jonassohn. *The History and Sociology of Genocide: Analyses and Case Studies*. New Haven, Conn. and London: Yale University Press, 1990.

Fackenheim, Emil L. *To Mend the World: Foundations of Future Jewish Thought*. New York: Schocken Books, 1982.

Haas, Peter J. *Morality After Auschwitz*. Philadelphia: Fortress Press, 1988.

Hallie, Philip. *Lest Innocent Blood Be Shed*. New York: Harper & Row, 1979; London: Joseph, 1979.

Hilberg, Raul. *The Destruction of the European Jews*. Rev. ed. 3 vols. New York and London: Holmes & Meier, 1985.

Kuper, Leo. *The Prevention of Genocide*. New Haven, Conn. and London: Yale University Press, 1985.

Lifton, Robert Jay. *The Nazi Doctors: Medical Killing and the Psychology of Genocide*. New York: Basic Books, 1986; London: Macmillan, 1986.

Oliner, Samuel P., and Pearl M. Oliner. *The Altruistic Personality: Rescuers of Jews in Nazi Europe*. New York: Free Press, 1988.

Rittner, Carol, and John K. Roth, eds. *Different Voices: Women and the Holocaust*. New York: Paragon House, 1993.

Roth, John K., and Michael Berenbaum, *Holocaust: Religious and Philosophical Reflections*. New York: Paragon House, 1989.

Rubenstein, Richard L. *The Age of Triage: Fear and Hope in an Overcrowded World*. Boston: Beacon Press, 1983.

————. *The Cunning of History: The Holocaust and the American Future*. Harper & Row, 1978.

Rubenstein, Richard L., and John K. Roth. *Approaches to Auschwitz*. Louisville: John Knox Press, 1987; London: SCM, 1987.

Sereny, Gitta. *Into That Darkness*. London: Deutsch, 1974; New York: Vintage, 1983.

Wiesel, Elie. *Night*. London: Penguin, 1981; New York: Bantam Books, 1986.

RR Ethics

LIST OF ENTRIES BY CATEGORY

HISTORY, RENAISSANCE AND
    RESTORATION

HUMAN RIGHTS

INTERNATIONAL RELATIONS

LEGAL AND JUDICIAL ETHICS

MEDIA ETHICS

MILITARY ETHICS

INDEX OF PERSONAGES

INDEX

Abelard, Peter, 1
ABM Treaty, 765
Abolition, 1-3, 255, 257, 810-814
Aborigines, 735-736
Abortion, 3-6, 214, 313, 699, 701-703, 757-760, 872
Absolutes and absolutism, 6-8, 243, 383, 534, 653
Absurd, The, 8, 117, 290
Abû Bakr, 8
Abû Ḥanîfa al-Nuʿman ibn Tabi, 8
Abuse, 8-9, 132-134, 298-299, 305, 668-670, 727-731, 792-793, 829-830, 875-876. *See also* Child abuse; Physical abuse; Psychological abuse; Sexual abuse and harassment
Academic freedom, 9-11, 670-671
Accountability, 11-12, 309-310
Accuracy in Media, 12-13
Acid rain, 87
Acquired immunodeficiency syndrome, 13-14, 798-799
Action, morality of, 1
Adultery, 14-15, 235-238, 797
Adventures of Ideas (Whitehead), 930
Adversary system, 15-16
Advertising, 764, 797
Affirmative action, 16, 553
African Americans, 1-3, 100, 105-106, 152-156, 161, 167-168, 186-187, 231-233, 241-242, 255, 257, 287-288, 348-349, 438-441, 480-481, 515-517, 524, 553, 587-590, 776-777, 779-780, 810-814, 924-926
African ethics, 16-21; ancestors, 20; child rearing, 20; marriage, 17, 19; morality, 19; punishment, 20; rites of passage, 19
African National Congress (ANC), 48
After Virtue (MacIntyre), 172, 442, 519
Agape, 129, 510
Ageism, 21-22, 359-360
Aggression, 22-23, 34-35, 907-911
Agreement for the Suppression of White Slave Traffic, 23-24
Ahiṁsā, 24, 316, 376, 460, 901-904

Aid to Families with Dependent Children (AFDC), 144
Akamba culture, initiations in, 19
Akbar, Jalâl al-Dîn, 24
ʿAlî ibn Abî Ṭâlib, 24-25, 310, 800
Alienation, 25-27
Althusser, Louis, 424
Altruism, 27-30, 511
Amato, Joseph, 359
American Association of Marriage and Family Therapists, Code of Ethics of, 306
American Association of University Professors (AAUP), 11
American Civil Liberties Union, 30
American Federation of Labor, 30-31
American Medical Association, 31
American Society for the Prevention of Cruelty to Animals (ASPCA), 206
American Society of Newspaper Editors, 31
Americans with Disabilities Act, 31, 229-230
Améry, Jean, 388
Amitābha, 70
Amnesty International, 31-32
Anabaptists, 636
Analects (Confucius), 186
Anarchy, 32-33, 63
Anger, 34-35
Animal consciousness, 35-36, 789
Animal Liberation (Singer), 38-39
Animal Liberation Front (ALF), 38
Animal research, 36-37, 90, 206, 208, 589, 650-651, 714, 916
Animal rights, 36-40, 206, 299, 411, 605-606, 875-876, 903, 916, 945. *See also* Moral status of animals
Anonymity, 827-828
Anscombe, G. E. M., 861
Anthropocentrism, 268
Anthropological ethics, 7, 41-42, 596-597, 817-818
Anthropomorphism, 42
Antigone (Sophocles), 190
Anti-Religionism, 98
Anti-Semitism, 42-44, 347-350, 381-384, 386, 388-389, 458-459, 667-668, 947

Antislavery, 811-812. *See also* Abolition
Antitrust legislation, 45-46
Apartheid, 47-48, 81, 526-527
Apel, Karl-Otto, 451, 622
Apology (Plato), 48-49
Applied ethics, 49-50
Aquinas, Thomas. *See* Thomas Aquinas
Arbitration, 51, 445
Arendt, Hannah, 51
Areopagitica (Milton), 328
Aristippus, 209-210, 373
Aristotelian ethics, 27-30, 51-52, 200-201, 292-293, 353-354, 577, 611-612, 654, 843, 913; influence on Islam of, 71
Aristotle, 29, 51-54, 197, 200-201, 333, 354-355, 357, 512, 565, 611-612, 654, 694, 781, 784, 843, 876
Arjuṅa, 376
Armenians, 348
Arminius, Jacobus, 807
Arms race, 54-55, 165-166
Art, 55-56; and public policy, 55-56, 58, 528-529, 575-577
Art of War, The (Sun Tzu), 58
Articles of Confederation, 196
Artificial intelligence, 59-60, 758-759
Arts and censorship, 55-56, 431
Asceticism, 60-61
Aśoka, 61
Assassination, 32, 61-63
Assertiveness training, 363
Atatürk, Mustafa Kemal, 63-64
Atheism, 64-65
Atkinson, Rita L., 418
Atom bomb, 65-66, 380-381, 527, 624-626
Atomic Energy Commission, 66-67
Attorney-client privilege, 67, 181
Augustine, Saint, 67-68, 227, 355, 784, 806, 908
Aurobindo Ghose, Sri, 68-69, 902
Austin, John, 468
Authenticity, 69
Authoritarianism, 324, 896

XXIX

Colorado Christian University
Library
180 S. Garrison
Lakewood, Colorado 80226